35,000+ BABY NAMES

Bruce Lansky

Meadowbrook Press
Distributed by Simon & Schuster
New York

Library of Congress Cataloging-in-Publication Data

Lansky, Bruce.
  35,000+ baby names / Bruce Lansky.
    p. cm.
  ISBN 0-88166-216-X (pbk.)
    1. Names, Personal—Dictionaries. I. Title.
  CS2377.L35 1995
  929.4'03—dc20

                                         95-10295
                                         CIP

Publisher's ISBN: 0-88166-216-X
Simon & Schuster Ordering # 0-671-51975-1

Editor: Bruce Lansky
Copyeditor: Liya Lev Oertel
Editorial Coordinator: Craig Hansen
Proofreaders: Tony Dierckens, Victoria Hall
Production Manager: Amy Unger
Desktop Publishing Manager: Patrick Gross
Cover Design: Erik Broberg
Cover Photography: Bill Gale

© 1995 by Bruce Lansky

Published by Meadowbrook Press, 5451 Smetana Drive, Minnetonka, MN 55343

BOOK TRADE DISTRIBUTION by Simon & Schuster, a division of Simon and Schuster, Inc., 1230 Avenue of the Americas, New York, NY 10020

99 98   10 9 8

Printed in the United States of America

Contents

Introduction

When you think about names for your baby, you'll find yourself daydreaming about what he or she may look like and be like. And you'll find yourself thinking about your hopes and dreams for the newest member of your family.

As you consider and discuss names, you will find that they conjure up pictures in your mind. Scarlett may bring to mind Scarlett O'Hara of Margaret Mitchell's *Gone with the Wind.* Ronald may call to mind Ronald Reagan or Ronald McDonald.

You will find yourself putting first, middle, and last names together and saying them out loud. Someone watching you may think you are talking to yourself. You probably are!

You will also find yourself fascinated by all the names you read in the birth announcements section of the newspaper; names of students in your local day care center, school, church, or favorite team; names you see or hear in the news; names you see in books, movies, or on television.

Don't be surprised to discover that you have developed a "fashion sense" about which names are currently "in" and which names are currently "out." As a result, you may find yourself considering:

- names from other countries
  and ethnic groups
- names that have been recently
  created (perhaps a name you've
  made up yourself)
- names that feature new spellings
  of familiar names
- names for a girl that once were more
  often used for boys
- names that are traditional surnames

The reasons you will probably consider some names
that your parents never did are simple. Pick up the
sports section of your local newspaper and you read
about Shaquille, Anfernee, and Hakeem on the basket-
ball court or Stefan, Boris, and Magnus on the tennis
court. Turn on the television and you'll see LaToya,
Danica, and Keisha perform. Go to the movies and you
can watch Whoopi, Demi, and Winona. Interesting,
unusual names from all around the world surround you.

This book was designed to open up the whole world
of names to you. I scoured the world for popular and
unusual names that just might work for your child.
Here are a few of the unusual names I find intriguing:

Native American: Cheyenne and Dakotah
Spanish: Nevada and Sierra
French: Brie and Chardonnay
African: Saki and Simba
Welsh: Bryn and Rhett
Russian: Sasha and Tamara
Gypsy: Chik and Tawny
Italian: Giulia and Matteo
Japanese: Kimiko and Ringo

I could go on for pages.

I created this book to give you the choice of a lifetime—more interesting and unusual names from all around the world than any other book.

My best advice is to:

a) Rate the names you are considering on the rating sheet that follows. It will help you make the very subjective process of selecting a name a little more objective.

b) "Go public" with the naming process. "Test" names you are considering on your friends and relatives. Find out how the names you are considering are perceived and received. What positive or negative associations come to mind?* How do your friends and relatives feel about the name?

Chances are, if a name survives this process, it may well be a name both you *and* your child can live with happily ever after.

Happy hunting,

Bruce Lansky

* If this factor intrigues you, consult *The Baby Name Personality Survey* to find how 1,400 popular names are perceived by a sample of 75,000 parents.

Ten Guidelines for Naming Your Baby

A Comparative Scoring System

If you have a name you like, you already know how pleasant it is going through life with a name that "fits" or "feels right." If you don't, you know how unpleasant it is to go through life with a name that, for any number of reasons, doesn't work for you.

It may help to test each name you are considering against the list of factors that could affect the way a name will work for your child. This will help make the subjective process of selecting a name more objective for you.

Scoring: In the chart on the following page, give each name two points for a positive rating on any criterion, one point for a medium rating, and no points for a negative rating.

I realize that this scoring system has a built-in bias toward names that are relatively common and familiar—and therefore easy to spell and pronounce. However, you are free to give extra weight to any factor you like. If, for example, you love exotic names that are unfamiliar (and potentially hard to spell and pronounce), you might want to double the weight of the "uniqueness" and/or "sound/rhythm" factors— in other words, give four points for a positive rating and two points for a medium rating.

Factors	Positive	Medium	Negative
1. Spelling	❑ easy	❑ medium	❑ hard
2. Pronunciation	❑ easy	❑ medium	❑ hard
3. Gender ID	❑ clear		❑ confusing
4. Stereotypes	❑ positive	❑ ok	❑ negative
5. Sound/Rhythm	❑ pleasing	❑ ok	❑ unpleasant
6. Nicknames	❑ appealing	❑ ok	❑ unappealing
7. Meaning	❑ positive	❑ ok	❑ negative
8. Popularity	❑ *not* too popular		❑ too popular
9. Uniqueness	❑ *not* too strange		❑ too strange
10. Initials	❑ pleasing	❑ ok	❑ unpleasant

Top Five Boys Names

Name 1: _____ Score_____

Name 2: _____ Score_____

Name 3: _____ Score_____

Name 4: _____ Score_____

Name 5: _____ Score_____

Top Five Girls Names

Name 1: _____ Score_____

Name 2: _____ Score_____

Name 3: _____ Score_____

Name 4: _____ Score_____

Name 5: _____ Score_____

Where in the World

35,000+ Baby Names includes names from over 160 different languages. Some of these languages are quite familiar, while others may be more obscure or exotic. In order to help identify where each language comes from, the following language chart has been provided.

In this chart, the languages used in *35,000+ Baby Names* have been divided up into general geographical categories. Upon encountering a name entry with an unfamiliar language citation, please refer to the chart below to discover what part of the world the name in question originated from.

Languages used in *35,000+ Baby Names:*

African

Abaluhya	Ga
African	Ghanian
Afrikaans	Hausa
Akan	Ibo
Ateso	Kakwa
Bambara	Kikuyu
Benin	Kiswahili
Dutooro	Lomwe
Egyptian	Luganda
Ethiopian	Lunyole
Ewe	Luo
Fanti	Musoga
	Mwera

Ngoni
Nigerian
North African
Nyakusa
Ochi
Rhodesian
Rukiga
Runyankore
Runyoro
Rutooro
Shona
Somali
South African
Swahili
Tanzanian
Tiv
Tswana
Twi
Ugandan
Umbundu
Uset
Xhosha
Yao
Yoruba
Zimbabwean
Zulu

Native American

Algonquin
Apache
Arapaho
Ashanti
Blackfoot
Carrier
Cherokee
Cheyenne

Chippewa
Choctaw
Comanche
Coos
Dakota
Dene
Eskimo
Fox
Hopi
Iroquois
Kiowa
Lakota
Mahona
Mohawk
Moquelumnan
Native American
Navajo
Omaha
Osage
Pawnee
Pomo
Ponca
Quiché
Sauk
Shoshone
Taos
Tupi-Guarani
Watamare
Winnebago
Zuni

East Asian and Pacific

Australian
Burmese
Cambodian
Chinese

Filipino
Fijian
Hawaiian
Japanese
Korean
Malayan
Maori
Polynesian
Samoan
Thai
Tibetan
Vietnamese
West Australian
Aboriginal

Eastern Europe and Northern Asia

Armenian
Basque
Bulgarian
Czech
Estonian
Hungarian
Latvian
Lithuanian
Mongolian
Polish
Romanian
Russian
Slavic
Turkish
Ukranian

West European

Cornish
Danish
Dutch
English
Finnish
French
German
Gypsy
Icelandic
Irish
Italian
Norwegian
Portugese
Scandinavian
Scottish
Spanish
Swedish
Swiss
Welsh
Yiddish

Middle and Near East

Afghani
Arabic
Hebrew
Hindi
Pakistani
Pashtu
Persian
Punjabi
Tamil
Todas
Urdu

South and North American

- American
- Brazilian
- Peruvian

Historical Languages

- Aramaic
- Assyrian
- Babylonian
- Greek
- Latin
- Phoenician
- Sanskrit
- Syrian
- Teutonic

Girls'
Names

Abbey, Abbie, Abby
(Hebrew) familiar forms
of Abigail.
Abbe, Abbi, Abbye, Abia

Abia (Arabic) great.
**Abbia, Abbiah, Abiah,
Abya**

Abida (Arabic) worshiper.
Abidah

Abigail (Hebrew) father's
joy. Bible: one of the wives
of King David. See also
Gail.
**Abagael, Abagail,
Abagale, Abagil,
Abbegail, Abbegale,
Abbegayle, Abbey,
Abbigail, Abbigale,
Abbigayle, Abbygail,
Abbygale, Abbygayle,
Abegail, Abegale,
Abegayle, Abgail, Abgale,
Abgayle, Abigael, Abigal,
Abigale, Abigayil,
Abigayle, Abigel, Avigail**

Abira (Hebrew) my
strength.

Abra (Hebrew) mother of
many nations. A feminine
form of Abraham.
Abree, Abri

Abrial (French) open;
secure, protected.
Abreal, Abreale, Abriale

Abriana (Italian) a form
of Abra.
**Abrianna, Abrielle,
Abrienne, Abrietta**

Acacia (Greek) thorny.
Mythology: the acacia
tree symbolizes immor-
tality and resurrection.
See also Casey.
**Acey, Acie, Cacia, Casia,
Kacia**

Ada (German) a short
form of Adelaide.
(English) prosperous;
happy. See also Aida.
**Adabelle, Adah, Adalee,
Adan, Adda, Addia,
Addie, Adia, Adiah, Auda,
Aude**

Adah (Hebrew) ornament.
Ada

Adalia (German, Spanish)
noble.
**Adal, Adala, Adalee,
Adali, Adalie, Adalin,
Adaly, Adalyn, Addal,
Addala, Addaly**

Adama (Phoenician)
woman, humankind.
(Hebrew) earth; woman
of the red earth. A femi-
nine form of Adam.

Adamma (Ibo) child
of beauty.

Adana (Spanish) a form of Adama.

Adanna (Nigerian) her father's daughter.
Adanya

Adara (Greek) beauty. (Arabic) virgin.
Adair, Adaira, Adaora, Adare, Adaria, Addie, Adra

Addie (Greek, German) a familiar form of Adelaide, Adrienne.
Adde, Addey, Addi, Addia, Addy, Adey, Adi, Adie, Ady, Atti, Attie, Atty

Adelaide (German) noble and serene. See also Ada, Adeline, Adelle, Ailis, Delia, Della, Ela, Elke, Heidi.
Adeela, Adelade, Adelaid, Adelaida, Adelei, Adelheid, Adeliade, Adelka, Aley, Laidey, Laidy

Adeline (English) a form of Adelaide. See also Delaney.
Adalina, Adaline, Addie, Adelina, Adelind, Adelita, Adeliya, Adelle, Adelyn, Adelynn, Adena, Adilene, Adina, Adinna, Adlena, Adlene, Adlin, Adline, Aline, Alita

Adelle (German, English) a short form of Adelaide, Adeline.
Adel, Adela, Adele, Adelia, Adelista, Adell, Adella

Adena (Greek, Hebrew) noble; adorned.
Adeana, Adeen, Adeena, Aden, Adene, Adenia, Adina

Adia (Swahili) gift.

Adila (Arabic) equal.
Adela, Adelah, Adilah

Adina (Hebrew) an alternate form of Adena. See also Dinah.
Adiana, Adiena, Adinah, Adinna

Adira (Hebrew) strong.
Adirah

Aditi (Hindi) unbound. Religion: the mother of Hindu gods.

Adonia (Spanish) beautiful. A feminine form of Adonis.
Adonya

Adora (Latin) beloved. See also Dora.
Adore, Adoree, Adoria

Adra (Arabic) virgin.
Adara

Adriana, Adrianna (Italian) forms of Adrienne.
Adrea, Adria

Adriane, Adrianne (English) forms of Adrienne.

Adrienne (Greek) rich. (Latin) dark. A feminine form of Adrian. See also Hadriane.
Addie, Adriana, Adriane,

**Adrianna, Adrianne,
Adrie, Adrien, Adriena,
Adrienna**

Adya (Hindi) Sunday.
Adia

Afi (African) born on Friday.
Affi, Afia, Efi, Efia

Afra (Hebrew) young doe.
(Arabic) earth color.
See also Aphra.
Affery, Affrey, Affrie

Africa (Irish) pleasant.
History: a twelfth-
century queen of the
Isle of Man. Geography:
one of the seven
continents.
**Affrica, Afric, Africah,
Afrika, Afrikah, Aifric**

Afton (English) from Afton,
England.
Aftan, Aftine, Aftyn

Agate (English) a semi-
precious stone.
Aggie

Agatha (Greek) good,
kind. Literature: Agatha
Christie was a British
writer of more than
seventy detective novels.
See also Gasha.
**Agace, Agasha, Agata,
Agathe, Agathi, Agatka,
Aggie, Ágota, Ágotha,
Agueda, Atka**

Aggie (Greek) a short form
of Agatha, Agnes.
Ag, Aggy, Agi

Agnes (Greek) pure.
See also Anice, Anissa,
Ina, Inez, Necha, Nessa,
Nessie, Neza, Nyusha,
Una, Ynez.
**Aganetha, Aggie,
Agna, Agne, Agneis,
Agnelia, Agnella, Agnés,
Agnesa, Agnesca,
Agnese, Agnesina,
Agness, Agnesse,
Agneta, Agneti, Agnetta,
Agnies, Agnieszka,
Agniya, Agnola, Aignéis,
Aneska, Anka**

Ahava (Hebrew) beloved.
Ahivla

Aida (Latin) helpful.
(English) an alternate
form of Ada.
Aidah

Aiko (Japanese) beloved.

Ailani (Hawaiian) chief.

Aileen (Scottish) light
bearer. (Irish) a form
of Helen.
**Ailean, Ailene, Aili, Ailina,
Ailinn, Aleen, Aleena,
Aleene, Alene, Aliana,
Alianna, Alina, Aline,
Allene, Alline, Allyn,
Alyna, Alyne, Alynne**

Aili (Scottish) a form
of Alice. (Finnish) a form
of Helen.
**Aila, Ailee, Ailey, Ailie,
Aily**

Ailis (Irish) a form
of Adelaide.

Ailsa (Scottish) island
dweller. Geography:
Ailsa Craig is an island
in Scotland.

Aimee (Latin) an alternate
form of Amy. (French)
loved.
**Aime, Aimée, Aimey,
Aimi, Aimia, Aimie, Aimy**

Ainsley (Scottish) my own
meadow.
**Ainslee, Ainsleigh, Ainslie,
Ainsly, Ansley, Aynslee,
Aynsley, Aynslie**

Aisha (Swahili) life. (Arabic)
woman. See also Asha,
Asia, Iesha, Isha, Yiesha.
**Aesha, Aeshah, Aiesha,
Aieshah, Aishah, Aishia,
Aishiah, Ayasha, Ayesha,
Ayeshah, Ayisha, Ayishah,
Aysa, Ayse, Aysha,
Ayshah, Ayshe, Ayshea,
Aytza, Azia**

Aiyana (Native American)
forever flowering.
Ayana

Aja (Hindi) goat.
Ajah, Ajaran, Ajha, Ajia

Akela (Hawaiian) noble.
Akeya, Akeyla, Akeylah

Aki (Japanese) born in
autumn.

Akiko (Japanese) bright
light.

Akilah (Arabic) intelligent.
Akia, Akiela, Akila, Akilka

Akili (Tanzanian) wisdom.

Alaina, Alayna (Irish)
alternate forms of Alana.
**Alaine, Alainna, Alainnah,
Alane, Alayne, Aleine,
Alleyna, Alleynah, Alleyne**

Alair (French) a form
of Hilary, Hillary.
Ali, Allaire

Alamea (Hawaiian) ripe;
precious.

Alameda (Spanish) poplar
tree.

Alana (Irish) attractive;
peaceful. (Hawaiian) offer-
ing. A feminine form of
Alan. See also Allena, Lana.
**Alaina, Alanah, Alani,
Alania, Alanis, Alanna,
Alannah, Alawna, Alayna,
Allana, Allanah, Allyn**

Alandra (Spanish) a form
of Alexandra.

Alani (Hawaiian) orange
tree.

Alanza (Spanish) noble
and eager. A feminine
form of Alphonse.

Alba (Latin) from Alba,
Italy, a city on a white hill.
A feminine form of Alban.
**Albina, Albine, Albinia,
Albinka**

Alberta (German, French) noble and bright. A feminine form of Albert. See also Auberte, Bertha, Elberta.
Albertina, Albertine, Albertyna, Albertyne, Alverta

Alcina (Greek) strong minded.
Alceena, Alcine, Alcinia, Alseena, Alsinia, Alsyna, Alzina

Alda (German) old; elder. A feminine form of Aldo.
Aldina, Aldine, Aldona, Aldyna, Aldyne

Alea, Aleah (Arabic) high, exalted. (Persian) God's being.
Aleea, Aleeah, Alia, Alleea, Alleeah, Allia

Alecia (Greek) a form of Alicia.
Alecea, Alesha

Aleela (Swahili) she cries.
Aleelah, Alila, Alile

Aleene (Dutch) alone.
Aleen, Alene

Aleeza (Hebrew) a form of Aliza. See also Leeza.
Aleezah, Aleezay, Alieza, Aliezah

Alegria (Spanish) cheerful.
Allegra, Allegria

Alejandra (Spanish) a form of Alexandra.
Alejanda, Alejandr, Alejandrea, Alejandria, Alejandrina

Aleka (Hawaiian) a form of Alice.
Aleeka, Alekah

Alena (Russian) a form of Helen.
Aleen, Aleena, Alenah, Alene, Alenka, Allene, Alyna

Alesha (Greek) an alternate form of Alecia, Alisha.
Aleasha, Aleashea, Aleasia, Aleesha, Aleeshah, Aleeshia, Aleeshya, Aleisha, Aleshia, Alesia

Alessandra (Italian) a form of Alexandra.
Alesandra, Alesandrea, Allesand, Allesia, Allessa

Aleta (Greek) a form of Alida. See also Leta.
Alita, Allita

Alethea (Greek) truth.
Alathea, Alathia, Aleta, Aletea, Aletha, Alethia, Aletia, Alithea, Alithia

Alette (Latin) wing.
Aletta

Alex, Alexa (Greek) short forms of Alexandra.
Alekia, Aleksa, Aleksha

Alexandra (Greek) defender of mankind. A feminine form of Alexander. History: the last czarina of Russia. See also Lexia, Olesia, Ritsa, Sandra,

Sasha, Shura, Sondra,
Xandra, Zandra.
**Alandra, Aleix, Alejandra,
Aleka, Aleks, Aleksandra,
Aleksasha, Alessandra,
Alexande, Alexina, Alexine,
Alexis, Alexx, Alexxandra,
Alexzand, Alexzandra, Ali,
Alix, Aljexi, Alla, Lexandra**

Alexandria (Greek) an alter-
nate form of Alexandra.
See also Drinka, Xandra,
Zandra.
**Alexanderia, Alexanderina,
Alexanderine, Alexandrea,
Alexandrena, Alexandrie,
Alexandrina, Alexandrine,
Alexia, Alexzandrea,
Alexzandria**

Alexia (Greek) a short form
of Alexandria. See also
Lexia.
**Aleksey, Aleksi, Aleska,
Alexey, Alexi, Alexie, Alka,
Alya**

Alexis (Greek) a short form
of Alexandra.
**Alexcis, Alexes, Alexi,
Alexiou, Alexisia, Alexius,
Alexsia, Alexus, Alexx,
Alexxis, Alexys, Alexyss,
Lexis**

Alfreda (English) elf
counselor; wise counselor.
A feminine form of Alfred.
See also Effie, Elfrida, Freda,
Frederica.
**Alfi, Alfie, Alfredda,
Alfreeda, Alfrieda, Alfy**

Ali (Greek) a familiar form
of Alicia, Alisha, Alison.
Allea, Alli, Allie, Ally, Aly

Alia (Hebrew) an alternate
form of Aliya. See also
Alea.
Aleana, Aliyah, Alya

Alice (Greek) truthful.
(German) noble. See also
Aili, Aleka, Alisa, Allie,
Allison, Alycia, Alysa,
Alyssa, Alysse, Elke.
**Adelice, Ailis, Alecia,
Aleece, Alica, Alican,
Alicie, Alicyn, Aliece,
Alies, Aliese, Alika, Alis,
Alison, Alix, Alize, Alla,
Alleece, Alles, Allesse,
Allice, Allie, Allis, Allisa,
Allise, Allisse, Allix**

Alicia (English) an alternate
form of Alice. See also
Elicia, Licia.
**Alecia, Aleecia, Ali,
Alicea, Alicha, Alichia,
Alician, Alicja, Alicya,
Aliecia, Alisha, Allicea,
Alycia, Ilysa**

Alida (Latin) small and
winged. (Spanish) noble.
See also Aleta, Lida,
Oleda.
**Aleda, Alidia, Alita,
Alleda, Allida, Allidah,
Alyda, Alydia, Elida**

Alika (Hawaiian) truthful.
(Swahili) most beautiful.
**Aleka, Alica, Alikah, Alike,
Alikee, Aliki**

Alima (Arabic) sea maiden; musical.

Alina, Aline (Slavic) bright. (Scottish) fair. (English) a short form of Adeline. See also Alena.
Allene, Allyna, Allyne, Alyna, Alyne

Alisa, Alissa (Greek) an alternate form of Alice. See also Elisa, Ilisa.
Alisia, Alise, Alisse, Alisza, Alisse, Alisza, Alyssa

Alisha (Greek) truthful. (German) noble. (English) an alternate form of Alicia. See also Elisha, Ilisha, Lisha.
Aleesha, Alesha, Ali, Aliesha, Alieshai, Aliscia, Alishah, Alishay, Alishaye, Alishea, Alishya, Alisia, Alissia, Alitsha, Alysha

Alison, Allison (English) a form of Alice. See also Lissie.
Ali, Alicen, Alicyn, Alisann, Alisanne, Alisen, Alisson, Alisun, Alisyn, Alles, Allesse, Allie, Allis, Allise, Allix, Allsun

Alita (Spanish) a form of Alida.

Alix (Greek) a short form of Alexandra, Alice.
Allix, Alyx

Aliya (Hebrew) ascender.
Alea, Aleah, Alee, Aleea, Aleia, Aleya, Alia, Aliyah, Aly

Aliye (Arabic) noble.

Aliza (Hebrew) joyful. See also Aleeza, Eliza.
Alieza, Aliezah, Alitza, Alizah

Allegra (Latin) cheerful.
Ali, Allie, Legra

Allena (Irish) an alternate form of Alana.
Ali, Alleen

Allie (Greek) a familiar form of Alice.
Ali, Aleni, Alenna, Alleen, Allene, Alline

Allyson, Alyson (English) alternate forms of Alison, Allison.
Allysen, Allyson, Allysun, Alyson

Alma (Arabic) learned. (Latin) soul.
Almah

Almeda (Latin) ambitious.
Allmeda, Allmedah, Allmeta, Allmita, Almea, Almedah, Almeta, Almida, Almita

Almira (Arabic) aristocratic, princess; exalted. (Spanish) from Almeíra, Spain. See also Elmira, Mira.
Allmeera, Allmeria, Allmira, Almeera, Almeeria, Almeira, Almeria, Almire

Aloha (Hawaiian) loving, kind hearted, charitable.
Alohi

Aloisa (German) famous warrior.
Aloisia, Aloysia

Aloma (Latin) a short form of Paloma.

Alonza (English) noble and eager. A feminine form of Alonzo.

Alpha (Greek) first-born. Linguistics: the first letter in the Greek alphabet.
Alphia

Alta (Latin) high; tall.
Allta, Altah, Alto

Althea (Greek) wholesome; healer. History: Althea Gibson was the first African-American to win a major tennis title. See also Thea.
Altha, Altheda, Altheya, Althia, Elthea, Eltheya, Elthia

Alva (Latin, Spanish) white; light skinned. See also Elva.
Alvana, Alvanna, Alvannah

Alvina (English) friend to all; noble friend; friend to elves. A feminine form of Alvin. See also Elva, Vina.
Alveanea, Alveen, Alveena, Alveenia, Alvenea, Alvie, Alvincia, Alvine, Alvinea, Alvinesha, Alvinia, Alvinna, Alvita, Alvona, Alvyna, Alwin, Alwina, Alwyn

Alycia (English) an alternate form of Alicia.
Allyce, Alycea, Lycia, Alyse

Alysa, Alyse, Alysse (Greek) alternate forms of Alice.
Allys, Allyse, Allyss, Alys, Alyss

Alysha, Alysia (Greek) alternate forms of Alisha.
Allysea, Allyscia, Alysea, Alyshia, Alyssha, Alyssia

Alyssa (Greek) rational. Botany: alyssum is a flowering herb. See also Alice, Elissa.
Alissa, Allissa, Allyssa, Ilyssa, Lyssa, Lyssah

Alysse (Greek) an alternate form of Alice.
Allyce, Allys, Allyse, Allyss, Alys, Alyss

Am (Vietnamese) lunar; female.

Ama (African) born on Saturday.

Amabel (Latin) lovable. See also Bel, Mabel.
Amabelle, Annaple

Amada (Spanish) beloved.
Amadea, Amadi, Amadia, Amadita

Amal (Arabic) hopeful.
Amala

Amalia (German) an alternate form of Amelia.
Amalea, Amalee, Amaleta, Amali, Amalie, Amalija,

Amalina, Amalisa, Amalita, Amaliya, Amaly, Amalyn

Amanda (Latin) lovable. See also Manda.
Amada, Amanada, Amandah, Amandalee, Amandalyn, Amandi, Amandie, Amandine, Amandy

Amara (Greek) eternally beautiful. See also Mara.

Amaranta (Spanish) a flower that never fades.

Amaris (Hebrew) promised by God.
Amarissa, Maris

Amaryllis (Greek) fresh; flower.
Amarillis, Amarylis

Amaui (Hawaiian) thrush.

Amaya (Japanese) night rain.

Amber (French) amber.
Amberia, Amberise, Amberly, Ambur

Amberly (American) a familiar form of Amber.
Amberle, Amberlea, Amberlee, Amberlie, Amberlyn

Amelia (Latin) an alternate form of Emily. (German) hardworking. History: Amelia Earhart, an American aviator, was the first woman to fly solo across the Atlantic Ocean. See also Ima, Melia, Millie, Nuela, Yamelia.
Amalia, Amaliya, Ameila, Ameley, Amelie, Amélie, Amelina, Ameline, Amelisa, Amelita, Amella, Amilia, Amilina, Amilisa, Amilita, Amillia, Amilyn, Amylia

Amelie (German) a familiar form of Amelia.
Amaley, Amalie, Amelee, Amy

Amina (Arabic) trustworthy, faithful. History: the mother of the prophet Mohammed.
Aminah, Aminda, Amindah, Aminta, Amintah

Amira (Hebrew) speech; utterance. (Arabic) princess. See also Mira.
Ameera, Ameerah, Amirah

Amissa (Hebrew) truth.
Amissah

Amita (Hebrew) truth.

Amity (Latin) friendship.
Amita, Amitha, Amitie

Amlika (Hindi) mother.
Amlikah

Amma (Hindi) god, godlike. Religion: another name for the Hindu goddess Shakti.

Amy (Latin) beloved. See also Aimee, Emma, Esmé.
Amata, Ame, Amey, Ami, Amia, Amie, Amiet, Amii, Amiiee, Amijo, Amiko, Amio, Ammie, Ammy, Amye, Amylyn

An (Chinese) peaceful.

Ana (Hawaiian, Spanish) a form of Hannah.
Anabela

Anaba (Native American) she returns from battle.

Anais (Hebrew) gracious.
Anaise, Anaïse

Anala (Hindi) fine.

Ananda (Hindi) blissful.

Anastasia (Greek) resurrection. See also Nastasia, Stacey, Stacia, Stasya, Tasha.
Ana, Anastace, Anastacia, Anastacie, Anastase, Anastasha, Anastashia, Anastasie, Anastassia, Anastassya, Anastatia, Anastazia, Anastice, Annstás

Anatola (Greek) from the east.

Anci (Hungarian) a form of Hannah.
Annus, Annushka

Andee (American) a short form of Andrea, Fernanda.
Ande, Andea, Andi, Andy

Andrea (Greek) strong; courageous. (Latin) feminine. A feminine form of Andrew. See also Ondrea.
Aindrea, Andee, Andera, Anderea, Andra, Andrah, Andraia, Andraya, Andreah, Andreaka, Andrean, Andreana, Andreane, Andreanna, Andreanne, Andree, Andrée, Andreea, Andreia, Andreja, Andreka, Andrel, Andrell, Andrelle, Andrena, Andrene, Andreo, Andressa, Andrette, Andrewina, Andreya, Andri, Andria, Andriana, Andriea, Andrieka, Andrienne, Andrietta, Andrija, Andrika, Andrina, Andris, Aundrea

Andromeda (Greek) rescued. Mythology: the daughter of Cassiopeia, rescued by Perseus.

Aneesa (Greek) an alternate form of Agnes.
Anee, Aneesah, Aneese, Aneesha, Aneeshah, Aneesia

Aneko (Japanese) older sister.

Anela (Hawaiian) angel.

Anetra (American) a form of Annette.
Anitra

Anezka (Czech) a form
of Hannah.

Angel (Greek) a short form
of Angela.
Angell, Angil, Anjel

Angela (Greek) angel;
messenger.
**Angala, Anganita, Ange,
Angel, Angelanell,
Angelanette, Angele,
Angèle, Angelea,
Angeleah, Angelee,
Angeleigh, Angeles,
Angeli, Angelia, Angelic,
Angelica, Angelina,
Angelique, Angelita,
Angella, Angelle,
Angellita, Angie, Anglea,
Anjela**

Angelica (Greek) an alter-
nate form of Angela.
**Angel, Angelici, Angelika,
Angeliki, Angellica,
Angilica, Anjelica,
Anjelika**

Angelina, Angeline
(Russian) alternate forms
of Angela.
**Angalena, Angalina,
Angeleen, Angelena,
Angelene, Angeliana,
Angeleana, Angellina,
Angelyn, Angelyna,
Angelyne, Angelynn,
Angelynne, Anhelina,
Anjelina**

Angelique (French) a form
of Angela.

**Angeliqua, Angélique,
Angilique, Anjelique**

Angeni (Native American)
spirit.
Ange, Angee, Angey

Angie (Greek) a familiar
form of Angela.
Angee, Angey, Angi, Angy

Ani (Hawaiian) beautiful.

Ania (Polish) a form
of Hannah.

Anice (English) an alternate
form of Agnes.
**Anesse, Anis, Anise,
Anisha, Annes, Annice,
Annis, Annissa, Annus**

Anika (Czech) a familiar
form of Anna.
**Anaka, Aneeky, Aneka,
Anekah, Anica, Anicka,
Anik, Anikah, Anikka,
Anikke, Aniko, Anneka,
Annik, Annika, Anouska,
Anuska**

Anila (Hindi) Religion:
a Hindu wind god.

Anisah (Arabic) friendly.
Anisa, Annissah

Anissa (English) a form
of Agnes, Ann.
**Anis, Anisa, Anise, Anisha,
Annissa**

Anita (Spanish) a form of
Ann, Anna. See also Nita.
**Aneeta, Aneetah,
Aneethah, Anetha,
Anitha, Anithah, Anitia,**

Anita *(cont.)*
Anitra, Anitte

Anka (Polish) a familiar
form of Hannah.

Ann, Anne (English)
gracious. A form of
Hannah. See also Nan.
**An, Ana, Anelle, Anice,
Anikó, Anissa, Anita,
Anke, Annalie, Annchen,
Annette, Annie, Annik,
Annika, Annze, Anouche,
Anouk**

Anna (German, Italian,
Czech, Swedish) gracious.
A form of Hannah.
Culture: Anna Pavlova
was a famous Russian
ballerina. See also Aneesa,
Anissa, Anika, Nana, Nina,
Nisa, Nita, Nona, Vanya.
**Ana, Anah, Ania, Anica,
Anita, Anja, Anka,
Annina, Annora, Anona,
Anya, Anyu, Aska**

Annabel (English) a combi-
nation of Anna + Bel.
**Amabel, Anabel, Anabela,
Anabella, Anabelle,
Annabal, Annabell,
Annabella, Annabelle**

Annalie (Finnish) a form
of Hannah.
**Analee, Annalee, Annali,
Anneli, Annelie**

Anneka (Swedish) a form
of Hannah.
**Annaka, Annika, Anniki,
Annikki**

Annelisa (English) a com-
bination of Anne + Lisa.
**Analiese, Analisa, Analise,
Anelisa, Anelise,
Annaliese, Annalisa,
Annalise, Anneliese,
Annelise**

**Annemarie, Annmarie,
Anne-Marie** (English)
combinations of
Anne + Marie.
**Annamaria, Anna-Maria,
Annamarie, Anna-Marie,
Annmaria**

Annette (French) a form
of Ann. See also Anetra,
Nettie.
**Anet, Aneta, Anetra,
Anett, Anetta, Anette,
Anneth, Annett, Annetta**

Annie (English) a familiar
form of Ann.
Anni, Anny

Annik, Annika (Russian)
forms of Ann.
**Aneka, Anekah, Anica,
Anika, Anninka**

Annjanette (American)
a combination of
Ann + Janette.
**Angen, Angenett,
Angenette, Anjane,
Anjanetta, Anjani**

Anona (English) pineapple.

Anouhea (Hawaiian) cool,
soft fragrance.

Anthea (Greek) flower.
**Antha, Anthe, Anthia,
Thia**

Antoinette (French) a
form of Antonia. See also
Nettie, Toinette, Toni.
**Anta, Antanette,
Antoinella, Antoinet,
Antonella, Antonetta,
Antonette, Antonice,
Antonieta, Antonietta,
Antonique**

Antonia (Greek) flourish-
ing. (Latin) praiseworthy.
A feminine form of
Anthony. See also Toni,
Tonya, Tosha.
**Ansonia, Ansonya,
Antania, Antoinette,
Antona, Antoñía,
Antonice, Antonie,
Antonina, Antonine,
Antonnea, Antonnia,
Antonya**

Antonice (Latin) an alter-
nate form of Antonia.
**Antanise, Antanisha,
Antonesha, Antoneshia,
Antonise, Antonisha**

Anya (Russian) a form
of Anna.
Anja

Aolani (Hawaiian) heavenly cloud.

Aphra (Hebrew) young
doe. See also Afra.
Aphrah, Aphrey, Aphrie

April (Latin) opening.
See also Avril.
**Aprele, Aprelle, Apriell,
Aprielle, Aprila, Aprile,
Aprilette, Aprili, Aprill,
Apryl**

Apryl (Latin) an alternate
form of April.
Apryle

Aquene (Native American)
peaceful.

Ara (Arabic) opinionated.
**Arae, Arah, Ari, Aria,
Arria**

Arabella (Latin) beautiful
altar. See also Belle,
Orabella.
**Ara, Arabela, Arabele,
Arabelle**

Ardelle (Latin) warm;
enthusiastic.
**Ardelia, Ardelis, Ardella,
Ardi**

Arden (English) valley
of the eagle. Literature:
in Shakespeare, a romantic
place of refuge.
**Ardeen, Ardeena, Ardena,
Ardene, Ardi, Ardenia,
Ardin, Ardine**

Ardi (Hebrew) a short form
of Arden, Ardice, Ardith.
Ardie, Arti, Artie

Ardice (Hebrew) an alter-
nate form of Ardith.
**Ardis, Artis, Ardiss,
Ardyce, Ardys**

Ardith (Hebrew) flowering field.
Ardath, Ardi, Ardice, Ardyth

Arella (Hebrew) angel; messenger.
Arela, Arelle, Orella, Orelle

Aretha (Greek) virtuous. See also Oretha.
Areatha, Areetha, Areta, Aretina, Aretta, Arette, Arita, Aritha, Retha, Ritha

Ariadne (Greek) holy. Mythology: the daughter of King Minos of Crete.
Ari, Ariana, Ariane

Ariana, Arianna (Italian) forms of Ariadne.
Aeriana, Aerianna, Airiana, Arieana

Ariane (French), **Arianne** (English) forms of Ariadne.
Aeriann, Airiann, Ari, Arianie, Ariann, Ariannie, Arieann, Arien, Arienne, Arieon, Aryane, Aryanna, Aryanne

Arica (Scandinavian) an alternate form of Erica.
Aricca, Aricka, Arika, Arikka

Ariel (Hebrew) lioness of God.
Aeriale, Aeriel, Aeriela, Aeryal, Aire, Aireal, Airial, Ari, Aria, Arial, Ariale, Arieal, Ariela, Arielle

Arielle (French) a form of Ariel.
Aeriell, Ariella

Arin (Hebrew) enlightened. (Arabic) messenger. A feminine form of Aaron. See also Erin.
Aaren, Arinn, Aryn

Arista (Greek) best.
Ari, Aris

Arla (German) an alternate form of Carla.

Arleigh (English) an alternate form of Harley.
Arlea, Arlee, Arley, Arlie, Arly

Arlene (Irish) pledge. A feminine form of Arlen. See also Lena, Lina.
Arla, Arlana, Arleen, Arleigh, Arlen, Arlena, Arlenis, Arlette, Arleyne, Arliene, Arlina, Arlinda, Arline, Arlis, Arly, Arlyn, Arlyne

Arlette (English) a form of Arlene.
Arleta, Arletta

Arlynn (American) a combination of Arlene + Lynn.
Arlyn, Arlynne

Armine (Latin) noble. (German) soldier. (French) a feminine form of Herman.
Armina

Artha (Hindi) wealthy, prosperous.
Arti, Artie

Artis (Irish) noble; lofty hill. (Scottish) bear. (English) rock. (Icelandic) follower of Thor. A feminine form of Arthur.
Arthea, Arthelia, Arthene, Arthette, Arthuretta, Arthurina, Arthurine, Artina, Artrice

Asa (Japanese) born in the morning.

Asha (Arabic, Swahili) an alternate form of Aisha, Ashia.
Ashia, Ashyah

Ashanti (Swahili) from a tribe in West Africa.
Ashanta, Ashantae, Ashante, Ashantee, Ashaunta, Ashauntae, Ashauntee, Ashaunti, Ashuntae, Ashunti

Ashia (Arabic) life.
Asha, Ayshia

Ashley (English) ash tree meadow. See also Lee.
Ashala, Ashalee, Ashalei, Ashaley, Ashelee, Ashelei, Asheleigh, Asheley, Ashely, Ashla, Ashlay, Ashlea, Ashleah, Ashleay, Ashlee, Ashlei, Ashleigh, Ashli, Ashlie, Ashly, Ashlye

Ashlyn, Ashlynn (English) ash tree pool. (Irish) vision, dream.
Ashlan, Ashleann, Ashleen, Ashleene, Ashlen, Ashlene, Ashliann, Ashlianne, Ashlin, Ashline, Ashling, Ashlyne, Ashlynne

Asia (Greek) resurrection. (English) eastern sunrise. (Swahili) an alternate form of Aisha.
Aisia, Asiah, Asian, Asya, Aysia, Aysiah, Aysian

Aspen (English) aspen tree.
Aspin, Aspyn

Aster (English) a form of Astra.
Astera, Asteria, Astyr

Astra (Greek) star.
Asta, Astara, Aster, Astraea, Astrea

Astrid (Scandinavian) divine strength.
Astri, Astrida, Astrik, Astrud, Atti, Estrid

Atalanta (Greek) mighty huntress. Mythology: an athletic young woman who refused to marry any man who could not outrun her in a footrace. See also Lani.
Addi, Addie, Atalaya, Atlanta, Atlante, Atlee, Atti, Attie

Atara (Hebrew) crown.
Atarah, Ataree

Athena (Greek) wise.
Mythology: the goddess
of wisdom.
**Athenea, Athene, Athina,
Atina**

Atira (Hebrew) prayer.

Auberte (French) a form
of Alberta.
**Auberta, Aubertha,
Auberthe, Aubine**

Aubrey (German) noble;
bearlike. (French) blond
ruler; elf ruler.
**Aubary, Auberi, Aubery,
Aubray, Aubre, Aubrea,
Aubreah, Aubree, Aubrei,
Aubreigh, Aubrette,
Aubria, Aubrie, Aubry,
Aubury**

Aubrie (French) an alternate form of Aubrey.
Aubri

Audra (French) a form
of Audrey.

Audrey (English) noble
strength.
**Aude, Audey, Audi, Audie,
Audra, Audray, Audre,
Audree, Audreen, Audri,
Audria, Audrianna,
Audrianne, Audrie,
Audrin, Audrina, Audriya,
Audry, Audrye**

Audris (German) fortunate,
wealthy.
Audrys

Augusta (Latin) a short
form of Augustine.
See also Gusta.
**Agusta, Auguste,
Augustia, Augustine,
Augustus, Austin,
Austina, Austine**

Augustine (Latin) majestic.
Religion: Saint Augustine
was the first Archbishop of
Canterbury. See also Tina.
**Augustina, Augustyna,
Augustyne**

'Aulani (Hawaiian) royal
messenger.
Lani, Lanie

Aura (Greek) soft breeze.
(Latin) golden. See also
Ora.

Aurelia (Latin) golden.
Mythology: the goddess
of dawn. See also Oralia.
**Auralea, Auralee, Auralei,
Auralia, Aurea, Aureal,
Aurel, Aurele, Aurelea,
Aurelee, Aurelei,
Aureliana, Aurelie, Auria,
Aurie, Auriel, Aurielle,
Aurilia, Aurita**

Aurora (Latin) dawn.
**Aurore, Ora, Ori, Orie,
Rora**

Autumn (Latin) autumn.
Autum

Ava (Greek) an alternate
form of Eva. (Latin) a short
form of Avis.
Avada, Avae, Ave, Aveen

Avalon (Latin) island.
Avallon

Avis (Latin) bird.
Avais, Avi, Avia, Aviana, Avianca, Aviance

Aviva (Hebrew) springtime.
See also Viva.
Avivah, Avivi, Avivice, Avni, Avnit, Avri, Avrit, Avy

Avril (French) a form of April.
Averil, Averyl, Avra, Avri, Avrilia, Avrill, Avrille, Avrillia, Avy

Aya (Hebrew) bird; fly swiftly.

Ayanna (Hindi) innocent.
Ayania

Ayasha (Persian) a form of Aisha.
Ayesha

Ayita (Cherokee) first in the dance.

Ayla (Hebrew) oak tree.
Aylana, Aylee, Ayleen, Aylene, Aylie

Aza (Arabic) comfort.

Aziza (Swahili) precious.
Azize

Baba (African) born on Thursday.
Aba

Babe (Latin) a familiar form of Barbara. (American) an alternate form of Baby.
Babby, Bebe

Babette (French, German) a familiar form of Barbara.
Babita, Barbette

Babs (American) a familiar form of Barbara.
Bab

Baby (American) baby.
Babby, Babe, Bebe

Bailey (English) bailiff.
Bailee, Bailley, Baillie, Bailly, Baily, Bali, Bayla, Baylee, Baylie, Bayly

Baka (Hindi) crane.

Bakula (Hindi) flower.

Bambi (Italian) child.
Bambee, Bambie, Bamby

Bandi (Punjabi) prisoner.
Banda, Bandy

Baptista (Latin) baptizer.
Baptiste, Batista, Battista, Bautista

Bara, Barra (Hebrew)
chosen.
Bára, Bari

Barb (Latin) a short form
of Barbara.
Barba, Barbe

Barbara (Latin) stranger,
foreigner. See also Bebe,
Varvara, Wava.
**Babara, Babb, Babbie,
Babe, Babette, Babina,
Babs, Barb, Barbara-Ann,
Barbarit, Barbarita,
Barbary, Barbeeleen,
Barbie, Barbora,
Barborka, Barbra,
Barbraann, Barbro,
Barùska, Basha, Bebe,
Bobbi, Bobbie**

Barbie (American) a famil-
iar form of Barbara.
**Barbee, Barbey, Barbi,
Barby, Baubie**

Barbra (American) a form
of Barbara.

Barrie (Irish) spear; marks-
woman. A feminine form
of Barry.
Bari, Barri

Basia (Hebrew) daughter
of God.
**Basya, Bathia, Batia,
Batya, Bitya, Bithia**

Bathsheba (Hebrew)
daughter of the oath;
seventh daughter. Bible:
a wife of King David.
See also Sheba.

**Bathshua, Batsheva,
Bersaba, Bethsabee,
Bethsheba**

Batini (Swahili) inner
thoughts.

Bayo (Yoruba) joy is found.

Bea, Bee (American) short
forms of Beatrice.

Beata (Latin) a short form
of Beatrice.
Beatta

Beatrice (Latin) blessed;
happy; bringer of joy.
See also Trish, Trixie.
**Bea, Beatrica, Béatrice,
Beatricia, Beatriks,
Beatris, Beatrisa, Beatrise,
Beatriss, Beatrissa,
Beatrix, Beatriz, Beattie,
Beatty, Bebe, Bee, Beitris,
Trice**

Bebe (Spanish) a form
of Barbara, Beatrice.
BB, Beebee, Bibi

Becca (Hebrew) a short
form of Rebecca.
Becka, Bekka

Becky (American) a familiar
form of Rebecca.
Becki, Beckie

Bedelia (Irish) an alternate
form of Bridget.
Bedeelia, Biddy, Bidelia

Bel (Hindi) sacred wood
of apple trees. A short
form of Amabel, Belinda,
Isabel.

Bela (Czech) white. (Hungarian) bright.
Belah

Belicia (Spanish) dedicated to God.
Beli, Belia, Belica

Belinda (Spanish) beautiful. Literature: a name coined by English poet Alexander Pope in *The Rape of the Lock.* See also Blinda, Linda.
Bel, Belindra, Belle, Belynda

Bella (Latin) beautiful.
Bell, Bellah

Belle (French) beautiful. A short form of Arabella, Belinda, Isabel. See also Billie.
Belita, Belli, Bellina, Belva, Belvia

Belva (Latin) beautiful view.

Bena (Native American) pheasant. See also Bina.
Benea, Beneta

Benecia (Latin) a short form of Benedicta.
Beneisha, Benish, Benisha, Benishia, Bennicia

Benedicta (Latin) blessed. A feminine form of Benedict.
Bendite, Benea, Benedetta, Benedikta, Bengta, Benicia, Benita, Benna, Benni, Bennicia, Benoîte, Binney

Benita (Spanish) a form of Benedicta.
Benetta, Benitta, Bennita, Neeta

Benni (Latin) a familiar form of Benedicta.
Bennie, Binni, Binnie, Binny

Bente (Latin) blessed.

Berget (Irish) an alternate form of Bridget.
Bergette, Bergit, Birgit, Birgita, Birgitta

Berit (German) glorious.
Beret, Berette, Berta

Berlynn (English) a combination of Bertha + Lynn.
Berla, Berlin, Berlinda, Berline, Berling, Berlyn, Berlyne, Berlynne

Bernadette (French) a form of Bernadine. See also Nadette.
Bera, Beradette, Berna, Bernadet, Bernadett, Bernadetta, Bernarda, Bernardette, Bernedet, Bernedette, Bernessa, Berneta

Bernadine (German) brave as a bear. (English) a feminine form of Bernard.
Bernadene, Bernadette, Bernadin, Bernadina, Bernardina, Bernardine, Berni

Berneta (French) a short form of Bernadette.

Berneta *(cont.)*
Bernatta, Bernetta, Bernette, Bernita

Berni (English) a familiar form of Bernadine, Bernice.
Bernie, Berny

Bernice (Greek) bringer of victory. See also Bunny, Vernice.
Berenice, Berenike, Bernessa, Berneta, Berni, Bernise, Brona, Nixie

Bertha (German) bright; illustrious; brilliant ruler. A short form of Alberta. A feminine form of Berthold. See also Birdie, Peke.
Barta, Bartha, Berlynn, Berta, Berte, Berthe, Bertita, Bertrona, Bertus

Berti (German, English) a familiar form of Gilberte, Bertina.
Berte, Bertie, Berty

Bertille (French) a form of Bertha.

Bertina (English) bright, shining. A feminine form of Bert.
Bertine

Beryl (Greek) sea green jewel.
Berri, Berrie, Berry, Beryle

Bess, Bessie (Hebrew) familiar forms of Elizabeth.
Bessi, Bessy

Beth (Hebrew, Aramaic) house of God. A short form of Bethany, Elizabeth.
Betha, Bethe, Bethia

Bethann (English) a combination of Beth + Ann.
Beth-Ann, Beth, Bethan, Bethanne, Beth-Anne

Bethany (Aramaic) house of figs. Bible: a village near Jerusalem where Lazarus lived.
Beth, Bethane, Bethanee, Bethaney, Bethani, Bethania, Bethanie, Bethann, Bethanney, Bethannie, Bethanny, Bethena, Betheny, Bethia, Bethina, Bethney

Betsy (American) a familiar form of Elizabeth.
Betsey, Betsi, Betsie

Bette (French) a form of Betty.
Beta, Beti, Betka, Bett, Betta, Betti, Bettie

Bettina (American) a combination of Beth + Tina.
Betina, Betine, Betti, Bettine

Betty (Hebrew) consecrated to God. (English) a familiar form of Elizabeth.
Bette, Bettye, Bettyjean, Betty-Jean, Bettyjo, Betty-Jo, Bettylou, Betty-Lou, Betuska, Bety, Biddy, Boski, Bözsi

Betula (Hebrew) girl, maiden.

Beulah (Hebrew) married. Bible: the Land of Beulah is a name for Israel.
Beula, Beulla, Beullah

Bev (English) a short form of Beverly.

Beverly (English) beaver field. See also Buffy.
Bev, Bevalee, Bevan, Bevann, Bevanne, Bevany, Beverle, Beverlee, Beverley, Beverlie, Beverlyann, Bevlyn, Bevlynn, Bevlynne, Bevvy, Verly

Beverlyann (American) a combination of Beverly + Ann.
Beverliann, Beverlianne, Beverlyanne

Bian (Vietnamese) hidden; secretive.

Bianca (Italian) white. See also Blanca, Vianca.
Bellanca, Beonca, Beyonca, Biancha, Biancia, Bianey, Binney, Bionca, Bioncha, Blanche

Bibi (Latin) a short form of Bibiana. (Arabic) lady. (Spanish) an alternate form of Bebe.

Bibiana (Latin) lively.
Bibi

Biddy (Irish) a familiar form of Bedelia.
Biddie

Billie (German, French) a familiar form of Belle, Wilhelmina. (English) strong willed.
Bilee, Bili, Billi, Billy, Billye

Billie-Jean (American) a combination of Billie + Jean.
Billiejean, Billyjean, Billy-Jean

Billie-Jo (American) a combination of Billie + Jo.
Billiejo, Billyjo, Billy-Jo

Bina (Hebrew) wise; understanding. (Latin) a short form of Sabina. (Swahili) dancer. See also Bena.
Binah, Binney, Binta, Bintah

Binney (English) a familiar form of Benedicta, Bianca, Bina.
Binnee, Binnie, Binny

Birdie (German) a familiar form of Bertha. (English) bird.
Bird, Birdee, Birdella, Birdena, Birdey, Birdi, Birdy, Byrd, Byrdey, Byrdie, Byrdy

Birgitte (Swedish) a form of Bridget.
Birgit, Birgita

Blaine (Irish) thin.
Blane, Blayne

Blair (Scottish) plains
dweller.
Blaire, Blayre

Blaise (French) one who
stammers.
**Blasha, Blasia, Blaza,
Blaze, Blazena**

Blake (English) dark.
**Blakelee, Blakeley,
Blakesley**

Blanca (Italian) an alternate
form of Bianca.
Bellanca, Blancka, Blanka

Blanche (French) a form
of Bianca.
**Blanca, Blanch, Blancha,
Blinney**

Blinda (American) a short
form of Belinda.
Blynda

Bliss (English) blissful,
joyful.
Blisse, Blyss, Blysse

Blodwyn (Welsh) flower.
See also Wynne.
**Blodwen, Blodwynne,
Blodyn**

Blondelle (French) blond,
fair haired.
Blondell, Blondie

Blondie (American) a familiar form of Blondell.
Blondee, Blondey, Blondy

Blossom (English) flower.

Blum (Yiddish) flower.
Bluma

Blythe (English) happy,
cheerful.
Blithe, Blyth

Bo (Chinese) precious.

Boacha (Hebrew) blessed.
A feminine form of Baruch.

Bobbette (American)
a familiar form of Roberta.
Bobbet, Bobbetta

Bobbi, Bobbie (American)
familiar forms of Barbara,
Roberta.
**Baubie, Bobbisue, Bobby,
Bobbye, Bobi, Bobie,
Bobina, Bobbie-Jean,
Bobbie-Lynn, Bobbie-Sue**

Bobbi-Ann, Bobbie-Ann
(American) combinations
of Bobbi + Ann,
Bobbie + Ann.
**Bobbiann, Bobbi-Anne,
Bobbianne, Bobbie-Anne,
Bobby-Ann, Bobbyann,
Bobby-Anne, Bobbyanne**

Bobbi-Jo (American)
a combination of
Bobbi + Jo.
**Bobbiejo, Bobbie-Jo,
Bobbijo, Bobby-Jo, Bobijo**

Bobbi-Lee (American)
a combination of
Bobbi + Lee.
**Bobbie-Lee, Bobbilee,
Bobbylee, Bobby-Leigh,
Bobile**

Bonita (Spanish) pretty.
Bonnie, Bonny

Bonnie, Bonny (English, Scottish) beautiful, pretty. (Spanish) familiar forms of Bonita.
Boni, Bonie, Bonne, Bonnee, Bonnell, Bonnetta, Bonney, Bonni, Bonnin

Bonnie-Bell (American) a combination of Bonnie + Belle.
Bonnebell, Bonnebelle, Bonnibell, Bonnibelle, Bonniebell, Bonniebelle, Bonnybell, Bonnybelle

Branda (Hebrew) blessing.

Brandi, Brandie (Dutch) alternate forms of Brandy.
Brandice, Brandee, Brandii, Brandily, Brandin, Brandis, Brandise, Brani, Branndie

Brandy (Dutch) an after-dinner drink made from distilled wine.
Brand, Branda, Brandace, Brandaise, Brandala, Brande, Brandea, Brandee, Brandei, Brandeli, Brandell, Brandi, Brandye, Brandylee, Brandy-Lee, Brandy-Leigh, Brandyn, Brann, Brantley, Branyell

Brandy-Lynn (American) a combination of Brandy + Lynn.
Brandalyn, Brandalynn, Brandelyn, Brandelynn, Brandelynne, Brandilyn, Brandilynn, Brandilynne, Brandlin, Brandlyn, Brandlynn, Brandlynne, Brandolyn, Brandolynn, Brandolynne, Brandylyn, Brandy-Lyn, Brandylynne, Brandy-Lynne

Breana, Breanna (Irish) alternate forms of Briana.
Breanda, Bre-Anna, Breauna, Breawna, Breeana, Breeanna, Breeauna, Breiana, Breiann, Breila, Breina

Breann, Breanne (Irish) alternate forms of Briana.
Bre-Ann, Bre-Anne, Breaunne, Bree, Breean, Breeann, Breeanne, Breelyn, Breiann, Breighann, Brieann, Brieon

Breck (Irish) freckled.

Bree (Irish) a short form of Breann. (English) broth. See also Brie.
Brea, Breah, Breay, Breea, Brei, Breigh

Breena (Irish) fairy palace.
Breina, Brena, Brina

Brenda (Irish) little raven. (English) sword. A feminine form of Brendan.
Brendell, Brendelle, Brendette, Brendie, Brendyl

Brenda-Lee (American)
a combination of
Brenda + Lee.
**Brendalee, Brendaleigh,
Brendali, Brendaly,
Brendalys, Brenlee,
Brenley**

Brenna (Irish) an alternate
form of Brenda.
**Bren, Brenie, Brenin,
Brenn, Brennah,
Brennaugh**

Brett (Irish) a short form
of Brittany. See also Brita.
**Bret, Bretta, Brette,
Brettin, Bretton**

Briana, Brianna (Irish)
strong; virtuous, honor-
able. Feminine forms
of Brian.
**Brana, Breana, Breann,
Bria, Briah, Briahna,
Briand, Brianda, Brie-Ann,
Briannah, Brianne,
Brianni, Briannon,
Briauna, Brina, Briona,
Bryanna, Bryna**

Brianne (Irish) an alternate
form of Briana.
**Briane, Briann, Brienne,
Bryanne, Bryn, Brynn,
Brynne**

Briar (French) heather.
**Brear, Brier, Briet, Brieta,
Brietta, Brya, Bryar**

Bridey (Irish) a familiar
form of Bridget.
Bridi, Bridie, Brydie

Bridget (Irish) strong.
See also Bedelia, Bryga,
Gitta.
**Beret, Berget, Biddy,
Birgitte, Bride, Bridey,
Bridger, Bridgete,
Bridgett, Bridgid,
Bridgot, Brietta, Brigada,
Briget, Brigid, Brigida,
Brigitte, Brita**

Bridgett, Bridgette (Irish)
alternate forms of Bridget.
**Bridgitte, Brigette,
Briggitte, Brigitta**

Brie (French) a type
of cheese. Geography:
a region in France known
for its cheese. See also
Bree.
**Brielle, Briena, Brieon,
Briette**

Brie-Ann (American)
a combination of Brie +
Ann. See also Briana.
**Brieann, Brieanna,
Brieanne, Brie-Anne**

Brielle (French) a form
of Brie.

Brienne (French) a form
of Briana.
Brienn

Brigitte (French) a form
of Bridget.
**Brigette, Briggitte, Brigit,
Brigita**

Brina (Latin) a short form
of Sabrina. (Irish) a familiar
form of Briana.
Brin, Brinan, Brinda,

Brindi, Brindy, Briney,
Brinia, Brinlee, Brinly,
Brinn, Brinna, Brinnan,
Briona, Bryn, Bryna

Briona (Irish) an alternate
form of Briana.
Breona, Brione, Brionna,
Brionne, Briony, Bryony

Brisa (Spanish) beloved.
Mythology: Briseis was the
Greek name of Achilles's
beloved.
Breezy, Breza, Brisha,
Brishia, Brissa, Bryssa

Brita (Irish) an alternate
form of Bridget. (English)
a short form of Brittany.
Brit, Britta

Britaney, Brittaney
(English) alternate forms
of Britany, Brittany.
Britanee, Britanny,
Britenee, Briteny,
Britianey, British,
Britkney, Britley, Britlyn,
Britney, Briton

Britani, Brittanie
(English) alternate forms
of Britany, Brittany.
Brit, Britania, Britanica,
Britanie, Britanii,
Britanni, Britannia,
Britatani, Britia, Britini,
Brittanni, Brittannia,
Brittannie, Brittenie,
Brittiani, Brittianni

Britney, Brittney (English)
alternate forms of Britany,
Brittany.

Bittney, Bridnee, Bridney,
Britnay, Britne, Britnee,
Britnei, Britni, Britny,
Britnye, Brittnay,
Brittnaye, Brittne,
Brittnea, Brittnee,
Brittneigh, Brittny,
Brytnea, Brytni

Britni, Brittni (English)
alternate forms of Britney,
Britney.
Britnie, Brittnie

Britt, Britta (Latin) short
forms of Britany, Brittany.
(Swedish) strong.
Brett, Brit, Brita, Britte

Britany, Brittany (English)
from Britain. See also
Brett.
Brita, Britana, Britaney,
Britani, Britanie, Britann,
Britlyn, Britney, Britt,
Brittainny, Brittainy,
Brittamy, Brittan,
Brittana, Brittane,
Brittanee, Brittaney,
Brittani, Brittania,
Brittanica, Brittany-Ann,
Brittanyne, Brittell,
Britten, Brittenee,
Britteney, Britteny,
Brittiany, Brittlin,
Brittlynn, Britton,
Brittoni, Brittony,
Bryttany

Britin, Brittin (English)
from Britain.
Brittin, Brittina, Brittine,
Brittinee, Brittiney,

Britin, Brittin *(cont.)*
Brittini, Brittiny

Bronwyn (Welsh) white
breasted.
**Bron, Bronia, Bronney,
Bronnie, Brony,
Bronwen, Bronwin,
Bronwynn, Bronwynne,
Bronya**

Brooke (English) brook,
stream. A feminine form
of Brook.
**Brookelle, Brookie,
Brooks, Brooky**

Brooklyn (American)
a combination of
Brooke + Lynn.
**Brookellen, Brookelyn,
Brooklin, Brooklynn,
Brooklynne**

Bruna (German) a short
form of Brunhilda.

Brunhilda (German)
armored warrior.
**Brinhilda, Brinhilde,
Bruna, Brunhilde,
Brünnhilde, Brynhild,
Brynhilda, Brynhilde,
Hilda**

Bryanna, Bryanne (Irish)
alternate forms of Briana.
Bryana, Bryann

Bryga (Polish) a form
of Bridget.
Brygid, Brygida, Brygitka

Bryn, Brynn (Latin) from
the boundary line. (Welsh)
mound.
**Brinn, Brynan, Brynee,
Brynne**

Bryna (Latin, Irish) an
alternate form of Brina.
Brynan, Brynna, Brynnan

Bryttany (English) an
alternate form of Britany,
Brittany.
**Brittyne, Brityn, Brityne,
Bryton, Bryttani, Bryttine,
Bryttney**

Buffy (American) buffalo;
from the plains.
**Buffee, Buffey, Buffie,
Buffye**

Bunny (Greek) a familiar
form of Bernice. (English)
little rabbit. See also
Bonnie.
Bunni, Bunnie

Burgundy (French)
Geography: a region
of France known for its
burgundy wine.
**Burgandi, Burgandie,
Burgandy**

Cachet (French) prestigious; desirous.
Cache, Cachea, Cachee, Cachée

Cadence (Latin) rhythm.
Cadena, Cadenza, Kadena

Cady (English) an alternate form of Kady.
Cade, Cadee, Cadey, Cadi, Cadie, Cadine, Cadori, Cadye

Caeley, Cailey, Cayley (American) alternate forms of Kaylee, Kelly.
Caelee, Caelie, Cailee, Cailie, Caylee, Caylie

Cai (Vietnamese) feminine.
Cae, Cay, Caye

Cailida (Spanish) adoring.
Kailida

Cailin (American) a form of Caitlin.
Caileen, Cailene, Cailine, Cailyn, Cailynn, Cailynne, Cayleen, Caylene, Caylin, Cayline, Caylyn, Caylyne, Caylynne

Caitlin (Irish) pure. An alternate form of Cathleen. See also Kaitlin, Katelin.
Caeley, Cailey, Cailin,
Caitlan, Caitland, Caitlandt, Caitleen, Caitlen, Caitlene, Caitline, Caitlinn, Caitlon, Caitlyn, Caitria, Caitriona, Catlee, Catleen, Catleene, Catlin, Cayley

Caitlyn (Irish) an alternate form of Caitlin. See also Kaitlyn.
Caitlynn, Caitlynne, Catlyn, Catlynn, Catlynne

Cala (Arabic) castle, fortress. See also Callie, Kala.
Calah, Calan, Calla, Callah

Calandra (Greek) lark.
Caelan, Cailan, Calan, Calandria, Caleida, Calendra, Calendre, Caylan, Kalan, Kalandra, Kalandria

Caleigh, Caley (American) alternate forms of Caeley, Kaylee, Kelly.

Cali, Calli (Greek) alternate forms of Callie. See also Kali.

Calida (Spanish) warm; ardent.
Calina, Calinda, Callida, Callinda, Kalida

Callie (Greek, Arabic) a familiar form of Cala, Callista. See also Cayla, Kalli.
Cal, Caleigh, Caley, Cali, Calie, Callee, Calley, Calli, Cally

Callista (Greek) most beautiful. See also Kallista.
Calesta, Calista, Callie, Calysta

Calvina (Latin) bald. A feminine form of Calvin.
Calvine, Calvinetta, Calvinette

Calypso (Greek) concealer. Botany: a white orchid with purple or yellow markings. Mythology: the sea nymph who held Odysseus captive for seven years.
Cally, Caly, Lypsie, Lypsy

Cam (Vietnamese) sweet citrus.
Kam

Cambria (Latin) from Wales. See also Kambria.
Camber, Camberlee, Camberleigh, Camberly, Camberry, Cambie, Cambrea, Cambree, Cambrya, Cami

Camellia (Italian) evergreen tree or shrub.
Camala, Camalia, Camallia, Camela, Camelia, Camelita, Camella, Camellita, Cami, Kamelia, Kamellia

Cameo (Latin) gem or shell on which a portrait is carved.
Cami, Kameo

Cameron (Scottish) crooked nose. See also Kameron.
Camera, Cameran, Cameren, Cameri, Cameria, Camesha, Cameshia, Cami

Cami (French) a short form of Camille. See also Kami.
Camey, Camie, Cammi, Cammie, Cammy, Cammye

Camilla (Italian) a form of Camille. See also Kamila, Mila.
Camia, Camila, Camillia, Chamelea, Chamelia, Chamika, Chamila, Chamilia

Camille (French) young ceremonial attendant. See also Millie.
Cam, Cami, Camill, Camilla, Cammille, Cammillie, Cammilyn, Cammyl, Cammyll, Camylle, Chamelle, Chamille, Kamille

Candace (Greek) glittering white; glowing. History: the name and title of the queens of ancient Ethiopia. See also Dacey, Kandace.
Cace, Canace, Canda, Candas, Candelle, Candi, Candice, Candida, Candis, Candyce

Candi, Candy (American) familiar forms of Candace, Candice, Candida. See also Kandi.
Candee, Candie

Candice, Candis, Candyce (Greek) alternate forms of Candace.
Candes, Candi, Candias, Candies, Candise, Candiss, Candus, Candys, Candyse, Cyndyss

Candida (Latin) bright white.
Candeea, Candi, Candia, Candide, Candita

Candra (Latin) glowing.
Candrea, Candria, Kandra

Cantara (Arabic) small crossing.
Cantarah

Cantrelle (French) song.
Cantrella

Capri (Italian) a short form of Caprice. Geography: an island off the west coast of Italy. See also Kapri.
Caprie, Capris

Caprice (Italian) fanciful.
Cappi, Caprece, Capricia, Caprina, Caprise, Capritta

Cara (Latin) dear. (Irish) friend. See also Karah.
Caragh, Carah, Caralea, Caralee, Caralia, Caralie, Caralin, Caraline, Caralyn, Caranda, Carey, Carra

Caressa (French) a form of Carissa.
Caresa, Carese, Caresse, Carissa, Charessa, Charesse, Karessa

Carey (Welsh) a familiar form of Cara, Caroline, Karen, Katherine. See also Carrie, Kari.
Caree, Cari, Carrey, Cary

Cari, Carie (Welsh) alternate forms of Carey, Kari.

Carina (Greek) a familiar form of Cora. (Italian) dear little one. (Swedish) a form of Karen.
Carena, Carin, Carine, Caryn

Carissa (Greek) beloved.
Caressa, Carisa, Carrissa, Charisa, Charissa, Karissa

Carita (Latin) charitable.
Caritta, Charity, Karita, Karitta

Carla (Latin) an alternate form of Carol, Caroline. (German) farmer. (English) strong and womanly.
Carila, Carilla, Carlan, Carle, Carleah, Carleigh, Carlene, Carleta, Carletha, Carlethe, Carlia, Carlicia, Carliqua, Carlissa, Carlita, Carliyle, Carlonda, Carlotta, Carireca, Carlye, Carlyjo, Carlyle, Carlyse, Carlysle

Carlee, Carley (English)
alternate forms of Carly.

Carlene (English) a form
of Caroline.
Carlaen, Carlaena,
Carleen, Carleena, Carlen,
Carlena, Carlenna,
Carline, Carlyn, Carlyne,
Karlene

Carli, Carlie (English) alternate forms of Carly. See
also Karli.

Carlin (Latin) a short form
of Caroline. (Irish) little
champion.
Carlan, Carlana,
Carlandra, Carlen,
Carlina, Carlinda, Carline,
Carling, Carllan, Carllen,
Carrlin

Carlissa (American) a com-
bination of Carla + Lissa.
Carleesia, Carleeza,
Carlesia, Carlis, Carlise,
Carlisha, Carlisia, Carliss,
Carlisse, Carlissia, Carlista

Carlotta (Italian) a form
of Charlotte.
Carletta, Carlota,
Karletta, Karlotta

Carly (English) a familiar
form of Caroline,
Charlotte. See also Karli.
Carlee, Carley, Carli,
Carlie, Carlye

Carmela, Carmella
(Hebrew) garden; vine-
yard. Bible: Mount Carmel

in Israel is often thought
of as paradise. See also
Karmel.
Carma, Carmaletta,
Carmalit, Carmalita,
Carmalla, Carmarit,
Carmel, Carmeli,
Carmelia, Carmelina,
Carmelit, Carmelita,
Carmelitha, Carmelitia,
Carmelle, Carmellia,
Carmellina, Carmellit,
Carmellita, Carmellitha,
Carmellitia, Carmesa,
Carmesha, Carmi, Carmie,
Carmiel, Carmil, Carmila,
Carmilla, Carmisha,
Leeta, Lita

Carmen (Latin) song.
Religion: Santa Maria
del Carmen—Saint Mary
of Mount Carmel—is one
of the titles of the Virgin
Mary. See also Karmen.
Carma, Carmaine,
Carman, Carmelina,
Carmelita, Carmencita,
Carmene, Carmi, Carmia,
Carmin, Carmina,
Carmine, Carmita,
Carmon, Carmynn,
Charmaine

Carol (German) farmer.
(French) song of joy.
(English) strong and
womanly. A feminine
form of Carl, Charles.
See also Carlene,
Charlene, Charlotte,
Kalle, Karoll.

Carel, Carely, Cariel,
Carilis, Carilise, Carilyse,
Carle, Carley, Carlita,
Caro, Carola, Carole,
Caroleen, Carolenia,
Carolinda, Caroline,
Caroll, Carolyn, Carrie,
Carrol, Carroll, Caryl

Carolann (American)
a form of Caroline.
Carolan, Carolane,
Carolanne,

Carole (English) an alternate form of Carol.
Carolee, Karole, Karrole

Carolina (Italian) a form
of Caroline.
Carilena, Carlena,
Carlina, Carlita, Carlota,
Carrolena, Karolina

Caroline (French) little and
womanly. See also Carla,
Carlin, Karoline.
Caralin, Caraline,
Carileen, Carilene, Carilin,
Cariline, Carling, Carly,
Caro, Carolann, Carolin,
Carolina, Carrie,
Carroleen, Carrolene,
Carrolin, Carroline, Cary,
Charlene

Carolyn (English) a form of
Caroline. See also Karolyn.
Caralyn, Caralynn,
Caralynne, Carilyn,
Carilynn, Carilynne,
Carlyn, Carlynn, Carlynne,
Carolyne, Carolynn,

Carolynne, Carrolyn,
Carrolynn, Carrolynne

Caron (Welsh) loving,
kind-hearted, charitable.
Carron, Carrone

Carra (Irish) an alternate
form of Cara.

Carrie (English) a familiar
form of Carol, Caroline.
See also Carey, Kari, Karri.
Carree, Carri, Carria,
Carry

Caryl (Latin) a form
of Carol.
Caryle, Caryll, Carylle

Caryn (Danish) a form
of Karen.
Caren, Caron, Caronne,
Carren, Carrin, Carron,
Caryna, Caryne, Carynn

Carys (Welsh) love.
Caris, Caryse, Ceris, Cerys

Casey (Greek) a familiar
form of Acacia. (Irish)
brave. See also Kasey.
Cacy, Cascy, Casie, Cass,
Casse, Cassee, Cassey,
Cassye, Casy, Cayce,
Cayse, Caysee, Caysy

Casie (Irish) an alternate
form of Casey.
Caci, Casci, Cascie, Casi,
Cass, Cayci, Caysi, Caysie,
Cazzi

Cass (Greek) a short form
of Cassandra.

Cassandra (Greek) helper
of men. Mythology:
a prophetess of ancient
Greece whose prophesies
were not believed. See
also Kassandra, Sandra,
Sandy, Zandra.
**Casandera, Casandra,
Casandre, Casandrey,
Casandri, Casandria,
Casaundra, Casaundre,
Casaundri, Casaundria,
Casondra, Casondre,
Casondri, Casondria,
Cass, Cassandre,
Cassandri, Cassandry,
Cassaundra, Cassaundre,
Cassaundri, Cassie,
Cassondra, Cassondre,
Cassondri, Cassondria,
Cassundra, Cassundre,
Cassundri, Cassundria**

Cassia (Greek) spicy cinna-
mon. See also Kasia.
Casia, Cass

Cassidy (Irish) clever.
See also Kassidy.
**Casadee, Casadi, Casadie,
Cass, Cassadi, Cassadie,
Cassadina, Cassady,
Casseday, Cassiddy,
Cassidee, Cassidi, Cassidie,
Cassity**

Cassie (Greek) a familiar
form of Cassandra,
Catherine. See also Kassie.
Cassey, Cassi, Cassy

Cassiopeia (Greek) clever.
Mythology: the wife of the

Ethiopian king Cepheus;
the mother of Andromeda.
Cass, Cassio

Catalina (Spanish) a form
of Catherine.
**Cataleen, Catalena,
Catalene, Catalin,
Catalyn, Catalyna,
Cateline, Kataleena,
Katalina, Katalyn**

Catherine (Greek) pure.
(English) a form of
Katherine.
**Cat, Catalina, Catarina,
Catarine, Cate, Caterina,
Catha, Cathann,
Cathanne, Catharina,
Catharine, Cathenne,
Catheren, Catherene,
Catheria, Catherin,
Catherina, Catheryn,
Cathi, Cathleen, Cathrine,
Cathryn, Cathy, Catlaina,
Catreeka, Catrelle,
Catrice, Catricia, Catrika,
Catrin, Catrina, Catryn,
Catteeka, Cattiah**

Cathi, Cathy (Greek)
familiar forms of
Catherine, Cathleen.
See also Kathy.
**Catha, Cathe, Cathee,
Cathey, Cathie**

Cathleen (Irish) a form
of Catherine. See also
Caitllin, Katelin, Kathleen.
**Cathaleen, Cathelin,
Cathelina, Cathelyn,
Cathi, Cathleana,**

**Cathlene, Cathleyn,
Cathlin, Cathlyn,
Cathlyne, Cathy**

Cathrine, Cathryn
(Greek) alternate forms
of Catherine.

Catrina (Slavic) a form
of Catherine, Katrina.
**Catina, Catreen, Catreena,
Catrene, Catrenia,
Catrine, Catrinia,
Catriona, Catroina**

Cayla (Hebrew) an alter-
nate form of Kayla.
**Cailee, Cailey, Cailie, Caily,
Calee, Caly, Caylee, Cayley,
Caylie, Cayly**

Cecilia (Latin) blind.
A feminine form of Cecil.
See also Cicely, Cissy,
Sela, Sheila, Sissy.
**Cacelia, Cacilia, Cacilie,
Caecilia, Cece, Ceceilia,
Ceceli, Cecelia, Cecely,
Cecelyn, Cecette, Cecil,
Cecila, Cecile, Cecilea,
Ceciley, Cecilija, Cecilla,
Cecille, Cecillia, Cecily,
Ceclia, Cecylia, Cee, Ceil,
Ceila, Ceilagh, Ceileh,
Ceileigh, Ceilena, Celia,
Cescelia, Cescelie, Cescily,
Cesia, Cesya, Cicelia,
Cicely, Cilley, Secilia, Selia**

Ceil (Latin) a short form
of Cecilia.
Ceel, Ciel

Celena (Greek) an alternate
form of Selena.

**Celeen, Celeena, Celene,
Celenia**

Celeste (Latin) celestial,
heavenly.
**Cele, Celense, Celes,
Celesia, Celesley, Celest,
Celesta, Celestia,
Celestial, Celestin,
Celestina, Celestine,
Celestinia, Celestyn,
Celestyna, Celina, Celine,
Selestina**

Celia (Latin) a short form
of Cecilia.
Ceilia, Celie

Celina (Greek) an alternate
form of Celena.
**Caleena, Calena, Calina,
Celena, Celinda, Celinka,
Celka, Selina**

Celine (Greek) an alternate
form of Celena.
**Caline, Celeen, Celene,
Céline, Cellina, Cellinn**

Cerella (Latin) springtime.
Cerelisa, Ceres

Cerise (French) cherry;
cherry red.
**Cera, Cerea, Cerese, Ceri,
Ceria, Cerice, Cericia,
Cerissa, Cerria, Cerrice,
Cerrina, Cerrita, Cerryce,
Ceryce, Cherise**

Chablis (French) a dry,
white wine. Geography:
a region in France where
wine grapes are grown.
Chabley, Chabli

Chadee (French) from Chad, a country in north central Africa. See also Sade.
Chaday, Chadday, Chade, Chadea,

Chai (Hebrew) life.
Chae, Chaela, Chaeli, Chaella, Chaena

Chaka (Sanskrit) an alternate form of Chakra. See also Shaka.
Chakai, Chakia, Chakka, Chakkah

Chakra (Sanskrit) circle of energy.
Chaka, Chakara, Chakaria, Chakeitha, Chakena, Chakeria, Chakila, Chakina, Chakira, Chakrah, Chakria, Chakriya, Chakyra

Chalice (French) goblet.
Chalace, Chalcie, Chalece, Chalie, Chaliese, Chalise, Chalisk, Chalissa, Challa, Challaine, Challis, Challisse, Challysse, Chalsey, Chalyce, Chalyn, Chalyse, Chalysse

Chalina (Spanish) a form of Rose.

Chalonna (American) a combination of the prefix Cha + Lona.
Chalon, Chalonn, Chalonne, Shalon

Chambray (French) a lightweight fabric.
Chambre, Chambree, Chambrée

Chan (Cambodian) sweet-smelling tree.
Chanae

Chana (Hebrew) an alternate form of Hannah.

Chanda (Sanskrit) great goddess. Religion: the name assumed by the Hindu goddess Devi. See also Shanda.
Chandee, Chandey, Chandi, Chandie

Chandelle (French) candle.
Chandal, Chandel, Shandal, Shandel

Chandra (Sanskrit) moon. Religion: one of the names of the Hindu goddess Shakti. See also Shandra.
Chandre, Chandrea, Chandrelle, Chandria

Chanel (English) channel. See also Shanel.
Chaneel, Chaneil, Chanell, Chanelle, Channel

Chanell, Chanelle (English) alternate forms of Chanel.
Shanell

Channa (Hindi) chickpea.

Chantal (French) song.
Chandal, Chanta, Chantaal, Chantae,

**Chantael, Chantai,
Chantale, Chantall,
Chantalle, Chantara,
Chantarai, Chantasia,
Chantay, Chantaye,
Chanteau, Chantel,
Chantiel, Chantielle,
Chantil, Chantila,
Chantill, Chantille,
Chantle, Chantoya,
Chantra, Chantri,
Chantrice, Chantrill,
Chaunta, Chauntay**

Chantel, Chantelle
(French) alternate forms
of Chantal. See also
Shantel.
**Chante, Chantea,
Chantee, Chantée,
Chanteese, Chantela,
Chantele, Chantell,
Chantella, Chanter,
Chantey, Chantez,
Chantrel, Chantrell,
Chantrelle, Chantress,
Chaunte, Chauntea,
Chauntéa, Chauntee,
Chauntel, Chauntell,
Chauntelle, Chawntel,
Chawntell, Chawntelle,
Chontelle**

Chantilly (French) fine
lace. See also Shantille.

Chantrea (Cambodian)
moon; moonbeam.
Chantria

Chantrice (French) singer.
See also Shantrice.
Chantreese

Chardae, Charde
(Punjabi) charitable.
(French) short forms
of Chardonnay.
See also Shardae.
**Charda, Chardai, Charday,
Chardea, Chardee,
Chardée, Chardese**

Chardonnay (French)
a dry white wine.
Geography: a wine-mak-
ing region in France.
**Char, Chardae, Chardon,
Chardonay, Chardonee,
Chardonnee, Chardonnée,
Shardonay, Shardonnay**

Charis (Greek) grace;
kindness.
**Chari, Charice, Charie,
Charish, Charisse**

Charissa, Charisse
(Greek) forms of Charity.
**Charesa, Charese, Charis,
Charisa, Charise,
Charisha, Charissee,
Charista**

Charity (Latin) charity,
kindness.
**Carisa, Carisia, Carissa,
Carita, Chariety, Charis,
Charissa, Charisse,
Charista, Charita, Chariti,
Sharity**

Charla (French, English)
a short form of Charlene,
Charlotte.
Char

Charlaine (English) an alternate form of Charlene.
Charlane, Charlanna, Charlayne

Charlene (English) little and womanly. A form of Caroline. See also Carol, Karla, Sharlene.
Charla, Charlaina, Charlaine, Charleen, Charleesa, Charlena, Charlesena, Charline, Charlyn, Charlyne, Charlynn, Charlynne, Charlzina

Charlie (German, English) strong and womanly. A feminine form of Charles.
Charla, Charle, Charlea, Charlee, Charleigh, Charley, Charli, Charyl, Chatty, Sharli, Sharlie

Charlotte (French) little and womanly. A form of Caroline. Literature: Charlotte Brontë was a British novelist and poet best known for her novel *Jane Eyre*. See also Karlotte, Lotte, Sharlotte, Sherry, Tottie.
Carla, Carlotta, Carly, Char, Chara, Charil, Charl, Charla, Charle, Charlene, Charlet, Charlett, Charletta, Charlette, Charlie, Charlisa, Charlita, Charlott, Charlotta, Charlotty, Charmaine, Charo, Charolet,
Charolette, Charoline, Charolot, Charolotte

Charmaine (French) a form of Carmen. See also Sharmaine.
Charamy, Charma, Charmain, Charmalique, Charman, Charmane, Charmar, Charmara, Charmayane, Charmeen, Charmene, Charmese, Charmian, Charmin, Charmine, Charmion, Charmisa, Charmon, Charmyn

Charo (Spanish) a familiar form of Rosa.

Chasity (Latin) an alternate form of Chastity.
Chasa Dee, Chasadie, Chasady, Chasidy, Chasiti, Chassedi, Chassey, Chassidy, Chassie, Chassity, Chassy

Chastity (Latin) pure.
Chasity, Chasta, Chastady, Chastidy, Chastin, Chastitie, Chastney, Chasty

Chava (Hebrew) life. (Yiddish) bird. Bible: the original name of Eve.
Chabah, Chavah, Chavalah, Chavarra, Chavarria, Chave, Chavé, Chavel, Chaveli, Chavette, Chaviva, Chavonne, Chavvis, Hava, Kaÿa

Chavella (Spanish) an alternate form of Isabel.
Chavelle, Chevelle, Chevie

Chavi (Gypsy) girl.
Chavali

Chavon (Hebrew) an alternate form of Jane.
Chavonn, Chavonne, Shavon

Chavonne (Hebrew) an alternate form of Chavon. (American) a combination of the prefix Cha + Yvonne.
Chavondria, Chavonna, Chevon, Chevonn, Chevonna

Chaya (Hebrew) life; living.
Chaike, Chayka, Chayla, Chaylea, Chaylene, Chayra

Chelsea (English) seaport. See also Kelsi, Shelsea.
Chelese, Chelesia, Chelsa, Chelsae, Chelse, Chelsee, Chelsei, Chelsey, Chelsie, Chesea, Cheslee

Chelsey (English) an alternate form of Chelsea. See also Kelsey.
Chelcy, Chelsay, Chelsy, Chesley

Chelsie (English) an alternate form of Chelsea.
Chelcie, Chelli, Chellie, Chellise, Chellsie, Chelsi, Chelsia, Cheslie, Chessie

Chenoa (Native American) white dove.

Chenee, Chenice, Chenika, Chenita, Chenna

Cher (French) beloved, dearest. (English) a short form of Cherilyn.
Chere, Cheree, Chereen, Chereena, Cheri, Cherice, Cherie, Cherise, Cherish, Cherrelle, Cherrie, Cherry, Cherye, Sher

Cherelle, Cherrelle (French) alternate forms of Cheryl. See also Sherelle.
Charell, Charelle

Cheri, Cherie (French) familiar forms of Cher.
Chérie

Cherilyn (English) a combination of Cheryl + Lynn.
Cher, Cheralyn, Cherilynn, Cherralyn, Cherrilyn, Cherrylyn, Cherylin, Cheryl-Lyn, Cheryl-Lynn, Cheryl-Lynne, Cherylyn, Cherylynn, Cherylynne, Sherilyn

Cherise (French) a form of Cherish. See also Sharice.
Charisa, Charise, Cherece, Chereese, Cheresa, Cherese, Cheresse, Cherice

Cherish (English) dearly held, precious.
Charish, Charisha, Cheerish, Cherise, Cherishe, Cherrish, Sherish

Cherokee (Native American) a tribal name.
Cherika, Cherkita, Sherokee

Cherry (Latin) a familiar form of Charity. (French) cherry; cherry red.
Chere, Cheree, Cherey, Cherida, Cherise, Cherita, Cherrey, Cherri, Cherrie, Cherrise, Cherrita, Cherry-Ann, Cherry-Anne, Cherrye, Chery

Cheryl (French) beloved. See also Sheryl.
Charel, Charil, Charyl, Cherelle, Cherilyn, Cherrelle, Cheryl-Ann, Cheryl-Anne, Cheryle, Cherylee, Cherylene, Cheryll, Cherylle, Cheryl-Lee, Cheryline, Cheryn

Chesna (Slavic) peaceful.
Chesnee, Chesney, Chesnie, Chesny

Cheyenne (Cheyenne) a tribal name. See also Sheyenne.
Chey, Cheyan, Cheyana, Cheyann, Cheyanne, Cheyene, Cheyenna, Chi, Chi-Anna, Chie, Chyann, Chyanna, Chyanne

Chiara (Italian) a form of Clara.
Cheara

Chika (Japanese) near and dear.

Chikaka, Chikako, Chikara, Chikona

Chiku (Swahili) chatterer.

China (Chinese) fine porcelain. Geography: a country in eastern Asia. See also Ciana, Shina.
Chinaetta, Chinasa, Chinda, Chinea, Chinesia, Chinita, Chinna, Chinwa, Chyna, Chynna

Chinira (Swahili) God receives.
Chinarah, Chinirah

Chinue (Ibo) God's own blessing.

Chiquita (Spanish) little one. See also Shiquita.
Chaqueta, Chaquita, Chica, Chickie, Chicky, Chikata, Chikita, Chiqueta, Chiquila, Chiquite, Chiquitha, Chiquithe, Chiquitia, Chiquitta

Chiyo (Japanese) eternal.
Chiya

Chloe (Greek) blooming, verdant. Mythology: the goddess of agriculture.
Chloé, Chlöe, Chloee, Clo, Cloe, Cloey, Kloe

Chloris (Greek) pale. Mythology: the only daughter of Niobe to escape the vengeful arrows of Apollo and Artemis. See also Loris.
Cloris, Clorissa

Cho (Korean) beautiful.
Choe

Cholena (Native American) bird.

Chriki (Swahili) blessing.

Chris (Greek) a short form of Christina. See also Kris.
Chrys, Cris

Chrissa (Greek) a short form of Christina. See also Khrissa.
Chryssa, Crissa, Cryssa

Chrissy (English) a familiar form of Christina.
Chrisie, Chrissee, Chrissie, Crissie, Khrissy

Christa (German) a short form of Christina. History: Christa McAuliffe, an American school teacher, was the first civilian on a U.S. space flight. See also Krista.
Chrysta, Crista, Crysta

Christabel (Latin, French) beautiful Christian.
Christabella, Christable, Cristabel, Kristabel

Christal (Latin) an alternate form of Crystal. (Scottish) a form of Christina.
Christalene, Christalin, Christaline, Christall, Christalle, Christalyn, Christel, Christelle, Chrystal

Christen, Christin (Greek) alternate forms of Christina.
Christan, Christyn, Chrystan, Chrysten, Chrystin, Chrystyn, Crestienne, Kristen

Christi, Christie (Greek) short forms of Christina, Christine.
Christy, Chrysti, Chrystie, Chrysty, Kristi

Christian, Christiana (Greek) alternate forms of Christina. See also Kristian, Krystian.
Christiane, Christiann, Christi-Ann, Christianna, Christianne, Christi-Anne, Christianni, Christienne, Christy-Ann, Christy-Anne, Chrystyann, Chrystyanne, Crystiann, Crystianne

Christin (Greek) a short form of Christina.
Christen

Christina (Greek) Christian; anointed. See also Khristina, Kristina, Stina, Tina.
Chris, Chrissa, Chrissy, Christa, Christeena, Christella, Christena, Christi, Christian, Christiana, Christie, Christin, Christine, Christinea, Christinna, Christna, Christy, Christyna, Chrys,

Christina (cont.)
Chrystena, Chrystina, Chrystyna, Cristeena, Cristena, Cristina, Cristy, Crystal, Crystina, Crystyna

Christine (French, English) forms of Christina. See also Kirsten, Kristen, Kristine.
Chrisa, Christeen, Christen, Christene, Christi, Christie, Christin, Christy, Chrys, Chrystine, Cristeen, Cristene, Cristine, Crystine

Christy (English) a short form of Christina, Christine.
Cristy

Chrys (English) a form of Chris.
Krys

Chu Hua (Chinese) chrysanthemum.

Chumani (Lakota) dewdrops.

Chun (Burmese) nature's renewal.

Ciana (Chinese) an alternate form of China. (Italian) a form of Jane.
Ciandra

Ciara, Cierra (Irish) black. See also Sierra.
Ceara, Cearaa, Cearia, Cearra, Cera, Ciaara, Ciarra, Ciarrah, Cieara, Ciearra, Ciearria, Ciera, Cierrah

Cicely (English) a form of Cecilia. See also Sissy.
Cicelie, Cicilie, Cicily, Cile, Cilka, Cilla, Cilli, Cillie, Cilly

Cinderella (French, English) little cinder girl. Literature: a fairy tale heroine.

Cindy (Greek) moon. (Latin) a familiar form of Cynthia. See also Sindy.
Cindee, Cindi, Cindl, Cynda, Cyndal, Cyndale, Cyndall, Cyndee, Cyndel, Cyndi, Cyndia, Cyndie, Cyndle, Cyndy

Cira (Spanish) a form of Cyrilla.

Cissy (American) a familiar form of Cecelia, Cicely.
Cissey, Cissi, Cissie

Claire (French) a form of Clara.
Clair, Clairette, Klaire, Klarye

Clara (Latin) clear; bright. Music: Clara Shumann was a famous nineteenth-century German composer. See also Chiara, Klara.
Claire, Clarabelle, Clare, Claresta, Clarette, Clarey, Clari, Claribel, Clarice, Clarie, Clarina, Clarinda, Clarine, Clarissa, Clarita, Claritza, Clarizza, Clary

Clarabelle (Latin) bright and beautiful.
Clarabella, Claribel

Clare (English) a form of Clara.

Clarice (Italian) a form of Clara.
Claris, Clarise, Clarisse, Claryce, Cleriese, Klarice, Klarise

Clarissa (Greek) brilliant. (Italian) a form of Clara. See also Klarissa.
Clarecia, Claresa, Claressa, Claresta, Clarisa, Clarissia, Clarrisa, Clarrissa, Clerissa

Clarita (Spanish) a form of Clara.
Clareta, Claretta

Claudette (French) a form of Claudia.
Clauddetta

Claudia (Latin) lame. A feminine form of Claude. See also Gladys, Klaudia.
Claudee, Claudeen, Claudelle, Claudette, Claudex, Claudiane, Claudie, Claudie-Anne, Claudina, Claudine

Clea (Greek) an alternate form of Cleo, Clio.

Clementine (Latin) merciful. A feminine form of Clement.
Clemence, Clemencie, Clemency, Clementia,
Clementina, Clemenza, Clemette

Cleo (Greek) a short form of Cleopatra.
Clea

Cleone (Greek) glorious.
Cleonie, Cliona

Cleopatra (Greek) her father's fame. History: a great Egyptian queen.
Cleo

Cleta (Greek) illustrious.

Clio (Greek) proclaimer; glorifier. Mythology: the muse of history.
Clea

Clotilda (German) heroine.

Coco (Spanish) coconut. See also Koko.

Codi, Cody (English) cushion.
Coady, Codee, Codey, Codie, Kodi

Colby (English) coal town. Geography: a region in England known for cheese-making.
Cobi, Cobie, Colbi, Colbie, Kolby

Colette (Greek, French) a familiar form of Nicole.
Coe, Coetta, Coletta, Collet, Collete, Collett, Colletta, Collette, Kolette, Kollette

Colleen (Irish) girl. See also
Kolina.
**Coe, Coel, Cole, Coleen,
Colena, Colene, Coley,
Colina, Colinda, Coline,
Colleene, Collen, Collene,
Collie, Collina, Colline,
Colly**

Concetta (Italian) pure.
Religion: refers to the
Immaculate Conception.
Concettina

Conchita (Spanish)
conception.
**Chita, Con, Conceptia,
Concha, Conciana**

Concordia (Latin) harmonious. Mythology:
the goddess governing
the peace after war.
Con, Cordae, Cordaye

Connie (Latin) a familiar
form of Constance.
**Con, Connee, Conni,
Conny, Konnie, Konny**

Constance (Latin)
constant; firm. History:
Constance Motley was
the first African-American
woman to be appointed
as a U.S. federal judge.
See also Kosta.
**Connie, Constancia,
Constancy, Constanta,
Constantia, Constantina,
Constantine, Constanza,
Konstance**

Constanza (Spanish)
a form of Constance.
Constanz, Constanze

Consuelo (Spanish) con-
solation. Religion: Santa
Maria del Consuelo—Saint
Mary of Consolation—is a
name for the Virgin Mary.
**Consolata, Consuela,
Consuella, Consula,
Konsuela, Konsuelo**

Cora (Greek) maiden.
Mythology: the daughter
of Demeter, the goddess
of agriculture.
**Coralee, Coretta, Corey,
Corissa, Corey, Corra,
Kora**

Coral (Latin) coral.
**Corabel, Corabella,
Corabelle, Coralee,
Coraline, Coralyn, Corral,
Koral**

Coralee (American) a com-
bination of Cora + Lee.
**Coralea, Cora-Lee,
Coralena, Coralie, Corella,
Corilee, Koralie**

Corazon (Spanish) heart.

Cordelia (Latin) warm
hearted. (Welsh) sea jewel.
See also Delia, Della.
**Cordae, Cordelie, Cordett,
Cordette, Cordey, Cordi,
Cordia, Cordie, Cordilia,
Cordula, Cordy, Kordelia,
Kordula**

Coretta (Greek) a familiar
form of Cora.
**Coreta, Corette, Correta,
Corretta, Corrette,
Koretta, Korretta**

Corey, Cory (Greek) famil-
iar forms of Cora. (Irish)
from the hollow. See also
Kori.
**Coree, Cori, Correy,
Correye, Corry**

Cori, Corie, Corrie (Irish)
alternate forms of Corey.
**Corian, Coriann, Cori-Ann,
Corianne, Corri, Corrie-
Ann, Corrie-Anne**

Corina, Corinna (Greek)
familiar forms of Corinne.
See also Korina.
**Coreena, Corinda,
Correna, Corrina,
Corrinna**

Corinne (Greek) maiden.
**Coreen, Coren, Corin,
Corina, Corinda, Corine,
Corinee, Corinn, Corinna,
Correen, Corren,
Corrianne, Corrin,
Corrinn, Corrinne, Corryn,
Coryn, Corynn, Corynna**

Corissa (Greek) a familiar
form of Cora.
**Coresa, Coressa, Corisa,
Korissa**

Corliss (English) cheerful;
good hearted.
**Corlisa, Corlise, Corlissa,
Corly, Korliss**

Cornelia (Latin) horn
colored. A feminine form
of Cornelius. See also
Kornelia, Nelia, Nellie.
**Carna, Carniella,
Corneilla, Cornela,
Cornelie, Cornella,
Cornelle, Cornie,
Cornilear, Cornisha, Corny**

Cortney (English) an alter-
nate form of Courtney.
**Cortnea, Cortnee,
Cortneia, Cortni, Cortnie,
Cortny, Corttney**

Cosette (French) a familiar
form of Nicole.
**Cosetta, Cossetta,
Cossette, Cozette**

Courtenay (English)
an alternate form of
Courtney.
Courteney

Courtney (English) from
the court. See also
Kortney, Kourtney.
**Cortney, Courtena,
Courtenay, Courtene,
Courtnae, Courtnay,
Courtnee, Courtnée,
Courtnei, Courtni,
Courtnie, Courtny,
Courtonie**

Crista (Italian) a form
of Christa.

Cristen, Cristin (Irish)
forms of Christen, Christin.
See also Kristin.
**Cristan, Cristyn, Crystan,
Crysten, Crystin, Crystyn**

Cristina (Greek) an alternate form of Christina.
See also Kristina.
Cristiona, Cristy

Cristy (English) a familiar form of Cristina. An alternate form of Christy.
See also Kristy.
Cristey, Cristi, Cristie, Crysti, Crystie, Crysty

Crystal (Latin) clear, brilliant glass. See also Krystal.
Christal, Chrystal, Chrystal-Lynn, Chrystel, Cristal, Cristalie, Cristalina, Cristalle, Cristel, Cristela, Cristelia, Cristella, Cristelle, Cristhie, Cristle, Crystala, Crystal-Ann, Crystal-Anne, Crystale, Crystalee, Crystalin, Crystall, Crystaly, Crystel, Crystelia, Crysthelle, Crystl, Crystle, Crystol, Crystole, Crystyl

Crystalin (American) a form of Crystal.
Cristilyn, Crystalina, Crystal-Lee, Crystal-Lynn, Crystalyn, Crystalynn

Cybele (Greek) an alternate form of Sybil.
Cybel, Cybil, Cybill, Cybille

Cynthia (Greek) moon. Mythology: another name for Artemis, the moon goddess. See also Hyacinth, Kynthia.
Cindy, Cyneria, Cynethia, Cynithia, Cynthea, Cynthiana, Cynthiann, Cynthie, Cynthria, Cynthy, Cynthya, Cyntreia, Cythia

Cyrilla (Greek) ladylike. A feminine form of Cyril.
Cerelia, Cerella, Cira, Cirilla, Cyrella

Dacey (Greek) a familiar form of Candace. (Irish) southerner. See also Daisy.
Dacee, Daci, Dacia, Dacie, Dacy, Daicee, Daicie, Daicy, Daycee, Daycie, Daycy

Dae (English) day. See also Dai.
Daeleen, Daelena, Daesha

Daelynn (American) a combination of Dae + Lynn.
Daelin, Daelyn, Daelynne

Daeshawna (American) a combination of Dae + Shawna.
Daeshan, Daeshanda, Daeshandra, Daeshandria,

**Daeshaun, Daeshauna,
Daeshaundra,
Daeshaundria, Daeshavon,
Daeshawn, Daeshawnda,
Daeshawndra,
Daeshawndria,
Daeshawntia, Daeshon,
Daeshona, Daeshonda,
Daeshondra, Daeshondria**

Dafny (American) a form
of Daphne.
**Dafany, Daffany, Daffie,
Daffy, Dafna, Dafne,
Dafney, Dafnie**

Dagmar (German)
glorious.
Dagmara

Dagny (Scandinavian) day.
**Dagna, Dagnanna, Dagne,
Dagney**

Dahlia (Scandinavian)
valley. Botany: a perennial
flower. See also Daliah.

Dai (Japanese) great.
See also Dae.
Daija, Daijon, Day, Daye

Daisy (English) day's eye.
Botany: a white and yellow
flower. See also Dacey.
**Daisee, Daisey, Daisi,
Daisia, Daisie, Dasey, Dasi,
Dasie, Dasy, Daysee,
Daysie, Daysy**

Dakota (Native American)
tribal name.
**Dakotah, Dakotha,
Dekoda, Dekota, Dekotah,
Dekotha**

Dale (English) valley.
**Dael, Dahl, Daile,
Daleleana, Dalena, Dalina,
Dayle**

Daliah (Hebrew) branch.
See also Dahlia.
Dalia, Dalialah, Daliyah

Dalila (Swahili) gentle.
Dalida, Dalilah, Dalilia

Dallas (Irish) wise.
**Dalishya, Dalisia, Dalissia,
Dallys, Dalyce, Dalys**

Damaris (Greek) gentle
girl. See also Maris.
**Damar, Damara,
Damarius, Damary,
Damarys, Dameress,
Dameris, Damiris,
Dammaris, Dammeris,
Damris, Demaras, Demaris**

Damiana (Greek) tamer,
soother. A feminine form
of Damian.
**Damiann, Damianna,
Damianne**

Damica (French) friendly.
**Damee, Dameeka,
Dameka, Damekah,
Damicah, Damie, Damika,
Damikah, Demeeka,
Demeka, Demekah,
Demica, Demicah**

Damita (Spanish) small
noblewoman.
**Damee, Damesha,
Dameshia, Damesia,
Dametia, Dametra,
Dametrah**

Dana (English) from Denmark; bright as day.
Daina, Dainna, Danae, Danah, Danai, Danaia, Danalee, Danan, Danarra, Danayla, Dane, Danean, Danee, Daniah, Danie, Danja, Danna, Dayna

Danae (Greek) Mythology: the mother of Perseus.
Danaë, Danay, Danayla, Danays, Danea, Danee, Dannae, Denae, Denee

Daneil (Hebrew) an alternate form of Danielle.
Daneal, Daneala, Daneale, Daneel, Daneela, Daneila

Danella (American) a form of Danielle.
Danela, Danelia, Danelle, Donella, Donnella

Danelle (Hebrew) an alternate form of Danielle.
Danael, Danalle, Danel, Danele, Danell, Danella, Donelle, Donnelle

Danessa (American) a combination of Danielle + Vanessa.
Danesa, Danesha, Danessia, Daniesa, Daniesha, Danisa, Danisha, Danissa

Danessia (American) an alternate form of Danessa.
Danesia, Danieshia, Danisia, Danissia

Danette (American) a form of Danielle.
Danetra, Danett, Danetta

Dani (Hebrew) a familiar form of Danielle.
Danee, Danie, Danne, Dannee, Danni, Dannie, Danny, Dannye, Dany

Dania, Danya (Hebrew) short forms of Danielle.
Daniah

Danica, Danika (Hebrew) alternate forms of Danielle. (Slavic) morning star.
Daneeka, Danikla, Danneeka, Dannica, Dannika

Danice (American) a combination of Danielle + Janice.
Daniah

Danielan (Spanish) a form of Danielle.

Daniella (Italian) a form of Danielle.
Daniela, Dannilla, Danijela

Danielle (Hebrew, French) God is my judge. A feminine form of Daniel.
Danae, Daneen, Daneil, Daneille, Danelle, Dani, Danial, Danialle, Danica, Danie, Danielan, Daniele, Danielka, Daniell, Daniella, Danilka, Danille, Danit, Danniele, Danniell, Danniella, Dannielle, Danya, Danyel, Donniella

Danille (American) a form of Danielle.
Danila, Danile, Danilla, Dannille

Danit (Hebrew) an alternate form of Danielle.
Danett, Danis, Danisha, Daniss, Danita, Danitra, Danitza, Daniz, Danni

Danna (Hebrew) a short form of Danella, Daniella. (English) an alternate form of Dana.
Danka, Dannae, Dannah, Danne, Danni, Dannia, Dannon, Danya

Danyel, Danyell (American) forms of Danielle.
Daniyel, Danya, Danyae, Danyail, Danyaile, Danyal, Danyale, Danyea, Danyele, Danyella, Danyelle, Danyle, Donnyale, Donnyell, Donyale, Donyell

Daphne (Greek) laurel tree.
Dafny, Daphane, Daphaney, Daphanie, Daphany, Dapheney, Daphna, Daphnee, Daphney, Daphnie, Daphnique, Daphnit, Daphny

Dara (Hebrew) compassionate.
Dahra, Darah, Daraka, Daralea, Daralee, Darda, Darice, Darilyn, Darilyn,

Darisa, Darissa, Darja, Darra, Darrah

Darby (Irish) free. (Scandinavian) deer estate.
Darb, Darbi, Darbie, Darbra

Darcelle (French) a form of Darci.
Darcel, Darcell, Darcella, Darselle

Darci, Darcy (Irish) dark. (French) fortress.
Darcee, Darcelle, Darcey, Darcie, Darsey, Darsi, Darsie

Daria (Greek) wealthy. A feminine form of Darius.
Dari, Darian, Darianne, Darria, Darya

Darielle (French) an alternate form of Daryl.
Dariel, Darriel, Darrielle

Darilynn (American) a form of Darlene.
Daralin, Daralynn, Daralynne, Darilin, Darilyn, Darilynne, Darlin, Darlyn, Darlynn, Darlynne, Darylin, Darylyn, Darylynn, Darylynne

Darla (English) a short form of Darlene.
Darli, Darlice, Darlie, Darlis, Darly, Darlys

Darlene (French) little darling. See also Daryl.
Darilynn, Darla, Darlean,

Darlene (cont.)
Darleen, Darlena,
Darlenia, Darletha, Darlin,
Darline, Darling

Darnelle (Irish) an alternate form of Daron.
Darnel, Darnell, Darnella,
Darnesha, Darnetta,
Darnette, Darnice,
Darniece, Darnita,
Darnyell

Darnesha (American) an alternate form of Darnelle.
Darneshia, Darnesia,
Darnisha, Darnishia,
Darnisia

Daron (Irish) great. A feminine form of Darren.
Daronica, Daronice,
Darnelle, Daryn

Darselle (French) an alternate form of Darcelle.
Darsel, Darsell, Darsella

Daru (Hindi) pine tree.

Daryl (French) a short form of Darlene. (English) beloved.
Darelle, Darielle, Daril,
Darilynn, Darrel, Darrell,
Darrelle, Darreshia,
Darryl, Darryll

Daryn (Greek) gifts. (Irish) great. A feminine form of Darren.
Daron, Daryan, Darynn,
Darynne

Dasha (Russian) a form of Dorothy.
Dashenka, Dasia

Dashawna (American) a combination of the prefix Da + Shawna.
Dashawn, Dashawnda,
Dashay, Dashell,
Deshawna

Dashiki (Swahili) loose-fitting shirt worn in Africa.
Dashi, Dashika, Dashka,
Desheka, Deshiki

Davalinda (American) a combination of Davida + Linda. A form of Davina.
Davalynda, Davelinda,
Davilinda, Davylinda

Davalynda (American) an alternate form of Davalinda.
Davelynda, Davilynda,
Davylynda

Davalynn (American) a combination of Davida + Lynn. A form of Davina.
Davalin, Davalyn,
Davalynne, Davelin,
Davelyn, Davelynn,
Davelynne, Davilin,
Davilyn, Davilynn,
Davilynne

Davida (Hebrew) beloved. A feminine form of David. See also Vida.
Daveisha, Davesia,
Daveta, Davetta, Davette,
Davika, Davisha, Davita

Davina (Scottish) a form
of Davida. See also Vina.
Dava, Davalinda,
Davalynn, Davannah,
Davean, Davee, Daveen,
Daveena, Davene, Daveon,
Davey, Davi, Daviana,
Davie, Davin, Davinder,
Davine, Davineen,
Davinia, Davinna,
Davonna, Davria, Devean,
Deveen, Devene, Devina

Davonna (Scottish,
English) an alternate form
of Davina, Devonna.
Davon, Davona, Davonda

Dawn (English) sunrise,
dawn.
Dawana, Dawandrea,
Dawanna, Dawin, Dawna,
Dawne, Dawnee,
Dawnele, Dawnell,
Dawnelle, Dawnetta,
Dawnisha, Dawnlynn,
Dawnn, Dawnrae,
Dawnyel, Dawnyella,
Dawnyelle

Dawna (English) an alternate form of Dawn.
Dawnna, Dawnya

Dawnisha (American)
a form of Dawn.
Dawni, Dawniell,
Dawnielle, Dawnisia,
Dawniss, Dawnita,
Dawnysha, Dawnysia

Dayna (Scandinavian)
a form of Dana.
Dayne, Daynna

Deana (Latin) divine.
(English) valley. A feminine
form of Dean.
Deane, Deanielle,
Deanisha, Deanna, Deena

Deandra (American)
a combination of
Dee + Andrea.
Deandre, Deandré,
Deandrea, Deandree,
Deandria, Deanndra,
Diandra, Diandre,
Diandrea

Deanna (Latin) an alternate
form of Deana, Diana.
De, Dea, Deaana,
Deahana, Deandra,
Deandre, Deann, Déanna,
Deannia, Deeanna, Deena

Deanne (Latin) an alternate
form of Diane.
Dea, Deahanne, Deane,
Deann, Déanne, Dee,
Deeann, Deeanne

Debbie (Hebrew) a short
form of Deborah.
Debbee, Debbey, Debbi,
Debby, Debee, Debi, Debie

Deborah (Hebrew) bee.
Bible: a great Hebrew
prophetess.
Deb, Debbie, Debbora,
Debborah, Deberah,
Debor, Debora, Deboran,
Deborha, Deborrah,
Debra, Debrea, Debrena,
Debria, Debrina, Debroah,
Devora, Dobra

Debra (American) a short form of Deborah.
Debbra, Debbrah, Debrah

Dedra (American) a form of Deirdre.
Deeddra, Deedra, Deedrea, Deedrie

Dee (Welsh) black, dark.
Dea, Deah, Dede, Dedie, Deea, Dee-Ann, Deedee, Dee Dee, Didi

Deena (American) a form of Deana, Dena, Dinah.

Deidra, Deidre (Irish) alternate forms of Deirdre.
Dedra, Deidrea, Deidrie, Diedra, Diedre, Dierdra

Deirdre (Irish) sorrowful; wanderer.
Dedra, Dee, Deerdra, Deerdre, Deidra, Deidre, Deirdree, Didi, Dierdre, Diérdre, Dierdrie

Deitra (Greek) a short form of Demetria.
Deetra, Detria

Déja (French) before.
Daija, Daisia, Daja, Dasha, Deejay, Dejanelle, Dejon

Dejon (French) an alternate form of Déja.
Daijon, Dajan, Dajona

Deka (Somali) pleasing.
Dekah

Delana (German) noble protector.
Dalanna, Dalayna, Daleena, Dalena, Dalenna, Dalina, Dalinda, Dalinna, Delaina, Delani, Delania, Delany, Delanya, Deleena, Delena, Delenya, Delina, Dellaina

Delaney (Irish) descendant of the challenger. (English) an alternate form of Adeline.
Dalaney, Dalania, Dalene, Daleney, Daline, Del, Delaine, Delainey, Delane, Delanie, Delayne, Delaynie, Deleani, Déline, Dell, Della, Dellaney

Delfina (Greek) an alternate form of Delphine. (Spanish) dolphin.
Delfeena, Delfine

Delia (Greek) visible; from Delos. (German, Welsh) a short form of Adelaide, Cordelia. Mythology: a festival of Apollo held every five years in ancient Greece.
Dee, Dehlia, Del, Delea, Deli, Delinda, Dellia, Dellya, Delya

Delicia (English) delightful.
Delesha, Delice, Delisa, Delise, Delisha, Delisiah, Delya, Delys, Delyse, Delysia

Delilah (Hebrew) brooder. Bible: the companion of Samson. See also Lila.
Dalia, Dalialah, Dalila, Daliliah, Delila, Delilia

Della a short form of Adelaide, Cordelia, Delaney.
Del, Dela, Dell, Delle, Delli, Dellie, Dells

Delores (Spanish) an alternate form of Dolores.
Del, Delora, Delore, Deloria, Delories, Deloris, Delorise, Delorita

Delphine (Greek) from Delphi. See also Delfina.
Delpha, Delphe, Delphi, Delphia, Delphina, Delphinia, Delvina

Delsie (English) a familiar form of Deloris.

Delta (Greek) door. Linguistics: the fourth letter in the Greek alphabet. Geography: a triangular land mass at the mouth of a river.
Delte, Deltora, Deltoria, Deltra

Demetria (Greek) cover of the earth. Mythology: Demeter was the Greek goddess of the harvest.
Deitra, Demeta, Demeteria, Demetra, Demetrice, Demetris, Demetrish, Demetrius, Demi, Demita, Demitra, Dymitra

Demi (Greek) a short form of Demetria. (French) half.
Demiah

Dena (Hebrew) an alternate form of Dinah. (English, Native American) valley. See also Deana.
Deane, Deena, Deeyn, Denae, Dene, Denea, Deney, Denna

Denae (Hebrew) an alternate form of Dena.
Denaé, Denay, Denee, Deneé

Denise (French) Mythology: follower of Dionysus, the god of wine. A feminine form of Dennis.
Danice, Danise, Denese, Deney, Deni, Denica, Denice, Denie, Deniece, Denisha, Denisse, Denize, Denni, Dennie, Dennise, Denny, Dennys, Denyce, Denys, Denyse, Dinnie, Dinny

Denisha (American) a form of Denise.
Deneesha, Deneichia, Denesha, Deneshia, Deniesha, Denishia

Derika (German) ruler of the people. A feminine form of Derek.
Dereka, Derekia, Derica, Dericka, Derrica, Derricka, Derrika

Derry (Irish) redhead.
Deri, Derie

Deryn (Welsh) bird.
Derren, Derrin, Derrine, Deryne

Deshawna (American)
a combination of the
prefix De + Shawna.
**Dashawna, Deshan,
Deshanda, Deshandra,
Deshane, Deshaun,
Deshaundra, Deshawn,
Deshawndra, Desheania,
Deshona, Deshonda,
Deshonna**

Desi (French) a short form
of Desiree.
**Désir, Desira, Dezi, Dezia,
Dezzia, Dezzie**

Desiree (French) desired,
longed for. See also Dessa.
**Desara, Desarae, Desarai,
Desaraie, Desaray, Desare,
Desaré, Desarea, Desaree,
Desarie, Desera, Deserae,
Deserai, Deseray, Desere,
Deseree, Deseret, Deseri,
Deserie, Deserrae,
Deserray, Deserré, Desi,
Desirae, Desirah, Desirai,
Desiray, Desire, Desirea,
Desirée, Désirée, Desirey,
Desiri, Desray, Desree,
Dessie, Dessirae, Dessire,
Dezarae, Dezeray, Dezere,
Dezerea, Dezerie, Dezirae,
Deziree, Dezirée, Dezorae,
Dezra, Dezrae, Dezyrae**

Dessa (Greek) wanderer.
(French) an alternate form
of Desiree.

Desta (Ethiopian) happy.
(French) a short form of
Destiny.
Desti, Destie, Desty

Destiny (French) fate.
**Desnine, Desta, Destanee,
Destanie, Destannie,
Destany, Desteni, Destin,
Destinee, Destinée,
Destiney, Destini,
Destinie, Destnie, Desty,
Destyn, Destyne, Destyni**

Deva (Hindi) divine.
Religion: the Hindu moon
goddess.

Devi (Hindi) goddess.
Religion: the Hindu
goddess of power and
destruction.

Devin (Irish) poet. An alter-
nate form of Devon.
**Devan, Devane, Devanie,
Devany, Deven, Devena,
Devenje, Deveny, Deveyn,
Devina, Devine, Devinne,
Devyn**

Devon (English) a short
form of Devonna.
Devonne

Devonna (English) from
Devonshire.
**Davonna, Devon, Devona,
Devonda, Devondra**

Devora (Hebrew) an alter-
nate form of Deborah.
**Deva, Devorah, Devra,
Devrah**

Dextra (Latin) adroit,
skillful.
Dekstra, Dextria

Di (Latin) a short form
of Diana, Diane.
Dy

Dia (Latin) a short form
of Diana, Diane.

Diamond (Latin) precious
gem.
**Diamonda, Diamonia,
Diamonique, Diamonte,
Diamontina**

Diana (Latin) divine.
Mythology: the goddess
of the hunt, the moon,
and fertility. See also Dee,
Deanna, Deanne, Dona,
Dyan.
**Daiana, Daianna, Dayana,
Dayanna, Di, Dia, Dianah,
Dianalyn, Dianarose,
Dianatris, Dianca,
Diandra, Diane, Dianelis,
Diania, Dianielle, Dianita,
Dianna, Dianys, Didi, Dina**

Diane (Latin) an alternate
form of Diana.
**Deane, Deanne, Deeane,
Deeanne, Di, Dia,
Diahann, Dian, Diani,
Dianie, Diann, Dianne**

Dianna (Latin) an alternate
form of Diana.
Diahanna

Diantha (Greek) divine
flower.
Diandre, Dianthe

Dilys (Welsh) perfect; true.

Dina (Hebrew) a short form
of Dinah.

Dinah (Hebrew) vindicated.
Bible: a daughter of Jacob
and Leah.
Dina, Dyna, Dynah

Dinka (Swahili) people.

Dionne (Greek) divine
queen. Mythology: the
mother of Aphrodite, the
goddess of love.
**Deona, Deondra, Deonia,
Deonjala, Deonna,
Deonne, Deonyia, Dion,
Diona, Diondra, Diondrea,
Dione, Dionee, Dionis,
Dionna, Dionte**

Dior (French) golden.
**Diora, Diore, Diorra,
Diorre**

Dita (Spanish) a form
of Edith.
Ditka, Ditta

Divinia (Latin) divine.
**Devina, Devinia, Diveena,
Diviniea**

Dixie (French) tenth.
(English) wall; dike.
Geography: a nickname
for the American South.
Dix, Dixee, Dixi, Dixy

Diza (Hebrew) joyful.
Ditza, Ditzah, Dizah

Dodie (Greek) a familiar
form of Dorothy. (Hebrew)
beloved.
**Doda, Dode, Dodee,
Dodi, Dody**

Dolly (American) a short form of Dolores, Dorothy.
Dol, Doll, Dollee, Dolley, Dolli, Dollie, Dollina

Dolores (Spanish) sorrowful. Religion: Santa Maria de los Dolores—Saint Mary of the Sorrows—is a name for the Virgin Mary. See also Lola.
Delores, Deloria, Dolly, Dolorcitas, Dolorita, Doloritas

Dominica, Dominika (Latin) belonging to the Lord. A feminine form of Dominic. See also Mika.
Domenica, Domenika, Domineca, Domineka, Dominga, Domini, Dominique, Dominixe, Domino, Dominyika, Domka, Domnicka, Domonica, Domonice, Domonika, Domonique

Dominique, Domonique (French) forms of Dominica, Dominika.
Domanique, Domeneque, Domenique, Domineque, Dominiqua, Domino, Dominoque, Dominuque, Domique, Domminique, Domoniqua

Domino (English) a short form of Dominica, Dominique.

Dona (Italian) an alternate form of Donna. (English)
world leader; proud ruler. A feminine form of Donald.
Donalda, Donaldina, Donaleen, Donelda, Donella, Donellia, Donette, Doni, Donita, Donnella, Donnelle

Doña (Italian) an alternate form of Donna.
Donail, Donalea, Donalisa, Donay, Donella, Donelle, Donetta, Doni, Donia, Donica, Donice, Donie, Donika, Donise, Donisha, Donishia, Donita, Donitrae

Donata (Latin) gift.
Donatha, Donatta

Dondi (American) a familiar form of Donna.
Dondra, Dondrea, Dondria

Donna (Italian) lady.
Doña, Dondi, Donnaica, Donnalee, Donnalen, Donnay, Donnell, Donnella, Donni, Donnica, Donnie, Donnika, Donnise, Donnisha, Donnita, Donny, Dontia, Donya

Donniella (American) a form of Daniella.
Doniella, Donielle, Donnielle, Donnyella, Donyelle

Dora (Greek) gift. A short
form of Adora, Eudora,
Pandora, Theodora.
**Doralia, Doralie, Doralisa,
Doraly, Doralynn, Doran,
Dorchen, Dore, Dorece,
Doree, Doreece, Doreen,
Dorelia, Dorella, Dorelle,
Doresha, Doressa,
Doretta, Dori, Dorika,
Doriley, Dorilis, Dorinda,
Dorion, Dorita, Doro,
Dory**

Doralynn (English) a com-
bination of Dora + Lynn.
**Doralin, Doralyn,
Doralynne**

Doreen (Greek) an
alternate form of Dora.
(Irish) moody, sullen.
(French) golden.
**Doreena, Dorena, Dorene,
Dorina, Dorine**

Doretta (American) a form
of Dora, Dorothy.
**Doretha, Dorette,
Dorettie**

Dori, Dory (American)
familiar forms of Dora,
Doria, Doris, Dorothy.
**Dore, Dorey, Dorie,
Dorinda, Dorree, Dorri,
Dorrie, Dorry**

Doria (Greek) from Doris,
Greece. A feminine form
of Dorian.
**Dori, Doriana, Doriann,
Dorianna, Dorianne, Dory**

Dorinda (Spanish) a form
of Dori.

Doris (Greek) sea.
Mythology: the wife of
Nereus and mother of the
Nereids, or sea nymphs.
**Dori, Dorice, Dorisa,
Dorise, Dorris, Dorrise,
Dorrys, Dory, Dorys**

Dorothea (Greek) an alter-
nate form of Dorothy.
**Dorethea, Dorotea,
Doroteya, Dorotha,
Dorothia, Dorotthea,
Dorthea, Dorthia**

Dorothy (Greek) gift
of God. See also Dasha,
Dodie, Lolotea, Theodora,
Thea.
**Dasha, Dasya, Do, Doa,
Doe, Dolly, Doortje,
Dorathy, Dordei, Dordi,
Doretta, Dori, Dorika,
Doritha, Dorka, Dorle,
Dorlisa, Doro, Dorolice,
Dorosia, Dorota,
Dorothea, Dorothee,
Dorottya, Dorrit, Dorte,
Dortha, Dorthy, Dory,
Dosi, Dossie, Dosya,
Dottie, Dotty**

Dorrit (Greek) dwelling.
(Hebrew) generation.
Dorit, Dorita, Doritt

Dottie, Dotty (Greek)
familiar forms of Dorothy.
Dot, Dottee

Drew (Greek) courageous; strong. (Latin) a short form of Drusilla.
Dru, Drue

Drinka (Spanish) a form of Alexandria.
Dreena, Drena, Drina

Drusi (Latin) a short form of Drusilla.
Drucey, Druci, Drucie, Drucy, Drusey, Drusie, Drusy

Drusilla (Latin) descendant of Drusus, the strong one. See also Drew.
Drewsila, Drucella, Drucill, Drucilla, Druscilla, Druscille, Drusi

Dulcie (Latin) sweet.
Delcina, Delcine, Douce, Doucie, Dulce, Dulcea, Dulci, Dulcia, Dulciana, Dulcibel, Dulcibella, Dulcine, Dulcinea, Dulcy, Dulsea

Dulcinea (Spanish) sweet. Literature: Don Quixote's love interest.

Duscha (Russian) soul; sweetheart; term of endearment.
Duschah, Dusha, Dushenka

Dustine (German) valiant fighter. (English) brown rock, quarry. A feminine form of Dustin.
Dustee, Dusti, Dustie, Dustina, Dusty, Dustyn

Dyan (Latin) an alternate form of Diana. (Native American) deer.
Dyana, Dyane, Dyani, Dyann, Dyanna, Dyanne

Dyllis (Welsh) sincere.
Dilys, Dylis, Dylys

Dyshawna (American) a combination of the prefix Dy + Shawna.
Dyshanta, Dyshawn, Dyshonda, Dyshonna

Earlene (Irish) pledge. (English) noblewoman. A feminine form of Earl.
Earla, Earlean, Earlecia, Earleen, Earlena, Earlina, Earlinda, Earline, Erla, Erlana, Erlene, Erlenne, Erlina, Erlinda, Erline, Erlisha

Eartha (English) earthy.
Ertha

Easter (English) Easter time. History: a name for a child born on Easter.
Eastan, Eastlyn, Easton

Eboni, Ebonie (Greek) alternate forms of Ebony.

Ebony (Greek) a hard, dark wood.
Eban, Ebanee, Ebanie, Ebany, Ebbony, Ebone, Ebonee, Eboney, Eboni, Ebonie, Ebonique, Ebonisha, Ebonnee, Ebonni, Ebonnie, Ebonye, Ebonyi

Echo (Greek) repeated sound. Mythology: the nymph who pined for the love of Narcissus until only her voice remained.
Echoe, Ekko, Ekkoe

Eda (Irish, English) a short form of Edana, Edith

Edana (Irish) ardent; flame.
Eda, Edan, Edanna

Edda (German) an alternate form of Hedda.
Etta

Eddy (American) a familiar form of Edwina.
Eddi, Eddie, Edy

Edeline (English) noble; kind.
Adeline, Edelyne, Ediline, Edilyne

Eden (Babylonian) a plain. (Hebrew) delightful. Bible: the earthly paradise.
Ede, Edena, Edene, Edenia, Edin, Edyn

Edie (English) a familiar form of Edith.
Eadie, Edi, Edy, Edye, Eyde, Eydie

Edith (English) rich gift. See also Dita.
Eadith, Eda, Ede, Edetta, Edette, Edie, Edit, Edita, Edite, Editha, Edithe, Editta, Ediva, Edka, Edyta, Edyth, Edytha, Edythe

Edna (Hebrew) rejuvenation. Mythology: the wife of Enoch, according to ancient eastern legends.
Ednah, Edneisha, Ednita

Edwina (English) prosperous friend. A feminine form of Edwin. See also Winnie.
Eddy, Edina, Edweena, Edwena, Edwine, Edwyna

Effia (Ghanian) born on Friday.
Effi, Effy

Effie (Greek) spoken well of. (English) a short form of Alfreda, Euphemia.
Effi, Effia, Effy, Ephie

Eileen (Irish) a form of Helen. See also Aileen, Ilene.
Eilean, Eilena, Eilene, Eiley, Eilidh, Eilleen, Eillen, Eilyn, Eleen, Elene

Ela (Polish) a form of Adelaide.

Elaine (French) a form of Helen. See also Laine.
Elain, Elaina, Elainia, Elainna, Elan, Elana, Elane, Elania, Elanie,

Elaine *(cont.)*
Elanit, Elanna, Elauna, Elayn, Elayna, Elayne, Ellaine

Elana (Greek) a short form of Eleanor. See also Ilana, Lana.
Elan, Elani, Elanie

Elberta (English) a form of Alberta.
Elbertha, Elberthina, Elberthine, Elbertina, Elbertine

Eldora (Spanish) golden, gilded.
Eldoree, Eldorey, Eldori, Eldoria, Eldorie, Eldory

Eleanor (Greek) light. An alternate form of Helen. History: Anna Eleanor Roosevelt was a U.S. delegate to the United Nations, a writer, and the thirty-second First Lady of the U.S. See also Elana, Ella, Ellen, Leanore, Lena, Lenore, Leonore, Leora, Nellie, Nora, Noreen.
Elana, Elanor, Elanore, Eleanora, Eleanore, Elena, Elenor, Elenorah, Elenore, Eleonor, Eleonore, Elianore, Elinor, Elinore, Elladine, Ellenor, Ellie, Elliner, Ellinor, Ellinore, Elna, Elnore, Elynor, Elynore

Eleanora (Greek) an alternate form of Eleanor. See also Lena.
Elenora, Eleonora, Eleora, Elianora, Eliora, Ellenora, Ellenorah, Elnora, Elora, Elynora

Electra (Greek) shining; brilliant. Mythology: the daughter of Agamemnon, leader of the Greeks in the Trojan War.
Elektra

Elena (Greek) an alternate form of Eleanor. (Italian) a form of Helen.
Eleana, Eleen, Eleena, Elen, Elene, Eleni, Elenitsa, Elenka, Elenoa, Elenola, Elina, Ellena, Lena

Eleora (Hebrew) the Lord is my light.
Eliora

Elfrida (German) peaceful. See also Freda.
Elfrea, Elfreda, Elfredda, Elfreeda, Elfreyda, Elfrieda, Elfryda

Elga (German) an alternate form of Helga. (Norwegian) pious.
Elgiva

Eliana (Hebrew) my God has answered me. A feminine form of Eli, Elijah. See also Iliana.
Elianna, Elianne, Elliane, Ellianna, Ellianne, Liana, Liane

Elicia (Hebrew) an alternate
form of Elisha. See also
Alicia.
Ellicia

Elisa (Spanish, Italian,
English) a short form
of Elizabeth. See also
Alisa, Ilisa.
**Elecea, Eleesa, Elesa,
Elesia, Elisia, Elisya, Ellisa,
Ellisia, Ellissa, Ellissia,
Ellissya, Ellisya, Elysa,
Elysia, Elyssia, Elyssya,
Elysya, Lisa**

Elise (French, English)
a short form of Elizabeth,
Elysia. See also Ilise, Liese,
Lisette, Lissie.
**Eilis, Eilise, Elese, Élise,
Elisee, Elisie, Elisse, Elizé,
Ellice, Ellise, Ellyce, Ellyse,
Ellyze, Elsey, Elsie, Elsy,
Elyce, Elyci, Elyse, Elyze,
Lisel, Lisl, Lison**

Elisha (Greek) an alternate
form of Alisha. (Hebrew)
consecrated to God.
See also Ilisha, Lisha.
**Eleacia, Eleasha, Elecia,
Eleesha, Eleisha, Elesha,
Eleshia, Eleticia, Elicia,
Eliscia, Elishia, Elishua,
Eliska, Elitia, Ellecia,
Ellesha, Ellexia, Ellisha,
Elsha, Elysha**

Elissa, Elyssa (Greek,
English) forms of Elizabeth.
Short forms of Melissa. See
also Alissa, Alyssa, Lissa.
Ellissa, Ellyssa, Ilissa, Ilyssa

Elita (Latin, French)
chosen. See also Lida, Lita.
**Elida, Elitia, Elitie, Ellita,
Ellitia, Ellitie, Ilida, Ilita,
Litia**

Eliza (Hebrew) a short form
of Elizabeth. See also Aliza.
**Elizaida, Elizalina, Elize,
Elizea**

Elizabeth (Hebrew)
consecrated to God.
Bible: the mother of John
the Baptist. See also Bess,
Beth, Betsy, Betty, Elsa,
Ilse, Libby, Liese, Liesel,
Lisa, Lisette, Lissa,
Lissie, Liz, Liza, Lizabeta,
Lizabeth, Lizina, Lizzy,
Tetty, Veta, Yelisabeta, Zizi.
**Eliabeth, Elisa, Elisabet,
Elisabeta, Elisabeth,
Elisabethe, Elisabetta,
Elisabette, Elise, Elisebet,
Elisheba, Elisheva, Elissa,
Eliz, Eliza, Elizabee,
Elizabet, Elizabete,
Elizaveta, Elizebeth, Elka,
Ellice, Elsabeth, Elsbet,
Elsbeth, Elsbietka,
Elschen, Else, Elspet,
Elspeth, Elspie, Elsy,
Elysabeth, Elyssa, Elzbieta,
Erzsébet, Helsa, Ilizzabet,
Lusa**

Elizaveta (Polish, English)
a form of Elizabeth.
**Elisavet, Elisaveta,
Elisavetta, Elisveta,
Elizavet, Elizavetta,
Elizveta, Elsveta, Elzveta**

Elka (Polish) a form
of Elizabeth.
Ilka

Elke (German) a form
of Adelaide, Alice.
Elki, Ilki

Ella (Greek) a short form
of Eleanor. (English) elfin;
beautiful fairy-woman.
Ellamae, Ellia, Ellie, Elly

Ellen (English) a form
of Eleanor, Helen.
**Elen, Elenee, Eleny, Elin,
Elina, Elinda, Ellan, Elle,
Ellena, Ellene, Ellie, Ellin,
Ellon, Elly, Ellyn, Ellynn,
Elyn**

Ellice (English) an alternate
form of Elise.
Ellecia, Ellyce, Elyce

Ellie, Elly (English) short
forms of Eleanor, Ella,
Ellen.
Ele, Elie, Elli

Elma (Turkish) sweet fruit.

Elmira (Arabic, Spanish) an
alternate form of Almira.
**Elmeera, Elmera, Elmeria,
Elmyra**

Elnora (American) a combination of Ella + Nora.

Eloise (French) a form
of Louise.
Elois, Eloisa, Eloisia

Elsa (Hebrew) a short form
of Elizabeth. (German)
noble. See also Ilse.
**Ellsa, Ellse, Ellsey, Ellsie,
Ellsy, Else, Elsie, Elsje, Elsy**

Elsbeth (German) a form
of Elizabeth.
**Elsbet, Elspet, Elspeth,
Elspie, Elzbet, Elzbieta**

Elsie (German) a familiar
form of Elsa, Helsa.
Elsi, Elsy

Elspeth (Scottish) a form
of Elizabeth.
Elspet, Elspie

Elva (English) elfin. See also
Alva, Alvina.
**Elvenea, Elvia, Elvie,
Elvina, Elvinea, Elvinia,
Elvinna**

Elvina (English) an alternate form of Alvina.

Elvira (Latin) white;
blond. (German) closed
up. (Spanish) elfin.
Geography: the town
in Spain that hosted
the first Ecumenical
Council in 300 A.D.
**Elva, Elvera, Elvina, Elvire,
Elwira, Vira**

Elysia (Latin) sweet; blissful.
Mythology: Elysium was
the dwelling place of
happy souls.
Elise, Elysha, Ilysha, Ilysia

Emerald (French) bright
green gemstone.
Emelda, Esmeralda

Emilee, Emilie (English)
forms of Emily.
Émilie, Emméie

Emilia (Italian) a form
of Amelia, Emily.
Emalia, Emelia, Emila

Emily (Latin) flatterer.
(German) industrious.
A feminine form of Emil.
See also Amelia, Emma,
Millie.
**Eimile, Em, Emaili, Emaily,
Emalia, Emalie, Emeli,
Emelia, Emelie, Emeline,
Emelita, Emely, Emilee,
Emiley, Emili, Emilia,
Emilie, Émilie, Emilienne,
Emilis, Emilka, Emillie,
Emilly, Emmalee,
Emmalou, Emmaly,
Emmalynn, Emmélie,
Emmey, Emmi, Emmie,
Emmilly, Emmy, Emmye,
Emyle**

Emilyann (American)
a combination of
Emily + Ann.
**Emileane, Emileann,
Emileanna, Emileanne,
Emiliana, Emiliann,
Emilianna, Emilianne,
Emillyane, Emillyann,
Emillyanna, Emillyanne,
Emliana, Emliann,
Emlianna, Emlianne**

Emma (German) a short
form of Emily. See also
Amy.
Em, Ema, Emi, Emiy,

**Emmaline, Emmi, Emmie,
Emmy, Emmye**

Emmalee (American)
a combination of Emma +
Lee. A form of Emily.
**Emalea, Emalee, Emilee,
Emmaleigh, Emmali,
Emmaliese, Emmalyse,
Emylee**

Emmaline (French) a form
of Emily.
**Emalina, Emaline,
Emelina, Emeline, Emilina,
Emiline, Emmalina,
Emmalene, Emmeline,
Emmiline**

Emmalynn (American)
a combination of
Emma + Lynn.
**Emelyn, Emelyne,
Emelynne, Emilyn,
Emilynn, Emilynne, Emlyn,
Emlynn, Emlynne,
Emmalyn, Emmalynne**

Emmanuelle (Hebrew)
God is with us. A feminine
form of Emmanuel.
Emmanuela, Emmanuella

Emmylou (American)
a combination of
Emmy + Lou.
**Emlou, Emmelou,
Emmilou, Emylou**

Ena (Irish) a form of Helen.

Enid (Welsh) life; spirit.

Enrica (Spanish) a form
of Henrietta. See also Rica.
Enrieta, Enrietta, Enriqua,

Enrica (cont.)
**Enriqueta, Enriquetta,
Enriquette**

Eppie (English) a familiar
form of Euphemia.
Effie, Effy, Eppy

Erica (Scandinavian) ruler
of all. (English) brave ruler.
A feminine form of Eric.
See also Arica, Rica, Ricki.
**Ericca, Ericha, Ericka,
Erika, Erikka, Errica,
Errika, Eryka, Erykka**

Erin (Irish) peace. History:
another name for Ireland.
See also Arin.
**Eran, Eren, Erena, Erene,
Ereni, Eri, Erian, Erina,
Erine, Erinetta, Erinn,
Erinna, Erinne, Eryn,
Erynn, Erynne**

Erma (Latin) a short form
of Ermine, Hermina.
See also Irma.
Ermelinda

Ermine (Latin) an alternate
form of Hermina.
**Erma, Ermin, Ermina,
Erminda, Erminia, Erminie**

Erna (English) a short form
of Ernestine.

Ernestine (English) earnest,
sincere. A feminine form
of Ernest.
**Erna, Ernaline, Ernesia,
Ernesta, Ernestina,
Ernesztina**

Eryn (Irish) an alternate
form of Erin.

Eshe (Swahili) life.
Esha

Esmé (French) a familiar
form of Esmeralda. A form
of Amy.
Esma, Esme, Esmēe

Esmeralda (Greek,
Spanish) a form of
Emerald.
**Emelda, Esmé, Esmerelda,
Esmerilda, Esmiralda,
Ezmerelda, Ezmirilda**

Esperanza (Spanish) hope.
See also Speranza.
**Espe, Esperance, Esperans,
Esperanta, Esperanz,
Esperenza**

Essie (English) a short form
of Estelle, Esther.
Essa, Essey, Essie, Essy

Estee (English) a short form
of Estelle, Esther.
Esta, Estée, Esti

Estelle (French) a form
of Esther. See also Stella,
Trella.
**Essie, Estee, Estel, Estela,
Estele, Estelina, Estelita,
Estell, Estella, Estellina,
Estellita, Esthella, Estrela,
Estrelinha, Estrell,
Estrella, Estrelle, Estrellita**

Esther (Persian) star. Bible:
the Jewish captive whom
Ahasuerus made his
queen. See also Hester.

Essie, Estee, Ester, Esthur, Eszter, Eszti

Ethana (Hebrew) strong; firm. A feminine form of Ethan.

Ethel (English) noble.
Ethelda, Ethelin, Etheline, Ethelle, Ethelyn, Ethelynn, Ethelynne, Ethyl

Étoile (French) star.

Etta (German) little. (English) a short form of Henrietta.
Etka, Etke, Etti, Ettie, Etty, Itke, Itta

Eudora (Greek) honored gift. See also Dora.

Eugenia (Greek) born to nobility. A feminine form of Eugene. See also Gina.
Eugenie, Eugénie, Eugenina, Eugina, Evgenia

Eulalia (Greek) well spoken. See also Ula.
Eula, Eulalee, Eulalie, Eulalya, Eulia

Eun (Korean) silver.

Eunice (Greek) happy; victorious. Bible: the mother of Saint Timothy. See also Unice.
Euna, Eunique, Eunise, Euniss

Euphemia (Greek) spoken well of, in good repute. History: a fourth-century Christian martyr.

Effam, Effie, Eppie, Eufemia, Euphan, Euphemie, Euphie

Eurydice (Greek) wide, broad. Mythology: the wife of Orpheus.
Euridice, Euridyce, Eurydyce

Eustacia (Greek) productive. (Latin) stable; calm. A feminine form of Eustace. See also Stacey.

Eva (Greek) a short form of Evangelina. (Hebrew) an alternate form of Eve. See also Ava, Chava.
Éva, Evah, Evalea, Evalee, Evike

Evaline (French) a form of Evelyn.
Evalin, Evalina, Evalyn, Eveleen, Evelene, Evelina, Eveline

Evangelina (Greek) bearer of good news.
Eva, Evangelia, Evangelica, Evangeline, Evangelique

Evania (Greek) a feminine form of Evan. (Irish) young warrior.
Evana, Evann, Evanna, Evanne, Evany, Eveania, Evvanne, Evvunea, Evyan

Eve (Hebrew) life. An alternate form of Chava. Bible: the first woman created by God. (French) a short form

of Evonne. See also Hava,
Naeva, Vica, Yeva.
**Eva, Evelyn, Evey, Evi,
Evita, Evuska, Evvie, Evvy,
Evy, Evyn, Ewa, Yeva**

Evelyn (English) hazelnut.
**Aveline, Evaleen, Evalene,
Evaline, Evalyn, Evalynn,
Evalynne, Eveleen, Eveline,
Evelyne, Evelynn,
Evelynne, Evline, Ewalina**

Evette (French) an alter-
nate form of Yvette.
A familiar form of Evonne.
See also Ivette.
Evett

Evi (Hungarian) a form
of Eve.
**Evicka, Evie, Evike, Evka,
Evuska, Evy, Ewa**

Evita (Spanish) a form
of Eve.

Evline (English) an alter-
nate form of Evelyn.
**Evleen, Evlene, Evlin,
Evlina, Evlyn, Evlynn,
Evlynne**

Evonne (French) an alter-
nate form of Yvonne.
See also Ivonne.
**Evanne, Eve, Evenie,
Evenne, Eveny, Evette,
Evon, Evonnie, Evony**

Fabia (Latin) bean grower.
A feminine form of Fabian.
**Fabiana, Fabiann,
Fabianne, Fabiene,
Fabienne, Fabiola, Fabra,
Fabreanne, Fabria**

Faith (English) faithful;
fidelity. See also Faye,
Fidelity.
Fayth, Faythe

Faizah (Arabic) victorious.

Falda (Icelandic) folded
wings.
Faida, Fayda

Faline (Latin) catlike.
**Faleen, Falena, Falene,
Falina, Faylina, Fayline,
Faylyn, Faylynn, Faylynne,
Felina**

Fallon (Irish) grandchild
of the ruler.
**Falan, Falen, Falin, Fallan,
Fallonne, Fallyn, Falyn,
Falynn, Falynne**

Fancy (French) betrothed.
(English) whimsical;
decorative.
**Fanchette, Fanchon, Fanci,
Fancia, Fancie**

Fanny (American) a familiar
form of Frances.
**Fan, Fanette, Fani, Fania,
Fannee, Fanney, Fanni,
Fannia, Fannie, Fanya**

Farah, Farrah (English)
beautiful; pleasant.
Fara, Farra, Fayre

Faren, Farren (English)
wanderer.
**Faran, Fare, Farin, Faron,
Farrahn, Farran, Farrand,
Farrin, Farron, Farryn,
Farye, Faryn, Feran, Ferin,
Feron, Ferran, Ferren,
Ferrin, Ferron, Ferryn**

Fātima (Arabic) daughter
of the Prophet. History: the
daughter of Muhammad.
**Fatema, Fathma, Fatimah,
Fatime, Fatma, Fattim**

Fawn (French) young deer.
**Faun, Fauna, Fawna,
Fawne, Fawnia, Fawnna**

Faye (French) fairy; elf.
(English) an alternate form
of Faith.
**Fae, Fay, Fayann, Fayanna,
Fayette, Fayina, Fayla, Fey,
Feyla**

Fayola (Nigerian) lucky.

Felecia (Latin) an alternate
form of Felicia.
Flecia

Felica (Spanish) a short
form of Felicia.
**Falisa, Felisa, Felisca,
Felissa, Feliza**

Felice (Latin) a short form
of Felicia.
**Felece, Felise, Felize,
Felysse**

Felicia (Latin) fortunate;
happy. A feminine form
of Felix. See also Lecia,
Phylicia.
**Falecia, Faleshia, Falicia,
Falleshia, Fela, Felecia,
Felica, Felice, Felicidad,
Felicie, Feliciona, Felicity,
Felicya, Felisha, Felishia,
Felisiana, Felita, Felixia,
Felizia, Felka, Fellcia,
Fellishia, Felysia, Fleasia,
Fleichia, Fleishia, Flichia**

Felicity (English) a form
of Felicia.
**Falicity, Felicita, Felicitas,
Félicité, Feliciti**

Felisha (Latin) an alternate
form of Felicia.
**Faleisha, Falesha, Falisha,
Feleasha, Feleisha, Felesha,
Flisha**

Femi (French) woman.
(Nigerian) love me.
Femie, Femmi, Femmie

Feodora (Greek) gift
of God. A feminine form
of Theodore.
Fedora, Fedoria

Fern (German) a short form
of Fernanda. (English) fern.
**Ferne, Ferni, Fernlee,
Fernleigh, Fernley, Fernly**

Fernanda (German) daring, adventurous. A feminine form of Ferdinand. See also Andee, Nan.
Ferdie, Ferdinanda, Ferdinande, Fern, Fernande, Fernandette, Fernandina, Nanda

Fiala (Czech) violet flower.

Fidelia (Latin) an alternate form of Fidelity.
Fidela, Fidele, Fidelina

Fidelity (Latin) faithful, true. See also Faith.
Fidelia, Fidelita

Fifi (French) a familiar form of Josephine.
Feef, Feefee, Fifine

Filippa (Italian) a form of Philippa.
Felipa, Filipa, Filippina, Filpina

Filomena (Italian) a form of Philomena.
Filemon

Fiona (Irish) fair, white.
Fionna

Fionnula (Irish) white shouldered. See also Nola, Nuala.
Fenella, Fenula, Finella, Finola, Finula

Flair (English) style; verve.
Flaire, Flare

Flannery (Irish) redhead. Literature: Flannery O'Connor was a renowned American writer.
Flan, Flann, Flanna

Flavia (Latin) blond, golden haired.
Flavere, Flaviar, Flavie, Flavien, Flavienne, Flaviere, Flavio, Flavyere, Fulvia

Fleur (French) flower.
Fleure

Flo (American) a short form of Florence.

Flora (Latin) flower. A short form of Florence. See also Lore.
Fiora, Fiore, Fiorenza, Fleur, Flo, Flor, Florann, Florella, Florelle, Floren, Floria, Floriana, Florianna, Florica, Florie, Florimel

Florence (Latin) blooming; flowery; prosperous. History: Florence Nightingale, a British nurse, is considered the founder of modern nursing. See also Florida.
Fiorenza, Flo, Flora, Florance, Florencia, Florency, Florendra, Florentia, Florentina, Florentyna, Florenza, Floretta, Florette, Florie, Florina, Florine, Floris, Flossie

Floria (Basque) a form of Flora.
Flori, Florria

Florida (Spanish) a form
of Florence.
Floridia, Florinda, Florita

Florie (English) a familiar
form of Florence.
**Flore, Flori, Florri, Florrie,
Florry, Flory**

Floris (English) a form
of Florence.
Florisa, Florise

Flossie (English) a familiar
form of Florence.
Floss, Flossi, Flossy

Fola (Yoruba) honorable.

Fonda (Latin) foundation.
(Spanish) inn.
Fondea, Fonta

Fontanna (French)
fountain.
**Fontaine, Fontana,
Fontane, Fontanne,
Fontayne**

Fortuna (Latin) fortune;
fortunate.
Fortoona, Fortune

Fran (Latin) a short form
of Frances.
Frain, Frann

Frances (Latin) free; from
France. A feminine form
of Francis. See also
Paquita.
**Fanny, Fran, Franca,
France, Francee, Francena,
Francesca, Francess,
Francesta, Franceta,
Francetta, Francette,
Franci, Francine, Francise,**

**Françoise, Francyne,
Frankie, Frannie, Franny**

Francesca (Italian) a form
of Frances.
**Franceska, Francessca,
Francesta, Franchesca,
Francisca, Franciska,
Franciszka, Frantiska,
Franzetta, Franziska**

Franchesca (Italian)
an alternate form
of Francesca.
**Cheka, Chekka, Chesca,
Cheska, Francheca,
Francheka, Franchelle,
Franchesa, Francheska,
Franchessca, Franchesska**

Franci (Hungarian) a familiar form of Francine.
Francey, Francie, Francy

Francine (French) a form
of Frances.
**Franceen, Franceine,
Franceline, Francene,
Francenia, Franci, Francin,
Francina**

Françoise (French) a form
of Frances.

Frankie (American) a famil-
iar form of Frances.
**Francka, Francki, Franka,
Frankeisha, Frankey,
Franki, Frankia, Franky**

Frannie, Franny (English)
familiar forms of Frances.
Frania, Franney, Franni

Freda, Freida (German)
short forms of Alfreda,
Elfrida, Frederica, Sigfreda.
**Frayda, Fredda, Fredella,
Fredia, Freeda, Freeha,
Freia, Frida, Frideborg,
Frieda**

Freddi, Freddie (English)
familiar forms of Frederica,
Winifred.
**Fredda, Freddy, Fredi,
Fredia, Fredy, Frici**

Frederica (German) peace-
ful ruler. A feminine form
of Frederick. See also
Alfreda, Ricki, Rica.
**Farica, Federica, Freda,
Fredalena, Fredaline,
Freddi, Freddie,
Fredericka, Frederickina,
Frederika, Frederina,
Frederine, Frederique,
Fredith, Fredora, Fredra,
Fredreca, Fredreka,
Fredrica, Fredricia,
Fredrika, Freida, Fritzi,
Fryderica, Fryderyka**

Frederique (French)
a form of Frederica.
**Frederike, Frédérique,
Friederike, Rike**

Freja (Scandinavian) noble-
woman. Mythology: the
Norse goddess of love.
Fraya, Freya

Fritzi (German) a familiar
form of Frederica.
**Friezi, Fritze, Fritzie,
Fritzinn, Fritzline, Fritzy**

Gabriela, Gabriella
(Italian) alternate forms
of Gabrielle.
**Gabriala, Gabrialla,
Gabrielia, Gabriellia,
Gabrila, Gabrilla**

Gabrielle (French) devoted
to God. A feminine form
of Gabriel.
**Gabielle, Gabreil, Gabrial,
Gabriana, Gabriela,
Gabriele, Gabriell,
Gabriella, Gabrille,
Gabrina, Gaby, Gavriella**

Gaby (French) a familiar
form of Gabrielle.
**Gabbey, Gabbi, Gabbie,
Gabey, Gabi, Gabie, Gavi,
Gavy**

Gada (Hebrew) lucky.
Gadah

Gaea (Greek) planet Earth.
Mythology: the Greek
goddess of Earth.
Gaia, Gaiea, Gaya

Gaetana (Italian) from
Gaeta. Geography:
a region in southern Italy.
**Gaetan, Gaétane,
Gaetanne**

Gail (Hebrew) a short form of Abigail. (English) merry, lively.
Gael, Gaela, Gaelen, Gaelle, Gaellen, Gaila, Gaile, Gale, Galyn, Gayla, Gayle

Gala (Norwegian) singer.
Galla

Galena (Greek) healer; calm.
Galen

Gali (Hebrew) hill; fountain; spring.
Galice, Galie

Galina (Russian) a form of Helen.
Galayna, Galenka, Galiana, Galiena, Galinka, Galka, Galochka, Galya, Galyna

Ganesa (Hindi) fortunate. Religion: the Hindu god of wisdom and luck.

Ganya (Hebrew) garden of the lord.
Gana, Gani, Gania, Ganice, Ganit

Gardenia (English) Botany: a sweet-smelling flower.
Deeni, Denia, Gardena

Garland (French) wreath of flowers.

Garnet (English) dark red gem.
Garnetta, Garnette

Garyn (English) spear carrier. A feminine form of Gary.
Garan, Garen, Garra, Garryn

Gasha (Russian) a familiar form of Agatha.
Gashka

Gavriella (Hebrew) a form of Gabrielle.
Gavila, Gavilla, Gavrid, Gavrieela, Gavriela, Gavrielle, Gavrila, Gavrilla

Gay (French) merry.
Gae, Gai, Gaye, Gayla, Gaylaine, Gayle, Gayleen, Gaylen, Gaylene, Gaylyn

Gayle (English) an alternate form of Gail.

Gayna (English) a familiar form of Guinevere.
Gaynah, Gayner, Gaynor

Geela (Hebrew) joyful.
Gela, Gila

Geena (American) a form of Gena.

Gelya (Russian) angelic.

Gemini (Greek) twin.
Gemelle, Gemima, Gemina, Geminine, Gemmina

Gemma (Latin, Italian) jewel, precious stone. See also Jemma.
Gem, Gemmey, Gemmie, Gemmy

Gen (Japanese) spring.
A short form of names
beginning with "Gen."
Gena, Genna

Gena (French) a form
of Gina. A short form
of Geneva, Genevieve,
Iphigenia.
**Geanna, Geena, Geenah,
Gen, Genah, Genea, Geni,
Genia, Genice, Genie,
Genita**

Geneen (Scottish) an alter-
nate form of Jeanine.
**Geanine, Geannine, Gen,
Genene, Genine, Gineen,
Ginene**

Geneva (French) juniper
tree. A short form of
Genevieve. Geography:
a city in Switzerland.
**Geena, Gen, Gena,
Geneive, Geneve, Genever,
Genevera, Genevra,
Ginevra, Ginneva, Janeva,
Jeaneva, Jeneva**

Genevieve (German,
French) an alternate form
of Guinevere. See also
Gwendolyn.
**Gen, Gena, Genaveve,
Genavieve, Genavive,
Geneva, Geneveve,
Genevie, Geneviéve,
Genevievre, Genevive,
Genna, Genovieve,
Ginette, Gineveve,
Ginevieve, Ginevive,
Guinevieve, Guinivive,
Gwenevieve, Gwenivive**

Genevra (French, Welsh)
an alternate form of
Guinevere.
Gen, Ginevra

Genice (American) a form
of Janice.
**Gen, Genece, Geneice,
Genesa, Genesee,
Genessia, Genis, Genise**

Genita (American) an alternate form of Janita.
Gen, Genet, Geneta

Genna (English) a form
of Jenna.
**Gen, Gennae, Gennay,
Genni, Gennie, Genny**

Gennifer (American)
a form of Jennifer.
**Gen, Genifer, Genny,
Ginnifer**

Genovieve (French)
an alternate form
of Genevieve.
**Genoveva, Genoveve,
Genovive**

Georgeanna (Latin) a form
of Georgeanne. (English)
a combination of
Georgia + Anna.
**Georgana, Georganna,
Georgeana, Georgiana,
Georgianna, Georgyanna**

Georgeanne (English)
a combination of
Georgia + Anne.
**Georgann, Georganne,
Georgean, Georgeann,
Georgianne, Georgyann,
Georgyanne**

Georgene (English) a familiar form of Georgia.
Georgeina, Georgena, Georgenia, Georgiena, Georgienne, Georgina, Georgine

Georgette (French) a form of Georgia.
Georgeta, Georgett, Georgetta, Georjetta

Georgia (Greek) farmer. A feminine form of George. Art: Georgia O'Keeffe was an American painter known especially for her paintings of flowers. Geography: a southern American state; a country in Eastern Europe. See also Jirina, Jorja.
Georgene, Georgette, Georgi, Georgie, Giorgi, Giorgia

Georgina (English) a form of Georgia.
Georgena, Georgene, Georgine, Giorgina

Geraldine (German) mighty with a spear. A feminine form of Gerald. See also Dena, Jeraldine.
Geralda, Geraldina, Geraldyna, Geraldyne, Gerhardine, Geri, Gerianna, Gerianne, Gerrilee, Giralda

Geralyn (American) a combination of Geraldine + Lynn.
Geralynn, Gerilyn, Gerrilyn

Gerda (German) a familiar form of Gertrude. (Norwegian) protector.
Gerta

Geri (American) a familiar form of Geraldine. See also Jeri.
Gerri, Gerrie, Gerry

Germaine (French) from Germany. See also Jermaine.
Germain, Germana, Germanie, Germaya, Germine

Gertrude (German) beloved warrior. See also Trudy.
Gerda, Gert, Gerta, Gertey, Gerti, Gertie, Gertina, Gertraud, Gertrud, Gertruda, Gerty

Gervaise (French) skilled with a spear. A feminine form of Jarvis.

Gessica (Italian) a form of Jessica.
Gesica, Gess, Gesse, Gessy

Geva (Hebrew) hill.
Gevah

Ghada (Arabic) young; tender.
Gada

Ghita (Italian) pearly.
  Gita

Gianna (Italian) a short form of Giovanna. See also Jianna, Johana, Johnna.
  Geona, Geonna, Giana, Gianella, Gianetta, Gianina, Giannella, Giannetta, Gianni, Giannina, Gianny, Gianoula

Gigi (French) a familiar form of Gilberte.
  Geegee, G.G.

Gilana (Hebrew) joyful.
  Gilah

Gilberte (German) brilliant; pledge; trustworthy. A feminine form of Gilbert. See also Berti.
  Gigi, Gilberta, Gilbertina, Gilbertine, Gill

Gilda (English) covered with gold.
  Gilde, Gildi, Gildie, Gildy

Gill (Latin, German) a short form of Gilberte, Gillian.
  Gilli, Gillie, Gilly

Gillian (Latin) an alternate form of Jillian.
  Gila, Gilana, Gilenia, Gili, Gilian, Gill, Gilliana, Gilliane, Gilliann, Gillianna, Gillianne, Gillie, Gilly, Gillyan, Gillyane, Gillyann, Gillyanne, Gyllian, Lian

Gin (Japanese) silver. A short form of names beginning with "Gin."

Gina (Italian) a short form of Angelina, Eugenia, Regina, Virginia. See also Jina.
  Gena, Gin, Ginah, Ginea, Gini, Ginia

Ginette (English) a form of Genevieve.
  Gin, Ginetta, Ginnetta, Ginnette

Ginger (Latin) flower; spice. A familiar form of Virginia.
  Gin, Ginata, Ginja, Ginjer, Ginny

Ginia (Latin) a familiar form of Virginia.
  Gin, Ginata

Ginnifer (Welsh) an alternate form of Jennifer. (English) white; smooth; soft.
  Gin, Ginifer

Ginny (English) a familiar form of Ginger, Virginia. See also Jin, Jinny.
  Gin, Gini, Ginney, Ginni, Ginnie, Giny

Giordana (Italian) a form of Jordana.

Giovanna (Italian) a form of Jane.
  Giavanna, Giavonna, Giovana

Gisa (Hebrew) carved
stone.
Gazit, Gissa

Giselle (German) pledge;
hostage. See also Jizelle.
**Gisel, Gisela, Gisele,
Giséle, Gisell, Gisella,
Gissell, Gissella, Gisselle,
Gizela**

Gita (Polish) a short form
of Margaret. (Yiddish)
good.
Gitka, Gitta, Gituska

Gitana (Spanish) gypsy;
wanderer.

Gitta (Irish) a short form
of Bridget.
Getta

Giulia (Italian) a form
of Julia.
**Giuliana, Giulianna, Guila,
Guiliana, Guilietta**

Gizela (Czech) a form
of Giselle.
**Gizella, Gizelle, Gizi,
Giziki, Gizus**

Gladys (Latin) small sword
(Irish) princess. (Welsh)
a form of Claudia. Botany:
a gladiolus flower.
**Glad, Gladi, Gladis, Gladiz,
Gladness, Gladwys,
Gwladys**

Glenda (Welsh) a form
of Glenna.
Glanda, Glennda, Glynda

Glenna (Irish) valley, glen.
A feminine form of Glenn.
See also Glynnis.
**Glenda, Glenetta, Glenina,
Glenine, Glenn,
Glennesha, Glennie,
Glenora, Gleny, Glyn**

Glennesha (American)
a form of Glenna.
**Glenesha, Glenisha,
Glennisha, Glennishia**

Gloria (Latin) glory.
History: Gloria Steinem,
a leading American
feminist, founded
Ms. magazine.
**Gloresha, Gloriah,
Glorianne, Gloribel,
Gloriela, Gloriella,
Glorielle, Gloris, Glorisha,
Glorvina, Glory**

Glorianne (American)
a combination of
Gloria + Anne.
**Gloriana, Gloriane,
Glorianna**

Glory (Latin) an alternate
form of Gloria.
Glorey, Glori, Glorie

Glynnis (Welsh) a form
of Glenna.
**Glenice, Glenis, Glenise,
Glenyse, Glennis, Glennys,
Glenwys, Glenys, Glenyss,
Glinnis, Glinys, Glynesha,
Glynice, Glynis, Glynisha,
Glyniss, Glynitra, Glynys,
Glynyss**

Golda (English) gold.
History: Golda Meir was
a Russian-born politician
who served as Prime
Minister of Israel.
**Goldarina, Golden, Goldi,
Goldie, Goldina, Goldy**

Goma (Swahili) joyful
dance.

Grace (Latin) graceful.
**Engracia, Graca, Gracea,
Graceanne, Gracey, Graci,
Gracia, Gracie, Graciela,
Graciella, Gracinha, Gracy,
Grata, Gratia, Gray,
Grayce**

Graceanne (English)
a combination of
Grace + Ann.
**Graceann, Graceanna,
Graciana, Gratiana**

Gracia (Spanish) a form
of Grace.

Grazia (Latin) an alternate
form of Grace.
**Graziella, Grazielle,
Graziosa, Grazyna**

Greer (Scottish) vigilant.
A feminine form of
Gregory.
Grear, Grier

Greta (German) a short
form of Gretchen,
Margaret.
**Greatal, Greatel, Greeta,
Gretal, Grete, Gretel,
Gretha, Grethal, Grethe,
Grethel, Gretta, Grette,
Grieta, Gryta, Grytta**

Gretchen (German) a form
of Margaret.
Greta, Gretchin

Griselda (German) gray
woman warrior. See also
Selda, Zelda.
**Grisel, Griseldis, Griseldys,
Griselys, Grishilda,
Grishilde, Grissel, Grissele,
Grissely, Grizel, Grizelda**

Guadalupe (Arabic) river
of black stones. See also
Lupe.
Guadulupe

Gudrun (Scandinavian)
battler. See also Runa.
**Gudren, Gudrin, Gudrinn,
Gudruna**

Guillerma (Spanish) a form
of Wilhelmina.
Guilla

Guinevere (French, Welsh)
white wave; white phan-
tom. Literature: the wife
of King Arthur. See also
Gayna, Genevieve,
Genevra, Jennifer,
Winifred, Wynne.
**Gayna, Generva, Genn,
Ginetta, Guenevere,
Guenna, Guinivere,
Guinna, Gwen,
Gwenevere, Gwenivere,
Gwynnevere**

Gunda (Norwegian) female
warrior.
Gundala, Gunta

Gurit (Hebrew) innocent baby.

Gurpreet (Punjabi) religion.

Gusta (Latin) a short form of Augusta.
Gus, Gussi, Gussie, Gussy, Gusti, Gustie, Gusty

Gwen (Welsh) a short form of Guinevere, Gwendolyn.
Gwenesha, Gweness, Gweneta, Gwenetta, Gwenette, Gweni, Gwenisha, Gwenita, Gwenith, Gwenn, Gwenna, Gwennie, Gwenny, Gwyn

Gwenda (Welsh) a familiar form of Gwendolyn.
Gwinda, Gwynda, Gwynedd

Gwendolyn (Welsh) white wave; white browed; new moon. Literature: the wife of Merlin, the magician. See also Genevieve, Gwyneth, Wendy, Wynne.
Guendolen, Gwen, Gwendalin, Gwenda, Gwendalee, Gwendaline, Gwendalyn, Gwendela, Gwendolen, Gwendolene, Gwendolin, Gwendoline, Gwendolyne, Gwendolynn, Gwendolynne, Gwendylan

Gwyn (Welsh) a short form of Gwyneth.
Gwinn, Gwinne, Gwynn, Gwynne

Gwyneth (Welsh) an alternate form of Gwendolyn. See also Winnie, Wynne.
Gweneth, Gwenneth, Gwennyth, Gwenyth, Gwyn

Gypsy (English) wanderer.
Gipsy, Gypsie

Habiba (Arabic) beloved.

Hachi (Japanese) eight thousand; good luck.
Hachiko, Hachiyo

Hadara (Hebrew) adorned with beauty.
Hadarah

Hadassah (Hebrew) myrtle tree.

Hadiya (Swahili) gift.

Hadley (English) field of heather.
Hadlea, Hadlee, Hadleigh

Hadriane (Greek, Latin) an alternate form of Adrienne.
Hadriana, Hadrianna Hadrianne, Hadriene, Hadrienne

Hagar (Hebrew) forsaken; stranger. Bible: Sarah's handmaiden, the mother of Ishmael.
Haggar

Haidee (Greek) modest.

Hailey (English) an alternate form of Hayley.
Hailea, Hailee, Haili, Hailie, Hailley, Hailly

Haldana (Norwegian) half-Danish.

Haley (Scandinavian) heroine. See also Hailey, Hayley.
Halee, Haleigh, Hali, Halie, Hallie

Halia (Hawaiian) in loving memory.

Halimah (Arabic) gentle; patient.
Halima, Halime

Halina (Russian) a form of Helen.
Haleena, Halena, Halinka

Halla (African) unexpected gift.
Hala, Halle

Hallie (Scandinavian) an alternate form of Haley.
Hallee, Hallei, Halley, Halli, Hally, Hallye

Halona (Native American) fortunate.
Haleen, Halena, Halina, Haloona, Haona

Hama (Japanese) shore.

Hana (Japanese) flower. (Arabic) happiness. (Slavic) a form of Hannah.
Hanan, Haneen, Hania, Hanicka, Hanin, Hanita, Hanja, Hanka

Hanako (Japanese) flower child.

Hania (Hebrew) resting place.
Haniya

Hanna (Hebrew) an alternate form of Hannah.

Hannah (Hebrew) gracious. Bible: the mother of Samuel. See also Anci, Anezka, Ania, Anka, Ann, Anna, Anneka, Chana, Nina, Nusi.
Hana, Hanna, Hannalore, Hanneke, Hannele, Hanni, Hannon, Honna

Hanni (Hebrew) a familiar form of Hannah.
Hani, Hanne, Hannie, Hanny

Happy (English) happy.

Hara (Hindi) tawny. Religion: another name for the Hindu goddess Shiva, the destroyer.

Harley (English) meadow of the hare. See also Arleigh.
Harlee, Harleen, Harleigh, Harlene, Harleyann, Harli, Harlie, Harlina, Harline, Harly

Harleyann (English) a combination of Harley + Ann.
Harlann, Harlanna, Harlanne, Harleyanna, Harleyanne, Harliann, Harlianna, Harlianne

Harmony (Latin) harmonious.
Harmon, Harmoni, Harmonia, Harmonie

Harpreet (Punjabi) devoted to God.

Harriet (French) ruler of the household. (English) an alternate form of Henrietta. Literature: Harriet Beecher Stowe was an American writer noted for her novel *Uncle Tom's Cabin.*
Harri, Harrie, Harriett, Harrietta, Harriette, Harriot, Harriott, Hattie

Haru (Japanese) spring.

Hasana (Swahili) she arrived first. A name used for the first-born female twin. See also Huseina.

Hasina (Swahili) good.
Haseena, Hasena, Hassina

Hateya (Moquelumnan) footprints.

Hattie (English) familiar forms of Harriet, Henrietta.
Hatti, Hatty, Hetti, Hettie, Hetty

Hausu (Moquelumnan) like a bear yawning upon awakening.

Hava (Hebrew) an alternate form of Chava. See also Eve.

Haviva (Hebrew) beloved.
Hava, Havah, Havalee, Havelah, Havi, Havvah, Hayah

Hayfa (Arabic) shapely.

Hayley (English) hay meadow. See also Hailey, Haley.
Haylee, Hayli, Haylie, Hayly

Hazel (English) hazelnut tree; commanding authority.
Hazal, Hazaline, Haze, Hazeline, Hazell, Hazelle, Hazen, Hazyl

Heather (English) flowering heather.
Heath, Heatherlee, Heatherly

Heaven (English) place of beauty and happiness. Bible: where God and angels are said to dwell.
Heavenly, Heavin, Heavyn, Heven

Hedda (German) battler. See also Edda, Hedy.
Heda, Hedaya, Hede, Hedia, Hedvick, Hedvig, Hedvika, Hedwig, Hedwiga, Heida, Hetta

Hedy (Greek) delightful; sweet. (German) a familiar form of Hedda.
Heddey, Heddi, Heddie, Heddy, Hedi

Heidi (German) a short form of Adelaide.
Heida, Heide, Heidie, Hidee, Hidi, Hiede, Hiedi

Helen (Greek) light. See also Aileen, Aili, Alena, Eileen, Elaine, Eleanor, Ellen, Galina, Ila, Ilene, Ilona, Jelena, Leanore, Leena, Lelya, Lenci, Lene, Liolya, Nellie, Nitsa, Olena, Onella, Yalena, Yelena.
Elana, Ena, Halina, Hela, Hele, Helena, Helene, Helle, Hellen, Helli, Hellin, Hellon, Helon, Heluska

Helena (Greek) an alternate form of Helen. See also Ilena.
Halena, Halina, Helaina, Helana, Helayna, Heleana, Heleena, Helenka, Helenna, Helina, Hellanna, Hellenna, Helona, Helonna

Helene (French) a form of Helen.
Helaine, Helayne, Heleen, Hèléne, Helenor, Heline, Hellenor

Helga (German) pious. (Scandinavian) an alternate form of Olga. See also Elga.

Helki (Native American) touched.
Helkey, Helkie, Helky

Helma (German) a short form of Wilhelmina.
Halma, Helme, Helmi, Helmine, Hilma

Heloise (French) a form of Louise.
Héloïse, Helse, Helsey, Helsie, Helsy

Helsa (Danish) a form of Elizabeth.
Helsey, Helsi, Helsy

Heltu (Moquelumnan) like a bear reaching out.

Henrietta (English) ruler of the household. A feminine form of Henry. See also Enrica, Etta, Yetta.
Harriet, Hattie, Hatty, Hendrika, Heneretta, Henia, Henka, Henna, Hennrietta, Hennriette, Henny, Henrica, Henrie, Henrieta, Henriete, Henriette, Henrika, Henrique, Henriquetta, Henryetta, Henya, Hetta, Hetti, Hettie, Hetty

Hera (Greek) queen; jealous. Mythology: the queen of heaven and the wife of Zeus.

Hermia (Greek) messenger. A feminine form of Hermes.

Hermina (Latin) noble.
(German) soldier.
A feminine form
of Herman. See also
Erma, Ermine, Irma.
Herma, Hermia

Hermione (Greek) earthy.
**Hermalina, Hermia,
Hermina, Hermine,
Herminia**

Hermosa (Spanish)
beautiful.

Hertha (English) child
of the earth.
Heartha, Hirtha

Hester (Dutch) a form
of Esther.
**Hessi, Hessie, Hessye,
Hesther, Hettie, Hetty**

Hestia (Persian) star.
Mythology: the Greek
goddess of the hearth
and home.
**Hestea, Hesti, Hestie,
Hesty**

Heta (Native American)
racer.

Hetta (German) an alternate form of Hedda.
(English) a familiar form
of Henrietta.
Hettie

Hilary, Hillary (Greek)
cheerful, merry. See also
Alair.
**Hilaree, Hilari, Hilaria,
Hilarie, Hilery, Hiliary,
Hillaree, Hillari, Hillarie,**
**Hilleary, Hilleree, Hilleri,
Hillerie, Hillery, Hillianne,
Hilliary, Hillory**

Hilda (German) a short
form of Brunhilda,
Hildegarde.
**Helle, Hilde, Hildey, Hildie,
Hildur, Hildy, Hulda, Hylda**

Hildegarde (German)
fortress.
**Hilda, Hildagard,
Hildagarde, Hildegard,
Hildred**

Hinda (Hebrew) hind; doe.
**Hindey, Hindie, Hindy,
Hynda**

Hisa (Japanese) long-
lasting.
Hisae, Hisako, Hisay

Hiti (Eskimo) hyena.
Hitty

Hoa (Vietnamese) flower;
peace.
Ho, Hoai

Hola (Hopi) seed-filled club.

Holley, Holli, Hollie
(English) alternate forms
of Holly.

Hollis (English) near the
holly bushes.
Hollise, Hollyce, Holyce

Holly (English) holly tree.
**Hollee, Holley, Holli,
Hollie, Hollinda, Hollis,
Hollyann**

Hollyann (English) a com-
bination of Holly + Ann.
**Holliann, Hollianna,
Hollianne, Hollyanne**

Honey (Latin) a familiar
form of Honora. (English)
sweet.
Honalee, Hunney, Hunny

Hong (Vietnamese) pink.

Honora (Latin) honorable.
See also Nora, Onora.
**Honey, Honner, Honnor,
Honnour, Honor,
Honorah, Honorata,
Honore, Honoree,
Honoria, Honorina,
Honorine, Honour,
Honoure**

Hope (English) hope.
Hopey, Hopi, Hopie

Hortense (Latin) gardener.
See also Ortensia.
Hortensia

Hoshi (Japanese) star.
Hoshie, Hoshiko, Hoshiyo

Hua (Chinese) flower.

Huata (Moquelumnan)
basket carrier.

Huong (Vietnamese)
flower.

Huseina (Swahili) an alternate form of Hasana.

Hyacinth (Greek) Botany:
a plant with colorful,
fragrant flowers. See also
Cynthia, Jacinda.
Giacinta, Hyacintha,

**Hyacinthe, Hyacinthia,
Hyacinthie, Hycinth,
Hycynth**

Hye (Korean) graceful.

Ianthe (Greek) violet
flower.
Ianthia, Ianthina

Ida (German) hardworking.
(English) prosperous.
**Idaia, Idaleena, Idaleene,
Idalena, Idalene, Idalia,
Idalina, Idaline, Idamae,
Idania, Idarina, Idarine,
Idaya, Ide, Idelle, Idette,
Iduska, Idys**

Idelle (Welsh) a form
of Ida.
Idell, Idella

Iesha (American) a form
of Aisha.
**Ieachia, Ieaisha, Ieasha,
Ieesha, Ieeshia, Ieisha,
Ieishia, Ieshia**

Ignacia (Latin) fiery,
ardent. A feminine form
of Ignatius.
**Ignacie, Ignasha,
Ignashia, Ignatia, Ignatzia**

Ikia (Hebrew) God is my
salvation. (Hawaiian) a
feminine form of Isaiah.

Ikaisha, Ikea, Ikeisha, Ikeishi, Ikeishia, Ikesha, Ikeshia

Ila (Hungarian) a form of Helen.

Ilana (Hebrew) tree.
Ilane, Ilani, Ilainie, Illana, Illane, Illani, Ilania, Illanie, Ilanit

Ilena (Greek) an alternate form of Helena.
Ileana, Ileena, Ilina, Ilyna

Ilene (Irish) a form of Helen. See also Aileen, Eileen.
Ileane, Ileen, Ileene, Iline, Ilyne

Iliana (Greek) from Troy.
Ileana, Ileane, Ileanne, Ili, Ilia, Iliani, Illiana, Illiani

Ilima (Hawaiian) flower of Oahu.

Ilisa (Scottish, English) an alternate form of Alisa, Elisa.
Ilissa, Illisa, Illissa, Illysa, Illyssa, Ilysa, Ilyssa

Ilise (German) a form of Elise.
Ilese, Ileshia, Ilicia, Ilissa, Illytse, Ilycia, Ilyse, Ilyssa

Ilisha (Hebrew) an alternate form of Alisha, Elisha. See also Lisha.
Ilishia, Ilycia, Ilysha, Ilyshia

Ilka (Hungarian) a familiar form of Ilona.
Ilke, Milka, Milke

Ilona (Hungarian) a form of Helen.
Ilka, Illona, Illonia, Illonya, Ilonka, Iluska, Ilyona

Ilse (German) a form of Elizabeth. See also Elsa.
Ilsa, Ilsey, Ilsie, Ilsy

Ima (German) a familiar form of Amelia. (Japanese) presently.

Imala (Native American) strong minded.

Iman (Arabic) believer.
Imani

Imelda (German) warrior.
Imalda, Irmhilde, Melda

Imena (African) dream.
Imee, Imene

Imogene (Latin) image, likeness.
Emogen, Emogene, Imogen, Imogenia, Imojean, Imojeen, Innogen, Innogene

Ina (Irish) a form of Agnes.
Ena, Inanna, Inanne

India (Hindi) from India.
Indi, Indie, Indy, Indya

Indigo (Latin) dark blue color.

Indira (Hindi) splendid. Religion: the god of heaven. History: Indira

Nehru Gandi was an Indian politician and prime minister.
Indra

Inez (Spanish) a form of Agnes. See also Ynez.
Ines, Inés, Inesa, Inesita, Inésita, Inessa

Inga (Scandinavian) a short form of Ingrid.
Ingaberg, Ingaborg, Inge, Ingeberg, Ingeborg, Ingela

Ingrid (Scandinavian) hero's daughter; beautiful daughter.
Inga, Inge, Inger

Inoa (Hawaiian) name.

Ioana (Romanian) a form of Joan.
Ioani, Ioanna

Iola (Greek) dawn; violet colored. (Welsh) worthy of the Lord.
Iole, Iolee, Iolia

Iolana (Hawaiian) soaring like a hawk.

Iolanthe (English) a form of Yolanda. See also Jolanda.
Iolanda, Iolande

Iona (Greek) violet flower.
Ione, Ioney, Ioni, Ionia

Iphigenia (Greek) sacrifice. Mythology: the daughter of the Greek leader Agamemnon. See also Gena.

Irene (Greek) peaceful. Mythology: the goddess of peace. See also Orina, Rena, Rene, Yarina.
Eirena, Erena, Ira, Irana, Iranda, Iranna, Irén, Irena, Irenea, Irenka, Iriana, Irien, Irina, Jereni

Irina (Russian) a form of Irene.
Ira, Irena, Irenka, Irin, Irinia, Irinka, Irona, Ironka, Irusya, Iryna, Irynka, Rina

Iris (Greek) rainbow. Mythology: the goddess of the rainbow and messenger of the gods.
Irisa, Irisha, Irissa, Irita

Irma (Latin) an alternate form of Erma.
Irmina, Irminia

Isabeau (French) a form of Isabel.

Isabel (Spanish) conse-crated to God. A form of Elizabeth. See also Bel, Belle, Chavella, Ysabel.
Isa, Isabal, Isabeau, Isabela, Isabeli, Isabelita, Isabella, Ishbel, Isobel, Issi, Issie, Issy, Iza, Izabel, Izabele

Isabella (Italian) a form of Isabel.
Isabelle, Isabello, Izabella

Isadora (Latin) gift of Isis.
Isidora

Isha (American) a form
of Aisha.
**Ishana, Ishanda, Ishaney,
Ishani, Ishaun, Ishenda**

Ishi (Japanese) rock.
Ishiko, Ishiyo, Shiko, Shiyo

Isis (Egyptian) supreme
goddess. Mythology:
the goddess of the moon,
maternity, and fertility.

Isla (Scottish) Geography:
the Isla River in Scotland.

Isoka (Benin) gift from
god.
Soka

Isolde (Welsh) fair lady.
Literature: a princess in
the Arthurian legends;
a heroine in the medieval
romance *Tristan and Isolde*.
See also Yseult.
Isolda, Isolt

Ita (Irish) thirsty.

Italia (Italian) from Italy.
Italie

Iva (Slavic) a short form
of Ivana.

Ivana (Slavic) God is gracious. A feminine form
of Ivan. See also Yvanna.
Iva, Ivania, Ivanka, Ivanna

Ivette (French) an alternate
form of Yvette. See also
Evette.
**Ivete, Iveth, Ivetha, Ivetta,
Ivey**

Ivonne (French) an alter-
nate form of Yvonne.
See also Evonne.
**Ivon, Ivona, Ivone, Ivonna,
Iwona, Iwonka, Iwonna,
Iwonne**

Ivory (Latin) made of ivory.
Ivori, Ivorine, Ivree

Ivria (Hebrew) from
the land of Abraham.
Ivriah, Ivrit

Ivy (English) ivy tree.
Ivey, Ivie

Iyabo (Yoruba) mother
has returned.

Izusa (Native American)
white stone.

Jacalyn (American) a form
of Jacqueline.
**Jacelyn, Jacelyne, Jacelynn,
Jacilyn, Jacilyne, Jacilynn,
Jacolyn, Jacolyne,
Jacolynn, Jacylyn,
Jacylyne, Jacylynn**

Jacey (Greek) a familiar
form of Jacinda.
(American) a combination
of the initials J. + C.
**Jace, Jac-E, Jacee, Jacia,
Jacie, Jaciel, Jacy, Jacylin**

Jacinda, Jacinta (Greek)
beautiful, attractive.
(Spanish) a form of
Hyacinth.
**Jacenda, Jacenta, Jacey,
Jacinth, Jacintha, Jacinthe,
Jacynth, Jakinda, Jaxine**

Jackalyn (American) a form
of Jacqueline.
**Jackalene, Jackalin,
Jackaline, Jackalynn,
Jackalynne, Jackelin,
Jackeline, Jackelyn,
Jackelynn, Jackelynne,
Jackilin, Jackilyn,
Jackilynn, Jackilynne,
Jackolin, Jackoline,
Jackolyn, Jackolynn,
Jackolynne**

Jacki, Jackie (American)
familiar forms of
Jacqueline.
**Jackee, Jackia, Jackielee,
Jacky**

Jacklyn (American) a short
form of Jacqueline.
**Jacklin, Jackline, Jacklyne,
Jacklynn, Jacklynne**

Jackquel (French) an alter-
nate form of Jacqueline.
**Jackquelin, Jackqueline,
Jackquelyn, Jackquelynn,
Jackquetta, Jackquilin,
Jackquiline, Jackquilyn,
Jackquilynn, Jackquilynne**

Jaclyn (American) a short
form of Jacqueline.
**Jacleen, Jaclin, Jacline,
Jaclyne, Jaclynn**

Jacobi (Hebrew)
supplanter, substitute.
A feminine form of Jacob.
**Coby, Jacoba, Jacobette,
Jacobia, Jacobina, Jacolbi,
Jacolbia, Jacolby**

Jacqueline (French)
supplanter, substitute;
little Jacqui. A feminine
form of Jacques.
**Jacalyn, Jackalyn, Jackie,
Jacklyn, Jaclyn, Jacqualin,
Jacqualine, Jacqualyn,
Jacqualyne, Jacqualynn,
Jacqueena, Jacqueine,
Jacquel, Jacqueleen,
Jacquelene, Jacquelin,
Jacquelyn, Jacquelynn,
Jacquena, Jacquene,
Jacquenetta, Jacquenette,
Jacqui, Jacquil, Jacquilin,
Jacquiline, Jacquilyn,
Jacquilyne, Jacquilynn,
Jacquine, Jaquelin,
Jaqueline, Jaquelyn,
Jaquelyne, Jaquelynn,
Jockeline, Jocqueline**

Jacquelyn, Jacquelynn
(French) alternate forms
of Jacqueline.
Jacquelyne

Jacqui (French) a short
form of Jacqueline.
**Jacquay, Jacqué, Jacquee,
Jacqueta, Jacquete,
Jacquetta, Jacquette,
Jacquie, Jacquise, Jacquita,
Jaquay, Jaqui, Jaquice,
Jaquie, Jaquiese, Jaquina,
Jaquinta, Jaquita**

Jade (Spanish) jade.
Jada, Jadah, Jadda, Jadea,
Jadeann, Jadee, Jaden,
Jadera, Jadi, Jadie,
Jadielyn, Jadienne, Jady,
Jadzia, Jadziah, Jaeda,
Jaedra, Jaida, Jaide, Jaiden

Jae (Latin) jaybird.
(French) a familiar form
of Jacqueline.
Jaea, Jaela, Jaya, Jayla,
Jaylee, Jayleen, Jaylyn,
Jaylynn, Jaylynne

Jael (Hebrew) mountain
goat; climber. See also
Yael.
Jaela, Jaelee, Jaeleen, Jaeli,
Jaelie, Jaelle, Jaelynn,
Jahla, Jahlea

Jaffa (Hebrew) an alternate
form of Yaffa.
Jaffice, Jaffit, Jafit, Jafra

Jaha (Swahili) dignified.
Jahaida, Jahaira, Jaharra,
Jahayra, Jahida, Jahira,
Jahitza

Jaime (French) I love.
Jaima, Jaimee, Jaimey,
Jaimi, Jaimini, Jaimmie,
Jaimy

Jaimee (French) an alternate form of Jaime.

Jaira (Spanish) Jehovah
teaches.

Jakki (American) an alter-
nate form of Jacki, Jackie.
Jakala, Jakea, Jakeela,
Jakeida, Jakeisha, Jakeisia,
Jakeita, Jakela, Jakelia,
Jakell, Jakena, Jakesha,
Jaketta, Jakevia, Jakia,
Jakira, Jakisha, Jakiya,
Jakkia

Jalena (American) a combi-
nation of Jane + Lena.
Jalayna, Jalean, Jaleen,
Jalene, Jalina, Jaline,
Jalyna, Jelayna, Jelena,
Jelina, Jelyna

Jalila (Arabic) great.
Jalile

Jamaica (Spanish)
Geography: an island
in the Caribbean.
Jameca, Jameka, Jamica,
Jamika, Jamoka, Jemaica,
Jemika, Jemyka

Jamesha (American) a form
of Jami.
Jameisha, Jamese,
Jameshia, Jameshyia,
Jamesia, Jamesica,
Jamesika, Jamesina,
Jamessa, Jameta, Jametta,
Jamisha, Jammisha

Jami, Jamie (Hebrew)
supplanter, substitute.
(English) feminine forms
of James.
Jama, Jamay, Jamea,
Jamee, Jameka, Jamesha,
Jamia, Jamielee, Jamiesha,
Jamii, Jamika, Jamilynn,
Jamis, Jamise, Jammie,
Jamy, Jamya, Jamye,
Jayme, Jaymee, Jaymie

Jamila (Arabic) beautiful.
See also Yamila.
Jahmela, Jahmelia, Jahmil,
Jahmilla, Jamee, Jameela,
Jameelah, Jameeliah,
Jameila, Jamela, Jamelia,
Jameliah, Jamell, Jamella,
Jamelle, Jamely, Jamelya,
Jamiela, Jamilah, Jamilee,
Jamilia, Jamiliah, Jamilla,
Jamillah, Jamille, Jamillia,
Jamilya, Jamyla, Jemeela,
Jemelia, Jemila, Jemilla

Jamilynn (English) a com-
bination of Jami + Lynn.
Jamielin, Jamieline,
Jamielyn, Jamielyne,
Jamielynn, Jamielynne,
Jamilin, Jamiline, Jamilyn,
Jamilyne, Jamilynne

Jammie (American) a form
of Jami.
Jammesha, Jammi,
Jammice, Jammise,
Jammisha

Jamylin (American) a form
of Jamilynn.
Jamylin, Jamyline,
Jamylyn, Jamylyne,
Jamylynn, Jamylynne,
Jaymylin, Jaymyline,
Jaymylyn, Jaymylyne,
Jaymylynn, Jaymylynne

Jan (English) a short form
of Jane, Janet, Janice.
Jani, Jania, Jandy, Jannie

Jana (Slavic) a form of Jane.
See also Yana.
Janaca, Janalee, Janalisa,
Janalynn, Janika, Janka,
Janna, Janne

Janae, Janay (American)
forms of Jane.
Janaé, Janaea, Janaeh,
Janah, Janai, Janaya,
Janaye, Janea, Janee,
Janée, Jannae, Jannay,
Jenae, Jenay, Jenaya,
Jennae, Jennay, Jennaya,
Jennaye

Janalynn (American)
a combination of
Jana + Lynn.
Janalin, Janaline, Janalyn,
Janalyne, Janalynne

Janan (Arabic) heart; soul.
Janani, Jananie

Jane (Hebrew) God is gra-
cious. A feminine form
of John. See also Chavon,
Jean, Joan, Juanita, Seana,
Shauna, Shawna, Sheena,
Shunta, Sinead, Zaneta,
Zanna.
Jaine, Jan, Jana, Janae,
Janay, Janean, Janeann,
Janeen, Janelle, Janene,
Jannessa, Janet, Jania,
Janice, Janie, Janika,
Janine, Janique, Janis,
Janka, Janna, Jannie, Jasia,
Jayna, Jayne, Jenica, Jenny,
Joanna, Joanne

Janel, Janell (French) alternate forms of Janelle.
Jannel, Jaynel, Jaynell

Janelle (French) a form
of Jane.

Janel, Janela, Janele,
Janelis, Janell, Janella,
Janelli, Janellie, Janelly,
Janely, Janelys, Janiel,
Janielle, Janille, Jannel,
Jannell, Jannelle,
Jannellies, Janyll, Jaynelle

Janessa (American) a form
of Jane.
Janesha, Janeska, Janiesa,
Janiesha, Janisha, Janissa,
Jannesa, Jannesha,
Jannessa, Jannisa,
Jannisha, Jannissa

Janet (English) a form
of Jane. See also Jessie.
Jan, Janeta, Janete, Janett,
Janetta, Janette, Janita,
Janith, Janitza, Jannet,
Janneta, Janneth,
Jannetta, Jannette, Janot,
Jante, Janyte

Janice (Hebrew) God is
gracious. (English) a famil-
iar form of Jane. See also
Genice.
Jan, Janece, Janecia,
Janeice, Janiece, Janika,
Janitza, Janizzette,
Jannice, Janniece, Jannika,
Janyce, Jynice

Janie (English) a familiar
form of Jane.
Janey, Jani, Jany

Janika (Slavic) a form
of Jane.
Janeca, Janecka, Janeika,
Janeka, Janica, Janick,
Janicka, Janieka, Janikka,

Janikke, Janka, Jenica,
Jenicka, Jenika, Jeniqua,
Jenique, Jennica, Jennika

Janine (French) a form
of Jane.
Janeen, Janenan, Janene,
Janina, Jannina, Jannine,
Jannyne, Janyne, Jenine

Janis (English) a form
of Jane.
Janees, Janeesa, Janesa,
Janese, Janesey, Janesia,
Janessa, Janesse, Janise,
Janisha, Janissa, Jannis,
Jannisa, Jannisha,
Jannissa, Jenesa, Jenessa,
Jenesse, Jenice, Jenis,
Jenisha, Jenissa, Jennisa,
Jennise, Jennisha,
Jennissa, Jennisse

Janita (American) a form
of Juanita. See also Genita.
Janitra, Janitza, Jenita,
Jennita

Janna (Hebrew) a short
form of Johana. (Arabic)
harvest of fruit.
Janaya, Janaye

Jannie (English) a familiar
form of Jan, Jane.
Janney, Janny

Jardena (Hebrew) an
alternate form of Jordan.
(French, Spanish) garden.
Jardan, Jardane, Jarden,
Jardenia, Jardine, Jardyne

Jarita (Arabic) earthen
water jug.

Jarita *(cont.)*
Jara, Jari, Jaria, Jarica,
Jarida, Jarietta, Jarika,
Jarina, Jaritta, Jaritza,
Jarixa, Jarnita, Jarrika,
Jarrine

Jas (American) a short form
of Jasmine.
Jass, Jaz, Jazz, Jazze, Jazzi

Jasia (Polish) a form
of Jane.
Jas, Jasha, Jashae, Jashala,
Jashona, Jashonte, Jasie

Jasmine (Persian) jasmine
flower. See also Jessamine,
Yasmin.
Jas, Jasma, Jasmain,
Jasmaine, Jasman, Jasme,
Jasmeen, Jasmeet,
Jasmene, Jasmin, Jasmina,
Jasmira, Jasmit, Jasmon,
Jasmyn, Jassma, Jassmain,
Jassmaine, Jassmin,
Jassmine, Jassmit,
Jassmon, Jassmyn, Jazmin

Jaspreet (Punjabi) virtuous.
Jas, Jaspar, Jasparit,
Jasparita, Jasper, Jasprit,
Jasprita, Jasprite

Jatara (American) a combi-
nation of Jane + Tara.
Jataria, Jatarra, Jatori,
Jatoria

Javana (Malayan) from
Java.
Javanna, Javanne, Javon,
Javonda, Javonna,
Javonne, Javonya, Jawana,
Jawanna, Jawn

Javiera (Spanish) owner
of a new house. A femi-
nine form of Javier.
See also Xaviera.
Javeera, Viera

Jaya (Hindi) victory.
Jaea, Jaia, Jayla

Jaycee (American) a combi-
nation of the initials J. + C.
Jacee, Jacey, Jaci, Jacie,
Jacy, Jaycey, Jayci, Jaycie,
Jaycy

Jaydee (American) a com-
bination of the initials
J. + D.
Jadee, Jadey, Jadi, Jadie,
Jady, Jaydey, Jaydi, Jaydie,
Jaydy

Jaye (Latin) jaybird.
Jae, Jay, Jaylene

Jaylene (American) a form
of Jaye.
Jayelene, Jayla, Jaylah,
Jaylan, Jayleana, Jaylee,
Jayleen

Jaylynn (American) a com-
bination of Jaye + Lynn.
Jaelin, Jaeline, Jaelyn,
Jaelyne, Jaelynn, Jaelynne,
Jalin, Jaline, Jalyn, Jalyne,
Jalynn, Jalynne, Jaylin,
Jayline, Jaylyn, Jaylyne,
Jaylynne

Jayme, Jaymie (English)
alternate forms of Jami.
Jaymi, Jaymia, Jaymine,
Jaymini

Jayna (Hebrew) an alternate form of Jane.
Jaynae

Jayne (Hindi) victorious. (English) a form of Jane.
Jayn, Jaynee, Jayni, Jaynie, Jaynita, Jaynne

Jazlyn (American) a combination of Jazmin + Lynn.
Jazleen, Jazlene, Jazlin, Jazline, Jazlynn, Jazlynne, Jazzleen, Jazzlene, Jazzlin, Jazzline, Jazzlyn, Jazzlynn, Jazzlynne

Jazmin, Jazmine (Persian) alternate forms of Jasmine.
Jazman, Jazmen, Jazminn, Jazmon, Jazmyn, Jazmyne, Jazzman, Jazzmen, Jazzmin, Jazzmine, Jazzmit, Jazzmon, Jazzmyn

Jean, Jeanne (Scottish) God is gracious. Forms of Jane, Joan. See also Kini.
Jeana, Jeanann, Jeancie, Jeane, Jeaneane, Jeaneen, Jeaneia, Jeanell, Jeanelle, Jeanette, Jeaneva, Jeanice, Jeanie, Jeanine, Jeanmarie, Jeanna, Jeanné, Jeannee, Jeanney, Jeannie, Jeannita, Jeannot, Jeanny, Jeantelle

Jeana, Jeanna (Scottish) alternate forms of Jean.

Jeanette (French) a form of Jean.
Jeanete, Jeanett, Jeanetta, Jeanita, Jeannete, Jeannett, Jeannetta, Jeannette, Jeannita, Jenet, Jenett, Jenette, Jennet, Jennett, Jennetta, Jennette, Jennita, Jinetta, Jinette

Jeanie (Scottish) a familiar form of Jean.
Jeani, Jeanny, Jeany

Jeanine, Jenine (Scottish) alternate forms of Jean.
Jeanene, Jeanina, Jeannina, Jeannine, Jennine

Jelena (Russian) a form of Helen. See also Yelena.
Jalaine, Jalane, Jalanna, Jalayna, Jalayne, Jaleen, Jaleena, Jaleene, Jalena, Jalene, Jelaina, Jelaine, Jelane, Jelani, Jelayna, Jelayne, Jelean, Jeleen, Jeleena, Jelene

Jelisa (American) a combination of Jean + Lisa.
Jelissa

Jem (Hebrew) a short form of Jemima.
Gem, Jemi, Jemie

Jemima (Hebrew) dove.
Jamim, Jamima, Jem, Jemimah, Jemma, Jemmia, Jemmiah, Jemmie, Jemmy

Jemma (Hebrew) a short form of Jemima. (English) a form of Gemma.
Jem, Jemmia, Jemmiah

Jena (Arabic) an alternate form of Jenna.
Jenae, Jenah, Jenai, Jenal, Jenay

Jendaya (Zimbabwean) thankful.
Daya, Jenda, Jendayah

Jenelle (American) a combination of Jenny + Nell.
Jenall, Jenalle, Jenel, Jenell, Jenille, Jennel, Jennell, Jennelle, Jennielle, Jennille

Jenica (Romanian) a form of Jane.
Jenika, Jennica, Jennika

Jenifer, Jeniffer (Welsh) alternate forms of Jennifer.

Jenilee (American) a combination of Jennifer + Lee.
Jenalea, Jenalee, Jenaleigh, Jenaly, Jenelea, Jenelee, Jeneleigh, Jenely, Jenelly, Jenileigh, Jenily, Jennely, Jennielee, Jennilea, Jennilee, Jennilie

Jenisa (American) a combination of Jennifer + Nisa.
Jenisha, Jenissa, Jennisa, Jennise, Jennisha, Jennissa, Jennisse, Jennysa, Jennyssa, Jenysa, Jenyse, Jenyssa, Jenysse

Jenka (Czech) a form of Jane.

Jenna (Arabic) small bird. (Welsh) a short form of Jennifer. See also Gen.
Jena, Jennah, Jennat, Jennay, Jhenna

Jenni, Jennie (Welsh) familiar forms of Jennifer.
Jeni, Jenica, Jenisa, Jenka, Jenne, Jenné, Jennee, Jenney, Jennia, Jennier, Jennita, Jennora, Jensine

Jennifer (Welsh) white wave; white phantom. An alternate form of Guinevere. See also Gennifer, Ginnifer.
Jen, Jenefer, Jenifer, Jeniffer, Jenipher, Jenna, Jennafer, Jenniferanne, Jenniferlee, Jenniffe, Jenniffer, Jenniffier, Jennifier, Jennilee, Jenniphe, Jennipher, Jenny, Jennyfer

Jennilee (American) a combination of Jenny + Lee.
Jennalea, Jennalee, Jennielee, Jennilea, Jennilie

Jennilynn (American) a combination of Jenni + Lynn.
Jennalin, Jennaline, Jennalyn, Jennalyne, Jennalynn, Jennalynne, Jennilin, Jenniline, Jennilyn, Jennilyne, Jennilynne

Jenny (Welsh) a familiar form of Jennifer.
Jenney, Jenni, Jennie, Jeny, Jinny

Jeraldine (English) a form
of Geraldine.
**Jeraldeen, Jeraldene,
Jeraldina, Jeraldyne,
Jeralee, Jeri**

Jereni (Russian) a form
of Irene.

Jeri, Jerri, Jerrie
(American) short forms
of Jeraldine.
**Jera, Jerae, JeRae, Jeree,
Jeriel, Jerilee, Jerilyn,
Jerina, Jerinda, Jerra,
Jerrece, Jerriann, Jerrilee,
Jerrine, Jerry, Jerrylee,
Jerryne, Jerzy**

Jerica (American) a combi-
nation of Jeri + Erica.
**Jerice, Jericka, Jerika,
Jerreka, Jerricca, Jerrice,
Jerricka, Jerrika**

Jerilyn (American) a combi-
nation of Jeri + Lynn.
**Jeralin, Jeraline, Jeralyn,
Jeralyne, Jeralynn,
Jeralynne, Jerelin, Jereline,
Jerelyn, Jerelyne, Jerelynn,
Jerelynne, Jerilin, Jeriline,
Jerilyne, Jerilynn,
Jerilynne, Jerrilin,
Jerriline, Jerrilyn,
Jerrilyne, Jerrilynn,
Jerrilynne**

Jermaine (French) an alter-
nate form of Germaine.
**Jermain, Jerman, Jermane,
Jermayne, Jermecia,
Jermia, Jermice, Jermicia,
Jermika, Jermila**

Jerusha (Hebrew)
inheritance.
Jerushah, Yerusha

Jessalyn (American) a com-
bination of Jessica + Lynn.
**Jesalin, Jesaline, Jesalyn,
Jesalyne, Jesalynn,
Jesalynne, Jesilin, Jesiline,
Jesilyn, Jesilyne, Jesilynn,
Jesilynne, Jessalin,
Jessaline, Jessalyne,
Jessalynn, Jessalynne,
Jesselin, Jesseline,
Jesselyn, Jesselyne,
Jesselynn, Jesselynne**

Jessamine (French) a form
of Jasmine.
**Jessamin, Jessamon,
Jessamy, Jessamyn,
Jessemin, Jessemine,
Jessimin, Jessimine,
Jessmin, Jessmine,
Jessmon, Jessmy, Jessmyn**

Jesse, Jessi (Hebrew) alternate forms of Jessie.
Jessey

Jessenia (Arabic) flower.
Jescenia, Jesenia

Jessica (Hebrew) wealthy.
A feminine form of Jesse.
Literature: a name perhaps
invented by Shakespeare
for a character in his play
The Merchant of Venice.
See also Gessica, Yessica.
**Jesi, Jesica, Jesika, Jess,
Jessa, Jessaca, Jessah,
Jessalyn, Jessca, Jesscia,
Jesseca, Jessia, Jessicca,**

Jessica (cont.)
Jessicia, Jessicka, Jessie,
Jessieka, Jessika, Jessiqua,
Jessiya, Jessy, Jessyca,
Jessyka, Jezeca, Jezica,
Jezika, Jezyca

Jessie (Hebrew) a short
form of Jessica. (Scottish)
a form of Janet.
Jescie, Jesey, Jess, Jesse,
Jessé, Jessee, Jessi, Jessia,
Jessiya, Jessy, Jessye

Jessika (Hebrew) an alternate form of Jessica.

Jésusa (Hebrew) God is
my salvation. (Spanish)
a feminine form of Jésus.

Jetta (English) jet black
gem. (American) a familiar
form of Jevette.
Jetje, Jette, Jettie

Jevette (American) a combination of Jean + Yvette.
Jetta, Jeva, Jeveta, Jevetta

Jewel (French) precious
gem.
Jewell, Jewelle, Jewellee,
Jewellie, Juel, Jule

Jezebel (Hebrew) unex-
alted; impure. Bible:
the wife of King Ahab.
Jessabel, Jessebel, Jez,
Jezabel, Jezabella,
Jezabelle, Jezebell,
Jezebella, Jezebelle, Jezel,
Jezell, Jezelle

Jianna (Italian) an alternate
form of Gianna.
Jiana, Jianina, Jianine

Jibon (Hindi) life.

Jill (English) a short form
of Jillian.
Jil, Jiline, Jilli, Jillie, Jilline,
Jillisa, Jillissa, Jilly, Jillyn

Jillaine (Latin) an alternate
form of Jillian.
Jilaine, Jilane, Jilayne,
Jillana, Jillane, Jillann,
Jillanne, Jillayne

Jilleen (Irish) a form
of Jillian.
Jileen, Jilene, Jillene,
Jillenne

Jillian (Latin) youthful.
An alternate form of Julia.
See also Gillian.
Jilian, Jiliana, Jiliann,
Jilianna, Jilianne, Jilienna,
Jilienne, Jill, Jillaine,
Jilliana, Jilliane, Jilliann,
Jillianne, Jillien, Jillienne,
Jillion, Jilliyn

Jimi (Hebrew) supplanter,
substitute. (American)
a feminine form of Jimmy.
Jimae, Jimaria, Jimella,
Jimena, Jimetrice,
Jimilonda, Jimisha,
Jimiyah, Jimmeka, Jimmet,
Jimmicia, Jimmie, Jimysha

Jin (Japanese) tender.
(American) a short form
of Ginny, Jinny.

Jina (Italian) an alternate form of Gina. (Swahili) baby with a name.
Jena, Jinae, Jinan, Jinda, Jinna, Jinnae

Jinny (Scottish) a familiar form of Jenny. (American) a familiar form of Virginia.
Jin, Jina, Jinae, Jinelle, Jinessa, Jinna, Jinnae, Jinnalee, Jinnee, Jinnell, Jinney, Jinni, Jinnie

Jirina (Czech) a form of Georgia.

Jizelle (American) a form of Giselle.
Jezel, Jezell, Jezella, Jezelle, Jisell, Jisella, Jiselle, Jissell, Jissella, Jisselle

Jo (American) a short form of Joanna, Jolene, Josephine.
Joangie, Joetta, Joette, Joey

Joan (Hebrew) God is gracious. An alternate form of Jane. History: Joan of Arc was a fifteenth-century heroine and resistance fighter. See also Ioana, Jean, Juanita, Siobahn.
Joane, Joaneil, Joanel, Joanelle, Joanie, Joanmarie, Joann, Joannanette, Joannel

Joanie (Hebrew) a familiar form of Joan.

Joani, Joanni, Joannie, Joany, Joenie, Joni

Joanna (English) a form of Joan. See also Yoanna.
Janka, Jo, Joana, Jo-Ana, Joandra, Joanka, Joananna, Joananne, Jo-Anie, Joanka, Jo-Anna, Joannah, Jo-Annie, Joayn, Joeana, Joeanna, Johana, Johanna, Johannah

Joanne (English) a form of Joan.
Joanann, Joananne, Joann, Jo-Ann, Jo-Anne, Joeann, Joeanne

Joaquina (Hebrew) God will establish.
Joaquine

Jobeth (English) a combination of Jo + Beth.
Joby

Joby (Hebrew) afflicted. A feminine form of Job. (English) a familiar form of Jobeth.
Jobey, Jobi, Jobie, Jobina, Jobita, Jobrina, Jobye, Jobyna

Jocelyn (Latin) joyous.
Jocelin, Joceline, Jocelle, Jocelyne, Jocelynn, Jocelynne, Joci, Jocia, Jocinta, Joscelin, Jossalin, Josilin, Joycelyn

Jodi, Jodie, Jody (American) familiar forms of Judith.

Jodi, Jodie, Jody *(cont.)*
**Jodee, Jodele, Jodell,
Jodelle, Jodene, Jodevea,
Jodilee, Jodi-Lee, Jodilynn,
Jodi-Lynn, Jodine, Jodyne**

Jodiann (American) a combination of Jodi + Ann.
**Jodi-Ann, Jodianna, Jodi-
Anna, Jodianne, Jodi-
Anne, Jodyann, Jody-Ann,
Jodyanna, Jody-Anna,
Jodyanne, Jody-Anne**

Joelle (Hebrew) God is willing. A feminine form of Joel.
**Joela, Joelee, Joeleen,
Joelene, Joeli, Joeline,
Joell, Joella, Joëlle, Joellen,
Joelly, Joellyn, Joelyn,
Joelyne, Joelynn**

Johana, Johanna
(German) forms of Joanna.
**Janna, Johanah, Johani,
Johanie, Johanka,
Johannah, Johanne,
Johanni, Johannie, Johnna,
Johonna, Jonna**

Johnna, Jonna (American)
forms of Johana, Joanna.
See also Gianna.
**Jahna, Jahnaya, Jhona,
Jhonna, Jianna, Jianni,
Jiannini, Johna, Johnda,
Johneatha, Johnetta,
Johnette, Johni, Johnica,
Johnie, Johnique, Johnita,
Johnittia, Johnnessa,
johnni, Johnnie,
Johnnielynn, Johnnie-
Lynn, Johnnquia, Johnny,**

**Johnquita, Joncie, Jonda,
Jondell, Jondrea, Jonni,
Jonnica, Jonnie, Jonnika,
Jonnita, Jonny, Jonyelle,
Jutta**

Johnnessa (American)
a combination of
Johnna + Nessa.
**Jahnessa, Johnecia,
Johnesha, Johnetra,
Johnisha, Johnishi,
Johnnise, Jonyssa**

Jokla (Swahili) beautiful
robe.

Jolanda (Greek) an alternate form of Yolanda.
See also Iolanthe.
**Jola, Jolan, Jolán, Jolande,
Jolander, Jolanka, Jolánta,
Jolantha, Jolanthe, Joli**

Joleen, Joline (English)
alternate forms of Jolene.

Jolene (Hebrew) God will
add, God will increase.
(English) a form of
Josephine.
**Jo, Jolaine, Jolana, Jolane,
Jolanna, Jolanne, Jolanta,
Jolayne, Jole, Jolean,
Joleane, Jolee, Joleen,
Jolena, Joléne, Jolenna,
Joley, Jolin, Jolina, Jolinda,
Joline, Jolinna, Jolisa,
Jolleane, Jolleen, Jollene,
Jolline, Jolye**

Jolie (French) pretty.
**Jole, Jolea, Jolee, Joleigh,
Joley, Joli, Jolibeth, Jollee,
Jollie, Jolly, Joly, Jolye**

Jolisa (American) a combination of Jo + Lisa.
Joleesa, Jolissa, Jolysa, Jolyssa

Jolynn (American) a combination of Jo + Lynn.
Joline, Jolinn, Jolyn, Jolyne, Jolynne

Jonelle (American) a combination of Joan + Elle.
Jahnel, Jahnell, Jahnelle, Johnel, Johnell, Johnella, Johnelle, Jonel, Jonell, Jonella, Jynell, Jynelle

Joni (American) a familiar form of Joan.
Jona, Jonae, Jonai, Jonann, Jonati, Joncey, Jonci, Joncie, Joneeka, Joneen, Joneika, Joneisha, Jonelle, Jonessa, Jonetia, Jonetta, Jonette, Jonica, Jonice, Jonie, Jonika, Jonilee, Jonilee, Jonina, Joniqua, Jonique, Jonis, Jonisa, Jonisha, Jonit, Jony

Jonina (Hebrew) dove. A feminine form of Jonah. See also Yonina.
Jona, Jonika, Joniqua, Jonita, Jonnina

Jonita (Hebrew) an alternate form of Jonina. See also Yonita.
Jonati, Jonit, Jonta, Jontae, Jontaé, Jontaya

Jonquil (Latin, English) Botany: an ornamental plant with fragrant yellow flowers.
Jonquille

Jontel (American) an alternate form of Johnna.
Jontaya, Jonteil, Jontelle, Jontia, Jontila, Jontrice

Jora (Hebrew) autumn rain.
Jorah

Jordan (Hebrew) descending.
Jordain, Jordana, Jordane, Jordanna, Jorden, Jordenne, Jordi, Jordin, Jordine, Jordon, Jordonna, Jordyn, Jordyne, Jori, Jorie

Jordana, Jordanna (Hebrew) alternate forms of Jordan. See also Giordana, Yordana.
Jordann, Jordanne, Jourdana, Jourdann, Jourdanna, Jourdanne

Jori, Jorie (Hebrew) familiar forms of Jordan.
Jorai, Jorea, Joree, Jorée, Jorey, Jorian, Jorin, Jorina, Jorine, Jorita, Jorrian, Jorrie, Jorry, Jory

Joriann (American) a combination of Jori + Ann.
Jori-Ann, Jorianna, Jori-Anna, Jorianne, Jori-Anne, Jorriann, Jorrianna, Jorrianne, Jorryann, Jorryanna, Jorryanne, Joryann, Joryanna, Joryanne

Jorja (American) a form
of Georgia.
**Jeorgi, Jeorgia, Jorgana,
Jorgi, Jorgia, Jorgina,
Jorjana, Jorji**

Joscelin (Latin) an alternate
form of Jocelyn.
**Josceline, Joscelyn,
Joscelyne, Joscelynn,
Joscelynne, Joselin,
Joseline, Joselyn, Joselyne,
Joselynn, Joselynne,
Joshlyn**

Josee, Josée (American)
familiar forms of Josephine.
**Joesee, Joesell, Joesette,
Joselle, Josette, Josey, Josi,
Josiane, Josiann, Josianne,
Josielina, Josina, Josy,
Jozee, Jozelle, Jozette, Jozie**

Josefina (Spanish) a form
of Josephine.

Joselyn, Joslyn (Latin) alter-
nate forms of Jocelyn.
**Josalene, Joselene, Joseline,
Josiline, Josilyn**

Josephine (French) God
will add, God will increase.
A feminine form of Joseph.
See also Fifi, Pepita,
Yosepha.
**Fina, Jo, Joey, Josee, Josée,
Josefa, Josefena, Josefina,
Josefine, Josepha, Josephe,
Josephene, Josephin,
Josephina, Josephyna,
Josephyne, Josette, Josie,
Sefa**

Josette (French) a familiar
form of Josephine.
Josetta

Joshlyn (Latin) an alternate
form of Jocelyn. (Hebrew)
God is my salvation. A fem-
inine form of Joshua.
**Jesusa, Joshalin, Joshalyn,
Joshalynn, Joshalynne,
Joshana, Joshann,
Joshanna, Joshanne,
Joshelle, Joshetta,
Joshleen, Joshlene, Joshlin,
Joshline, Joshlyne,
Joshlynn, Joshlynne**

Josie (Hebrew) a familiar
form of Josephine.
Josee, Josey, Josi, Josy, Josye

Josilin, Joslin (Latin) alter-
nate forms of Jocelyn.
**Josielina, Josiline, Josilyn,
Josilyne, Josilynn,
Josilynne, Joslin, Josline,
Joslyn, Joslyne, Joslynn,
Joslynne**

Jossalin an alternate form
of Jocelyn.
**Jossaline, Jossalyn,
Jossalynn, Jossalynne,
Josseline, Jossellen,
Jossellin, Jossellyn,
Josselyn, Josselyne,
Josselynn, Josselynne,
Jossie, Josslin, Jossline,
Josslyn, Josslyne, Josslynn,
Josslynne**

Jovanna (Latin) majestic.
A feminine form of Jovan.
(Italian) an alternate form

of Giovanna. Mythology:
Jove, also known as
Jupiter, was the supreme
Roman god.
**Jeovana, Jeovanna,
Jouvan, Jovado, Joval,
Jovan, Jovana, Jovanie,
Jovann, Jovanne, Joveda,
Jovena, Jovian, Jovida,
Jovon, Jovonda, Jovonna,
Jovonne, Jowanna**

Jovita (Latin) jovial.
**Jovena, Joveta, Jovetta,
Jovida, Jovina, Jovitta**

Joy (Latin) joyous.
**Joi, Joie, Joya, Joyan,
Joyann, Joyanna,
Joyanne, Joye, Joyeeta,
Joyelle, Joyhanna,
Joyhannah, Joyia, Joylin,
Joyline, Joylyn, Joylyne,
Joylynn, Joylynne, Joyous,
Joyvina**

Joyce (Latin) joyous.
A short form of Jocelyn.
**Joice, Joycey, Joycie,
Joyous, Joysel**

Joycelyn (American)
a form of Jocelyn.
**Joycelin, Joyceline,
Joycelyne, Joycelynn,
Joycelynne**

Joylyn (American) a combi-
nation of Joy + Lynn.
**Joyleen, Joylene, Joylin,
Joyline, Joylyne, Joylynn,
Joy-Lynn, Joylynne**

Juandalyn (Spanish) an
alternate form of Juanita.

**Juandalin, Juandaline,
Juandalyne, Juandalynn,
Juandalynne**

Juanita (Spanish) a form
of Jane, Joan. See also
Kwanita, Nita, Waneta
Wanika.
**Juana, Juandalyn,
Juaneice, Juanequa,
Juanesha, Juanice,
Juanicia, Juaniqua,
Juanisha, Juanishia,
Juanna**

Juci (Hungarian) a form
of Judy.

Judith (Hebrew) praised.
Mythology: the slayer
of Holofernes, according
to ancient eastern legend.
A feminine form of Judah.
See also Yehudit, Yudita.
**Giuditta, Ioudith, Jodi,
Jodie, Jody, Jucika, Judana,
Jude, Judine, Judit, Judita,
Judite, Juditha, Judithe,
Judy, Judyta, Jutka**

Judy (Hebrew) a familiar
form of Judith.
Juci, Judi, Judie, Judye

Judyann (American)
a combination of
Judy + Ann.
**Judiann, Judianna,
Judianne, Judyanna,
Judyanne**

Jula (Polish) a form of Julia.
Julca, Julcia, Juliska, Julka

Julene (Basque) a form
of Julia. See also Yulene.
**Julina, Juline, Julinka,
Juliska, Julleen, Jullena,
Jullene, Julyne**

Julia (Latin) youthful.
A feminine form of Julius.
See also Giulia, Jill, Jillian,
Sulia, Yulia.
**Iulia, Jula, Julene, Juliana,
Juliann, Julica, Julie, Juliet,
Julija, Julina, Juline, Julisa,
Julissa, Julita, Julka,
Julyssa**

Juliana (Czech, Spanish),
Julianna (Hungarian)
forms of Julia.
Julliana, Jullianna

Juliann, Julianne (English)
forms of Julia.
**Juliane, Julieann,
Julie-Ann, Julieanne,
Julie-Anne**

Julie (English) a form
of Julia.
**Juel, Jule, Julee, Juli,
Julie-Lynn, Julie-Mae,
Julien, Juliene, Julienne,
Jullie, July**

Juliet, Juliette (French)
forms of Julia.
**Julet, Julieta, Julietta,
Jullet, Julliet, Jullietta**

Julita (Spanish) a form
of Julia.
Julitta, Julyta

Jun (Chinese) truthful.

June (Latin) born in the
sixth month.
**Juna, Junell, Junelle,
Junette, Junia, Junie,
Juniet, Junieta, Junietta,
Juniette, Junina, Junita**

Juno (Latin) queen.
Mythology: the goddess
of heaven.

Justina (Italian) a form
of Justine.
**Jestena, Jestina, Justinna,
Justyna**

Justine (Latin) just,
righteous. A feminine
form of Justin.
**Giustina, Jestine, Juste,
Justi, Justie, Justina,
Justinn, Justy, Justyne**

Kacey, Kacy (Irish) brave.
(American) alternate forms
of Casey. A combination
of the initials K. + C.
**K. C., Kace, Kacee, Kaci,
Kacie, Kaicee, Kaicey,
Kasey, Kasie, Kaycee,
Kayci, Kaycie**

Kachina (Native American)
sacred dancer.
Kachine

Kaci, Kacie (American) alternate forms of Kacey, Kacy.
Kasci, Kaycie, Kaysie

Kacia (Greek) a short form of Acacia.
Kaycia, Kaysia

Kady (English) an alternate form of Katy. A combination of the initials K. + D. See also Cady.
K. D., Kade, Kadee, Kadey, Kadi, Kadie, Kayde, Kaydee, Kaydey, Kaydi, Kaydie, Kaydy

Kaedé (Japanese) maple leaf.

Kaela (Hebrew, Arabic) beloved sweetheart. A short form of Kalila, Kelila.
Kaelah, Kayla, Kaylah, Keyla, Keylah, Kaelyn

Kaelyn (American) a combination of Kae + Lynn. See also Kaylyn.
Kaelan, Kaelen, Kaelin, Kaelinn, Kaelynn, Kaelynne

Kagami (Japanese) mirror.

Kahsha (Native American) fur robe.
Kasha, Kashae, Kashia

Kai (Hawaiian) sea. (Hopi, Navaho) willow tree.

Kaia (Greek) earth. Mythology: Gaia was the goddess of the earth.
Kaija, Kaiya

Kaila (Hebrew) laurel; crown.
Kailah, Kailee, Kailey, Kayla

Kailee, Kailey (American) familiar forms of Kaila. Alternate forms of Kaylee.
Kaile, Kaili

Kairos (Greek) last, final, complete. Mythology: the last goddess born to Jupiter.
Kaira, Kairra

Kaitlin (Irish) pure. An alternate form of Caitlin. See also Katelin.
Kaitlan, Kaitland, Kaitleen, Kaitlen, Kaitlind, Kaitlinn, Kaitlon, Kalyn

Kaitlyn (Irish) an alternate form of Caitlyn.
Kaitlynn, Kaitlynne

Kala (Arabic) a short form of Kalila. An alternate form of Cala.

Kalama (Hawaiian) torch.

Kalani (Hawaiian) chieftain; sky.
Kailani, Kalanie, Kaloni

Kalare (Latin, Basque) bright; clear.

Kalea (Hawaiian) bright; clear.
Kahlea, Kahleah, Kailea, Kaileah, Kallea, Kalleah, Kaylea, Kayleah, Khalea, Khaleah

Kalei (Hawaiian) flower wreath.
Kahlei, Kailei, Kallei, Kaylei, Khalei

Kalena (Hawaiian) pure. See also Kalina.
Kaleena

Kalere (Swahili) short woman.
Kaleer

Kaley (American) an alternate form of Caley, Kaylee.
Kalee, Kaleigh, Kalleigh

Kali (Sanskrit) energy; black goddess; time the destroyer. (Hawaiian) hesitating. Religion: a name for the Hindu goddess Shakti. See also Cali.
Kala, Kalee, Kaleigh, Kaley, Kalie, Kallee, Kalley, Kalli, Kallie, Kally, Kallye, Kaly

Kalifa (Somali) chaste; holy.

Kalila (Arabic) beloved, sweetheart.
Kahlila, Kala, Kaleela, Kaley, Kalilla, Kaylee, Kaylil, Kaylila, Kelila, Khalila, Khalilah, Khalillah, Kyla, Kylila, Kylilah, Kylillah

Kalina (Slavic) flower. (Hawaiian) a form of Karen. See also Kalena.
Kalinna, Kalynna

Kalinda (Hindi) sun.
Kaleenda, Kalindi, Kalynda, Kalyndi

Kalisa (American) a combination of Kate + Lisa.
Kaleesha, Kalisha, Kalissa, Kalysa, Kalyssa

Kaliska (Moquelumnan) coyote chasing deer.

Kallan (Slavic) stream, river.
Kalahn, Kalan, Kalen, Kallen, Kalin, Kallin, Kallon, Kalon, Kallyn, Kalyn

Kalle (Finnish) a form of Carol.
Kaille, Kaylle

Kalli, Kallie (Greek) an alternate form of Callie. A familiar form of Kalliope, Kallista, Kalliyan.
Kalle, Kallee, Kalley, Kallita, Kally

Kalliope (Greek) beautiful voice. Mythology: Calliope was the muse of epic poetry.
Kalli, Kallie, Kallyope

Kallista (Greek) an alternate form of Callista.
Kalesta, Kalista, Kallesta,

Kalli, Kallie, Kallysta, Kaysta

Kalliyan (Cambodian) best.
Kalli, Kallie

Kaltha (English) marigold, yellow flower.

Kaluwa (Swahili) forgotten one.
Kalua

Kalyca (Greek) rosebud.
Kali, Kalica, Kalika, Kaly

Kalyn (American) an alternate form of Kaylyn.

Kama (Sanskrit) loved one. Religion: the Hindu god of love.

Kamala (Hindi) lotus.
Kamalah

Kamali (Mahona) spirit guide; protector.
Kamalie

Kamaria (Swahili) moonlight.
Kamara, Kamarie

Kamata (Moquelumnan) gambler.

Kambria (Latin) an alternate form of Cambria.
Kambra, Kambrie, Kambriea, Kambry

Kamea (Hawaiian) one and only; precious.
Kameo

Kameke (Swahili) blind.

Kameko (Japanese) turtle child. Mythology: the turtle symbolizes longevity.

Kameron (American) a form of Cameron.
Kamren, Kamrin, Kamron, Kamryn

Kami (Italian, North African) a short form of Kamila, Kamilah. (Japanese) divine aura. See also Cami.
Kammi, Kammie, Kammy, Kamy

Kamila (Slavic) a form of Camilla. See also Millie.
Kameela, Kameelah, Kami, Kamilka, Kamilla, Kamille, Kamma, Kamyla

Kamilah (North African) perfect.
Kameela, Kameelah, Kami, Kammilah

Kanani (Hawaiian) beautiful.
Kana, Kanae, Kanan

Kanda (Native American) magical power.

Kandace, Kandice (Greek) glittering white; glowing. (American) alternate forms of Candace, Candice.
Kandas, Kandess, Kandi, Kandis, Kandise, Kandiss, Kandus, Kandyce, Kandys, Kandyse

Kandi (American) a familiar form of Kandace, Kandice. See also Candi.
Kanda, Kandhi, Kandia, Kandie, Kandy

Kane (Japanese) two right hands.

Kaneisha (American) an alternate form of Keneisha.
Kaneasha, Kaneesha, Kanesha, Kaneshia, Kanisha, Kanishia

Kanene (Swahili) a little important thing.

Kani (Hawaiian) sound.

Kanika (Mwera) black cloth.

Kannitha (Cambodian) angel.

Kanoa (Hawaiian) free.

Kanya (Hindi) virgin. (Thai) young lady. Religion: a name for the Hindu goddess Shakti.
Kania

Kapri (American) an alternate form of Capri.
Kaprice, Kapricia, Kaprisha, Kaprisia

Kapua (Hawaiian) blossom.

Kapuki (Swahili) first-born daughter.

Kara (Greek, Danish) pure. An alternate form of Katherine.
Kaira, Kairah, Karah,
Karalea, Karaleah, Karalee, Karalie, Kari

Karah (Greek, Danish) an alternate form of Kara. (Irish, Italian) an alternate form of Cara.
Karrah

Karalynn (English) a combination of Kara + Lynn.
Karalin, Karaline, Karalyn, Karalyne, Karalynne

Karen (Greek) pure. An alternate form of Katherine. See also Carey, Carina, Caryn.
Kaaren, Kaarin, Kaarina, Kalina, Karaina, Karan, Karena, Karin, Karina, Karine, Karna, Karon, Karren, Karrin, Karrina, Karrine, Karron, Karyn, Kerrin, Kerron, Kerrynn, Kerrynne, Koren

Karena (Scandinavian) a form of Karen.
Kareen, Kareena, Kareina, Karenah, Karene, Karreen, Karreena, Karrena, Karrene

Karessa (French) an alternate form of Caressa.
Karese, Karess, Karesse

Kari (Greek) pure. (Danish) a form of Caroline, Katherine. See also Carey, Cari, Carrie.
Karee, Karey, Kariann, Karianna, Karianne, Karie,

Karrey, Karri, Karrie, Karry, Kary

Karida (Arabic) untouched, pure.
Kareeda, Karita

Karilynn (American) a combination of Kari + Lynn.
Kareelin, Kareeline, Kareelinn, Kareelyn, Kareelyne, Kareelynn, Kareelynne, Karilin, Kariline, Karilinn, Karilyn, Karilyne, Karilynne, Karylin, Karyline, Karylinn, Karylyn, Karylyne, Karylynn, Karylynne

Karimah (Arabic) generous.
Kareema, Kareemah, Karima, Karime

Karin (Scandinavian) a form of Karen.
Karina, Karine, Karinne

Karina (Russian) a form of Karen.
Karinna, Karrina, Karryna, Karyna

Karine (Russian) a form of Karen.
Karrine, Karryne, Karyne

Karis (Greek) graceful.
Karess, Karice, Karise, Karris, Karys, Karyss

Karissa (Greek) an alternate form of Carissa.
Karese, Karessa, Karesse,

Karisa, Karisha, Karishma, Karisma, Karissimia, Kariza, Karrisa, Karrissa, Karyssa

Karla (German) an alternate form of Carla. (Slavic) a short form of Karoline.
Karila, Karilla, Karle, Karleen, Karleigh, Karlen, Karlena, Karlene, Karlenn, Karletta, Karley, Karlicka, Karlign, Karlin, Karlina, Karling, Karlinka, Karlisha, Karlisia, Karlita, Karlitha, Karlla, Karlon, Karlyan, Karlye, Karlyn, Karlynn, Karlynne

Karli, Karly (Latin) little and womanly. (American) forms of Carly.
Karlee, Karley, Karlie, Karlye

Karlotte (American) a form of Charlotte.
Karletta, Karlette, Karlotta

Karma (Hindi) fate, destiny; action.

Karmel (Hebrew) an alternate form of Carmela.
Karmeita, Karmela, Karmelina, Karmella, Karmelle, Karmiella, Karmielle, Karmyla

Karmen (Hebrew) song. A form of Carmen.
Karman, Karmencita, Karmin, Karmina, Karmine, Karmita,

Karmen *(cont.)*
Karmon, Karmyn,
Karmyne

Karoline (Slavic) a form
of Caroline.
Karaleen, Karalena,
Karalene, Karalin,
Karaline, Karileen,
Karilena, Karilene, Karilin,
Karilina, Kariline, Karleen,
Karlen, Karlena, Karlene,
Karling, Karoleena,
Karolena, Karolina,
Karolinka, Karroleen,
Karrolena, Karrolene,
Karrolin, Karroline

Karoll (Slavic) a form
of Carol.
Karel, Karilla, Karily,
Karola, Karole, Karoly,
Karlyan, Karlye, Karrol,
Karyl, Kerril

Karolyn (American) a form
of Carolyn.
Karalyn, Karalyna,
Karalynn, Karalynne,
Karilyn, Karilyna,
Karilynn, Karilynne,
Karlyn, Karlynn, Karlynne,
Karolyna, Karolynn,
Karolynne, Karrolyn,
Karrolyna, Karrolynn,
Karrolynne

Karri, Karrie (American)
forms of Carrie.
Kari, Karie, Karry

Karuna (Hindi) merciful.

Karyn (American) a form
of Karen.
Karyna, Karyne, Karynn

Kasa (Hopi) fur robe.

Kasey, Kasie (Irish) brave.
(American) forms of Casey,
Kacey.
Kaisee, Kaisie, Kasci,
Kascy, Kasee, Kasi, Kasy,
Kasya, Kaysci, Kaysea,
Kaysee, Kaysey, Kaysi,
Kaysie, Kaysy

Kashawna (American)
a combination of
Kate + Shawna.
Kashana, Kashawn,
Kashonda, Kashonna

Kashmir (Sanskrit)
Geography: a state
in India.
Cashmere, Kashmear,
Kashmere, Kashmia,
Kashmira, Kasmir,
Kasmira, Kazmir, Kazmira

Kasi (Hindi) from the holy
city.

Kasia (Polish) a form of
Katherine. See also Cassia.
Kasha, Kashia, Kasienka,
Kasja, Kaska, Kassa,
Kassia, Kassya, Kasya

Kasinda (Umbundu) our
last baby.

Kassandra (Greek)
an alternate form
of Cassandra.
Kasander, Kasandria,
Kasandra, Kasaundra,

**Kasondra, Kasoundra,
Kassandr, Kassandre,
Kassandré, Kassaundra,
Kassi, Kazandra,
Khrisandra, Krisandra,
Krissandra**

Kassi, Kassie (American)
familiar forms of
Kassandra, Kassidy.
See also Cassie.
Kassey, Kassia, Kassy

Kassidy (Irish) clever.
(American) an alternate
form of Cassidy.
**Kassadee, Kassadi,
Kassadie, Kassadina,
Kassady, Kasseday,
Kassedee, Kassi, Kassiddy,
Kassidee, Kassidi,
Kassidie, Kassity**

Katarina (Czech) a form
of Katherine.
**Kata, Katarin, Kataryna,
Katenka, Katerina,
Katerine, Katerini,
Katerinka, Katinka,
Katrika, Katrina, Katrine,
Katrinka**

Kate (Greek) pure. (English)
a short form of Katherine.
**Kait, Kata, Kati, Katica,
Katja, Katka, Katy, Katya**

Katelin, Katelyn (Irish)
alternate forms of Caitlin.
See also Kaitlin.
**Kaetlin, Kaetlyn,
Kaetlynn, Kaetlynne,
Katalin, Katelan,
Kateland, Kateleen,**

**Katelen, Katelene,
Katelind, Katelinn,
Katelun, Katelyne, Katlyn,
Kaytlin, Kaytlyn,
Kaytlynn, Kaytlynne**

Katharine (Greek) an alternate form of Katherine.
**Katharaine, Katharin,
Katharina, Katharyn**

Katherine (Greek) pure.
See also Carey, Catherine,
Kara, Karen, Kari, Kasia,
Katie, Yekaterina.
**Ekaterina, Ekatrinna,
Kasienka, Kasin, Kat,
Katarina, Katchen, Kate,
Katha, Kathann,
Kathanne, Katharine,
Kathereen, Katheren,
Katherene, Katherenne,
Katherin, Katherina,
Katheryn, Katheryne,
Kathi, Kathleen, Kathryn,
Kathy, Kathyrine, Katina,
Katlaina, Katoka,
Katreeka, Katrina, Kay,
Kitty**

Kathi, Kathy (English)
familiar forms of
Katherine, Kathleen.
See also Cathi.
**Kaethe, Katha, Kathe,
Kathee, Kathey, Kathi,
Kathie, Katka, Katla, Kató**

Kathleen (Irish) a form
of Katherine. See also
Cathleen.
**Katheleen, Kathelene,
Kathileen, Kathlyn,**

Kathleen (cont.)
**Kathlyne, Kathlynn,
Kathy, Katleen, Katlin,
Katlyn, Katlynn**

Kathryn (English) a form
of Katherine.
**Kathren, Kathrine,
Kathryne**

Kati (Estonian) a form
of Kate.
Katia, Katja, Katya, Katye

Katie (English) a familiar
form of Kate.
**Kady, Katee, Kati, Kātia,
Katy, Kayte, Kaytee,
Kaytie**

Katlyn (Greek) pure.
(Irish) an alternate form
of Katelin.
**Kaatlain, Katland,
Katlynd, Katlynn,
Katlynne**

Katriel (Hebrew) God
is my crown.
**Katri, Katrie, Katry,
Katryel**

Katrina (German) a form
of Katherine. See also
Catrina, Trina.
**Katja, Katreen, Katreena,
Katrelle, Katrene, Katri,
Katrice, Katricia, Katrien,
Katrin, Katrine, Katrinia,
Katriona, Katryn,
Katryna, Kattiah,
Kattrina, Kattryna, Katus,
Katuska, Katya**

Katy (English) a familiar
form of Kate. See also
Cady.
Kady, Katey, Katya, Kayte

Kaulana (Hawaiian)
famous.
Kaula, Kauna, Kahuna

Kaveri (Hindi) Geographical: a sacred river in India.

Kavindra (Hindi) poet.

Kawena (Hawaiian) glow.

Kay (Greek) rejoicer.
(Teutonic) a fortified place.
(Latin) merry. A short form
of Katherine.
**Caye, Kae, Kai, Kaye,
Kayla**

Kaya (Hopi) wise child.
(Japanese) resting place.
Kaja, Kayia

Kaycee (American) a combination of the initials
K. + C.

Kayla (Arabic, Hebrew)
laurel; crown. An alternate
form of Kaela, Kaila.
**Kaela, Kaila, Kayle,
Kaylee, Kayleen, Kaylene,
Kaylia, Kaylin**

Kaylee (American) a form
of Kayla. See also Caeley.
**Kaelea, Kaeleah, Kaelee,
Kaeli, Kaelie, Kaelee,
Kaeli, Kaelie, Kailea,
Kaileah, Kailee, Kayle,
Kaylea, Kayleah, Kaylei,
Kayleigh, Kayley, Kayli,
Kaylie**

Kayleen, Kaylene
(Hebrew) beloved,
sweetheart. Alternate
forms of Kayla.
**Kaeleen, Kaelen, Kaelene,
Kailen, Kaileen, Kailene,
Kaylen**

Kayleigh (American) an
alternate form of Kaylee.
Kaeleigh, Kaileigh

Kaylin (American) an alternate form of Kaylyn.
Kaylan, Kaylon

Kaylyn (American) a combi-
nation of Kay + Lynn.
See also Kaelyn.
**Kailyn, Kailynn, Kailynne,
Kayleen, Kaylene, Kaylynn,
Kaylynne**

Keala (Hawaiian) path.

Keara (Irish) dark; black.
Religion: an Irish saint.
**Kearia, Kearra, Keera,
Keerra, Keira, Keirra, Kera,
Kiara, Kiarra, Kiera, Kierra**

Keeley, Keely (Irish) alter-
nate forms of Kelly.
**Kealee, Kealey, Keali,
Kealie, Keallie, Kealy,
Kealyn, Keela, Keelan,
Keelee, Keeleigh, Keeli,
Keelie, Keelin, Keellie,
Keelyn, Keighla, Keilan,
Keilee, Keileigh, Keiley,
Keilly, Kiela, Kiele, Kieley,
Kielly, Kiely, Kielyn**

Keena (Irish) brave.
Keenya, Kina

Kei (Japanese) reverent.
**Keiana, Keikann,
Keikanna, Keionna**

Keiki (Hawaiian) child.
Keikana, Keikanne

Keiko (Japanese) happy
child.
Kei

Keilani (Hawaiian) glorious
chief.
Keilan, Keilana

Keira (Irish) an alternate
form of Kiara.
Kera

Keisha (American) a short
form of Keneisha.
**Keesha, Keishaun,
Keishauna, Keishawn,
Kesha, Keysha, Kiesha,
Kisha, Kishanda**

Keita (Scottish) woods;
enclosed place.
Keiti

Kekona (Hawaiian) second-
born child.

Kelila (Hebrew) crown,
laurel. See also Kaela,
Kayla, Kalila.
Kelilah, Kelula

Kelley (Irish) an alternate
form of Kelly.

Kelli, Kellie (Irish) familiar
forms of Kelly.
**Keli, Kelia, Kellia, Kelliann,
Kellianne, Kellisa**

Kelly (Irish) brave warrior.
See also Caeley.

Kelly *(cont.)*
Keeley, Keely, Kelley,
Kellyann, Kellyanne,
Kelley, Kelli, Kellie, Kellye

Kellyn (Irish) a combination
of Kelly + Lyn.
Kelleen, Kellen, Kellene,
Kellina, Kelline, Kellynn,
Kellynne

Kelsey (Scandinavian,
Scottish) ship island.
(English) an alternate
form of Chelsey.
Kelcey, Kelcy, Kelda,
Kellsee, Kellsei, Kellsey,
Kellsie, Kellsy, Kelsa,
Kelsea, Kelsei, Kelsey,
Kelsi, Kelsie, Kelsy, Keslie

Kelsi, Kelsie (Scottish)
forms of Chelsea.
Kelci, Kelcie

Kenda (English) water
baby. (Dakota) magical
power. Astrology: a child
born under Cancer,
Scorpio, or Pisces.
Kendi, Kendie, Kendy,
Kennda, Kenndi, Kenndie,
Kenndy

Kendall (English) ruler
of the valley.
Kendahl, Kendal,
Kendalla, Kendalle,
Kendel, Kendele, Kendell,
Kendelle, Kendera,
Kendia, Kendyl, Kendyle,
Kendyll, Kinda, Kindal,
Kindall, Kindi, Kindle,
Kynda, Kyndal, Kyndall

Kendra (English) an alternate form of Kenda.
Kendre, Kenna, Kenndra,
Kentra, Kentrae, Kindra,
Kyndra

Keneisha (American)
a combination of the
prefix Ken + Aisha.
Kaneisha, Keneesha,
Kenesha, Keneshia,
Kenisha, Kenishia,
Kennesha, Kenneshia,
Kennisa, Kennisha,
Kineisha

Kenenza (English) an alternate form of Kennice.
Kenza

Kenna (Irish) a short form
of Kennice.
Kennia

Kennice (English) beautiful.
A feminine form of
Kenneth.
Kanice, Keneese, Kenese,
Kennise

Kenya (Hebrew) animal
horn. Geography:
a country in Africa.
Keenya, Kenia, Kenja

Kenzie (Scottish) light
skinned. (Irish) a short
form of Mackenzie.
Kenzy, Kinzie

Kerani (Sanskrit) sacred
bells. See also Rani.
Kera, Keri, Kerie, Kery

Keren (Hebrew) animal's horn.
Kerrin, Keryn

Kerensa (Cornish) loving, affectionate.
Karensa, Karenza, Kerenza

Kerri, Kerrie (Irish) alternate forms of Kerry.
Keri, Keriann, Kerianne, Kerriann, Kerrianne

Kerry (Irish) dark haired. Geography: a county in Ireland.
Keree, Kerey, Kerri, Kerrie, Kerryann, Kerryanne, Kiera, Kierra

Kerstin (Scandinavian) an alternate form of Kirsten.
Kersten, Kerston, Kerstyn

Kesare (Latin) long haired. (Basque) a feminine form of Caesar.

Keshia (American) an alternate form of Keisha. A short form of Keneisha.
Kecia, Keishia, Keschia, Kesia, Kesiah, Kessiah

Kesi (Swahili) born during difficult times.

Kessie (Ashanti) chubby baby.
Kess, Kessa, Kesse, Kessey, Kessi, Kessia, Kessiah

Kevyn (Irish) beautiful. A feminine form of Kevin.
Keva, Kevan, Kevina, Kevone, Kevonna, Kevynn

Keziah (Hebrew) cinnamonlike spice. Bible: one of the daughters of Job.
Kazia, Kaziah, Ketzi, Ketzia, Ketziah, Kezi, Kezia, Kissie, Kizzie, Kizzy

Khadijah (Arabic) trustworthy. History: Muhammed's first wife.
Khadeeja, Khadeja, Khadejha, Khadija

Khalida (Arabic) immortal, everlasting.
Khali, Khalia, Khalita

Khrissa (American) a form of Chrissa.
Khrishia, Khryssa, Krisha, Krisia, Krissa, Krysha, Kryssa

Khristina (Russian, Scandinavian) a form of Kristina, Christina.
Khristeen, Khristen, Khristin, Khristine, Khyristya, Khristyana, Khristyna, Khrystyne

Ki (Korean) arisen.

Kia (African) season's beginning. (American) a short form of Kiana.
Kiah

Kiana (American) a combination of the prefix Ki + Ana.

Kiana (cont.)
**Keanna, Keiana, Kiani,
Kiahna, Kianna, Kianni,
Kiauna, Kiandra, Kiandria,
Kiauna, Kiaundra, Kiona,
Kionah, Kioni, Kionna**

Kiara (Irish) little and dark.
A feminine form of Kieran.

Kiaria, Kiarra, Kichi
(Japanese) fortunate.

Kiele (Hawaiian) gardenia;
fragrant blossom.
**Kiela, Kieley, Kieli, Kielli,
Kielly**

Kiera, Kierra (Irish) alternate forms of Kerry.
Kierana, Kieranna, Kierea

Kiki (Spanish) a familiar
form of names ending
in "queta."

Kiku (Japanese)
chrysanthemum.
Kiko

Kiley (Irish) attractive;
from the straits.
**Kilee, Kilie, Kylee, Kyli,
Kylie**

Kim (Vietnamese) needle.
(English) a short form
of Kimberly.
**Kimba, Kimbra, Kimee,
Kimette, Kimme, Kimmee,
Kimmi, Kimmie, Kimmy,
Kimy, Kym**

Kimana (Shoshone)
butterfly.

Kimberlee, Kimberley
(English) alternate forms
of Kimberly.
**Kimbalee, Kimberlea,
Kimberlei, Kimberleigh,
Kimbley**

Kimberly (English) chief,
ruler.
**Cymbre, Kim, Kimba,
Kimbely, Kimber,
Kimbereley, Kimberely,
Kimberlee, Kimberli,
Kimberlie, Kimberlyn,
Kimbery, Kimbria,
Kimbrie, Kimbry,
Kymberly**

Kimi (Japanese) righteous.
**Kimia, Kimika, Kimiko,
Kimiyo**

Kina (Hawaiian) from
China.

Kineisha (American) an
alternate form of Keneisha.
**Kineesha, Kinesha,
Kineshia, Kinisha, Kinishia**

Kineta (Greek) energetic.
Kinetta

Kini (Hawaiian) a form
of Jean.
Kina

Kinsey (English) offspring;
relative.
Kinsee

Kioko (Japanese) happy
child.
Kiyo, Kiyoko

Kiona (Native American)
brown hills.

Kira (Persian) sun. (Latin)
light. A feminine form
of Cyrus.
Kiran, Kiri, Kiria

Kirima (Eskimo) hill.

Kirsi (Hindi) amaranth
blossoms.

Kirsta (Scandinavian) an
alternate form of Kirsten.

Kirsten (Greek) Christian;
annointed. (Scandinavian)
a form of Christine.
**Karsten, Keirstan, Kerstin,
Kiersten, Kirsteni, Kirsta,
Kirstan, Kirsteen,
Kirstene, Kirstin, Kirston,
Kirsty, Kirstyn, Kjersten,
Kursten, Kyrsten**

Kirstin (Scandinavian)
an alternate form
of Kirsten.
Karstin, Kirstien, Kirstine

Kirsty (Scandinavian)
a familiar form of Kirsten.
**Kerstie, Kirsta, Kirstee,
Kirsti, Kirstie, Kjersti,
Kyrsty**

Kisa (Russian) kitten.
Kisha, Kiska, Kissa, Kiza

Kishi (Japanese) long and
happy life.

Kissa (Ugandan) born
after twins.

Kita (Japanese) north.

Kitra (Hebrew) crowned.

Kitty (Greek) a familiar
form of Katherine.
**Ketter, Ketti, Ketty, Kit,
Kittee, Kitteen, Kittey,
Kitti, Kittie**

Kiwa (Japanese) borderline.

Kizzy (American) a familiar
form of Keziah.
Kissie, Kizzi, Kizzie

Klara (Hungarian) a form
of Clara.
**Klára, Klari, Klarice,
Klarika, Kláris**

Klarissa (German) clear,
bright. (Italian) an alternate form of Clarissa.
**Klarisa, Klarise, Klarrisa,
Klarisza, Klarysa, Kleresa**

Klaudia (American) a form
of Claudia.
Klaudija

Kodi (American) a form
of Codi.
Kodee, Kodie, Kody, Koedi

Koffi (Swahili) born
on Friday.
Kaffe, Kaffi, Koffe, Koffie

Koko (Japanese) stork.
See also Coco.

Kolby (American) a form
of Colby.
**Kobie, Koby, Kolbee,
Kolbie**

Kolina (Swedish) a form
of Katherine. See also
Colleen.
Koleen, Kolena, Kolene,

Kolina *(cont.)*
Koli, Kolleen, Kollene,
Kolyn, Kolyna

Kona (Hawaiian) lady.
(Hindi) angular. Astrology:
born under the sign of
Capricorn.
Koni, Konia

Konstance (Latin) an alter-
nate form of Constance.
Konstantina, Konstantine,
Konstanza, Konstanze

Kora (Greek) an alternate
form of Cora.
Kore, Korella, Koren,
Koressa, Koretta, Korey,
Kori, Korie, Korilla, Kory,
Korra, Korri, Korrie, Korry

Koral (American) a form
of Coral.
Korel, Korele, Korral,
Korrel, Korrell, Korrelle

Kori (American) a short
form of Korina. See also
Corey, Cori.
Koree, Korey, Koria, Korie,
Korri, Korrie, Korry, Kory

Korina (Greek) an alternate
form of Corina, Corinna.
Koreen, Koreena, Korena,
Korin, Korine, Korinna,
Korreena, Korrin, Korrina,
Korrine, Korrinna,
Korrinne, Koryn, Koryna

Kornelia (Latin) an alter-
nate form of Cornelia.
Karniela, Karniella,
Karnis, Kornelija,
Kornelis, Kornelya, Korny

Kortney (English) an alter-
nate form of Courtney.
Kortnay, Kortnee, Kortni,
Kortnie, Kortny

Kosma (Greek) order;
universe.
Cosma

Kosta (Latin) a short form
of Constance.
Kostia, Kostusha, Kostya

Koto (Japanese) harp.

Kourtney (American)
a form of Courtney.
Kourtni, Kourtny,
Kourtynie

Kris (American) a short
form of Kristine. An alternate form of Chris.
Khris, Krissy

Krissy (American) a familiar
form of Kris.
Krissey, Krissi, Krissie

Krista (Czech) a form of
Christina. See also Christa.
Khrissa, Khrista, Khryssa,
Khrysta, Krissa, Kryssa,
Krysta

Kristen (Greek) Christian;
annointed. (Scandinavian)
a form of Christine.
Christen, Kristan, Kristin,
Krysten

Kristi, Kristie
(Scandinavian) short forms
of Kristine.
Christi

Kristian, Kristiana
(Greek) Christian;
anointed. Alternate
forms of Christian.
**Khristian, Kristian,
Kristiann, Kristi-Ann,
Kristianna, Kristianne,
Kristi-Anne, Kristien,
Kristienne, Kristiin,
Kristyan, Kristyana,
Kristy-Ann, Kristy-Anne**

Kristin (Scandinavian)
an alternate form of
Kristen. See also Cristen.
Kristyn, Kristin

Kristina (Greek) Christian;
annointed. (Scandinavian)
a form of Christina.
See also Cristina.
**Khristina, Kristina,
Kristeena, Kristena,
Kristiana, Kristianna,
Kristinka, Krysteena,
Krystena, Krystiana,
Krystianna, Krystina,
Krystyna, Krystynka**

Kristine (Scandinavian)
a form of Christine.
**Kristeen, Kristene, Kristi,
Kristiane, Kristie, Kristy,
Krystine, Krystyne**

Kristy (American) a familiar
form of Kristine, Krystal.
See also Cristy.
**Kristi, Kristia, Kristie,
Krysia, Krysti**

Krysta (Polish) a form
of Krista.
Krystka

Krystal (American) clear,
brilliant glass. A form of
Crystal.
**Kristabel, Kristal, Kristale,
Kristall, Kristel, Kristell,
Kristelle, Kristill, Kristl,
Kristle, Kristy, Krystalann,
Krystalanne, Krystale,
Krystaleen, Krystalina,
Krystall, Krystel,
Krystelle, Krystil, Krystle,
Krystol**

Krystalee (American)
a combination of
Krystal + Lee.
**Kristalea, Kristaleah,
Kristalee, Krystalea,
Krystaleah, Krystlea,
Krystleah, Krystlee,
Krystlelea, Krystleleah,
Krystlelee**

Krystalynn (American)
a combination of
Krystal + Lynn.
**Kristaline, Kristalyn,
Kristalynn, Kristilyn,
Kristilynn, Kristlyn,
Krystalin, Krystalyn**

Krystian, Krystiana
(Greek) alternate forms
of Christian.
**Krystiana, Krystianne,
Krysty-Ann, Krystyan,
Kristyana, Krystyanna,
Krystyanne, Krysty-Anne,
Krystyen**

Krystin (Czech) a form
of Kristin.

Krystle (American)
an alternate form
of Krystal.
Krystl, Krystyl

Kudio (Swahili) born
on Monday.

Kuma (Japanese) bear.

Kumiko (Japanese) girl
with braids.
Kumi

Kumuda (Sanskrit) lotus
flower.

Kuniko (Japanese) child
from the country.

Kuri (Japanese) chestnut.

Kusa (Hindi) God's grass.

Kwanita (Zuni) a form
of Juanita.

Kwashi (Swahili) born
on Sunday.

Kwau (Swahili) born
on Thursday.

Kyla (Irish) attractive.
(Yiddish) crown; laurel.
**Kylen, Kylene, Kylia,
Kylynn**

Kyle (Irish) attractive.
**Kial, Kiele, Kylee, Kylene,
Kylie**

Kylee (Irish) a familiar form
of Kyle.
**Kylea, Kyleah, Kyleigh,
Kylie**

Kylene (Irish) an alternate
form of Kyle.
Kylen, Kylyn

Kylie (West Australian
Aboriginal) curled stick;
boomerang. (Irish)
a familiar form of Kyle.
**Keiley, Keilley, Keilly,
Keily, Kiley, Kye, Kylee**

Kymberly (English)
an alternate form
of Kimberly.
**Kymberlee, Kymberley,
Kymberlie, Kymberlyn**

Kynthia (Greek) an alternate form of Cynthia.
Kyndi

Kyoko (Japanese) mirror.

Kyra (Greek) ladylike.
An alternate form
of Cyrilla.
**Keera, Keira, Kira, Kyrah,
Kyrene, Kyria, Kyriah,
Kyriann, Kyrie**

Lacey, Lacy (Greek)
a familiar form of Larissa.
(Latin) cheerful.
Lacee, Laci, Lacie

Lachandra (American)
a combination of the
prefix La + Chandra.
Lachanda, Lachandice

Laci, Lacie (Latin) alternate forms of Lacey.
Lacia, Laciann, Lacianne

Lacrecia (Latin) an alternate form of Lucretia.
Lacrasha, Lacreash, Lacreasha, Lacreashia, Lacresha, Lacreshia, Lacresia, Lacretia, Lacricia, Lacrisha, Lacrishia

Lada (Russian) Mythology: the goddess of beauty.

Ladasha (American) a combination of the prefix La + Dasha.
Ladaisa, Ladaishia, Ladaseha, Ladashia, Ladassa, Ladaysha, Ladesha

Ladonna (American) a combination of the prefix La + Donna.
Ladon, Ladona, Ladonne, Ladonya

Laela (Arabic, Hebrew) an alternate form of Leila.
Layla, Laylah

Lahela (Hawaiian) a form of Rachel.

Laila (Arabic) an alternate form of Leila.
Laili, Lailie

Laine (French) a short form of Elaine.
Laina, Lainee, Lainey, Layney

Lajila (Hindi) shy, coy.

Lajuana (American) a combination of the prefix La + Juana.
Lajuanna, Lawana, Lawanna, Lawanne, Lawanza, Lawanze, Laweania

Laka (Hawaiian) attractive; seductive; tame. Mythology: the goddess of the hula dance.

Lakeishia (American) a combination of the prefix La + Keisha. See also Lekasha.
Lakaiesha, Lakaisha, Lakasha, Lakecia, Lakeesh, Lakeesha, Lakesha, Lakeshia, Lakeshya, Lakesia, Laketia, Lakeysha, Lakeyshia, Lakezia, Lakicia, Lakiesha, Lakieshia, Lakisha, Lakitia

Lakendra (American) a combination of the prefix La + Kendra.
Lakanda, Lakedra

Lakenya (American) a combination of the prefix La + Kenya.
Lakeena, Lakeenna, Lakeenya, Lakena, Lakenia, Lakin, Lakinja, Lakinya, Lakwanya, Lekenia, Lekenya

Lakesha, Lakeshia, Lakisha (American) alternate forms of Lakeishia.
Lakecia, Lakeesha, Lakeseia, Lakiesha

Laketa (American) a combination of the prefix La + Keita.
Lakeeta, Lakeetah, Lakeita, Lakeitha, Lakeithia, Laketha, Laketia, Laketta, Lakietha, Lakita, Lakitra, Lakitri, Lakitta

Lakia (Arabic) found treasure.
Lakita

Lakresha (American) a form of Lucretia.
Lacresha, Lacreshia, Lacresia, Lacretia, Lacrisha, Lakreshia, Lakrisha, Lekresha, Lekresia

Lakya (Hindi) born on Thursday.

Lala (Slavic) tulip.
Lalla

Lalasa (Hindi) love.

Laleh (Persian) tulip.
Lalah

Lali (Spanish) a form of Lulani.
Lala, Lalia, Lalla, Lalli, Lally

Lalita (Greek) talkative. (Sanskrit) charming; candid. Religion: a name for the Hindu goddess Shakti.

Lallie (English) babbler.
Lalli, Lally

Lamesha (American) a combination of the prefix La + Mesha.
Lamees, Lameise, Lameshia, Lamisha, Lemisha

Lamia (German) bright land. A feminine form of Lambert.
Lama

Lamis (Arabic) soft to the touch.

Lamya (Arabic) dark lipped.
Lama

Lan (Vietnamese) flower.

Lana (Latin) woolly. (Irish) attractive, peaceful. A short form of Alana, Elana. (Hawaiian) floating; bouyant.
Lanae, Lanata, Lanay, Laneetra, Lanette, Lanna, Lannah, Lanny

Landa (Basque) another name for the Virgin Mary.

Landra (German, Spanish) counselor.
Landrea

Lane (English) narrow road.
Laina, Laney, Lanie, Lanni, Lanny, Lany, Layne

Laneisha (American)
a combination of the
prefix La + Keneisha.
**Lanecia, Laneesha,
Laneise, Lanesha,
Laneshe, Lanessa, Lanesse,
Lanisha**

Lani (Hawaiian) sky;
heaven. A short form of
Atalanta, 'Aulani, Leilani.
Lanita, Lannie

Laqueena (American)
a combination of the
prefix La + Queenie.
**Laqueen, Laquena,
Laquenetta**

Laquinta (American)
a combination of the
prefix La + Quintana.
**Laquanta, Laqueinta,
Laquenda, Laquenta,
Laquinda**

Laquisha (American)
a combination of the
prefix La + Queisha.
**Laquasha, Laquaysha,
Laqueisha, Laquesha,
Laquiesha**

Laquita (American)
a combination of the
prefix La + Quintana.
**Laqeita, Laqueta,
Laquetta, Laquia,
Laquiata, Laquinta,
Laquitta**

Lara (Greek) cheerful.
(Latin) shining; famous.
Mythology: the daughter
of the river god Almo.

A short form of Laraine,
Larissa, Laura.
Larah, Laretta, Larette

Laraine (Latin) an alternate
form of Lorraine.
**Lara, Laraene, Larain,
Larayne, Larein, Lareina,
Lareine, Larena**

Larina (Greek) seagull.
Larena, Larine

Larissa (Greek) cheerful.
See also Lacey.
Laris, Larisa, Laryssa

Lark (English) skylark.

Lashanda (American)
a combination of the
prefix La + Shanda.
**Lashana, Lashanay,
Lashandra, Lashane,
Lashanna, Lashannon,
Lashanta, Lashante**

Lashawna (American)
a combination of the
prefix La + Shawna.
**Lashaun, Lashauna,
Lashaune, Lashaunna,
Lashaunta, Lashawn,
Lashawnd, Lashawnda,
Lashawndra, Lashawne,
Lashawnia, Leshawn,
Leshawna**

Lashonda (American)
a combination of the
prefix La + Shonda.
**Lachonda, Lashaunda,
Lashaundra, Lashon,
Lashona, Lashond,
Lashonde, Lashondia,
Lashondra, Lashonna,**

Lashonda *(cont.)*
Lashonta, Lashunda, Lashundra, Lashunta, Lashunte, Leshande, Leshandra, Leshondra, Leshundra

Latanya (American) a combination of the prefix La + Tanya.
Latana, Latandra, Latania, Latanja, Latanna, Latanua, Latona, Latoni, Latonia, Latonna, Latonshia, Latonya

Latara (American) a combination of the prefix La + Tara.

Latasha (American) a combination of the prefix La + Tasha.
Latacha, Latacia, Latai, Lataisha, Latashia, Lataysha, Letasha, Letashia, Leteshia, Letasiah, Leteisha

Lateefah (Arabic) pleasant. (Hebrew) pat, caress.
Latifa, Latifah, Latipha

Latesha (American) a form of Letitia.
Lataeasha, Lateashia, Latecia, Lateesha, Lateicia, Lateisha, Latesa, Lateshia, Latessa, Latisa, Latissa

Latia (American) a combination of the prefix La + Tia.
Latea, Lateia, Lateka

Latika (Hindi) small creeper.

Latisha (Latin) joy. An alternate form of Leticia. (American) a combination of the prefix La + Tisha.
Laetitia, Laetizia, Latashia, Latia, Latice, Laticia, Lateasha, Lateashia, Latecia, Lateesha, Lateicia, Lateisha, Lateshia, Latiesha, Latishia, Latissha, Latitia

Latona (Latin) Mythology: the powerful goddess who bore Apollo and Diana.

Latonya (Latin) an alternate form of Latona. (American) a combination of the prefix La + Tonya.
Latoni, Latonia, Latonna

Latoria (American) a combination of the prefix La + Tori.
Latorio, Latorja, Latorray, Latorreia, Latory, Latorya, Latoyra, Latoyria

Latosha (American) a combination of the prefix La + Tosha.
Latoshia, Latosia

Latoya (American) a combination of the prefix La + Toya.
Latoia, Latoira, Latoiya, LaToya, Latoyia, Latoye, Latoyia, Latoyita, Latoyo, Latoyra, Latoyria

Latrice (American)
a combination of the
prefix La + Trice.
**Latrece, Latreece,
Latreese, Latresa, Latrese,
Latressa, Letreece, Letrice**

Latricia (American)
a combination of the
prefix La + Tricia.
**Latrecia, Latresh,
Latresha, Latreshia,
Latrica, Latrisha, Latrishia**

Laura (Latin) crowned
with laurel. A feminine
form of Laurence.
**Lara, Lauralee,
Laureana, Laurel,
Laurelen, Laurella,
Lauren, Lauriana,
Lauriane, Lauricia, Laurie,
Laurina, Laurka, Lavra,
Lolly, Lora, Loretta, Lori,
Lorinda, Lorina, Lorinda,
Lorita, Lorna, Loura**

Laurel (Latin) laurel tree.
**Laural, Laurell, Laurelle,
Lorel, Lorelle**

Lauren (English) a form
of Laura.
**Laureen, Laurena,
Laurene, Laurin, Lauryn,
Laurynn, Loren**

Laurie (English) a familiar
form of Laura.
**Lari, Larilia, Laure, Lauré,
Lauri, Lawrie, Lori**

Laveda (Latin) cleansed,
purified.
Lavare, Lavetta, Lavette

Lavelle (Latin) cleansing.
Lavella

Lavena (Latin) an alternate
form of Lavina. (Irish,
French) joy.

Laverne (Latin) springtime.
(French) grove of alder
trees. See also Verna.
**Laverine, Lavern, Laverna,
La Verne**

Lavina (Latin) purified;
woman of Rome.
See also Vina.
**Lavena, Lavenia, Lavinia,
Lavinie, Levenia, Levinia,
Livinia, Louvinia, Lovina,
Lovinia**

Lavonna (American)
a combination of the
prefix La + Yvonne.
**Lavon, Lavonda,
Lavonder, Lavondria,
Lavone, Lavonia,
Lavonica, Lavonn,
Lavonne, Lavonnie,
Lavonya**

Lawan (Thai) pretty.

Lawanda (American)
a combination of the
prefix La + Wanda.
Lawynda

Layla (Hebrew, Arabic)
an alternate form of Leila.
Layli, Laylie

Le (Vietnamese) pearl.

Lea (Hawaiian) Mythology: the goddess of canoe makers.

Leah (Hebrew) weary. Bible: the wife of Jacob. See also Lia.
Lea, Léa, Lee, Leea, Leeah, Leia, Leigh

Leala (French) faithful, loyal.
Lealia, Lealie, Leial

Lean, Leanne (English) forms of Leeann, Lian.
Leana, Leane, Leann, Leanna

Leandra (Latin) like a lioness.
Leanda, Leandre, Leandrea, Leandria, Leeanda, Leeandra

Leanna (English) an alternate form of Liana.
Leana

Leanore (Greek) an alternate form of Eleanor. (English) a form of Helen.
Leanora, Lanore

Lecia (Latin) a short form of Felecia.
Leecia, Leesha, Leesia, Lesha, Leshia, Lesia

Leda (Greek) lady. Mythology: the Queen of Sparta and the mother of Helen of Troy.
Ledah, Lida, Lidah, Lita, Litah, Lyda, Lydah

Lee (Chinese) plum. (Irish) poetic. (English) meadow. A short form of Ashley, Leah.
Lea, Leigh

Leeann, Leeanne (English) a combination of Lee + Ann. A form of Lian.
Leane, Leanna, Leean, Leeanna, Leian, Leiann, Leianna, Leianne

Leena (Estonian) a form of Helen.

Leeza (Hebrew) a short form of Aleeza. (English) an alternate form of Lisa, Liza.

Lei (Hawaiian) a familiar form of Leilani.

Leigh (English) an alternate form of Lee.
Leigha, Leighann, Leighanna, Leighanne

Leiko (Japanese) arrogant.

Leila (Hebrew) dark beauty; night. (Arabic) born at night. Literature: the heroine of the epic Persian poem *Leila and Majnum*. See also Laela, Layla, Lila.
Laila, Layla, Leela, Leelah, Leilah, Leilia, Lela, Lelah, Leland, Lelia, Leyla

Leilani (Hawaiian) heavenly flower; heavenly child.
Lani, Lei, Lelani, Lelania

Leire (Basque) Religion: another name for the Virgin Mary.

Lekasha (American) an alternate form of Lakeishia.
Lekeesha, Lekeisha, Lekesha, Lekeshia, Lekesia, Lekicia, Lekisha

Leli (Swiss) a form of Magdalen.

Lelia (Greek) fair speech.
Lelie, Lelika, Lelita, Lellia

Lelya (Russian) a form of Helen.
Leka

Lena (Greek) a short form of Eleanor. (Hebrew) dwelling or lodging. (Latin) temptress. (Norwegian) illustrious. Music: Lena Horne, a well-known African-American singer.
Lenah, Lene, Lenea, Lenee, Lenette, Leni, Lenka, Lina, Linah

Lenci (Hungarian) a form of Helen.

Lene (German) a form of Helen.
Leni, Line

Leneisha (American) a combination of the prefix Le + Keneisha.
Lenece, Lenesha, Lenisa, Lenise, Lenisha

Lenia (German) an alternate form of Leona.
Lenda, Leneen, Lenette, Lenna, Lennah, Lennette

Lenita (Latin) gentle.
Leneta

Lenore (Greek, Russian) a form of Eleanor.
Lenni, Lenor, Lenora, Lenorah

Leona (German) brave as a lioness. A feminine form of Leon. See also Lona.
Leoine, Leola, Leolah, Leone, Leonelle, Leonia, Leonice, Leonicia, Léonie, Leonine, Leonissa, Liona

Leonore (Greek) an alternate form of Eleanor. See also Nora.
Leonor, Leonora, Leonorah, Léonore

Leontine (Latin) like a lioness.
Leona, Leontyne, Léontyne

Leora (Greek) a familiar form of Eleanor. (Hebrew) light.
Leorah, Leorit, Liora

Leotie (Native American) prairie flower.

Lera (Russian) a short form of Valera.
Lerka

Lesley (Scottish) gray fortress.

Lesley (cont.)
**Leslea, Leslee, Leslie,
Leslye, Lezlee, Lezley,
Lezli, Lezly**

Leslie (Scottish) an alternate
form of Lesley.
Lesli, Lesslie

Leta (Greek) a short form
of Aleta. (Latin) glad.
(Swahili) bringer.
Lita, Lyta

Leticia (Latin) joy. See also
Latisha, Tisha.
**Leisha, Leshia, Let, Leta,
Letha, Lethia, Letice,
Letichia, Letisha, Letisia,
Letita, Letiticia, Letiza,
Letizia, Letty, Letycia,
Loutitia**

Letty (English) a familiar
form of Leticia.
Letta, Letti, Lettie

Levana (Hebrew) moon;
white. (Latin) risen.
Mythology: the goddess
of newborn babies.
See also Lewana.
**Lévana, Levania, Levanna,
Levenia, Livana**

Levani (Fijian) anointed
with oil.

Levia (Hebrew) joined,
attached.

Levina (Latin) flash
of lightning.
Levene

Levona (Hebrew) spice,
incense.
Leavonia, Levonat, Livona

Lewana (Hebrew) an alternate form of Levana.
Lebhanah, Lewanna

Lexandra (Greek) a short
form of Alexandra.
Lisandra

Lexia (Greek) a familiar
form of Alexandra.
**Leksi, Leska, Lesya, Lexa,
Lexane, Lexey, Lexi, Lexie,
Lexina, Lexine, Lexy**

Leya (Spanish) loyal. (Tamil)
the constellation Leo.
Leyla

Lia (Greek) bringer of good
news. (Hebrew, Dutch,
Italian) dependent.
See also Leah.
Liah

Lian (Chinese) graceful
willow. (Latin) a short form
of Gillian, Lillian.
Lean, Leeann

Liana (Hebrew) a short form
of Eliana. (Latin) youth.
(French) bound, wrapped
up; tree covered with vines.
(English) meadow.
**Leanna, Liane, Lianna,
Lianne**

Liane, Lianne (Hebrew)
a short form of Eliane.
(English) forms of Lian.
Liana

Libby (Hebrew) a familiar
form of Elizabeth.
Lib, Libbee, Libbey, Libbie

Liberty (Latin) free.

Licia (Greek) a short form
of Alicia.
**Licha, Lisha, Lishia, Lisia,
Lycia**

Lida (Greek) happy. (Latin)
a short form of Alida, Elita.
(Slavic) loved by people.
Leeda, Lyda

Lide (Latin, Basque) life.

Lidia (Greek) an alternate
form of Lydia.
Lidi, Lidka, Lyda

Lien (Chinese) lotus.
Lienne

Liese (German) a familiar
form of Elise, Elizabeth.
**Liesa, Liesabet, Liesbeth,
Lieschen, Lisbete, Lise**

Liesel (German) a familiar
form of Elizabeth.
**Leesel, Leesl, Leezel, Leezl,
Liesl, Liezel, Liezl, Lisel**

Lila (Arabic) night. (Hindi)
free will of god. (Persian)
lilac. A short form of
Dalila, Delilah, Lillian.
Lilah, Lilia, Lyla, Lylah

Lilac (Sanskrit) lilac;
blue-purple.

Lilibeth (English) a combi-
nation of Lilly + Beth.
**Lilibet, Lillibeth, Lillybeth,
Lilybet**

Lilith (Arabic) of the night;
night demon. Mythology:
the first wife of Adam,
according to ancient
eastern legends.
Lillis, Lilly, Lily

Lillian (Latin) lily flower.
**Lian, Lil, Lila, Lilas,
Lileana, Lileane, Lilia,
Lilian, Liliana, Liliane,
Lilias, Liliha, Lilja, Lilla,
Lilli, Lillia, Lillianne, Lis,
Liuka**

Lily (Latin, Arabic) a familiar
form of Lilith, Lillian.
**Lil, Líle, Lili, Lilie, Lilijana,
Lilika, Lilike, Liliosa,
Lilium, Lilka, Lille, Lilli,
Lillie, Lilly**

Lillyann (Latin) an alter-
nate form of Lilian.
(English) a combination
of Lilly + Ann.
**Lillyan, Lillyanne, Lily,
Lilyan, Lilyann, Lilyanne**

Limber (Tiv) joyful.

Lin (Chinese) beautiful
jade. (English) a short
form of Lynn.
Linn, Lyn

Lina (Greek) light. (Latin)
an alternate form of Lena.
(Arabic) tender.
Lin

Linda (Spanish) pretty.
**Lin, Lind, Lindee, Lindey,
Lindi, Lindie, Lindy, Linita,
Lynda**

Lindsay (English) an alternate form of Lindsey.
Lin, Lindsi, Lyndsay, Lyndsaye, Linsay

Lindsey (English) linden tree island; camp near the stream.
Lin, Lind, Lindsea, Lindsee, Lindsi, Linsey, Lyndsey, Lynsey

Lindsi (American) a familiar form of Lindsay, Lindsey.
Lin, Lindsie, Lindsy, Lindzy

Linette (Welsh) idol. (French) bird.
Lanette, Lin, Linet, Linnet, Linnetta, Linnette, Lynette, Lynnet, Lynnette

Ling (Chinese) delicate, dainty.

Linnea (Scandinavian) lime tree. History: the national flower of Sweden.
Lin, Linea, Linnaea, Lynea, Lynnea

Linsey (English) an alternate form of Lindsey.
Lin, Linsi, Linsie, Linsy, Linzee, Linzey, Linzi, Linzy, Lynsey

Liolya (Russian) a form of Helen.
Lenuschka, Lenushka, Lenusya

Liora (Hebrew) light.

Lirit (Hebrew) poetic; lyrical, musical.

Liron (Hebrew) my song.
Leron, Lerone, Lirone

Lisa (Hebrew) consecrated to God. (English) a short form of Elizabeth.
Leesa, Leeza, Liesa, Liisa, Lisanne, Lise, Lisenka, Lisette, Liszka, Litsa, Liza, Lysa

Lise (German) a form of Lisa.

Lisette (French) a form of Lisa. (English) a familiar form of Elise, Elizabeth.
Liseta, Lisetta, Lisettina, Lissette

Lisha (Hebrew) a short form of Alisha, Elisha, Ilisha. (Arabic) darkness before midnight.
Lishe

Lissa (Greek) honey bee. A short form of Elissa, Elizabeth, Melissa, Millicent.
Lissi, Lyssa

Lissie (American) a familiar form of Allison, Elise, Elizabeth.
Lissee, Lissey, Lissi, Lissy, Lissye

Lita (Latin) a familiar form of names ending in "lita".
Leta

Litonya (Moquelumnan) darting hummingbird.

Liv (Latin) a short form of Livia, Olivia.

Livana (Hebrew) an alternate form of Levana. Astrological: born under the sign of Cancer.
Livna, Livnat

Livia (Hebrew) crown. A familiar form of Olivia. (Latin) olive.
Levia, Liv, Livie, Livy, Livya, Livye

Liviya (Hebrew) brave lioness; royal crown.
Leviya, Levya, Livya

Livona (Hebrew) an alternate form of Levona.

Liz (English) a short form of Elizabeth.
Lizanka, Lizanne, Lizina

Liza (American) a short form of Elizabeth.
Leeza, Lizete, Lizette, Lizka, Lizzie, Lyza

Lizabeta (Russian) a form of Elizabeth.
Lizabetah, Lizaveta, Lizonka

Lizabeth (English) a short form of Elizabeth.
Lisabet, Lisabeth, Lisabette, Lisbet, Lizabette, Lizbeth, Lizbett

Lizina (Latvian) a familiar form of Elizabeth.

Lizzy (American) a familiar form of Elizabeth.
Lizzie

Lois (German) famous warrior. An alternate form of Louise.

Lola (Spanish) a familiar form of Carlota, Dolores, Louise.
Lolita

Lolita (Spanish) sorrowful. A familiar form of Lola.
Lita, Lulita

Lolly (English) a familiar form of Laura.

Lolotea (Zuni) a form of Dorothy.

Lomasi (Native American) pretty flower.

Lona (Latin) lioness. (German) a short form of Leona. (English) solitary.
Loni, Lonna

Loni (American) a form of Lona.
Lonee, Lonie, Lonni, Lonnie

Lora (Latin) crowned with laurel. (American) a form of Laura.
Lorah, Lorane, Lorann, Lorra, Lorrah, Lorrane

Lore (Latin) a short form of Flora.
Lor

Lorelei (German) alluring. Mythology: the sirens of the Rhine River who lured sailors to their deaths. See also Lurleen.

Lorelei *(cont.)*
Loralee, Loralie, Loralyn, Lorilee, Lorilyn

Lorelle (American) a form of Laurel.

Loren (American) an alternate form of Lauren.
Loreen, Lorena, Lorin, Lorine, Lorne, Lorren, Lorrin, Lorryn, Loryn, Lorynn, Lorynne

Lorena (English) an alternate form of Lauren, Loren.
Loreen, Lorene, Lorenia, Lorenna, Lorrina, Lorrine

Lorenza (Latin) an alternate form of Laura.
Laurencia, Laurentia, Laurentina

Loretta (English) a familiar form of Laura.
Larretta, Lauretta, Laurette, Loretah, Lorette, Lorita, Lorretta, Lorrette

Lori (Latin) crowned with laurel. (French) a short form of Lorraine. (American) a familiar form of Laura.
Laurie, Loree, Lorey, Loria, Lorianna, Lorianne, Lorie, Lorree, Lorrie, Lory

Lorinda (Spanish) a form of Laura.

Loris (Greek) a short form of Chloris. (Latin) thong. (Dutch) clown.
Laurice, Laurys, Lorice

Lorna (Latin) crowned with laurel. An alternate form of Laura. Literature: probably coined by Richard Blackmore in his novel *Lorna Doone.*
Lorrna

Lorraine (Latin) sorrowful. (French) from Lorraine. See also Rayna.
Laraine, Lauraine, Laurraine, Lorain, Loraine, Lorayne, Lorein, Loreine, Lori, Lorine, Lorrain, Lorraina, Lorrayne, Lorreine

Lotte (German) a short form of Charlotte.
Lotie, Lotta, Lottchen, Lottey, Lottie, Lotty, Loty

Lotus (Greek) lotus.

Lou (American) a short form of Louise, Luella.

Louam (Ethiopian) sleep well.

Louisa (English) a familiar form of Louise. Literature: Louisa May Alcott was an American writer and reformer best known for her novel *Little Women.*
Aloisa, Eloisa, Heloisa, Lou, Louisian, Louisane, Louisina, Louiza, Lovisa,

**Ludovica, Ludovika,
Ludwiga, Luisa, Luiza,
Lujza, Lujzika, Lula, Lulita**

Louise (German) famous
warrior. A feminine form
of Louis. See also Alison,
Eloise, Heloise, Lois, Lola,
Luella, Lulu.
**Loise, Lou, Louisa,
Louisette, Louisiane,
Louisine, Lowise, Loyce,
Loyise, Lu, Luisa, Luise**

Love (English) love; kind-
ness; charity.
**Lovely, Lovena, Lovewell,
Lovey, Lovie, Lovina, Lovy,
Luv, Luvvy**

Lovisa (German) an alternate form of Louise.

Luann (Hebrew, German)
graceful woman warrior.
(Hawaiian) happy; relaxed.
(American) a combination
of Louise + Anne.
**Lewanna, Louann,
Louanna, Louanne, Lu,
Lua, Luan, Luana, Luane,
Luanne, Luanni, Luannie,
Luwana**

Lucerne (Latin) lamp;
circle of light. Geography:
a lake in Switzerland.
Lucerna

Lucetta (English) a familiar
form of Lucy.
Lucette

Lucia (Italian, Spanish)
a form of Lucy.
Luciana, Lucianna

Lucie (French) a familiar
form of Lucy.

Lucille (English) a familiar
form of Lucy.
Lucila, Lucile, Lucilla

Lucinda (Latin) a familiar
form of Lucy. See also
Cindy.
Lucka, Lucky

Lucine (Basque) a form
of Lucy. (Arabic) moon.
**Lucina, Lucyna, Lukene,
Lusine, Luzine**

Lucita (Spanish) a form
of Lucy.
Lusita

Lucretia (Latin) rich;
rewarded.
**Lacrecia, Lucrece, Lucrèce,
Lucrecia, Lucreecia,
Lucresha, Lucreshia,
Lucrezia, Lucrisha,
Lucrishia**

Lucrezia (Italian) a form of
Lucretia. History: Lucrezia
Borgia was the Duchess of
Ferrara and a patron of
learning and the arts.

Lucy (Latin) light; bringer
of light. A feminine form
of Lucius.
**Lou, Lu, Luca, Luce,
Lucetta, Luci, Lucia,
Lucida, Lucie, Lucienne,
Lucija, Lucika, Lucille,
Lucinda, Lucine, Lucita,
Luciya, Lucya, Luzca, Luz,
Luzi**

Ludmilla (Slavic) loved by the people. See also Mila.
Ludie, Ludka, Ludmila, Ludovika, Lyuba, Lyudmila

Luella (German) a familiar form of Louise. (English) elf.
Loella, Lou, Louella, Lu, Ludella, Luelle, Lula, Lulu

Luisa (Spanish) a form of Louisa.

Lulani (Polynesian) highest point of heaven.

Lulu (Arabic) pearl. (German) a familiar form of Louise, Luella. (English) soothing, comforting. (Native American) hare.
Loulou, Lula, Lulie

Luna (Latin) moon.
Lunetta, Lunette, Lunneta, Lunnete

Lupe (Latin) wolf. (Spanish) a short form of Guadalupe.
Lupita

Lurleen, Lurlene (German) alternate forms of Lorelei. (Scandinavian) war horn.
Lura, Lurette, Lurline

Lusa (Finnish) a form of Elizabeth.

Lusela (Moquelumnan) like a bear swinging its foot when licking it.

Luvena (Latin, English) little; beloved.

Luyu (Moquelumnan) like a pecking bird.

Luz (Spanish) light. Religion: Santa Maria de Luz is another name for the Virgin Mary.
Luzi, Luzija

Lycoris (Greek) twilight.

Lyda (Greek) a short form of Lidia, Lydia.

Lydia (Greek) from Lydia, an ancient land once ruled by Midas. (Arabic) strife.
Lida, Lidi, Lidia, Lidija, Lidiya, Lidka, Lidochka, Lyda, Lydie, Lydië

Lyla (French) island. (English) a feminine form of Lyle.
Lila, Lilah

Lynda (Spanish) pretty. (American) a form of Linda.
Lyndall, Lynde, Lyndee, Lyndi, Lyndy, Lynnda, Lynndie, Lynndy

Lyndsay (American) a form of Lindsay.

Lyndsey (English) linden tree island; camp near the stream. (American) a form of Lindsey.
Lyndsea, Lyndsee, Lyndsi, Lyndsie, Lyndsy, Lynndsie

Lynelle (English) pretty.
Linel, Linell, Linnell, Lynell

Lynette (Welsh) idol.
(English) a form of Linette.
Lynett, Lynetta, Lynnette

Lynn, Lynne (English)
waterfall; pool below
a waterfall.
**Lin, Lina, Linn, Lyn,
Lyndel, Lyndell, Lyndella,
Lynette, Lynlee, Lynley,
Lynna, Lynnell**

Lynnell (English) an alter-
nate form of Lynn.
**Linell, Linnell, Lynell,
Lynella, Lynelle, Lynnelle**

Lynsey (American) an alter-
nate form of Lyndsey.
**Lynnsey, Lynnzey, Lynsie,
Lynsy, Lynzey, Lynzi,
Lynzie, Lynzy**

Lyra (Greek) lyre player.
Lyre, Lyris

Lysandra (Greek) liberator.
A feminine form of
Lysander.
Lisandra, Lytle

Mab (Irish) joyous. (Welsh)
baby. Literature: the name
of the Fairy Queen in
Edmund Spenser's epic
romance *The Faerie Queene.*
Mabry

Mabel (Latin) lovable.
A short form of Amabel.
**Mab, Mabelle, Mable,
Mabyn, Maible, Maybel,
Maybelle, Maybull**

Macawi (Dakota) generous;
motherly.

Machiko (Japanese)
fortunate child.
Machi

Macia (Polish) a form
of Miriam.
**Macelia, Macey, Machia,
Maci, Macy, Masha, Mashia**

Mackenzie (Irish) daughter
of the wise leader. See also
Kenzie.
**Macenzie, Mackensi,
Mackensie, Mackenzee,
Mackenzi, Mackenzia,
Mackenzy, McKenzie,
Mekenzie, Mykenzie**

Mada (English) a short form
of Madeline, Magdalen.
Madda, Mahda

Maddie (English) a familiar
form of Madeline.
Maddi, Maddy, Mady

Madeleine (French) a form
of Madeline.
Madelaine, Madelayne

Madeline (Greek) high
tower. (English) from
Magdala, England.
An alternate form of
Magdalen. See also
Lena, Lina, Maud.
**Mada, Madailéin,
Madalaina, Madaleine,
Madalena, Madaline,
Maddalena, Maddie,
Madel, Madeleine,
Madelena, Madelene,
Madelia, Madelina,
Madella, Madelle,
Madelon, Madelyn,
Madge, Madlen, Madlin,
Madline, Madoline,
Maida, Malena**

Madelyn (Greek) an alter-
nate form of Madeline.
**Madalyn, Madalynn,
Madalynne, Madelynn,
Madelynne, Madlyn,
Madolyn**

Madge (Greek) a familiar
form of Madeline,
Margaret.
Madgi, Madgie, Mady

Madison (English) good;
son of Maud.
**Madisen, Madissen,
Madisyn, Madysen,
Madyson**

Madonna (Latin) my lady.
Madona

Madrona (Spanish)
mother.
Madre, Madrena

Mae (English) an alternate
form of May. History:
Mae Jemison was the first
African-American woman
in space.
**Maelea, Maeleah, Maelen,
Maelle, Maeona**

Maegan (Irish) an alternate
form of Megan.
Maeghan

Maeko (Japanese) honest
child.
Mae, Maemi

Maeve (Irish) joyous.
History: a first-century
queen of Ireland.
See also Mavis.
**Maevi, Maevy, Maive,
Mayve**

Magan, Magen (Greek)
short forms of Margaret.

Magda (Czech, Polish,
Russian) a form of
Magdalen.

Magdalen (Greek) high
tower. Bible: Magdala was
the home of Saint Mary
Magdalen. See also
Madeline, Malena,
Marlene.
**Mada, Magda, Magdala,
Magdalena, Magdalene,
Magdalina, Magdaline,**

**Magdalyn, Magdelana,
Magdelane, Magdelene,
Magdelina, Magdeline,
Magdelyn, Magdlen,
Magdolna, Maggie,
Magola, Mahda,
Maighdlin, Makda, Mala,
Malaine, Maudlin**

Magena (Native American)
coming moon.

Maggie (Greek) pearl.
(English) a familiar form
of Magdalen, Margaret.
**Mag, Magge, Maggee,
Maggen, Maggey, Maggi,
Maggia, Maggiemae,
Maggin, Maggy, Mags**

Magnolia (Latin) flowering
tree. See also Nollie.
Nola

Mahal (Filipino) love.

Mahala (Arabic) fat,
marrow; tender.
(Native American)
powerful woman.
**Mahalah, Mahalar,
Mahalla, Mahela, Mahila,
Mahlah, Mahlaha,
Mehala, Mehalah**

Mahalia (American) a form
of Mahala.
**Mahaliah, Mahelea,
Maheleah, Mahelia,
Mahilia, Mehalia**

Maharene (Ethiopian)
forgive us.

Mahesa (Hindi) great lord.
Religion: a name for the
Hindu goddess Shiva.
Maheesa, Mahisa

Mahila (Sanskrit) woman.

Mahina (Hawaiian) moon
glow.

Mahira (Hebrew)
energetic.
Mahri

Mahogony (Spanish) rich;
strong.
**Mahagony, Mahogani,
Mahoganie, Mahogny,
Mohogany, Mohogony**

Mai (Japanese) brightness.
(Vietnamese) flower.
(Navajo) coyote.

Maia (Greek) mother;
nurse. (English)
kinswoman; maiden.
Mythology: the loveliest
of the Pleiades, the seven
daughters of Atlas, and
the mother of Hermes.
See also Maya.
**Maiah, Maie, Maya,
Mayam, Mya**

Maida (Greek) a short form
of Madeline. (English)
maiden.
**Maddie, Maddy, Mady,
Magda, Maidel, Maidie,
Mayda, Maydena, Maydey**

Maija (Finnish) a form
of Mary.
Maiji, Maikki

Maire (Irish) a form
of Mary.
**Mair, Maira, Mairi,
Mairim, Mairin, Mairona,
Mairwen**

Maisie (Scottish) a familiar
form of Margaret.
**Maisa, Maisey, Maisi,
Maisy, Maizie, Maysie,
Mayzie, Mazey, Mazie,
Mazy, Mazzy, Mysie, Myzie**

Maita (Spanish) a form
of Martha.
Maite, Maitia

Maja (Arabic) a short form
of Majidah.
**Majal, Majalisa, Majalyn,
Majalynn**

Majidah (Arabic) splendid.
Maja, Majida

Makala (Hawaiian) myrtle.

Makana (Hawaiian) gift,
present.

Makani (Hawaiian) wind.

Makara (Hindi) born
during the lunar month
of Capricorn.

Makayla (American)
an alternate form
of Michaela.
Mikayla

Mala (Greek) a short form
of Magdalen.
Malana, Malee, Mali

Malana (Hawaiian)
bouyant, light.

Malaya (Filipino) free.
Malayna, Malea

Malena (Swedish) a famil-
iar form of Magdalen.
**Malen, Malenna, Malin,
Malina, Maline, Malini,
Malinna**

Malha (Hebrew) queen.
**Maliah, Malkah, Malkia,
Malkiah, Malkie, Malkiya,
Malkiyah, Miliah**

Mali (Thai) jasmine flower.
(Hungarian) a short form
of Malika.
Malea, Malee, Maley

Malia (Hawaiian, Zuni)
a form of Mary. (Spanish)
a form of Maria.
**Malea, Maleah, Maleia,
Maliaka, Maliasha, Malie,
Maliea, Malli, Mally**

Malika (Hungarian)
industrious.
Maleeka, Maleka, Mali

Malina (Hebrew) tower.
(English) from Magdala,
England. (Native
American) soothing.
**Malin, Maline, Malina,
Malinna, Mallie**

Malinda (Greek) an alter-
nate form of Melinda.
**Malinde, Malinna,
Malynda**

Malini (Hindi) gardener.
Religion: the Hindu god
of the earth.

Malissa (Greek) an alternate form of Melissa.

Mallalai (Pashto) beautiful.

Malley (American) a familiar form of Mallory.
Mallee, Malli, Mallie, Mally, Maly

Mallorie (French) an alternate form of Mallory.

Mallory (German) army counselor. (French) unlucky.
Malerie, Maliri, Mallari, Mallary, Mallauri, Mallerie, Mallery, Malley, Malloree, Malloreigh, Mallorey, Mallori, Mallorie, Malori, Malorie, Malorym, Malree, Malrie, Mellory, Melorie, Melory

Malva (English) a form of Melba.
Malvi, Malvy

Malvina (Scottish) a form of Melvina. Literature: a name created by the eighteenth-century romantic poet James MacPherson.
Malvane, Malvi

Mamie (American) a familiar form of Margaret.
Mame, Mamee, Mamy

Mamo (Hawaiian) saffron flower; yellow bird.

Mana (Hawaiian) psychic; sensitive.
Manal, Manali

Manar (Arabic) guiding light.
Manayra

Manda (Latin) a short form of Amanda. (Spanish) woman warrior.
Mandee, Mandy

Mandara (Hindi) calm. Religion: a Hindu mythical tree that makes worries disappear.

Mandeep (Punjabi) enlightened.

Mandisa (Xhosa) sweet.

Mandy (Latin) lovable. A familiar form of Amanda, Manda, Melinda.
Mandee, Mandi, Mandie

Manette (French) a form of Mary.

Mangena (Hebrew) song, melody.
Mangina

Mani (Chinese) a mantra repeated in Tibetan Buddhist prayer to impart understanding.
Manee

Manka (Polish, Russian) a form of Mary.

Manon (French) a familiar form of Marie.

Manpreet (Punjabi) mind full of love.

Mansi (Hopi) plucked flower.
Mancey, Manci, Mancie,

Mansi (cont.)
Mansey, Mansie, Mansy

Manuela (Spanish) a form
of Emmanuelle.
Manuelita

Manya (Russian) a form
of Mary.

Mara (Greek) a short form
of Amara. (Slavic) a form
of Mary.
**Mahra, Marah, Maralina,
Maraline, Marra**

Marabel (English) a form
of Mirabel.
Marabella, Marabelle

Maranda (Latin) an alternate form of Miranda.

Marcelen (English) a form
of Marcella.
**Marcelen, Marcelin,
Marcelina, Marceline,
Marcellin, Marcellina,
Marcelline, Marcelyn,
Marcilen**

Marcella (Latin) martial,
warlike. Mythology: Mars
was the god of war. A fem-
inine form of Marcellus.
**Mairsil, Marca, Marce,
Marceil, Marcela, Marcele,
Marcelen, Marcelia,
Marcell, Marcelle,
Marcello, Marcena,
Marchella, Marchelle,
Marci, Marcie, Marciella,
Marcile, Marcilla, Marcille,
Marcy, Marella, Marsella,
Marselle, Marsiella**

Marcena (Latin) an alter-
nate form of Marcella,
Marcia.
**Maracena, Marceen,
Marcene, Marcenia,
Marceyne, Marcina**

Marci, Marcie (English)
familiar forms of Marcella,
Marcia.
**Marcee, Marcita, Marcy,
Marsi, Marsie**

Marcia (Latin) martial,
warlike. An alternate form
of Marcella. See also
Marquita.
**Marcena, Marchia, Marci,
Marciale, Marcie, Marcsa,
Marsha, Martia**

Marciann (American)
a form of Marcella.
**Marciane, Marcianna,
Marcianne, Marcyane,
Marcyanna, Marcyanne**

Marcilynn (American)
a combination of
Marci + Lynn.
**Marcilen, Marcilin,
Marciline, Marcilyn,
Marcilyne, Marcilynne,
Marcylen, Marcylin,
Marcyline, Marcylyn,
Marcylyne, Marcylynn,
Marcylynne**

Marcy (English) an alternate form of Marci.
Marsey, Marsy

Mardi (French) born on
Tuesday. (Aramaic) a familiar form of Martha.

Mare (Irish) a form of Mary.
Mair, Maire

Marelda (German)
renowned warrior.
Marella, Marilda

Maren (Latin) sea.
(Aramaic) a form of Mary.
See also Marina.
**Marena, Marin, Marina,
Miren, Mirena**

Maretta (English) a familiar
form of Margaret.
Maret, Marette

Margaret (Greek) pearl.
History: Margaret Hilda
Thatcher served as British
prime minister. See also
Gita, Greta, Gretchen,
Marjorie, Markita, Meg,
Megan, Peggy, Reet, Rita.
**Madge, Maergrethe,
Magan, Magen, Maggie,
Maisie, Mamie, Maretta,
Marga, Margalide,
Margalit, Margalith,
Margalo, Marganit,
Margara, Maretha,
Margarett, Margaretta,
Margarette, Margarid,
Margarida, Margaro,
Margaux, Marge,
Margeret, Margeretta,
Margerette, Margerie,
Margerite, Marget,
Margetta, Margette,
Margiad, Margie,
Margisia, Margit, Margo,
Margot, Margret,
Marguerite, Meta**

Margarita (Italian,
Spanish) a form
of Margaret.
**Margareta, Margarit,
Margaritis, Margaritt,
Margaritta, Margharita,
Margherita, Margrieta,
Margrita, Marguarita,
Marguerita, Margurita**

Margaux (French) a form
of Margaret.
Margeaux

Marge (English) a short
form of Margaret,
Marjorie.
Margie

Margie (English) a familiar
form of Marge, Margaret.
Margey, Margi, Margy

Margit (Hungarian) a form
of Margaret.
Margita

Margo, Margot (French)
forms of Margaret.
Mago, Margaro

Margret (German) a form
of Margaret.
**Margreta, Margrete,
Margreth, Margrett,
Margretta, Margrieta,
Margrita**

Marguerite (French)
a form of Margaret.
**Margarete, Margaretha,
Margarethe, Margarite,
Margerite, Marguaretta,
Marguarette, Marguarite,
Marguerette, Margurite**

Mari (Japanese) ball.
(Spanish) a form of Mary.

Maria (Hebrew) bitter;
sea of bitterness. (Italian,
Spanish) a form of Mary.
**Maie, Malia, Marea,
Mareah, Maree,
Mariabella, Mariae, Marie,
Mariesa, Mariessa,
Mariha, Marija, Mariya,
Marja, Marya**

Mariah (Hebrew)
an alternate form of
Mary. See also Moriah.
**Maraia, Maraya, Mariyah,
Marriah, Meriah**

Mariam (Hebrew) an alter-
nate form of Miriam.
**Maryam, Mariem,
Meryam**

Marian (English) an alter-
nate form of Maryann.
**Mariana, Mariane,
Mariann, Marianne,
Mariene, Marion, Marrian,
Marriann, Marrianne,
Maryann, Maryanne**

Mariana (Spanish) a form
of Marian.
**Marianna, Marriana,
Marrianna, Maryana,
Maryanna**

Maribel (French) beautiful.
(English) a combination
of Maria + Bell.
**Marabel, Marbelle,
Mariabella, Maribella,
Maribelle, Maridel,**

**Marybel, Marybella,
Marybelle**

Marice (Italian) a form
of Mary. See also Maris.
Marica, Marise, Marisse

Maridel (English) a form
of Maribel.

Marie (French) a form
of Mary.
**Manon, Maree, Marietta,
Marrie**

Mariel (German, Dutch)
a form of Mary.
**Marial, Marieke, Mariela,
Mariele, Marieline,
Mariella, Marielle,
Mariellen, Marielsie,
Mariely, Marielys**

Marietta (Italian) a familiar
form of Marie.
**Maretta, Marette, Mariet,
Mariette, Marrietta**

Marigold (English) Botany:
a plant with yellow or
orange flowers.
Marygold

Marika (Dutch, Slavic)
a form of Mary.
**Marica, Marieke, Marija,
Marijke, Marike, Marikia,
Mariska, Mariske,
Marrika, Maryk, Maryka,
Merica, Merika**

Mariko (Japanese) circle.

Marilee (American) a combination of Mary + Lee.
Marrilee, Marylea,

Marylee, Merrilee, Merrili, Merrily

Marilla (Hebrew, German) a form of Mary.
Marella, Marelle

Marilyn (Hebrew) Mary's line or descendants. See also Merilyn.
Maralin, Maralyn, Maralyne, Maralynn, Maralynne, Marelyn, Marilin, Marillyn, Marilynn, Marilynne, Marlyn, Marolyn, Marralynn, Marrilin, Marrilyn, Marrilynn, Marrilynne, Marylin, Marylinn, Marylyn, Marylyne, Marylynn, Marylynne

Marina (Latin) sea. See also Maren, Marnie.
Marena, Marenka, Marinda, Marindi, Marine, Marinka, Marrina, Maryna, Merina

Marini (Swahili) healthy; pretty.

Marion (French) a form of Mary.
Marrian, Marrion, Maryon, Maryonn

Maris (Greek) a short form of Amaris. (Latin) sea. See also Marice.
Maries, Marise, Marris, Marys, Meris

Marisa (Latin) sea.
Mariesa, Mariessa, Marisela, Marissa, Marita, Mariza, Marrisa, Marrissa, Marysa, Maryse, Maryssa, Merisa

Marisela (Latin) an alternate form of Marisa.
Mariseli, Marisella, Marishelle

Marisha (Russian) a familiar form of Mary.
Marishenka, Marishka, Mariska

Marisol (Spanish) sunny sea.
Marise, Marizol

Marissa (Latin) an alternate form of Maris, Marisa.
Maressa, Marisa, Marisha, Marisse, Marrissa, Marrissia, Merissa, Morissa

Marit (Aramaic) lady.
Marita

Marita (Spanish) a form of Marissa.
Maritha

Maritza (Arabic) blessed.

Mariyan (Arabic) purity.
Mariya

Marja (Finnish) a form of Mary.
Marjae, Marjatta, Marjie

Marjan (Persian) coral. (Polish) a form of Mary.
Marjaneh, Marjanna

Marjie (Scottish) a familiar
form of Marjorie.
**Marje, Marjey, Marji,
Marjy**

Marjolaine (French)
marjoram.

Marjorie (Greek) a familiar
form of Margaret.
(Scottish) a form of Mary.
**Majorie, Marge,
Margeree, Margerey,
Margerie, Margery,
Margorie, Margory,
Marjarie, Marjary,
Marjerie, Marjery, Marjie,
Marjorey, Marjori,
Marjory**

Markeisia (English) a com-
bination of Mary + Keisha.
**Markesha, Markesia,
Markiesha, Markisha,
Markishia**

Markita (Czech) a form
of Margaret.
**Marka, Markeda, Markee,
Markeeta, Marketa,
Marketta, Markia, Markie,
Markieta, Markita,
Markitha, Markketta**

Marla (English) a short
form of Marlena, Marlene.
Marlah, Marlea, Marleah

Marlana (English) a form
of Marlena.
Marlania, Marlanna

Marlee (English) a form
of Marlene.
Marlea, Marleah

Marlena (German) a form
of Marlene.
**Marla, Marlaina, Marlana,
Marlanna, Marleena,
Marlina, Marlinda,
Marlyna, Marna**

Marlene (Greek) high
tower. (Slavic) a form
of Magdalen.
**Marla, Marlaine,
Marlane, Marlayne,
Marlee, Marleen,
Marlena, Marlenne,
Marley, Marline,
Marlyne**

Marley (English) a familiar
form of Marlene.
**Marlee, Marli, Marlie,
Marly**

Marlis (English) a combina-
tion of Maria + Lisa.
**Marles, Marlisa, Marlise,
Marlys, Marlyse, Marlyssa**

Marlo (English) a form
of Mary.
Marlon, Marlow, Marlowe

Marlyn (Hebrew) a short
form of Marilyn.
Marlynn, Marlynne

Marmara (Greek)
sparkling, shining.
Marmee

Marni (Hebrew) an alter-
nate form of Marnie.
**Marnia, Marnina,
Marnique**

Marnie (Hebrew) a short
form of Marnina.

Marna, Marne, Marnee, Marney, Marni, Marnja, Marnya

Marnina (Hebrew) rejoice.

Maroula (Greek) a form of Mary.

Marquise (French) noble-woman.
Markese, Marquees, Marquese, Marquice, Marquies, Marquiese, Marquisa, Marquisee, Marquiste

Marquita (Spanish) a form of Marcia.
Marqueda, Marquedia, Marquee, Marqueita, Marquet, Marqueta, Marquetta, Marquette, Marquia, Marquida, Marquietta, Marquitra, Marquitia, Marquitta

Marrim (Chinese) tribal name in Manpur state.

Marsala (Italian) from Marseille, Italy.
Marsali, Marseilles

Marsha (English) a form of Marcia.
Marcha, Marshae, Marshay, Marshayly, Marshel, Marshele, Marshell, Marshia, Marshiela

Marta (English) a short form of Martha, Martina.
Martá, Martä, Marte, Marttaha, Merta

Martha (Aramaic) lady; sorrowful. Bible: a sister of the Virgin Mary. See also Mardi.
Maita, Marta, Martaha, Marth, Marthan, Marthe, Marthena, Marthina, Marthine, Marthy, Marti, Marticka, Martita, Matti, Mattie, Matty, Martus, Martuska, Masia

Marti (English) a familiar form of Martha, Martina.
Martie, Marty

Martina (Latin) martial, warlike. A feminine form of Martin. See also Tina.
Marta, Martel, Martella, Martelle, Martene, Marthena, Marthina, Marthine, Marti, Martine, Martinia, Martino, Martisha, Martiza, Martosia, Martoya, Martricia, Martrina, Martyna, Martyne, Martynne

Martiza (Arabic) blessed.

Maru (Japanese) round.

Maruca (Spanish) a form of Mary.
Maruja, Maruska

Marvella (French) marvelous.
Marva, Marvel, Marvela, Marvele, Marvelle, Marvely, Marvetta, Marvette, Marvia, Marvina

Mary (Hebrew) bitter; sea of bitterness. An alternate form of Miriam. Bible: the mother of Jesus. See also Maija, Malia, Maren, Mariah, Marjorie, Maura, Maureen, Miriam, Mitzi, Moira, Molly, Muriel.
Maire, Manette, Manka, Manon, Manya, Mara, Marabel, Mare, Maree, Maren, Marella, Marelle, Mari, Maria, Mariam, Marian, Maricara, Marice, Maridel, Marie, Mariel, Marika, Marilee, Marilla, Marilyn, Marion, Mariquilla, Mariquita, Marisha, Marita, Marité, Maritsa, Maritza, Marja, Marjan, Marje, Marlo, Maroula, Maruca, Marye, Maryla, Marynia, Maryse, Marysia, Masha, Maurise, Maurizia, Mavra, Mendi, Mérane, Meridel, Merrili, Mhairie, Mirja, Mirjam, Molara, Morag, Moya, Muire

Marya (Arabic) purity; bright whiteness.

Maryann, Maryanne (English) combinations of Mary + Ann.
Mariann, Marianne, Maryanna

Marybeth (American) a combination of Mary + Beth.
Maribeth, Maribette

Maryellen (American) a combination of Mary + Ellen.
Mariellen

Maryjo (American) a combination of Mary + Jo.
Marijo

Marylou (American) a combination of Mary + Lou.
Marilou, Marilu

Masago (Japanese) sands of time.

Masani (Luganda) gap toothed.

Masha (Russian) a form of Mary.
Mashka, Mashenka

Mashika (Swahili) born during the rainy season.
Masika

Matana (Hebrew) gift.
Matat

Mathena (Hebrew) gift of God. (English) a feminine form of Matthau.
Mäite, Marité

Matilda (German) powerful battler. See also Maud, Tilda, Tillie.
Máda, Mahaut, Maitilde, Malkin, Mat, Matelda, Mathilda, Mathilde, Matilde, Matti, Mattie, Matty, Matusha, Matuxa, Matya, Matylda

Matrika (Hindi) mother.
Religion: a name for the
Hindu goddess Shakti.

Matsuko (Japanese) pine
tree.

Mattea (Hebrew) gift
of God.
**Matea, Mathea, Mathia,
Matia, Matte, Matthea,
Matthia, Mattia**

Mattie, Matty (English)
familiar forms of Martha,
Matilda.
**Matte, Mattey, Matti,
Mattye**

Matusha (Spanish) a form
of Matilda.
Matuja, Matuxa

Maud, Maude (English)
short forms of Madeline,
Matilda. See also Madison.
**Maudie, Maudine,
Maudlin**

Maura (Irish) dark. An
alternate form of Mary,
Maureen. See also Moira.
**Maure, Maurette,
Mauricette, Maurita**

Maureen (French) dark.
(Irish) a form of Mary.
**Maura, Maurene,
Maurine, Mo, Moreen,
Morena, Morene, Morine,
Morreen, Moureen**

Maurelle (French) dark;
elfin.
**Mauriel, Mauriell,
Maurielle**

Maurise (French) dark
skinned; moor; marshland.
A feminine form of
Maurice.
**Maurisa, Maurissa,
Maurita, Maurizia**

Mausi (Native American)
plucked flower.

Mauve (French) violet
colored.
Malva

Mavis (French) song thrush
bird. See also Maeve.
**Mavies, Mavin, Mavine,
Mavon, Mavra**

Maxine (Latin) greatest.
A feminine form of
Maximillian.
**Max, Maxa, Maxeen,
Maxena, Maxene, Maxi,
Maxie, Maxima, Maxime,
Maximiliane, Maxina,
Maxna, Maxy, Maxyne**

May (Latin) great. (Arabic)
discerning. (English)
flower; month of May.
See also Mae, Maia.
**Maj, Maybelle, Mayberry,
Maybeth, Mayday,
Maydee, Maydena, Maye,
Mayela, Mayella, Mayetta,
Mayrene**

Maya (Hindi) God's creative
power. (Greek) mother;
grandmother. (Latin)
great. An alternate form
of Maia.

Maybeline (Latin)
a familiar form of Mabel.
Maybel, Maybelle

Maylyn (American) a combination of May + Lynn.
**Mayelene, Mayleen,
Maylen, Maylene, Maylin,
Maylon, Maylynn,
Maylynne**

Mayoree (Thai) beautiful.
Mayra, Mayree, Mayariya

Maysa (Arabic) walks with
a proud stride.

Maysun (Arabic) beautiful.

Mazel (Hebrew) lucky.
Mazal, Mazala, Mazella

McKenzie (Scottish) a form
of Mackenzie.
McKensi, McKinzie

Mead, Meade (Greek)
honey wine.

Meagan (Irish) an alternate
form of Megan.
**Maegan, Meagain,
Meagann, Meagen,
Meagin, Meagnah,
Meagon**

Meaghan (Welsh) a form
of Megan.
**Maeghan, Meaghann,
Meaghen, Meahgan**

Meara (Irish) mirthful.

Meda (Native American)
prophet; priestess.

Medea (Greek) ruling.
(Latin) middle. Mythology:
a sorceress who helped

Jason get the Golden
Fleece.
Medeia

Medina (Arabic) History:
the site of Muhammed's
tomb.

Medora (Greek) mother's
gift. Literature: a character
in Lord Byron's poem
"Corsair."

Meena (Hindi) blue semi-
precious stone; bird.

Meg (English) a familiar
form of Margaret, Megan.
Meggi, Meggie, Meggy

Megan (Greek) pearl;
great. (Irish) a form
of Margaret.
**Maegan, Magan, Meagan,
Meaghan, Magen, Meg,
Megean, Megen, Meggan,
Meggen, Meghan, Megyn,
Meygan**

Megara (Greek) first.
Mythology: Hercules's
first wife.

Meghan (Welsh) a form
of Megan.
**Meeghan, Meehan,
Megha, Meghana,
Meghane, Meghann,
Meghanne, Meghean,
Meghen, Mehgan,
Mehgen**

Mehadi (Hindi) flower.

Mehira (Hebrew) speedy;
energetic.
Mahira

Mehitabel (Hebrew) benefited by trusting God.
Mehetabel, Mehitabelle, Hetty, Hitty

Mehri (Persian) kind; lovable; sunny.

Mei (Chinese) a short form of Meiying. (Hawaiian) great.
Meiko

Meira (Hebrew) light.
Meera

Meit (Burmese) affectionate.

Meiying (Chinese) beautiful flower.

Meka (Hebrew) a familiar form of Michaela.

Mel (Portuguese, Spanish) sweet as honey.

Mela (Hindi) religious service. (Polish) a form of Melanie.

Melana (Russian) a form of Melanie.
Melanenka, Melanna, Melenka

Melanie (Greek) dark skinned.
Malania, Malanie, Meila, Meilani, Meilin, Meladia, Melaine, Melainie, Melana, Melane, Melanee, Melaney, Melani, Melania, Mélanie, Melanka, Melanney, Melannie, Melantha, Melany,

Melanya, Melashka, Melasya, Melayne, Melenia, Melina, Mella, Mellanie, Melonie, Melya, Melyn, Melyne, Melynn, Melynne, Milana, Milena, Milya

Melantha (Greek) dark flower.

Melba (Greek) soft; slender. (Latin) mallow flower.
Malva, Melva

Mele (Hawaiian) song; poem.

Melesse (Ethiopian) eternal.
Mellesse

Melia (German) a short form of Amelia.
Melcia, Melea, Meleah, Meleia, Meleisha, Meli, Meliah, Melida, Melika, Mema, Milia, Milica, Milka

Melina (Latin) canary yellow. (Greek) a short form of Melinda.
Melaina, Meleana, Meleena, Melena, Meline, Melinia, Melinna, Melynna

Melinda (Greek) honey. See also Linda, Melina, Mindy.
Maillie, Malinda, Melinde, Melinder, Mellinda, Melynda, Milinda, Milynda, Mylinda, Mylynda

Meliora (Latin) better.
Melior, Meliori, Mellear,
Melyor, Melyora

Melisande (French) a form
of Melissa, Millicent.
Lisandra, Malisande,
Malissande, Malyssandre,
Melesande, Melisandra,
Melisandre, Mélisandré,
Melisenda, Melissande,
Melissandre, Mellisande,
Melond, Melysande,
Melyssandre

Melissa (Greek) honey bee.
See also Elissa, Lissa,
Melisande, Millicent.
Malissa, Mallissa,
Melesa, Melessa, Meleta,
Melisa, Mélisa, Melise,
Melisha, Melishia, Melisia,
Mélissa, Melisse, Melissia,
Meliza, Melizah, Mellie,
Mellisa, Mellissa, Melly,
Melosa, Milisa, Milissa,
Millie, Milly, Misha, Missy,
Molissia, Mollissa, Mylisa,
Mylisia, Mylissa, Mylissia

Melita (Greek) a form of
Melissa. (Spanish) a short
form of Carmelita.
Malita, Meleeta, Melitta,
Melitza, Melletta, Molita

Melly (American) a familiar
form of names beginning
with "Mel." See also Millie.
Meli, Melie, Melli, Mellie

Melonie (American) an
alternate form of Melanie.
Melloney, Mellonie,

Mellony, Melonee,
Meloney, Meloni, Melonie,
Melonnie, Melony

Melody (Greek) melody.
Melodee, Melodey,
Melodi, Melodia, Melodie,
Melodye

Melosa (Spanish) sweet;
tender.

Melvina (Irish) armored
chief. A feminine form of
Melvin. See also Malvina.
Melevine, Melva, Melveen,
Melvena, Melvene,
Melvonna

Mena (Greek) a short form
of Philomena. (German,
Dutch) strong. History:
Mena was the first king
of Egypt.
Menah

Mendi (Basque) a form
of Mary.
Menda, Mendy

Mérane (French) a form
of Mary.
Meraine, Merrane

Mercedes (Latin) reward,
payment. (Spanish)
merciful.
Merced, Mercede,
Mersade

Mercia (English) a form
of Marcia. History: the
name of an ancient British
kingdom.

Mercy (English) compassionate, merciful. See also Merry.
Mercey, Merci, Mercie, Mercille, Mersey

Meredith (Welsh) protector of the sea.
Meredithe, Meredy, Meredyth, Meredythe, Meridath, Merideth, Meridie, Meridith, Merridie, Merridith, Merry

Meri (Finnish) sea. (Irish) a short form of Meriel.

Meriel (Irish) shining sea.
Meri, Merial, Meriol, Meryl

Merilyn (English) a combination of Merry + Lynn. See also Marilyn.
Merelyn, Merlyn, Merralyn, Merrelyn, Merrilyn

Merle (Latin, French) blackbird.
Merl, Merla, Merlina, Merline, Merola, Murle, Myrle, Myrleen, Myrlene, Myrline

Merry (English) cheerful, happy. A familiar form of Mercy, Meredith.
Merie, Merree, Merri, Merrie, Merrielle, Merrile, Merrilee, Merrilyn, Merris, Merrita

Meryl (German) famous. (Irish) shining sea. An alternate form of Meriel, Muriel.
Meral, Merel, Merrall, Merrell, Merril, Merrill, Merryl, Meryle, Meryll

Mesha (Hindi) born in the lunar month of Aries.
Meshal

Meta (German) a short form of Margaret.
Metta, Mette, Metti

Mhairie (Scottish) a form of Mary.
Mhaire, Mhairi, Mhari, Mhary

Mia (Italian) mine. A familiar form of Michaela, Michelle.
Mea, Meah, Miah

Micah (Hebrew) a short form of Michaela. Bible: one of the Old Testament prophets.
Mica, Mika, Myca, Mycah

Michaela (Hebrew) who is like God? A feminine form of Michael.
Machaela, Makayla, Meecah, Mia, Micaela, Michael, Michaelann, Michealia, Michaelina, Michaeline, Michaell, Michaella, Michaelle, Michaelyn, Michaila, Michal, Michala, Micheal, Micheala, Michela, Michelia, Michelina,

Michaela (cont.)
**Michelle, Michely,
Michelyn, Micheyla,
Micheline, Micki, Micquel,
Miguela, Mikaela, Miquel,
Miquela, Miquelle,
Mycala, Mychael, Mychal**

Michala (Hebrew) an alter-
nate form of Michaela.
**Michalann, Michale,
Michalene, Michalin,
Mchalina, Michalisha,
Michalla, Michalle,
Michayla, Michayle**

Michele (Italian) a form
of Michaela.
Michela

Michelle (French) who
is like God? A form of
Michaela. See also Shelley.
**Machealle, Machele,
Machell, Machella,
Machelle, Mechelle,
Meichelle, Meschell,
Meshell, Meshelle, Mia,
Michel, Michele, Michèle,
Michell, Michella,
Michellene, Michellyn,
Mischel, Mischelle, Misha,
Mishae, Mishael,
Mishaela, Mishayla,
Mishell, Mishelle,
Mitchele, Mitchelle**

Michi (Japanese) righteous
way.
Miche, Michee, Michiko

Micki (American) a familiar
form of Michaela.
Mickee, Mickeeya, Mickia,

**Mickie, Micky, Mickya,
Miquia**

Midori (Japanese) green.

Mieko (Japanese)
prosperous.
Mieke

Mielikki (Finnish) pleasing.

Miette (French) small;
sweet.

Migina (Omaha) new
moon.

Mignon (French) cute;
graceful.
**Mignonette, Minnionette,
Minnonette, Minyonette,
Minyonne**

Miguela (Spanish) a form
of Michaela.
Miguelina, Miguelita

Mika (Hebrew) an alternate
form of Micah. (Latin)
a short form of Dominica,
Dominika. (Russian) God's
child. (Native American)
wise racoon.
Mikah

Mikaela (Hebrew) an alter-
nate form of Michaela.
**Mekaela, Mekala,
Mekayla, Mickael,
Mickaela, Mickala,
Mickalla, Mickayla,
Mickeel, Mickell, Mickelle,
Mikail, Mikaila, Mikal,
Mikalene, Mikalovna,
Mikalyn, Mikayla,
Mikayle, Mikea, Mikeisha,**

**Mikeita, Mikel, Mikela,
Mikele, Mikell, Mikella,
Mikesha, Mikeya,
Mikhaela, Mikie, Mikiela,
Mikkel, Mikyla, Mykaela**

Mikhaela (American) an
alternate form of Mikaela.
**Mikhail, Mikhaila,
Mikhala, Mikhalea,
Mikhelle**

Miki (Japanese) flower
stem.
**Mika, Mikia, Mikiala,
Mikie, Mikita, Mikiyo,
Mikka, Mikki, Mikkie,
Mikkiya, Mikko, Miko**

Mila (Italian, Slavic) a short
form of Camilla, Ludmilla.
(Russian) dear one.
Milah, Milla

Milada (Czech) my love.
Mila, Milady

Milagros (Spanish)
miracle.
**Mila, Milagritos, Milagro,
Milagrosa, Mirari**

Milana (Italian) from Milan,
Italy.
**Mila, Milan, Milane,
Milani, Milanka, Milanna,
Milanne**

Mildred (English) gentle
counselor.
**Mil, Mila, Mildrene,
Mildrid, Millie, Milly**

Milena (Greek, Hebrew,
Russian) a form of
Ludmilla, Magdalen,
Melanie.

**Mila, Milène, Milenia,
Milenny, Milini, Millini**

Mileta (German) generous,
merciful. A feminine form
of Milo.
Mila, Milessa, Mylie

Milia (German) industrious.
A short form of Amelia,
Emily.
**Mila, Mili, Milica, Milika,
Milla, Milya**

Miliani (Hawaiian) caress.
Mila, Milanni

Mililani (Hawaiian) heavenly caress.
Mila, Milliani

Milissa (Greek) an alternate
form of Melissa.
Milisa, Millisa, Millissa

Milka (Czech) a form
of Amelia.

Millicent (Greek) an
alternate form of Melissa.
(English) industrious.
See also Lissa, Melisande.
**Melicent, Meliscent,
Mellicent, Mellisent,
Melly, Milicent, Milisent,
Millie, Milliestone,
Millisent, Milly, Milzie,
Missie, Missy**

Millie, Milly (English)
familiar forms of Amelia,
Camille, Emily, Kamila,
Melissa, Mildred, Millicent.
**Mili, Milla, Millee, Milley,
Millie**

Mima (Burmese) woman.
  Mimma

Mimi (French) a familiar
  form of Miriam.

Mina (German) love.
  (Persian) blue sky. (Hindi)
  born in the lunar month
  of Pisces. (Arabic) harbor.
  (Japanese) south. A short
  form of names ending in
  "mina."
  Meena, Mena, Min

Minal (Native American)
  fruit.

Minda (Hindi) knowledge.

Mindy (Greek) a familiar
  form of Melinda.
  **Mindee, Mindi, Mindie,
  Mindyanne, Mindylee,
  Myndy**

Miné (Japanese) peak;
  mountain range.
  Minéko

Minerva (Latin) wise.
  Mythology: the goddess
  of wisdom.
  **Merva, Minivera, Minnie,
  Myna**

Minette (French) faithful
  defender.
  Minnette, Minnita

Minka (Polish) a short form
  of Wilhelmina.

Minna (German) a short
  form of Wilhelmina.
  **Mina, Minka, Minnie,
  Minta**

Minnie (American) a famil-
  iar form of Mina, Minerva,
  Minna, Wilhelmina.
  **Mini, Minie, Minne, Minni,
  Minny**

Minowa (Native American)
  singer.
  Minowah

Minta (English) Literature:
  originally coined by
  playwright Sir John
  Vanbrugh in his comedy
  The Confederacy.
  Minty

Minya (Osage) older sister.

Mio (Japanese) three times
  as strong.

Mira (Latin) wonderful.
  (Spanish) look, gaze.
  A short form of Almira,
  Amira, Mirabel, Miranda.
  Mirae, Mirra, Mirah

Mirabel (Latin) beautiful.
  **Mira, Mirabell, Mirabella,
  Mirabelle, Mirable**

Miranda (Latin) strange;
  wonderful; admirable.
  Literature: the heroine of
  Shakespeare's *The Tempest*.
  See also Randi.
  **Maranda, Marenda,
  Meranda, Mira, Miran,
  Miranada, Mirandia,
  Mirinda, Mirindé,
  Mironda, Mirranda,
  Muranda, Myranda**

Mireil (Hebrew) God
  spoke. (Latin) wonderful.

Mirella, Mirelle, Mirelys, Mireya, Mireyda, Mirielle, Mirilla, Myrella, Myrilla

Miri (Gypsy) a short form of Miriam.
Miria, Miriah

Miriam (Hebrew) bitter, sea of bitterness. Bible: the original form of Mary. See also Macia, Mimi, Mitzi.
Mairona, Mairwen, Marca, Marcsa, Mariam, Mariame, Maroula, Maruca, Maruja, Maruska, Meryem, Miram, Mirham, Miri, Miriain, Miriama, Miriame, Mirian, Mirit, Mirjam, Mirjana, Mirra, Mirriam, Mirrian, Miryam, Miryan, Myriam

Missy (English) a familiar form of Melissa, Millicent.
Missi, Missie

Misty (English) shrouded by mist.
Missty, Mistee, Mistey, Misti, Mistie, Mistin, Mistina, Mistral, Mistylynn, Mystee, Mysti, Mystie

Mitra (Hindi) god of daylight. (Persian) angel.
Mita

Mituna (Moquelumnan) like a fish wrapped up in leaves.

Mitzi (German) a form of Mary, Miriam.
Mieze, Mitzee, Mitzie

Miwa (Japanese) wise eyes.
Miwako

Miya (Japanese) temple.
Miyana, Miyanna

Miyo (Japanese) beautiful generation.
Miyoko, Miyuki, Miyuko

Miyuki (Japanese) snow.

Moana (Hawaiian) ocean; fragrance.

Mocha (Arabic) chocolate-flavored coffee.
Moka

Modesty (Latin) modest.
Modesta, Modeste, Modestia, Modestie, Modestina, Modestine, Modestus

Mohala (Hawaiian) flowers in bloom.
Moala

Moira (Irish) great. A form of Mary. See also Maura.
Moirae, Moirah, Moire, Moya, Moyra, Moyrah

Molara (Basque) a form of Mary.

Molly (Irish) a familiar form of Mary.
Moll, Mollee, Molley, Molli, Mollie, Mollissa

Mona (Greek) a short form of Monica, Ramona, Rimona. (Irish) noble.

Mona *(cont.)*
**Moina, Monah, Mone,
Monea, Monna, Moyna**

Monet (French) Art:
Claude Monet was a lead-
ing French impressionist
remembered for his paint-
ings of water lilies.
Monae, Monay, Monee

Monica (Greek) solitary.
(Latin) advisor.
**Mona, Monca, Monee,
Monia, Monic, Monice,
Monicia, Monicka,
Monika, Monique,
Monise, Monn, Monnica,
Monnie, Monya**

Monifa (Yoruba) I have
my luck.

Monika (German) a form
of Monica.
**Moneeke, Moneik,
Moneka, Monieka,
Monike, Monnika**

Monique (French) a form
of Monica.
**Moniqua, Moniquea,
Moniquie, Munique**

Montana (Spanish)
mountain.
Montanna

Mora (Spanish) blueberry.
Morea, Moria, Morita

Morela (Polish) apricot.

Morena (Irish) a form
of Maureen.

Morgan (Welsh) seashore.
Literature: Morgan
Le Fay was the half-
sister of King Arthur.
**Morgana, Morgance,
Morgane, Morganetta,
Morganette, Morganica,
Morgann, Morganna,
Morganne, Morgen,
Morgyn, Morrigan**

Moriah (Hebrew) God is
my teacher. (French) dark
skinned. Bible: the name
of the mountain on which
the temple of Solomon
was built. See also Mariah.
**Moria, Moriel, Morit,
Morria, Morriah**

Morie (Japanese) bay.

Morowa (Akan) queen.

Morrisa (Latin) dark
skinned; moor; marshland.
A feminine form of Morris.
Morisa, Morissa, Morrissa

Moselle (Hebrew) drawn
from the water. A feminine
form of Moses. (French)
a white wine.
Mozelle

Mosi (Swahili) first-born.

Moswen (Tswana) white.

Mouna (Arabic) wish,
desire.
**Moona, Moonia, Mounia,
Muna, Munia**

Mrena (Slavic) white eyes.
Mren

Mura (Japanese) village.

Muriel (Arabic) myrrh.
(Irish) shining sea. A form
of Mary. See also Meryl.
**Merial, Meriel, Meriol,
Merrial, Merriel, Murial,
Muriell, Murielle**

Musetta (French) little
bagpipe.
Musette

Muslimah (Arabic) devout
believer.

Mya (Burmese) emerald.

Mykaela (American) a form
of Mikaela.
**Mykael, Mykal, Mykala,
Mykaleen, Mykel, Mykela**

Myla (English) merciful.

Mylene (Greek) dark.
**Mylaine, Mylana, Mylee,
Myleen, Mylenda, Mylinda**

Myra (Latin) fragrant
ointment. A feminine
form of Myron.
Myrena, Myria

Myriam (American) a form
of Miriam.
Myriame, Myryam

Myrna (Irish) beloved.
**Merna, Mirna, Morna,
Muirna**

Myrtle (Greek) dark green
shrub.
**Mertis, Mertle, Mirtle,
Myrta, Myrtia, Myrtias,
Myrtice, Myrtie, Myrtilla,
Myrtis**

Nabila (Arabic) born
to nobility.
Nabeela, Nabiha, Nabilah

Nadda (Arabic) generous;
dewy.
Nada

Nadette (French) a short
form of Bernadette.

Nadia (French, Slavic)
hopeful.
**Nada, Nadea, Nadenka,
Nadezhda, Nadie, Nadine,
Nadiya, Nadja, Nadka,
Nadusha, Nady, Nadya**

Nadine (French, Slavic)
a form of Nadia.
**Nadean, Nadeana,
Nadeen, Nadena, Nadene,
Nadien, Nadina, Nadyne,
Naidene, Naidine**

Nadira (Arabic) rare,
precious.
Nadirah

Naeva (French) a form
of Eve.
Nahvon

Nafuna (Luganda) born
feet first.

Nagida (Hebrew) noble; prosperous.
Nagda, Nageeda

Nahid (Persian) Mythology: another name for Venus, the goddess of love and beauty.

Nahimana (Dakota) mystic.

Naida (Greek) water nymph.
Naia, Naiad, Naya, Nayad, Nyad

Naila (Arabic) successful.
Nailah

Nairi (Armenian) land of canyons. History: a name for ancient Armenia.

Najam (Arabic) star.
Naja, Najma

Najila (Arabic) brilliant eyes.
Naja, Najah, Najia, Najla

Nakeisha (American) a combination of the prefix Na + Keisha.
Nakeesha, Nakesha, Nakeshea, Nakeshia, Nakeysha, Nakiesha, Nakisha, Nekeisha

Nakeita (American) a form of Nikita.
Nakeeta, Nakeitha, Nakeithra, Nakeitra, Nakeitress, Nakeitta, Nakeittia, Naketta,
Nakieta, Nakitha, Nakitia, Nakitta, Nakyta

Nakia (Arabic) pure.
Nakea, Nakeia

Nakita (American) a form of Nicole, Nikita.
Nakia, Nakkita, Naquita

Nalani (Hawaiian) calm as the heavens.
Nalanie, Nalany

Nami (Japanese) wave.
Namika, Namiko

Nan (German) a short form of Fernanda. (English) an alternate form of Ann.
Nana, Nanette, Nani, Nanice, Nanine, Nanna, Nannie, Nanny, Nanon

Nana (Hawaiian) spring.

Nancy (English) gracious. A familiar form of Nan.
Nainsi, Nance, Nancee, Nancey, Nanci, Nancie, Nancine, Nancsi, Nancye, Nanette, Nanice, Nanine, Nanncey, Nanncy, Nanouk, Nansee, Nansey, Nanuk, Noni, Nonie

Nanette (French) a form of Nancy.
Nan, Nanete, Nannette, Neti, Netti, Nettie, Netty, Ninette, Nini, Ninon

Nani (Greek) charming. (Hawaiian) beautiful.
Nanni, Nannie, Nanny

Naomi (Hebrew) pleasant, beautiful. Bible: a friend of Ruth.
Naoma, Naomia, Naomie, Naomy, Navit, Neoma, Neomi, Noami, Noemi, Noemie, Noma, Nomi, Nyome, Nyomi

Nara (Greek) happy. (English) north. (Japanese) oak.
Narah

Narcissa (Greek) daffodil. A feminine form of Narcissus. Mythology: the youth who fell in love with his own reflection.
Narcisa, Narcisse, Narcyssa, Narkissa

Narelle (Australian) woman from the sea.

Nari (Japanese) thunder.
Nariko

Narmada (Hindi) pleasure giver.

Nashawna (American) a combination of the prefix Na + Shawna.
Nashana, Nashanda, Nashauna, Nashaunda, Nashawn, Nashounda, Nashuana

Nashota (Native American) double; second-born twin.

Nastasia (Greek) an alternate form of Anastasia.
Nastasha, Nastashia, Nastasja, Nastassa, Nastassia, Nastassiya, Nastassja, Nastassya, Nastasya, Nastazia, Nastisija, Nastka, Nastusya, Nastya

Nasya (Hebrew) miracle.
Nasia

Nata (Sanskrit) dancer. (Latin) swimmer. (Polish, Russian) a form of Natalie. (Native American) speaker; creator. See also Nadia.
Natia, Natka, Natya

Natalia (Russian) a form of Natalie. See also Talia.
Nacia, Natala, Nataliia, Natalina, Natalja, Natalka, Natalya, Nathalia, Natka

Natalie (Latin) born on Christmas day. See also Nata, Natasha, Nettie, Noel, Talia.
Nat, Natalea, Natalee, Natalene, Natalène, Natali, Natalia, Natalija, Nataline, Natalle, Nataly, Natalya, Natalyn, Natelie, Nathalia, Nathalie, Nathaly, Nati, Natie, Natilie, Natlie, Nattalie, Natti, Nattie, Nattilie, Nattlee, Natty

Natalle (French) a form of Natalie.
Natale, Natallia, Natallie, Natallye

Natane (Arapaho) daughter.
Natanne

Natania (Hebrew) gift
of God. A feminine form
of Nathan.
**Natée, Nathania,
Nathenia, Netania,
Nethania**

Natara (Arabic) sacrifice.

Natasha (Russian) a form
of Natalie. See also Stacey,
Tasha.
**Nahtasha, Natacha,
Natachia, Natacia, Natasa,
Natascha, Natashah,
Natashea, Natashenka,
Natashia, Natashiea,
Natashja, Natashka,
Natasia, Natassija,
Natassja, Natasza,
Natausha, Natawsha,
Nathasha, Nathassha,
Naticha, Natisha, Natishia,
Natosha, Natoshia,
Netasha, Netosha,
Notasha, Notosha**

Natesa (Hindi) godlike;
goddess. Religion:
another name for the
Hindu goddess Shakti.
Natisa, Natissa

Nava (Hebrew) beautiful;
pleasant.
Navah, Naveh, Navit

Neala (Irish) an alternate
form of Neila.
**Nayela, Naylea, Naylia,
Nealee, Nealia, Nealie,
Nealy, Neela, Neelia, Neeli,
Neelie, Neely, Neila**

Necha (Spanish) a form
of Agnes.
Necho

Neci (Hungarian) fiery,
intense.
Necia, Necie

Neda (Slavic) born
on Sunday.
Nedi

Nedda (English) prosperous
guardian. A feminine form
of Edward.
Neddi, Neddie, Neddy

Neely (Irish) a familiar form
of Neila, Nelia.
**Neelee, Neeley, Neelia,
Neelie, Neili, Neilie**

Neema (Swahili) born
during prosperous times.

Neila (Irish) champion.
A feminine form of Neil.
See also Neala, Neely.
Neile, Neilla, Neille

Nekeisha (American)
an alternate form of
Nakeisha.
**Nechesa, Neikeishia,
Nekesha, Nekeshia,
Nekiesha, Nekisha,
Nekysha**

Nelia (Spanish) yellow.
(Latin) a familiar form
of Cornelia.
**Neelia, Neely, Neelya,
Nela, Neli, Nelka, Nila**

Nelle (Greek) stone.

Nellie (English) a familiar
form of Cornelia, Eleanor,
Helen, Prunella.
**Nel, Neli, Nell, Nella,
Nelley, Nelli, Nellianne,
Nellice, Nellis, Nelly,
Nelma**

Nenet (Egyptian) born near
the sea. Mythology: the
goddess of the sea.

Neola (Greek) youthful.

Neona (Greek) new moon.

Nerine (Greek) sea nymph.
**Nereida, Nerida, Nerina,
Nerita, Nerline**

Nerissa (Greek) sea nymph.
See also Rissa.
**Narice, Narissa, Nerice,
Nerisse, Nerys, Neryssa**

Nessa (Greek) a short form
of Agnes. (Scandinavian)
promontory. See also
Nessie.
**Nesa, Nesha, Neshia,
Nesiah, Nessia, Nesta,
Nevsa, Neya, Neysa,
Nyusha**

Nessie (Greek) a familiar
form of Agnes, Nessa,
Vanessa.
**Nese, Neshie, Nesho, Nesi,
Ness, Nessi, Nessy, Nest,
Neys**

Neta (Hebrew) plant,
shrub. See also Nettie.
Netia, Netta, Nettia

Netis (Native American)
trustworthy.

Nettie (French) a familiar
form of Annette, Nanette,
Antoinette.
**Neti, Netie, Netta, Netti,
Netty, Nety**

Neva (Spanish) snow.
(English) new. (Russian)
Geography: a river in
Russia.
**Neiva, Nevada, Neve,
Nevein, Nevia, Nevin,
Neyva, Nieve**

Nevada (Spanish) snow.
Geography: a western
American state.
Neiva, Neva

Nevina (Irish) worshipper
of the saint. A feminine
form of Nevin. History:
a well-known Irish saint.
Nevena, Nivena

Neylan (Turkish) fulfilled
wish.
Neya, Neyla

Neza (Slavic) a form
of Agnes.

Nia (Irish) a familiar form
of Neila. Mythology: a legendary Welsh woman.
Niah, Nya, Nyah

Niabi (Osage) fawn.

Nichelle (American)
a combination of
Nicole + Michelle. Culture:
Nichelle Nichols was the
first African-American

woman featured in a television drama *Star Trek*.
Nichele, Nishelle

Nichole (French) an alternate form of Nicole.
Nichol, Nichola

Nicki (French) a familiar form of Nicole.
Nicci, Nickey, Nickeya, Nickia, Nickie, Nickiya, Nicky, Niki

Nicola (Italian) a form of Nicole.
Nacola, Necola, Nichola, Nickola, Nicolea, Nicolla, Nikkola, Nikola, Nikolia, Nykola

Nicole (French) victorious people. A feminine form of Nicholas. See also Colette, Cosette, Nikita.
Nacole, Nakita, Necole, Nica, Nichol, Nichole, Nicholette, Nicia, Nicki, Nickol, Nickole, Nicol, Nicola, Nicolette, Nicoli, Nicolie, Nicoline, Nicolle, Nikki, Niquole, Nocole

Nicolette (French) an alternate form of Nicole.
Nettie, Nicholette, Nicoletta, Nikkolette, Nikoleta, Nikoletta, Nikolette

Nicoline (French) a familiar form of Nicole.
Nicholine, Nicholyn, Nicoleen, Nicolene, Nicolina, Nicolyn,
Nicolyne, Nicolynn, Nicolynne, Nikolene, Nikolina, Nikoline

Nicolle (French) an alternate form of Nicole.
Nicholle

Nida (Omaha) Mythology: an elflike creature.

Nidia (Latin) nest.
Nidi, Nidya

Niesha (Scandinavian) an alternate form of Nissa. (American) pure.
Neisha, Neishia, Neissia, Nesha, Neshia, Nesia, Nessia, Niessia, Nisha

Nika (Russian) belonging to God.

Nike (Greek) victorious. Mythology: the goddess of victory.

Niki (Russian) a short form of Nikita.
Nikia

Nikita (Russian) victorious people. A form of Nicole.
Niki, Nikki, Nikkita, Niquita, Niquitta

Nikki (American) a familiar form of Nicole, Nikita.
Nicki, Nikia, Nikka, Nikkey, Nikkia, Nikkie, Nikky

Nikole (French) an alternate form of Nicole.
Nikkole, Nikola, Nikole, Nikolle

Nila (Latin) Geography:
the Nile River in Egypt.
(Irish) an alternate form
of Neila.
Nilesia

Nili (Hebrew) Botany:
a pea plant that yields
indigo.

Nima (Hebrew) thread.
(Arabic) blessing.
Nema, Nimali

Nina (Hebrew) a familiar
form of Hannah. (Spanish)
girl. (Native American)
mighty.
**Neena, Nena, Ninacska,
Nineta, Ninete, Ninetta,
Ninette, Ninita, Ninja,
Ninnetta, Ninnette,
Ninon, Ninosca, Ninoshka,
Nynette**

Ninon (French) a form
of Nina.

Nirel (Hebrew) light
of God.

Nirveli (Hindi) water child.

Nisa (Arabic) woman.

Nisha (American) an alternate form of Niesha, Nissa.

Nishi (Japanese) west.

Nissa (Hebrew) sign,
emblem. (Scandinavian)
friendly elf; brownie.
See also Nyssa.
Nisha, Nisse, Nissie, Nissy

Nita (Hebrew) planter.
(Spanish) a short form
of Anita, Juanita.
(Choctaw) bear.
Nitika

Nitara (Hindi) deeply
rooted.

Nitasha (American) a form
of Natasha.
**Nitasha, Niteisha, Nitisha,
Nitishia**

Nitsa (Greek) a form
of Helen.

Nituna (Native American)
daughter.

Nitza (Hebrew) flower bud.
**Nitzah, Nitzana, Nitzanit,
Niza, Nizah**

Nixie (German) water
sprite.

Nizana (Hebrew) an alternate form of Nitza.
Nitzana, Nitzania, Zana

Noel (Latin) Christmas.
**Noël, Noela, Noeleen,
Noelene, Noelia, Noeline,
Noelle, Noelyn, Noelynn,
Noleen, Novelenn,
Novelia, Nowel, Noweleen,
Nowell**

Noelani (Hawaiian) beautiful one from heaven.
Noela

Noelle (French) Christmas.
A form of Noel.
**Noell, Noella, Noelleen,
Noellyn**

Noemi (Hebrew) an alternate form of Naomi.
Noemie, Nohemi, Nomi

Noga (Hebrew) morning light.

Nokomis (Dakota) moon daughter.

Nola (Latin) small bell. (Irish) famous; noble. A short form of Fionnula. A feminine form of Nolan.
Nuala

Noleta (Latin) unwilling.
Nolita

Nollie (English) a familiar form of Magnolia.
Nolley, Nolli, Nolly

Noma (Hawaiian) a form of Norma.

Nona (Latin) ninth.
Nonah, Noni, Nonia, Nonie, Nonna, Nonnah, Nonya

Nora (Greek) light. A familiar form of Eleanor, Honora, Leonore.
Norah, Noreen

Noreen (Irish) a form of Eleanor, Nora. (Latin) a familiar form of Norma.
Noorin, Noreena, Noren, Norene, Norina, Norine, Nureen

Norell (Scandinavian) from the north.
Narell, Narelle, Norelle

Nori (Japanese) law, tradition.
Noria, Norico, Noriko, Norita

Norma (Latin) rule, precept.
Noma, Noreen, Normi, Normie

Nova (Latin) new. A short form of Novella, Novia. (Hopi) butterfly chaser. Astronomy: a star that releases bright bursts of energy.

Novella (Latin) newcomer.
Nova, Novela

Novia (Spanish) sweetheart.
Nova, Novka, Nuvia

Nu (Burmese) tender. (Vietnamese) girl.
Nue

Nuala (Irish) a short form of Fionnula.
Nola, Nula

Nuela (Spanish) a form of Amelia.

Nuna (Native American) land.

Nunciata (Latin) messenger.
Nunzia

Nura (Aramaic) light.
Noor, Nour, Noura, Nur, Nureen

Nuria (Aramaic) the Lord's light.
Nuri, Nuriel, Nurin

Nurita (Hebrew) Botany: a flower with red and yellow blossoms.
Nurit

Nuru (Swahili) daylight.

Nusi (Hungarian) a form of Hannah.

Nuwa (Chinese) mother goddess. Mythology: the creator of mankind and order.

Nydia (Latin) nest.
Nyda

Nyla (Irish) an alternate form of Nila.
Nylah

Nyoko (Japanese) gem, treasure.

Nyree (Maori) sea.
Nyra, Nyrie

Nyssa (Greek) beginning. See also Nissa.
Nisha, Nissi, Nissy, Nysa

Nyusha (Russian) a form of Agnes.
Nyushenka, Nyushka

Oba (Yoruba) Mythology: the goddess who rules the rivers.

Obelia (Greek) needle.

Oceana (Greek) ocean. Mythology: Oceanus was the god of water.
Ocean, Oceanne, Oceon

Octavia (Latin) eighth. A feminine form of Octavio. See also Tavia.
Octavice, Octavie, Octavienne, Octavise, Octivia, Ottavia

Odeda (Hebrew) strong; courageous.

Odele (Greek) melody, song.
Odela, Odelet, Odelette, Odella, Odelle

Odelia (Greek) ode; melodic. (Hebrew) I will praise God. (French) wealthy. A feminine form of Odell. See also Odetta.
Oda, Odeelia, Odele, Odeleya, Odelina, Odelinda, Odell, Odelyn, Odila, Odile, Odilia

Odella (English) wood hill.
Odelle, Odelyn

Odera (Hebrew) plough.

Odessa (Greek) odyssey,
long voyage.

Odetta (German, French)
a form of Odelia.
Oddetta, Odette

Odina (Algonquin)
mountain.

Ofira (Hebrew) gold.
Ofarrah, Ophira

Ofra (Hebrew) an alternate
form of Aphra.
Ofrat

Ogin (Native American)
wild rose.

Ohanna (Hebrew) God's
gracious gift.

Okalani (Hawaiian)
heaven.
Okilani

Oki (Japanese) middle
of the ocean.

Ola (Greek) a short form
of Olesia. (Scandinavian)
ancestor. A feminine form
of Olaf.

Olathe (Native American)
beautiful.
Olathia

Oleda (Spanish) an alter-
nate form of Alida.
See also Leda.
Oleta, Olida, Olita

Olena (Russian) a form
of Helen.
Olenka, Olenya, Olya

Olesia (Greek) an alternate
form of Alexandra.
**Cesya, Ola, Olecia, Olesya,
Olexa, Olicia, Ollicia**

Oletha (Scandinavian)
nimble.

Olethea (Latin) truthful.
See also Alethea.
Oleta

Olga (Scandinavian) holy.
See also Helga, Olivia.
Olenka, Olia, Olva

Oliana (Polynesian)
oleander.

Olina (Hawaiian) filled
with happiness.

Olinda (Greek) an alternate
form of Yolanda. (Latin)
scented. (Spanish) protector of property.

Olisa (Ibo) God.

Olive (Latin) olive tree.
**Oliff, Oliffe, Olivet,
Olivette**

Olivia (Latin) olive tree.
(English) a form of Olga.
See also Livia.
**Oliva, Olive, Olivea,
Olivetta, Olivianne,
Oliwia, Ollie, Olly, Ollye,
Olva, Olyvia**

Olwen (Welsh) white
footprint.
**Olwenn, Olwin, Olwyn,
Olwyne, Olwynne**

Olympia (Greek) heavenly.
Olimpia, Olympe, Olympie

Oma (Hebrew) reverent.
(German) grandmother.
(Arabic) highest. A femi-
nine form of Omar.

Omaira (Arabic) red.
Omara

Omega (Greek) last,
final, end. Linguistics:
the last letter in the
Greek alphabet.

Ona (Latin, Irish) an alternate form of Oona, Una.
(English) river.

Onatah (Iroquois) daughter of the earth and the
corn spirit.

Onawa (Native American)
wide awake.
Onaja, Onajah

Ondine (Latin) an alternate
form of Undine.
Ondina, Ondyne

Ondrea (Czech) a form
of Andrea.
**Ohndrea, Ohndreea,
Ohndreya, Ohndria,
Ondreea, Ondreya,
Ondria, Ondriea**

Oneida (Native American)
eagerly awaited.
Onida, Onyda

Onella (Hungarian) a form
of Helen.

Oni (Yoruba) born on holy
ground.

Onora (Latin) an alternate
form of Honora.
Onoria, Onorine, Ornora

Oona (Latin, Irish) an alter-
nate form of Una.
**Ona, Onna, Onnie,
Oonagh, Oonie**

Opa (Choctaw) owl.

Opal (Hindi) precious
stone.
Opale, Opalina, Opaline

Ophelia (Greek) helper.
Literature: Hamlet's
love interest in the
Shakespearean play
Hamlet.
**Filia, Ofeelia, Ofelia,
Ofilia, Ophélie, Ophilia,
Phelia**

Oprah (Hebrew) an alternate form of Orpah.
Ophra, Ophrah, Opra

Ora (Greek) an alternate
form of Aura. (Latin)
prayer. (Spanish) gold.
(English) seacoast.
**Orabel, Orabelle, Orah,
Orlice, Orra**

Orabella (Latin) an alternate form of Arabella.
Orabel, Orabela, Orabelle

Oralee (Hebrew) the Lord is my light.
Orali, Oralit, Orlee, Orli, Orly

Oralia (French) a form of Aurelia. See also Oriana.
Oralis, Orelie, Oriel, Orielda, Orielle, Oriena, Orlena, Orlene

Orea (Greek) mountains.
Oreal

Orela (Latin) announcement from the gods; oracle.
Oreal, Orella, Oriel, Orielle

Orenda (Iroquois) magical power.

Oretha (Greek) an alternate form of Aretha.
Oreta, Oretta, Orette

Oriana (Latin) dawn, sunrise. (Irish) golden.
Orane, Orania, Orelda, Orelle, Ori, Oria, Oriane, Orianna

Orina (Russian) a form of Irene.
Orya, Oryna

Orinda (Hebrew) pine tree. (Irish) light skinned, white. A feminine form of Oren.
Orenda

Orino (Japanese) worker's field.
Ori

Oriole (Latin) golden; black and orange bird.
Auriel, Oriel, Oriella, Oriola

Orla (Irish) golden woman.
Orlagh, Orlie, Orly

Orlanda (German) famous throughout the land. A feminine form of Orlando.
Orlantha

Orlenda (Russian) eagle.

Orli (Hebrew) light.
Orlice, Orlie, Orly

Ormanda (Latin) noble. (German) mariner, seaman. A feminine form of Orman.
Orma

Ornice (Hebrew) cedar tree. (Irish) pale; olive colored.
Orna, Ornah, Ornat, Ornette, Ornit

Orpah (Hebrew) runaway. See also Oprah.
Orpa, Orpha, Orphie

Orquidea (Spanish) orchid.
Orquidia

Orsa (Greek) an alternate form of Ursula. (Latin) bearlike. A feminine form of Orson. See also Ursa.
Orsaline, Orse, Orsel, Orselina, Orseline, Orsola

Ortensia (Italian) a form
of Hortense.

Orva (French) golden;
worthy. (English) brave
friend.

Osanna (Latin) praise
the Lord.

Osen (Japanese) one
thousand.

Oseye (Benin) merry.

Osma (English) devine
protector. A feminine
form of Osmond.
Ozma

Otilie (Czech) lucky
heroine.
Otila, Otka, Ottili, Otylia

Ovia (Latin, Danish) egg.

Owena (Welsh) born to
nobility; young warrior.
A feminine form of Owen.

Oya (Moquelumnan) called
forth.

Oz (Hebrew) strength.

Ozara (Hebrew) treasure,
wealth.

Paca (Spanish) a short form
of Pancha. See also Paka.

Padma (Hindi) lotus.

Page (French) young
assistant.
**Padget, Padgett, Pagen,
Paget, Pagett, Pagi,
Payge**

Paige (English) young
child.

Paisley (Scottish) patterned
fabric made in Paisley,
Scotland.
Paisleyann, Paisleyanne

Paka (Swahili) kitten.
See also Paca.

Pakuna (Moquelumnan)
deer bounding while
running downhill.

Palila (Polynesian) bird.

Pallas (Greek) wise.
Mythology: another name
for Athena, the goddess
of wisdom.

Palma (Latin) palm tree.
**Pallma, Pallmirah,
Pallmyra, Palmer,
Palmira, Palmyra**

Paloma (Spanish) dove.
See also Aloma.
**Palloma, Palometa,
Palomita, Peloma**

Pamela (Greek) honey.
**Pam, Pama, Pamala,
Pamalla, Pamelia,
Pamelina, Pamella,
Pamilla, Pammela,
Pammi, Pammie, Pammy,
Pamula**

Pancha (Spanish) free;
from France. A feminine
form of Pancho.
Paca, Panchita

Pandita (Hindi) scholar.

Pandora (Greek) highly
gifted. Mythology:
a young woman who
received many gifts from
the gods, such as beauty,
wisdom, and creativity.
See also Dora.
**Pandi, Pandorah,
Pandorra, Pandorrah,
Pandy, Panndora,
Panndorah, Panndorra,
Panndorrah**

Pansy (Greek) flower;
fragrant. (French)
thoughtful.
Pansey, Pansie

Panthea (Greek) all the
gods.
Pantheia, Pantheya

Panya (Swahili) mouse; tiny
baby. (Russian) a familiar
form of Stephanie.

Panyin (Fanti) older twin.

Paola (Italian) a form
of Paula.
Paolina

Papina (Moquelumnan)
vine growing on an oak
tree.

Paquita (Spanish) a form
of Frances.
Panchita, Paqua

Pari (Persian) fairy eagle.

Paris (French) Geography:
the capital of France.
Mythology: the Trojan
prince who started the
Trojan war by abducting
Helen.
**Parice, Paries, Parisa,
Pariss, Parissa, Parris**

Parthenia (Greek) virginal.
**Partheenia, Parthenie,
Parthinia, Pathina**

Parveneh (Persian)
butterfly.

Pascale (French) born
on Easter or Passover.
A feminine form of Pascal.
**Pascalette, Pascaline,
Pascalle, Paschale, Paskel**

Pasha (Greek) sea.
Palasha, Pashel, Pashka

Pasua (Swahili) born by
Caesarean section.

Pat (Latin) a short form
of Patricia, Patsy.

Pati (Moquelumnan) fish baskets made of willow branches.

Patia (Latin, English) a familiar form of Patience, Patricia. (Gypsy, Spanish) leaf.

Patience (English) patient.
Paciencia, Patia, Patty

Patrice (French) a form of Patricia.
Patrease, Patrece, Patresa, Patriece, Patryce, Pattrice

Patricia (Latin) noble-woman. A feminine form of Patrick. See also Payton, Tricia, Trisha, Trissa.
Pat, Patia, Patreece, Patreice, Patrica, Patrice, Patriceia, Patricja, Patricka, Patrickia, Patrisha, Patrishia, Patrizia, Patrizzia, Patsy, Patty

Patsy (Latin) a familiar form of Patricia.
Pat, Patsey, Patsi

Patty (English) a familiar form of Patricia.
Patte, Pattee, Patti

Paula (Latin) small. A femi-nine form of Paul. See also Pavla, Polly.
Pali, Paliki, Paola, Paulane, Paulann, Paule, Paulette, Pauli, Paulie, Pauline, Paulla, Pauly, Pavia

Paulette (Latin) a familiar form of Paula.
Pauletta, Paulita, Paullette

Pauline (Latin) a familiar form of Paula.
Pauleen, Paulene, Paulina, Paulyne, Pawlina

Pausha (Hindi) lunar month of Capricorn.

Pavla (Czech, Russian) a form of Paula.
Pavlina, Pavlinka

Payton (Irish) a form of Patricia.
Peyton

Paz (Spanish) peace.

Pazi (Ponca) yellow bird.

Pazia (Hebrew) golden.
Paz, Paza, Pazice, Pazit

Peace (English) peaceful.

Pearl (Latin) jewel. See also Peninah.
Pearla, Pearle, Pearleen, Pearlena, Pearlene, Pearlette, Pearlie, Pearline, Perlette, Perlie, Perline, Perlline, Perry

Peggy (Greek) a familiar form of Margaret.
Peg, Pegeen, Pegg, Peggey, Peggi, Peggie, Pegi

Peke (Hawaiian) a form of Bertha.

Pela (Polish) a short form of Penelope.

Pelagia (Greek) sea.
  Pelage, Pelageia, Pelagie,
  Pelga, Pelgia, Pellagia

Pelipa (Zuni) a form
  of Philippa.

Pemba (Bambara) the
  power that controls all life.

Penda (Swahili) loved.

Penelope (Greek) weaver.
  Mythology: the clever and
  loyal wife of Odysseus,
  a Greek hero.
  Pela, Pen, Penelopa,
  Penina, Penna,
  Pennelope, Penny,
  Pinelopi, Popi

Peni (Carrier) mind.

Peninah (Hebrew) pearl.
  Peni, Penina, Peninit,
  Peninnah, Penny

Penny (Greek) a familiar
  form of Penelope,
  Peninah.
  Penee, Penney, Penni,
  Pennie

Peony (Greek) flower.
  Peonie

Pepita (Spanish) a familiar
  form of Josephine.
  Pepa, Pepi, Peppy, Peta

Pepper (Latin) condiment
  from the pepper plant.

Perah (Hebrew) flower.

Perdita (Latin) lost.
  Literature: a character

in Shakespeare's play
  The Winter's Tale.
  Perdida, Perdy

Perfecta (Spanish) flawless.

Peri (Greek) mountain
  dweller. (Persian) fairy
  or elf.
  Perita

Perlie (Latin) a familiar
  form of Pearl.
  Pearley, Pearly, Perl,
  Perla, Perle, Perley, Perli,
  Perly, Purley, Purly

Pernella (Greek, French)
  rock. (Latin) a short form
  of Petronella.
  Parnella, Pernel, Pernelle

Perri (Greek, Latin) small
  rock; traveler. (French)
  pear tree. (Welsh) daughter of Harry. A feminine
  form of Perry.
  Perrey, Perriann, Perrie,
  Perrin, Perrine, Perry

Persephone (Greek)
  springtime. Mythology:
  the goddess of spring.

Persis (Latin) from Persia.
  Perssis, Persy

Peta (Blackfoot) golden
  eagle.

Petra (Greek, Latin) small
  rock. A short form of
  Petronella. A feminine
  form of Peter.
  Pet, Peta, Petena,
  Peterina, Petrice, Petrina,

Petrine, Petrova, Petrovna, Pier, Pierette, Pierrette, Pietra

Petronella (Greek) small rock. (Latin) of the Roman clan Petronius.
Pernella, Peternella, Petra, Petrona, Petronela, Petronella, Petronelle, Petronia, Petronija, Petronilla, Petronille

Petula (Latin) seeker.
Petulah

Petunia (Native American) flower.

Phaedra (Greek) bright.
Faydra, Phae, Phaidra, Phe, Phedre

Pheodora (Greek, Russian) an alternate form of Feodora.
Phedora, Phedorah, Pheodorah, Pheydora, Pheydorah

Philana (Greek) lover of mankind. A feminine form of Philander.
Phila, Philene, Philiane, Philina, Philine

Philantha (Greek) lover of flowers.

Philippa (Greek) lover of horses. A feminine form of Philip. See also Filippa.
Phil, Philipa, Philippe, Phillipina, Phillippine, Phillie, Philly, Pippa, Pippy

Philomena (Greek) love song; loved one. Bible: a first-century saint. See also Filomena, Mena.
Philomène, Philomina

Phoebe (Greek) shining.
Phaebe, Pheba, Phebe, Pheby, Phoebey

Phylicia (Greek) a form of Felicia. (Latin) fortunate; happy.
Philica, Philycia, Phylecia, Phylesia, Phylisha, Phylisia, Phyllecia, Phyllicia, Phyllisia

Phyllida (Greek) an alternate form of Phyllis.
Fillida, Philida, Phillida, Phillyda

Phyllis (Greek) green bough.
Filise, Fillys, Fyllis, Philis, Phillis, Philliss, Philys, Philyss, Phylis, Phyllida, Phyllis, Phylliss, Phyllys

Pia (Italian) devout.

Piedad (Spanish) devoted; pious.

Pier (French) a form of Petra.

Pilar (Spanish) pillar, column. Religion: honoring the Virgin Mary, the pillar of the Catholic Church.
Peelar, Pilár

Ping (Chinese) duckweed. (Vietnamese) peaceful.

Pinga (Hindi) bronze; dark. Religion: another name for the Hindu goddess Shakti.

Piper (English) pipe player.

Pippa (English) a short form of Phillipa.

Pippi (French) rosy cheeked.
Pippen, Pippie, Pippin, Pippy

Pita (African) fourth daughter.

Placidia (Latin) serene.
Placida

Pleasance (French) pleasant.
Pleasence

Polla (Arabic) poppy.
Pola

Polly (Latin) a familiar form of Paula.
Paili, Poll, Pollee, Polley, Polli, Pollie

Pollyam (Hindi) goddess of the plague. Religion: the Hindu name invoked to ward off bad spirits.

Pollyanna (English) a combination of Polly + Anna. Literature: an overly optimistic heroine created by Eleanor Poiter.

Poloma (Choctaw) bow.

Pomona (Latin) apple. Mythology: the goddess of fruit and fruit trees.

Poni (African) second daughter.

Poppy (Latin) poppy flower.
Poppey, Poppi, Poppie

Pora, Poria (Hebrew) fruitful.

Porsche (German) a form of Portia.
Porcha, Porchai, Porcsha, Porcshe, Porscha, Porsché, Porschea, Porschia, Pourche

Porsha (Latin) an alternate form of Portia.
Porshai, Porshay, Porshe, Porshia

Portia (Latin) offering. Literature: the heroine of Shakespeare's play *The Merchant of Venice*.
Porsche, Porsha, Portiea

Precious (French) precious; dear.

Prima (Latin) first, beginning; first child.
Primalia, Primetta, Primina, Priminia

Primavera (Italian, Spanish) spring.

Primrose (English) primrose flower.
Primula

Princess (English) daughter of royalty.
Princcess, Princetta, Princie, Princilla

Priscilla (Latin) ancient.
Cilla, Piri, Piroshka,
Precilla, Prescilla, Pricila,
Pricilla, Pris, Prisca,
Priscella, Priscila, Priscill,
Priscille, Prisella, Prisila,
Prisilla, Prissilla, Prissy,
Prysilla

Prissy (Latin) a familiar
form of Priscilla.
Prisi, Priss, Prissi, Prissie

Priya (Hindi) beloved;
sweet natured.

Procopia (Latin) declared
leader. A feminine form
of Prokopius.

Pru (Latin) a short form
of Prudence.
Prue

Prudence (Latin) cautious;
discreet.
Pru, Prudencia, Prudy

Prudy (Latin) a familiar
form of Prudence.
Prudee, Prudi, Prudie

Prunella (Latin) brown;
little plum. See also Nellie.
Prunela

Psyche (Greek) soul.
Mythology: a beautiful
mortal loved by Eros,
the Greek god of love.

Pua (Hawaiian) flower.

Pualani (Hawaiian)
heavenly flower.
Puni

Purity (English) purity.
Pura, Pureza, Purisima

Pyralis (Greek) fire.
Pyrene

Qadira (Arabic) powerful.
Kadira

Qamra (Arabic) moon.
Kamra

Qitarah (Arabic) fragrant.

Quaashie (Ewe) born
on Sunday.

Quaneisha (American)
a combination of the
prefix Qu + Aisha.
Quanecia, Quanesha,
Quanesia, Quanisha,
Quanishia, Quansha,
Quarnisha, Queisha,
Quenisha, Quenishia,
Qynisha

Quanika (American)
a combination of the
prefix Qu + Nika.
Quanikka, Quanikki,
Quanique, Quantenique,
Quawanica

Quartilla (Latin) fourth.
Quantilla

Qubilah (Arabic)
agreeable.

Queenie (English) queen.
See also Quinn.
**Queen, Queena,
Queenation, Queeneste,
Queenetta, Queenette,
Queenika, Queenique,
Queeny, Quenna**

Queisha (African) a short
form of Quaneisha.
Qeysha, Queshia

Quenby (Scandinavian)
feminine.

Quenna (English) an alter-
nate form of Queenie.
**Quenell, Quenessa,
Quenetta**

Querida (Spanish) dear;
beloved.

Questa (French) searcher.

Queta (Spanish) a short
form of names ending
in "queta" or "quetta."

Quiana (American)
a combination of the
prefix Qu + Anna.
Quian, Quianna

Quinby (Scandinavian)
queen's estate.

Quincy (Irish) fifth.
Quinci, Quincie

Quinella (Latin) an alter-
nate form of Quintana.
**Quinetta, Quinette,
Quinita, Quinnette**

Quinn (German, English)
queen. See also Queenie.
Quin, Quinna

Quintana (Latin) fifth.
(English) queen's lawn.
A feminine form of
Quentin, Quintin.
See also Quinella.
**Quinntina, Quinta,
Quintanna, Quintara,
Quintarah, Quintia,
Quintila, Quintilla,
Quintina, Quintona,
Quintonice**

Quintessa (Latin) essence.
See also Tess.
Quintice

Quiterie (Latin, French)
tranquil.
Quita

Rabi (Arabic) breeze.
Rabiah

Rachael (Hebrew) an alternate form of Rachel.
Rachaele

Rachel (Hebrew) female
sheep. Bible: the wife
of Jacob. See also Lahela,
Rae, Rochelle, Shelley.
Racha, Rachael, Rachal,

**Racheal, Rachela,
Rachelann, Rachele,
Rachelle, Rackel, Raechel,
Raechele, Rahel, Rahela,
Rahil, Rakel, Rakhil,
Raquel, Ray, Raycene,
Rey, Ruchel**

Rachelle (French) a form
of Rachel. See also Shelley.
**Rachalle, Rachell, Rachella,
Raechell, Raechelle,
Raeshelle, Rashel, Rashele,
Rashell, Rashelle, Raychell,
Rayshell, Rochell, Ruchelle**

Racquel (French) a form
of Rachel.
**Racquell, Racquella,
Racquelle**

Radella (German)
counselor.

Radeyah (Arabic) content,
satisfied.
**Radeeyah, Radhiya,
Radiah, Radiyah**

Radinka (Slavic) full of life;
happy, glad.

Radmilla (Slavic) worker for
the people.

Radwa (Arabic) Geography:
a mountain in Medina,
Saudi Arabia.

Rae (English) doe. (Hebrew)
a short form of Rachel.
**Raeda, Raedeen, Raeden,
Raeh, Raelene, Raena,
Raenah, Raeneice,
Raeneisha, Raesha,**

**Raewyn, Ralina, Ray,
Raye, Rayetta, Rayette,
Rayma, Rayna, Rayona,
Rey**

Raeann (American)
a combination of
Rae + Ann. See also
Rayanne.
**Raea, Raeanna, Reanna,
Raeanne**

Raelene (American) a com-
bination of Rae + Lee.
**Raela, Raelee, Raeleen,
Raeleigh, Raeleigha,
Raelene, Raelesha,
Raelina, Raelyn,
Raelynn**

Rafa (Arabic) happy;
prosperous.

Rafaela (Hebrew) an alternate form of Raphaela.
Rafaelia, Rafaella

Ragnild (Scandinavian)
Mythology: a warrior
goddess.
**Ragna, Ragnell, Ragnhild,
Rainell, Renilda, Renilde**

Ráidah (Arabic) leader.

Raina (German) mighty.
(English) a short form
of Regina. See also Rayna.
**Raenah, Raheena, Raine,
Rainna, Reanna**

Rainbow (English) rainbow.
**Rainbeau, Rainbeaux,
Rainbo, Raynbow**

Raine (Latin) a short form
of Regina. An alternate
form of Raina, Rane.
**Rainey, Raini, Rainie,
Rainy**

Raisa (Russian) a form
of Rose.
**Raisah, Raissa, Raiza,
Raysa, Rayza, Razia**

Raizel (Yiddish) a form
of Rose.
Rayzil, Razil

Raja (Arabic) hopeful.
Raia

Raku (Japanese) pleasure.

Rama (Hebrew) lofty,
exalted. (Hindi) godlike.
Religion: another name for
the Hindu goddess Shiva.
Ramah

Ramla (Swahili) fortune-
teller.
Ramlah

Ramona (Spanish) mighty;
wise protector. See also
Mona.
**Ramonda, Raymona,
Romona, Romonda**

Ran (Japanese) water lily.
(Scandinavian) destroyer.
Mythology: the sea
goddess who destroys.

Rana (Sanskrit) royal.
(Arabic) gaze, look.
Rahna, Rahni, Rani

Ranait (Irish) graceful;
prosperous.
Renny

Randall (English)
protected.
**Randa, Randah, Randai,
Randalee, Randel,
Randell, Randelle, Randi,
Randilee, Randilynn,
Randlyn, Randy, Randyl**

Randi, Randy (English)
familiar forms of Miranda,
Randall.
**Rande, Randee, Randeen,
Randene, Randey, Randie,
Randii**

Rane (Scandinavian)
queen.
Raine

Rani (Sanskrit) queen.
(Hebrew) joyful. A short
form of Kerani.
**Rahni, Ranee, Rania,
Ranice, Ranique**

Ranita (Hebrew) song;
joyful.
**Ranata, Ranice, Ranit,
Ranite, Ranitta, Ronita**

Raniyah (Arabic) gazing.

Rapa (Hawaiian)
moonbeam.

Raphaela (Hebrew) healed
by God. Bible: one of the
four archangels.
Rafaella

Raquel (French) a form
of Rachel.
**Rakel, Rakhil, Rakhila,
Raqueal, Raquela,
Raquella, Raquelle,
Rickquel, Ricquel,**

Ricquelle, Rikell, Rikelle, Rockell

Rasha (Arabic) young gazelle.
Rahshea, Rahshia, Rashea

Rashawna (American) a combination of the prefix Ra + Shawna.
Rashana, Rashanda, Rashani, Rashanta, Rashaunda, Rashaundra, Rashawn, Rashon, Rashona, Rashonda, Rashunda

Rashida (Swahili, Turkish) righteous.
Rahshea, Rahsheda, Rahsheita, Rashdah, Rasheda, Rashedah, Rasheeda, Rasheeta, Rasheida, Rashidi

Rashieka (Arabic) descended from royalty.
Rasheeka, Rasheika, Rasheka, Rashika, Rasika

Rasia (Greek) rose.

Ratana (Thai) crystal.
Ratania, Ratanya, Ratna, Rattan, Rattana

Ratri (Hindi) night. Religion: another name for the Hindu goddess Shakti.

Raula (French) wolf counselor. A feminine form of Raoul.
Raoula, Raulla, Raulle

Raven (English) blackbird.
Raveen, Raveena, Ravena, Ravennah, Ravi, Ravin, Ravine, Ravyn, Rayven, Rayvin

Rawnie (Gypsy) fine lady.
Rawna, Rhawnie

Raya (Hebrew) friend.
Raia, Raiah, Ray, Rayah

Rayanne (American) an alternate form of Raeann.
Ray-Ann, Rayan, Rayana, Rayann, Rayanna, Rayona, Reyana, Reyann, Reyanna, Reyanne

Rayleen (American) a combination of Rae + Lyn.
Rayel, Rayele, Rayelle, Raylena, Raylene, Raylin, Raylona, Raylyn, Raylynn, Raylynne

Raymonde (German) wise protector. A feminine form of Raymond.
Rayma, Raymae, Raymie

Rayna (Scandinavian) mighty. (Yiddish) pure, clean. (French) a familiar form of Lorraine. (English) king's advisor. A feminine form of Reynold. See also Raina.
Rayna, Rayne, Raynell, Raynelle, Raynette, Rayona, Rayonna, Reyna

Rayya (Arabic) thirsty no longer.

Razi (Aramaic) secretive.
**Rayzil, Rayzilee, Raz,
Razia, Raziah, Raziela,
Razilee, Razili**

Raziya (Swahili) agreeable.

Rea (Greek) poppy flower.
Reah

Reanna (German, English)
an alternate form of Raina.
(American) an alternate
form of Raeann.
Reannah

Reanne (American)
an alternate form
of Raeann, Reanna.
**Reana, Reane, Reann,
Reannan, Reanne,
Reannen, Reannon,
Reeana**

Reba (Hebrew) fourth-born
child. A short form of
Rebecca. See also Reva,
Riva.
Rabah, Reeba, Rheba

Rebecca (Hebrew) tied,
bound. Bible: the wife
of Isaac. See also Becca,
Becky.
**Rabecca, Rabecka, Reba,
Rebbecca, Rebeca,
Rebeccah, Rebeccea,
Rebeccka, Rebecha,
Rebecka, Rebeckah,
Rebeckia, Rebecky,
Rebekah, Rebeque, Rebi,
Reveca, Riva, Rivka**

Rebekah (Hebrew) an
alternate form of Rebecca.

**Rebeka, Rebekha,
Rebekka, Rebekkah,
Rebekke, Revecca, Reveka,
Revekka, Rifka**

Rebi (Hebrew) a familiar
form of Rebecca.
**Rebbie, Rebe, Reby, Ree,
Reebie**

Reena (Greek) peaceful.
Reen, Reenie, Rena, Reyna

Reet (Estonian) a form
of Margaret.
Reatha, Reta, Retha

Reganne (Irish) little ruler.
A feminine form of
Reagan.
Ragan, Reagan, Regin

Regina (Latin) queen.
(English) king's advisor.
A feminine form of
Reginald. Geography: the
capital of Saskatchewan.
See also Gina.
**Ragina, Raina, Raine,
Rane, Rega, Regena,
Regennia, Reggi, Reggie,
Reggy, Regi, Regia, Regie,
Regiena, Regin, Regine,
Reginia, Regis, Reina,
Rena**

Rei (Japanese) polite,
well behaved.
Reiko

Reina (Spanish) a short
form of Regina. See also
Reyna.
**Reine, Reinette, Reiny,
Reiona, Renia, Rina**

Rekha (Hindi) thin line.
**Reka, Rekia, Rekiah,
Rekiya**

Remedios (Spanish)
remedy.

Remi (French) from
Rheims.
Remee, Remie, Remy

Ren (Japanese) arranger;
water lily; lotus.

Rena (Hebrew) song; joy.
A familiar form of Irene,
Regina, Renata, Sabrina,
Serena.
**Reena, Rina, Rinna,
Rinnah**

Renae (French) an alternate
form of Renée.
Renay

Renata (French) an alter-
nate form of Renée.
**Ranata, Rena, Renada,
Renita, Rennie, Renyatta,
Rinada, Rinata**

Rene (Greek) a short form
of Irene, Renée.
**Reen, Reenie, Renae,
Reney, Rennie**

Renée (French) born again.
**Renae, Renata, Renay,
Rene, Renell, Renelle**

Renita (French) an alternate form of Renata.
Reneeta, Renetta, Renitza

Rennie (English) a familiar
form of Renata.
Reni, Renie, Renni

Reseda (Spanish) fragrant
mignonette blossom.

Reshawna (American)
a combination of the
prefix Re + Shawna.
**Resaunna, Reshana,
Reshaunda, Reshawnda,
Reshawnna, Reshonda,
Reshonn, Reshonta**

Resi (German) a familiar
form of Theresa.
**Resel, Ressie, Reza, Rezka,
Rezi**

Reta (African) shaken.
**Reeta, Retta, Rheta,
Rhetta**

Reubena (Hebrew) behold
a daughter. A feminine
form of Reuben.
**Reubina, Reuvena,
Rubena, Rubenia, Rubina,
Rubine, Rubyna**

Reva (Latin) revived.
(Hebrew) rain; one-
fourth. An alternate
form of Reba, Riva.
Ree, Reeva, Revia, Revida

Reveca, Reveka (Slavic)
forms of Rebecca,
Rebekah.
Reve, Rivka

Rexanne (American)
queen. A feminine form
of Rex.
**Rexan, Rexana, Rexann,
Rexanna**

Reyhan (Turkish) sweet-
smelling flower.

Reyna (Greek) peaceful.
(English) an alternate form
of Reina.
Reyne

Reynalda (German) king's
advisor. A feminine form
of Reynold.

Réz (Latin, Hungarian)
copper-colored hair.

Reza (Czech) a form
of Theresa.
Rezi, Rezka

Rhea (Greek) brook,
stream. Mythology:
the mother of Zeus.
**Rheá, Rhéa, Rhealyn,
Rheana, Rheann,
Rheanna, Rheannan,
Rheanne, Rheannon**

Rhiannon (Welsh) witch;
nymph; goddess.
**Rhian, Rhiana, Rhianen,
Rhianna, Rhianne,
Rhiannen, Rhianon,
Rhianwen, Rhiauna,
Rhinnon, Rhyan, Rhyanna,
Rian, Riana, Riane, Riann,
Rianna, Rianne, Riannon,
Rianon, Riayn**

Rhoda (Greek) from
Rhodes.
**Rhode, Rhodeia, Rhodie,
Rhody, Roda, Rodi, Rodie,
Rodina**

Rhona (Scottish) powerful,
mighty. (English) king's
advisor. A feminine form
of Ronald.

Rhonda (Welsh) grand.
**Rhondelle, Rhondene,
Rhondiesha, Rhonnie,
Ronda, Ronelle, Ronnette**

Ria (Spanish) river.
Riah

Riana (Irish) a short form
of Briana.
Reana, Reanna, Rianna

Rica (Spanish) a short form
of Erica, Frederica, Ricarda.
See also Enrica, Sandrica,
Terrica, Ulrica.
**Ricca, Rieca, Riecka,
Rieka, Rikka, Riqua, Rycca**

Ricarda (Spanish) rich and
powerful ruler. A feminine
form of Richard.
**Rica, Richanda, Richarda,
Richi**

Richael (Irish) saint.

Richelle (German, French)
a form of Ricarda.
**Richel, Richela, Richele,
Richell, Richella, Richia**

Ricki, Rikki (American)
familiar forms of Erica,
Frederica, Ricarda.
**Rica, Rici, Ricka, Rickia,
Rickie, Rickilee, Rickina,
Rickita, Ricky, Ricquie,
Riki, Rikia, Rikita, Rikky**

Ricquel (American) a form
of Raquel.
**Rickquell, Ricquelle,
Rikell, Rikelle**

Rida (Arabic) favored by God.

Rihana (Arabic) sweet basil.
Rhiana, Rhianna, Riana, Rianna

Rika (Swedish) ruler.

Riley (Irish) valiant.
Rileigh, Rilie

Rilla (German) small brook.

Rima (Arabic) white antelope.
Reem, Reema, Rema, Remah, Rim, Ryma

Rimona (Hebrew) pomegranate. See also Mona.

Rin (Japanese) park. Geography: a Japanese village.
Rini, Rynn

Rina (English) a short form of names ending in "rina."
Reena, Rena

Rinah (Hebrew) joyful.
Rina

Riona (Irish) saint.

Risa (Latin) laughter.
Reesa, Resa

Risha (Hindi) born during the lunar month of Taurus.
Rishah, Rishay

Rishona (Hebrew) first.

Rissa (Greek) a short form of Nerissa.
Risa, Rissah, Ryssa, Ryssah

Rita (Sanskrit) brave; honest. (Greek) a short form of Margarita.
Reatha, Reda, Reeta, Reida, Reitha, Rheta, Riet, Ritamae, Ritamarie

Ritsa (Greek) a familiar form of Alexandra.
Ritsah, Ritsi, Ritsie, Ritsy

Riva (Hebrew) a short form of Rebecca. (French) river bank. See also Reba, Reva.
Rivalee, Rivana, Rivi, Rivvy

River (Latin, French) stream, water.
Rivana, Rivers, Riviane

Rivka (Hebrew) a short form of Rebecca.
Rivca, Rivcah, Rivkah

Riza (Greek) a form of Theresa.
Riesa, Rizus, Rizza

Roanna (American) a combination of Rose + Anna.
Ranna, Roana, Roanda, Roanne

Roberta (English) famous brilliance. A feminine form of Robert. See also Bobbette, Bobbi, Robin.
Roba, Robbi, Robbie, Robby, Robena, Robertena, Robertina

Robin (English) robin. An alternate form of Roberta.
Robann, Robbi, Robbie, Robbin, Robby, Robena,

Robin *(cont.)*
Robina, Robine,
Robinette, Robinia,
Robinn, Robinta, Robyn

Robinette (English) a
familiar form of Robin.
Robernetta, Robinet,
Robinett, Robinita

Robyn (English) an alter-
nate form of Robin.
Robbyn, Robyne, Robynn,
Robynne

Rochelle (Hebrew) an
alternate form of Rachel.
(French) large stone.
See also Shelley.
Roch, Rochele, Rochell,
Rochella, Rochette,
Rockelle, Roshele, Roshell,
Roshelle

Rocio (Spanish) dewdrops.
Rocío

Roderica (German) famous
ruler. A feminine form
of Roderick.
Rica, Rika, Rodericka,
Roderika, Rodreicka,
Rodricka, Rodrika

Rodnae (English) island
clearing.
Rodna, Rodneisha,
Rodnesha, Rodnetta,
Rodnicka

Rohana (Hindi) sandalwood. (American)
a combination of
Rose + Hannah.
Rochana, Rohena

Rohini (Hindi) woman.

Rolanda (German) famous
throughout the land.
A feminine form of Roland.
Ralna, Rolaine, Rolande,
Rolene, Rollande, Rolleen

Roma (Latin) from Rome.
Romeise, Romeka,
Romelle, Romesha,
Rometta, Romi, Romie,
Romilda, Romilla,
Romina, Romini, Romma,
Romonia

Romaine (French) from
Rome.
Romana, Romanda,
Romanelle, Romanique,
Romayne

Romy (French) a familiar
form of Romaine.
(English) a familiar
form of Rosemary.
Romi

Rona (Scandinavian)
a short form of Rhona.
Rhona, Roana, Ronalda,
Ronalee, Ronella, Ronelle,
Ronna, Ronne, Ronni,
Ronsy

Ronaele (Greek) Eleanor
spelled backwards.
Ronni, Ronnie, Ronny

Ronda (Welsh) an alternate
form of Rhonda.
Rondai, Rondel, Rondelle,
Rondesia, Rondi, Ronelle,
Ronndelle, Ronnette,
Ronni, Ronnie, Ronny

Roneisha (American) a combination of Rhonda + Aisha.
Ronecia, Ronee, Roneeka, Roneice, Roneshia, Ronessa, Ronichia, Ronicia, Roniesha, Ronisha, Ronnesa, Ronnesha, Ronni, Ronnie, Ronnise, Ronnisha, Ronnishia, Ronny

Ronelle (Welsh) an alternate form of Rhonda, Ronda.
Ranell, Ranelle, Ronella, Ronnella, Ronnelle

Ronli (Hebrew) joyful.
Roni, Ronia, Ronice, Ronit, Ronlee, Ronlie, Ronni, Ronnie, Ronny

Ronnette (Welsh) a familiar form of Rhonda, Ronda.
Ronetta, Ronit, Ronita, Ronni, Ronnie, Ronny

Ronni, Ronnie, Ronny (American) familiar forms of Veronica and names beginning with "Ron."
Ronee, Roni, Ronnee, Ronney

Rori, Rory (Irish) famous brilliance; famous ruler. Feminine forms of Robert, Roderick.

Ros, Roz (English) short forms of Rosalind, Rosalyn.

Rozz, Rozzey, Rozzi, Rozzie, Rozzy

Rosa (Italian, Spanish) a form of Rose. History: Rosa Parks inspired the American civil rights movement by refusing to give up her bus seat to a white man in Montgomery, Alabama. See also Charo, Roza.

Rosabel (French) beautiful rose.
Rosabella, Rosabelle

Rosalba (Latin) white rose.

Rosalie (English) a form of Rosalind.
Rosalea, Rosalee, Rosaleen, Rosalene, Rosalia, Roselia, Rosilee, Rosli, Rozali, Rozalie, Rozália, Rozele

Rosalind (Spanish) fair rose.
Ros, Rosalina, Rosalinda, Rosalinde, Rosalyn, Rosalynd, Rosalynde, Roselind, Rosie, Rozalind

Rosalyn (Spanish) an alternate form of Rosalind.
Ros, Rosaleen, Rosalin, Rosaline, Rosalyne, Rosalynn, Rosalynne, Roseleen, Roselin, Roseline, Roselyn, Roselynn, Roselynne, Rosilyn, Roslin, Roslyn, Roslyne, Roslynn, Rozalyn, Rozland, Rozlyn

Rosamond (German)
famous guardian.
**Rosamund, Rosamunda,
Rosemonde, Rozamond**

Rosanna, Roseanna
(English) combinations
of Rose + Anna.
**Ranna, Roanna, Rosana,
Rosannah, Roseana,
Roseannah, Rosehanah,
Rosehannah, Rosie,
Rossana, Rossanna,
Rozana, Rozanna**

Rosanne, Roseanne
(English) combinations
of Rose + Ann.
**Roanne, Rosan, Rosann,
Roseann, Rose Ann, Rose
Anne, Rossann, Rossanne,
Rozann, Rozanne**

Rosario (Filipino, Spanish)
rosary.

Rose (Latin) rose. See also
Chalina, Raisa, Raizel,
Roza.
**Rada, Rasia, Rasine, Rois,
Róise, Rosa, Rosella,
Roselle, Roseta, Rosetta,
Rosette, Rosie, Rosina,
Rosita, Rosse**

Roselani (Hawaiian)
heavenly rose.

Rosemarie (English)
a combination of
Rose + Marie.
**Romy, Rosemaria, Rose
Marie**

Rosemary (English) a combination of Rose + Mary.
Romi, Romy

Rosetta (Italian) a form
of Rose.

Roshan (Sanskrit) shining
light.

Roshawna (American)
a combination of
Rose + Shawna.
**Roshan, Roshanda,
Roshani, Roshanna,
Roshanta, Roshaun,
Roshaunda, Roshawn,
Roshawnda, Roshawnna,
Roshona, Roshonda**

Rosie (English) a familiar
form of Rosalind, Rosanna,
Rose.
**Rosey, Rosi, Rosio, Rosse,
Rosy, Rozsi, Rozy**

Rosina (English) a familiar
form of Rose.
**Rosena, Rosenah, Rosene,
Rosheen, Rozena, Rozina**

Rosita (Spanish) a familiar
form of Rose.
**Roseeta, Roseta, Rozeta,
Rozita**

Rossalyn (Scottish) cape;
promontory.
**Rosselyn, Rosslyn,
Rosslynn**

Rowan (English) tree with
red berries. (Welsh) an
alternate form of Rowena.

Rowena (Welsh) fair haired. (English) famous friend. Literature: Ivanhoe's love interest in Sir Walter Scott's novel *Ivanhoe*.
Ranna, Ronni, Row, Rowan, Rowe, Roweena, Rowina

Roxana, Roxanna (Persian) alternate forms of Roxann, Roxanne.
Rocsana

Roxann, Roxanne (Persian) sunrise. Literature: the heroine of Edmond Rostand's play *Cyrano de Bergerac*.
Rocxann, Roxana, Roxane, Roxanna, Roxianne, Roxy

Roxy (Persian) a familiar form of Roxann.
Roxi, Roxie

Royale (English) royal.
Royal, Royalle, Ryal, Ryale

Royanna (English) queenly, royal. A feminine form of Roy.
Roya, Royalene, Roylee, Roylene

Roza (Slavic) a form of Rosa.
Roz, Rozalia, Roze, Rozele, Rozella, Rozsa, Rozsi, Rozyte, Ruza, Ruzena, Ruzenka, Ruzha, Ruzsa

Rozene (Native American) rose blossom.
Rozena, Rozina, Rozine

Ruana (Hindi) stringed musical instrument.
Ruan, Ruon

Rubena (Hebrew) an alternate form of Reubena.
Rubenia, Rubina, Rubine, Rubinia, Rubyn, Rubyna

Ruby (French) precious stone.
Rubetta, Rubette, Rubey, Rubi, Rubia, Rubiann, Rubie, Rubyann, Rubye

Ruchi (Hindi) one who wishes to please.

Rudee (German) famous wolf. A feminine form of Rudolph.
Rudeline, Rudell, Rudella, Rudi, Rudie, Rudina, Rudy

Rudra (Hindi) seeds of the rudraksha plant.

Rue (German) famous. (French) street. (English) regretful; strong-scented herbs.
Ru, Ruey

Ruffina (Italian) redhead.
Rufeena, Rufeine, Rufina, Ruphyna

Rui (Japanese) affectionate.

Rukan (Arabic) steady; confident.

Rula (Latin, English) ruler.

Runa (Norwegian) secret; flowing.
Runna

Ruperta (Spanish) a form of Roberta.

Ruri (Japanese) emerald.
Ruriko

Rusalka (Czech) wood nymph. (Russian) mermaid.

Russhell (French) redhead; fox colored. A feminine form of Russell.
Rushell, Rushelle, Russellynn, Russhelle

Rusti (English) redhead.
Russet, Rustie, Rusty

Ruth (Hebrew) friendship. Bible: friend of Naomi.
Rutha, Ruthalma, Ruthe, Ruthella, Ruthetta, Ruthi, Ruthie, Ruthina, Ruthine, Ruthven, Ruthy

Ruthann (American) a combination of Ruth + Ann.
Ruthan, Ruthanne

Ruthie (Hebrew) a familiar form of Ruth.
Ruthey, Ruthi, Ruthy

Ruza (Czech) rose.
Ruzena, Ruzenka, Ruzha, Ruzsa

Ryann (Irish) little ruler. A feminine form of Ryan.
Raiann, Raianne, Rhyann, Riana, Riane, Ryana, Ryanna, Ryanne, Rye, Ryen, Ryenne

Ryba (Czech) fish.

Rylee (Irish) valiant.
Rye, Ryley, Rylie, Rylina, Ryllie, Rylly, Rylyn

Ryo (Japanese) dragon.
Ryoko

Saarah (Arabic) princess.

Saba (Greek) a form of Sheba. (Arabic) morning.
Sabah, Sabbah

Sabi (Arabic) young girl.

Sabina (Latin) History: the Sabine were a tribe in ancient Italy. See also Bina.
Sabienne, Sabine, Sabinka, Sabinna, Sabiny, Saby, Sabyne, Savina, Sebina, Sebinah

Sabiya (Arabic) morning; eastern wind.
Saba, Sabaya

Sable (English) sable; sleek.
Sabel, Sabela, Sabella

Sabra (Hebrew) thorny cactus fruit. History: a name for native-born Israelis, who were said to be hard on the outside and soft and sweet on the inside. (Arabic) resting.

Sabira, Sabrah, Sabriya, Sebra

Sabrina (Latin) boundary line. (Hebrew) a familiar form of Sabra. (English) princess. See also Bree, Brina, Rena, Zabrina.
Sabre, Sabreena, Sabrinia, Sabrinna, Sabryna, Sebree, Sebrina

Sacha (Russian) an alternate form of Sasha.

Sachi (Japanese) blessed; lucky.
Sachiko

Sada (Japanese) chaste. (English) a form of Sadie.
Sadá, Sadako

Sade (Hebrew) an alternate form of Chadee, Sarah, Shardae, Sharday.
Sáde, Sadé, Sadee

Sadhana (Hindi) devoted.

Sadie (Hebrew) a familiar form of Sarah. See also Sada.
Sadah, Sadella, Sadelle, Sady, Sadye, Saidee, Saydie, Sydel, Sydell, Sydella, Sydelle

Sadira (Persian) lotus tree. (Arabic) star.
Sadra

Sadiya (Arabic) lucky, fortunate.
Sadi, Sadia, Sadya

Sadzi (Carrier) sunny disposition.

Saffron (English) Botany: a plant with purple or white flowers whose orange stigmas are used as a spice.

Safiya (Arabic) pure; serene; best friend.
Safa, Safeya, Saffa, Safia, Safiyah

Sagara (Hindi) ocean.

Sage (English) wise. Botany: an herb with healing powers.
Sagia, Saige

Sahara (Arabic) desert; wilderness.
Sahar, Saharah

Sai (Japanese) talented.
Saiko

Saida (Hebrew) an alternate form of Sarah. (Arabic) happy; fortunate.
Saidah

Sakaë (Japanese) prosperous.

Sakari (Hindi) sweet.
Sakkara

Saki (Japanese) cloak; rice wine.

Sakti (Hindi) energetic. An alternate form of Shakti.

Sakuna (Native American) bird.

Sakura (Japanese) cherry blossom; wealthy; prosperous.

Sala (Hindi) sala tree. Religion: the sacred tree under which Buddha died.

Salali (Cherokee) squirrel.

Salama (Arabic) peaceful. See also Zulima.

Salima (Arabic) safe and sound; healthy.
Saleema, Salema, Salim, Salimah, Salma

Salina (French) solemn, dignified.
Salena, Saleena, Salinda

Salliann (English) an alternate form of Sally.
Sallian, Sallianne, Sallyann, Sally-Ann, Sallyanne, Sally-Anne

Sally (English) princess. A familiar form of Sarah. History: Sally Ride, an American astronaut, became the first U.S. woman in space.
Sal, Salaid, Sallee, Salletta, Sallette, Salley, Salli, Salliann, Sallie

Salome (Hebrew) peaceful. History: Salome Alexandra was a ruler of ancient Judea. Bible: the sister of King Herod.
Saloma, Salomé, Salomey, Salomi

Salvadora (Spanish) savior.

Salvia (Latin) a form of Sage. (Spanish) healthy; saved.
Sallvia, Salviana, Salviane, Salvina, Salvine

Samala (Hebrew) asked of God.
Samale, Sammala

Samantha (Aramaic) listener. (Hebrew) told by God.
Sam, Samana, Samanath, Samanatha, Samanitha, Samanithia, Samanta, Samanth, Samanthe, Samanthi, Samanthia, Sami, Sammanth, Sammantha, Sammatha, Semantha, Simantha, Smanta, Smantha, Symantha

Samara (Latin) elm tree seed.
Sam, Samaria, Samarie, Samarra, Samera, Sameria, Samira, Sammar, Sammara, Samora

Sameh (Hebrew) listener. (Arabic) forgiving.
Samaiya, Samaya

Sami (Hebrew) a short form of Samantha, Samuela. (Arabic) praised.
Samia, Samiha, Samina, Sammey, Sammi, Sammijo, Sammy, Sammyjo, Samya, Samye

Samira (Arabic)
entertaining.
Sami

Samuela (Hebrew) heard
God, asked of God. A fem-
inine form of Samuel.
**Samala, Samelia, Samella,
Samielle, Samille,
Sammile, Samuella,
Samuelle**

Sana (Arabic) mountaintop;
splendid; brilliant.
Sanaa, Sanáa

Sancia (Spanish) holy,
sacred.
**Sanceska, Sancha,
Sancharia, Sanchia,
Sancie, Santsia, Sanzia**

Sandeep (Punjabi)
enlightened.

Sandi (Greek) a familiar
form of Sandra.
**Sandee, Sandia, Sandie,
Sandiey, Sandine, Sanndie**

Sandra (Greek) defender
of mankind. A short form
of Alexandra, Cassandra.
History: Sandra Day
O'Connor was the first
woman appointed to the
U.S. Supreme Court.
See also Zandra.
**Sahndra, Sandi, Sandira,
Sandrea, Sandria,
Sandrica, Sandy, Saundra,
Shandra, Sondra**

Sandrea (Greek) an alternate form of Sandra.

**Sandreea, Sandreia,
Sandrell, Sandrenna,
Sandria, Sandrina,
Sandrine, Sanndra,
Sanndria**

Sandrica (Greek) an alter-
nate form of Sandra.
See also Rica.
Sandricka, Sandrika

Sandy (Greek) a familiar
form of Cassandra, Sandra.
Sandya, Sandye

Sanne (Hebrew, Dutch) lily.
Sanneen

Santana (Spanish) saint.
**Santa, Santaniata,
Santanna, Santanne,
Santena, Santenna,
Santina, Shantana**

Santina (Spanish) little
saint.
Santinia

Sanura (Swahili) kitten.
Sanora

Sanuye (Moquelumnan)
red clouds at sunset.

Sanya (Sanskrit) born on
Saturday.

Sanyu (Luganda)
happiness.

Sapata (Native American)
dancing bear.

Sapphira (Hebrew) a form
of Sapphire.
Safira, Saphira, Sephira

Sapphire (Greek) blue gemstone.
Saffire, Saphyre, Sapphira

Sara (Hebrew) an alternate form of Sarah.
Saralee, Sarra

Sarah (Hebrew) princess. Bible: the wife of Abraham and mother of Isaac. See also Sadie, Saida, Sally, Saree, Sharai, Shari, Zara, Zarita.
Sahra, Sara, Saraha, Sarahann, Sarai, Sarann, Sarina, Sarita, Sarolta, Sarotte, Sarrah, Sasa, Sayre, Sorcha

Saree (Hebrew) a familiar form of Sarah. (Arabic) noble.
Sareeka, Sareka, Sari, Sarika, Sarka, Sarri, Sarrie, Sary

Sarila (Turkish) waterfall.

Sarina (Hebrew) a familiar form of Sarah.
Sareen, Sarena, Sarene, Sarinna, Sarinne

Sarita (Hebrew) a familiar form of Sarah.
Saretta, Sarette, Saritia, Sarolta, Sarotte

Sarolta (Hungarian) a form of Sarah.

Sarotte (French) a form of Sarah.

Sasa (Hungarian) a form of Sarah, Sasha. (Japanese) assistant.

Sasha (Russian) defender of mankind. A short form of Alexandra. See also Zasha.
Sacha, Sahsha, Sasa, Sascha, Saschae, Sashah, Sashana, Sashel, Sashenka, Sashia, Sashira, Sashsha, Sasjara, Sasshalai, Sausha, Shasha, Shashi, Shashia, Shura, Shurka

Satara (American) a combination of Sarah + Tara.
Sataria, Satarra, Sateriaa, Saterra, Saterria

Satin (French) smooth, shiny.
Satinder

Satinka (Native American) sacred dancer.

Sato (Japanese) sugar.
Satu

Saundra (English) a form of Sandra, Sondra.
Saundee, Saundi, Saundie, Saundy

Saura (Hindi) sun worshiper. Astrology: born under the sign of Leo.

Sass (Irish) Saxon.
Sassie, Sassoon, Sassy

Savannah (Spanish) treeless plain.
Sahvannah, Savana,

**Savanah, Savanha,
Savanna, Savannha,
Savauna, Sevan, Sevanah,
Sevanh, Sevann, Sevanna,
Svannah**

Sawa (Japanese) swamp.
(Moquelumnan) stone.

Sayo (Japanese) born
at night.

Scarlett (English) bright
red. Literature: Scarlett
O'Hara is the heroine
of Margaret Mitchell's
novel *Gone with the Wind.*
**Scarlet, Scarlette,
Scarlotte, Skarlette**

Scotti (Scottish) from
Scotland. A feminine form
of Scott.
**Scota, Scotia, Scottie,
Scotty**

Seana (Irish) a form of Jane.
See also Shauna, Shawna.
**Seaana, Seandra, Seane,
Seanette, Seann, Seanna,
Seannalisa, Seanté,
Seantelle, Sina**

Sebastiane (Greek)
venerable. (Latin) revered.
(French) a feminine form
of Sebastian.
**Sebastene, Sebastia,
Sebastiana, Sebastienne**

Seble (Ethiopian) autumn.

Secilia (Latin) an alternate
form of Cecilia.
**Saselia, Sasilia, Sesilia,
Sileas**

Secunda (Latin) second.

Seda (Armenian) forest
voices.

Sedna (Eskimo) well-fed.
Mythology: the goddess
of sea animals.

Seelia (English) a form
of Sheila.

Seema (Greek) sprout.
(Afghani) sky; profile.
Seemah, Sima, Simah

Sefa (Swiss) a familiar form
of Josefina.

Seki (Japanese) wonderful.
Seka

Sela (English) a short form
of Selena.
Seeley, Selah

Selam (Ethiopian) peaceful.

Selda (German) a short
form of Griselda. (Yiddish)
an alternate form of Zelda.
**Seldah, Selde, Sellda,
Selldah**

Selena (Greek) moon.
Mythology: Selene was
the goddess of the moon.
See also Celena.
**Saleena, Sela, Selen,
Selene, Séléné, Selenia,
Selina, Sena, Syleena,
Sylena**

Selia (Latin) a short form
of Cecilia.
Seel, Seil, Sela

Selima (Hebrew) peaceful. A feminine form of Solomon.
Selema, Selemah, Selimah

Selina (Greek) an alternate form of Celina, Selena.
Selia, Selie, Selina, Selinda, Seline, Selinka, Selyna, Selyne, Sylina

Selma (German) devine protector. (Irish) fair, just. (Scandinavian) divinely protected. (Arabic) secure. A feminine form of Anselm. See also Zelma.
Sellma, Sellmah, Selmah

Sema (Turkish) heaven; divine omen.
Semaj

Sen (Japanese) Mythology: a magical forest elf that lives for thousands of years.

Senalda (Spanish) sign.
Sena, Senda, Senna

Septima (Latin) seventh.

Sequoia (Cherokee) giant redwood tree.
Sequora, Sequoya, Sikoya

Serafina (Hebrew) burning; ardent. Bible: Seraphim are the highest order of angels.
Sarafina, Serafine, Seraphe, Seraphin, Seraphina, Seraphine, Seraphita, Serapia, Serofina

Serena (Latin) peaceful. See also Rena.
Sarina, Saryna, Sereena, Serenah, Serene, Serenity, Serenna, Serina, Serrena, Serrin, Serrina, Seryna

Serilda (Greek) armed warrior woman.

Sevilla (Spanish) from Seville.
Seville

Shaba (Spanish) rose.
Shabana, Shabina

Shada (Native American) pelican.
Shadae, Shadea, Shadeana, Shadee, Shadi, Shadia, Shadiah, Shadie, Shadiya, Shaida, Shaiday

Shadrika (American) a combination of the prefix Sha + Rika.
Shadreka, Shadrica, Shadricka

Shae (Irish) an alternate form of Shea.
Shaeen, Shaeine, Shaela, Shaelea, Shaelee, Shaeleigh, Shaelie, Shaely, Shaelyn, Shaena, Shaenel, Shaeya, Shaia

Shaelyn (Irish) an alternate form of Shea.
Shaeleen, Shaelene, Shaelin, Shaeline, Shaelynn, Shaelynne

Shafira (Swahili) distinguished.

Shahar (Arabic) moonlit.
Shahara

Shahina (Arabic) falcon.
**Shaheen, Shaheena,
Shahi, Shahin**

Shahla (Afghani) beautiful
eyes.
Shaila, Shailah, Shalah

Shaina (Yiddish) beautiful.
**Shaena, Shainah, Shaine,
Shainna, Shajna, Shanie,
Shayna, Shayndel, Sheina,
Sheindel**

Shajuana (American)
a combination of the
prefix Sha + Juanita.
See also Shawanna.
**Shajuan, Shajuanda,
Shajuanita, Shajuanna,
Shajuanza**

Shaka (Hindi) an alternate
form of Shakti. A short
form of names beginning
with "Shak." See also
Chaka.
**Shakah, Shakha, Shikah,
Shikha**

Shakarah (American)
a combination of the
prefix Sha + Kara.
**Shacara, Shacari,
Shaccara, Shaka, Shakari,
Shakkara, Shikara**

Shakeena (American)
a combination of the
prefix Sha + Keena.
**Shaka, Shakeina,
Shakeyna, Shakina,
Shakyna**

Shakeita (American)
a combination of the
prefix Sha + Keita.
See also Shaqueita.
**Shaka, Shakeeta,
Shakeitha, Shakeithia,
Shaketa, Shaketha,
Shakethia, Shaketia,
Shakita, Shakitra,
Sheketa, Shekita, Shikita,
Shikitha**

Shakia (American)
a combination of the
prefix Sha + Kia.
**Shakeeia, Shakeeyah,
Shakeia, Shakeya,
Shakiya, Shekeia, Shekia,
Shekiah, Shikia**

Shakila (Arabic) pretty.
**Shaka, Shakeela,
Shakeena, Shakela,
Shakilah, Shekila,
Shekilla, Shikeela**

Shakira (Arabic) thankful.
A feminine form of Shakir.
**Shaakira, Shaka, Shakera,
Shakerah, Shakeria,
Shakeriay, Shakeyra,
Shakir, Shakirah,
Shakirat, Shakirra,
Shakyra, Shekiera,
Shekira, Shikira**

Shakti (Hindi) divine
woman. Religion:
the Hindu goddess
who controls time
and destruction.
Sakti, Shaka, Sita

Shalana (American)
a combination of the
prefix Sha + Lana.
**Shalaina, Shalaine,
Shaland, Shalanda,
Shalane, Shalann,
Shalaun, Shalauna,
Shallan, Shalyn, Shalyne,
Shelan, Shelanda**

Shaleah (American)
a combination of the
prefix Sha + Leah.
Shalea, Shalee, Shaleea

Shaleisha (American)
a combination of the
prefix Sha + Aisha.
**Shalesha, Shalesia,
Shalicia, Shalisha**

Shalena (American)
a combination of the
prefix Sha + Lena.
**Shaleana, Shaleen, Shalen,
Shálena, Shalene, Shalené,
Shalenna, Shelayna,
Shelayne, Shelena**

Shalisa (American)
a combination of the
prefix Sha + Lisa.
**Shalesa, Shalese, Shalice,
Shalise, Shalisia, Shalisse,
Shalys, Shalyse**

Shalita (American)
a combination of the
prefix Sha + Lita.
**Shaleta, Shaletta, Shalida,
Shalitta**

Shalonda (American)
a combination of the
prefix Sha + Ondine.
Shalonde, Shalondine

Shalona (American)
a combination of the
prefix Sha + Lona.
Shálonna, Shalonne

Shalyn (American)
a combination of the
prefix Sha + Lynn.
**Shalin, Shalina, Shalinda,
Shaline, Shalyna,
Shalynda, Shalynn,
Shalynne**

Shamara (Arabic) ready
for battle.
**Shamar, Shamarah,
Shamari, Shamaria,
Shamarra, Shamarri,
Shammara, Shamora,
Shamorra, Shamorria**

Shameka (American)
a combination of the
prefix Sha + Meka.
**Shameca, Shamecca,
Shamecha, Shameeka,
Shameika, Shameke,
Shamekia**

Shamika (American)
a combination of the
prefix Sha + Mika.
**Shamica, Shamicia,
Shamicka, Shamieka,
Shamikia**

Shamira (Hebrew) precious
stone. A feminine form of
Shamir.

Shamir, Shamiran, Shamiria

Shana (Hebrew) God is gracious (Irish) a form of Jane.
Shaana, Shan, Shanae, Shanay, Shanda, Shandi, Shane, Shanna, Shannah, Shauna, Shawna

Shanae (Irish) an alternate form of Shana.
Shanea

Shanda (American) a form of Chanda, Shana.
Shandah

Shandi (English) a familiar form of Shana.
Shandee, Shandeigh, Shandey, Shandi, Shandice, Shandie

Shandra (American) an alternate form of Shanda. See also Chandra.
Shandrea, Shandreka, Shandri, Shandria, Shandriah, Shandrice, Shandrie, Shandry

Shane (Irish) an alternate form of Shana.
Shanea, Shanee, Shanée, Shanie

Shaneisha (American) a combination of the prefix Sha + Aisha.
Shanesha, Shaneshia, Shanessa, Shanisha, Shanissha

Shaneka (American) an alternate form of Shanika.
Shanecka, Shaneikah, Shanekia, Shanequa, Shaneyka

Shanel, Shanell, Shanelle (American) forms of Chanel.
Schanel, Schanell, Shanella, Shannel, Shenel, Shenela, Shenell, Shenelle, Shonelle, Shynelle

Shaneta (American) a combination of the prefix Sha + Neta.
Shaneeta, Shanetha, Shanethis, Shanetta, Shanette

Shani (Swahili) marvelous.

Shanice (American) a form of Janice.
Shanece, Shaneese, Shaneice, Shanese, Shanise, Shanisse, Shanneice, Shannice, Sheneice

Shanida (American) a combination of the prefix Sha + Ida.
Shaneeda, Shannida

Shanika (American) a combination of the prefix Sha + Nika.
Shanica, Shanicca, Shanicka, Shanieka, Shanike, Shanikia, Shanikka, Shanikqua,

Shanika *(American)*
**Shanikwa, Shaniqua,
Shanique, Shenika**

Shanita (American)
a combination of the
prefix Sha + Nita.
**Shanitha, Shanitra,
Shanitta**

Shanley (Irish) hero's child.
**Shanlee, Shanleigh,
Shanlie, Shanly**

Shanna (Irish) an alternate
form of Shana, Shannon.
**Shanea, Shannah,
Shannda, Shannea**

Shannon (Irish) small and
wise.
**Shanan, Shann, Shanna,
Shannan, Shanneen,
Shannen, Shannie,
Shannin, Shannyn,
Shanon**

Shanta, Shantae, Shante
(French) alternate forms
of Chantal.
**Shantai, Shantay,
Shantaya, Shantaye,
Shantea, Shantee,
Shantée**

Shantana (American)
a form of Santana.
**Shantan, Shantanae,
Shantanell, Shantanickia,
Shantanika, Shantanna**

Shantara (American)
a combination of the
prefix Sha + Tara.
Shantaria, Shantarra,

**Shantera, Shanteria,
Shanterra, Shantieria,
Shantira, Shantirea**

Shanteca (American)
a combination of the
prefix Sha + Teca.
**Shantecca, Shanteka,
Shantika, Shantikia**

Shantel, Shantell
(American) song.
Forms of Chantel.
**Shanntell, Shanta,
Shantal, Shantae,
Shantale, Shante,
Shanteal, Shanteil,
Shantele, Shantella,
Shantelle, Shantrell,
Shantyl, Shantyle,
Shauntel, Shauntell,
Shauntelle, Shauntrel,
Shauntrell, Shauntrella,
Shentel, Shentelle,
Shontal, Shontalla,
Shontalle**

Shantesa (American)
a combination of the
prefix Sha + Tess.
**Shantese, Shantice,
Shantise, Shantisha**

Shantia (American)
a combination of the
prefix Sha + Tia.
**Shanteya, Shanti,
Shantida, Shantie,
Shaunteya, Shauntia**

Shantille (American)
a form of Chantilly.
**Shanteil, Shantil,
Shantille, Shantilli,**

Shantilly, Shantyl, Shantyle

Shantina (American) a combination of the prefix Sha + Tina. **Shanteena**

Shantora (American) a combination of the prefix Sha + Tory. **Shantoia, Shantori, Shantoria, Shantory, Shantorya, Shantoya, Shanttoria**

Shantrice (American) a combination of the prefix Sha + Trice. See also Chantrice. **Shantreece, Shantreese, Shantriece, Shantrisse**

Shappa (Native American) red thunder.

Shaquanda (American) a combination of the prefix Sha + Wanda. **Shaquan, Shaquana, Shaquand, Shaquandra, Shaquanera, Shaquani, Shaquanna, Shaquantia, Shaquonda**

Shaqueita (American) an alternate form of Shakeita. **Shaqueta, Shaquetta, Shaquita, Shequida, Shequita, Shequittia**

Shaquila (American) a form of Shakila. **Shaquille, Shequela,**

Shequele, Shequila, Shquiyla

Shara (Hebrew) a short form of Sharon. **Shaara, Sharal, Sharala, Sharalee, Sharlyn, Sharlynn, Sharra**

Sharai (Hebrew) princess. An alternate form of Sarah See also Sharon. **Sharae, Sharaé, Sharah, Sharaiah, Sharay, Sharaya**

Sharan (Hindi) protector. **Sharaine, Sharanda, Sharanjeet**

Shardae, Sharday (Punjabi) charity. (Yoruba) honored by royalty. (Arabic) runaway. An alternate form of Chardae. **Sade, Shadae, Sharda, Shar-Dae, Shardai, Shar-Day, Sharde, Shardea, Shardee, Shardée, Shardei, Shardeia, Shardey**

Sharee (English) a form of Shari. **Shareen, Shareena, Sharine**

Shari (French) beloved, dearest. An alternate form of Cheri. (Hungarian) a form of Sarah. See also Sharita, Sheree, Sherry. **Shara, Sharee, Sharian, Shariann, Sharianne, Sharie, Sharra, Sharree, Sharrie, Sharry, Shary**

Sharice (French) an alternate form of Cherise.
Shareese, Sharese,
Sharica, Sharicka,
Shariece, Sharis, Sharise,
Sharisha, Shariss,
Sharissa, Sharisse

Sharik (African) child
of God.

Sharissa (American) a form
of Sharice.
Sharesa, Sharisa, Sharisha,
Shereeza, Shericia,
Sherisa, Sherissa

Sharita (French) a familiar
form of Shari. (American)
a form of Charity. See also
Sherita.
Shareeta, Sharrita

Sharla (French) a short
form of Sharlene,
Sharlotte.

Sharlene (French) little
and womanly. A form
of Charlene.
Scharlane, Scharlene,
Shar, Sharla, Sharlaina,
Sharlaine, Sharlane,
Sharlanna, Sharlee,
Sharleen, Sharleine,
Sharlena, Sharleyne,
Sharline, Sharlyn,
Sharlynn, Sharlynne,
Sherlean, Sherleen,
Sherlene, Sherline

Sharlotte (American)
a form of Charlotte.
Sharla, Sharlet, Sharlett,
Sharlott, Sharlotta

Sharma (American) a short
form of Sharmaine.
Sharmae, Sharme

Sharmaine (American)
a form of Charmaine.
Sharmain, Sharman,
Sharmane, Sharmanta,
Sharmayne, Sharmeen,
Sharmene, Sharmese,
Sharmin, Sharmine,
Sharmon, Sharmyn

Sharna (Hebrew) an alternate form of Sharon.
Sharnae, Sharnay, Sharne,
Sharnea, Sharnease,
Sharnee, Sharneese,
Sharnell, Sharnelle,
Sharnese, Sharnett,
Sharnetta, Sharnise

Sharon (Hebrew) desert
plain. An alternate form
of Sharai.
Shaaron, Shara, Sharai,
Sharan, Shareen, Sharen,
Shari, Sharin, Sharna,
Sharonda, Sharran,
Sharren, Sharrin, Sharron,
Sharrona, Sharyn,
Sharyon, Sheren, Sheron,
Sherryn

Sharonda (Hebrew) an
alternate form of Sharon.
Sharronda, Sheronda,
Sherrhonda

Sharrona (Hebrew) an
alternate form of Sharon.
Sharona, Sharone,
Sharonia, Sharony,
Sharronne, Sheron,

Sherona, Sheronna, Sherron, Sherronna, Sherronne, Shirona

Shatara (Hindi) umbrella. (Arabic) good; industrious. (American) a combination of Sharon + Tara.
Shataria, Shatarra, Shataura, Shateira, Shaterah, Shateria, Shatherian, Shatierra, Shatiria

Shatoria (American) a combination of the prefix Sha + Tory.
Shatora, Shatorria, Shatorya, Shatoya

Shauna (Hebrew) God is gracious. (Irish) an alternate form of Shana.
Shaun, Shaunah, Shaune, Shaunee, Shauneen, Shaunelle, Shaunette, Shauni, Shaunice, Shaunicy, Shaunie, Shaunika, Shaunisha, Shaunna, Shaunnea, Shaunua, Shaunya

Shaunda (Irish) an alternate form of Shauna. See also Shanda, Shawnda, Shonda.
Shaundal, Shaundala, Shaundel, Shaundela, Shaundell, Shaundelle, Shaundra, Shaundrea, Shaundree, Shaundria, Shaundrice

Shaunta (Irish) an alternate form of Shauna. See also Shawnta.
Schunta, Shauntae, Shauntay, Shaunte, Shauntea, Shauntee, Shauntée, Shaunteena, Shauntei, Shauntia, Shauntier, Shauntrel, Shauntrell, Shauntrella

Shavonne (American) a combination of the prefix Sha + Yvonne. See also Siobhahn.
Schavon, Schevon, Shavan, Shavana, Shavanna, Shavaun, Shavon, Shavonda, Shavondra, Shavone, Shavonn, Shavonna, Shavonni, Shavontae, Shavonte, Shavonté, Shavoun, Shivani, Shivaun, Shivawn, Shivonne, Shyvon, Shyvonne

Shawanna (American) a combination of the prefix Sha + Wanda. See also Shawna.
Shawana, Shawanda, Shawante

Shawna (Hebrew) God is gracious. (Irish) a form of Jane. An alternate form of Shana, Shauna.
Sawna, Shawn, Shawnai, Shawnaka, Shawne, Shawnee, Shawneen, Shawneena, Shawnequa,

Shawna *(cont.)*
**Shawneika, Shawnell,
Shawnette, Shawni,
Shawnicka, Shawnie,
Shawnika, Shawnna,
Shawnra, Sheona, Siân,
Siana, Sianna**

Shawnda (Irish) an alter-
nate form of Shawna.
See also Shanda,
Shaunda, Shonda.
**Shawndal, Shawndala,
Shawndan, Shawndel,
Shawndra, Shawndrea,
Shawndree, Shawndreel,
Shawndrell, Shawndria**

Shawnta (Irish) an alter-
nate form of Shawna.
See also Shaunta, Shonta.
**Shawntae, Shawntay,
Shawnte, Shawnté,
Shawntee, Shawntell,
Shawntelle, Shawnteria,
Shawntia, Shawntil,
Shawntile, Shawntill,
Shawntille, Shawntina,
Shawntish, Shawntrese,
Shawntriece**

Shay (Irish) an alternate
form of Shea.
**Shaya, Shayda, Shaye,
Shayha, Shayia, Shey,
Sheye**

Shayla (Irish) an alternate
form of Shay.
**Shay, Shaylagh, Shaylah,
Shaylain, Shaylan,
Shaylea, Shaylee, Shayley,
Shayli, Shaylie, Shaylin,**
**Shaylla, Shayly, Shaylyn,
Shaylynn, Sheyla, Sheylyn**

Shayna (Hebrew) beautiful.
A form of Shaina.
**Shaynae, Shayne,
Shaynee, Shayney, Shayni,
Shaynie, Shayny**

Shea (Irish) fairy palace.
**Shae, Shay, Shealy,
Shealyn, Sheana, Sheann,
Sheanna, Sheannon,
Sheanta, Sheaon, Shearra,
Sheatara, Sheaunna,
Sheavon**

Sheba (Hebrew) a short
form of Bathsheba.
Geography: an ancient
country of South Arabia.
**Saba, Sabah, Shebah,
Sheeba**

Sheena (Hebrew) God is
gracious. (Irish) a form
of Jane.
**Sheenagh, Sheenah,
Sheenan, Sheeneal,
Sheenika, Sheenna,
Sheina, Shena, Shiona**

Sheila (Latin) blind. (Irish)
a form of Cecelia. See also
Zelizi.
**Seelia, Seila, Selia,
Shaylah, Sheela, Sheelagh,
Sheelah, Sheilagh,
Sheilah, Sheileen,
Sheiletta, Sheilia,
Sheillynn, Sheilya, Shela,
Shelagh, Shelah, Shelia,
Shiela, Shila, Shilah,
Shilea, Shyla**

Shelby (English) ledge
estate.
**Schelby, Shel, Shelbe,
Shelbee, Shelbey, Shelbi,
Shelbie, Shellby**

Shelee (English) an alter-
nate form of Shelley.
**Shelee, Sheleen, Shelena,
Sheley, Sheleza, Sheli,
Shelia, Shelica, Shelicia,
Shelina, Shelinda, Shelisa,
Shelise, Shelisse, Shelita,
Sheliza**

Shelley, Shelly (English)
meadow on the ledge.
(French) a familiar form
of Michelle.
**Shelee, Shell, Shella,
Shellaine, Shellana,
Shellany, Shellee,
Shellene, Shelli, Shellian,
Shellie, Shellina**

Shelsea (American) a form
of Chelsea.
Shellsea, Shellsey, Shelsey

Shena (Irish) an alternate
form of Sheena.
**Shenada, Shenae, Shenay,
Shenda, Shene, Shenea,
Sheneda, Shenee,
Sheneena, Shenica,
Shenika, Shenina,
Sheniqua, Shenita,
Shenna**

Shera (Aramaic) light.
**Sheera, Sheerah, Sherae,
Sherah, Sheralee, Sheralle,
Sheralyn, Sheralynn,
Sheralynne, Sheray,
Sheraya**

Sheree (French) beloved,
dearest. An alternate form
of Shari.
**Scherie, Sheeree, Shere,
Shereé, Sherrelle,
Shereen, Shereena**

Sherelle (French) an alter-
nate form of Cherelle,
Sheryl.
Sherrell

Sheri, Sherri (French)
alternate forms of Sherry.
**Sheria, Sheriah, Sherian,
Sherianne, Shericia,
Sherie, Sheriel, Sherrie,
Sherrina**

Sherice (French) an alter-
nate form of Sherry.
**Scherise, Sherece,
Shereece, Sherees,
Shereese, Sherese,
Shericia, Sherise, Sherisse,
Sherrish, Sherryse,
Sheryce**

Sherika (Punjabi) relative.
(Arabic) easterner.
**Shereka, Sherica,
Shericka, Sherrica,
Sherricka, Sherrika**

Sherissa (French) a form
of Sherry, Sheryl.
**Shereeza, Sheresa,
Shericia, Sherrish**

Sherita (French) a form
of Sherry, Sheryl. See also
Sharita.
**Shereta, Sheretta,
Sherette, Sherrita**

Sherleen (French, English) an alternate form of Sheryl, Shirley.
Sherileen, Sherlene, Sherline

Sherry (French) beloved, dearest. An alternate form of Shari. A familiar form of Sheryl. See also Sheree.
Sherey, Sheri, Sherissa, Sherrey, Sherri, Sherria, Sherriah, Sherrie, Sherye, Sheryy

Sheryl (French) beloved. An alternate form of Cheryl. A familiar form of Shirley. See also Sherry.
Sharel, Sharil, Sharilyn, Sharyl, Sharyll, Sheral, Sherell, Sheriel, Sheril, Sherill, Sherily, Sherilyn, Sherissa, Sherita, Sherleen, Sherral, Sherrel, Sherrell, Sherrelle, Sherril, Sherrill, Sherryl, Sherylly

Sherylyn (American) a combination of Sheryl + Lynn. See also Cherilyn.
Sharlyne, Sharolin, Sharolyn, Sharyl-Lynn, Sheralyn, Sherilyn, Sherilynn, Sherilynne, Sherralyn, Sherralynn, Sherrilyn, Sherrilynn, Sherrilynne, Sherrylyn, Sherryn, Sherylanne

Shevonne (American) a combination of the prefix She + Yvonne.
Shevaun, Shevon, Shevonda, Shevone

Sheyenne (Cheyenne) an alternate form of Cheyenne.
Sheyen, Shi, Shiana, Shianda, Shiana, Shiane, Shiann, Shianna, Shianne, Shiante, Shyan, Shyana, Shyann, Shyanne, Shye, Shyenna

Shifra (Hebrew) beautiful.
Schifra, Shifrah

Shika (Japanese) gentle deer.
Shi

Shilo (Hebrew) God's gift. Geography: a site near Jerusalem. Bible: a sanctuary for the Israelites where the Ark of the Covenant was kept.
Shiloh

Shina (Japanese) virtuous; wealthy. (Chinese) an alternate form of China.
Shine, Shineeca, Shineese, Shinelle, Shinequa, Shineta, Shiniqua, Shinita, Shiona

Shino (Japanese) bamboo stalk.

Shiquita (American) a form of Chiquita.
Shiquata, Shiquitta

Shira (Hebrew) song.
Shirah, Shiray, Shire, Shiree, Shiri, Shirit

Shirlene (English) an alternate form of Shirley.
Shirleen, Shirline, Shirlynn

Shirley (English) bright meadow. See also Sheryl.
Sherlee, Sherleen, Sherley, Sherli, Sherlie, Shir, Shirelle, Shirl, Shirlee, Shirlena, Shirlene, Shirlie, Shirlina, Shirly, Shirlyn, Shirlly, Shurlee, Shurley

Shizu (Japanese) silent.
Shizue, Shizuka, Shizuko, Shizuyo

Shona (Irish) a form of Jane. An alternate form of Shana, Shauna, Shawna.
Shonagh, Shonah, Shonalee, Shonda, Shone, Shonee, Shonelle, Shonetta, Shonette, Shoni, Shonna, Shonneka, Shonnika, Shonta

Shonda (Irish) an alternate form of Shona. See also Shanda, Shaunda, Shawnda.
Shondalette, Shondalyn, Shondel, Shondelle, Shondi, Shondia, Shondie, Shondra, Shondreka, Shounda

Shonta (Irish) an alternate form of Shona. See also Shaunta, Shawnta.
Shontá, Shontae, Shontai, Shontal, Shontalea, Shontara, Shontasia, Shontavia, Shontaviea, Shontay, Shontaya, Shonte, Shonté, Shontecia, Shontedra, Shontee, Shontel, Shontelle, Shonteral, Shonteria, Shontessia, Shonti, Shontia, Shontina, Shontol, Shontoy, Shontrail, Shontrice, Shountáe

Shoshana (Hebrew) lily. An alternate form of Susan.
Shosha, Shoshan, Shoshanah, Shoshane, Shoshanha, Shoshann, Shoshanna, Shoshannah, Shoshauna, Shoushan, Sosha, Soshana

Shu (Chinese) kind, gentle.

Shug (American) a short form of Sugar.

Shula (Arabic) flaming, bright.
Shulah

Shulamith (Hebrew) peaceful. See also Sula.
Shulamit, Sulamith

Shunta (Irish) an alternate form of Shonta.
Shuntae, Shunté, Shuntel, Shuntia

Shura (Russian) a form of Alexandra.

Shuree, Shureen, Shurelle, Shuritta, Shurka, Shurlana

Shyla (English) an alternate form of Sheila.

Sibeta (Moquelumnan) finding a fish under a rock.

Sibley (Greek) an alternate form of Sybil. (English) sibling; friendly.
Sybley

Sidonia (Hebrew) enticing.

Sidonie (French) from Saint Denis, France. Geography: an ancient Phoenician city. See also Sydney.
Sidaine, Sidanni, Sidelle, Sidney, Sidoine, Sidona, Sidonia, Sidony

Sidra (Latin) star child.
Sidrah, Sidras

Sierra (Irish) black. (Spanish) saw toothed. Geography: a rugged range of mountains that, when viewed from a distance, has a jagged profile. See also Ciara.
Seara, Searria, Seera, Seiarra, Seira, Seirra, Siara, Siarah, Siarra, Sieara, Siearra, Siera, Sieria, Sierrah, Sierre

Sigfreda (German) victorious peace. See also Freda.
Sigfreida, Sigfrida, Sigfrieda, Sigfryda

Sigmunda (German) victorious protector.
Sigmonda

Signe (Latin) sign, signal. (Scandinavian) a short form of Sigourney.
Sig, Signa, Signy, Singna, Singne

Sigourney (English) victorious conquerer.
Signe, Sigourny

Sigrid (Scandinavian) victorious counselor.
Siegrid, Siegrida, Sigritt

Sihu (Native American) flower; bush.

Siko (African) crying baby.

Silvia (Latin) an alternate form of Sylvia.
Silivia, Silva, Silvaine, Silvanna, Silvi, Silviane, Silva, Silvy

Simcha (Hebrew) joyful.

Simone (Hebrew) she heard. (French) a feminine form of Simon.
Siminie, Simmi, Simmie, Simmona, Simmone, Simoane, Simona, Simonetta, Simonette, Simonia, Simonina, Simonne, Somone, Symona, Symone

Sina (Irish) an alternate form of Seana.
Seena, Sinan

Sindy (American) a form
of Cindy.
**Sinda, Sindal, Sindee,
Sindia, Sindie, Synda,
Syndal, Syndee, Syndey,
Syndi, Syndia, Syndie,
Syndy**

Sinead (Irish) a form
of Jane.
**Seonaid, Sine, Sinéad,
Sinnedy**

Siobhan (Irish) a form of
Joan. See also Shavonne.
**Shibahn, Shibani,
Shibhan, Shioban,
Shobana, Shobha,
Shobhana, Siobahn,
Siobhana, Siobhann,
Siobhon, Siovaun, Siovhan**

Sirena (Greek) enchanter.
Mythology: sirens were
half-woman, half-bird
creatures whose singing
so enchanted sailors, they
crashed their ships into
nearby rocks.
**Sireena, Sirene, Sirine,
Syrena, Syrenia, Syrenna,
Syrina**

Sisika (Native American)
songbird.

Sissy (American) a familiar
form of Cecelia, Cicely.
Sisi, Sisie, Sissey, Sissie

Sita (Hindi) an alternate
form of Shakti.
**Sitah, Sitarah, Sitha,
Sithara**

Siti (Swahili) respected
woman.

Skye (Arabic) water giver.
(Dutch) a short form
of Skyler. Geography:
an island in the Hebrides,
Scotland.
Sky

Skyler (Dutch) sheltering.
**Schuyla, Schuyler,
Schuylia, Schyler, Skila,
Skilah, Skye, Skyla, Skylar,
Skylee, Skylena, Skyllar,
Skylynn, Skyra**

Sloane (Irish) warrior.
Sloan

Socorro (Spanish) helper.

Sofia (Greek) an alternate
form of Sophia. See also
Zofia, Zsofia.
**Sofeea, Sofeeia, Soffi,
Sofi, Soficita, Sofie, Sofija,
Sofiya, Sofka, Sofya**

Solada (Thai) listener.

Solana (Spanish) sunshine.
**Solande, Solanna, Soleil,
Solena, Solene, Soléne,
Soley, Solina, Solinda**

Solange (French) dignified.

Soledad (Spanish) solitary.
Sole, Soleda

Solenne (French) solemn,
dignified.
**Solaine, Solène, Solenna,
Solina, Soline, Solonez,
Souline, Soulle**

Soma (Hindi) lunar. Astrological: born under the sign of Cancer.

Sommer (English) summer; summoner. (Arabic) black. See also Summer.
Sommar, Sommara

Sondra (Greek) defender of mankind. A short form of Alexandra.
Saundra, Sondre, Sonndra, Sonndre

Sonia (Russian, Slavic) an alternate form of Sonya.
Sonica, Sonida, Sonita, Sonni, Sonnie, Sonny

Sonja (Scandinavian) a form of Sonya.
Sonjae, Sonjia

Sonya (Greek) wise. (Russian, Slavic) a form of Sophia.
Sonia, Sonja, Sunya

Sook (Korean) pure.

Sopheary (Cambodian) beautiful girl.

Sophia (Greek) wise. See also Sonya, Zofia.
Sofia, Sophie

Sophie (Greek) a familiar form of Sophia. See also Zocha.
Sophey, Sophi, Sophy

Sophronia (Greek) wise; sensible.
Soffrona, Sofronia

Sora (Native American) chirping songbird.

Soraya (Persian) princess.
Suraya

Sorrel (French) reddish brown. Botany: a wild herb.

Soso (Native American) tree squirrel dining on pine nuts; chubby-cheeked baby.

Souzan (Persian) burning fire.

Speranza (Italian) a form of Esperanza.
Speranca

Spring (English) springtime.

Stacey, Stacy (Greek) resurrection. (Irish) a short form of Anastasia, Eustacia, Natasha.
Stace, Stacee, Staceyan, Staceyann, Staicy, Stasya, Stayce, Staycee, Staci

Staci (Greek) an alternate form of Stacey.
Stacci, Stacia, Stacie, Stayci

Stacia (English) a short form of Anastasia.
Stasia, Staysha

Starleen (English) an alternate form of Starr.
Starleena, Starlena, Starlene, Starlin, Starlyn, Starlynn, Starrlen

Starling (English) bird.

Starr (English) star.
Star, Staria, Starisha,
Starla, Starle, Starlee,
Starleen, Starlet,
Starlette, Starley,
Starlight, Starly, Starri,
Starria, Starrika, Starrsha,
Starsha, Starshanna,
Starskysha, Startish

Stasya (Greek) a familiar
form of Anastasia.
(Russian) a form of Stacey.
Stasa, Stasha, Stashia,
Stasia, Stasja, Staska

Stefanie (Greek) an alter-
nate form of Stephanie.
Stafani, Stafanie,
Staffany, Stefaney,
Stefani, Stefania,
Stefanié, Stefanija,
Stefannie, Stefany,
Stefcia, Stefenie, Steffane,
Steffani, Steffanie,
Steffany, Steffi, Stefka

Steffi (Greek) a familiar
form of Stefanie,
Stephanie.
Stefa, Stefcia, Steffie,
Stefi, Stefka, Stepha,
Stephi, Stephie, Stephy

Stella (Latin) star. (French)
a familiar form of Estelle.
Steile, Stellina

Stepania (Russian) a form
of Stephanie.
Stepa, Stepahny,
Stepanida, Stepanie,
Stepanyda, Stepfanie

Stephanie (Greek)
crowned. A feminine
form of Stephan. See also
Panya, Stevie, Zephania.
Stamatios, Stefanie,
Steffie, Stepania,
Stephaija, Stephaine,
Stephana, Stephanas,
Stephane, Stephanee,
Stephaney, Stephani,
Stephania, Stephanida,
Stéphanie, Stephanine,
Stephann, Stephannie,
Stephany, Stephene,
Stephenie, Stephianie,
Stephney, Stesha, Steshka,
Stevanee

Stephene (Greek) an alter-
nate form of Stephanie.
Stephina, Stephine,
Stephyne

Stephenie (Greek) an alternate form of Stephanie.
Stephena

Stephney (Greek) an alter-
nate form of Stephanie.
Stephne, Stephni,
Stephnie, Stephny

Stevie (Greek) a familiar
form of Stephanie.
Steva, Stevana, Stevanee,
Stevee, Stevena, Stevey,
Stevi, Stevy, Stevye

Stina (German) a form
of Christina.
Steena, Stena, Stine,
Stinna

Stockard (English)
stockyard.

Stormy (English) impetuous by nature.
Storm, Storme, Stormi, Stormie

Suchin (Thai) beautiful thought.

Sue (Hebrew) a short form of Susan, Susanna.
Suann, Suanna, Suanne, Sueanne, Suetta

Suela (Spanish) consolation.
Suelita

Sugar (American) sweet as sugar.
Shug

Sugi (Japanese) cedar tree.

Suke (Hawaiian) a form of Susan.

Sukey (Hawaiian) a familiar form of Susan.
Suka, Sukee, Suki, Sukie, Suky

Suki (Japanese) loved one. (Moquelumnan) eagle eyed.
Sukie

Sula (Greek, Hebrew) a short form of Shulamith, Ursula. (Icelandic) large seabird.

Suletu (Moquelumnan) soaring bird.

Sulia (Latin) an alternate form of Julia.
Suliana

Sulwen (Welsh) bright as the sun.

Sumalee (Thai) beautiful flower.

Sumati (Hindi) unity.

Sumi (Japanese) elegant, refined.
Sumiko

Summer (English) summertime. See also Sommer.
Sumer, Summar, Summerbreeze, Summerhaze, Summerlee

Sun (Korean) obedient.
Suncance, Sundee, Sundeep, Sundi, Sundip, Sundrenea, Sunta, Sunya

Sunee (Thai) good.
Suni

Sun-Hi (Korean) good; joyful.

Suni (Zuni) native; member of our tribe.
Sunita, Sunitha, Suniti, Sunne, Sunni, Sunnie, Sunnilei

Sunki (Hopi) swift.
Sunkia

Sunny (English) bright, cheerful.
Sunni, Sunnie

Sunshine (English) sunshine.

Surata (Pakistani) blessed joy.

Suri (Todas) pointy nose.
Suree, Surena, Surenia

Surya (Pakistani) Mythology: a sun god.
Surra

Susammi (French) a combination of Susan + Aimee.
Suzami, Suzamie, Suzamy

Susan (Hebrew) lily.
See also Shoshana,
Sukey, Zsa Zsa, Zusa.
**Sawsan, Siusan, Sosana,
Sosanna, Sue, Suesan,
Sueva, Suisan, Suke,
Susann, Susanna, Suse,
Susen, Susette, Suson,
Sussi, Suzan, Suzane,
Suzette, Suzzane**

Susanna, Susannah
(Hebrew) alternate forms
of Susan. See also Xuxa,
Zsuzsanna, Zanna.
**Sonel, Sue, Suesanna,
Susana, Susanah, Susanka,
Susette, Susie, Suzana,
Suzanna, Suzanne**

Suse (Hawaiian) a form
of Susan.

Susette (French) a familiar
form of Susan, Susanna.
**Susetta, Suzetta, Suzette,
Suzzette**

Susie (American) a familiar
form of Susan, Susanna.
**Suse, Susey, Susi, Sussy,
Susy, Suze, Suzi, Suzie,
Suzy**

Suzanne (English) a form
of Susan.
**Susanne, Suszanne,
Suzane, Suzann, Suzzann,
Suzzanne**

Suzette (French) a form
of Susan.
Susetta, Susette, Suzetta

Suzu (Japanese) little bell.
Suzue, Suzuko

Suzuki (Japanese) bell tree.

Svetlana (Russian) bright
light.
Sveta, Svetochka

Syà (Chinese) summer.

Sybella (English) a form
of Sybil.
**Sibeal, Sibel, Sibell,
Sibella, Sibelle, Sybel,
Sybelle**

Sybil (Greek) prophet.
Mythology: sibyls were
oracles who relayed the
messages of the gods.
See also Cybele, Sibley.
**Sebila, Sib, Sibbel,
Sibbella, Sibbie, Sibbill,
Sibby, Sibeal, Sibel, Sibilla,
Sibyl, Sibylla, Sibylle,
Sibylline, Sybella, Sybila,
Sybilla, Sybille, Syble**

Sydney (French) from
Saint Denis, France.
A feminine form of Sidney.
See also Sidonie.
**Sy, Syd, Sydania, Sydel,
Sydelle, Sydna, Sydnee,
Sydni, Sydnie, Sydny,
Sydnye, Syndona,
Syndonah, Syndonia**

Sying (Chinese) star.

Sylvana (Latin) forest.
Sylva, Sylvaine, Sylvanna, Sylvi, Sylvie, Sylvina, Sylvinnia, Sylvonna

Sylvia (Latin) forest.
Literature: Sylvia Plath was a well-known American writer and poet. See also Silvia, Xylia.
Sylvana, Sylvette, Sylvie, Sylwia

Syreeta (Hindi) good traditions. (Arabic) companion.

Tabatha (Greek, Aramaic) an alternate form of Tabitha.
Tabathe, Tabathia, Tabbatha

Tabby (English) a familiar form of Tabitha.

Tabia (Swahili) talented.

Tabina (Arabic) follower of Muhammed.

Tabitha (Greek, Aramaic) gazelle.
Tabatha, Tabbee, Tabbetha, Tabbey, Tabbi, Tabbie, Tabbitha, Tabby, Tabetha, Tabithia, Tabotha, Tabtha, Tabytha

Tacey (English) a familiar form of Tacita.
Taci

Taci (Zuni) washtub. (English) an alternate form of Tacey.
Tacia, Taciana, Tacie

Tacita (Latin) silent.
Tace, Tacey, Tacy, Tacye

Tadita (Omaha) runner.
Tadeta, Tadra

Taesha (Latin) an alternate form of Tisha. (American) a combination of the prefix Ta + Aisha.
Taheisha, Tahisha, Taiesha, Taisha, Taishae, Teisha, Tesha, Tyeisha, Tyeishia, Tyeshia, Tyeyshia, Tyieshia, Tyishia

Taffy (Welsh) beloved.
Taffia, Taffine, Taffye, Tafia, Tafisa, Tafoya

Tahira (Arabic) virginal, pure.
Taheera, Taheria

Taima (Native American) loud thunder.
Taimy

Taipa (Moquelumnan) flying quail.

Taite (English) cheerful.
Tate, Tayte

Taja (Hindi) crown.
Taiajára, Taija, Teja, Tejah, Tejal

Taka (Japanese) honored.

Takala (Hopi) corn tassel.

Takara (Japanese) treasure.
Takra

Takeisha (American)
a combination of the
prefix Ta + Keisha.
**Takecia, Takesha,
Takeshia, Takesia,
Takisha, Takishea,
Takishia, Tekeesha,
Tekeisha, Tekeshi,
Tekeysia, Tekisha,
Tikesha, Tikisha, Tokesia,
Tykeisha, Tykeshia,
Tykeza, Tykisha**

Takenya (Hebrew) animal
horn. (Moquelumnan)
falcon. (American)
a combination of the
prefix Ta + Kenya.
Takenia, Takenja

Taki (Japanese) waterfall.
Tiki

Takia (Arabic) worshiper.
**Takeiyah, Takeya, Takija,
Takiya, Takiyah, Takkia,
Taqiyya, Taquaia,
Taquaya, Taquiia, Tekeyia,
Tekiya, Tikia, Tykeia,
Tykia**

Takila (American) a form
Tequila.
**Tatakyla, Takela, Takelia,
Takella, Takeyla, Takilla,
Takilya, Tekela, Tekelia,
Tekilaa, Tekla**

Takira (American)
a combination of the
prefix Ta + Kira.
**Takara, Takarra, Takeara,
Takiria, Taquera, Taquira,
Tekeria, Tikara, Tikira,
Tykera, Tykira**

Tala (Native American)
stalking wolf.

Talasi (Hopi) corn tassel.
Talasea, Talasia

Taleah (American)
a combination of the
prefix Ta + Leah.
**Talaya, Talea, Taleéi, Talei,
Talia, Tylea, Tylee**

Taleisha (American)
a combination of the
prefix Ta + Aisha.
**Taileisha, Taleesha,
Taleise, Talesa, Talesha,
Taleshia, Talesia, Talicia,
Taliesha, Talisa, Talisha,
Tallese, Tallesia, Talysha,
Teleisia, Teleshia, Telesia,
Telicia, Telisa, Telisha,
Telishia, Tellisa, Telsa,
Tilisha, Tyleasha, Tyleisha,
Tylicia, Tylisha, Tylishia**

Talena (American)
a combination of the
prefix Ta + Lena.
**Talayna, Talihna, Talin,
Talina, Talinda, Taline,
Tallenia, Talná, Tilena,
Tilene, Tylena, Tylina,
Tyline**

Talia (Greek) blooming. (Hebrew) dew from heaven. (Latin, French) birthday. A short form of Natalie, Taleah. See also Thalia.
Tahlia, Tali, Taliah, Taliatha, Talieya, Taliya, Talley, Tallia, Tallie, Tally, Tallya, Talya, Talyah, Tylia

Talitha (Arabic) young girl.
Taleetha, Taletha, Talethia, Taliatha, Talita, Talithia, Taliya, Telita, Tiletha

Tallis (French, English) forest.
Tallys

Tallulah (Choctaw) leaping water.
Talley, Tallie, Tallou, Tally, Talula

Tam (Vietnamese) heart.

Tama (Japanese) jewel.
Tamaa, Tamah, Tamaiah, Tamala

Tamaka (Japanese) bracelet.
Tamaki, Tamako, Timaka

Tamar (Hebrew) a short form of Tamara. (Russian) History: a twelfth-century Georgian queen.
Tamer, Tamor, Tamour

Tamara (Hebrew) palm tree. See also Tammy.
Tamar, Tamará, Tamarah, Tamaria, Tamarin,
Tamarla, Tamarra, Tamarria, Tamarrian, Tamarsha, Tamary, Tamer, Tamera, Tamerai, Tameria, Tameriás, Tamma, Tammara, Tammera, Tamora, Tamoya, Tamra, Tamura, Tamyra, Temara, Temarian, Thama, Thamar, Thamara, Thamarra, Thamer, Timara, Timera, Tomara, Tymara

Tamassa (Hebrew) an alternate form of Thomasina.
Tamasin, Tamasine, Tamsen, Tamsin, Tamzen, Tamzin

Tameka (Aramaic) twin.
Tameca, Tamecia, Tamecka, Tameeka, Tamekia, Tamiecka, Tamieka, Temeka, Timeeka, Timeka, Tomeka, Tomekia, Trameika, Tymeka, Tymmeeka, Tymmeka

Tamesha (American) a combination of the prefix Ta + Mesha.
Tameshia, Tameshkia, Tamisha, Tamishia, Tamnesha, Temisha, Timesha, Timisha, Tomesha, Tomiese, Tomise, Tomisha, Tramesha, Tramisha, Tymesha

Tamiko (Japanese) child
of the people.
**Tami, Tamica, Tamieka,
Tamika, Tamike, Tamikia,
Tamikka, Tamiqua,
Tamiyo, Timika, Timikia,
Tomika, Tymika,
Tymmicka**

Tamila (American)
a combination of the
prefix Ta + Mila.
**Tamala, Tamela, Tamelia,
Tamilla, Tamille, Tamillia,
Tamilya**

Tammi, Tammie (English)
alternate forms of Tammy.
**Tameia, Tamia, Tamiah,
Tamie, Tamijo, Tamiya**

Tammy (Hebrew) a familiar
form of Tamara. (English)
twin.
**Tamilyn, Tamlyn,
Tammee, Tammey,
Tammi, Tammie, Tamy,
Tamya**

Tamra (Hebrew) a short
form of Tamara.
Tammra, Tamrah

Tana (Slavic) a short form
of Tanya.
**Taina, Tanae, Tanaeah,
Tanah, Tanairi, Tanairy,
Tanalia, Tanara, Tanas,
Tanasha, Tanashea,
Tanavia, Tanaya, Tanaz,
Tanea, Tania, Tanna,
Tannah**

Tandy (English) team.
**Tanda, Tandalaya, Tandi,
Tandie, Tandis, Tandra,
Tandrea, Tandria**

Taneisha, Tanesha
(American) a combination
of the prefix Ta + Nesha.
**Tahniesha, Tanasha,
Tanashia, Taneesha,
Taneshea, Taneshia,
Tanesia, Tanesian,
Tanessa, Tanessia,
Taniesha, Tanneshia,
Tanniecia, Tanniesha,
Tantashea**

Taneya (Russian, Slavic)
an alternate form of Tanya.
**Tanea, Tanee, Taneé,
Taneia**

Tangia (American)
a combination of the
prefix Ta + Angela.
**Tangela, Tangi, Tangie,
Tanja, Tanji, Tanjia, Tanjie**

Tani (Japanese) valley.
(Slavic) stand of glory.
A familiar form of Tania.
**Tahni, Tahnie, Tanee,
Taney, Tanie, Tany**

Tania (Russian, Slavic) fairy
queen. A form of Tanya,
Titania.
**Taneea, Tanija, Tanika,
Tanis, Taniya, Tannia,
Tannica, Tannis, Tanniya,
Tannya, Tarnia**

Taniel (American)
a combination of
Tania + Danielle.

Taniel *(cont.)*
**Taniele, Tanielle, Teniel,
Teniele, Tenielle**

Tanis, Tannis (Slavic)
forms of Tania, Tanya.
**Tanesa, Tanese, Taniese,
Tanisa, Tanissa, Tanka,
Tannesa, Tannese,
Tanniece, Tanniese,
Tannisa, Tannise, Tannus,
Tannyce, Tenice, Tenise,
Tennessa, Tonise, Tranice,
Tranise, Tranissa, Tynice,
Tyniece, Tyniese, Tynise**

Tanisha (American)
a combination of the
prefix Ta + Nisha.
**Tahniscia, Tahnisha,
Tanicha, Taniesha, Tanish,
Tanishah, Tanishia,
Tanitia, Tannicia,
Tannisha, Tenisha,
Tenishka, Tinisha,
Tonisha, Tonnisha,
Tynisha**

Tanita (American)
a combination of the
prefix Ta + Nita.
**Taneta, Tanetta, Tanitra,
Tanitta, Teneta, Tenetta,
Tenita, Tenitta, Tyneta,
Tynetta, Tynette, Tynita,
Tynitra, Tynitta**

Tanith (Phoenician)
Mythology: the goddess
of love.
Tanitha

Tansy (Greek) immortal.
(Latin) tenacious,
persistent.
**Tancy, Tansee, Tansey,
Tanshay, Tanzey**

Tanya (Russian, Slavic)
fairy queen. A short form
of Tatiana.
**Tahnee, Tahnya, Tana,
Tanaya, Taneya, Tania,
Tanis, Taniya, Tanka,
Tannis, Tanoya, Tany,
Tanyia, Taunya, Tawnya,
Thanya**

Tao (Chinese, Vietnamese)
peach.

Tara (Aramaic) throw;
carry. (Irish) rocky hill.
(Arabic) a measurement.
**Taira, Tairra, Taraea,
Tarah, Taráh, Tarai,
Taralee, Tarali, Taralyn,
Taran, Tarasa, Tarasha,
Taraya, Tarha, Tari, Tarra,
Taryn, Tayra, Tehra**

Taraneh (Persian) melody.

Taree (Japanese) arching
branch.
Tarea, Tareya, Tari, Taria

Tari (Irish) a familiar form
of Tara.
**Taria, Tarika, Tarila,
Tarilyn, Tarin, Tarina,
Taris, Tarisa, Tarise,
Tarisha, Tarissa, Tarita**

Tarra (Irish) an alternate
form of Tara.
Tarrah

Taryn (Irish) an alternate
form of Tara.
**Taran, Tareen, Tareena,
Taren, Tarene, Tarin,
Tarina, Tarren, Tarrena,
Tarrin, Tarron, Tarryn,
Taryna**

Tasarla (Gypsy) dawn.

Tasha (Greek) born on
Christmas day. (Russian)
a short form of Natasha.
See also Tashi, Tosha.
**Tacha, Tachia, Tachiana,
Tachika, Tahsha, Tasenka,
Tashana, Tashka, Tasia,
Taska, Thasha, Tysha**

Tashana (American)
a combination of the
prefix Ta + Shana.
**Tashanda, Tashani,
Tashanika, Tashanna,
Tashiana, Tishana,
Tishani, Tishanna,
Tishanne, Toshanna,
Toshanti, Tyshana**

Tashawna (American)
a combination of the
prefix Ta + Shawna.
**Tashauna, Tashawanna,
Tashonda, Tashondra,
Tiashauna, Tishawn,
Tishunda, Tishunta,
Toshauna, Toshawna,
Tyshauna, Tyshawna**

Tasheena (American)
a combination of the
prefix Ta + Sheena.
Tasheeni, Tashena,
**Tashenna, Tashina,
Tisheena, Tosheena,
Tysheana, Tysheena,
Tyshyna**

Tashelle (American)
a combination of the
prefix Ta + Shelley.
**Tachell, Tashell, Techell,
Techelle, Teshell, Teshelle,
Tochell, Tochelle, Toshelle,
Tychell, Tychelle, Tyshell,
Tyshelle**

Tashi (Slavic) a form
of Tasha. (Hausa) a bird
in flight.
**Tashia, Tashiana, Tashika,
Tashima, Tashina, Tashira**

Tasia (Slavic) a familiar
form of Tasha.
**Tasiya, Tassi, Tassia,
Tassiana, Tassie, Tasya**

Tasida (Sarcee) horse rider.

Tassos (Greek) an alternate
form of Theresa.

Tata (Russian) a familiar
form of Tatiana.
Tatia

Tate (English) a short form
of Tatum. An alternate
form of Taite, Tata.

Tatiana (Slavic) fairy
queen. A feminine form
of Tatius. See also Tiana,
Tanya.
**Taitiann, Taitianna, Tata,
Tatania, Tatanya, Tati,
Tatia, Tatie, Tatihana,**

Tatiana (cont.)
Tatjana, Tatyana,
Tatyanah, Tatyanna,
Tiana, Tiatiana

Tatum (English) cheerful.
Tate, Tatumn

Taura (Latin) bull.
Astrology: Taurus is
a sign of the zodiac.
Taurina

Tavia (Latin) a short form
of Octavia. See also Tawia.
Taiva, Tauvia, Tava, Tavah,
Tavie, Tavita

Tavie (Scottish) twin.
A feminine form of Tavish.

Tawanna (American)
a combination of the
prefix Ta + Wanda.
Taiwana, Taiwanna,
Taquana, Taquanna,
Tawan, Tawana, Tawanda,
Tawanne, Tequana,
Tequanna, Tequawna,
Tewanna, Tewauna,
Tiquana, Tiwanna,
Tiwena, Towanda,
Towanna, Tywania,
Tywanna

Tawia (African) born
after twins. (Polish)
a form of Tavia.

Tawny (Gypsy) little one.
(English) brownish yellow,
tan.
Tahnee, Tany, Tauna,
Tauné, Tauni, Taunia,
Taunisha, Tawna, Tawnee,
Tawnesha, Tawney, Tawni,
Tawnia, Tawnie, Tawnyell,
Tiawna, Tiawni

Tawnya (American)
a combination of
Tawny + Tonya.

Taye (English) a short form
of Taylor.
Tay, Taya, Tayah, Tayana,
Tayiah, Tayna, Tayra,
Taysha, Taysia, Tayva,
Tayvonne, Teyanna,
Teyona, Teyuna, Tiaya,
Tiya, Tiyah, Tiyana, Tye

Taylor (English) tailor.
Tailor, Taiylor, Talor,
Talora, Taye, Tayla, Taylar,
Tayler, Tayllor, Taylore

Tazu (Japanese) stork;
longevity.
Taz, Tazi, Tazia

Teagan (Welsh) beautiful,
attractive.
Taegen, Teaghen, Teegan,
Teeghan, Tega, Tegan,
Teghan, Tegin, Tegwen,
Teigan, Tejan, Tiegan,
Tigan, Tijan, Tijana

Teal (English) river duck;
blue green.
Teala, Teale, Tealia,
Tealisha

Teanna (American)
a combination of the
prefix Te + Anna. An alternate form of Tina.
Teana, Teann, Teanne,
Teaunna, Teena, Teuana

Teca (Hungarian) a form
of Theresa.
Techa, Teka, Tica, Tika

Tecla (Greek) God's fame.
Tekla

Teddi (Greek) a familiar
form of Theodora.
**Tedde, Teddey, Teddie,
Teddy**

Tedra (Greek) a short form
of Theodora.
**Teddra, Teddreya, Tedera,
Teedra, Teidra**

Temira (Hebrew) tall.
Temora, Timora

Tempest (French) stormy.
**Tempeste, Tempestt,
Tempistt, Tempress,
Tempteste**

Tenesha (American)
a combination of the
prefix Te + Nesha.
**Tenecia, Teneesha,
Teneisha, Tenesha,
Teneshia, Tenesia,
Tenessa, Teneusa,
Tenezya, Teniesha**

Tennille (American)
a combination of the
prefix Te + Nellie.
**Taniel, Tanille, Teneal,
Teneil, Teneille, Teniel,
Tenille, Tenneal, Tenneill,
Tenneille, Tennia, Tennie,
Tennielle, Tennile, Tineal,
Tiniel, Tonielle, Tonille**

Teodora (Czech) a form
of Theodora.
Teadora

Tequila (Spanish)
an alcoholic cocktail.
See also Takila.
**Taquela, Taquella,
Taquila, Taquilla, Tequilia,
Tequilla, Tiquila, Tiquilia**

Tera, Terra (Latin) earth.
(Japanese) swift arrow.
Teria, Terria

Teralyn (American)
a combination of
Terri + Lynn.
**Teralyn, Teralynn,
Terralin, Terralyn**

Teresa (Greek) reaper.
An alternate form of
Theresa. See also Tressa.
**Taresa, Tarese, Taress,
Taressa, Taris, Tarisa,
Tarise, Tarissa, Teca,
Terasa, Tercza, Tereasa,
Tereatha, Tereese, Tereka,
Terese, Teresea, Teresha,
Teresia, Teresina, Teresita,
Tereska, Tereson, Teress,
Teressa, Teretha, Terez,
Tereza, Terezia, Terezie,
Terezilya, Terezinha,
Terezka, Terezsa, Teri,
Teris, Terisa, Terisha,
Teriza, Terrasa, Terresa,
Terresia, Terrosina, Tersa,
Teruska, Terza, Teté**

Teri (Greek) reaper.
A familiar form of Theresa.
Terie

Terrelle (Greek) an alternate form of Theresa.
Teral, Terall, Terel, Terell, Teriel, Terral, Terrall, Terrell, Terrella, Terriel, Terrill, Terryl, Terryll, Terrylle, Teryl, Tyrell, Tyrelle

Terrene (Latin) smooth. A feminine form of Terrence.
Tareena, Tarena, Teran, Teranee, Tereena, Terena, Terencia, Terene, Terenia, Terentia, Terina, Terran, Terren, Terrena, Terrin, Terrina, Terron, Terrosina, Terryn, Terun, Teryn, Teryna, Terynn, Tyreen, Tyrene

Terri (Greek) reaper. A familiar form of Theresa.
Terree, Terria, Terrie

Terriann (American) a combination of Terri + Ann.
Terian, Teriana, Teriann, Terianna, Terianne, Terria, Terrian, Terrianna, Terrianne, Terriyanna

Terrica (American) a combination of Terri + Erica. See also Rica.
Terica, Tericka, Terika, Terreka, Terricka, Terrika, Tyrica, Tyricka, Tyrika, Tyrikka

Terry (Greek) a short form of Theresa.
Tere, Teree, Terelle, Terene, Teri, Terie, Terrey, Terri, Terrie, Terrye, Tery

Terry-Lynn (American) a combination of Terry + Lynn.
Terelyn, Terelynn, Terri-Lynn, Terrilynn, Terrylynn

Tertia (Latin) third.
Tercia, Tercina, Tercine, Terecena, Tersia, Terza

Tess (Greek) a short form of Quintessa, Theresa.

Tessa (Greek) reaper. A short form of Theresa.
Tesa, Tesha, Tesia, Tessia, Tezia

Tessie (Greek) a familiar form of Theresa.
Tessey, Tessi, Tessy, Tezi

Tetsu (Japanese) strong as iron.

Tetty (English) a familiar form of Elizabeth.

Tevy (Cambodian) angel.
Teva

Thaddea (Greek) courageous. (Latin) praiser. A feminine form of Thaddeus.
Thada, Thadda

Thalassa (Greek) sea, ocean.

Thalia (Greek) an alternate form of Talia. Mythology: the Muse of comedy.
Thaleia, Thalie, Thalya

Thana (Arabic) happy occasion.
Thaina

Thanh (Vietnamese) bright blue. (Punjabi) good place.
Thantra, Thanya

Thao (Vietnamese) respectful of parents.

Thea (Greek) goddess. A short form of Althea.
Theo

Thelma (Greek) willful.
Thelmalina

Thema (African) queen.

Theodora (Greek) gift of God. See also Dora, Dorothy, Feodora.
Taedra, Teddy, Tedra, Teodora, Teodory, Teodosia, Theda, Thedorsha, Thedrica, Theo, Theodosia, Theodra

Theone (Greek) gift of God.
Theondra, Theoni, Theonie

Theophania (Greek) God's appearance. See also Tiffany.
Theo, Theophanie

Theophila (Greek) loved by God.
Theo

Theresa (Greek) reaper. See also Resi, Reza, Riza, Tassos, Teca, Tracey, Tracy, Zilya.
Teresa, Terri, Terry, Tess, Tessa, Tessie, Theresina, Theresita, Theressa, Thereza, Thersa, Thersea, Tresha, Tressa, Trice

Therese (Greek) an alternate form of Theresa.
Terese, Terise, Terrise, Thérèse, Theresia, Theressa, Therra, Therressa, Thersa

Theta (Greek) Linguistics: a letter in the Greek alphabet.

Thetis (Greek) disposed. Mythology: the mother of Achilles.

Thi (Vietnamese) poem.
Thia, Thy, Thya

Thirza (Hebrew) pleasant.
Therza, Thirsa, Thirzah, Thursa, Thurza, Thyrza, Tirshka, Tirza

Thomasina (Hebrew) twin. A feminine form of Thomas. See also Tamassa, Tammy.
Thomasa, Thomasia, Thomasin, Thomasine, Thomazine, Thomencia, Thomethia, Thomisha, Thomsina, Toma, Tomasa, Tomasina, Tomasine, Tomina, Tommie, Tommina

Thora (Scandinavian)
thunder. A feminine form
of Thor.
**Thordia, Thordis, Thorri,
Thyra, Tyra**

Thuy (Vietnamese) gentle.

Tia (Greek) princess.
(Spanish) aunt.
**Ti, Téa, Teah, Teeya,
Teia, Tiaisha, Tiajuanna,
Tiakeisha, Tialeigh,
Tiamarie, Tianda,
Tiandria, Tianeka,
Tianika, Tiante,
Tiashauna, Tiawanna, Tiia**

Tiana (Greek) princess.
(Latin) a short form of
Tatiana.
**Teana, Teanna, Tia,
Tiahna, Tianna, Tiaon**

Tiara (Latin) crowned.
**Teair, Teaira, Teairra,
Teara, Téare, Tearra,
Tearia, Tearria, Teearia,
Teira, Teirra, Tiaira,
Tiairra, Tiarra, Tiera,
Tiéra, Tierra, Tierre,
Tierrea, Tierria, Tyara,
Tyarra**

Tiberia (Latin) Geography:
the Tiber River in Italy.
Tib, Tibbie, Tibby

Tida (Thai) daughter.

Tierney (Irish) noble.
Tiernan

Tiff (Latin) a short form
of Tiffanie.

Tiffani, Tiffanie (Latin)
alternate forms of Tiffany.
**Tephanie, Tifanee, Tifani,
Tifanie, Tiff, Tiffanee,
Tiffayne, Tiffeni, Tiffenie,
Tiffennie, Tiffiani,
Tiffianie, Tiffine, Tiffini,
Tiffinie, Tiffni, Tiffy,
Tiffynie, Tifni, Tiphani,
Tiphanie**

Tiffany (Greek) a short
form of Theophania.
(Latin) trinity. See also
Tyfany.
**Taffanay, Taffany, Tifaney,
Tifany, Tiff, Tiffaney,
Tiffani, Tiffanie, Tiffanny,
Tiffeney, Tiffiany, Tiffiney,
Tiffiny, Tiffnay, Tiffney,
Tiffny, Tiffy, Tiphany,
Triffany**

Tiffy (Latin) a familiar form
of Tiffani, Tiffany.
Tiffey, Tiffi, Tiffie

Tijuana (Spanish)
Geography: a border town
in Mexico.
**Tajuana, Tajuanna,
Thejuana, Tiajuana,
Tiawanna**

Tilda (German) a short
form of Matilda.
**Tilde, Tildie, Tildy, Tylda,
Tyldy**

Tillie (German) a familiar
form of Matilda.
Tilli, Tilly, Tillye

Timi (English) a familiar
form of Timothea.
Timia, Timie

Timothea (English) honoring God. A feminine form
of Timothy.
Thea, Timmi, Timmie

Tina (Spanish, American)
a short form of Augustine,
Martina, Christina,
Valentina.
**Teanna, Teena, Teina,
Tena, Tenae, Tine, Tinnia,
Tyna, Tynka**

Tinble (English) sound
bells make.
Tynble

Tinesha (American)
a combination of the
prefix Ti + Nesha.
**Timnesha, Tinecia,
Tinesha, Tineshia,
Tiniesha, Tinsia**

Tiponya (Native American)
great horned owl.
Tipper

Tipper (Irish) water pourer.
(Native American) a short
form of Tiponya.

Tira (Hindi) arrow.
Tirah, Tirea, Tirena

Tirtha (Hindi) ford.

Tirza (Hebrew) pleasant.
**Thersa, Thirza, Tierza,
Tirsa, Tirzah, Tirzha,
Tyrzah**

Tisa (Swahili) ninth-born.
Tisah, Tysa, Tyssa

Tish (Latin) an alternate
form of Tisha.

Tisha (Latin) joy. A short
form of Leticia.
**Taesha, Tesha, Teisha,
Tiesha, Tieshia, Tish,
Tishal, Tishia, Tysha,
Tyshia**

Tita (Greek) giant.
(Spanish) a short form
of names ending in "tita."
A feminine form of Titus.

Titania (Greek) giant.
Mythology: the Titans
were a race of giants.
**Tania, Teata, Tita,
Titanna, Titanya,
Titianna, Tiziana, Tytan,
Tytania**

Tivona (Hebrew) nature
lover.

Tiwa (Zuni) onion.

Tobi (Hebrew) God is
good. A feminine form
of Tobias.
**Tobe, Tobee, Tobey, Tobie,
Tobit, Toby, Tobye, Tova,
Tovah, Tove, Tovi, Tybi,
Tybie**

Tocarra (American)
a combination of the
prefix To + Cara.
Tocara, Toccara

Toinette (French) a short form of Antoinette.
Toinetta, Tola, Tonetta, Tonette, Toni, Toniette, Twanette

Toki (Japanese) hopeful.
Toko, Tokoya, Tokyo

Tola (Polish) a form of Toinette.
Tolsia

Tomi (Japanese) rich.
Tomie, Tomiju

Tommie (Hebrew) a short form of Thomasina.
Tomme, Tommi, Tommia, Tommy

Tomo (Japanese) intelligent.
Tomoko

Tonesha (American) a combination of the prefix To + Nesha.
Toneisha, Toneisheia, Tonesha, Tonesia, Toniece, Toniesha, Tonisa, Tonneshia

Toni (Greek) flourishing. (Latin) praiseworthy. A short form of Antoinette, Antonia, Toinette.
Tonee, Toney, Tonia, Tonie, Tony

Tonia (Latin, Slavic) an alternate form of Toni, Tonya.
Tonja, Tonje, Tonna,
Tonni, Tonnia, Tonnie, Tonnja

Tonya (Slavic) fairy queen.
Tonia, Tonnya, Tonyetta

Topaz (Latin) golden yellow gem.

Topsy (English) on top. Literature: a slave in Harriet Beecher Stowe's novel *Uncle Tom's Cabin*.
Topspsy, Topsey, Topsie

Tora (Japanese) tiger.

Tori (Japanese) bird. (English) an alternate form of Tory.
Toria, Toriana, Torie, Torri, Torria, Torrie, Torrina, Torrita

Toriana (English) an alternate form of Tory.
Torian, Toriann, Torianna, Torianne

Torilyn (English) an alternate form of Tory.
Torilynn, Torrilyn, Torrilynn

Tory (Latin) a short form of Victoria. (English) victorious.
Torey, Tori, Torrey, Torreya, Torrye, Torya, Torye, Toya

Tosha (Punjabi) armaments. (Polish) a familiar form of Antonia. (Russian) an alternate form of Tasha.

Toshea, Toshia, Toshiea, Toshke, Tosia, Toska

Toshi (Japanese) mirror image.
Toshie, Toshiko, Toshikyo

Toski (Hopi) squash bug.

Totsi (Hopi) moccasins.

Tottie (English) a familiar form of Charlotte.
Tota, Totti, Totty

Tovah (Hebrew) good.
Tova, Tovia

Toya (Spanish) a form of Tory.
Toia, Toyanika, Toyanna, Toyea, Toylea, Toyleah, Toylenn, Toylin, Toylyn

Tracey (Greek) a familiar form of Theresa. (Latin) warrior.
Trace, Tracee, Tracell, Traci, Tracie, Tracy, Traice, Trasey, Treesy

Traci, Tracie (Latin) alternate forms of Tracey.
Tracia, Tracilee, Tracilyn, Tracilynn, Tracina, Traeci

Tracy (Greek) a familiar form of Theresa. (Latin) warrior.
Treacy

Tralena (Latin) a combination of Tracy + Lena.
Traleen, Tralene, Tralin, Tralinda, Tralyn, Tralynn, Tralynne

Tranesha (American) a combination of the prefix Tra + Nesha.
Traneice, Traneis, Traneise, Traneisha, Traneshia

Trava (Czech) spring grasses.

Trella (Spanish) a familiar form of Estelle.

Tresha (Greek) an alternate form of Theresa.
Trescha, Trescia, Treshana, Treshia

Tressa (Greek) a short form of Theresa.
Treaser, Tresa, Tresca, Trese, Tresha, Treska, Tressia, Tressie, Trez, Treza, Trisa

Trevina (Irish) prudent. (Welsh) homestead. A feminine form of Trevor.
Treva, Trevanna, Trevenia, Trevonna

Triana (Greek) an alternate form of Trina. (Latin) third.
Tria, Triann, Trianna, Trianne

Trice (Greek) a short form of Theresa.
Treece

Tricia (Latin) an alternate form of Trisha.
Trica, Tricha, Trichelle, Tricina, Trickia

Trilby (English) soft hat.
Tribi, Trilbie, Trillby

Trina (Greek) pure. A short
form of Katrina. (Hindi)
points of sacred kusa
grass.
**Treena, Treina, Trenna,
Triana, Trinia, Trinchen,
Trind, Trinda, Trine,
Trinette, Trinica, Trinice,
Triniece, Trinika, Trinique,
Trinisa, Trinnette, Tryna**

Trinity (Latin) triad.
Religion: the Father, the
Son, and the Holy Spirit.
Trini, Trinita

Trish (Latin) a short form
of Beatrice, Trisha.
Trishell, Trishelle

Trisha (Latin) noblewoman.
A familiar form of Patricia.
(Hindi) thirsty. See also
Tricia.
**Treasha, Trish, Trishann,
Trishanna, Trishanne,
Trishara, Trishia, Trishna,
Trissha**

Trissa (Latin) a familiar
form of Patricia.
**Trisa, Trisanne, Trisia,
Trisina, Trissi, Trissie,
Trissy, Tryssa**

Trista (Latin) a short form
of Tristen.
**Trisatal, Tristess, Tristia,
Trysta, Trystia**

Tristen (Latin) bold. A feminine form of Tristan.

**Trista, Tristian, Tristiana,
Tristin, Tristina, Tristine,
Trystan**

Trixie (American) a familiar
form of Beatrice.
**Tris, Trissie, Trissina, Trix,
Trixi, Trixy**

Troya (Irish) foot soldier.
Troi, Troia, Troiana

Trudel (Dutch) a form
of Trudy.

Trudy (German) a familiar
form of Gertrude.
**Truda, Trude, Trudessa,
Trudey, Trudi, Trudie**

Tryna (Greek) an alternate
form of Trina.
Tryane, Tryanna, Trynee

Tsigana (Hungarian) an
alternate form of Zigana.
Tsigane, Tzigana, Tzigane

Tu (Chinese) jade.

Tuesday (English) second
day of the week.
Tuesdey

Tula (Hindi) born in the
lunar month of Capricorn.
Tulah, Tulla, Tullah, Tuula

Tullia (Irish) peaceful,
quiet.
Tulia, Tulliah

Tulsi (Hindi) basil,
a sacred Hindi herb.
Tulsia

Turquoise (French) blue
green, semi-precious stone

originally brought to
Europe through Turkey.
**Turkois, Turkoise,
Turkoys, Turkoyse**

Tusa (Zuni) prairie dog.

Tuyen (Vietnamese) angel.

Tuyet (Vietnamese) snow.

Twyla (English) woven
of double thread.
Twila, Twilla

Tyanna (American)
a combination of the
prefix Ty + Anna.
Tya, Tyana, Tyann, Tyanne

Tyesha (American)
a combination of the
prefix Ty + Aisha.
Tyisha

Tyfany (American) a short
form of Tiffany.
**Tyfani, Tyfanny, Tyffani,
Tyffanni, Tyffany, Tyffini,
Typhanie, Typhany**

Tyler (English) tailor.
Tyller, Tylor

Tyna (Czech) a short form
of Kristina.

Tyne (English) river.
**Tine, Tyna, Tynelle,
Tynessa, Tynetta**

Tynesha (American)
a combination of the
prefix Ty + Nesha.
**Tynaise, Tynece, Tyneicia,
Tynesa, Tynesha,
Tyneshia, Tyniesha,
Tynisha, Tyseisha**

Tyra (Scandinavian) battler.
Mythology: Tyr was the
god of battle.
**Tyraa, Tyrah, Tyran,
Tyree, Tyrell, Tyrelle,
Tyrena, Tyrene, Tyresa,
Tyresia, Tyria, Tyrica,
Tyricka, Tyrikka, Tyrina,
Tyronica**

U (Korean) gentle.

Udele (English) prosperous.
**Uda, Udella, Udelle,
Yudelle**

Ula (Basque) the Virgin
Mary. (Irish) sea jewel.
(Spanish) a short form
of Eulalia. (Scandinavian)
wealthy.
Uli, Ulla

Ulani (Polynesian) cheerful.
Ulana, Ulane

Ulima (Arabic) astute; wise.
Ullima

Ulla (Latin) a short form
of Ursula. (German,
Swedish) willful.
Ulli

Ulrica (German) wolf
ruler; ruler of all. A feminine form of Ulric. See
also Rica.

Ulrica (cont.)
Ulka, Ullrica, Ullricka, Ullrika, Ulrika, Ulrike

Ultima (Latin) last, endmost, farthest.

Ululani (Hawaiian) heavenly inspiration.

Ulva (German) wolf.

Uma (Hindi) mother. Religion: another name for the Hindu goddess Shakti.

Umay (Turkish) hopeful.

Umeko (Japanese) plum blossom child; patient.
Ume, Umeyo

Una (Latin) one; united. (Irish) a form of Agnes. (Hopi) good memory. See also Oona.
Unna, Uny

Undine (Latin) little wave. Mythology: the Undines were water sprites. See also Ondine.
Undeen, Undene

Unice (English) a form of Eunice.

Unique (Latin) only one.
Unica, Uniqua

Unity (English) unity.
Unita, Unitee

Unn (Norwegian) she who is loved.

Unna (German) woman.

Urania (Greek) heavenly. Mythology: the Muse of astronomy.
Urainia, Uranie, Uraniya, Uranya

Urbana (Latin) city dweller.
Urbanah, Urbanna

Urika (Omaha) useful to everyone.

Urit (Hebrew) bright.
Urice

Ursa (Greek) a short form of Ursula. (Latin) an alternate form of Orsa.
Ursey, Ursi, Ursie, Ursy

Ursula (Greek) little bear. See also Sula, Ulla, Vorsila.
Ursa, Ursala, Ursel, Ursela, Ursella, Ursely, Ursilla, Ursillane, Ursola, Ursule, Ursulina, Ursuline, Urszula, Urszuli, Urzula

Usha (Hindi) sunrise.

Ushi (Chinese) ox. Astrology: a sign of the zodiac.

Uta (German) rich. (Japanese) poem.
Utako

Utina (Native American) woman of my country.

Vail (English) valley.
Vale, Vayle

Val (Latin) a short form
of Valentina, Valerie.

Vala (German) singled out.
Valla

Valarie (Latin) an alternate
form of Valerie.
Valaria

Valda (German) famous
ruler. A feminine form
of Valdemar.
Valida, Velda

Valencia (Spanish) strong.
Geography: a region in
eastern Spain.
**Valecia, Valence, Valenica,
Valentia, Valenzia**

Valene (Latin) a short form
of Valentina.
**Valaine, Valean, Valeda,
Valeen, Valen, Valena,
Valeney, Valien, Valina,
Valine, Vallan, Vallen**

Valentina (Latin) strong.
History: Valentina
Tereshkova, a Soviet
cosmonaut, was the first
woman in space. See also
Tina, Valene, Valli.

**Val, Valantina, Vale,
Valentijn, Valentin,
Valentine, Valiaka, Valida,
Valka, Valtina, Valyn,
Valynn, Velora**

Valera (Russian) a form
of Valerie. See also Lera.

Valerie (Latin) strong.
**Vairy, Val, Valarae,
Valaree, Valarey, Valari,
Valaria, Valarie, Vale,
Valera, Valeree, Valeri,
Valeria, Valeriana,
Valeriane, Valérie, Valery,
Valerye, Valka, Vallarie,
Valleree, Valleri, Vallerie,
Vallery, Valli, Vallirie,
Valora, Valry, Valya,
Veleria, Velerie, Waleria**

Valeska (Slavic) glorious
ruler. A feminine form
of Vladislav.
**Valese, Valeshia, Valezka,
Valisha**

Valli (Latin) a familiar form
of Valentina, Valerie.
Botany: a plant native
to India.
Vallie, Vally

Valma (Finnish) loyal
defender.

Valonia (Latin) shadow
valley.
Vallon, Valona

Valora (Latin) an alternate
form of Valerie.
**Valori, Valoria, Valorie,
Valory, Valorya**

Vanda (German) an alternate form of Wanda.
Vandana, Vandella, Vandetta, Vandi, Vannda

Vanessa (Greek) butterfly. Literature: a name invented by Jonathan Swift as a nickname for Esther Vanhomrigh. See also Nessie.
Van, Vanassa, Vanesa, Vanesha, Vaneshia, Vanesia, Vanesse, Vanessia, Vanessica, Vanetta, Vaneza, Vania, Vaniece, Vaniessa, Vanija, Vanika, Vanisa, Vanissa, Vanita, Vanna, Vannessa, Vanneza, Vanni, Vannie, Vanny, Vanya, Varnessa, Venessa

Vanetta (English) a form of Vanessa.
Vaneta, Vanita, Vanneta, Vannetta, Vannita, Venetta

Vanity (English) vain.
Vanita, Vanitty

Vanna (Greek) a short form of Vanessa. (Cambodian) golden.
Vana, Vanae, Vannah, Vannalee, Vannaleigh

Vanora (Welsh) white wave.
Vannora

Vantrice (American) a combination of the prefix Van + Trice.

Vantrece, Vantricia, Vantrisa, Vantrissa

Vanya (Russian) a familiar form of Anna.
Vania, Vanina

Varda (Hebrew) rose.
Vadit, Vardia, Vardice, Vardina, Vardis, Vardit

Varvara (Latin) a form of Barbara.
Vara, Varenka, Varina, Varinka, Varya, Varyusha, Vava, Vavka

Vashti (Persian) lovely. Bible: the wife of Ahasuerus, king of Persia.
Vashtee, Vashtie

Veanna (American) a combination of the prefix Ve + Anna.
Veeana, Veena

Veda (Sanskrit) wise. Religion: the Vedas are the sacred writings of Hinduism.
Vedad, Vedis, Veeda, Veida, Veleda, Vida, Vita

Vedette (Italian) sentry; scout. (French) movie star.
Vedetta

Vega (Arabic) falling star.

Velda (German) an alternate form of Valda.

Velika (Slavic) great, wondrous.

Velma (German) a familiar form of Vilhelmina.

Valma, Vellma, Vilma, Vilna

Velvet (English) velvety.

Venecia (Italian) from Venice.
Vanecia, Vanetia, Veneise, Venesa, Venesha, Venesher, Venesse, Venessia, Venetia, Venette, Venezia, Venice, Venicia, Veniece, Veniesa, Venise, Venisha, Venishia, Venita, Venitia, Venize, Vennesa, Vennice, Vennisa, Vennise, Vonitia, Vonizia

Venessa (Latin) a form of Vanessa.
Venesa

Venus (Latin) love. Mythology: the goddess of love and beauty.
Venis, Venusa, Venusina, Vinny

Vera (Latin) true. (Slavic) faith. A short form of Elvera, Veronica. See also Verena, Wera.
Vara, Veera, Veira, Veradis, Verasha, Vere, Verka, Verla, Viera, Vira

Verbena (Latin) sacred plants including olive, laurel, and myrtle.
Verbeena, Verbina

Verda (Latin) young, fresh.
Verdi, Verdie, Viridiana, Viridis

Verdad (Spanish) truthful.

Verena (Latin) truthful. A familiar form of Vera, Verna.
Verene, Verenis, Vereniz, Verina, Verine, Verinka, Veroshka, Verunka, Verusya, Virna

Verity (Latin) truthful.
Verita, Veritie

Verlene (Latin) a combination of Veronica + Lena.
Verleen, Verlena, Verlin, Verlina, Verlinda, Verline, Verlyn

Verna (Latin) springtime. (French) a familiar form of Laverne. See also Verena, Wera.
Verasha, Verka, Verla, Verne, Vernese, Vernesha, Verneshia, Vernessa, Vernetia, Vernetta, Vernette, Vernia, Vernice, Vernis, Vernisha, Vernisheia, Vernita, Verusya, Viera, Virida, Virna, Virnell

Vernice (Latin) a form of Bernice, Verna.
Vernica, Vernicca, Vernique

Veronica (Latin) true image. See also Ronni, Weronika.
Varonica, Vera, Veranique, Verenice, Verhonica, Verinica, Verohnica,

Veronica *(cont.)*
Veron, Verona, Verone, Veronic, Véronic, Veronice, Veronika, Veronique, Véronique, Veronne, Veronnica, Veruszhka, Vironica, Vonni, Vonnie, Vonny, Vron, Vronica

Veronika (Latin) an alternate form of Veronica.
Varonika, Veronick, Véronick, Veronik, Veronike, Veronka, Veronkia, Veruka

Veronique, Véronique (French) forms of Veronica.

Vespera (Latin) evening star.

Vesta (Latin) keeper of the house. Mythology: the goddess of the home.
Vessy, Vest, Vesteria

Veta (Slavic) a familiar form of Elizabeth.
Veeta, Vita

Vi (Latin, French) a short form of Viola, Violet.
Vye

Vianca (Spanish) a form of Bianca.
Vianeca, Vianica

Vianna (American) a combination of Vi + Anna.
Viana, Viann, Vianne

Vica (Hungarian) a form of Eve.

Vicki (Latin) a familiar form of Victoria.
Vic, Vicci, Vicke, Vickee, Vickiana, Vickie, Vickilyn, Vickki, Vicky, Vika, Viki, Vikie, Vikki

Vicky (Latin) a familiar form of Victoria.
Viccy, Vickey, Viky, Vikkey, Vikky

Victoria (Latin) victorious. See also Tory, Wicktoria, Wisia.
Vicki, Vicky, Victoire, Victoriana, Victorie, Victorina, Victorine, Victory, Viktoria, Vitoria, Vyctoria

Vida (Sanskrit) an alternate form of Veda. (Hebrew) a short form of Davida.
Vidamarie

Vidonia (Portuguese) branch of a vine.
Vedonia, Vidonya

Vienna (Latin) Geography: the capital of Austria.
Veena, Vena, Venna, Vienette, Vienne, Vina

Viktoria (Latin) an alternate form of Victoria.
Viktorie, Viktorija, Viktorina, Viktorine, Viktorka

Vilhelmina (German) an alternate form of Wilhelmina.
Velma, Vilhelmine, Vilma

Villette (French) small town.
Vietta

Vilma (German) a short form of Vilhemina.

Vina (Hebrew) a short form of Davina. (Hindi) Mythology: a musical instrument played by the Hindu goddess of wisdom. (Spanish) vineyard. See also Lavina. (English) a short form of Alvina.
Veena, Vena, Viña, Vinesha, Vinessa, Vinia, Viniece, Vinique, Vinisha, Vinita, Vinna, Vinni, Vinnie, Vinny, Vinora, Vyna

Vincentia (Latin) victor, conqueror. A feminine form of Vincent.
Vicenta, Vincenta, Vincentena, Vincentina, Vincentine, Vincenza, Vincy, Vinnie

Viñita (Spanish) an alternate form of Vina.
Viñeet, Viñeeta, Viñetta, Viñette, Viñitha, Viñta, Viñti, Viñtia, Vyñetta, Vyñette

Viola (Latin) violet; stringed instrument in the violin family. Literature: the heroine of Shakespeare's play *Twelfth Night*.
Vi, Violaine, Violanta, Violante, Viole, Violeine

Violet (French) Botany: a plant with purplish blue flowers.
Vi, Violetta, Violette, Vyolet, Vyoletta, Vyolette

Virgilia (Latin) rod bearer, staff bearer. A feminine form of Virgil.
Virgillia

Virginia (Latin) pure, virginal. Literature: Virginia Woolf was a well-known British writer. See also Gina, Ginger, Ginny, Jinny.
Verginia, Verginya, Virge, Virgen, Virgenia, Virgenya, Virgie, Virgine, Virginie, Virginië, Virginio, Virginnia, Virgy, Virjeana

Viridis (Latin) green.
Virdis, Virida, Viridia, Viridiana

Virtue (Latin) virtuous.

Vita (Latin) life.
Veeta, Veta, Vitaliana, Vitalina, Vitel, Vitella, Vitia, Vitka, Vitke

Vitoria (Spanish) a form of Victoria.
Vittoria

Viv (Latin) a short form of Vivian.

Viva (Latin) a short form of Aviva, Vivian.
Vica, Vivan, Vivva

Viveca (Latin) an alternate form of Vivian.

Viveca (cont.)
Viv, Vivecca, Vivecka, Viveka, Vyveca

Vivian (Latin) full of life.
Vevay, Vevey, Viv, Viva, Viveca, Vivee, Vivi, Vivia, Viviana, Viviane, Vivie, Vivien, Vivienne, Vivina, Vivion, Vivyan, Vyvyan

Viviana (Latin) an alternate form of Vivian.
Viv, Viviann, Vivianna, Vivianne, Vivyana, Vivyann, Vivyanne, Vyvyana, Vyvyann, Vyvyanne

Vondra (Czech) loving woman.
Vonda, Vondrea

Voneisha (American) a combination of Yvonne + Aisha.
Voneishia, Vonesha, Voneshia

Vonna (French) an alternate form of Yvonne.
Vona, Vonni, Vonnie, Vonny

Vontricia (American) a combination of Yvonne + Tricia.
Vontrece, Vontrese, Vontrice, Vontriece

Vorsila (Greek) an alternate form of Ursula.
Vorsilla, Vorsula, Vorsulla, Vorsyla

Wadd (Arabic) beloved.

Wainani (Hawaiian) beautiful water.

Wakana (Japanese) plant.

Wakanda (Dakota) magical power.
Wakenda

Wakeisha (American) a combination of the prefix Wa + Keisha.
Wakeishia, Wakesha, Wakeshia, Wakesia

Walad (Arabic) newborn.
Waladah, Walidah

Walda (German) powerful; famous. A feminine form of Waldo.
Waldina, Waldine, Walida, Wallda, Welda

Waleria (Polish) a form of Valerie.
Wala

Walker (English) cloth; walker.
Wallker

Wallis (English) from Wales. A feminine form of Wallace.
Wallie, Walliss, Wally, Wallys

Wanda (German) wanderer. See also Wendy.
Vanda, Wahnda, Wandah, Wandely, Wandi, Wandie, Wandis, Wandja, Wandy, Wandzia, Wannda, Wonda, Wonnda

Waneta (Native American) charger. See also Juanita.
Waneeta, Wanita, Wanite, Wanneta, Waunita, Wonita, Wonnita, Wynita

Wanetta (English) pale face.
Wanette, Wannetta, Wannette

Wanika (Hawaiian) a form of Juanita.

Warda (German) guardian. A feminine form of Ward.
Wardia, Wardine

Washi (Japanese) eagle.

Wattan (Japanese) homeland.

Wauna (Moquelumnan) snow geese honking.
Waunakee

Wava (Slavic) a form of Barbara.

Waynette (English) wagon maker. A feminine form of Wayne.
Waynel, Waynelle, Waynlyn

Weeko (Dakota) pretty girl.

Wehilani (Hawaiian) heavenly adornment.

Wenda (Welsh) an alternate form of Wendy.
Wendaine, Wendayne,

Wendelle (English) wanderer.
Wendaline, Wendall, Wendalyn, Wendeline, Wendella, Wendelline

Wendi (Welsh) an alternate form of Wendy.
Wendie

Wendy (Welsh) white; light skinned. A familiar form of Gwendolyn, Wanda.
Wenda, Wende, Wendee, Wendey, Wendi, Wendye

Wera (Polish) a form of Vera.
Wiera, Wiercia, Wierka

Weronika (Polish) a form of Veronica.
Weronikra

Wesisa (Musoga) foolish.

Weslee (English) western meadow. A feminine form of Wesley.
Weslea, Weslene, Wesley, Weslia, Weslie, Weslyn

Whitley (English) white field.
Whitely

Whitney (English) white island.
Whiteney, Whitne, Whitné, Whitnee, Whitneigh, Whitnie, Whitny, Whitnye, Whittany, Whitteny,

Whitney *(cont.)*
**Whittney, Whytne,
Whytney, Witney**

Whitnie (English) an alternate form of Whitney.
**Whitani, Whitnei, Whitni,
Whittnie, Whytnie**

Whoopi (English) happy; excited.
Whoopie, Whoopy

Wicktoria (Polish) a form of Victoria.
**Wicktorja, Wiktoria,
Wiktorja**

Wilda (German) untamed. (English) willow.
Willda, Wylda

Wileen (English) a short form of Wilhelmina.
Wilene, Willeen, Willene

Wilhelmina (German) determined guardian. A feminine form of Wilhelm, William. See also Billie, Guillerma, Helma, Minka, Minna, Minnie.
**Vilhelmina, Wileen,
Wilhelmine, Willa,
Willamina, Willamine,
Willemina, Willette,
Williamina, Willie,
Willmina, Willmine,
Wilma, Wimina, Winnie**

Wilikinia (Hawaiian) a form of Virginia.

Willa (German) a short form of Wilhelmina.

**Willabella, Willette,
Williabelle**

Willette (English) a familiar form of Wilhelmina, Willa.
**Wiletta, Wilette, Willetta,
Williette**

Willie (English) a familiar form of Wilhelmina.
**Willi, Willina, Willisha,
Willishia, Willy**

Willow (English) willow tree.

Wilma (German) a short form of Wilhelmina.
**Williemae, Wilmanie,
Wilmayra, Wilmetta,
Wilmette, Wilmina,
Wilmyne, Wylma**

Wilona (English) desired.
Willona, Willone, Wilone

Win (German) a short form of Winifred. See also Edwina.
Wyn

Winda (Swahili) hunter.

Windy (English) windy.
**Windee, Windey, Windi,
Windie, Wyndee, Wyndy**

Winema (Moquelumnan) woman chief.

Winifred (German) peaceful friend. (Welsh) an alternate form of Guinevere. See also Freddi, Una, Winnie.
**Win, Winafred, Winefred,
Winefride, Winfreda,**

**Winfrieda, Winiefrida,
Winifrid, Winifryd,
Winnafred, Winnefred,
Winniefred, Winnifred,
Winnifrid, Wynafred,
Wynifred, Wynnifred**

Winna (African) friend.
Winnah

Winnie (English) a familiar
form of Edwina, Gwyneth,
Winnifred, Winona,
Wynne. History: Winnie
Mandela kept the anti-
aparteid movement alive
in South Africa while her
husband, Nelson Mandela,
was imprisoned. Literature:
the lovable bear in
A. A. Milne's children's
story *Winnie the Pooh*.
**Wina, Winne, Winney,
Winni, Winny, Wynnie**

Winola (German) charming friend.
Wynola

Winona (Lakota) oldest
daughter.
**Wanona, Wenona,
Wenonah, Winnie,
Winonah, Wynnona,
Wynona**

Winter (English) winter.
Wintr, Wynter

Wira (Polish) a form
of Elvira.
Wiria, Wirke

Wisia (Polish) a form
of Victoria.
Wicia, Wikta

Wren (English) wren,
songbird.

Wyanet (Native American)
legendary beauty.
**Wyaneta, Wyanita,
Wynette**

Wynne (Welsh) white,
light skinned. A short form
of Blodwyn, Guinivere,
Gwyneth.
Winnie, Wyn, Wynn

Wyoming (Native
American) Geography:
a western American state.
Wy, Wye, Wyoh, Wyomia

Xandra (Greek) an alternate form of Zandra.
(Spanish) a short form
of Alexandra.
Xander, Xandrea, Xandria

Xanthe (Greek) yellow,
blond. See also Zanthe.
**Xanne, Xantha, Xanthia,
Xanthippe**

Xanthippe (Greek) an
alternate form of Xanthe.
History: Socrates's wife.
Xantippie

Xaviera (Basque) owner
of the new house. (Arabic)
bright. A feminine form

of Xavier. See also Javiera, Zaviera.
Xavia, Xavière, Xavyera

Xela (Quiché) my mountain home.

Xenia (Greek) hospitable. See also Zena, Zina.
Xeenia, Xena

Xiang (Chinese) fragrant.

Xiu Mei (Chinese) beautiful plum.

Xuan (Vietnamese) spring.

Xuxa (Brazilian) a familiar form of Susanna.

Xylia (Greek) a form of Sylvia.
Xylina, Xylona

Yachne (Hebrew) hospitable.

Yael (Hebrew) strength of God. See also Jael.
Yaeli, Yaella, Yeala

Yaffa (Hebrew) beautiful. See also Jaffa.
Yafeal, Yaffit, Yafit

Yalanda (Greek) an alternate form of Yolanda.
Yalando, Yalonda, Ylana, Ylanda

Yalena (Greek, Russian) an alternate form of Helen. See also Lena, Yelena.

Yamary (American) a combination of the prefix Ya + Mary.
Yamairy, Yamarie, Yamaris, Yamayra

Yamelia (American) an alternate form of Amelia.
Yameily, Yamelya, Yamelys

Yamila (Arabic) an alternate form of Jamila.
Yamile, Yamilla, Yamille

Yaminah (Arabic) right, proper.
Yamina, Yamini, Yemina, Yeminah, Yemini

Yamka (Hopi) blossom.

Yamuna (Hindi) sacred river.

Yana (Slavic) an alternate form of Jana.
Yanae, Yanah, Yanet, Yaneth, Yanik, Yanina, Yanis, Yanisha, Yanitza, Yanixia, Yanna, Yannah, Yannica, Yannick, Yannina

Yanaba (Navajo) brave.

Yáng (Chinese) sun.

Yarina (Slavic) a form of Irene.
Yaryna

Yarkona (Hebrew) green.

Yarmilla (Slavic) market trader.

Yasmin, Yasmine (Persian)
alternate forms of Jasmine.
**Yashmine, Yasiman,
Yasimine, Yasma,
Yasmain, Yasmaine,
Yasmeen, Yasmene,
Yasmina, Yasminda,
Yasmon, Yasmyn, Yazmen,
Yazmin, Yazmina,
Yazmine, Yesmean,
Yesmeen, Yesmin,
Yesmina, Yesmine,
Yesmyn**

Yasu (Japanese) resting,
calm.
Yasuko, Yasuyo

Yehudit (Hebrew) an alternate form of Judith.
Yudit, Yudita, Yuta

Yei (Japanese) flourishing.

Yeira (Hebrew) light.

Yekaterina (Russian)
a form of Katherine.

Yelena (Russian) a form
of Helen, Jelena. See also
Lena.
**Yeleana, Yelen, Yelenne,
Yelina, Ylena, Ylenia,
Ylenna**

Yelisabeta (Russian) a form
of Elizabeth.
Yelizaveta

Yemena (Arabic) from
Yemen.
Yemina

Yen (Chinese) yearning;
desirous.
Yeni, Yenih, Yenny

Yenene (Native American)
shaman.

Yeo (Korean) mild.
Yee

Yepa (Native American)
snow girl.

Yera (Basque) Religion:
a name for the Virgin
Mary.

Yesenia (Arabic) flower.
**Yesnia, Yessena, Yessenia,
Yissenia**

Yessica (Hebrew) an alternate form of Jessica.
Yessika, Yesyka

Yetta (English) a short form
of Henrietta.
Yette, Yitta

Yeva (Ukrainian) a form
of Eve.

Yiesha (Arabic, Swahili)
an alternate form of Aisha.

Yín (Chinese) silver.

Ynez (Spanish) a form
of Agnes. See also Inez.
Ynes, Ynesita

Yoanna (Hebrew) an alter-
nate form of Joanna.
**Yoana, Yohana, Yohanka,
Yohanna, Yohannah**

Yoi (Japanese) born in the
evening.

Yoki (Hopi) bluebird.
Yokie

Yoko (Japanese) good girl.
Yo

Yola (Greek) a short form
of Yolanda.
Yoley, Yoli, Yolie, Yoly

Yolanda (Greek) violet
flower. See also Iolanthe,
Jolanda, Olinda.
**Yalanda, Yola, Yolaine,
Yolana, Yoland, Yolande,
Yolane, Yolanna,
Yolantha, Yolanthe,
Yolette, Yolonda,
Yorlanda, Youlanda,
Yulanda, Yulonda**

Yoluta (Native American)
summer flower.

Yon (Burmese) rabbit.
(Korean) lotus blossom.
Yona, Yonna

Yoné (Japanese) wealth;
rice.

Yonina (Hebrew) an alternate form of Jonina.
Yona, Yonah

Yonita (Hebrew) an alternate form of Jonita.
Yonat, Yonati, Yonit

Yoomee (Coos) star.
Yoome

Yordana (Basque) descendant. See also Jordana.

Yori (Japanese) reliable.
Yoriko, Yoriyo

Yosepha (Hebrew) a form
of Josephine.
Yosefa, Yosifa, Yuseffa

Yoshi (Japanese) good;
respectful.
Yoshie, Yoshiko, Yoshiyo

Yovela (Hebrew) joyful
heart; rejoicer.

Ysabel (Spanish) an alter-
nate form of Isabel.
**Ysabell, Ysabella,
Ysabelle, Ysbel, Ysbella,
Ysobel**

Ysanne (American) a combination of Ysabel + Ann.
Ysande, Ysann, Ysanna

Yseult (German) ice rule.
(Irish) fair; light skinned.
(Welsh) an alternate form
of Isolde.
Yseulte, Ysolt

Yuana (Spanish) an alternate form of Juana.
Yuan, Yuanna

Yudelle (English) an alternate form of Udele.
Yudela, Yudell, Yudella

Yudita (Russian) a form
of Judith.

Yuki (Japanese) snow.
Yukie, Yukiko, Yukiyo

Yulene (Basque) a form
of Julia.
Yuleen

Yulia (Russian) a form
of Julia.
**Yula, Yulenka, Yulinka,
Yulka, Yulya**

Yuri (Japanese) lily.
Yuriko, Yuriyo

Yvanna (Slavic) an alternate form of Ivana.
Yvan, Yvana, Yvannia

Yvette (French) a familiar form of Yvonne. See also Evette, Ivette.
Yavette, Yevett, Yevette, Yevetta, Yvetta

Yvonne (French) young archer. (Scandanavian) yew wood; bow wood. A feminine form of Ivar. See also Evonne, Ivonne, Vonna, Yvette.
Yavanda, Yavanna, Yavanne, Yavonda, Yavonna, Yavonne, Yveline, Yvon, Yvone, Yvonna, Yvonny

Zabrina (American) an alternate form of Sabrina.
Zabreena, Zabrinia, Zabrinna, Zabryna

Zacharie (Hebrew) God remembered. A feminine form of Zachariah.
Zacari, Zacceaus, Zacchaea, Zachoia, Zackeisha, Zackery, Zakaria, Zakaya, Zakeshia, Zakiah, Zakir, Zakiya, Zakiyah, Zechari

Zada (Arabic) fortunate, prosperous.
Zaida, Zayda, Zayeda

Zafirah (Arabic) successful; victorious.

Zahar (Hebrew) daybreak; dawn.
Zahera, Zahira, Zahirah

Zahavah (Hebrew) golden.
Zachava, Zachavah, Zechava, Zechavah, Zehava, Zehavi, Zehavit, Zeheva, Zehuva

Zahra (Swahili) flower. (Arabic) white.
Zahara, Zahrah

Zakia (Swahili) smart. (Arabic) chaste.
Zakiah, Zakiyah

Zalika (Swahili) born to royalty.
Zuleika

Zaltana (Native American) high mountain.

Zandra (Greek) an alternate form of Sandra.
Zahndra, Zandrea, Zandria, Zandy, Zanndra, Zondra

Zaneta (Spanish) a form of Jane. A feminine form of Zane.
Zanita, Zanitra

Zanna (Spanish) a form of Jane. (English) a short form of Susanna.
Zana, Zanella, Zanette, Zannah, Zannette

Zanthe (Greek) an alternate form of Xanthe.
Zanth, Zantha

Zara (Hebrew) an alternate form of Sarah, Zora.
Zaira, Zarah, Zaree, Zareen, Zareena, Zaria

Zarifa (Arabic) successful.

Zarita (Spanish) a form of Sarah.

Zasha (Russian) an alternate form of Sasha.
Zascha, Zashenka, Zashka, Zasho

Zaviera (Spanish) a form of Xaviera.
Zavera, Zavirah

Zawati (Swahili) gift.

Zayit (Hebrew) olive.

Zaynah (Arabic) beautiful.
Zayn, Zayna

Zea (Latin) grain.

Zelda (German) a short form of Griselda. (Yiddish) gray haired. See also Selda.
Zelde, Zella, Zellda

Zelene (English) sunshine.
Zeleen, Zelena, Zeline

Zelia (Spanish) sunshine.
Zele, Zelene, Zelie, Zélie, Zelina

Zelizi (Basque) a form of Sheila.

Zelma (German) an alternate form of Selma.

Zemirah (Hebrew) song of joy.

Zena (Greek) an alternate form of Xenia. (Ethiopian) news. (Persian) woman. See also Zina.
Zeena, Zeenat, Zeenet, Zeenia, Zeenya, Zein, Zeina, Zenah, Zenana, Zenea, Zenia, Zenya

Zenaide (Greek) Mythology: a daughter of Zeus.
Zenaida, Zenaïde, Zenayda, Zenochka

Zenda (Persian) sacred; feminine.

Zenobia (Greek) sign, symbol. History: a queen who ruled the city of Palmyra in the Arabian desert.
Zeba, Zeeba, Zenobie, Zenovia

Zephania, Zephanie (Greek) alternate forms of Stephanie.
Zepania, Zephanas, Zephany

Zephyr (Greek) west wind.
Zefiryn, Zephra, Zephria, Zephyer, Zephyrine

Zera (Hebrew) seeds.

Zerdali (Turkish) wild apricot.

Zerlina (Latin, Spanish)
beautiful dawn. Music:
a character in Mozart's
opera *Don Giovanni*.
Zerla, Zerlinda

Zerrin (Turkish) golden.
Zerren

Zeta (English) rose.
Linguistics: the last letter
in the Greek alphabet.
Zayit, Zetana, Zetta

Zetta (Portuguese) rose.

Zhen (Chinese) chaste.

Zia (Latin) grain. (Arabic)
light.
Zea

Zigana (Hungarian) gypsy
girl. See also Tsigana.
Zigane

Zihna (Hopi) one who
spins tops.

Zilla (Hebrew) shadow.
Zila, Zillah, Zylla

Zilpah (Hebrew) dignified.
Bible: Jacob's wife.
Zilpha, Zylpha

Zilya (Russian) a form
of Theresa.

Zimra (Hebrew) song
of praise.
**Zamora, Zemira, Zemora,
Zimria**

Zina (Greek) an alternate
form of Xenia, Zena.
(African) secret spirit.
(English) hospitable.
Zinah, Zine

Zinnia (Latin) Botany:
a plant with beautiful,
rayed, colorful flowers.
**Zinia, Zinny, Zinnya,
Zinya**

Zipporah (Hebrew) bird.
Bible: Moses' wife.
**Zipora, Ziporah, Zipporia,
Ziproh**

Zita (Spanish) rose.
(Arabic) mistress. A short
form of names ending in
"sita" or "zita."
Zeeta, Zyta, Zytka

Ziva (Hebrew) bright;
radiant.
Zeeva, Ziv, Zivanka, Zivit

Zizi (Hungarian) a familiar
form of Elizabeth.
Zsi Zsi

Zocha (Polish) an alternate
form of Sophie.

Zoe (Greek) life.
**Zoé, Zoë, Zoee, Zoelie,
Zoeline, Zoelle, Zoey,
Zoie, Zooey, Zoya**

Zofia (Slavic) an alternate
form of Sophia.
Zofka, Zsofia

Zohar (Hebrew) shining,
brilliant.
Zoheret

Zohra (Hebrew) blossom.

Zohreh (Persian) happy.
Zahreh, Zohrah

Zola (Italian) piece of earth.
Zoela

Zona (Latin) belt, sash.
 Zonia

Zondra (Greek) an alternate form of Zandra.
 Zohndra

Zora (Slavic) aurora; dawn. See also Zara.
 Zorah, Zorana, Zoreen, Zoreena, Zorna, Zorra, Zorrah, Zorya

Zorina (Slavic) golden.
 Zorana, Zori, Zorie, Zorine, Zorna, Zory

Zoya (Slavic) a form of Zoe.
 Zoia, Zoyara, Zoyechka, Zoyenka, Zoyya

Zsa Zsa (Hungarian) a familiar form of Susan.
 Zhazha

Zsofia (Hungarian) a form of Sofia.
 Zofia, Zsofi, Zsofika

Zsuzsanna (Hungarian) a form of Susanna.
 Zsuska, Zsuzsa, Zsuzsi, Zsuzsika, Zsuzska

Zudora (Sanskrit) laborer.

Zuleika (Arabic) brilliant.
 Zeleeka, Zul, Zulay, Zulekha, Zuleyka

Zulima (Arabic) an alternate form of Salama.
 Zuleima, Zulema, Zulemah, Zulimah

Zurafa (Arabic) lovely.
 Ziraf, Zuruf

Zuri (Basque) white; light skinned. (Swahili) beautiful.
 Zuria, Zurisha

Zusa (Czech, Polish) a form of Susan.
 Zuzana, Zuzanka, Zuzia, Zuzka, Zuzu

Zytka (Polish) rose.

Boys' Names

Aaron (Hebrew) enlightened. (Arabic) messenger. Bible: the brother of Moses and the first high priest of the Jews.
Aahron, Aaran, Aaren, Aareon, Aarin, Aaronn, Aarron, Aaryn, Aeron, Aharon, Ahran, Ahren, Aranne, Arek, Aren, Ari, Arin, Aron, Aronek, Aronne, Aronos, Arran, Arron

Aban (Persian) Mythology: a figure associated with water and the arts.

Abasi (Swahili) stern.

Abbey (Hebrew) a familiar form of Abe.
Abbie, Abby

Abbott (Hebrew) father; abbot.
Ab, Abba, Abbah, Abbán, Abbé, Abbot, Abott

Abbud (Arabic) devoted.

Abdul (Arabic) servant.
Abdal, Abdeel, Abdel, Abdoul, Abdual, Abul

Abdulaziz (Arabic) servant of the Mighty.
Abdelazim, Abdelaziz, Abdulazaz, Abdulazeez

Abdullah (Arabic) servant of Allah.
Abdalah, Abdalla, Abdallah, Abdualla, Abdulah, Abdulahi

Abdulrahman (Arabic) servant of the Merciful.
Abdelrahim, Abdelrahman, Abdirahman, Abdolrahem, Abdularahman, Abdurrahman, Abdurram

Abe (Hebrew) a short form of Abel, Abraham.
Abey

Abel (Hebrew) breath. (Assyrian) meadow. (German) a short form of Abelard. Bible: Adam and Eve's second son.
Abe, Abele, Abell, Able, Adal, Avel

Abelard (German) noble; resolute.
Ab, Abalard, Abelhard, Abilard, Adalard, Adelard

Abi (Turkish) older brother.

Abiah (Hebrew) God is my father.
Abia, Abiel, Abija, Abijah, Abisha, Abishai, Aviya, Aviyah

Abie (Hebrew) a familiar form of Abraham.

Abiel (Hebrew) an alternate form of Abiah.

Abir (Hebrew) strong.

Abisha (Hebrew) gift of God.
Abijah, Abishai

Abner (Hebrew) father of light. Bible: the commander of King Saul's army.
Ab, Avner, Ebner

Abraham (Hebrew) father of many nations. Bible: the first Hebrew patriarch. See also Avram, Bram, Ibrahim.
Abarran, Abe, Aberham, Abey, Abhiram, Abie, Abrahamo, Abrahán, Abrahim, Abrahm, Abram, Abramo, Abrán, Abrao, Arram, Avram

Abram (Hebrew) a short form of Abraham. See also Bram.
Abramo, Abrams, Avram

Absalom (Hebrew) father of peace. Bible: the son of King David. See also Avshalom, Axel.
Absalon

Acar (Turkish) bright.

Ace (Latin) unity.
Acer, Acey, Acie

Achilles (Greek) Mythology: a hero of the Trojan war. Literature: the hero of Homer's epic *The Iliad*.

Achill, Achille, Achillea, Achillios, Akil, Akili, Akilles

Ackerley (English) meadow of oak trees.
Accerley, Ackerlea, Ackerleigh, Ackersley, Acklea, Ackleigh, Ackley, Acklie

Acton (English) oak-tree settlement.

Adahy (Cherokee) in the woods.

Adair (Scottish) oak-tree ford.
Adaire, Adare

Adam (Phoenician) man; mankind. (Hebrew) earth; man of the red earth. Bible: the first man created by God. See also Adamson, Addison, Damek, Keddy, Macadam.
Ad, Adama, Adamec, Adamo, Adão, Adas, Addam, Addams, Addis, Addy, Adem, Adham, Adhamh, Adné, Adok, Adomas

Adamec (Czech) a form of Adam.
Adamek, Adamik, Adamka, Adamko, Adamok

Adamson (Hebrew) son of Adam.
Adams, Adamsson, Addamson

Adar (Syrian) ruler, prince. (Hebrew) noble; exalted.
Addar

Addison (English) son of Adam.
Addis, Adison, Adisson

Addy (Hebrew) a familiar form of Adam, Adlai. (German) a familiar form of Adelard.
Addey, Addi, Addie, Ade, Adi

Ade (Yoruba) royal.

Adelard (German) noble; courageous.
Adal, Adalar, Adalard, Addy, Adel, Adél, Adelar

Aden (Arabic) Geography: a region in southern Yemen. (Irish) an alternate form of Aidan.
Aiden

Adham (Arabic) black.

Adil (Arabic) just; wise.
Adeel, Adeele

Adin (Hebrew) pleasant.

Adir (Hebrew) majestic; noble.
Adeer

Adiv (Hebrew) pleasant; gentle.
Adeev

Adlai (Hebrew) my ornament.
Ad, Addy, Adley

Adler (German) eagle.
Ad, Addler, Adlar

Adli (Turkish) just; wise.

Admon (Hebrew) peony.

Adnan (Arabic) pleasant.
Adnaan

Adney (English) noble's island.

Adolf (German) noble wolf. History: Adolf Hitler led Germany to defeat in World War II. See also Dolf.
Ad, Adolfo, Adolfus, Adolph

Adolph (German) an alternate form of Adolf.
Adolphe, Adolpho, Adolphus, Adulphus

Adom (Akan) help from God.

Adon (Greek) a short form of Adonis. (Hebrew) Lord.

Adonis (Greek) highly attractive. Mythology: the attractive youth loved by Aphrodite.
Adon, Adonnis, Adonys

Adri (Indo-Pakistani) rock. (Hindi) Religion: a minor Hindu god.

Adrian (Greek) rich. (Latin) dark. (Swedish) a short form of Hadrian.
Adarian, Ade, Adorjan, Adrain, Adreian, Adreyan, Adri, Adriaan, Adriane, Adriano, Adrien, Adrik, Adrion, Adron, Adryan, Adryon

Adriano (Italian) a form of Adrian.
Adrianno

Adriel (Hebrew) member of God's flock.
Adrial

Adrien (French) a form of Adrian.
Adriene

Adrik (Russian) a form of Adrian.
Adric

Aeneas (Greek) praised. Literature: the Trojan hero of Virgil's epic *Aeneid*. See also Eneas.

Afram (African) Geography: a river in Ghana, Africa.

Afton (English) from Afton, England.
Affton

Agamemnon (Greek) resolute. Mythology: the King of Argos who led the Greeks in the Trojan War.

Agni (Hindi) Religion: the Hindu fire god.

Agu (Ibo) leopard.

Ahab (Hebrew) father's brother. Literature: the captain of the *Pequod* in Herman Melville's novel *Moby Dick*.

Ahanu (Native American) laughter.

Ahdik (Native American) caribou; reindeer.

Ahearn (Scottish) lord of the horses. (English) heron.
Ahearne, Aherin, Ahern, Aherne, Hearn

Ahir (Turkish) last.

Ahmad, Ahmed (Arabic) most highly praised. See also Muhammad.
Achmad, Achmed, Ahamad, Ahamada, Ahamed, Ahmaad, Ahmaud, Amad, Amahd, Amed

Ahmed (Swahili) praise-worthy.

Ahsan (Arabic) charitable.

Aidan (Irish) fiery.
Aden, Adin, Aiden, Aydan, Ayden, Aydin

Aiken (English) made of oak.
Aicken, Aikin, Ayken, Aykin

Aimery (German) an alternate form of Emery.
Aime, Aimerey, Aimeric, Amerey, Aymeric, Aymery

Aimon (French) house. (Irish) an alternate form of Eamon.

Aindrea (Irish) a form of Andrew.
Aindreas

Ainsley (Scottish) my own meadow.
Ainsleigh, Ainslie, Ansley, Aynslee, Aynsley, Aynslie

Aizik (Russian) a form of Isaac.

Ajala (Yoruba) potter.

Ajay (Punjabi) victorious; undefeatable. (American) a combination of the initials A. + J.
Aj, Aja, Ajai, Ajaz, Ajit

Akar (Turkish) flowing stream.
Akara

Akash (Hindi) sky.
Akasha

Akbar (Arabic) great.

Akecheta (Lakota) warrior.

Akemi (Japanese) dawn.

Akil (Arabic) intelligent. Geography: a river in the Basque region.
Ahkeel, Akeel, Akeyla, Akhil, Akiel, Akili

Akim (Hebrew) a short form of Joachim.
Achim, Ackeem, Ackim, Ahkieme, Akeam, Akee, Akeem, Akiem, Akima, Arkeem

Akins (Yoruba) brave.

Akira (Japanese) intelligent.
Akihito, Akio, Akiyo

Akiva (Hebrew) an alternate form of Jacob.
Akiba, Kiva

Akmal (Arabic) perfect.

Aksel (Norwegian) father of peace.

Akule (Native American) he looks up.

Al (Irish) a short form of Alan, Albert, Alexander.

Aladdin (Arabic) height of faith. Literature: the hero of a story in the *Arabian Nights*.
Ala, Alaa, Alaaddin, Aladean, Aladino

Alain (French) a form of Alan.
Alaen, Alainn, Alayn, Allain

Alaire (French) joyful.

Alam (Arabic) universe.

Alan (Irish) handsome; peaceful.
Ailan, Ailin, Al, Alain, Alair, Aland, Alani, Alano, Alanson, Alao, Allan, Allen, Alon, Alun

Alaric (German) ruler of all. See also Ulrich.
Alarick, Alarico, Alarik, Aleric, Allaric, Allarick, Alric, Alrick, Alrik

Alastair (Scottish) a form of Alexander.
Alaisdair, Alaistair, Alaister, Alasdair, Alasteir, Alaster, Alastor, Aleister, Alester, Alistair, Allaistar, Allastair, Allaster, Allastir, Allysdair, Alystair

Alban (Latin) from Alba,
Italy, a city on a white hill.
**Albain, Albany, Albean,
Albein, Alby, Auban,
Auben**

Albern (German) noble;
courageous.

Albert (German, French)
noble and bright. See also
Elbert, Ulbrecht.
**Adelbert, Ailbert, Al,
Albertik, Alberto, Alberts,
Albie, Albrecht, Alvertos,
Aubert**

Alberto (Italian) a form
of Albert.
Berto

Albie, Alby (German,
French) familiar forms
of Albert.

Albin (Latin) an alternate
form of Alvin.
**Alben, Albeno, Albinek,
Albino, Albins, Albinson,
Alby, Auben**

Albion (Latin) white cliffs.
Geography: a reference to
the white cliffs in Dover,
England.

Alcott (English) old
cottage.
**Alcot, Alkot, Alkott,
Allcot, Allcott, Allkot,
Allkott**

Alcandor (Greek) manly;
strong.

Alden (English) old; wise
protector.
Aldin, Aldous, Elden

Alder (German, English)
alder tree.

Aldo (Italian) old; elder.

Aldous (German) a form
of Alden.
Aldis, Aldo, Aldon, Aldus

Aldred (English) old; wise
counselor.
Alldred, Eldred

Aldrich (English) wise
counselor.
**Aldric, Aldrick, Aldridge,
Aldrige, Aldritch, Alldric,
Alldrich, Alldrick,
Alldridge, Eldridge**

Aldwin (English) old friend.
Aldwyn, Eldwin

Alec (Greek) a short form
of Alexander.
**Aleck, Alek, Alekko, Alic,
Elek**

Alejándro (Spanish) a form
of Alexander.
**Alejándra, Aléjo,
Alexjándro**

Aleksei (Russian) a form
of Alexander.
**Aleks, Aleksey, Aleksi,
Aleksis, Aleksy**

Alem (Arabic) wise.

Aleric (German) an alternate form of Alaric.
Alerick, Alleric, Allerick

Aleron (Latin) winged.

Alessandro (Italian) a form of Alexander.
Alessand, Allessandro

Alex (Greek) a short form of Alexander.
Alax, Alix, Allax, Allex, Elek

Alexander (Greek) defender of mankind. History: Alexander the Great was the conquerer of the Greek Empire. See also Alastair, Alistair, Iskander, Jando, Leks, Lex, Macallister, Olés, Oleksandr, Sasha, Sander, Sándor, Sandro, Sandy, Xan, Zander, Zindel.
Al, Alec, Alecsandar, Alejandro, Alekos, Aleksandar, Aleksander, Aleksandr, Aleksandras, Aleksandur, Aleksei, Alessandro, Alex, Alexandar, Alexandor, Alexandr, Alexandre, Alexandros, Alexis, Alexxander, Alexzander, Alick, Alisander, Alixander, Alixandre

Alexandre (French) a form of Alexander.

Alexandros (Greek) an alternate form of Alexander.
Alexandras, Alexandro, Alexandru

Alexis (Greek) a short form of Alexander.
Alexei, Alexes, Alexey, Alexi, Alexie, Alexio, Alexios, Alexius, Alexiz, Alexy

Alfie (English) a familiar form of Alfred.
Alfy

Alfonso (Italian, Spanish) a form of Alphonse.
Affonso, Alfons, Alfonse, Alfonsus, Alfonza, Alfonzo, Alfonzus

Alford (English) old river ford.

Alfred (English) elf counselor; wise counselor. See also Fred.
Ailfrid, Ailfryd, Alf, Alfeo, Alfie, Alfredo, Alured

Alfredo (Italian, Spanish) a form of Alfred.
Alfrido

Alger (German) noble spearman. (English) a short form of Algernon. See also Elgar.
Algar, Allgar

Algernon (English) bearded, wearing a moustache.
Algenon, Alger, Algie, Algin, Algon

Algie (English) a familiar form of Algernon.
Algy

Algis (German) spear.

Ali (Arabic) greatest.
(Swahili) exalted.
Aly

Alim (Arabic) scholar.

Alisander (Greek) an alternate form of Alexander.
Alisander, Alissander, Alissandre, Alsandair, Alsandare, Alsander

Alistair (English) a form of Alexander.
Alisdair, Alistaire, Alistar, Alister, Allister, Allistir

Allan (Irish) an alternate form of Alan.
Allayne

Allard (English) noble, brave.
Alard, Ellard

Allen (Irish) an alternate form of Alan.
Alen, Alley, Alleyn, Alleyne, Allie, Allin, Allon, Allyn

Almon (Hebrew) widower.

Alois (German) a short form of Aloysius.
Aloys

Aloisio (Spanish) a form of Louis.

Alon (Hebrew) oak.

Alonzo (Spanish) a form of Alphonse.
Alano, Alanzo, Alon, Alonso, Alonza, Elonzo, Lon, Lonnie

Aloysius (German) famous warrior. An alternate form of Louis.
Alaois, Alois, Aloisius, Aloisio

Alphonse (German) noble and eager.
Alf, Alfie, Alfonso, Alonzo, Alphons, Alphonsa, Alphonso, Alphonsus, Alphonza, Alphonzus, Fonzie

Alphonso (Italian) a form of Alphonse.
Alphanso, Alphonzo, Fonso

Alpin (Irish) attractive.
Alpine

Alroy (Spanish) king.

Alston (English) noble's settlement.
Allston

Altair (Greek) star.
(Arabic) flying eagle.

Altman (German) old man.
Altmann, Atman

Alton (English) old town.
Alten

Alva (Hebrew) sublime.

Alvan (German) an alternate form of Alvin.
Alvand

Alvar (Swedish) Botany: a small shrub native to Sweden. (English) army of elves.

Alvaro (Spanish) just; wise.

Alvern (Latin) spring.
Elvern

Alvin (Latin) white; light skinned. (German) friend to all; noble friend; friend of elves. See also Albin, Elvin.
Aloin, Aluin, Aluino, Alvan, Alven, Alvie, Alvino, Alvy, Alvyn, Alwin, Elwin

Alvis (Scandinavian) all-knowing.

Alwin (German) an alternate form of Alvin.
Ailwyn, Alwyn, Alwynn, Aylwin

Amadeo (Italian) a form of Amadeus.

Amadeus (Latin) loves God. Music: Wolfgang Amadeus Mozart was a famous eighteenth-century Austrian composer.
Amad, Amadeaus, Amadée, Amadeo, Amadei, Amadio, Amadis, Amado, Amador, Amadou, Amando, Amedeo, Amodaos

Amal (Hebrew) worker. (Arabic) hopeful.

Amandeep (Punjabi) light of peace.
Amandip, Amanjit, Amanjot, Amanpreet

Amando (French) a form of Amadeus.
Amand, Amandio, Amaniel, Amato

Amar (Punjabi) immortal. (Arabic) builder.
Amari, Amario, Amaris, Amarjit, Amarpreet, Ammar, Ammer

Amato (French) loved.

Ambrose (Greek) immortal.
Ambie, Ambroise, Ambros, Ambrosi, Ambrosio, Ambrosius, Ambrus, Amby

Amerigo (Teutonic) industrious. History: Amerigo Vespucci was the explorer for whom America is named.

Ames (French) friend.

Amicus (English, Latin) beloved friend.
Amico

Amiel (Hebrew) God of my people.
Ammiel

Amin (Hebrew, Arabic) trustworthy; honest. (Hindi) faithful.

Amir (Hebrew) proclaimed. (Punjabi) wealthy; king's minister. (Arabic) prince.
Ameer

Amit (Punjabi) unfriendly. (Arabic) highly praised.

Amit *(cont.)*
Amitan, Amreet, Amrit

Ammon (Egyptian) hidden.
Mythology: the ancient
god associated with
reproduction and life.

Amon (Hebrew) trust-
worthy; faithful.

Amory (German) an alternate form of Emory.
Amery, Amor

Amos (Hebrew) burdened,
troubled. Bible: an Old
Testament prophet.

Amram (Hebrew) mighty
nation.
Amarien, Amran, Amren

An (Chinese, Vietnamese)
peaceful.
Ana

Anand (Hindi) blissful.
Ananda, Anant, Ananth

Anastasius (Greek)
resurrection.
**Anas, Anastagio, Anastas,
Anastase, Anastasi,
Anastasio, Anastasios,
Anastice, Anastisis,
Anaztáz, Athanasius**

Anatole (Greek) east.
**Anatol, Anatoli,
Anatolijus, Anatolio,
Anatoly, Anitoly**

Anchali (Taos) painter.

Anders (Swedish) a form
of Andrew.

**Ander, Andersen,
Anderson**

Andonios (Greek) an alternate form of Anthony.
Andonis

Andor (Hungarian) a form
of Andrew.

András (Hungarian) a form
of Andrew.
**Andri, Andris, Andrius,
Andriy, Aundras,
Aundreas**

André (French) a form
of Andrew.
**Andra, Andrae, Andre,
Andrecito, Andree,
Andrei, Aundré**

Andreas (Greek) an alternate form of Andrew.
Andres, Andries

Andrei (Bulgarian,
Romanian, Russian)
a form of Andrew.
**Andreian, Andrej, Andrey,
Andreyan, Andrie,
Aundrei**

Andres (Spanish) a form
of Andrew.
Andras, Andrés, Andrez

Andrew (Greek) strong;
manly; courageous.
Bible: one of the Twelve
Apostles. See also Bandi,
Drew, Endre, Evangelos,
Kendew, Ondro.
**Aindrea, Anders, Andery,
Andonis, Andor, András,
André, Andreas, Andrei,**

**Andres, Andrews, Andru,
Andrue, Andrus, Andy,
Anker, Anndra, Antal,
Audrew**

Andros (Polish) sea.
Mythology: the god
of the sea.
Andris, Andrius, Andrus

Andy (Greek) a short form
of Andrew.
Andino, Andis, Andje

Aneurin (Welsh) honorable; gold. See also Nye.
Aneirin

Angel (Greek) angel.
(Latin) messenger.
See also Gotzon.
**Ange, Angell, Angelo,
Angie, Angy**

Angelo (Italian) a form
of Angel.
Angelito, Angelos, Anglo

Angus (Scottish) excep-
tional; outstanding.
Mythology: Angus Og was
the Celtic god of laughter,
love, and wisdom. See also
Ennis, Gus.
Aeneas, Aonghas

Anh (Vietnamese) peace;
safety.

Anibal (Phoenician) an
alternate form of Hannibal.

Anil (Hindi) wind god.
Aneel, Anel, Aniel, Aniello

Anka (Turkish) phoenix.

Anker (Danish) a form
of Andrew.
Ankur

Annan (Scottish) brook.
(Swahili) fourth-born son.

Annas (Greek) gift from
God.
Anis, Anna, Annais

Anno (German) a familiar
form of Johann.

Anoki (Native American)
actor.

Ansel (French) follower
of a nobleman.
Ancell, Ansa, Ansell

Anselm (German) divine
protector. See also Elmo.
**Anse, Anselme,
Anselmi, Anselmo**

Ansis (Latvian) an alternate
form of Janis.

Ansley (Scottish) an alter-
nate form of Ainsley.
**Anslea, Anslee, Ansleigh,
Anslie, Ansly, Ansy**

Anson (German) divine.
(English) Anne's son.
Ansun

Antal (Hungarian) a form
of Anthony.
Antek, Anti, Antos

Antares (Greek) giant,
red star. Astronomy:
the brightest star in the
constellation Scorpio.
Antarr

Antavas (Lithuanian)
a form of Anthony.
**Antae, Antaeus, Antavius,
Ante, Anteo**

Anthony (Latin) praise-
worthy. (Greek) flourish-
ing. See also Tony.
**Anathony, Andonios,
Andor, András, Anothony,
Antal, Antavas, Anfernee,
Anferny, Anthawn,
Anthey, Anthian, Anthino,
Anthoney, Anthoni,
Anthonie, Anthonio,
Anthonu, Anthonysha,
Anthoy, Anthyoine,
Anthyonny, Antjuan,
Antoine, Anton, Antonio,
Antony, Antwan**

Antjuan (Spanish) a form
of Anthony.
**Antajuan, Anthjuan,
Antuan, Antuane**

Antoan (Vietnamese) safe,
secure.

Antoine (French) a form
of Anthony.
**Anntoin, Antionne,
Antoiné, Atoine**

Anton (Slavic) a form
of Anthony.
Antone, Antons, Antos

Antonio (Italian) a form
of Anthony. See also Tino.
**Antinio, Antonello,
Antoino, Antonin,
Antonín, Antonino,
Antonnio, Antonios,**

**Antonius, Antonyia,
Antonyio, Antonyo**

Antony (Latin) an alternate
form of Anthony.
**Antin, Antini, Antius,
Antoney, Antoni, Antonie,
Antonin, Antonios,
Antonius, Antonyia,
Antonyio, Antonyo, Anty**

Antti (Finnish) manly.
Anthey, Anthi, Anti

Antwan (Arabic) a form
of Anthony.
**Antaw, Antawan,
Antawn, Anthawn,
Antowine, Antowne,
Antowyn, Antwain,
Antwaina, Antwaine,
Antwaion, Antwane,
Antwann, Antwanne,
Antwarn, Antwaun,
Antwen, Antwian,
Antwine, Antwion,
Antwoan, Antwoin,
Antwoine, Antwon,
Antwone, Antwonn,
Antwonne, Antwuan,
Antwyon, Antyon,
Antywon**

Anwar (Arabic) luminous.
Anour, Anouar, Anwi

Apiatan (Kiowa)
wooden lance.

Apollo (Greek) manly.
Mythology: the god of
prophecy, healing, music,
poetry, truth, and the sun.
See also Polo.
Appollo, Apolinar,

Apolinario, Apollos, Apolo, Apolonio

Aquila (Latin, Spanish) eagle.
Acquilla, Aquil, Aquilas, Aquilla, Aquillino

Araldo (Spanish) a form of Harold.
Aralodo, Aralt, Aroldo, Arry

Aram (Syrian) high, exalted.
Ara, Aramia, Arra

Aramis (French) Literature: one of the title characters in Alexandre Dumas's novel *The Three Musketeers*.
Airamis, Aramith, Aramys

Aran (Thai) forest.

Archer (English) bowman. See also Ivar, Ives, Ivo.
Archie

Archibald (German) bold. See also Arkady.
Arch, Archaimbaud, Archambault, Archibaldo, Archibold, Archie

Archie (German, English) a familiar form of Archer, Archibald.
Archy

Ardal (Irish) a form of Arnold.

Ardell (Latin) eager; industrious.

Arden (Latin) ardent; fiery.
Ard, Ardie, Ardin, Arduino

Ardon (Hebrew) bronzed.

Aren (Danish) eagle; ruler.

Aretino (Greek, Italian) victorious.

Argus (Danish) watchful, vigilant.
Agos

Ari (Greek) a short form of Aristotle. (Hebrew) a short form of Ariel.
Aria, Arias, Arie, Arih, Arij, Ario, Arri

Aric (German) an alternate form of Richard. (Scandinavian) an alternate form of Eric.
Aaric, Areck, Arick, Arik, Arric, Arrick, Arrik

Ariel (Hebrew) lion of God. Bible: another name for Jerusalem. Literature: the name of a spirit in the Shakespearean play *The Tempest*.
Airel, Arel, Areli, Ari, Ariya, Ariyel, Arrial, Arriel

Aries (Greek) Mythology: Ares was the Greek god of war. (Latin) ram.
Arie, Ariez

Arif (Arabic) knowledgeable.
Areef

Arion (Greek) enchanted.
Mythology: a magic horse.
(Hebrew) melodious.
**Arian, Ariane, Arien,
Arrian**

Aristides (Greek) son
of the best.
Aris, Aristidis

Aristotle (Greek) best;
wise. History: a third-
century B.C. philosopher
who tutored Alexander
the Great.
**Ari, Aris, Aristito, Aristo,
Aristokles, Aristotelis**

Arkady (Russian) a form
of Archibald.
Arkadi, Arkadij, Arkadiy

Arkin (Norwegian) son
of the eternal king.
Aricin, Arkeen, Arkyn

Arledge (English) lake
with the hares.
Arlidge, Arlledge

Arlen (Irish) pledge.
**Arlan, Arland, Arlend,
Arlin, Arlyn, Arlynn**

Arley (English) a short
form of Harley.
Arleigh, Arlie, Arly

Arlo (German) an alternate
form of Charles. (Spanish)
barberry. (English)
fortified hill.

Arman (Persian) desire,
goal.
Armaan

Armand (Latin) noble.
(German) soldier. An alter-
nate form of Herman.
See also Mandek.
**Armad, Arman, Armanda,
Armando, Armands,
Armanno, Armaude,
Armenta, Armond**

Armando (Spanish) a form
of Armand.
Armondo

Armon (Hebrew) high
fortress, stronghold.
**Arman, Armen, Armin,
Armino, Armoni, Armons**

Armstrong (English)
strong arm.

Arnaud (French) a form
of Arnold.
Arnauld, Arnault, Arnoll

Arne (German) an alternate
form of Arnold.
Arna, Arnel, Arnell

Arnette (English) little
eagle.
**Arnat, Arnet, Arnot,
Arnott**

Arnie (German) a familiar
form of Arnold.
Arney, Arni, Arnny, Arny

Arno (German) eagle wolf.
(Czech) a short form
of Ernest.
Arnou, Arnoux

Arnold (German) eagle
ruler.
**Ardal, Arnald, Arnaldo,
Arnaud, Arne, Arnie,**

Arno, Arnoldo, Arnoll, Arndt

Arnon (Hebrew) rushing river.
Arnan

Aron, Arron (Hebrew) alternate forms of Aaron.

Aroon (Thai) dawn.

Arran (Hebrew) an alternate form of Aaron. (Scottish) island dweller. Geography: an island off the coast of Scotland.
Arren, Arrin

Arrigo (Italian) a form of Harry.
Alrigo, Arrighetto

Arrio (Spanish) warlike.
Ario, Arrow, Arryo, Aryo

Arsenio (Greek) masculine; virile. History: Saint Arsenius was a teacher in the Roman Empire.
Arsen, Arsène, Arsenius, Arseny, Arsinio

Arsha (Persian) venerable.

Art (English) a short form of Arthur.

Artemus (Greek) gift of Artemis. Mythology: Artemis was the goddess of the hunt and the moon.
Artemas, Artemio, Artemis, Artimas, Artimis, Artimus

Artie (English) a familiar form of Arthur.

Arte, Artian, Artis, Arty, Atty

Arthur (Irish) noble; lofty hill. (Scottish) bear. (English) rock. (Icelandic) follower of Thor. See also Turi.
Art, Artair, Artek, Arth, Arther, Arthor, Artie, Artor, Arturo, Artus, Aurthar, Aurther, Aurthur

Arturo (Italian) a form of Arthur.
Arthuro, Artur

Arun (Cambodian, Hindi) sun.
Aruns

Arundel (English) eagle valley.

Arve (Norwegian) heir, inheritor.

Arvel (Welsh) wept over.
Arval, Arvell, Arvelle

Arvid (Hebrew) wanderer. (Norwegian) eagle tree. See also Ravid.
Arv, Arvad, Arve, Arvie, Arvind, Arvinder, Arvydas

Arvin (German) friend of the people; friend of the army.
Arv, Arvie, Arvind, Arvinder, Arvon, Arvy

Aryeh (Hebrew) lion.

Asa (Hebrew) physician, healer. (Yoruba) falcon.
Ase

Asád (Arabic) lion.
**Asaad, Asad, 'Asid, Assad,
Azad**

Asadel (Arabic) prosperous.
Asadour, Asadul, Asael

Ascot (English) eastern
cottage; style of necktie.
Geography: a famous
racetrack near Windsor
castle.

Asgard (Scandinavian)
court of the gods.

Ash (Hebrew) ash tree.
Ashby

Ashby (Scandinavian)
ash-tree farm. (Hebrew)
an alternate form of Ash.
Ashbey

Asher (Hebrew) happy;
blessed.
Ashar, Ashor, Ashur

Ashford (English) ash-tree
ford.
Ash, Ashtin

Ashley (English) ash-tree
meadow.
**Ash, Asheley, Ashelie,
Ashely, Ashlan, Ashleigh,
Ashlen, Ashlie, Ashlin,
Ashling, Ashlinn, Ashlone,
Ashly, Ashlyn, Ashlynn,
Aslan**

Ashon (Swahili) seventh-
born son.

Ashton (English) ash-tree
settlement.
Ashtin

Ashur (Swahili) Mythology:
the principle Assyrian
deity.

Ashwani (Hindi) first.
Religion: the first of the
twenty-seven galaxies
revolving around the
moon.

Ashwin (Hindi) star.

Asiel (Hebrew) created
by God.

Asker (Turkish) soldier.

Aston (English) eastern
town.
Asten, Astin

Aswad (Arabic) dark
skinned, black.

Ata (Fanti) twin.

Atek (Polish) a form
of Tanek.

Athan (Greek) immortal.

Atherton (English) town
by a spring.

Atid (Thai) sun.

Atif (Arabic) caring.
Ateef, Atef

Atlas (Greek) lifted; carried.
Mythology: Atlas was
forced to carry the world
on his shoulders as a punishment for feuding with
Zeus.

Atley (English) meadow.
**Atlea, Atlee, Atleigh, Atli,
Attley**

Attila (Gothic) little father.
History: the Hun leader
who conquered the Goths.
Atalik, Atilio, Atiya

Atwater (English) at the
water's edge.

Atwell (English) at the
well.

Atwood (English) at the
forest.

Atworth (English) at the
farmstead.

Auberon (German) an
alternate form of Oberon.
Auberron, Aubrey

Aubrey (German) noble;
bearlike. (French) a famil-
iar form of Auberon.
See also Avery.
**Aubary, Aube, Aubery,
Aubry, Aubury**

Auburn (Latin) reddish
brown.

Auden (English) old friend.

Audie (German) noble;
strong. (English) a familiar
form of Edward.
Audi, Audiel, Audley

Audon (French) old; rich.
Audelon

Audric (English) wise ruler.

Audun (Scandinavian)
deserted, desolate.

Augie (Latin) a familiar
form of August.
Auggie, Augy

August (Latin) a short form
of Augustine, Augustus.
**Agosto, Augie, Auguste,
Augusto**

Augustine (Latin) majestic.
Religion: Saint Augustine
was the first Archbishop
of Canterbury. See also
Austin, Gus, Tino.
**Agostino, Agoston,
Aguistin, August, Agustin,
Augustin, Austin**

Augustus (Latin) majestic;
venerable. History:
a name used by Roman
emperors such as
Augustus Caesar.
August

Aukai (Hawaiian) seafarer.

Aurek (Polish) golden
haired.

Aurelius (Latin) golden.
History: Marcus Aurelius
Antoninus was a second-
century A.D. philosopher
and emperor of Rome.
**Arelian, Areliano, Aurel,
Aurele, Aurèle, Aureli,
Aurélien, Aurelio, Aurey,
Auriel, Aury**

Aurick (German) protecting ruler.

Austin (Latin) a short form
of Augustine.
**Astin, Austen, Austine,
Auston, Austyn, Oistin,
Ostin**

Avel (Greek) breath.

Avent (French) born during
Advent.
Aventin, Aventino

Averill (French) born in
April. (English) boar-
warrior.
**Ave, Averel, Averell,
Averiel, Averil, Averyl,
Averyll, Avrel, Avrell,
Avrill, Avryll**

Avery (English) a form
of Aubrey.
**Avary, Aveary, Averey,
Averie, Avry**

Avi (Hebrew) God is my
father.
**Avian, Avidan, Avidor,
Aviel, Avion**

Aviv (Hebrew) youth;
springtime.

Avner (Hebrew) an alternate form of Abner.
Avneet, Avniel

Avram (Hebrew) an alter-
nate form of Abraham,
Abram.
**Arram, Avraham, Avrom,
Avrum**

Avshalom (Hebrew) father
of peace. See also
Absalom.
Avsalom

Awan (Native American)
somebody.

Axel (Latin) axe. (German)
small oak tree; source of
life. (Scandinavian) a form
of Absalom.
**Aksel, Ax, Axe, Axell, Axil,
Axill**

Aydin (Turkish) intelligent.

Ayers (English) heir
to a fortune.

Ayinde (Yoruba) we gave
praise and he came.

Aylmer (English) an alter-
nate form of Elmer.
**Aillmer, Ailmer, Allmer,
Ayllmer**

Aymil (Greek) an alternate
form of Emil.

Aymon (French) a form
of Raymond.

Azad (Turkish) free.

Azeem (Arabic) an alternate form of Azim.
Aseem, Asim

Azi (Nigerian) youth.

Azim (Arabic) defender.

'Aziz (Arabic) strong.

Azizi (Swahili) precious.

Azriel (Hebrew) God is
my aid.

Azuriah (Hebrew) aided
by God.
Azaria, Azariah, Azuria

Baden (German) bather.
Bayden

Bahir (Arabic) brilliant,
dazzling.

Bahram (Persian) ancient
king.

Bailey (French) bailiff,
steward.
**Bail, Bailie, Bailio, Baillie,
Baily, Bayley, Bayly**

Bain (Irish) a short form
of Bainbridge.

Bainbridge (Irish) fair
bridge.
**Bain, Baynbridge, Bayne,
Baynebridge**

Baird (Irish) bard, traveling
minstrel; poet.
Bairde, Bard

Bakari (Swahili) noble
promise.

Baker (English) baker.
See also Baxter.

Bal (Sanskrit) child born
with lots of hair.

Balasi (Basque) flat footed.

Balbo (Latin) stammerer.
Bailby, Balbi, Ballbo

Baldemar (German) bold;
famous.
**Baldemer, Baldomero,
Baumar, Baumer**

Balder (Scandinavian) bald.
Mythology: the Norse god
of light, summer, and
innocence.
Baldier, Baldur, Baudier

Baldric (German) brave
ruler.
Baldrick, Baudric

Baldwin (German) bold
friend.
**Bald, Baldovino, Balduin,
Baldwinn, Baldwyn,
Baldwynn, Balldwin,
Baudoin**

Balfour (Scottish) pasture
land.
Balfor, Balfore

Balin (Hindi) mighty
soldier.
Bali, Valin

Ballard (German) brave;
strong.
Balard

Balthasar (Greek) God
save the king. Bible:
one of the Three Wise
Men.
**Badassare, Baldassare,
Baltasar, Baltazar,
Balthasaar, Balthazar,
Baltsaros, Belshazar,
Belshazzar, Boldizsár**

Bancroft (English) bean
field.
**Ban, Bancrofft, Bank,
Bankroft, Banky, Binky**

Bandi (Hungarian) a form
of Andrew.
Bandit

Bane (Hawaiian) a form
of Bartholomew.

Banner (Scottish, English)
flag bearer.
Bannor, Banny

Banning (Irish) small and
fair.
Banny

Barak (Hebrew) lightning
bolt. Bible: the valiant warrior who helped Deborah.
Barrak

Baran (Russian) ram.
Baren

Barasa (Kikuyu) meeting
place.

Barclay (Scottish, English)
birch tree meadow.
**Bar, Barcley, Barklay,
Barkley, Barklie, Barrclay,
Berkeley**

Bard (Irish) an alternate
form of Baird.
**Bar, Barde, Bardia,
Bardiya, Barr**

Bardolf (German) bright
wolf. Literature: the name
of a drunken fool who
appeared in four
Shakespearean plays.

**Bardo, Bardolph, Bardou,
Bardoul, Bardulf,
Bardulph**

Bardrick (Teutonic)
axe ruler.
Bardric, Bardrik

Baris (Turkish) peaceful.

Barker (English)
lumberjack; advertiser
at a carnival.

Barlow (English) bare
hillside.
**Barlowe, Barrlow,
Barrlowe**

Barnabas (Greek, Hebrew,
Aramaic, Latin) son of the
missionary. Bible: disciple
of Paul.
**Bane, Barna, Barnaba,
Barnabus, Barnaby,
Barnebas, Barnebus,
Barney**

Barnaby (English) a form
of Barnabas.
**Barnabe, Barnabé,
Barnabee, Barnabey,
Barnabie, Bernabé,
Burnaby**

Barnard (English) a form
of Bernard.
**Barn, Barnard, Barnhard,
Barnhardo**

Barnes (English) bear;
son of Barnett.

Barnett (English) nobleman; leader.
Barn, Barnet, Barney,

Baronet, Baronett, Barrie, Barron, Barry

Barney (English) a familiar form of Barnabas, Barnett.
Barnie, Barny

Barnum (German) barn; storage place. (English) baron's home.
Barnham

Baron (German, English) nobleman, baron.
Baaron, Baronie, Barrion, Barron, Baryn

Barrett (German) strong as a bear.
Bar, Baret, Barrat, Barret, Barrette, Barry

Barric (English) grain farm.
Barrick, Beric

Barrington (English) Geography: a town in England.

Barry (Welsh) son of Harry. (Irish) spear, marksman. (French) gate, fence.
Baris, Barri, Barrie, Barris, Bary

Bart (Hebrew) a short form of Bartholomew, Barton.
Barrt, Bartel, Bartie, Barty

Bartholomew (Hebrew) son of Talmaí. Bible: one of the Twelve Apostles. See also Jerney, Parlan, Parthalán.
Balta, Bane, Bart, Bartek, Barth, Barthel,

Barthelemy, Barthélemy, Barthélmy, Bartho, Bartholo, Bartholomaus, Bartholome, Bartholomeo, Bartholomeus, Bartholomieu, Bartimous, Bartlet, Barto, Bartolome, Bartolomé, Bartolomeo, Bartolomeô, Bartolommeo, Bartome, Bartz, Bat

Bartlet (English) a form of Bartholomew.
Bartlett, Bartley

Barto (Spanish) a form of Bartholomew.
Bardo, Bardol, Bartol, Bartoli, Bartolo, Bartos

Barton (English) barley farm; Bart's town.
Barrton, Bart

Bartram (English) an alternate form of Bertram.
Barthram

Baruch (Hebrew) blessed.
Boruch

Basam (Arabic) smiling.
Basem, Basim, Bassam

Basil (Greek, Latin) royal, kingly. Religion: a saint and leading scholar of the early Christian Church. Botany: an herb used in cooking. See also Vasilis, Wasili.
Bas, Base, Baseal, Basel, Basle, Basile, Basilio,

Basil (cont.)
Basilios, Basilius, Bassel, Bazek, Bazel, Bazil, Bazyli

Basir (Turkish) intelligent, discerning.
Bashar, Basheer, Bashir, Bashiyr, Bechir, Bhasheer

Bassett (English) little person.
Basett, Basset

Bastien (German) a short form of Sebastian.
Baste, Bastiaan

Bat (English) a short form of Bartholomew.

Baul (Gypsy) snail.

Bavol (Gypsy) wind; air.

Baxter (English) an alternate form of Baker.
Bax, Baxie, Baxty, Baxy

Bay (Vietnamese) seventh son. (French) chestnut brown color; evergreen tree. (English) howler.

Bayard (English) reddish brown hair.
Baiardo, Bay, Bayerd, Bayrd

Beacan (Irish) small.
Beacán, Becan

Beacher (English) beech trees.
Beach, Beachy, Beech, Beecher, Beechy

Beagan (Irish) small.
Beagen, Beagin

Beale (French) an alternate form of Beau.
Beal, Beall, Bealle, Beals

Beaman (English) beekeeper.
Beamann, Beamen, Beeman, Beman

Beamer (English) trumpet player.

Beasley (English) field of peas.

Beattie (Latin) blessed; happy; bringer of joy. A masculine form of Beatrice.
Beatie, Beatty, Beaty

Beau (French) handsome.
Beale, Bo

Beaufort (French) beautiful fort.

Beaumont (French) beautiful mountain.

Beauregard (French) handsome; beautiful; well regarded.

Beaver (English) beaver.
Beav, Beavo, Beve, Bevo

Bebe (Spanish) baby.

Beck (English, Scandinavian) brook.
Beckett

Bede (English) prayer. Religion: the patron saint of scholars.

Bela (Czech) white. (Hungarian) bright.
Béla, Belal, Bellal

Belden (French, English)
pretty valley.
**Beldin, Beldon, Bellden,
Belldon**

Belen (Greek) arrow.

Bell (French) handsome.
(English) bell ringer.

Bellamy (French) beautiful
friend.
**Belamy, Bell, Bellamey,
Bellamie**

Bello (African) helper or
promoter of Islam

Belmiro (Portuguese)
good looking; attractive.

Bem (Tiv) peace.
Behm

Ben (Hebrew) a short
form of Benjamin.
**Behn, Benio, Benn,
Benne, Benno**

Ben-ami (Hebrew) son
of my people.
Baram, Barami

Benedict (Latin) blessed.
See also Venedictos,
Venya.
**Benci, Bendick, Bendict,
Bendix, Benedetto,
Benedick, Benedicto,
Benedictus, Benedikt,
Bengt, Benito, Benoist**

Benedikt (German, Slavic)
a form of Benedict.
**Bendek, Bendik, Benedek,
Benedik**

Bengt (Scandinavian)
a form of Benedict.
Beng, Benke, Bent

Beniam (Ethiopian) a form
of Benjamin.
Beniamino

Benito (Italian) a form of
Benedict. History: Benito
Mussolini led Italy during
World War II.
**Benedo, Benino, Benno,
Beno, Betto**

Benjamin (Hebrew) son
of my right hand. See also
Peniamina, Veniamin.
**Behnjamin, Bejamin,
Bemjiman, Ben,
Benejamen, Benejaminas,
Beniam, Benja, Benjaim,
Benjamaim, Benjaman,
Benjamen, Benjamine,
Benjamino, Benjamon,
Benjamyn, Benjemin,
Benjermain, Benji, Benjie,
Benjiman, Benjimen,
Benjjmen, Benjy,
Benkamin, Benny,
Benyamin, Benyamino,
Binyamin, Mincho**

Benjiro (Japanese) enjoys
peace.

Bennett (Latin) little
blessed one.
Benet, Benett, Bennet

Benny (Hebrew) a familiar
form of Benjamin.
Bennie

Beno (Hebrew) son.
(Mwera) band member.

Benoit (French) a form
of Benedict. (English)
Botany: a yellow, flowering
rose plant.

Benoni (Hebrew) son
of my sorrow. Bible:
Ben-Oni was the son
of Jacob and Rachel.
Ben-Oni

Benson (Hebrew) son
of Ben. A short form
of Ben Zion.
Bensen, Benssen, Bensson

Bentley (English) moor;
coarse grass meadow.
**Bent, Bentlea, Bentlee,
Bentlie, Lee**

Benton (English) Ben's
town; town on the moors.
Bent

Benzi (Hebrew) a familiar
form of Ben Zion.

Ben Zion (Hebrew) son
of Zion.
Benson

Beppe (Italian) a form
of Joseph.
Beppy

Ber (English) boundary.
(Yiddish) bear.

Beredei (Russian) a form
of Hubert.
**Berdry, Berdy, Beredej,
Beredy**

Berg (German) mountain.
Berdj, Bergh, Berje

Bergen (German, Scandinavian) hill dweller.
Bergin, Birgin

Berger (French) shepherd.

Bergren (Scandinavian)
mountain stream.
Berg

Berk (Turkish) solid,
rugged.

Berkeley (English) an alter-
nate form of Barclay.
**Berk, Berkie, Berkley,
Berklie, Berkly, Berky**

Berk (Turkish) solid,
rugged.

Berl (German) an alternate
form of Burl.

Bern (German) a short
form of Bernard.
Berne

Bernal (German) strong
as a bear.
**Bernald, Bernaldo, Bernel,
Bernhald, Bernhold,
Bernold**

Bernard (German) brave
as a bear. See also Bjorn.
**Bear, Bearnard, Benek,
Ber, Berend, Bern,
Bernabé, Bernadas,
Bernal, Bernardel,
Bernardin, Bernardo,
Bernardus, Bernardyn,
Bernarr, Bernat, Bernek,
Bernel, Bernerd,
Berngards, Bernhard,
Bernhards, Bernhardt,
Bernie, Bjorn, Burnard**

Bernardo (Spanish) a form of Bernard.
Barnardino, Barnardo, Barnhardo, Benardo, Bernhardo, Berno, Burnardo, Nardo

Bernie (German) a familiar form of Bernard.
Berney, Berni, Berny, Birney, Birnie, Birny, Burney

Berry (English) berry; grape.

Bersh (Gypsy) one year.

Bert (German, English) bright, shining. A short form of Berthold, Berton, Bertram, Bertrand.
Bertie, Bertus, Birt, Burt

Berthold (German) bright; illustrious; brilliant ruler.
Bert, Berthoud, Bertold, Bertolde

Bertie (English) a familiar form of Bert.
Bertie, Berty, Birt, Birtie, Birty

Bertín (Spanish) distinguished friend.
Berti

Berto (Spanish) a short form of Alberto.

Berton (English) bright settlement; fortified town.
Bert

Bertram (German) bright; illustrious.

(English) bright raven. See also Bartram.
Beltran, Beltrán, Beltrano, Bert, Berton

Bertrand (German) bright shield.
Bert, Bertran, Bertrando, Bertranno

Berwyn (English) harvest son; powerful friend. Astrology: a name for babies born under the signs of Virgo, Capricorn, and Taurus.
Berwin, Berwynn, Berwynne

Bevan (Welsh) son of Evan.
Beavan, Beaven, Beavin, Bev, Beve, Beven, Bevin, Bevo, Bevon

Beverly (English) beaver meadow.
Beverlea, Beverleigh, Beverley, Beverlie

Bevis (French) from Beauvais, France; bull.
Beauvais, Bevys

Bhagwandas (Hindi) servant of God.

Bickford (English) axeman's ford.

Bienvenido (Filipino) welcome.

Bijan (Persian) ancient hero.
Bihjan, Bijann

Bilal (Arabic) chosen.
Bila, Billal

Bill (German) a short form of William.
Bil, Billijo, Byll, Will

Billy (German) a familiar form of Bill, William.
Bille, Billey, Billie, Billy, Bily, Willie

Binah (Hebrew) understanding; wise.
Bina

Bing (German) kettle-shaped hollow.

Binh (Vietnamese) peaceful.

Binkentios (Greek) a form of Vincent.

Binky (English) a familiar form of Bancroft, Vincent.
Bink, Binkentios, Binkie

Birch (English) white; shining; birch tree.
Birk, Burch

Birger (Norwegian) rescued.

Birkey (English) island with birch trees.
Birk, Birkie, Birky

Birkitt (English) birch-tree coast.
Birk, Birket, Birkit, Burket, Burkett, Burkitt

Birley (English) meadow with the cow barn.
Birlee, Birlie, Birly

Birney (English) island with a brook.
Birne, Birnie, Birny, Burney, Burnie, Burny

Birtle (English) hill with birds.

Bishop (Greek) overseer. (English) bishop.
Bish

Bjorn (Scandinavian) a form of Bernard.
Bjarne

Blackburn (Scottish) black brook.

Blade (English) knife, sword.
Blae, Blaed, Blayde

Blaine (Irish) thin, lean. (English) river source.
Blane, Blaney, Blayne, Blayney

Blair (Irish) plain, field. (Welsh) place.
Blaire, Blayr, Blayre

Blaise (French) a form of Blaze.
Ballas, Balyse, Blaisot, Blas, Blase, Blasi, Blasien, Blasius

Blake (English) attractive; dark.
Blakely, Blakeman, Blakey

Blakely (English) dark meadow.
Blakelee, Blakeleigh, Blakeley, Blakelie, Blakeny

Blanco (Spanish) light skinned, white, blond.

Blaze (Latin) stammerer. (English) flame; trail mark made on a tree.
Balázs, Biaggio, Biagio, Blaise, Blaize, Blayze

Blayne (Irish) an alternate form of Blaine.
Blain, Blaine, Blane

Bliss (English) blissful; joyful.

Bly (Native American) high.

Blythe (English) carefree; merry, joyful.
Blithe, Blyth

Bo (English) a form of Beau, Beauregard.

Boaz (Hebrew) swift; strong.
Bo, Boas, Booz, Bos, Boz

Bob (English) a short form of Robert.
Bobb, Bobby, Bobek, Rob

Bobby (English) a familiar form of Bob, Robert.
Bobbey, Bobbi, Bobbie, Boby

Bobek (Czech) a form of Bob, Robert.

Boden (Scandinavian) sheltered. (French) messenger, herald.
Bodee, Bodie, Bodin, Bodine, Boe, Boedee

Bodil (Norwegian) mighty ruler.

Bodua (Akan) animal's tail.

Bogart (German) strong as a bow. (Irish, Welsh) bog, marshland.
Bo, Bogey, Bogie, Bogy

Bohdan (Ukranian) a form of Donald.
Bogdan, Bogdashka, Bohdon

Bonaro (Italian, Spanish) friend.
Bona, Bonar

Bonaventure (Italian) good luck.

Bond (English) tiller of the soil.
Bondie, Bondon, Bonds, Bondy

Boniface (Latin) do-gooder.
Bonifacio, Bonifacius, Bonifacy

Booker (English) bookmaker; book lover; Bible lover.
Bookie, Books, Booky

Boone (Latin, French) good. History: Daniel Boone was an American frontiersman.
Bon, Bone, Bonne, Boonie, Boony

Booth (English) hut. (Scandinavian) temporary dwelling.
Boot, Boote, Boothe

Borak (Arabic) lightning.
Mythology: the horse that
carried Muhammed
to seventh heaven.

Borden (French) cottage.
(English) valley of the
boar; boar's den.
Bord, Bordie, Bordy

Borg (Scandinavian) castle.

Boris (Slavic) battler,
warrior. Religion: the
patron saint of Moscow.
**Boriss, Borja, Borris,
Borya, Boryenka, Borys**

Borka (Russian) fighter.
Borkinka

Bosley (English) grove
of trees.

Botan (Japanese) blossom,
bud.

Bourey (Cambodian)
country.

Bourne (Latin, French)
boundary. (English) brook,
stream. See also Burne.
Byrn

Boutros (Arabic) a form
of Peter.

Bowen (Welsh) son of
Owen.
Bow, Bowe, Bowie

Bowie (Irish) yellow haired.
History: Colonel James
Bowie was an American
scout.
Bow, Bowen

Boyce (French) woods,
forest.
**Boice, Boise, Boy, Boycey,
Boycie**

Boyd (Scottish) yellow
haired.
Boid, Boyde

Brad (English) a short form
of Bradford, Bradley.
Bradd, Brade

Bradburn (English) broad
stream.

Braden (English) broad
valley.
**Bradan, Bradden, Bradin,
Bradine, Bradyn, Braeden,
Braiden, Brayden**

Bradford (English) broad
river crossing.
Brad, Braddford, Ford

Bradley (English) broad
meadow.
**Brad, Bradlay, Bradlea,
Bradlee, Bradleigh,
Bradlie, Bradly, Bradney**

Bradly (English) an alternate form of Bradley.

Bradon (English) broad hill.
**Braedon, Braidon,
Braydon**

Bradshaw (English) broad
forest.

Brady (Irish) spirited.
(English) broad island.
Bradey

Bragi (Scandinavian) poet. Mythology: the god of poetry and music.
Brage

Braham (Hindi) creator.
Braheem, Braheim, Brahiem, Brahima, Brahm

Brainard (English) bold raven; prince.
Brainerd

Bram (Hebrew) a short form of Abraham, Abram. (Scottish) bramble, brushwood.
Bramm, Bramdon

Bramwell (English) bramble-bush spring.
Brammel, Brammell, Bramwel, Bramwyll

Branch (Latin) paw; claw; tree branch.

Brand (English) firebrand; sword. A short form of Brandon.
Brandall, Brande, Brandel, Brandell, Brander, Brandley, Brandol, Brandt, Brandy, Brann

Brandeis (Czech) dweller on a burned clearing.
Brandis

Branden (English) beacon valley.

Brandon (English) beacon hill.
Bran, Brand, Brandan, Branddon, Brandin, Brandone, Brandonn,

Brandyn, Branndan, Brannon

Brandt (English) an alternate form of Brant.

Brandy (Dutch) brandy.
Brandey, Brandi, Brandie

Brannon (Irish) a form of Brandon.
Branen, Brannan, Branon

Branson (English) son of Brandon, Brant.
Bransen, Bransin, Brantson

Brant (English) proud.
Brandt, Brannt, Brantley, Brantlie

Brawley (English) meadow on the hillside.
Brawlee, Brawly

Braxton (English) Brock's town.

Breck (Irish) freckled.
Brec, Breckie, Brexton

Brede (Scandinavian) iceberg, glacier.

Brencis (Latvian) a form of Lawrence.

Brendan (Irish) little raven. (English) sword.
Breandan, Bren, Brenden, Brendis, Brendon, Brenn, Brennan, Brenndan, Bryn

Brenden (Irish) an alternate form of Brendan.
Bren, Brendene, Brendin, Brendine

Brennan, Brennen
(English, Irish) alternate
forms of Brendan.
Bren, Brennin, Brennon

Brent (English) a short
form of Brenton.
Brendt, Brentson

Brenton (English) steep
hill.
**Brent, Brentan, Brenten,
Brentin, Brentton,
Brentyn**

Bret, Brett (Scottish) from
Great Britain.
**Bhrett, Braten, Braton,
Brayton, Breton, Brette,
Bretten, Bretton, Brit**

Brit, Britt (Scottish) alter-
nate forms of Bret, Brett.
**Brit, Britain, Briton,
Brittain, Brittan, Britten,
Britton, Brityce**

Brewster (English) brewer.
Brew, Brewer, Bruwster

Brian (Irish, Scottish)
strong; virtuous; honor-
able. History: Brian Boru
was the most famous Irish
king. See also Palaina.
**Briano, Briant, Briante,
Brien, Brience, Brient,
Brin, Briny, Brion, Bryan**

Brice (Welsh) alert;
ambitious. (English) son
of Rice.
Bricen, Briceton, Bryce

Brick (English) bridge.
Brickman, Brik

Bridger (English) bridge
builder.
Bridd, Bridgeley, Bridgely

Brigham (English) covered
bridge. (French) troops,
brigade.
**Brig, Brigg, Briggs,
Brighton**

Brock (English) badger.
**Broc, Brocke, Brockett,
Brockie, Brockley,
Brockton, Brocky, Brok,
Broque**

Brod (English) a short form
of Broderick.

Broderick (Welsh) son
of the famous ruler.
(English) broad ridge.
See also Roderick.
**Brod, Broddie, Broddy,
Broderic, Brodric,
Brodrick, Brodryck**

Brodie (Irish) an alternate
form of Brody.
Brodi

Brody (Irish) ditch;
canal builder.
**Brodee, Broden, Brodey,
Brodie, Broedy**

Bromley (English) brushwood meadow.

Bron (Afrikaans) source.

Bronislaw (Polish) weapon
of glory.

Bronson (English) son
of Brown.
**Bransen, Bransin,
Branson, Bron, Bronnie,**

**Bronnson, Bronny,
Bronsen, Bronsin,
Bronsonn, Bronsson,
Bronsun**

Brook (English) brook,
stream.
**Brooke, Brooker, Brookin,
Brooklyn**

Brooks (English) son
of Brook.
Brookes, Broox

Brown (English) brown;
bear.

Bruce (French) brushwood
thicket; woods.
Brucey, Brucy, Brue, Bruis

Bruno (German, Italian)
brown haired; brown
skinned.
Brunon, Bruns

Bryan (Irish) strong; virtuous; honorable. An alter-
nate form of Brian.
Bryant, Bryen

Bryant (Irish) an alternate
form of Bryan.
Bryent

Bryce (Welsh) an alternate
form of Brice.
**Brycen, Bryceton, Bryson,
Bryston**

Bryon (German) cottage.
(English) bear.

Bryson (Welsh) son
of Brice.

Bubba (American) good
old boy.

Buck (German, English)
male deer.
**Buckie, Buckley, Buckner,
Bucko, Bucky**

Buckley (English) deer
meadow.
Bucklea, Bucklee

Buckminster (English)
preacher.

Bud (English) herald,
messenger.
Budd, Buddy

Buddy (American) a familiar form of Bud.
Budde, Buddey, Buddie

Buell (German) hill dweller.
(English) bull.

Buford (English) ford
near the castle.
Burford

Burgess (English) town
dweller; shopkeeper.
**Burg, Burges, Burgh,
Burgiss, Burr**

Burian (Ukrainian) lives
near weeds.

Burke (German, French)
fortress, castle.
**Berk, Berke, Birk, Bourke,
Burk, Burkley**

Burl (German) a short
form of Berlyn. (English)
cup bearer; wine servant;
knot in a tree.
**Burley, Burlie, Burlin,
Byrle**

Burleigh (English) meadow with knotted tree trunks.
Burlee, Burley, Burlie, Byrleigh, Byrlee

Burne (English) brook. See also Bourne.
Beirne, Burn, Burnell, Burnett, Burney, Byrne

Burney (English) island with a brook. A familiar form of Rayburn.

Burr (Swedish) youth. (English) prickly plant.

Burris (English) town dweller.

Burt (English) an alternate form of Bert. A short form of Burton.
Burrt, Burtt, Burty

Burton (English) fortified town.
Berton, Burt

Busby (Scottish) village in the thicket; tall, military hat made of fur.
Busbee, Buzby, Buzz

Butch (American) a short form of Butcher.

Butcher (English) butcher.
Butch

Buster (American) hitter, puncher.

Buzz (Scottish) a short form of Busby.
Buzzy

Byford (English) by the ford.

Byram (English) cattleyard.

Byrd (English) birdlike.
Bird, Birdie, Byrdie

Byrne (English) an alternate form of Burne.
Byrn, Byrnes

Byron (French) cottage. (English) barn.
Beyren, Beyron, Biren, Biron, Buiron, Byram, Byran, Byrann, Byren, Byrom, Byrone

Cable (French, English) rope maker.

Cadao (Vietnamese) folk song.

Cadby (English) warrior's settlement.

Caddock (Welsh) eager for war.

Cade (Welsh) a short form of Cadell.

Cadell (Welsh) battler.
Cade, Cadel, Cedell

Cadmus (Greek) from the east. Mythology: the founder of the city of Thebes.

Caelan (Scottish) a form
of Nicholas.
**Cael, Caelin, Cailan,
Cailean, Cailen, Cailin,
Caillan, Caillin, Calan,
Caleon, Caley, Calin,
Callan, Callen, Callon,
Calyn, Caylan, Cayley**

Caesar (Latin) long haired.
History: a title for Roman
emperors. See also Kaiser,
Kesar, Sarito.
**Caezar, Caseare, Ceasar,
Cesar, Ceseare, Cezar,
Cézar, Czar, Seasar**

Cahil (Turkish) young,
naive.

Cai (Welsh) a form of Gaius.
Caio, Caius, Caw

Cain (Hebrew) spear;
gatherer. Bible: Adam
and Eve's oldest son.
See also Kabil, Kane.
Cainan, Caine, Caineth

Cairn (Welsh) landmark
made of piled-up stones.
Cairne, Carn, Carne

Cairo (Arabic) Geography:
the capital of Egypt.
Kairo

Cal (Latin) a short form
of Calvert, Calvin.

Calder (Welsh, English)
brook, stream.

Caldwell (English) cold
well.

Cale (Hebrew) a short form
of Caleb.

Caleb (Hebrew) dog; faith-
ful. (Arabic) bold, brave.
Bible: a companion of
Moses and Joshua.
See also Kaleb.
Caeleb, Calab, Cale, Caley

Caley (Irish) a familiar form
of Caleb.

Calhoun (Irish) narrow
woods. (Scottish) warrior.
Colhoun, Colquhoun

Callahan (Irish) Religion:
a Catholic saint.
Calahan, Callaghan

Callum (Irish) dove.
Callam, Calum, Calym

Calvert (English) calf
herder.
Cal, Calbert, Calvirt

Calvin (Latin) bald.
See also Kalvin, Vinny.
Cal, Calv

Cam (Gypsy) beloved.
(Scottish) a short form
of Cameron.
**Camm, Cammie, Cammy,
Camy**

Camden (Scottish) winding
valley.

Cameron (Scottish)
crooked nose. See also
Kameron.
**Cam, Camar, Camaron,
Cameran, Camerson,
Camiren, Camron**

Camilo (Latin) child
born to freedom; noble.
Camiel, Camillo, Camillus

Campbell (Latin, French)
beautiful field. (Scottish)
crooked mouth.
Cam, Camp, Campy

Camron (Scottish) a short
form of Cameron.
Camren

Candide (Latin) pure;
sincere.
**Candid, Candido,
Candonino**

Cannon (French) church
official; large gun.
Cannan, Canning, Canon

Canute (Latin) white
haired. (Scandinavian)
knot. History: an ancient
Danish king who won
a battle at Knutsford.
See also Knute.
Cnut, Cnute

Cappi (Gypsy) good
fortune.

Car (Irish) a short form
of Carney.

Carey (Greek) pure.
(Welsh) castle; rocky
island. See also Karey.
Care, Cary

Carl (German) farmer.
(English) strong and
manly. An alternate form
of Charles. A short form
of Carlton. See also
Carroll, Karl.

**Carle, Carles, Carless,
Carlis, Carll, Carlo, Carlos,
Carlson, Carlston, Carlus,
Carolos**

Carlin (Irish) little
champion.
**Carlan, Carlen, Carley,
Carlie, Carling, Carlino,
Carly**

Carlisle (English) Carl's
island.
Carlyle, Carlysle

Carlo (Italian) a form
of Carl, Charles.
Carolo

Carlos (Spanish) a form
of Carl, Charles.

Carlton (English) Carl's
town.
**Carl, Carleton, Carllton,
Carlston, Carltonn,
Carltton, Charlton**

Carmel (Hebrew) vineyard,
garden. See also Carmine.
**Carmello, Carmelo,
Karmel**

Carmichael (Scottish)
follower of Michael.

Carmine (Latin) song;
crimson. (Italian) a form
of Carmel.
Carman, Carmen, Carmon

Carnell (English) defender
of the castle.

Carney (Irish) victorious.
(Scottish) fighter. See also
Kearney.
Car, Carny, Karney

Carr (Scandinavian) marsh. See also Kerr.
Karr

Carrick (Irish) rock.
Carooq, Carricko

Carroll (German) an alternate form of Carl. (Irish) champion.
Carel, Carell, Cariel, Cariell, Carol, Carole, Carolo, Carols, Carollan, Carolus, Carrol, Cary, Caryl

Carson (English) son of Carr.
Carrson

Carter (English) cart driver.
Cart

Cartwright (English) cart builder.

Carvell (French, English) village on the marsh.
Carvel

Carver (English) woodcarver; sculptor.

Case (Irish) a short form of Casey. (English) a short form of Casimir.

Casey (Irish) brave.
Case, Casie, Casy, Cayse, Caysey, Kacey

Cash (Latin) vain. (Slavic) a short form of Casimir.
Cashe

Casimir (Slavic) peacemaker.
Cachi, Cas, Case, Cash, Cashi, Casimire, Casimiro, Castimer, Kasimir

Casper (Persian) treasurer. (German) imperial. See also Gaspar, Jasper, Kasper.
Caspar, Cass

Cass (Irish, Persian) a short form of Casper, Cassidy.

Cassidy (Irish) clever; curly haired. See also Kazio.
Cass, Cassady, Cassie, Kassidy

Cassie (Irish) a familiar form of Cassidy.
Casi, Casie, Cassy

Cassius (Latin, French) box; protective cover.
Cassia, Cassio, Cazzie

Castle (Latin) castle.
Cassle, Castel

Castor (Greek) beaver. Astrology: one of the twins in the constellation Gemini. Mythology: one of the patron saints of sailors.
Caston

Cater (English) caterer.

Cato (Latin) knowledgeable, wise.
Caton, Catón

Cavan (Irish) handsome. See also Kevin.
Caven, Cavin

Cazzie (American) a familiar form of Cassius.
Caz, Cazz

Cecil (Latin) blind.
Cece, Cecile, Cecilio,
Cecilius, Cecill, Celio,
Siseal

Cedric (English) battle
chieftain. See also Kedrick,
Rick.
Cad, Caddaric, Ced,
Cedrec, Cédric, Cedrick,
Cedryche, Sedric

Cedrick (English) an alternate form of Cedric.
Cederick, Cedirick, Cedrik

Ceejay (American) a com-
bination of the initials
C. + J.
Cejay, C.J.

Cemal (Arabic) attractive.

Cephas (Latin) small rock.
Bible: the term used by
Jesus to describe Peter.
Cephus

Cerdic (Welsh) beloved.
Caradoc, Caradog,
Ceredig, Ceretic

Cerek (Greek) an alternate
form of Cyril. (Polish)
lordly.

Cesar (Spanish) a form
of Caesar.
Casar, César, Cesare,
Cesareo, Cesario, Cesaro

Cestmir (Czech) fortress.

Cezar (Slavic) a form
of Caesar.
Cézar, Cezary, Cezek,
Chezrae, Sezar

Chad (English) warrior.
A short form of Chadwick.
Geography: a country
in north-central Africa.
Ceadd, Chaad, Chadd,
Chaddie, Chaddy, Chade,
Chadleigh, Chadler,
Chadley, Chadlin,
Chadlyn, Chadmen,
Chado, Chadron, Chady

Chadrick (German)
mighty warrior.
Chaderick, Chadric

Chadwick (English)
warrior's town.
Chad, Chadvic, Chadwyck

Chago (Spanish) a form
of Jacob.
Chango, Chanti

Chaim (Hebrew) life.
See also Hyman.
Chai, Chaimek, Haim,
Khaim

Chal (Gypsy) boy; son.
Chalie, Chalin

Chalmers (Scottish) son
of the lord.
Chalmer, Chalmr, Chamar,
Chamarr

Cham (Vietnamese) hard
worker.
Chams

Chan (Sanskrit) shining.
(Spanish) an alternate
form of Juan.
Chann, Chano, Chayo

Chanan (Hebrew) cloud.

Chance (English) a short form of Chancellor, Chauncey.
Chanc, Chancey, Chancy, Chanse, Chansy, Chants, Chantz, Chanz

Chancellor (English) recordkeeper.
Chance, Chancelen

Chander (Hindi) moon.
Chand, Chandan, Chandany, Chandara, Chandaravth, Chandon

Chandler (English) candle maker.
Chand, Chandlan

Chane (Swahili) dependable.

Chaney (French) oak.
Chayne, Cheney, Cheyn, Cheyne, Cheyney

Chankrisna (Cambodian) sweet-smelling tree.

Channing (English) wise. (French) canon; church official.
Chane, Chann

Chante (French) singer.
Chant, Chantha, Chanthar, Chantra, Chantry, Shantae

Chapman (English) merchant.
Chap, Chappie, Chappy

Charles (German) farmer. (English) strong and manly. See also Carl, Searles, Tearlach, Xarles.
Carlo, Carlos, Charl, Charle, Charlen, Charlie, Charlot, Charlzell, Chick, Chip, Chuck

Charlie (German, English) a familiar form of Charles.
Charley, Charly

Charlton (English) a form of Carlton.
Charlesten, Charleston, Charleton, Charlotin

Charro (Spanish) cowboy.

Chase (French) hunter.
Chasen, Chason, Chass, Chasten, Chaston, Chasyn

Chauncey (English) chancellor; church official.
Chan, Chance, Chancey, Chaunce, Chauncei, Chauncy

Chayton (Lakota) falcon.

Chaz (English) a familiar form of Charles.
Chas, Chazwick, Chazz

Ché (Spanish) a familiar form of José. History: Ché Guevarra was a revolutionary who fought at Fidel Castro's side in Cuba.
Chay

Checha (Spanish) a familiar form of Jacob.

Cheche (Spanish) a familiar form of Joseph.

Chen (Chinese) great, tremendous.

Chencho (Spanish) a familiar form of Lawrence.

Chepe (Spanish) a familiar form of Joseph.
Cepito

Cherokee (Cherokee) people of a different speech.

Chesmu (Native American) gritty.

Chester (English) a short form of Rochester.
Ches, Cheslav, Cheston, Chet

Chet (English) a short form of Chester.

Cheung (Chinese) good luck.

Chevalier (French) horseman, knight.
Chev, Chevy

Chevy (French) a familiar form of Chevalier. Geography: Chevy Chase is a town in Maryland. Culture: a short form of Chevrolet, an American automobile.
Chev, Chevi, Chevie, Chevvy

Chi (Chinese) younger generation. (Nigerian) personal guardian angel.

Chick (English) a familiar form of Charles.
Chic, Chickie, Chicky

Chico (Spanish) boy.

Chik (Gypsy) earth.

Chike (Ibo) God's power.

Chiko (Japanese) arrow; pledge.

Chilo (Spanish) a familiar form of Francisco.

Chilton (English) farm by the spring.
Chil, Chill, Chilt

Chim (Vietnamese) bird.

Chinua (Ibo) God's blessing.
Chino, Chinou

Chioke (Ibo) gift of God.

Chip (English) a familiar form of Charles.
Chipman, Chipper

Chiram (Hebrew) exalted; noble.

Chris (Greek) a short form of Christian, Christopher. See also Kris.
Chriss, Christ, Chrys, Cris, Crist

Christian (Greek) follower of Christ; anointed. See also Jaan, Kerstan, Kit, Krister, Khristian, Kristian, Krystian.
Chretien, Chris, Christa, Christai, Christain, Christé, Christen,

Christensen, Christiaan, Christiana, Christiano, Christianos, Christin, Christino, Christion, Christon, Christos, Christyan, Chritian, Chrystian, Cristian, Crystek

Christoff (Russian) a form of Christopher.
Chrisof, Christif

Christophe (French) a form of Christopher.
Christoph

Christopher (Greek) Christ-bearer. Religion: the patron saint of travelers and drivers. See also Kester, Kit, Kristopher, Risto, Stoffel, Tobal, Topher.
Chris, Chrisopherson, Christafer, Christepher, Christhoper, Christifer, Christipher, Christobal, Christofer, Christoff, Christoffer, Christofper, Christoher, Christopehr, Christoper, Christophe, Christopherr, Christophoros, Christorpher, Christos, Christovao, Christpher, Christphere, Christpor, Christrpher

Christophoros (Greek) an alternate form of Christopher.
Christoforo, Christoforos, Christophor, Christophorus, Christphor, Cristoforo, Cristopher

Christos (Greek) an alternate form of Christopher. See also Khristos.

Chucho (Hebrew) a familiar form of Jesus.

Chuck (American) a familiar form of Charles.
Chuckey, Chuckie, Chucky

Chui (Swahili) leopard.

Chul (Korean) firm.

Chuma (Ibo) having many beads, wealthy. (Swahili) iron.

Chuminga (Spanish) a familiar form of Dominic.
Chumin

Chumo (Spanish) a familiar form of Thomas.

Chung (Chinese) intelligent.
Chungo, Chuong

Churchill (English) church on the hill. History: Sir Winston Churchill served as British prime minister and won a Nobel Prize for literature.

Cian (Irish) ancient.
Céin, Cianán, Kian

Cicero (Latin) chickpea. History: a famous Roman orator and statesman.
Cicerón

Cid (Spanish) lord. History:
an eleventh-century
Spanish soldier and
national hero.
Cyd

Ciqala (Dakota) little.

Cirrillo (Italian) a form
of Cyril.
Cirilio, Cirilo, Ciro

Cisco (Spanish) a short
form of Francisco.

Clancy (Irish) red-headed
fighter.
Clancey, Claney

Clare (Latin) a short form
of Clarence.
Clair, Clarey, Clary

Clarence (Latin) clear;
victorious.
**Clarance, Clare, Clarrance,
Clarrence, Clearence**

Clark (French) cleric;
scholar.
Clarke, Clerc, Clerk

Claude (Latin, French)
lame.
**Claud, Claudan, Claudel,
Claudell, Claudian,
Claudianus, Claudien,
Claudin, Claudio, Claudius**

Claudio (Italian) a form
of Claude.

Claus (German) a short
form of Nicholas. See also
Klaus.
Claas, Claes, Clause

Clay (English) clay pit.
A short form of Clayborne,
Clayton.

Clayborne (English) brook
near the clay pit.
**Claiborn, Claiborne, Clay,
Clayborn, Claybourne,
Clayburn**

Clayton (English) town
built on clay.
Clay

Cleary (Irish) learned.

Cleavon (English) cliff.

Clem (Latin) a short form
of Clement.
Cleme, Clemmy, Clim

Clement (Latin) merciful.
Bible: a disciple of Paul.
See also Klement, Menz.
**Clem, Clemens, Clément,
Clemente, Clementius,
Clemmons**

Clemente (Italian, Spanish)
a form of Clement.
Clemento, Clemenza

Cleon (Greek) famous.
Kleon

Cletus (Greek) illustrious.
History: a Roman pope
and martyr.
Cledis, Cleotis, Cletis

Cleveland (English) land
of cliffs.
**Cleaveland, Cleavland,
Cleavon, Cleve, Clevelend,
Clevelynn, Clevey, Clevie,
Clevon**

Cliff (English) a short form
of Clifford, Clifton.
**Clif, Clift, Clive, Clyff,
Clyph**

Clifford (English) cliff at
the river crossing.
Cliff, Cliford, Clyfford

Clifton (English) cliff town.
**Cliff, Cliffton, Clift,
Cliften, Clyfton**

Clint (English) a short
form of Clinton.

Clinton (English) hill town.
**Clint, Clinten, Clintton,
Clynton**

Clive (English) an alternate
form of Cliff.
**Cleve, Clivans, Clivens,
Clyve**

Clovis (German) famous
soldier. See also Louis.

Cluny (Irish) meadow.

Clyde (Welsh) warm.
(Scottish) Geography:
a river in Scotland.
Cly, Clywd

Coby (Hebrew) a familiar
form of Jacob.
Cob, Cobe, Cobey, Cobie

Cochise (Apache) History:
a famous Apache warrior
and chief.

Coco (French) a familiar
form of Jacques.
Coko, Koko

Codey (English) an alternate form of Cody.
Coday

Cody (English) cushion.
History: William Cody
(Buffalo Bill) was a sharp-
shooter and showman in
the American "Wild" West.
See also Kody.
**Code, Codee, Codell,
Codey, Codi, Codiak,
Codie, Coedy**

Coffie (Ewe) born on
Friday.

Cola (Italian) a familiar form
of Nicola, Nicholas.
Colas

Colar (French) a form
of Nicholas.

Colbert (English) famous
seafarer.
**Cole, Colt, Colvert,
Culbert**

Colby (English) dark;
dark haired.
Colbey, Collby, Kolby

Cole (Greek) a short form
of Nicholas. (Latin)
cabbage farmer. (English)
a short form of Coleman.
Colet, Coley, Colie

Coleman (Latin) cabbage
farmer. (English) coal
miner.
**Cole, Colemann, Colm,
Colman**

Colin (Greek) a short
form of Nicholas.
(Irish) young cub.
**Cailean, Colan, Cole,
Colen, Collin, Colyn**

Colley (English) black
haired; swarthy.
Collie, Collis

Collier (English) miner.
**Colier, Collayer, Collie,
Collyer, Colyer**

Collin (Scottish) a form
of Colin, Collins.
Collen, Collon, Collyn

Collins (Greek) son of
Colin. (Irish) holly.
Coilin, Coilis

Colson (Greek, English)
son of Nicholas.
Coulson

Colt (English) young horse;
frisky. A short form of
Colter, Colton.

Colter (English) herd
of colts.
Colt

Colton (English) coal town.
**Colt, Colten, Coltin,
Coltrane, Kolton**

Columba (Latin) dove.
Coim, Columbus

Colwyn (Welsh)
Geography: a river in
Wales.
Colwin, Colwinn

Coman (Arabic) noble.
(Irish) bent.
Comán

Conall (Irish) high, mighty.
Connell

Conan (Irish) praised;
exalted. (Scottish) wise.
**Conant, Conary, Connie,
Connor, Conon**

Conary (Irish) an alternate
form of Conan.
Conaire

Conlan (Irish) hero.
**Conlen, Conley, Conlin,
Conlyn**

Connie (English, Irish)
a familiar form of Conan,
Conrad, Constantine,
Conway.
Con, Conn, Conney, Conny

Connor (Scottish) wise.
(Irish) an alternate form
of Conan.
Conner, Conor, Konnor

Conor (Irish) an alternate
form of Connor.

Conrad (German) brave
counselor.
**Connie, Conrade,
Conrado, Corrado,
Konrad**

Conroy (Irish) wise.
Conry, Roy

Constant (Latin) a short
form of Constantine.

Constantine (Latin)
firm, constant. History:
Constantine the Great
was one of the most
famous Roman emperors.
See also Dinos, Konstantin,
Stancio.
**Connie, Constadine,
Constandine,
Constandios,
Constanstine, Constant,
Constantin, Constantino,
Constantinos,
Constantios, Costa**

Conway (Irish) hound
of the plain.
Connie, Conwy

Cook (English) cook.
Cooke

Cooper (English) barrel
maker. See also Keiffer.
Coop, Couper

Corbett (Latin) raven.
Corbet, Corbit, Corbitt

Corbin (Latin) raven.
**Corban, Corben, Corbey,
Corbie, Corby, Korbin**

Corcoran (Irish) ruddy.

Cordaro (Spanish) an alter-
nate form of Cordero.
**Coradaro, Cordairo,
Cordara, Cordarell,
Cordareo, Cordarin,
Cordario, Cordarius,
Cordarrel, Cordarrell,
Cordarro, Cordarrol,
Cordarryl, Cordaryal,
Corddarro, Corrdarl**

Cordell (French) rope
maker.
**Cord, Cordae, Cordale,
Corday, Cordeal, Cordel,
Cordelle, Cordie, Cordy,
Kordell**

Cordero (Spanish) little
lamb.
**Cordaro, Cordeal,
Cordeara, Cordearo,
Cordeiro, Cordelro,
Cordera, Corderall,
Corderro, Corderun,
Cordiaro, Cordy,
Corrderio**

Corey (Irish) hollow.
See also Kory.
**Core, Coreaa, Cori,
Corian, Corie, Corio,
Correy, Corria, Corrie,
Corry, Corrye, Cory**

Cormac (Irish) raven's son.
History: a third-century
king of Ireland who
founded schools.
Cormack, Cormick

Cornelius (Greek) cornel
tree. (Latin) horn colored.
See also Kornel, Kornelius,
Nelek.
**Carnelius, Conny,
Cornealous, Corneili,
Corneilius, Corneliaus,
Cornelious, Cornelis,
Corneliu, Cornell,
Cornellis, Cornellius,
Cornelus, Corney, Cornie,
Corniellus, Corny,
Cournelius, Nelius, Nellie**

Cornell (French) a form
of Cornelius.
**Carnell, Cornail, Corney,
Cornie, Corny, Nellie**

Cornwallis (English) from
Cornwall.

Corrado (Italian) a form
of Conrad.
Carrado

Corrigan (Irish) spearman.
**Corrigon, Corrigun,
Korrigan**

Corrin (Irish) spear carrier.

Corry (Latin) a form of
Corey.

Cort (German) bold.
(Scandinavian) short.
(English) a short form
of Courtney.
Cortie, Corty, Kort

Cortez (Spanish)
conqueror. History:
Hernando Cortez was an
explorer who conquered
the Aztecs in Mexico.
Cartez, Cortes, Courtez

Corwin (English) heart's
companion; heart's
delight.
**Corwinn, Corwyn,
Corwynn**

Cory (Latin) a form of
Corey. (French) a familiar
form of Cornell.

Corydon (Greek) helmet,
crest.

**Coridon, Corradino, Cory,
Coryden, Coryell**

Cosgrove (Irish) victor,
champion.

Cosmo (Greek) orderly;
harmonious; universe.
**Cos, Cosimo, Cosme,
Cosmé, Cozmo, Kosmo**

Costa (Greek) a short form
of Constantine.
**Costandinos, Costantinos,
Costas, Costes**

Coty (French) slope,
hillside.
Cotee, Cotey, Cotie, Cotty

Courtland (English) court's
land.
**Court, Courtlana,
Courtlandt, Courtlin,
Courtlyn**

Courtney (English) court.
**Cort, Cortnay, Cortne,
Cortney, Court,
Courteney, Courtnay, Curt**

Cowan (Irish) hillside
hollow.
Coe, Cowey, Cowie

Coy (English) woods.
Coyie, Coyt

Coyle (Irish) leader in
battle.

Coyne (French) modest.
Coyan

Craddock (Welsh) love.
Caradoc, Caradog

Craig (Irish, Scottish) crag;
steep rock.
**Crag, Craige, Craigen,
Craigery, Craigon, Creag,
Cregg, Creig, Criag, Kraig**

Crandall (English) crane's
valley.
**Cran, Crandal, Crandell,
Crendal**

Crawford (English) ford
where crows fly.
Craw, Crow, Ford

Creed (Latin) belief.
Creedon

Creighton (English) town
near the rocks.
**Cray, Crayton, Creighm,
Creight, Creighto,
Crichton**

Crepin (French) a form
of Crispin.

Crispin (Latin) curly haired.
**Crepin, Cris, Crispian,
Crispino, Crispo, Krispin**

Cristian (Greek) an alter-
nate form of Christian.
**Crétien, Cristhian,
Cristiano, Cristino, Cristle,
Criston, Cristos, Cristy,
Crystek**

Cristoforo (Italian) a form
of Christopher.
Cristofor

Cristopher (Greek)
an alternate form of
Christopher.
Cristaph, Cristóbal,

**Cristobál, Cristofer,
Cristoph, Cristophe,
Cristoval, Cristovao**

Crofton (Irish) town
with cottages.

Cromwell (English)
crooked spring, winding
spring.

Crosby (Scandinavian)
shrine of the cross.
Crosbey, Crosbie, Cross

Crosley (English) meadow
of the cross.
Cross

Crowther (English) fiddler.

Cruz (Portuguese, Spanish)
cross.
Kruz

Crystek (Polish) a form
of Christian.

Csaba (Hungarian)
Geography: a city in
southwestern Hungary.

Cullen (Irish) handsome.
Cull, Cullan, Cullie, Cullin

Culley (Irish) woods.
Cullie, Cully

Culver (English) dove.
Colver, Cull, Cullie, Cully

Cunningham (Irish) village
of the milk pail.

Curran (Irish) hero.
**Curan, Curr, Currey,
Currie, Curry**

Currito (Spanish) a form
of Curtis.
Curcio

Curt (Latin) a short form
of Courtney, Curtis.
See also Kurt.

Curtis (Latin) enclosure.
(French) courteous.
See also Kurtis.
**Curio, Currito, Curt,
Curtice, Curtiss, Curtus**

Cuthbert (English)
brilliant.

Cutler (English) knife
maker.
Cut, Cuttie, Cutty

Cy (Persian) a short form
of Cyrus.

Cyprian (Latin) from the
island of Cyprus.
Cipriano, Ciprien, Cyprien

Cyrano (Greek) from
Cyrene, an ancient Greek
city. Literature: *Cyrano
de Bergerac* is a play by
Edmond Rostand about
a great swordsman whose
large nose prevented him
from pursuing the woman
he loved.

Cyril (Greek) lordly.
See also Kiril.
**Cerek, Cerel, Ceril, Ciril,
Cirillo, Cyra, Cyrel, Cyrell,
Cyrelle, Cyrill, Cyrille,
Cyrillus**

Cyrus (Persian) sun.
Historial: Cyrus the Great
was a king in ancient
Persia. See also Kir.
Ciro, Cy, Cyris

Dabi (Basque) a form
of David.

Dabir (Arabic) tutor.

Dacey (Latin) from Dacia,
an area now in Romania.
(Irish) southerner.
**Dace, Dache, Dacian,
Dacias, Dacio, Dacy,
Daicey, Daicy**

Dada (Yoruba) curly haired.
Dadi

Daegel (English) from
Daegel, England.

Dafydd (Welsh) a form
of David.

Dag (Scandinavian) day;
bright.
**Daeg, Daegan, Dagen,
Dagny, Deegan**

Dagan (Hebrew) corn;
grain.
Dagon

Dagwood (English) shining
forest.

Dai (Japanese) big.

Dajuan (American) a combination of the prefix Da + Juan. See also Dejuan.
Da Jon, Da-Juan, Dawan, Dawaun, Dawawn, Dawon, Dawoyan, Dijuan, Diuan, Dujuan, D'Juan, D'juan, Dwaun

Dakarai (Shona) happy.

Dakota (Dakota) friend; partner; tribal name.
Dac, Dack, Dacoda, Dacota, DaCota, Dak, Dakoata, Dakotah, Dakotha, Dekota, Dekotes

Daksh (Hindi) efficient.

Dalal (Sanskrit) broker.

Dalbert (English) bright, shining. See also Delbert.

Dale (English) dale, valley.
Dael, Dal, Dalen, Daley, Dalibor, Daly, Dayl, Dayle

Dalen (English) an alternate form of Dale.
Daelan, Daelen, Daelin, Dailin, Dalan, Dalian, Dalibor, Dalin, Dalione, Dallan, Dalyn, Daylan, Daylen, Daylin, Daylon

Daley (Irish) assembly. (English) a familiar form of Dale.
Daily, Daly, Dawley

Dallan (English) an alternate form of Dale.

Dallen, Dallin, Dallon, Dallyn

Dallas (Scottish) Geography: a town in Scotland; a city in Texas.
Dal, Dalieass, Dall, Dalles, Dallis, Dalys, Dellis

Dalston (English) Daegel's place.
Dalis, Dallon

Dalton (English) town in the valley.
Dal, Dallton, Dalt, Dalten

Dalziel (Scottish) small field.

Damek (Slavic) a form of Adam.
Damick, Damicke

Damian (Greek) tamer; soother.
Daemean, Daemon, Daemyen, Daimean, Daimen, Daimon, Daimyan, Damaiaon, Dame, Damean, Dameion, Dameon, Dameone, Damián, Damiann, Damiano, Damianos, Damien, Damion, Damján, Damyan, Daymian, Dema, Demyan

Damien (Greek) an alternate form of Damian. Religion: Father Damien spent his life serving the leper colony on Molokai island, Hawaii.

Damien (cont.)
Daemien, Daimien, Damie, Damyen

Damion (Greek) an alternate form of Damian.
Damin, Damyon

Damon (Greek) constant, loyal. (Latin) spirit, demon.
Daemen, Daemon, Daemond, Daimon, Daman, Damen, Damonn, Damonta, Damontez, Damontis, Daymon, Daymond

Dan (Hebrew) a short form of Daniel. (Vietnamese) yes.
Dahn, Danh, Danne

Dana (Scandinavian) from Denmark.
Dain, Daina

Dandin (Hindi) holy man.

Dandré (French) a combination of the prefix De + André.
D'André, Dandrae, D'andrea, Dandras, Dandray, Dandre, Dondrea

Dane (English) from Denmark. See also Halden.
Daine, Danie, Dayne, Dhane

Danek (Polish) a form of Daniel.

Danforth (English) a form of Daniel.

Danial (Hebrew) an alternate form of Daniel.
Danal, Daneal, Danieal

Daniel (Hebrew) God is my judge. Bible: a great Hebrew prophet. See also Danno, Kanaiela.
Dacso, Dan, Daneel, Daneil, Danek, Danel, Danforth, Danial, Dániel, Daniël, Daniele, Danielius, Daniell, Daniels, Danielson, Danila, Danilka, Danilo, Daniyel, Dan'l, Dannel, Danniel, Dannil, Danno, Danny, Danukas, Danyel, Dasco, Dayne, Deniel, Doneal, Doniel, Donois, Dusan, Nelo

Daniele (Hebrew) an alternate form of Daniel.

Danior (Gypsy) born with teeth.

Danladi (Hausa) born on Sunday.

Danno (Hebrew) a familiar form of Daniel. (Japanese) gathering in the meadow.
Dannon, Dano

Dannon (American) a form of Danno.
Daenan, Daenen, Dainon, Danaan, Danen, Danon

Danny (Hebrew) a familiar form of Daniel.
Dani, Dannee, Dannie, Dannye, Dany

Dano (Czech) a form
of Daniel.
Danko

Dante (Latin) lasting,
enduring.
**Danatay, Danaté,
Dant, Danté, Dauntay,
Dauntaye, Daunté,
Dauntrae, Deanté,
De Anté, Deaunta,
Dontae, Donté**

Danyel (Hebrew) an alter-
nate form of Daniel.
**Danya, Danyal, Danyale,
Danyele, Danyell, Danyiel,
Danyl, Danyle, Danylets,
Danylo, Donyell**

Daoud (Arabic) a form
of David.
**Daudi, Daudy, Dauod,
Dawud**

Daquan (American)
a combination of the
prefix Da + Quan.
**Daquain, Daquann,
Daquawn, Daqwan,
Dequain, Dequan,
Dequann, Dequaun**

Dar (Hebrew) pearl.

Dara (Cambodian) stars.

Daran (Irish) an alternate
form of Darren.
**Darann, Darawn, Darian,
Darran, Dayran, Deran**

Darby (Irish) free.
(English) deer park.
**Dar, Darb, Darbee,
Darbey, Darbie, Derby**

Darcy (Irish) dark.
(French) from Arcy.
**Dar, Daray, D'Aray, Darce,
Darcee, Darcel, Darcey,
Darcio, D'Arcy, Darsey,
Darsy**

Dareh (Persian) wealthy.

Darell (English) a form
of Darrell.
Daralle, Dareal

Daren (Irish) an alternate
form of Darren. (Hausa)
born at night.
Dare, Dayren, Dheren

Darick (German) an alter-
nate form of Derek.
**Daric, Darico, Darek,
Darik**

Darin (Irish) an alternate
form of Darren.
**Darian, Darien, Darion,
Darrian, Darrin, Daryn,
Darynn, Dayrin, Dearin,
Dharin**

Dario (Spanish) affluent.

Darius (Greek) wealthy.
**Dairus, Dare, Darieus,
Darioush, Darrias,
Darrious, Darris, Darrius,
Darrus, Derrious, Derris,
Derrius**

Darnell (English) hidden
place.
Dar, Darn, Darnall, Darnel

Daron (Irish) an alternate
form of Darren.
**Darron, Dayron, Dearon,
Dharon, Diron**

Darrell (French) darling, beloved; grove of oak trees.
Dare, Darel, Darell, Darral, Darrel, Darrill, Darrol, Darryl, Derrell

Darren (Irish) great. (English) small; rocky hill.
Daran, Dare, Daren, Darin, Daron, Darran, Darrian, Darrien, Darrience, Darrin, Darrion, Darron, Darryn, Darun, Daryn, Dearron, Deren, Dereon, Derren, Derron

Darrick (German) an alternate form of Derek.
Darrec, Darrik, Darryk

Darrion (Irish) an alternate form of Darren.
Darian, Darien, Darion, Darrian, Darrien, Derrian, Derrion

Darryl (French) darling, beloved; grove of oak trees. An alternate form of Darrell.
Dahrll, Darryle, Darryll, Daryl, Daryle, Daryll, Derryl

Darshan (Hindi) god; godlike. Religion: another name for the Hindu god Shiva.

Darton (English) deer town.
Dartel, Dartrel

Darwin (English) dear friend. History: Charles Darwin was the naturalist who established the theory of evolution.
Darwyn, Derwin, Derwynn, Durwin

Daryl (French) an alternate form of Darryl.
Darel, Daril, Darl, Darly, Daryell, Daryle, Daryll, Darylle, Daroyl

Dasan (Pomo) leader of the bird clan.
Dassan

Dauid (Swahili) a form of David.

Dave (Hebrew) a short form of David, Davis.

Davey (Hebrew) a familiar form of David.
Davee, Davi, Davie, Davy

David (Hebrew) beloved. Bible: the first king of Israel. See also Dov, Havika, Kawika, Taaveti, Taffy, Tevel.
Dabi, Daevid, Dafydd, Dai, Daivid, Daoud, Dauid, Dav, Dave, Daved, Daveed, Daven, Davey, Davidde, Davide, Davidek, Davido, Davon, Davoud, Davyd, Dawid, Dawit, Dawud, Dayvid, Dodya, Dov

Davin (Scandinavian) brilliant Finn.
Daevin, Davinte, Davon, Dawin, Dawine

Davis (Welsh) son of David.
**Dave, Davidson, Davies,
Davison**

Davon (American) a form
of Davin.
**Daevon, Davon, Davone,
Davonn, Davonne,
Davonte, Dayvon, Devon**

Dawit (Ethiopian) a form
of David.

Dawson (English) son of
David.

Dax (French, English) water.

Dayne (Scandinavian)
a form of Dane.

Dayton (English) day town;
bright, sunny town.
Daeton, Daiton, Deyton

De (Chinese) virtuous.

Deacon (Greek) one who
serves.
Deke

Dean (French) leader.
(English) valley. See also
Dino.
Deane, Deen, Dene, Deyn

Deandre (French)
a combination of the
prefix De + André.
**D'andre, D'andré,
D'André, D'andrea,
Deandrae, Déandre,
Deandré, Deandra,
De André, Deandrea,
De Andrea, Deaundera,
Deaundra, Deaundre,
De Aundre, Deaundrey,**

**Deondray, Deondre,
Deondré**

Deangelo (Italian)
a combination of the
prefix De + Angelo.
**Dang, Dangelo, D'Angelo,
Danglo, Deaengelo,
Déangelo, De Angelo,
Deangleo, Deanglo,
Diangelo, Di'angelo**

Deanthony (Italian)
a combination of the
prefix De + Anthony.
**D'anthony, Danton,
Dianthony**

Dearborn (English) deer
brook.
**Dearbourn, Dearburne,
Deerborn**

Decarlos (Spanish)
a combination of the
prefix De + Carlos.
**Dacarlos, Decarlo,
Di'carlos**

Decha (Thai) strong.

Decimus (Latin) tenth.

Declan (Irish) man of
prayer. Religion: Saint
Declan was a fifth-century
Irish bishop.

Dedrick (German) ruler
of the people.
**Deadrick, Dederick,
Dedric, Dedrix, Diedrich,
Diedrick, Dietrich, Detrick**

Deems (English) judge's
child.

Dejuan (American)
a combination of the
prefix De + Juan. See also
Dajuan.
**Dejan, Dejon, Dejun,
Dewan, Dewaun, Dewon,
Dijaun, D'Juan, Dujuan,
D'Won**

Dekel (Hebrew, Arabic)
palm tree, date tree.

Del (English) a short form
of Delbert, Delvin, Delwin.

Delaney (Irish) descendant
of the challenger.
**Delaine, Delainey, Delainy,
Delan, Delane, Delanny,
Delany**

Delano (French) nut tree.
(Irish) dark.
Delayno

Delbert (English) bright as
day. See also Dalbert.
Bert, Del, Dilbert

Delfino (Latin) dolphin.

Déli (Chinese) virtuous.

Dell (English) small valley.
A short form of Udell.

Delling (Scandinavian)
scintillating.

Delmar (Latin) sea.
**Dalmar, Dalmer, Delmer,
Delmor, Delmore**

Delroy (French) belonging
to the king. See also Elroy,
Leroy.
Delray, Delree, Delroi

Delsin (Native American)
he is so.
Delsy

Delvin (English) proud
friend; friend from the
valley.
**Del, Delavan, Delvyn,
Delwin**

Delwin (English) an alter-
nate form of Delvin.
**Dalwin, Dalwyn, Del,
Dellwin, Dellwyn, Delwyn,
Delwynn**

Deman (Dutch) man.

Demarco (Italian)
a combination of the
prefix De + Marco.
Damarco, D'Marco

Demarcus (American)
a combination of the
prefix De + Marcus.
**Damarcius, Damarcus,
Demarkes, Demarkis,
Demarkus, D'Marcus**

Demario (Italian)
a combination of the
prefix De + Mario.
**Demarreio, Demarrio,
Demerrio**

Dembe (Luganda)
peaceful.
Damba

Demetris (Greek) a short
form of Demetrius.
**Demeatric, Demeatrice,
Demeatris, Demetres,
Demetress, Demetric,
Demetrice, Demetrick,**

Demetrics, Demetricus, Demetrik, Demitrez

Demetrius (Greek) lover of the earth. Mythology: a follower of Demeter, the goddess of the harvest and fertility. See also Dimitri, Mimis, Mitsos.
Damitriuz, Demeitrius, Demeterious, Demetreus, Demetrias, Demetrio, Demetrios, Demetrious, Demetris, Demetriu, Demetrium, Demetrois, Demetruis, Demetrus, Demitirus, Demitri, Demitrias, Demitriu, Demitrius, Demitrus, Demtrius, Demtrus, Dimitri, Dimitrios, Dimitrius, Dmetrius, Dymek

Demichael (American) a combination of the prefix De + Michael.
Dumichael

Demitri (Greek) a short form of Demetrius.
Dametri, Damitré, Demeter, Demetre, Demetrea, Demetri, Demetriel, Demitre, Domotor

Demond (Irish) a short form of Desmond.
Demonde, Demonds, Demone, Dumonde

Demont (French) mountain.

Démont, Demonta, Demonte, Demontez, Demontre

Demorris (American) a combination of the prefix De + Morris.
Demoris, DeMorris, Demorus

Demos (Greek) people.
Demas, Demosthenes

Demothi (Native American) talks while walking.

Dempsey (Irish) proud.
Demp, Demps, Dempsie, Dempsy

Dempster (English) one who judges.
Demster

Denby (Scandinavian) Geography: a Danish village.
Danby, Den, Denbey, Denney, Dennie, Denny

Denham (English) village in the valley.

Denholm (Scottish) Geography: a town in Scotland.

Denis (Greek) an alternate form of Dennis.

Denley (English) meadow; valley.
Denlie, Denly

Denman (English) man from the valley.

Dennis (Greek) Mythology: a follower of Dionysius, the god of wine. See also Dion, Nicho.
Den, Dénes, Denies, Denis, Deniz, Dennes, Dennet, Denny, Dennys, Denya, Denys, Deon, Dinis

Dennison (English) son of Dennis. See also Dyson, Tennyson.
Den, Denison, Denisson, Dennyson

Denny (Greek) a familiar form of Dennis.
Den, Denney, Dennie, Deny

Denton (English) happy home.
Dent, Denten, Dentin

Denver (English) green valley. Geography: the capital of Colorado.

Denzil (Cornish) Geography: a location in Cornwall, England.
Danzel, Danzell, Dennzel, Dennzil, Dennzyl, Denzel, Denzell, Denziel, Denzill, Denzyl, Donzell

Deon (Greek) an alternate form of Dennis. See also Dion.
Deion, Deone, Deonno

Deontae (American) a combination of the prefix De + Dontae.
D'Ante, Deante, Deonta,

Deonte, Deonté, Deontée, Deontie, Deontre, Deontrea, Deontrez, Diante, Diontae, Diontay

Dequan (American) a combination of the prefix De + Quan.
Dequain, Dequan, Dequann, Dequaun

Derek (German) ruler of the people. A short form of Theodoric. See also Dietrich, Dirk.
Darek, Darick, Darrick, Derak, Dereck, Derecke, Derele, Derick, Derk, Derke, Derrek, Derrick, Deryek

Derick (German) an alternate form of Derek.
Deric, Dericka, Derico, Deriek, Derik, Derikk, Derique, Deryck, Deryk, Deryke, Detrek

Dermot (Hebrew) a short form of Jeremiah. (Irish) free from envy. (English) free. See also Kermit.
Der, Dermod, Dermott, Diarmid, Diarmuid

Deron (Hebrew) bird; freedom. (American) a combination of the prefix De + Ron.
Daaron, Daron, Da-Ron, Darone, Darron, Dayron, Dereon, Deronn, Deronne, Derrin, Derrion, Derron,

Derronn, Derronne, Derryn, Diron, Duron, Durron, Dyron

Deror (Hebrew) lover of freedom.
Derori, Derorie

Derrek (German) an alternate form of Derek.
Derrec, Derreck

Derrell (French) an alternate form of Darrell.
Derrel, Dérrell, Derriel, Derril, Derrill

Derren (Irish) great. An alternate form of Darren.
Deren, Derran, Derrien, Derrin, Derryn

Derrick (German) ruler of the people. An alternate form of Derek.
Derric, Derrik, Derryck, Derryk

Derry (Irish) redhead. Geography: a city in Northern Ireland.
Darrie, Darry, Derrie, Derrye

Derryl (French) an alternate form of Darryl.
Deryl, Deryll

Derward (English) deer keeper.

Derwin (English) an alternate form of Darwin.
Derwyn

Deshane (American) a combination of the prefix De + Shane.
Deshan, Deshayne

Deshawn (American) a combination of the prefix De + Shawn.
Dasean, Dashaun, Dashawn, Desean, Deshaun, Deshaune, Deshauwn, Deshawan, D'Sean, D'shaun, D'Shaun, D'shawn, D'Shawn, Dusean, Dushan, Dushaun, Dushawn

Deshea (American) a combination of the prefix De + Shea.
Deshay

Déshì (Chinese) virtuous.

Deshon (American) an alternate form of Deshawn.
Deshondre, Deshone, Deshonte, Deshun

Desiderio (Spanish) desired.

Desmond (Irish) from south Munster.
Demond, Des, Desi, Desmon, Desmund, Dezmon, Dezmond

Destin (French) destiny, fate.
Destine, Deston, Destry

Destry (American) a form of Destin.
Destrey, Destrie

Detrick (German) an alternate form of Dedrick.
Detric

Devayne (American) an alternate form of Dewayne.
Devain, Devaine, Devan, Devane, Devayn, Devein, Deveion

Deven (Hindi) for God. (Irish) an alternate form of Devin.
Deaven, Deiven

Deverell (English) riverbank.

Devin (Irish) poet.
Deavin, Deivin, Dev, Devan, Deven, Devlyn, Devy, Dyvon

Devine (Latin) divine. (Irish) ox.
Davon, Devinn, Devon, Devyn, Devyne

Devlin (Irish) brave, fierce.
Dev, Devland, Devlen, Devlyn

Devon (Irish) an alternate form of Devin.
Deavon, Deivon, Deivone, Deivonne, Devoen, Devohn, Devone, Devonn, Devonne, Devontae, Devontaine, Devontay, Devyn

Dewayne (Irish) an alternate form of Dwayne. (American) a combination of the prefix De + Wayne.

Deuwayne, Devayne, Dewain, Dewaine, Dewan, Dewon, Dewune

Dewei (Chinese) highly virtuous.

Dewey (Welsh) prized.
Dew, Dewi, Dewie

DeWitt (Flemish) blond.
Dewitt, Dwight, Wit

Dexter (Latin) dexterous, adroit. (English) fabric dyer.
Daxter, Decca, Deck, Decka, Dekka, Dex, Dextar, Dextor, Dextrel, Dextron

Diamond (English) brilliant gem; bright guardian.
Diamend, Diamenn, Diamont

Dick (German) a short form of Frederick, Richard.
Dic, Dicken, Dickens, Dickenson, Dickerson, Dickie, Dickon, Dickson, Dicky, Dik, Dikerson

Dickran (Armenian) History: an ancient Armenian king.
Dicran, Dikran

Didi (Hebrew) a familiar form of Jedidiah, Yedidyah.

Didier (French) desired, longed for. A masculine form of Desiree.

Diedrich (German) an
alternate form of Dedrick,
Dietrich.
**Didrich, Didrick, Didrik,
Diederick**

Diego (Spanish) a form
of Jacob, James.
Iago, Diaz, Jago

Dietbald (German)
an alternate form
of Theobald.
Dietbalt, Dietbolt

Dieter (German) army
of the people.
Deiter

Dietrich (German) an alter-
nate form of Dedrick.
**Deitrich, Deitrick, Deke,
Diedrich, Dierck, Dieter,
Dieterich, Dieterick, Dietz**

Digby (Irish) ditch town;
dike town.

Dillon (Irish) loyal, faithful.
See also Dylan.
**Dil, Dilan, Dill, Dillan,
Dillen, Dillie, Dillin,
Dillion, Dilly, Dillyn, Dilon,
Dilyn**

Dilwyn (Welsh) shady
place.
Dillwyn

Dima (Russian) a familiar
form of Vladimir.
Dimka

Dimitri (Russian) a form
of Demetrius.
Dimetra, Dimetri,
Dimetric, Dimetrie,
Dimitr, Dimitric, Dimitrie,
Dimitrik, Dimitris,
Dimitry, Dimmy, Dmitri,
Dymitr, Dymitry

Dimitrios (Greek) an alter-
nate form of Demetrius.
**Dhimitrios, Dimitrius,
Dimos, Dmitrios**

Dimitrius (Greek) an alter-
nate form of Demetrius.
**Dimetrius, Dimitricus,
Dimitrius, Dimetrus,
Dmitrius**

Dingbang (Chinese)
protector of the country.

Dinh (Vietnamese) calm,
peaceful.
Din

Dino (German) little sword.
(Italian) a form of Dean.
Deano

Dinos (Greek) a familiar
form of Constantine,
Konstantin.

Dinsmore (Irish) fortified
hill.
Dinnie, Dinny, Dinse

Diogenes (Greek) honest.
History: an ancient phil-
osopher who searched the
streets for an honest man.

Dion (Greek) a short form
of Dennis, Dionysus.
**Deon, Dio, Dione, Dionigi,
Dionis, Dionn, Diontae,
Dionte, Diontray**

Dionysus (Greek) celebration. Mythology: the god of wine.
Dion, Dionesios, Dionicio, Dionisio, Dionisios, Dionusios, Dionysios, Dionysius, Dunixi

Dirk (German) a short form of Derek, Theodoric.
Derk, Dirck, Dirke, Durc, Durk, Dyrk

Dixon (English) son of Dick.
Dickson, Dix

Dmitri (Russian) an alternate form of Dimitri.
Dmitiri, Dmitrik

Doane (English) low, rolling hills.
Doan

Dob (English) a familiar form of Robert.
Dobie

Dobry (Polish) good.

Doherty (Irish) harmful.
Docherty, Dougherty, Douherty

Dolan (Irish) dark haired.
Dolin, Dolyn

Dolf, Dolph (German) short forms of Adolf, Adolph, Rudolf, Rudolph.
Dolfe, Dolfi, Dolphe, Dolphus

Dom (Latin) a short form of Dominic.
Dome, Domó

Domenico (Italian) a form of Dominic.
Domenic, Domicio, Dominico, Menico

Domingo (Spanish) born on Sunday.
Demingo, Domingos

Dominic (Latin) belonging to the Lord. See also Chuminga.
Deco, Demenico, Dom, Domanic, Domeka, Domenic, Domenico, Domini, Dominie, Dominique, Dominitric, Dominy, Domnenique, Domonic, Nick

Dominick (Latin) an alternate form of Dominic.
Domenick, Domiku, Domineck, Dominick, Dominicke, Dominiek, Dominik, Domminick, Domnick, Domokos, Domonick, Donek, Dumin

Dominique (French) a form of Dominic.
Domeniqu, Domenque, Dominiqu, Dominiqueia, Domnenique, Domnique, Domoniqu, Domonique

Domokos (Hungarian) a form of Dominic.
Dedo, Dome, Domek, Domok, Domonkos

Don (Scottish) a short form of Donald. See also Kona.
Donn

Donahue (Irish) dark
warrior.
Donohoe, Donohue

Donal (Irish) a form
of Donald.

Donald (Scottish) world
leader; proud ruler. See
also Bohdan, Tauno.
**Don, Donal, Dónal,
Donaldo, Donall, Donalt,
Donát, Donaugh, Donnie**

Donatien (French) gift.
Donathan, Donathon

Donato (Italian) gift.
**Dodek, Donatello, Donati,
Donatien, Donatus**

Dong (Vietnamese)
easterner.
Duong

Donkor (Akan) humble.

Donnell (Irish) brave; dark.
**Doneal, Donell, Donelle,
Donnelly, Doniel, Donielle,
Donnel, Donnelle, Donniel**

Donnelly (Irish) an alternate form of Donnell.
Donelly, Donlee, Donley

Donnie, Donny (Irish)
familiar forms of Donald.

Donovan (Irish) dark
warrior.
**Dohnovan, Donavan,
Donavin, Donavon,
Donavyn, Donevon,
Donoven, Donovin,
Donovon, Donvan**

Dontae, Donté (American)
forms of Dante.
**Donta, Dontai, Dontao,
Dontate, Dontay,
Dontaye, Dontea, Dontee,
Dontez**

Dooley (Irish) dark hero.
Dooly

Dor (Hebrew) generation.

Doran (Greek, Hebrew)
gift. (Irish) stranger; exile.
**Dore, Dorin, Dorran,
Doron, Dorren, Dory**

Dorian (Greek) from Doris,
Greece. See also Isidore.
**Dore, Dorey, Dorie,
Dorien, Dorion, Dorján,
Dorrian, Dorrien,
Dorryen, Dory**

Dorrell (Scottish) king's
doorkeeper.
Dorrel, Dorrelle, Durrell

Dotan (Hebrew) law.
Dothan

Doug (Scottish) a short
form of Dougal, Douglas.
**Dougie, Dougy, Dugey,
Dugie, Dugy**

Dougal (Scottish) dark
stranger. See also Doyle.
**Doug, Dougall, Dugal,
Dugald, Dugall, Dughall**

Douglas (Scottish) dark
river, dark stream. See
also Koukalaka.
**Doug, Douglass, Dougles,
Dugaid, Dughlas**

Dov (Hebrew) a familiar form of David. (Yiddish) bear.
Dovid, Dovidas, Dowid

Dovev (Hebrew) whisper.

Dow (Irish) dark haired.

Doyle (Irish) a form of Dougal.
Doy, Doyal, Doyel

Drago (Italian) a form of Drake.

Drake (English) dragon; owner of the inn with the dragon trademark.
Drago

Draper (English) fabric maker.
Dray, Draypr

Dreng (Norwegian) hired hand; brave.

Drew (Welsh) wise. (English) a short form of Andrew.
Drewe, Dru

Dru (English) an alternate form of Drew.
Druan, Drud, Drue, Drugi, Drui

Drummond (Scottish) druid's mountain.
Drummund, Drumond, Drumund

Drury (French) loving. Geography: Drury Lane is a street in London's theater district. Literature: according to a nursery rhyme, Drury Lane is where the Muffin Man lives.

Dryden (English) dry valley.
Dry

Duane (Irish) an alternate form of Dwayne.
Deune, Duain, Duaine, Duana

Duarte (Portuguese) rich guard.

Duc (Vietnamese) moral.
Duoc, Duy

Dudd (English) a short form of Dudley.
Dud, Dudde, Duddy

Dudley (English) common field.
Dudd, Dudly

Duer (Scottish) heroic.

Duff (Scottish) dark.
Duffey, Duffie, Duffy

Dugan (Irish) dark.
Doogan, Dougan, Douggan, Duggan

Duke (French) leader; duke.
Dukey, Dukie, Duky

Dukker (Gypsy) fortune-teller.

Dulani (Ngoni) cutting.

Dumaka (African) helping hand.

Duman (Turkish) misty, smoky.

Duncan (Scottish) brown warrior. Literature: King Duncan was MacBeth's victim in Shakespeare's play *MacBeth*.
Dunc, Dunn

Dunham (Scottish) brown.

Dunixi (Basque) a form of Dionysus.

Dunley (English) hilly meadow.

Dunlop (Scottish) muddy hill.

Dunmore (Scottish) fortress on the hill.

Dunn (Scottish) a short form of Duncan.
Dun, Dune, Dunne

Dunstan (English) brown-stone fortress.
Dun

Dunton (English) hill town.

Dur (Hebrew) stacked up.

Durand (Latin) an alternate form of Durant.

Durant (Latin) enduring.
Duran, Durance, Durand, Durante, Durontae, Durrant

Durell (Scottish, English) king's doorkeeper.
Dorrell, Durel, Durial, Durreil, Durrell, Durrelle

Durko (Czech) a form of George.

Durriken (Gypsy) fortune-teller.

Durril (Gypsy) gooseberry.

Durward (English) gate-keeper.
Dur, Ward

Durwin (English) an alternate form of Darwin.

Dustin (German) valiant fighter. (English) brown rock quarry.
Dust, Dustan, Dusten, Dustie, Dustine, Duston, Dusty, Dustyn

Dusty (English) a familiar form of Dustin.

Dustyn (English) an alternate form of Dustin.

Dutch (Dutch) from the Netherlands; from Germany.

Duval (French) a combination of the prefix Du + Val.
Duvall, Duveuil

Dwaun (American) an alternate form of Dajuan.
Dwan, Dwaunn, Dwawn, Dwon, Dwuann

Dwayne (Irish) dark. See also Dewayne.
Dawayne, Dawyne, Duane, Duwain, Duwan, Duwane, Duwayn, Duwayne, Dwain, Dwaine, Dwan, Dwane, Dwyane, Dywane

Dwight (English) a form of DeWitt.

Dyami (Native American) soaring eagle.

Dyer (English) fabric dyer.

Dyke (English) dike; ditch.
Dike

Dylan (Welsh) sea. See also Dillon.
Dyllan, Dyllon, Dylon

Dyre (Norwegian) dear heart.

Dyson (English) a short form of Dennison.
Dysen, Dysonn

Ea (Irish) a form of Hugh.

Eachan (Irish) horseman.

Eagan (Irish) very mighty.
Egan, Egon

Eamon (Irish) a form of Edmond, Edmund.
Eammon, Eamonn

Ean (English) a form of Ian.
Eaen, Eann, Eion, Eon, Eyan, Eyon

Earl (Irish) pledge. (English) nobleman.
Airle, Earld, Earle, Earlie, Earlson, Early, Eorl, Erl, Erle, Errol

Earnest (English) an alternate form of Ernest.
Earn, Earnesto, Earnie, Eranest

Easton (English) eastern town.
Eason

Eaton (English) estate on the river.
Eatton, Eton, Eyton

Eb (Hebrew) a short form of Ebenezer.
Ebbie, Ebby

Eben (Hebrew) rock.
Eban

Ebenezer (Hebrew) foundation stone. Literature: Ebenezer Scrooge is a character in Charles Dickens's *A Christmas Carol.*
Eb, Ebbaneza, Eben, Ebeneezer, Ebeneser, Ebenezar, Eveneser

Eberhard (German) courageous as a boar.
Eberhardt, Evard, Everard, Everardo, Everhardt, Everhart

Ebner (English) a form of Abner.

Ebo (Fanti) born on Tuesday.

Ed (English) a short form of Edgar, Edsel, Edward.
Edd

Edan (Scottish) fire.

Edbert (English) wealthy; bright.
Ediberto

Eddie (English) a familiar form of Edgar, Edsel, Edward.
Eddee, Eddy

Eddy (English) an alternate form of Eddie.
Eddye, Edy

Edel (German) noble.
Adel, Edelmar, Edelweiss

Eden (Hebrew) delightful. Bible: the earthly paradise.
Eaden, Eadin, Edan, Edenson, Edin, Edyn

Eder (Hebrew) flock.
Ederick

Edgar (English) successful spearman. See also Garek, Gerik, Medgar.
Ed, Eddie, Edek, Edgard, Edgardo, Edgars

Edison (English) son of Edward.
Eddison, Edisen, Edson

Edmond (English) an alternate form of Edmund.
Eamon, Edmon, Edmonde, Edmondo, Edmondson, Esmond

Edmund (English) prosperous protector.
Eadmund, Eamon, Edmond, Edmundo, Edmunds

Edmundo (Spanish) a form of Edmund.
Mundo

Edo (Czech) a form of Edward.

Edoardo (Italian) a form of Edward.

Edorta (Basque) a form of Edward.

Édouard (French) a form of Edward.
Édoard

Edric (English) prosperous ruler.
Eddrick, Ederick, Edrice, Edrick

Edsel (English) rich man's house.
Ed, Eddie

Edson (English) a short form of Edison.

Eduardo (Spanish) a form of Edward.

Edur (Basque) snow.

Edward (English) prosperous guardian. See also Audie, Duarte, Ned, Ted, Teddy.
Ed, Eddie, Edik, Edko, Edo, Edoardo, Edorta, Édouard, Eduard, Eduardo, Edus,

Edward (cont.)
Edvard, Edvardo, Edwardo, Edwards, Edwy, Edzio, Ekewaka, Etzio, Ewart

Edwin (English) prosperous friend. See also Ned, Ted.
Eadwinn, Edik, Edlin, Eduino, Edwyn

Efrain (Hebrew) fruitful.
Efrane

Efrat (Hebrew) honored.

Efrem (Hebrew) a short form of Ephraim.
Efe, Efren, Efrim, Efrum

Egan (Irish) ardent, fiery.
Egann, Egen, Egon

Egbert (English) bright sword. See also Bert, Bertie.

Egerton (English) Edgar's town.
Edgarton, Edgartown, Edgerton, Egeton

Egil (Norway) awe-inspiring.
Eigil

Eginhard (German) power of the sword.
Eginhardt, Einhard, Einhardt, Enno

Egon (German) formidable.

Egor (Russian) a form of George. See also Igor, Yegor.

Ehren (German) honorable.

Eikki (Finnish) ever-powerful.

Einar (Scandinavian) individualist.
Ejnar, Inar

Eion (Irish) a form of Ean, Ian.
Eann, Ein

Ejau (Ateso) we have received.

Ekewaka (Hawaiian) a form of Edward.

Ekon (Nigerian) strong.

Elam (Hebrew) highlands.

Elan (Hebrew) tree. (Native American) friendly.
Elann

Elbert (English) a form of Albert.

Elchanan (Hebrew) an alternate form of John.
Elhanan, Elhannan

Elden (English) an alternate form of Alden, Aldous.
Eldin

Elder (English) dweller near the elder trees.

Eldon (English) holy hill.

Eldred (English) an alternate form of Aldred.
Eldrid

Eldridge (English) an alternate form of Aldrich.
El, Eldred, Eldredge,

Eldrege, Eldrid, Eldrige, Elric

Eldwin (English) an alternate form of Aldwin.
Eldwinn, Eldwyn, Eldwynn

Eleazar (Hebrew) God has helped. See also Lazarus.
Elazar, Elazaro, Eleasar, Eléazar, Eliasar, Eliazar, Elieser, Eliezer, Elizar, Elizardo

Elek (Hungarian) a form of Alec, Alex.
Elec, Elic, Elik

Elger (German) an alternate form of Alger.
Elger, Ellgar, Ellger

Elgin (English) noble; white.
Elgan, Elgen

Eli (Hebrew) uplifted. A short form of Elijah, Elisha. Bible: the high priest who trained the prophet Samuel. See also Elliot.
Elie, Elier, Eloi, Eloy, Ely

Elia (Zuni) a short form of Elijah.
Eliya, Elya

Elian (English) a form of Elijah. See also Trevelyan.

Elias (Greek) a form of Elijah.
Elia, Eliasz, Elice, Ellice, Ellis, Elyas

Elihu (Hebrew) a short form of Eliyahu.
Elih, Eliu, Ellihu

Elijah (Hebrew) the Lord is my God. An alternate form of Eliyahu. Bible: a great Hebrew prophet. See also Eli, Elliot, Elisha, Ilias, Ilya.
El, Elia, Elias, Elija, Elijuo, Elisjsha, Eliya, Eliyahu, Ellis

Elika (Hawaiian) a form of Eric.

Elisha (Hebrew) God is my salvation. Bible: a great Hebrew prophet, successor to Elijah. See also Eli.
Elijsha, Elisee, Elisée, Eliseo, Elish, Elisher, Elishia, Elishua, Lisha

Eliyahu (Hebrew) the Lord is my God. The original form of Elijah.
Elihu

Elkan (Hebrew) God is jealous.
Elkana, Elkanah, Elkin, Elkins

Elki (Moquelumnan) hanging over the top.

Ellard (German) sacred; brave.
Allard, Ellerd

Ellery (English) elder tree island.
Ellary, Ellerey

Elliot, Elliott (English)
forms of Eli, Elijah.
**Elio, Eliot, Eliott, Eliud,
Eliut, Elyot, Elyott**

Ellis (English) a form
of Elias.

Ellison (English) son of Ellis.
**Elison, Ellson, Ellyson,
Elson**

Ellsworth (English) nobleman's estate.
Ellswerth, Elsworth

Elman (German) like an
elm tree.
Elmen

Elmer (English) noble;
famous.
**Aylmer, Elemér, Ellmer,
Elmir, Elmo**

Elmo (Latin) a familiar
form of Anselm. (Greek)
lovable, friendly. (Italian)
guardian. (English) an
alternate form of Elmer.

Elmore (English) moor
where the elm trees grow.

Elonzo (Spanish) an alternate form of Alonzo.
Elon, Élon, Elonso

Eloy (Latin) chosen.

Elrad (Hebrew) God rules.
Rad, Radd

Elroy (French) an alternate
form of Delroy, Leroy.
Elroi

Elsdon (English) nobleman's hill.

Elston (English) noble's
town.
Ellston

Elsu (Native American)
swooping, soaring falcon.

Elsworth (English) noble's
estate.

Elton (English) old town.
Alton, Eldon, Ellton

Elvern (Latin) an alternate
form of Alvern.

Elvin (English) a form
of Alvin. See also Elvis.
**El, Elvyn, Elwin, Elwyn,
Elwynn**

Elvio (Spanish) light
skinned; blond.

Elvis (Scandinavian) wise.
El, Elvys

Elvy (English) elfin warrior.

Elwell (English) old well.

Elwood (English) old forest.
See also Wood, Woody.

Ely (Hebrew) an alternate
form of Eli. Geography:
a river in Wales.
Elya

Eman (Czech) a form
of Emmanuel.

Emanuel (Hebrew)
an alternate form
of Emmanuel.
**Emaniel, Emanual,
Emanuele**

Emerson (German, English)
son of Emery.
Emmerson, Emreson

Emery (German) industrious leader.
Emari, Emeri, Emerich, Emerio, Emmerich, Emmerie, Emmery, Emmo, Emory, Inre, Imrich

Emil (Latin) flatterer.
(German) industrious.
See also Amal.
Aymil, Émile, Emilek, Emiliano, Emilio, Emill, Emils, Emilyan, Emlyn

Émile (French) a form of Emil.
Emiel, Emile, Emille

Emiliano (Italian) a form of Emil.
Emilian, Emilion

Emilio (Italian, Spanish) a form of Emil.
Emilio, Emilios, Emilo

Emlyn (Welsh) a form of Emil.
Emelen, Emlen, Emlin

Emmanuel (Hebrew)
God is with us. See also
Immanuel, Maco, Manuel,
Mango.
Eman, Emanuel, Emanuell, Emek, Emmaneuol, Emmanle, Emmanueal, Emmanuele, Emmanuil

Emmett (German) industrious; strong. (English) ant.

History: Robert Emmett
was an Irish patriot.
Em, Emitt, Emmet, Emmit, Emmot, Emmott, Emmy

Emory (German) an alternate form of Emery.
Emmory, Emrick

Emre (Turkish) brother.
Emra, Emrah, Emreson

Emrick (German) an alternate form of Emery.
Emryk

Enapay (Lakota) brave appearance; he appears.

Endre (Hungarian) a form of Andrew.
Ender

Eneas (Greek) an alternate form of Aeneas.
Eneias, Enné

Engelbert (German) bright as an angel. See also Inglebert.
Bert, Englebert

Enli (Dene) that dog over there.

Ennis (Greek) mine.
(Scottish) an alternate form of Angus.
Eni, Enni

Enoch (Hebrew) dedicated, consecrated. Bible:
the father of Methuselah.
Enoc, Enock, Enok

Enos (Hebrew) man.
Enosh

Enric (Romanian) a form
of Henry.
Enrica

Enrico (Italian) a form
of Henry.
Enzio, Enzo, Rico

Enrikos (Greek) a form
of Henry.

Enrique (Spanish) a form
of Henry. See also Quiqui.
**Enrigué, Enriqué,
Enriquez, Enrrique**

Enver (Turkish) bright;
handsome.

Enyeto (Native American)
walks like a bear.

Enzi (Swahili) powerful.

Eoin (Welsh) a form
of Evan.

Ephraim (Hebrew) fruitful.
Bible: the second son of
Joseph.
**Efraim, Efrayim, Efrem,
Efren, Ephraen, Ephrain,
Ephrem**

Erasmus (Greek) lovable.
Érasme, Erasmo, Rasmus

Erastus (Greek) beloved.
**Éraste, Erastious, Ras,
Rastus**

Erbert (German) a short
form of Herbert.
Ebert, Erberto

Ercole (Italian) splendid
gift.

Erhard (German) strong;
resolute.
Erhardt, Erhart

Eric (German) a short
form of Frederick.
(Scandinavian) ruler of all.
(English) brave ruler.
History: Eric the Red was
a Norse hero and explorer.
**Ehrich, Elika, Erek, Éric,
Erica, Erich, Erick,
Erickson, Erico, Ericson,
Erik, Erric, Eryc, Eryk, Rick**

Erich (Czech, German)
a form of Eric.

Erik (Scandinavian) an
alternate form of Eric.
**Erek, Eriks, Erikson,
Erikur, Errick**

Erikur (Icelandic) a form
of Eric, Erik.

Erin (Irish) peaceful.
History: another name
for Ireland.
**Erine, Erinn, Erino, Eryn,
Erynn**

Erland (English) nobleman's land.
Erlend

Erling (English) nobleman's
son.

Ermanno (Italian) a form
of Herman.
Erman

Ermano (Spanish) a form
of Herman.
Ermin

Ernest (English) earnest, sincere. See also Arne.
Earnest, Ernestino, Ernesto, Ernestus, Ernie, Erno, Ernst

Ernesto (Spanish) a form of Ernest.
Ernester, Neto

Ernie (English) a familiar form of Ernest.
Earnie, Erney, Erny

Erno (Hungarian) a form of Ernest.
Ernö

Ernst (German) a form of Ernest.
Erns

Erol (Turkish) strong, courageous.

Errando (Basque) bold.

Errol (Latin) wanderer. (English) an alternate form of Earl. See also Rollo.
Erol, Erold, Erroll, Erryl

Erroman (Basque) from Rome.

Erskine (Scottish) high cliff. (English) from Ireland.
Ersin, Erskin, Kinny

Ervin, Erwin (English) sea friend. Alternate forms of Irwin.
Earvin, Erv, Erven, Ervyn, Erwan, Erwinek, Erwinn, Erwyn, Erwynn

Ervine (English) a form of Irving.

Erv, Ervin, Ervince, Erving, Ervins

Esau (Hebrew) rough; hairy. Bible: Jacob's twin brother.
Esaw

Eshkol (Hebrew) grape clusters.

Eskil (Norwegian) god vessel.

Esmond (English) rich protector.

Espen (Danish) god-bear.

Essien (Ochi) sixth-born son.

Este (Italian) east.
Estes

Estéban (Spanish) a form of Stephen.
Estabon, Estefan, Estephan

Estebe (Basque) a form of Steven.

Estevao (Spanish) a form of Stephen.
Estevan, Esteven, Estevez, Estiven

Ethan (Hebrew) strong; firm.
Eathan, Etan, Ethe

Étienne (French) a form of Stephen.
Etian, Étienn

Ettore (Italian) steadfast.
Etor, Etore

Etu (Native American) sunny.

Euclid (Greek) intelligent. History: the founder of Euclidean geometry.

Eugen (German) a form of Eugene.

Eugene (Greek) born to nobility. See also Ewan, Gene, Gino, Iukini, Jenö, Yevgenyi, Zenda.
Eoghan, Eugen, Eugéne, Eugeni, Eugenio, Eugenius, Evgeny, Ezven

Eugenio (Spanish) a form of Eugene.

Eustace (Greek) productive. (Latin) stable, calm. See also Stacey.
Eustache, Eustachius, Eustachy, Eustashe, Eustasius, Eustatius, Eustazio, Eustis, Eustiss

Evagelos (Greek) an alternate form of Andrew.
Evaggelos, Evangelo, Evangelos

Evan (Irish) young warrior. (English) a form of John. See also Bevan, Owen.
Eoin, Ewan, Ewen, Ev, Evann, Evans, Even, Evens, Evin, Evyn

Evelyn (English) hazelnut.
Evelin

Everett (English) a form of Eberhard.
Ev, Evered, Everet, Everette, Everitt, Evert, Evrett

Everley (English) boar meadow.
Everlea, Everlee

Everton (English) boar town.

Evgeny (Russian) a form of Eugene. See also Zhek.
Evgenij, Evgenyi

Ewald (German) always powerful. (English) powerful lawman.

Ewan (Scottish) a form of Eugene, Evan.
Euan, Euann, Euen, Ewen, Ewhen

Ewert (English) ewe herder, shepherd.
Ewart

Ewing (English) friend of the law.
Ewin, Ewynn

Eyota (Native American) great.

Ezekiel (Hebrew) strength of God. Bible: a Hebrew prophet. See also Haskel, Zeke.
Ezéchiel, Ezeck, Ezeeckel, Ezekeial, Ezekial, Ezell, Ezequiel, Eziakah, Eziechiele, Eziequel

Ezer (Hebrew) an alternate form of Ezra.

Ezra (Hebrew) helper; strong. Bible: a prophet and leader of the Israelites.
Esdras, Esra, Ezer, Ezera, Ezri

Ezven (Czech) a form of Eugene.
Esven, Esvin

Faber (German) a form of Fabian.

Fabian (Latin) bean grower.
Fabayan, Fabe, Fabek, Fabeon, Faber, Fabert, Fabi, Fabiano, Fabien, Fabio, Fabius, Fabiyan, Fabiyus, Fabyan, Fabyen, Faybian, Faybien

Fabiano (Italian) a form of Fabian.
Fabianno, Fabio

Fabio (Latin) an alternate form of Fabian. (Italian) a short form of Fabiano.

Fabrizio (Italian) craftsman.
Fabrice, Fabrizius

Fabron (French) little blacksmith; apprentice.
Fabre, Fabroni

Fadey (Ukrainian) a form of Thaddeus.
Faday, Faddei, Faddey, Fadeyka, Fadie, Fady

Fadi (Arabic) redeemer.

Fadil (Arabic) generous.

Fagan (Irish) little fiery one.
Fagin

Fahd (Arabic) lynx.
Fahad

Fai (Chinese) beginning.

Fairfax (English) blond.
Fair, Fax

Faisal (Arabic) decisive.
Faisel, Faisil, Faisl, Faizal, Fasel, Fasil, Faysal, Fayzal, Fayzel

Fakhir (Arabic) excellent.
Fahkry

Fakih (Arabic) thinker; reader of the Koran.

Falco (Latin) falconer.
Falcon, Falk, Falke, Falken

Falito (Italian) a familiar form of Rafael.

Falkner (English) trainer of falcons.
Falconer, Falconner, Faulconer, Faulconner, Faulkner

Fane (English) joyful, glad.
Fanes, Faniel

Faraji (Swahili) consolation.

Farid (Arabic) unique.

Faris (Arabic) horseman.

Farley (English) bull meadow; sheep meadow.
Fairlay, Fairlee, Fairleigh, Fairley, Fairlie, Far, Farlay,

Farley *(cont.)*
Farlee, Farleigh, Farlie, Farly, Farrleigh, Farrley

Farnell (English) fern-covered hill.
Farnall, Fernald, Fernall, Furnald

Farnham (English) field of ferns.
Farnam, Farnum, Fernham

Farnley (English) fern meadow.
Farnlea, Farnlee, Farnleigh, Farnly, Fernlea, Fernlee, Fernleigh, Fernley

Faroh (Latin) an alternate form of Pharoh.

Farold (English) mighty traveler.

Farquhar (Scottish) dear.
Fark, Farq, Farquar, Farquarson, Farque, Farquharson, Farquy, Farqy

Farr (English) traveler.
Faer, Farran, Farren, Farrin, Farrington, Farron

Farrell (Irish) heroic.
Farrel, Farrill, Farryll, Ferrell

Farrow (English) piglet.

Farruco (Spanish) a form of Francis, Francisco.
Frascuelo

Faruq (Arabic) honest.
Farook, Farooq, Farouk, Faruqh

Faste (Norwegian) firm.

Fath (Arabic) victor.

Fatin (Arabic) clever.

Faust (Latin) lucky, fortunate. History: the sixteenth-century German doctor who inspired many legends.
Faustino, Faustis, Fausto, Faustus

Fausto (Italian) a form of Faust.

Favian (Latin) understanding.

Faxon (German) long haired.

Federico (Italian, Spanish) a form of Frederick.
Federic, Federigo, Federoquito

Feivel (Yiddish) God aids.

Feliks (Russian) a form of Felix.

Felipe (Spanish) a form of Philip.
Feeleep, Felipino, Felo, Filip, Filippo, Filips, Fillip, Flip

Felippo (Italian) a form of Philip.
Felip, Filippo, Lipp, Lippo, Pip, Pippo

Felix (Latin) fortunate; happy. See also Pitin.
Fee, Felic, Félice, Feliciano, Felicio, Felike, Feliks, Felo, Félix, Felizio, Phelix

Felton (English) field town.
Felten, Feltin

Fenton (English) marshland
farm.
Fen, Fennie, Fenny

Feodor (Slavic) a form
of Theodore.
**Dorek, Fedar, Fedinka,
Fedor, Fedya, Fyodor**

Feoras (Greek) smooth
rock.

Ferdinand (German)
daring, adventurous.
See also Hernando.
**Feranado, Ferd, Ferda,
Ferdie, Ferdinánd, Ferdy,
Ferdynand, Fernando,
Nando**

Ferenc (Hungarian) a form
of Francis.
Feri, Ferke, Ferko

Fergus (Irish) strong;
manly.
**Fearghas, Fearghus,
Feargus, Fergie, Ferguson,
Fergusson**

Fermin (French, Spanish)
firm, strong.
Ferman, Firmin, Furman

Fernando (Spanish) a form
of Ferdinand.
**Ferdinando Ferdnando,
Ferdo, Fernand,
Fernandez**

Feroz (Persian) fortunate.

Ferran (Arabic) baker.
**Feran, Feron, Ferrin,
Ferron**

Ferrand (French) iron
gray hair.
**Farand, Farrand, Farrant,
Ferrant**

Ferrell (Irish) an alternate
form of Farrell.
Ferrel, Ferrill, Ferryl

Ferris (Irish) a form
of Peter.
**Fares, Faris, Fariz, Farris,
Farrish, Feris, Ferriss**

Fico (Spanish) a familiar
form of Frederick.

Fidel (Latin) faithful.
**Fidele, Fidèle, Fidelio,
Fidelis, Fido**

Field (English) a short form
of Fielding.
Fields

Fielding (English) field;
field worker.
Field

Fife (Scottish) from Fife,
Scotland.
Fyfe

Fifi (Fanti) born on Friday.

Fil (Polish) a form of Phil.
Filipek

Filbert (English) brilliant.
**Bert, Filberte, Filberto,
Philbert**

Fillipp (Russian) a form
of Philip.
**Filip, Filipe, Filipek, Filips,
Fill, Fillip, Filya**

Filmore (English) famous.
Fillmore, Filmer, Fyllmer, Fylmer

Filya (Russian) a form of Philip.

Fineas (Irish) a form of Phineas.
Finneas

Finian (Irish) light skinned; white.
Finnian, Fionan, Fionn, Phinean

Finlay (Irish) blond-haired soldier.
Findlay, Findley, Finlea, Finlee, Finley, Finn, Finnlea, Finnley

Finn (German) from Finland. (Irish) blond haired; light skinned. A short form of Finlay. (Norwegian) from the Lapland.
Fin, Finnie, Finnis, Finny

Finnegan (Irish) light skinned; white.
Finegan

Fiorello (Italian) little flower.

Firas (Arabic) persistent.

Firman (French) firm; strong.
Ferman

Firth (English) woodland.

Fischel (Yiddish) a form of Phillip.

Fiske (English) fisherman.
Fisk

Fitch (English) weasel, ermine.
Fitche

Fitz (English) son.
Filz

Fitzgerald (English) son of Gerald.

Fitzhugh (English) son of Hugh.
Hugh

Fitzpatrick (English) son of Patrick.

Fitzroy (Irish) son of Roy.

Flaminio (Spanish) Religion: a Roman priest.

Flann (Irish) redhead.
Flainn, Flannan, Flannery

Flavian (Latin) blond, yellow haired.
Flavel, Flavelle, Flavien, Flavio, Flawiusz

Flavio (Italian) a form of Flavian.
Flabio, Flavious, Flavius

Fleming (English) from Denmark; from Flanders.
Flemming, Flemmyng, Flemyng

Fletcher (English) arrow featherer, arrow maker.
Flecher, Fletch

Flint (English) stream; flintstone.
Flynt

Flip (Spanish) a short form of Felipe. (American) a short form of Philip.

Florent (French) flowering.
Florenci, Florencio, Florentin, Florentino, Florentyn, Florentz, Florinio, Florino

Florian (Latin) flowering, blooming.
Florien, Florrian, Flory, Floryan

Floyd (English) a form of Lloyd.

Flurry (English) flourishing, blooming.

Flynn (Irish) son of the red-haired man.
Flin, Flinn, Flyn

Folke (German) an alternate form of Volker.
Folker

Foluke (Yoruba) given to God.

Foma (Bulgarian, Russian) a form of Thomas.
Fomka

Fonso (German, Italian) a short form of Alphonso.
Fonzo

Fontaine (French) fountain.

Fonzie (German) a familiar form of Alphonse.
Fons, Fonsie, Fonz

Forbes (Irish) prosperous.
Forbe

Ford (English) a short form of names ending in "ford."

Fordel (Gypsy) forgiving.

Forest (French) an alternate form of Forrest.

Forester (English) forest guardian.
Forrester, Forrie, Forry, Forster, Foss, Foster

Forrest (French) forest; woodsman.
Forest, Forester, Forrie

Fortino (Italian) fortunate, lucky.

Fortune (French) fortunate, lucky.
Fortun, Fortunato, Fortuné, Fortunio

Foster (Latin) a short form of Forester.

Fowler (English) trapper of wild fowl.

Fran (Latin) a short form of Francis.
Franh

Francesco (Italian) a form of Francis.

Franchot (French) a form of Francis.

Francis (Latin) free; from France. Religion: Saint Francis of Assisi was the founder of the Franciscan order. See also Farruco, Ferenc.
Fran, France, Francessco, Franchot, Francisco,

Francis *(cont.)*
**Franciskus, François,
Frang, Frank, Frannie,
Franny, Frans, Franscis,
Fransis, Franta, Frantisek,
Frants, Franus, Franz,
Frantisek, Frencis**

Francisco (Portuguese,
Spanish) a form of Francis.
See also Chilo, Cisco,
Farruco, Paco, Pancho.
**Franco, Fransisco, Frasco,
Frisco**

François (French) a form
of Francis.

Frank (English) a short
form of Francis, Franklin.
See also Palani, Pancho.
**Franc, Franck, Franek,
Frang, Franio, Franke,
Frankie, Franko**

Frankie (English) a familiar
form of Frank.
Franky

Franklin (English) free
landowner.
**Fran, Francklin, Francklyn,
Frank, Frankin, Franklinn,
Franklyn, Franquelin**

Franklyn (English) an alternate form of Franklin.
Franklynn

Frans (Swedish) a form
of Francis.
Frants

Frantisek (Czech) a form
of Francis.
Franta

Franz (German) a form
of Francis.
**Frantz, Franzen, Franzin,
Franzl, Franzy**

Fraser (French) strawberry.
(English) curly haired.
**Fraizer, Frasier, Fraze,
Frazer, Frazier**

Frayne (French) dweller
at the ash tree. (English)
stranger.
**Fraine, Frayn, Frean,
Freen, Freyne**

Fred (German) a short form
of Frederick. See also
Alfred, Manfred.
Fredd, Fredo, Fredson

Freddie (German) a famil-
iar form of Frederick.
**Freddi, Freddy, Fredi,
Fredy**

Frederic (German) an alter-
nate form of Frederick.
**Frédéric, Frederich,
Frederric, Fredric,
Fredrich**

Frederick (German) peace-
ful ruler. See also Dick,
Eric, Fico, Peleke, Rick.
**Federico, Fico, Fred,
Fredderick, Freddie,
Freddrick, Fredek,
Frederic, Fréderick,
Frédérick, Frederik,
Frédérik, Frederrick,
Fredo, Fredrick, Fredricka,
Fredrik, Fredwick,
Fredwyck, Friedrich, Fritz**

Frederico (Spanish) a form of Frederick.
Fredrico, Frederigo

Fredo (Spanish) a form of Fred.

Freeborn (English) child of freedom.
Free

Freeman (English) free.
Free, Freedman, Freemon, Friedman, Friedmann

Fremont (German) free; noble protector.

Frewin (English) free; noble friend.
Frewen

Frey (English) lord. (Scandinavian) Mythology: god of prosperity.

Frick (English) bold.

Fridolf (English) peaceful wolf.
Freydolf, Freydulf, Fridulf

Friedrich (German) a form of Frederick.
Friedel, Friedrick, Fridrich, Fridrick, Friedrike, Fryderyk

Frisco (Spanish) a short form of Francisco.

Fritz (German) a familiar form of Frederick.
Fritson, Fritts, Fritzchen, Fritzl

Frode (Norwegian) wise.

Fulbright (German) very bright.
Fulbert

Fuller (English) cloth thickener.

Fulton (English) field near town.

Funsoni (Ngoni) requested.

Fyfe (Scottish) an alternate form of Fife.
Fyffe

Fynn (Ghanian) Geography: another name for the Offin river.

Fyodor (Russian) an alternate form of Theodore.

Gabby (American) a familiar form of Gabriel.
Gabbi, Gabbie, Gabi, Gabie, Gaby

Gabe (Hebrew) a short form of Gabriel.

Gábor (Hungarian) God is my strength.
Gabbo, Gabko, Gabo

Gabriel (Hebrew) devoted to God. Bible: the Archangel of Annunciation.

Gabriel *(cont.)*
Gab, Gabe, Gabby,
Gaberial, Gabin, Gabino,
Gabis, Gábor, Gabrail,
Gabreil, Gabriël, Gabriele,
Gabriell, Gabrielli, Gabris,
Gabys, Gavril, Gebereal,
Ghabriel, Riel

Gabrielli (Italian) a form
of Gabriel.
Gabriello

Gadi (Arabic) God is my
fortune.
Gad, Gaddy, Gadiel

Gaetan (Italian) from
Gaeta, a region in south-
ern Italy.
Gaetano, Gaetono

Gage (French) pledge.
Gager

Gair (Irish) small.
Gaer, Gearr, Geir

Gaius (Latin) rejoicer.
See also Cai.

Galbraith (Irish) Scotsman
in Ireland.
Galbrait, Galbreath

Gale (Greek) a short form
of Galen.
Gael, Gail, Gaile, Gayle

Galen (Greek) healer; calm.
(Irish) little and lively.
Gaelan, Gaelen, Galan,
Gale, Galeno, Galin,
Gaylen

Galeno (Spanish) illumi-
nated child.

Gallagher (Irish) eager
helper.

Galloway (Irish) Scotsman
in Ireland.
Gallway, Galway

Galt (Norwegian) high
ground.

Galton (English) owner
of a rented estate.
Gallton

Galvin (Irish) sparrow.
Gal, Gall, Gallven, Gallvin,
Galvan, Galven

Gamal (Arabic) camel.
See also Jamal.
Gamall, Gamil

Gamble (Scandinavian)
old.

Gan (Chinese) daring,
adventurous. (Vietnamese)
near.

Gannon (Irish) light
skinned, white.
Gannie, Ganny

Ganya (Zulu) clever.

Gar (English) a short form
of Gareth, Garnett,
Garrett, Garvin.
Garr

Garcia (Spanish) mighty
with a spear.

Gardner (English)
gardener.
Gard, Gardener, Gardie,
Gardiner, Gardy

Garek (Polish) a form of Edgar.

Gareth (Welsh) gentle.
Gar, Garith, Garreth, Garth, Garyth

Garett (Irish) an alternate form of Garrett.
Gared, Garet

Garfield (English) field of spears; battlefield.

Garland (French) wreath of flowers; prize. (English) land of spears; battle-ground.
Garlan, Garlen, Garllan, Garlund, Garlyn

Garman (English) spearman.
Garmann, Garrman

Garner (French) army guard, sentry.
Garnier

Garnett (Latin) pomegranate seed; garnet stone. (English) armed with a spear.
Gar, Garnet, Garnie

Garnock (Welsh) dweller by the alder river.

Garrad (English) a form of Garrett.
Gared, Garrard, Garred, Garrod, Gerred, Jared

Garrett (Irish) brave spearman. See also Jarrett.
Gar, Gareth, Garett, Garrad, Garret, Garrette, Gerret, Gerrett, Gerrit, Gerritt, Gerrot, Gerrott

Garrick (English) oak spear.
Gaerick, Garek, Garick, Garik, Garreck, Garrek, Garrik, Garryck, Garryk, Gerreck, Gerrick

Garrin (English) an alternate form of Garry.
Garran, Garren, Garron, Garyn

Garrison (French) troops stationed at a fort; garrison.
Garris

Garroway (English) spear fighter.
Garraway

Garry (English) an alternate form of Gary.
Garrey, Garri, Garrie, Garrin

Garson (English) son of Gar.

Garth (Scandinavian) garden, gardener. (Welsh) a short form of Gareth.

Garvey (Irish) rough peace.
Garbhán, Garrvey, Garrvie, Garv, Garvan, Garvie, Garvy

Garvin (English) comrade in battle.
Gar, Garvan, Garven, Garvyn, Garwen, Garwin, Garwyn, Garwynn

Garwood (English) evergreen forest. See also Wood, Woody.
Garrwood

Gary (German) mighty spearman. (English) a familiar form of Gerald. See also Kali.
Gare, Garey, Gari, Garry

Gaspar (French) a form of Casper.
Gáspár, Gaspard, Gaspare, Gasparo, Gasper, Gazsi

Gaston (French) from Gascony, France.
Gascon

Gaute (Norwegian) great.

Gautier (French) a form of Walter.
Galtero, Gaulterio, Gaultier, Gaultiero, Gauthier

Gavin (Welsh) white hawk.
Gav, Gavan, Gaven, Gavinn, Gavino, Gavyn, Gavynn, Gawain

Gavriel (Hebrew) man of God.
Gav, Gavi, Gavrel, Gavril, Gavy

Gavril (Russian) a form of Gavriel.
Ganya, Gavrilo, Gavrilushka

Gawain (Welsh) an alternate form of Gavin.
Gawaine, Gawayn, Gawayne, Gawen, Gwayne

Gaylen (Greek) an alternate form of Galen.
Gaylin, Gaylinn, Gaylon, Gaylyn

Gaylord (French) merry lord; jailer.
Gaillard, Gallard, Gay, Gayelord, Gayler, Gaylor

Gaynor (Irish) son of the fair-skinned man.
Gainer, Gainor, Gay, Gayner, Gaynnor

Geary (English) variable, changeable.
Gearey, Gery

Gedeon (Bulgarian, French) a form of Gideon.

Geffrey (English) an alternate form of Geoffrey. See also Jeffrey.
Geff, Geffery, Geffrard

Gellert (Hungarian) a form of Gerald.

Gena (Russian) a short form of Yevgenyi.
Genka, Genya, Gine

Gene (Greek) born to nobility. A short form of Eugene.
Genek

Genek (Polish) a form of Gene.

Geno (Italian) a form of John. A short form of Genovese.
Genio, Jeno

Genovese (Italian) from
Genoa, Italy.
Geno

Gent (English) gentleman.
Gentle, Gentry

Genty (Irish, English) snow.

Geoff (English) a short
form of Geoffrey.

Geoffrey (English) divinely
peaceful. A form of Jeffrey.
See also Giotto, Godfrey,
Gottfried, Jeff.
**Geffrey, Geoff, Geoffery,
Geoffre, Geoffroi,
Geoffroy, Geoffry,
Geofrey, Geofri, Gofery**

Geordan (Scottish) a form
of Gordon.
Geordann, Geordon

Geordie (Scottish) a form
of George.
Geordi

Georg (Scandinavian)
a form of George.

George (Greek) farmer.
See also Durko, Egor,
Iorgos, Jerzy, Jiri, Joji, Jörg,
Jorge, Jorgen, Joris, Jorrín,
Jur, Jurgis, Keoki, Mahiái,
Semer, Yegor, Yoyi, Yrjo,
Yuri, Zhora.
**Geordie, Georg, Georgas,
Georges, Georget, Georgi,
Georgii, Georgio,
Georgios, Georgiy,
Georgy, Gevork,
Gheorghe, Giorgio,**

**Giorgos, Goerge, Goran,
Gordios, Gorge, Gorje,
Gorya, Grzegorz, Gyorgy**

Georges (French) a form
of George.
Geórges

Georgio (Italian) a form
of George.

Georgios (Greek) an alternate form of George.
Georgious, Georgius

Georgy (Greek) a familiar
form of George.
Georgie

Geovanni (Italian) an alter-
nate form of Giovanni.
**Geovan, Geovani,
Geovannee, Geovanny**

Geraint (English) old.

Gerald (German) mighty
spearman. See also
Fitzgerald, Jarell, Jarrell,
Jerald, Jerry, Kharald.
**Garald, Garold, Garolds,
Gary, Gearalt, Gellert,
Gérald, Geralde, Geraldo,
Gerale, Geraud, Gerek,
Gerick, Gerik, Gerold,
Gerrald, Gerrell, Gérrick,
Gerrild, Gerrin, Gerrit,
Gerrold, Gerry, Geryld,
Giraldo, Giraud, Girauld**

Geraldo (Italian, Spanish)
a form of Gerald.

Gerard (English) brave
spearman. See also
Jerard, Jerry.

Gerard *(cont.)*
Garrard, Garrat, Garratt, Gearard, Gerad, Gerar, Gérard, Gerardo, Geraro, Géraud, Gerd, Gerek, Gerhard, Gerrard, Gerrit, Gerry, Gherardo, Girard

Gerardo (Spanish) a form of Gerard.

Géraud (French) a form of Gerard.

Gerek (Polish) a form of Gerard.

Geremia (Hebrew) exalted by God. (Italian) a form of Jeremiah.

Geremiah (Italian) a form of Jeremiah.
Geremia, Gerimiah

Gerhard (German) a form of Gerard.
Garhard

Gerik (Polish) a form of Edgar.

Germain (French) from Germany. (English) sprout, bud. See also Jermaine.
Germaine, German, Germane, Germano, Germayn, Germayne

Gerome (English) a form of Jerome.

Geronimo (Greek, Italian) a form of Jerome. History: a famous Apache chief.
Geronemo

Gerrit (Dutch) a form of Gerald.

Gerry (English) a familiar form of Gerald, Gerard. See also Jerry.
Geri, Gerre, Gerri, Gerrie, Gerryson

Gershom (Hebrew) exiled. (Yiddish) stranger in exile.
Gersham, Gersho, Gershon, Gerson, Geurson, Gursham, Gurshan

Gert (German, Danish) fighter.

Gervaise (French) honorable. See also Jervis.
Garvais, Garvaise, Garvey, Gervais, Gervasio, Gervaso, Gervayse, Gervis, Gerwazy

Gerwin (Welsh) fair love.

Gethin (Welsh) dusky.
Geth

Ghazi (Arabic) conqueror.

Ghilchrist (Irish) servant of Christ. See also Gil.
Gilchrist, Gilcrist, Gilie, Gill, Gilley, Gilly

Gi (Korean) brave.

Gia (Vietnamese) family.

Giacinto (Portuguese, Spanish) an alternate form of Jacinto.
Giacintho

Giacomo (Italian) a form of Jacob.
Gaimo, Giacamo, Giaco, Giacobbe, Giacobo, Giacopo

Gian (Italian) a form of Giovanni, John.
Gianetto, Giann, Giannes, Gianni, Giannis, Giannos, Ghian

Giancarlo (Italian) a combination of John + Charles.
Giancarlos

Gianni (Italian) a form of Johnny.

Gianpaolo (Italian) a combination of John + Paul.
Gianpaulo

Gib (English) a short form of Gilbert.
Gibb, Gibbie, Gibby

Gibor (Hebrew) powerful.

Gibson (English) son of Gilbert.
Gibbon, Gibbons, Gibbs, Gillson, Gilson

Gideon (Hebrew) tree cutter. Bible: the judge who delivered the Israelites from captivity.
Gedeon, Gideone, Gidon, Hedeon

Gidon (Hebrew) an alternate form of Gideon.

Gifford (English) bold giver.
Giff, Giffard, Gifferd, Giffie, Giffy

Gig (English) horse-drawn carriage.

Gil (Greek) shield bearer. (Hebrew) happy. (English) a short form of Gilbert.
Gili, Gill, Gilli, Gillie, Gillis, Gilly

Gilad (Arabic) camel hump; from Giladi, Saudi Arabia.
Giladi, Gilead

Gilamu (Basque) a form of William.
Gillen

Gilbert (English) brilliant pledge; trustworthy. See also Gil, Gillett.
Gib, Gilberto, Gilburt, Giselbert, Giselberto, Giselbertus, Guilbert

Gilberto (Spanish) a form of Gilbert.

Gilby (Scandinavian) hostage's estate. (Irish) blond boy.
Gilbey, Gillbey, Gillbie, Gillby

Gilchrist (Irish) an alternate form of Ghilchrist.

Gilen (Basque, German) illustrious pledge.

Giles (French) goatskin shield.
Gide, Gilles, Gyles

Gillean (Irish) Bible: Saint John's servant.
Gillan, Gillen, Gillian

Gillespie (Irish) son of the bishop's servant.
Gillis

Gillett (French) young Gilbert.
Gelett, Gelette, Gillette

Gilmer (English) famous hostage.

Gilmore (Irish) devoted to the Virgin Mary.
Gillmore, Gillmour, Gilmour

Gilon (Hebrew) circle.

Gilroy (Irish) devoted to the king.
Gilderoy, Gildray, Gildroy, Gillroy, Roy

Gino (Greek) a familiar form of Eugene. (Italian) a short form of names ending in "gene," "gino."
Ghino

Giona (Italian) a form of Jonah.

Giordano (Italian) a form of Jordan.
Giordan, Giordana, Guordan

Giorgio (Italian) a form of George.

Giorgos (Greek) an alternate form of George.
Georgos

Giosia (Italian) a form of Joshua.

Giotto (Italian) a form of Geoffrey.

Giovanni (Italian) a form of John. See also Jeovanni, Jiovanni.
Geovanni, Gian, Gianni, Giannino, Giavani, Giovani, Giovannie, Giovanno, Giovanny, Giovany, Giovonathon, Giovonni

Gipsy (English) wanderer.
Gipson, Gypsy

Girvin (Irish) small; tough.
Girvan, Girven, Girvon

Gitano (Spanish) gypsy.

Giulio (Italian) a form of Julius.
Giuliano, Guilano

Giuseppe (Italian) a form of Joseph.
Giuseppino

Giustino (Italian) a form of Justin.
Giusto

Givon (Hebrew) hill; heights.

Gladwin (English) cheerful. See also Win.
Glad, Gladdie, Gladdy, Gladwinn, Gladwyn, Gladwynne

Glanville (English) village with oak trees.

Glen (Irish) an alternate form of Glenn.
Glyn

Glendon (Scottish) fortress in the glen.

Glenden, Glendin, Glenn, Glenton

Glendower (Welsh) from Glyndwer, England.

Glenn (Irish) a short form of Glendon.
Gleann, Glen, Glennie, Glennis, Glennon, Glenny, Glynn

Glentworth (English) from Glenton, England.

Glenville (Irish) village in the glen.

Glyn (Welsh) a form of Glen.
Glin

Goddard (German) divinely firm.
Godard, Godart, Goddart, Godhardt, Godhart, Gothart, Gotthard, Gotthardt, Gotthart

Godfrey (German) a form of Jeffrey. (Irish) God's peace. See also Geoffrey, Gottfried.
Giotto, Godefroi, Godfree, Godfry, Godofredo, Godoired, Godrey, Goffredo, Gofraidh, Gofredo, Gorry

Godwin (English) friend of God. See also Win.
Godewyn, Godwinn, Godwyn, Goodwin, Goodwyn, Goodwynn, Goodwynne

Goel (Hebrew) redeemer.

Goldwin (English) golden friend. See also Win.
Goldewin, Goldewinn, Goldewyn, Goldwyn, Goldwynn

Goliath (Hebrew) exiled. Bible: the giant Phillistine whom David slew with a slingshot.
Golliath

Gomda (Kiowa) wind.

Gomer (Hebrew) completed, finished. (English) famous battle.

Gonza (Rutooro) love.

Gonzalo (Spanish) wolf.
Goncalve, Gonsalve, Gonzales

Gordon (English) triangular hill.
Geordan, Gord, Gordain, Gordan, Gorden, Gordy

Gordy (English) a familiar form of Gordon.
Gordie

Gore (English) triangular-shaped land; wedge-shaped land.

Gorman (Irish) small; blue eyed.

Goro (Japanese) fifth.

Gosheven (Native American) great leaper.

Gottfried (German) a form of Geoffrey, Godfrey.
Gotfrid, Gotfrids, Gottfrid

Gotzon (German) a form of Angel.

Govert (Dutch) heavenly peace.

Gower (Welsh) pure.

Gowon (Tiv) rainmaker.
Gowan

Gozol (Hebrew) soaring bird.
Gozal

Grady (Irish) noble; illustrious.
Gradea, Gradee, Gradey, Gradleigh, Graidey, Graidy

Graeme (Scottish) a form of Graham.
Graem

Graham (English) grand home.
Graeham, Graehame, Graehme, Graeme, Grahame, Grahme, Gram

Granger (French) farmer.
Grainger, Grange

Grant (English) a short form of Grantland.
Grand, Grantham, Granthem, Grantley

Grantland (English) great plains.
Grant

Granville (French) large village.
Gran, Granvel, Granvil, Granvile, Granvill, Grenville, Greville

Gray (English) gray haired.
Grey, Greye

Grayden (English) gray haired.
Graden

Graydon (English) gray hill.
Gradon, Greydon

Grayson (English) bailiff's son. See also Sonny.
Greydon, Greyson

Greeley (English) gray meadow.
Greelea, Greeleigh, Greely

Greenwood (English) green forest.
Green, Greener

Greg, Gregg (Latin) short forms of Gregory.
Graig, Greig, Gregson

Greggory (Latin) an alternate form of Gregory.
Greggery

Gregor (Scottish) a form of Gregory.
Gregoor, Grégor, Gregore

Gregorio (Italian, Portuguese) a form of Gregory.
Gregorios

Gregory (Latin) vigilant watchman. See also Jörn, Krikor.
Gergely, Gergo, Greagoir, Greagory, Greer, Greg, Gregary, Greger, Gregery, Greggory, Grégoire, Gregor, Gregori, Grégorie,

Gregorio, Gregorius, Gregors, Gregos, Gregrey, Gregroy, Gregry, Greogry, Gries, Grisha, Grzegorz

Gresham (English) village in the pasture.

Greyson (English) an alternate form of Grayson.
Greyston

Griffin (Latin) hooked nose.
Griff, Griffen, Griffie, Griffon, Griffy, Gryphon

Griffith (Welsh) fierce chief; ruddy.
Griff, Griffie, Griffy, Gryphon

Grigori (Bulgarian) a form of Gregory.
Grigoi, Grigor, Grigorios, Grigorov, Grigory

Grimshaw (English) dark woods.

Grisha (Russian) a form of Gregory.

Griswold (German, French) gray forest.
Gris, Griz

Grosvener (French) big hunter.

Grover (English) grove.
Grove

Gualberto (Spanish) a form of Walter.
Gualterio

Gualtiero (Italian) a form of Walter.
Gualterio

Guglielmo (Italian) a form of William.

Guido (Italian) a form of Guy.

Guilford (English) ford with yellow flowers.
Guildford

Guilherme (Portuguese) a form of William.

Guillaume (French) a form of William.
Guillaums

Guillermo (Spanish) a form of William.

Gunnar (Scandinavian) an alternate form of Gunther.
Gunner

Gunther (Scandinavian) battle army; warrior.
Guenter, Guenther, Gun, Gunnar, Guntar, Gunter, Guntero, Gunthar, Günther

Guotin (Chinese) polite; strong leader.

Gurion (Hebrew) young lion.
Gur, Guri, Guriel

Gurpreet (Punjabi) devoted to the guru; devoted to the Prophet.
Gurjeet, Gurmeet, Guruprit

Gus (Scandinavian) a short form of Gustave.
Guss, Gussie, Gussy, Gusti, Gustry, Gusty

Gustaf (Swedish) a form of Gustave.
Gustaaf

Gustave (Scandinavian) staff of the Goths. History: Gustavus Adolphus was a king of Sweden. See also Kosti, Tabo, Tavo.
Gus, Gustaf, Gustaff, Gustaof, Gustav, Gustáv, Gustava, Gustaves, Gustavo, Gustavs, Gustavus, Gustik, Gustus, Gusztav

Gustavo (Italian, Spanish) a form of Gustave.

Guthrie (German) war hero. (Irish) windy place.
Guthrey, Guthry

Gutierre (Spanish) a form of Walter.

Guy (Hebrew) valley. (German) warrior. (French) guide. See also Guido.
Guyon

Guyapi (Native American) candid.

Gwayne (Welsh) an alternate form of Gawain.
Gwaine, Gwayn

Gwidon (Polish) life.

Gwilym (Welsh) a form of William.
Gwillym

Gyasi (Akan) marvelous baby.

Gyorgy (Russian) a form of George.
Gyoergy, György, Gyuri, Gyurka

Gyula (Hungarian) youth.
Gyala, Gyuszi

Habib (Arabic) beloved.

Hackett (German, French) little woodcutter.
Hacket, Hackit, Hackitt

Hackman (German, French) woodcutter.

Hadar (Hebrew) glory.

Haddad (Arabic) blacksmith.

Hadden (English) heather-covered hill.
Haddan, Haddon, Haden, Hadon, Hadyn

Hadi (Arabic) guiding to the right.

Hadley (English) heather-covered meadow.
Had, Hadlea, Hadlee, Hadleigh, Hadly, Lee, Leigh

Hadrian (Latin, Swedish)
dark.
Adrian, Hadrien

Hadwin (English) friend
in a time of war.
**Hadwinn, Hadwyn,
Hadwynn, Hadwynne**

Hagan (German) strong
defense.
Haggan

Hagen (Irish) young,
youthful.

Hagley (English) enclosed
meadow.

Hagos (Ethiopian) happy.

Hahnee (Native American)
beggar.

Hai (Vietnamese) sea.

Haidar (Arabic) lion.

Haig (English) enclosed
with hedges.

Haji (Swahili) born during
the pilgrimage to Mecca.

Hakan (Native American)
fiery.

Hakim (Arabic) wise.
(Ethiopian) doctor.
Hakeem, Hakiem

Hakon (Scandinavian)
of Nordic ancestry.
**Haaken, Haakin, Haakon,
Haeo, Hak, Hakan, Hako**

Hal (English) a short form
of Halden, Hall, Harold.

Halbert (English) shining
hero.
Bert, Halburt

Halden (Scandinavian)
half-Danish. See also
Dane.
**Hal, Haldan, Haldane,
Halfdan, Halvdan**

Hale (English) a short form
of Haley. (Hawaiian)
a form of Harry.
Hayle, Heall

Halen (Swedish) hall.
Hale, Hallen, Haylan

Haley (Irish) ingenious.
**Hailey, Haily, Hale,
Haleigh, Hayleigh, Hayley**

Halford (English) valley
ford.

Hali (Greek) sea.

Halian (Zuni) young.

Halil (Turkish) dear friend.

Halim (Arabic) mild,
gentle.
Haleem

Hall (English) manor, hall.
Hal, Halstead, Halsted

Hallam (English) valley.

Hallan (Engish) dweller
at the hall; dweller at
the manor.
Halin, Hallene, Hallin

Halley (English) meadow
near the hall; holy.

Halliwell (English) holy well.
Hallewell, Hellewell, Helliwell

Hallward (English) hall guard.

Halsey (English) Hal's island.

Halstead (English) manor grounds.
Halsted

Halton (English) estate on the hill.

Halvor (Norwegian) rock; protector.
Halvard

Ham (Hebrew) hot. Bible: one of Noah's sons.

Hamal (Arabic) lamb. Astronomy: a bright star in the constellation of Aries.

Hamar (Scandinavian) hammer.

Hamid (Arabic) praised. See also Mohammed.
Haamid, Hamadi, Hamdrem, Hamed, Hameed, Hamidi, Hammad, Hammed, Humayd

Hamill (English) scarred.
Hamel, Hamell, Hammill

Hamilton (English) proud estate.
Hamel, Hamelton, Hamil, Hamill, Tony

Hamish (Scottish) a form of Jacob, James.

Hamisi (Swahili) born on Thursday.

Hamlet (German, French) little village; home. Literature: one of Shakespeare's tragic heroes.

Hamlin (German, French) loves his home.
Hamblin, Hamelen, Hamelin, Hamlen, Hamlyn, Lin

Hammet (English, Scandinavian) village.
Hammett, Hamnet, Hamnett

Hammond (English) village.

Hampton (English) Geography: a town in England.
Hamp

Hanale (Hawaiian) a form of Henry.
Haneke

Hanan (Hebrew) grace.
Hananel, Hananiah, Johanan

Hanbal (Arabic) pure. History: founder of Islamic school of thought.

Handel (German, English) a form of John.

Hanford (English) high ford.

Hanif (Arabic) true believer.
Haneef, Hanef

Hank (American) a familiar
form of Henry.

Hanley (English) high
meadow.
**Handlea, Handleigh,
Handley, Hanlea, Hanlee,
Hanleigh, Hanly, Henlea,
Henlee, Henleigh, Henley**

Hannes (Finnish) a form
of John.

Hannibal (Phoenician)
grace of God. History:
a famous Carthaginian
general who fought the
Romans.
Anibal

Hanno (German) a short
form of Johann.

Hans (Scanadinavian)
a form of John.
**Hanschen, Hansel, Hants,
Hanz**

Hansel (Scandinavian)
an alternate form of Hans.
Haensel, Hansl

Hansen (Scandinavian)
son of Hans.
Hanson

Hansh (Hindi) god; godlike. Religion: another
name for the Hindu god
Shiva.

Hanson (Scandinavian)
an alternate form of
Hansen.
Hansen, Hanssen, Hansson

Hanus (Czech) a form
of John.

Haoa (Hawaiian) a form
of Howard.

Hara (Hindi) seizer.
Religion: another name
for the Hindu god Shiva.

Harald (Scandinavian) an
alternate form of Harold.
**Haraldo, Haralds,
Haralpos**

Harb (Arabic) warrior.

Harbin (German, French)
little bright warrior.
Harben, Harbyn

Harcourt (French) fortified
dwelling.
Court, Harcort

Hardeep (Punjabi) an alternate form of Harpreet.

Harden (English) valley
of the hares.
Hardin

Harding (English) brave
man's son.
Hardin

Hardwin (English) brave
friend.

Hardy (German) bold,
daring.

Harel (Hebrew) mountain
of God.
Hariel, Harrell

Harford (English) ford
of the hares.

Hargrove (English) grove of the hares.
Hargreave, Hargreaves

Hari (Hindi) tawny. Religion: another name for the Hindu god Vishnu.
Hariel, Harin

Harith (Arabic) cultivator.

Harkin (Irish) dark red.
Harkan, Harken

Harlan (English) hare's land; army land.
Harland, Harlen, Harlenn, Harlin, Harlon, Harlyn, Harlynn

Harley (English) hare's meadow; army meadow.
Arley, Harlea, Harlee, Harleigh, Harly

Harlow (English) hare's hill; army hill. See also Arlo.

Harmon (English) a form of Herman.
Harm, Harman, Harmond, Harms

Harold (Scandinavian) army ruler. See also Jindra.
Araldo, Garald, Garold, Hal, Harald, Haraldas, Haraldo, Haralds, Harry, Heraldo, Herold, Heronim, Herrick, Herryck

Haroun (Arabic) lofty; exalted.
Haarun, Harin, Haron, Haroon, Harron, Harun

Harper (English) harp player.
Harp, Harpo

Harpreet (Punjabi) loves God, devoted to God.
Hardeep

Harris (English) a short form of Harrison.
Haris, Hariss

Harrison (English) son of Harry.
Harris, Harrisen

Harrod (Hebrew) hero; conqueror.

Harry (English) a familiar form of Harold. See also Arrigo, Hale, Parry.
Harm, Harray, Harrey, Harri, Harrie

Hart (English) a short form of Hartley.

Hartley (English) deer meadow.
Hart, Hartlea, Hartlee, Hartleigh, Hartly

Hartman (German) hard; strong.

Hartwell (English) deer well.
Harwell, Harwill

Hartwig (German) strong advisor.

Hartwood (English) deer forest.

Harvey (German) army warrior.
Harv, Hervé, Hervey, Hervy

Hasad (Turkish) reaper, harvester.

Hasani (Swahili) handsome.
Hasaan, Hasain, Hasan, Hashaan, Hason, Hassen, Hassian, Husani

Hashim (Arabic) destroyer of evil.
Haashim, Hasheem

Hasin (Hindi) laughing.
Hasen, Hassin

Haskel (Hebrew) an alternate form of Ezekiel.
Haskell

Haslett (English) hazel-tree land.
Haze, Hazel, Hazlett, Hazlitt

Hassan (Arabic) handsome.
Hasan

Hassel (German, English) witches' corner.
Hassal, Hassall, Hassell

Hastin (Hindi) elephant.

Hastings (Latin) spear. (English) house council.
Hastie, Hasty

Hatim (Arabic) judge.
Hateem, Hatem

Hauk (Norwegian) hawk.
Haukeye

Havelock (Norwegian) sea battler.

Haven (Dutch, English) harbor, port; safe place.
Haeven, Havin, Hovan

Havika (Hawaiian) a form of David.

Hawley (English) hedged meadow.
Hawleigh, Hawly

Hawthorne (English) hawthorn tree.

Hayden (English) hedged valley.
Haden, Haidyn, Haydn, Haydon

Hayes (English) hedged valley.
Hayse

Hayward (English) guardian of the hedged area.
Haward, Heyvard, Heyward

Haywood (English) hedged forest.
Heywood, Woody

Hearn (Scottish, English) a short form of Ahearn.
Hearne, Herin, Hern

Heath (English) heath.
Heathe, Heith

Heathcliff (English) cliff near the heath. Literature: the hero of Emily Brontë's novel *Wuthering Heights*.

Heaton (English) high place.

Heber (Hebrew) ally, partner.

Hector (Greek) steadfast. Mythology: the greatest hero of the Trojan war.

Hedley (English) heather-filled meadow.
Headley, Headly, Hedly

Heinrich (German) an alternate form of Henry.
Heindrick, Heiner, Heinrick, Heinrik, Hinrich

Heinz (German) a familiar form of Henry.

Helaku (Native American) sunny day.

Helge (Russian) holy.

Helki (Moquelumnan) touching.

Helmer (German) warrior's wrath.

Helmut (German) courageous.
Helmuth

Heman (Hebrew) faithful.

Henderson (Scottish, English) son of Henry.
Hendrie, Hendries, Hendron, Henryson

Hendrick (Dutch) a form of Henry.
Hendricks, Hendrickson, Hendrik, Hendriks, Hendrikus, Henning

Heniek (Polish) a form of Henry.
Henier

Henley (English) high meadow.

Henning (German) an alternate form of Hendrick, Henry.

Henoch (Yiddish) initiator.
Enoch

Henri (French) a form of Henry.
Henrico

Henrick (Dutch) a form of Henry.
Heinrick, Henerik, Henrich, Henrik, Henryk

Henrique (Portuguese) a form of Henry.

Henry (German) ruler of the household. See also Arrigo, Enric, Enrico, Enrikos, Enrique, Hanale, Honok, Kiki.
Hagan, Hank, Harro, Harry, Heike, Heinrich, Heinz, Hendrick, Henery, Heniek, Henning, Henraoi, Henri, Henrick, Henrim, Henrique, Henrry, Heromin, Hersz

Heraldo (Spanish) a form of Harold.
Herald, Hiraldo

Herb (German) a short form of Herbert.
Herbie, Herby

Herbert (German) glorious soldier.
Bert, Erbert, Harbert, Hebert, Hébert, Heberto, Herb, Heriberto, Hurbert

Hercules (Greek) glorious gift. Mythology: a famous Greek hero renowned for his twelve labors.
Herakles, Herc, Hercule, Herculie

Heriberto (Spanish) a form of Herbert.
Heribert

Herman (Latin) noble. (German) soldier. See also Armand, Ermanno, Ermano, Mandek.
Harmon, Hermann, Hermie, Herminio, Hermino, Hermon, Hermy, Heromin

Hermes (Greek) messenger. Mythology: the messenger for the Greek gods.

Hernando (Spanish) a form of Ferdinand.
Hernandes, Hernandez

Herrick (German) war ruler.
Herrik, Herryck

Herschel (Hebrew) an alternate form of Hershel.
Hersch, Herschell

Hersh (Hebrew) a short form of Hershel.
Hersch, Hirsch

Hershel (Hebrew) deer.
Herschel, Hersh, Hershell, Herzl, Hirschel, Hirshel

Hertz (Yiddish) my strife.
Herzel

Hervé (French) a form of Harvey.

Hesperos (Greek) evening star.
Hespero

Hesutu (Moquelumnan) picking up a yellow jacket's nest.

Hew (Welsh) a form of Hugh.
Hewe, Huw

Hewitt (German, French) little smart one.
Hewe, Hewet, Hewett, Hewie, Hewit, Hewlett, Hewlitt

Hewson (English) son of Hugh.

Hezekiah (Hebrew) God gives strength.

Hiamovi (Cheyenne) high chief.

Hibah (Arabic) gift.

Hideaki (Japanese) smart, clever.
Hideo

Hieremias (Greek) God will uplift.

Hieronymos (Greek) a form of Jerome.
Hierome, Hieronim,

Hieronymos (cont.)
**Hieronimo, Hieronimos,
Hieronymo, Hieronymus**

Hieu (Vietnamese)
respectful.

Hilario (Spanish) a form
of Hilary.

Hilary (Latin) cheerful.
See also Ilari.
**Hi, Hilaire, Hilarie, Hilario,
Hilarion, Hilarius, Hil, Hill,
Hillary, Hillery, Hilliary,
Hillie, Hilly**

Hildebrand (German)
battle sword.
Hildo

Hilel (Arabic) new moon.

Hillel (Hebrew) greatly
praised. Religion: Rabbi
Hillel originated the
Talmud.

Hilliard (German) brave
warrior.
**Hillard, Hiller, Hillier,
Hillierd, Hillyard, Hillyer,
Hillyerd**

Hilmar (Swedish) famous
noble.

Hilton (English) town on
a hill.
Hylton

Hinto (Dakota) blue.

Hinun (Native American)
spirit of the storm.

Hippolyte (Greek)
horseman.
Hipolito, Hippolit,

**Hippolitos, Hippolytus,
Ippolito**

Hiram (Hebrew) noblest;
exalted.
Hi, Hirom, Huram, Hyrum

Hiromasa (Japanese) fair,
just.

Hiroshi (Japanese)
generous.

Hisoka (Japanese) secretive, reserved.

Hiu (Hawaiian) a form
of Hugh.

Ho (Chinese) good.

Hoang (Vietnamese)
finished.

Hobart (German) Bart's
hill.
**Hobard, Hobbie, Hobby,
Hobie, Hoebart**

Hobert (German) Bert's
hill.
Hobey

Hobson (English) son
of Robert.

Hoc (Vietnamese) studious.

Hod (Hebrew) a short form
of Hodgson.

Hodgson (English) son
of Roger.
Hod

Hogan (Irish) youth.

Holbrook (English) brook
in the hollow.
Brook, Holbrooke

Holden (English) hollow in the valley.
Holdin, Holdun

Holic (Czech) barber.

Holleb (Polish) dove.
Hollub, Holub

Hollis (English) grove of holly trees.
Hollie, Holly

Holmes (English) river islands.

Holt (English) forest.
Holton

Homer (Greek) hostage; pledge; security. Literature: a renowned Greek poet.
Homere, Homère, Homero, Homeros, Homerus

Hondo (Shona) warrior.

Honesto (Filipino) honest.

Honi (Hebrew) gracious.
Choni

Honok (Polish) a form of Henry.

Honon (Moquelumnan) bear.

Honorato (Spanish) honorable.

Honoré (Latin) honored.
Honoratus, Honorius

Honovi (Native American) strong.

Honza (Czech) a form of John.

Hop (Chinese) agreeable.

Horace (Latin) keeper of the hours. Literature: a famous Latin poet.
Horacio, Horaz

Horatio (Latin) clan name. See also Orris.
Horatius, Oratio

Horst (German) dense grove; thicket.
Hurst

Horton (English) garden estate.
Hort, Horten, Orton

Hosea (Hebrew) salvation. Bible: a Hebrew prophet.
Hose, Hoseia, Hoshea, Hosheah

Hotah (Lakota) white.

Hototo (Native American) whistler.

Houghton (English) settlement on the headland.
Hoho

Houston (English) hill town. Geography: a city in Texas.
Huston

Howard (English) watchman. See also Haoa.
Howie, Ward

Howe (German) high.
Howey, Howie

Howell (Welsh) remarkable.
Howel

Howi (Moquelumnan)
turtle dove.

Howie (English) a familiar
form of Howard, Howland.
Howey

Howin (Chinese) loyal
swallow.

Howland (English) hilly
land.
Howie, Howlan, Howlen

Hoyt (Irish) mind; spirit.

Hu (Chinese) tiger.

Hubbard (German) an
alternate form of Hubert.

Hubert (German) bright
mind; bright spirit.
See also Beredei, Uberto.
**Bert, Hobart, Hubbard,
Hubbert, Huber,
Hubertek, Huberto,
Hubie, Huey, Hugh,
Hugibert, Humberto**

Huberto (Spanish) a form
of Hubert.
Humberto

Hubie (English) a familiar
form of Hubert.
Hube, Hubi

Hud (Arabic) Religion:
a Muslim prophet.
Hudson

Huey (English) a familiar
form of Hugh.
Hughey, Hughie, Hughy

Hugh (English) a short form
of Hubert. See also Ea,

Hewitt, Huxley, Maccoy,
Ugo.
**Fitzhugh, Hew, Hiu, Huey,
Hughes, Hugo, Hugues**

Hugo (Latin) a form
of Hugh.
Ugo

Hulbert (German) brilliant
grace.
**Bert, Hulbard, Hulburd,
Hulburt, Hull**

Humbert (German)
brilliant strength.
See also Umberto.
Hum, Humberto

Humberto (Portuguese)
a form of Humbert.

Humphrey (German)
peaceful strength. See also
Onofrio, Onufry.
**Hum, Humfredo, Humfrey,
Humfrid, Humfried,
Humfry, Hump, Humph,
Humphery, Humphry,
Humphrys, Hunfredo**

Hung (Vietnamese) brave.

Hunt (English) a short form
of names beginning with
"Hunt."

Hunter (English) hunter.
Hunt

Huntington (English)
hunting estate.
Hunt, Huntingdon

Huntley (English) hunter's
meadow.
**Hunt, Huntlea, Huntlee,
Huntleigh, Huntly**

Hurley (Irish) sea tide.
Hurlee, Hurleigh

Hurst (English) a form
of Horst.
Hearst, Hirst

Husam (Arabic) sword.

Husamettin (Turkish)
sharp sword.

Huslu (Native American)
hairy bear.

Hussein (Arabic) little;
handsome.
**Hossain, Hossein, Husain,
Husani, Husayn, Husein,
Husian, Hussain, Hussien**

Hutchinson (English) son
of the hutch dweller.
Hutcheson

Hute (Native American)
star. Astronomy: a star in
the Big Dipper.

Hutton (English) house
on the jutting ledge.
Hut, Hutt, Huttan

Huxley (English) Hugh's
meadow.
**Hux, Huxlea, Huxlee,
Huxleigh, Lee**

Huy (Vietnamese) glorious.

Hy (Vietnamese) hopeful.
(English) a short form
of Hyman.

Hyacinthe (French)
hyacinth.

Hyatt (English) high gate.
Hyat

Hyde (English) measure of
land equal to 120 acres.

Hyder (English) tanner,
preparer of animal hides
for tanning.

Hyman (English) a form
of Chaim.
**Haim, Hayim, Hayvim,
Hayyim, Hy, Hyam, Hymie**

Hyun-Ki (Korean) wise.

Hyun-Shik (Korean) clever.

Iago (Spanish, Welsh)
a form of Jacob, James.
Literature: the villain in
Shakespeare's *Othello*.
Jago

Iain (Scottish) an alternate
form of Ian.

Iakobos (Greek) a form
of Jacob.
Iakov, Iakovos, Iakovs

Ian (Scottish) a form of
John. See also Ean, Eion.
Iain

Ianos (Czech) a form
of John.

Ib (Phoenician, Danish)
oath of Baal.

Iban (Basque) a form
of John.

Ibon (Basque) a form
of Ivor.

Ibrahim (Arabic) a form
of Abraham. (Hausa) my
father is exalted.
Ibraham, Ibrahem

Ichabod (Hebrew) glory is
gone. Literature: Ichabod
Crane was the main
character of Washington
Irving's story "The Legend
of Sleepy Hollow."

Idi (Swahili) born during
the Idd festival.

Idris (Welsh) eager lord.
Religion: a Muslim
prophet.
Idriss, Idriys

Iestyn (Welsh) a form
of Justin.

Igashu (Native American)
wanderer; seeker.
Igasho

Iggy (Latin) a familiar form
of Ignatius.

Ignatius (Latin) fiery,
ardent. Religion: Saint
Ignatious of Loyola was
the founder of the Jesuit
order. See also Inigo, Neci.
**Iggie, Iggy, Ignac, Ignác,
Ignace, Ignacio, Ignacius,
Ignatious, Ignatz, Ignaz,
Ignazio**

Ignazio (Italian) a form
of Ignatius.
Ignacio

Igor (Russian) a form of
Inger, Ingvar. See also
Egor, Yegor.
Igoryok

Ihsan (Turkish) compassionate.

Ike (Hebrew) a familiar
form of Isaac. History:
the nickname of the
thirty-fourth U.S. president
Dwight D. Eisenhower.
Ikee, Ikey

Iker (Basque) visitation.

Ilan (Hebrew) tree.
(Basque) youth.

Ilari (Basque) a form
of Hilary.
Ilario

Ilias (Greek) a form
of Elijah.
Illyas

Illan (Basque, Latin) youth.

Ilom (Ibo) my enemies
are many.

Ilya (Russian) a form
of Elijah.
Ilia, Ilie, Ilija, Ilja, Illya

Imad (Arabic) supportive;
mainstay.

Immanuel (Hebrew)
an alternate form
of Emmanuel.
**Iman, Imanol, Imanuel,
Immanuele, Immuneal**

Imran (Arabic) host. Bible:
a character in the Old
Testament.

Imre (Hungarian) a form
of Emery.
Imri

Imrich (Czech) a form
of Emery.
Imrus

Inay (Hindi) god; godlike.
Religion: another name for
the Hindu god Shiva.

Ince (Hungarian) innocent.

Inder (Hindi) god; godlike.
Religion: another name for
the Hindu god Shiva.
**Inderjeet, Inderjit,
Inderpal, Indervir, Indra,
Indrajit**

Inek (Welsh) an alternate
form of Irvin.

Ing (Scandinavian) a short
form of Ingmar.
Inge

Ingelbert (German)
an alternate form
of Engelbert.
Inglebert

Inger (Scandinavian)
son's army.
Igor, Ingemar, Ingmar

Ingmar (Scandinavian)
famous son.
**Ing, Ingamar, Ingamur,
Ingemar**

Ingram (English) angel.
**Inglis, Ingra, Ingraham,
Ingrim**

Ingvar (Scandinavian)
Ing's soldier.
Igor, Ingevar

Inigo (Basque) a form
of Ignatius.
Iñaki, Iñigo

Iniko (Ibo) born during
bad times.

Innis (Irish) island.
Innes, Inness, Inniss

Innocenzio (Italian)
innocent.
**Innocenty, Inocenci,
Inocencio, Inocente,
Inosente**

Inteus (Native American)
proud; unashamed.

Ioakim (Russian) a form
of Joachim.
Ioachime, Iov

Ioan (Greek, Bulgarian,
Romanian) a form of John.
**Ioane, Ioann, Ioannes,
Ioannikios, Ioannis, Ionel**

Iokepa (Hawaiian) a form
of Joseph.
Keo

Iolo (Welsh) the Lord is
worthy.
Iorwerth

Ionakana (Hawaiian)
a form of Jonathan.

Iorgos (Greek) an alternate form of George.

Iosif (Greek, Russian) a form of Joseph.

Iosua (Romanian) a form of Joshua.

Ipyana (Nyakusa) graceful.

Ira (Hebrew) watchful.

Iram (English) bright.

Irumba (Rutooro) born after twins.

Irv (Irish, Welsh, English) a short form of Irvin, Irving.

Irvin (Irish, Welsh, English) a short form of Irving. See also Ervine.
Inek, Irv, Irvine

Irving (Irish) handsome. (Welsh) white river. (English) sea friend. See also Ervin, Ervine.
Irv, Irvin, Irvington

Irwin (English) an alternate form of Irving. See also Ervin.
Irwinn, Irwyn

Isa (Arabic) a form of Jesus.
Isaah

Isaac (Hebrew) he will laugh. Bible: the son of Abraham and Sarah. See also Itzak, Izak, Yitzchak.
Aizik, Icek, Ike, Ikey, Ikie, Isaak, Isaakios, Isac, Ishaq, Isacco, Isack, Isak, Isiac,

Isiacc, Issca, Issiac, Itzak, Izak, Izzy

Isaiah (Hebrew) God is my salvation. Bible: an influential Hebrew prophet.
Isa, Isai, Isaia, Isaid, Isaih, Isais, Isaish, Ishaq, Isia, Isiah, Isiash, Issia, Issiah, Izaiah, Izaiha

Isam (Arabic) safeguard.

Isas (Japanese) meritorious.

Isekemu (Native American) slow-moving creek.

Isham (English) home of the iron one.

Ishan (Hindi) direction.

Ishaq (Arabic) a form of Isaac.

Ishmael (Hebrew) God will hear. Literature: the narrator of Melville's novel *Moby Dick*.
Isamail, Ishma, Ishmeal, Ishmel, Ismael, Ismail

Isidore (Greek) gift of Isis. See also Dorian, Ysidro.
Isador, Isadore, Isadorios, Isidor, Isidoro, Isidro, Issy, Ixidor, Izadore, Izidor, Izidore, Izydor, Izzy

Iskander (Afghani) a form of Alexander.

Ismail (Arabic) a form of Ishmael.
Ismeal, Ismeil

Israel (Hebrew) prince of God; wrestled with God. History: the nation of Israel took its name from the name given Jacob after he wrestled with the Angel of the Lord.
Iser, Isser, Izrael, Izzy, Yisrael

Issa (Swahili) God is our salvation.

Istu (Native American) sugar pine.

István (Hungarian) a form of Stephen.
Isti, Istvan, Pista

Ithel (Welsh) generous lord.

Ittamar (Hebrew) island of palms.
Itamar

Itzak (Hebrew) an alternate form of Isaac.
Itzik

Iukini (Hawaiian) a form of Eugene.
Kini

Iustin (Bulgarian, Russian) a form of Justin.

Ivan (Russian) a form of John.
Iván, Ivanchik, Ivanichek, Ivano, Ivas, Vanya

Ivar (Scandinavian) an alternate form of Ivor. See also Yves.
Iv, Iva

Ives (English) young archer.
Ive, Iven, Ivey, Yves

Ivo (German) yew wood; bow wood. See also Archer.
Ibon, Ivar, Ives, Ivon, Ivonnie, Ivor, Yvo

Ivor (Scandinavian) a form of Ivo. See also Archer.
Ibon, Ifor, Ivar, Iver

Iwan (Polish) a form of John.

Iyapo (Yoruba) many trials; many obstacles.

Iye (Native American) smoke.

Izak (Czech) a form of Isaac.
Ixaka, Izaac, Izaak, Izac, izak, Izeke, Izik, Izsak, Izsák

Izzy (Hebrew) a familiar form of Isaac, Isidore, Israel.
Issy

J (American) an initial used as a first name.
J.

Ja (Korean) attractive, magnetic.

Jaali (Swahili) powerful.

Jaan (Estonian) a form of Christian.

Jaap (Dutch) a form of Jim.

Jabari (Swahili) fearless.
Jabaar, Jabare, Jabbar, Jabier

Jabez (Hebrew) born in pain.
Jabe, Jabes, Jabesh

Jabin (Hebrew) God has created.

Jabir (Arabic) consoler, comforter.
Jabiri, Jabori

Jabulani (Shona) happy.

Jacan (Hebrew) trouble.
Jachin

Jace (American) a combination of the initials J. + C.
JC, J.C., Jacey, Jaice, Jayce, Jaycee

Jacinto (Portuguese, Spanish) hyacinth. See also Giacinto.
Jacindo, Jacint

Jack (American) a familiar form of Jacob, John. See also Keaka.
Jackie, Jacko, Jackub, Jacque, Jak, Jax, Jock, Jocko

Jackie (American) a familiar form of Jack.
Jacky

Jackson (English) son of Jack.
Jacson, Jakson, Jaxon

Jaco (Portuguese) a form of Jacob.

Jacob (Hebrew) supplanter, substitute. Bible: son of Abraham, brother of Esau. See also Akiva, Chago, Checha, Coby, Diego, Giacomo, Hamish, Iago, Iakobos, James, Kiva, Koby, Kuba, Tiago, Yakov, Yasha, Yoakim.
Jaap, Jachob, Jack, Jackub, Jaco, Jacobb, Jacobe, Jacobi, Jacobis, Jacobo, Jacobs, Jacobus, Jacoby, Jacolby, Jacques, Jago, Jaime, Jake, Jakob, Jalu, Jasha, Jecis, Jeks, Jeska, Jim, Jocek, Jock, Jocoby, Jocolby, Jokubas

Jacques (French) a form of Jacob, James. See also Coco.

Jacot, Jacquan, Jacquees, Jacquet, Jacquez, Jaques, Jarques, Jarquis

Jacy (Tupi-Guarani) moon.
Jaicy, Jaycee

Jade (Spanish) jade, precious stone.

Jadon (Hebrew) God has heard.
Jaden, Jadin, Jaeden, Jaedon, Jaiden, Jaydon

Jadrien (American) a combination of Jay + Adrien.
Jad, Jada, Jadd, Jader

Jaegar (German) hunter.
Jaager, Jagur

Jae-Hwa (Korean) rich, prosperous.

Jael (Hebrew) mountain goat.
Yael

Ja'far (Sanskrit) little stream.
Jafar, Jafari, Jaffar

Jagger (English) carter.

Jago (English) an alternate form of James.

Jaguar (Spanish) jaguar.
Jagguar

Jahi (Swahili) dignified.

Jaime (Spanish) a form of Jacob, James.
Jaimey, Jaimie, Jaimito, Jayme, Jaymie

Jairo (Spanish) God enlightens.
Jairus, Jarius

Jaja (Ibo) honored.

Jajuan (American) a combination of the prefix Ja + Juan.
Ja Juan, Jauan, Jawaun, Jejuan, Jujuan, Juwan

Jake (Hebrew) a short form of Jacob.
Jakie, Jayk, Jayke

Jakeem (Arabic) uplifted.

Jakob (Hebrew) an alternate form of Jacob.
Jakab, Jakiv, Jakov, Jakovian, Jakub, Jakubek, Jekebs

Jakome (Basque) a form of James. Bible: another name for Saint James.
Xanti

Jal (Gypsy) wanderer.

Jalil (Hindi) god; godlike. Religion: another name for the Hindu god Shiva.
Jahlee, Jahleel, Jahlil, Jalaal, Jalal

Jam (American) a short form of Jamal, Jamar.
Jama

Jamaal (Arabic) an alternate form of Jamal.

Jamaine (Arabic) a form of Germain.

Jamal (Arabic) handsome.
See also Gamal.
Jahmal, Jahmall, Jahmalle,
Jahmel, Jahmil, Jahmile,
Jam, Jamaal, Jamael,
Jamahl, Jamail, Jamala,
Jamale, Jamall, Jamar,
Jamel, Jamil, Jammal,
Jarmal, Jaumal, Jemal,
Jermal

Jamar (American)
a form of Jamal.
Jam, Jamaar, Jamaari,
Jamahrae, Jamara, Jamarl,
Jamarr, Jamarvis, Jamaur,
Jarmar, Jarmarr, Jaumar,
Jemaar, Jemar, Jimar

Jamarcus (American)
a combination of the
prefix Ja + Marcus.
Jamarco, Jemarcus,
Jimarcus

Jamario (American)
a combination of the
prefix Ja + Mario.
Jamari, Jamariel, Jamarius,
Jemario, Jemarus

Jamel (Arabic) an alternate
form of Jamal.
Jameel, Jamele, Jamell,
Jamelle, Jammel, Jarmel,
Jaumell, Je-Mell, Jimell

James (Hebrew) supplanter,
substitute. (English) a form
of Jacob. Bible: James the
Great and James the Lesser
were two of the Twelve
Apostles. See also Diego,

Hamish, Iago, Kimo,
Santiago, Seumas, Yago,
Yasha.
Jacques, Jago, Jaime,
Jaimes, Jakome, Jamesie,
Jamesy, Jamie, Jas, Jasha,
Jay, Jaymes, Jem, Jemes,
Jim

Jameson (English) son
of James.
Jamerson, Jamesian,
Jamison, Jaymeson

Jamie (English) a familiar
form of James.
Jaime, Jaimey, Jaimie,
Jame, Jamee, Jamey,
Jameyel, Jami, Jamian,
Jammie, Jammy, Jayme,
Jaymee, Jaymie

Jamil (Arabic) an alternate
form of Jamal.
Jamiel, Jamiell, Jamielle,
Jamile, Jamill, Jamille,
Jamyl, Jarmil

Jamin (Hebrew) favored.
Jamian, Jamiel, Jamon,
Jarmin, Jarmon, Jaymin

Jamison (English) son of
James.
Jamiesen, Jamieson,
Jamisen

Jamond (American)
a combination of
James + Raymond.
Jamod, Jamon, Jamone,
Jarmond

Jamsheed (Persian) from
Persia.

Jan (Dutch, Slavic) a form
of John.
**Jaan, Janne, Jano, Janson,
Jenda, Yan**

Janco (Czech) a form
of John.
Jancsi

Jando (Spanish) a form
of Alexander.
Jandino

Janeil (American)
a combination of the
prefix Ja + Neil.
**Janel, Janielle, Janile,
Janille, Jarnail, Jarneil,
Jarnell**

Janek (Polish) a form
of John.
**Janik, Janika, Janka,
Jankiel, Janko**

Janis (Latvian) a form
of John.
Ansis, Jancis, Zanis

Janne (Finnish) a form
of John.
Jann, Jannes

János (Hungarian) a form
of John.
Jancsi, Jani, Jankia, Jano

Janson (Scandinavian)
son of Jan.
**Janse, Jansen, Janssen,
Janten, Jantzen, Janzen,
Jensen, Jenson**

Janus (Latin) gate, passage-
way; born in January.

Mythology: the Roman
god of beginnings.
Januario

Japheth (Hebrew) hand-
some. (Arabic) abundant.
Bible: a son of Noah.
See also Yaphet.
Japeth, Japhet

Jaquan (American)
a combination of the
prefix Ja + Quan.
**Ja'quan, Jaquin, Jaquon,
Jaqwan**

Jarah (Hebrew) sweet
as honey.
Jerah

Jareb (Hebrew)
contending.
Jarib

Jared (Hebrew)
descendant.
**Jahred, Jaired, Jarad,
Jareid, Jarid, Jarod, Jarred,
Jarrett, Jarrod, Jarryd,
Jerad, Jered, Jerod, Jerrad,
Jerred, Jerrod, Jerryd,
Jordan**

Jarek (Slavic) born
in January.
**Janiuszck, Januarius,
Januisz, Jarrek**

Jarell (Scandinavian)
a form of Gerald.
**Jairell, Jareil, Jarel, Jarelle,
Jarrell, Jarryl, Jayryl, Jerel,
Jerell, Jerrell, Jharell**

Jareth (American) a combination of Jared + Gareth.
Jarreth, Jereth

Jarl (Scandinavian) earl, nobleman.

Jarlath (Latin) in control.
Jarl, Jarlen

Jarman (German) from Germany.
Jerman

Jaron (Hebrew) he will sing; he will cry out.
Jaaron, Jairon, Jaren, Jarone, Jayron, Jayronn, Je Ronn, J'ron

Jaroslav (Czech) glory of spring.
Jarda

Jarred (Hebrew) an alternate form of Jared.
Ja'red, Jarrad, Jarrayd, Jarrid, Jarrod, Jarryd, Jerrid

Jarrell (English) a form of Gerald.
Jarel, Jarell, Jarrel, Jerall, Jerel, Jerell

Jarrett (English) a form of Garrett, Jared.
Jairett, Jaret, Jareth, Jaretté, Jarhett, Jarratt, Jarret, Jarrette, Jarrot, Jarrott, Jerrett

Jarrod (Hebrew) an alternate form of Jared.
Jarod, Jerod

Jarryd (Hebrew) an alternate form of Jared.
Jarrayd, Jaryd

Jarvis (German) skilled with a spear.
Jaravis, Jarv, Jarvaris, Jarvas, Jarvaska, Jarvey, Jarvie, Jarvorice, Jarvoris, Jarvous, Javaris, Jervey, Jervis

Jas (Polish) a form of John. (English) a familiar form of James.
Jasio

Jasha (Russian) a familiar form of Jacob, James.
Jascha

Jashawn (American) a combination of the prefix Ja + Shawn.
Jasean, Jashan, Jashon

Jason (Greek) healer. Mythology: the hero who led the Argonauts in search of the Golden Fleece.
Jacen, Jaeson, Jahson, Jaisen, Jaison, Jasan, Jase, Jasen, Jasin, Jasten, Jasun, Jay, Jayson

Jaspal (Punjabi) living a virtuous lifestyle.

Jasper (French) green ornamental stone. (English) a form of Casper. See also Kasper.
Jaspar, Jazper, Jespar, Jesper

Jatinra (Hindi) great
Brahmin sage.

Javan (Hebrew) Bible:
son of Japheth.
**Jaavon, Jahvaughan,
Jahvine, Jahvon,
JaVaughn, Javen, Javin,
Javine, Javion, Javoanta,
Javon, Javona, Javone,
Javoney, Javoni, Javonn,
Jayvin, Jayvion, Jayvon,
Jevan**

Javaris (English) a form
of Jarvis.
**Javaor, Javar, Javares,
Javario, Javarius, Javaro,
Javaron, Javarous, Javarre,
Javarrious, Javarro,
Javarte, Javarus, Javoris,
Javouris**

Javas (Sanskrit) quick, swift.
Jayvas, Jayvis

Javier (Spanish) owner of
a new house. See also
Xavier.
Jabier

Jawaun (American) an
alternate form of Jajuan.
**Jawaan, Jawan, Jawann,
Jawn, Jawon, Jawuan**

Jawhar (Arabic) jewel;
essence.

Jay (French) blue jay.
(English) a short form
of James, Jason.
**Jae, Jai, Jave, Jaye, Jeays,
Jeyes**

Jayce (American) a combination of the initials J. + C.
JC, J.C., Jaycee, Jay Cee

Jayde (American) a combination of the initials J. + D.
JD, J.D., Jayden

Jaylee (American) a combi-
nation of Jay + Lee.
**Jaylen, Jaylin, Jaylon,
Jaylun**

Jayme (English) an alternate form of Jamie.
Jaymes, Jayms

Jaymes (English) an alternate form of James.
Jayms

Jayson (Greek) an alternate
form of Jason.
**Jaycent, Jaysen, Jaysin,
Jayssen, Jaysson**

Jazz (American) jazz.
**Jazze, Jazzlee, Jazzman,
Jazzmen, Jazzmin,
Jazzmon, Jazztin, Jazzton**

Jean (French) a form
of John.
**Jéan, Jeannah, Jeannie,
Jeannot, Jeanot, Jeanty,
Jene**

Jeb (Hebrew) a short form
of Jebediah.
Jebi

Jebediah (Hebrew) an
alternate form of Jedidiah.
**Jeb, Jebadia, Jebadiah,
Jebidiah**

Jed (Hebrew) a short form
of Jedidiah. (Arabic) hand.
Jedd, Jeddy, Jedi

Jediah (Hebrew) hand
of God.
**Jedaia, Jedaiah, Jedeiah,
Jedi, Yedaya**

Jedidiah (Hebrew) friend
of God, beloved of God.
See also Didi.
**Jebediah, Jed, Jedediah,
Jedediha, Jedidia,
Jedidiah, Yedidya**

Jedrek (Polish) strong;
manly.
Jedrik, Jedrus

Jeff (English) a short form
of Jefferson, Jeffrey.
A familiar form of Geoffrey.
**Jefe, Jeffe, Jeffey, Jeffie,
Jeffy, Jhef**

Jefferson (English) son
of Jeff. History: Thomas
Jefferson was the third
U.S. president.
Jeferson, Jeff, Jeffers

Jeffery (English) an alter-
nate form of Jeffrey.
**Jefery, Jeffeory, Jefferay,
Jeffereoy, Jefferey,
Jefferie, Jeffory**

Jefford (English) Jeff's ford.

Jeffrey (English) divinely
peaceful. See also Geffrey,
Geoffrey, Godfrey.
**Jeff, Jefferies, Jeffery,
Jeffree, Jeffrery, Jeffrie,**

**Jeffries, Jeffry, Jefre, Jefry,
Jeoffroi, Joffre, Joffrey**

Jeffry (English) an alternate
form of Jeffrey.

Jehan (French) a form
of John.
Jehann

Jehu (Hebrew) God lives.
Bible: a military comman-
der and king of Israel.
Yehu

Jelani (Swahili) mighty.
Jel

Jem (English) a short form
of James, Jeremiah.
Jemmie, Jemmy

Jemal (Arabic) an alternate
form of Jamal.
**Jemaal, Jemael, Jemale,
Jemel**

Jemel (Arabic) an alternate
form of Jemal.
**Jemehyl, Jemell, Jemelle,
Jemeyle, Jemmy**

Jemond (French) worldly.
**Jemon, Jémond, Jemonde,
Jemone**

Jenkin (Flemish) little John.
**Jenkins, Jenkyn, Jenkyns,
Jennings**

Jenö (Hungarian) a form
of Eugene.
**Jenci, Jency, Jenoe, Jensi,
Jensy**

Jens (Danish) a form
of John.
Jensen, Jenson, Jensy

Jeovanni (Italian) an alternate form of Giovanni.
Jeovani, Jeovany

Jerad, Jered (Hebrew) alternate forms of Jared.
Jeread, Jeredd

Jerahmy (Hebrew) a form of Jeremy.
Jerahmeel, Jerahmeil, Jerahmey

Jerald (English) a form of Gerald.
Jeraldo, Jerold, Jerral, Jerrald, Jerrold, Jerry

Jerall (English) an alternate form of Jarrell.
Jerai, Jerail, Jeraile, Jerale, Jerall, Jerrail, Jerral, Jerrel, Jerrell, Jerrelle

Jeramie, Jeramy (Hebrew) alternate forms of Jeremy.
Jerame, Jeramee, Jeramey, Jerami, Jerammie

Jerard (French) a form of Gerard.
Jarard, Jarrard, Jerardo, Jeraude, Jerrard

Jere (Hebrew) a short form of Jeremiah, Jeremy.
Jeré, Jeree

Jerel, Jerell (English) forms of Jarell.
Jerelle, Jeril, Jerrail, Jerral, Jerrall, Jerrel, Jerrill, Jerrol, Jerroll, Jerryll, Jeryl

Jereme, Jeremey (Hebrew) alternate forms of Jeremy.
Jarame

Jeremiah (Hebrew) God will uplift. Bible: a great Hebrew prophet. See also Dermot, Yeremey, Yirmaya.
Geremiah, Jaramia, Jem, Jemeriah, Jemiah, Jeramiah, Jeramiha, Jere, Jereias, Jeremaya, Jeremi, Jeremia, Jeremial, Jeremias, Jeremija, Jeremy, Jerimiah, Jerimiha, Jerimya, Jermiah, Jermija, Jerry

Jeremie, Jérémie (Hebrew) alternate forms of Jeremy.
Jeremi, Jérémie, Jeremii

Jeremy (English) a form of Jeremiah.
Jaremay, Jaremi, Jaremy, Jem, Jemmy, Jerahmy, Jeramie, Jeramy, Jere, Jereamy, Jereme, Jeremee, Jeremey, Jeremie, Jérémie, Jeremry, Jérémy, Jeremye, Jereomy, Jeriemy, Jerime, Jerimy, Jermey, Jeromy, Jerremy

Jeriah (Hebrew) Jehovah has seen.

Jericho (Arabic) city of the moon. Bible: a city conquered by Joshua.
Jeric, Jerick, Jerico, Jerik,

Jericho (cont.)
Jerric, Jerrick

Jermaine (French) an alternate form of Germain. (English) sprout, bud.
Jarman, Jeremaine, Jeremane, Jerimane, Jermain, Jermane, Jermanie, Jermayn, Jermayne, Jermiane, Jermine, Jer-Mon, Jhirmaine

Jermal (Arabic) an alternate form of Jamal.
Jermael, Jermail, Jermal, Jermall, Jermaul, Jermel, Jermell

Jermey (English) an alternate form of Jeremy.
Jerme, Jermee, Jermere, Jermery, Jermie, Jhermie

Jermiah (Hebrew) an alternate form of Jeremiah.
Jermiha, Jermiya

Jerney (Slavic) a form of Bartholomew.

Jerod (Hebrew) an alternate form of Jarrod.

Jerolin (Basque, Latin) holy.

Jerome (Latin) holy. See also Geronimo, Hieronymos.
Gerome, Jere, Jeroen, Jerom, Jérome, Jérôme, Jeromo, Jeromy, Jeron, Jerónimo, Jerrome, Jerromy

Jeromy (Latin) an alternate form of Jerome.
Jeromey, Jeromie

Jeron (English) a form of Jerome.
Jéron, Jerone, Jeronimo, Jerron, J'ron

Jerrett (Hebrew) a form of Jarrett.
Jeret, Jerett, Jeritt, Jerret, Jerrette, Jerriot, Jerritt, Jerrot, Jerrott

Jerrick (American) a combination of Jerry + Derrick.
Jaric, Jarrick, Jerick

Jerry (German) mighty spearman. (English) a familiar form of Gerald, Gerard. See also Kele.
Jehri, Jere, Jeree, Jeris, Jerison, Jerri, Jerrie

Jervis (English) a form of Gervaise, Jarvis.

Jerzy (Polish) a form of George.
Jurek

Jess (Hebrew) a short form of Jesse.

Jesse (Hebrew) wealthy. Bible: the father of David. See also Yishai.
Jescey, Jesee, Jesi, Jesie, Jess, Jessé, Jessee, Jessey, Jessi, Jessie, Jessy

Jessie (Hebrew) an alternate form of Jesse.

Jestin (Welsh) a form
of Justin.
Jeston, Jesstin, Jessston

Jesus (Hebrew) God is my
salvation. An alternate
form of Joshua. Bible: son
of Mary and Joseph,
believed by Christians to
be the Son of God. See
also Chucho, Isa, Joshua,
Yosu.
Jecho, Jesús, Josu

Jesús (Hispanic) a form
of Jesus.

Jethro (Hebrew) abundant.
Bible: the father-in-law of
Moses. See also Yitro.
Jeth, Jetro, Jett

Jett (Hebrew) a short form
of Jethro. (English) hard,
black mineral.
Jet, Jetson, Jetter, Jetty

Jevan (Hebrew) an alter-
nate form of Javan.
**Jevaun, Jevin, Jevohn,
Jevon, Jevonne**

Jibade (Yoruba) born close
to royalty.

Jibben (Gypsy) life.

Jibril (Arabic) archangel
of Allah.

Jilt (Dutch) money.

Jim (Hebrew) supplanter,
substitute. (English)
a short form of James.
See also Jaap.
Jimbo, Jimi, Jimmy

Jimbo (American) a familiar
form of Jim.
Jimboo

Jimell (Arabic) an alternate
form of Jamel.
Jimel, Jimelle, Jimmil

Jimiyu (Abaluhya) born
in the dry season.

Jimmie (English) an alternate form of Jimmy.
Jimmee

Jimmy (English) a familiar
form of Jim.
**Jimmey, Jimmie, Jimmyjo,
Jimy**

Jimoh (Swahili) born on
Friday.

Jin (Chinese) gold.
Jinn

Jindra (Czech) a form
of Harold.

Jing-Quo (Chinese) ruler
of the country.

Jiovanni (Italian) an alternate form of Giovanni.
Jio, Jiovani, Jiovanny, Jivan

Jirair (Armenian) strong;
hard working.

Jiri (Czech) a form of
George.
Jirka

Jiro (Japanese) second son.

Jivin (Hindi) life giver.
Jivanta

Jo (Hebrew, Japanese) a form of Joe.

Joab (Hebrew) God is father. See also Yoav.
Joaby

Joachim (Hebrew) God will establish. See also Akim, Ioakim, Yehoyakem.
Joacheim, Joakim, Joaquim, Joaquín, Jokin, Jov

João (Portuguese) a form of John.

Joaquim (Portuguese) a form of Joachim.

Joaquín (Spanish) a form of Joachim, Yehoyakem.
Jehoichin, Joaquin, Jocquin, Jocquinn, Juaquin

Job (Hebrew) afflicted. Bible: a righteous man who endured many afflictions.
Jobe, Jobert, Jobey, Jobie, Joby

Joben (Japanese) enjoys cleanliness.

Jobo (Spanish) a familiar form of Joseph.

Joby (Hebrew) a familiar form of Job.

Jock (American) a familiar form of Jacob.
Jocko, Joco, Jocoby, Jocolby

Jodan (Hebrew) a combination of Jo + Dan.
Jodhan, Jodin, Jodon, Jodonnis

Jody (Hebrew) a familiar form of Joseph.
Jodey, Jodi, Jodie, Jodiha, Joedy

Joe (Hebrew) a short form of Joseph.
Jo, Joely, Joey

Joel (Hebrew) God is willing. Bible: an Old Testament Hebrew prophet.
Jôel, Joël, Joell, Joelle, Joely, Jole, Yoel

Joey (Hebrew) a familiar form of Joe, Joseph.

Johann (German) a form of John. See also Anno, Hanno, Yohann.
Joahan, Johan, Johanan, Johane, Johannas, Johannes, Johansen, Johanson, Johanthan, Johatan, Johathan, Johathon, Johaun, Johon, Johonson

John (Hebrew) God is gracious. Bible: name honoring John the Baptist and John the Evangelist. See also Elchanan, Evan, Geno, Gian, Giovanni, Handel, Hannes, Hans, Hanus, Honza, Ian, Ianos, Iban, Ioan, Ivan, Iwan, Keoni, Kwam, Ohannes, Owen,

Sean, Ugutz, Yan,
Yochanan, Yohance, Zane.
**Jack, Jacsi, Jaenda, Jahn,
Jan, Janak, Janco, Janek,
Janis, Janne, János, Jansen,
Jantje, Jantzen, Jas, Jean,
Jehan, Jen, Jenkin, Jenkyn,
Jens, Jhan, Jhanick, Jhon,
Jian, Joáo, João, Jock, Joen,
Johan, Johann, Johne,
Johnl, Johnlee, Johnnie,
Johnny, Johnson, Jon,
Jonam, Jonas, Jone, Jones,
Jonté, Jovan, Juan, Juhana**

Johnathan (Hebrew) an
alternate form of Jonathan.
**Jhonathan, Johathe,
Johnatan, Johnathaon,
Johnathen, Johnatten,
Johniathin, Johnothan,
Johnthan**

Johnathon (Hebrew)
an alternate form of
Jonathon. See also Yanton.

Johnnie (Hebrew) a familiar
form of John.
**Johnie, Johnier, Johnni,
Johnsie, Jonni, Jonnie**

Johnny (Hebrew) a familiar
form of John. See also
Gianni.
**Jantje, Jhonny, Johney,
Johnney, Johny, Jonny**

Johnson (English) son
of John.
Johnston, Jonson

Joji (Japanese) a form
of George.

Jojo (Fanti) born on
Monday.

Jokin (Basque) a form
of Joachim.

Jolon (Native American)
valley of the dead oaks.
Jolyon

Jomei (Japanese) spreads
light.

Jon (Hebrew) an alternate
form of John. A short form
of Jonathan.
**J'on, Joni, Jonn, Jonnie,
Jonny, Jony**

Jonah (Hebrew) dove.
Bible: an Old Testament
prophet who was swal-
lowed by a large fish.
Giona, Jona, Yonah

Jonas (Lithuanian) a form
of John. (Hebrew) he
accomplishes.
**Jonelis, Jonukas, Jonus,
Jonutis, Joonas**

Jonathan (Hebrew) gift
of God. Bible: the son
of King Saul who became
a loyal friend of David.
See also Ionakana,
Yonatan.
**Janathan, Johnathan, Jon,
Jonatan, Jonatane, Jonate,
Jonatha, Jonathen,
Jonathon, Jonattan,
Jonethen, Jonnatha,
Jonnathan, Jonnattan,
Jonothan**

Jonathon (Hebrew) an alternate form of Jonathan.
Joanathon, Johnathon, Jonothon, Jounathon, Yanaton

Jones (Welsh) son of John.
Joenns, Jonesy

Jontae (French) a combination of Jon + the letter "t."
Johntae, Jontay, Jontea, Jonteau, Jontez

Jontay (American) a form of Jontae.
Johntay, Johnte, Johntez, Jontai, Jonte, Jonté, Jontez

Joop (Dutch) a familiar form of Joseph.
Jopie

Joost (Dutch) just.

Jora (Hebrew) teacher.
Yora, Jorah

Joram (Hebrew) Jehovah is exalted.
Joran, Jorim

Jordan (Hebrew) descending. See also Giordano, Yarden.
Jared, Jordaan, Jordae, Jordain, Jordaine, Jordany, Jordáo, Jorden, Jordenn, Jordi, Jordie, Jordin, Jordon, Jordy, Jordyn, Jori, Jorrdan, Jory, Jourdain, Jourdan

Jordon (Hebrew) an alternate form of Jordan.
Jeordon, Johordan

Jordy (Hebrew) a familiar form of Jordan.

Jorell (American) he saves. Literature: a name inspired by the fictional character Jor-el, Superman's father.
Jorel, Jor-El, Jorelle, Jori, Jorrel, Jorrell

Jörg (German) a form of George.
Jeorg, Juergen, Jungen, Jürgen

Jorge (Spanish) a form of George.
Jorrín

Jorgen (Danish) a form of George.
Joergen, Jorgan, Jörgen

Joris (Dutch) a form of George.

Jörn (German) a familiar form of Gregory.

Jorrín (Spanish) a form of George.
Jorian, Jorje

Jory (Hebrew) a familiar form of Jordan.
Joar, Joary, Jori, Jorie

José (Spanish) a form of Joseph. See also Ché, Pepe.
Josean, Josecito, Josee, Joseito, Joselito, Josey

Josef (German, Portuguese, Czech, Scandinavian) a form of Joseph.

Joosef, Joseff, Josif, Jozef, József, Juzef

Joseph (Hebrew) God will add, God will increase. Bible: in the Old Testament, the son of Jesse who came to rule Egypt; in the New Testament, the husband of Mary. See also Beppe, Cheche, Chepe, Giuseppe, Iokepa, Iosif, Osip, Pepa, Peppe, Sepp, Yeska, Yosef, Yousef, Youssel, Yusif, Yusuf, Zeusef.
Jazeps, Jo, Jobo, Jody, Joe, Joeseph, Joey, Jojo, Joop, Joos, Jooseppi, Jopie, José, Joseba, Josef, Josep, Josephat, Josephe, Josephie, Josephus, Josheph, Josip, Jóska, Joza, Joze, Jozef, Jozhe, Jozio, Jozka, Jozsi, Jozzepi, Jupp, Juziu

Josh (Hebrew) a short form of Joshua.
Joshe

Josha (Hindi) satisfied.

Joshi (Swahili) galloping.

Joshua (Hebrew) God is my salvation. Bible: led the Israelites into the Promised Land. See also Giosia, Iosua, Jesus, Yehoshua.
Johsua, Johusa, Josh, Joshau, Joshaua, Joshauh, Joshawa, Joshawah,

Joshia, Joshu, Joshuaa, Joshuah, Joshuea, Joshula, Joshus, Joshusa, Joshuwa, Joshwa, Josue, Jousha, Jozshua, Jozsua, Jozua, Jushua

Josiah (Hebrew) fire of the Lord. See also Yoshiyahu.
Joshiah, Josia, Josiahs, Josian, Josias, Josie

Joss (Chinese) luck; fate.
Josse, Jossy

Josue (Hebrew) an alternate form of Joshua.
Joshue, Josu, Josua, Josuha, Jozus

Jotham (Hebrew) may God complete. Bible: a king of Judah.

Jovan (Latin) Jove-like, majestic. (Slavic) a form of John. Mythology: Jove, also known as Jupiter, was the supreme Roman god.
Jovaan, Jovani, Jovanic, Jovann, Jovanni, Jovannie, Jovannis, Jovanny, Jovany, Jovenal, Jovenel, Jovi, Jovian, Jovin, Jovito, Jovoan, Jovon, Jovonn, Jovonne, Yovan

Jr (Latin) a short form of Junior.
Jr.

Juan (Spanish) a form of John. See also Chan.
Juanch, Juanchito, Juanito, Juann, Juauん

Juaquin (Spanish) an alternate form of Joaquín.
Juaquine

Jubal (Hebrew) ram's horn. Bible: a musician and a descendant of Cain.

Judah (Hebrew) praised. Bible: the fourth of Jacob's sons. See also Yehudi.
Juda, Judas, Judd, Jude

Judas (Latin) a form of Judah. Bible: Judas Iscariot was the disciple who betrayed Jesus.
Jude

Judd (Hebrew) a short form of Judah.
Jud, Judson

Jude (Latin) a short form of Judah, Judas. Bible: one of the Christian apostles, author of the New Testament book, "The Epistle of Saint Jude."

Judson (English) son of Judd.

Juhana (Finnish) a form of John.
Juha, Juho

Juku (Estonian) a form of Richard.
Jukka

Jules (French) a form of Julius.
Joles, Jule

Julian (Greek, Latin) an alternate form of Julius.

Jolyon, Juliaan, Juliano, Julien, Jullian, Julyan

Julien (Latin) an alternate form of Julian.

Julio (Hispanic) a form of Julius.

Julius (Greek, Latin) youthful, downy bearded. History: Julius Caesar was a great Roman emperor. See also Giulio.
Jolyon, Julas, Jule, Jules, Julen, Jules, Julian, Julias, Julie, Julio, Juliusz

Jumaane (Swahili) born on Tuesday.

Jumah (Arabic, Swahili) born on Friday, a holy day in the Islamic religion.
Jimoh, Juma

Jumoke (Nigerian) loved by everyone.

Jun (Chinese) truthful. (Japanese) obedient; pure.
Junnie

Junior (Latin) young.
Jr, Junious, Junius

Jupp (German) a form of Joseph.

Jur (Czech) a form of George.
Juraz, Jurek, Jurik, Jurko, Juro

Jurgis (Lithuanian) a form of George.
Jurgi, Juri

Juro (Japanese) best wishes; long life.

Jurrien (Dutch) God will uplift.
Jore, Jurian, Jurre

Justin (Latin) just, righteous. See also Giustino, Iestyn, Iustin, Tutu, Ustin, Yustyn.
Jestin, Jobst, Joost, Jost, Jusa, Just, Justain, Justan, Justas, Justek, Justen, Justice, Justinas, Justine, Justinian, Justinius, Justinn, Justino, Justins, Justinus, Justo, Juston, Justton, Justukas, Justun, Justyn

Justis (French) just.
Justs, Justus

Justyn (Latin) an alternate form of Justin.
Justn

Juvenal (Latin) young. Literature: a Roman satiric poet.
Juvon, Juvone

Juwan (American) an alternate form of Jajuan.
Juwann, Juwaun, Juwon, Juwuan

Kabiito (Rutooro) born while foreigners are visiting.

Kabil (Turkish) a form of Cain.

Kabir (Hindi) History: a Hindu mystic.
Kabar

Kabonero (Runyankore) sign.

Kabonesa (Rutooro) difficult birth.

Kacancu (Rukonjo) firstborn child.

Kacey (Irish) an alternate form of Casey. (American) a combination of the initials K. + C. See also KC.
Kace, Kacee, Kacy, Kaesy, Kase, Kasey, Kasie, Kasy, Kaycee

Kadar (Arabic) powerful.
Kader

Kade (Scottish) wetlands. (American) a combination of the initials K. + D.
Kadee, Kaydee

Kadeem (Arabic) servant.
Kadim, Khadeem

Kadin (Arabic) friend, companion.

Kadir (Arabic) spring greening.
Kadeer

Kado (Japanese) gateway.

Kaelan (Irish) an alternate form of Kellen.
Kael, Kaelen, Kaelin, Kaelyn

Kaemon (Japanese) joyful; right handed.

Ka'eo (Hawaiian) victorious.

Kafele (Ngoni) worth dying for.

Kaga (Native American) writer.

Kahale (Hawaiian) home.

Kahil (Turkish) young; inexperienced; naive.
Cahil, Kale, Kayle

Kahlil (Arabic) an alternate form of Khalíl.
Kahleel, Kahleil, Kahlill, Kalel, Kalil

Kaholo (Hawaiian) runner.

Kahraman (Turkish) hero.

Kai (Welsh) keeper of the keys. (German) an alternate form of Kay. (Hawaiian) sea.

Kaikara (Runyoro) Religion: a Banyoro deity.

Kailen (Irish) an alternate form of Kellen.
Kail, Kailan, Kailey, Kailin

Kaili (Hawaiian) Religion: a Hawaiian deity.

Kainoa (Hawaiian) name.

Kaipo (Hawaiian) sweetheart.

Kairo (Arabic) an alternate form of Cairo.

Kaiser (German) a form of Caesar.
Kaisar

Kaj (Danish) earth.
Kai

Kakar (Hindi) grass.

Kala (Hindi) black; time. (Hawaiian) sun. Religion: another name for the Hindu god Shiva.

Kalama (Hawaiian) torch.
Kalam

Kalani (Hawaiian) heaven; chief.
Kalan

Kale (Arabic) a short form of Kahlil. (Hawaiian) a familiar form of Carl.
Kalee, Kaleu, Kaley, Kali, Kalin, Kayle

Kaleb (Hebrew) an alternate form of Caleb.
Kal, Kalab, Kalb, Kale, Kalev, Kalib, Kilab

Kalen, Kalin (Arabic) alternate forms of Kale. (Irish) alternate forms of Kellen.

Kalevi (Finnish) hero.

Kali (Arabic) a short form of Kalil. (Hawaiian) a form of Gary.

Kalil (Arabic) an alternate form of Khalîl.
Kali

Kaliq (Arabic) an alternate form of Khaliq.
Kalique

Kalkin (Hindi) tenth. Religion: the tenth incarnation of the Hindu god Vishnu.
Kalki

Kalle (Scandinavian) a form of Carl.

Kallen (Irish) an alternate form of Kellen.
Kallan, Kallin, Kallon, Kallun, Kalon, Kalun, Kalyn

Kaloosh (Armenian) blessed event.

Kalvin (Latin) an alternate form of Calvin.
Kal, Kalv, Vinny

Kamaka (Hawaiian) face.

Kamakani (Hawaiian) wind.

Kamal (Hindi) lotus. Religion: a Hindu god. (Arabic) perfect, perfection.
Kamaal, Kameel, Kamel, Kamil

Kamau (Kikuyu) quiet warrior.

Kameron (Scottish) an alternate form of Cameron.
Kam, Kamey, Kammy, Kamran, Kamren, Kamron

Kami (Hindi) loving.

Kamoga (Luganda) name of a royal Baganda family.

Kamuela (Hawaiian) a form of Samuel.

Kamuhanda (Runyankore) born on the way to the hospital.

Kamukama (Runyankore) protected by God.

Kamuzu (Nguni) medicine.

Kamya (Luganda) born after twin brothers.

Kana (Japanese) powerful; capable. (Hawaiian) Mythology: a god who took the form of a rope extending from Molokai to Hawaii.

Kanaiela (Hawaiian) a form of Daniel.
Kana, Kaneii

Kane (Welsh) beautiful. (Irish) tribute. (Japanese) golden. (Hawaiian) eastern sky. (English) an alternate form of Keene. See also Cain.

Kane *(cont.)*
Kahan, Kain, Kainan,
Kaine, Kainen, Kaney,
Kayne

Kange (Lakota) raven.
Kanga

Kaniel (Hebrew) stalk,
reed.
Kan, Kani, Kannie, Kanny

Kannan (Hindi) Religion:
another name for the
Hindu god Krishna.
Kannen

Kannon (Polynesian) free.
An alternate form of
Cannon.
Kanon

Kanoa (Hawaiian) free.
(Chinese) Religion: the
Chinese god of mercy.

Kantu (Hindi) happy.

Kanu (Swahili) wildcat.

Kaori (Japanese) strong.

Kapila (Hindi) ancient
prophet.
Kapil

Kapono (Hawaiian)
righteous.
Kapena

Kardal (Arabic) mustard
seed.

Kare (Norwegian)
enormous.
Karee

Kareem (Arabic) noble;
distinguished.

Karee, Karem, Kareme,
Karim, Karriem

Karel (Czech) a form
of Carl.
Karell

Karey (Greek) an alternate
form of Carey.
Karee, Kari, Karry, Kary

Karif (Arabic) born in
autumn.
Kareef

Kariisa (Runyankore)
herdsman.

Karim (Arabic) an alternate
form of Kareem.

Karl (German) an alternate
form of Carl.
Kaarle, Kaarlo, Kale, Kalle,
Kalman, Kálmán, Karcsi,
Karel, Kari, Karlen,
Karlitis, Karlo, Karlos,
Karlton, Karlus, Karol,
Kjell

Karlen (Latvian, Russian)
a form of Carl.
Karlan, Karlens, Karlik,
Karlin, Karlis

Karmel (Hebrew) an alternate form of Carmel.

Karney (Irish) an alternate
form of Carney.

Karol (Czech, Polish)
a form of Carl.
Karal, Karolek, Karolis,
Karalos, Károly, Karrel,
Karrol

Karr (Scandinavian) an alternate form of Carr.

Karsten (Greek) anointed.

Karu (Hindi) cousin. Bible: the cousin of Moses.
Karun

Karutunda (Runyankore) little.

Karwana (Rutooro) born during wartime.

Kaseem (Arabic) divided.
Kasceem, Kaseym, Kasim, Kazeem

Kaseko (Rhodesian) mocked, ridiculed.

Kasem (Thai) happiness.

Kasen (Basque) protected with a helmet.

Kasey (Irish) an alternate form of Casey.

Kasib (Arabic) fertile.

Kasim (Arabic) an alternate form of Kaseem.

Kasimir (Arabic) peace. (Slavic) an alternate form of Casimir.
Kasim, Kazimierz, Kazimir, Kazio, Kazmer, Kazmér, Kázmér

Kasiya (Ngoni) separate.

Kasper (Persian) treasurer. (German) an alternate form of Casper.
Kaspar, Kaspero

Kass (German) blackbird.
Kaese, Kasch, Kase

Kassidy (Irish) an alternate form of Cassidy.
Kassady, Kassie, Kassy

Kateb (Arabic) writer.

Kato (Runyankore) second of twins.

Katungi (Runyankore) rich.

Kavan (Irish) handsome.
Cavan, Kavanagh, Kavenaugh

Kaveh (Persian) ancient hero.

Kavi (Hindi) poet.

Kawika (Hawaiian) a form of David.

Kay (Greek) rejoicing. (German) fortified place. Literature: one of the knights of King Arthur's Round Table.
Kai, Kaycee, Kayson

Kayin (Nigerian) celebrated. (Yoruba) long-hoped-for child.

Kayle (Hebrew) faithful dog. (Arabic) a short form of Kahlil.

Kaylen (Irish) an alternate form of Kellen.
Kaylan, Kaylin, Kaylon, Kaylyn

Kayode (Yoruba) he brought joy.

Kayonga (Runyankore) ash. History: a great Ankole warrior.

Kazio (Polish) a form of Casimir, Kasimir.

Kazuo (Japanese) man of peace.

KC (American) a combination of the initials K. + C. See also Kacey.
Kc, K.C., Kcee, Kcey

Keahi (Hawaiian) flames.

Keaka (Hawaiian) a form of Jack.

Kealoha (Hawaiian) fragrant.
Ke'ala

Keandre (American) a combination of the prefix Ke + Andre.
Keondre

Keane (German) bold; sharp. (Irish) handsome. (English) an alternate form of Keene.
Kean

Kearn (Irish) a short form of Kearney.
Kearne

Kearney (Irish) an alternate form of Carney.
Kar, Karney, Karny, Kearn, Kearny

Keary (Irish) an alternate form of Kerry.
Kearie

Keaton (English) where hawks fly.
Keaten, Keeton, Keetun

Keawe (Hawaiian) strand.

Keb (Egyptian) earth. Mythology: an ancient earth god, also known as Geb.

Kedar (Hindi) mountain lord. (Arabic) powerful. Religion: another name for the Hindu god Shiva.
Keder, Kadar

Keddy (Scottish) a form of Adam.

Kedem (Hebrew) ancient.

Kedrick (English) an alternate form of Cedric.
Keddrick, Kedric

Keefe (Irish) handsome; loved.

Keegan (Irish) little; fiery.
Kaegan, Keagen, Kegan, Keghan, Kegun

Keelan (Irish) little; slender.

Keeley (Irish) handsome.
Kealey, Kealy, Keelen, Keelian, Keelie, Keely

Keenan (Irish) little Keene.
Keanan, Keanen, Keannan, Keenen, Keenon, Kenan, Keynan, Kienan, Kienen, Kienon

Keene (German) bold; sharp. (English) smart. See also Kane.
Keane, Keen, Keenan

Kees (Dutch) a form
of Kornelius.
Keese, Keesee, Keyes

Kehind (Yoruba) second-
born twin.

Keiffer (German) a form
of Cooper.
**Keefer, Keifer, Kiefer,
Kieffer**

Keiji (Japanese) cautious
ruler.

Keir (Irish) a short form
of Kieran.

Keitaro (Japanese) blessed.
Keita

Keith (Welsh) forest.
(Scottish) battle place.
See also Kika.
**Keath, Keeth, Keithen,
Keithon**

Kekapa (Hawaiian)
tapa cloth.

Kekipi (Hawaiian) rebel.

Kekoa (Hawaiian) bold,
courageous.

Kelby (German) farm
by the spring.
**Keelby, Kelbee, Kelbey,
Kellby**

Kele (Hawaiian) a form
of Jerry. (Hopi) sparrow
hawk.
Kelle

Kelemen (Hungarian)
gentle; kind.
Kellman

Kelevi (Finnish) hero.

Keli (Hawaiian) a form
of Terry.

Keli'i (Hawaiian) chief.

Kelile (Ethiopian)
protected.

Kell (Scandinavian) spring.

Kellen (Irish) mighty
warrior.
**Kaelan, Kailen, Kalan,
Kalen, Kalin, Kallen,
Kaylen, Keelan, Keilan,
Keillan, Kelden, Kellan,
Kelle, Kellin, Kelynn**

Keller (Irish) little
companion.

Kelly (Irish) warrior.
**Kelle, Kellen, Kelley, Kelli,
Kely**

Kelmen (Basque) merciful.

Kelsey (Scandinavian)
island of ships.
**Kelcy, Kelse, Kelsie, Kelsy,
Kesley, Kesly**

Kelton (English) keel town;
port.
**Kelden, Keldon, Kelson,
Kelten, Keltonn**

Kelvin (Irish, English)
narrow river. Geography:
a river in Scotland.
**Kelvan, Kelven, Kelvyn,
Kelwin, Kelwyn**

Kemal (Turkish) highest
honor.

Kemen (Basque) strong.

Kemp (English) fighter; champion.

Kempton (English) military town.

Ken (Japanese) one's own kind. (Scottish) a short form of Kendall, Kendrick, Kenneth.
Kena, Kenn, Keno

Kenaz (Hebrew) bright.

Kendall (English) valley of the river Kent.
Ken, Kendal, Kendale, Kendali, Kendel, Kendell, Kendrall, Kendrell, Kendryll

Kendrew (Scottish) a form of Andrew.

Kendrick (Irish) son of Henry. (Scottish) royal chieftain.
Ken, Kendric, Kendricks, Kendrik, Kendrix, Kendryck, Keondric, Keondrick

Kenley (English) royal meadow.
Kenlea, Kenlee, Kenleigh, Kenlie, Kenly

Kenn (Scottish) an alternate form of Ken.

Kennan (Scottish) little Ken.
Kenna, Kenan, Kennen, Kennon

Kennard (Irish) brave chieftain.
Kenner

Kennedy (Irish) helmeted chief. History: John F. Kennedy was the thirty-fifth U.S. president.
Kennedey

Kenneth (Irish) handsome. (English) royal oath.
Ken, Keneth, Kennet, Kennethen, Kennett, Kennieth, Kennith, Kennth, Kenny, Kennyth

Kenny (Scottish) a familiar form of Kenneth.
Keni, Kenney, Kennie, Kinnie

Kenrick (English) bold ruler; royal ruler.
Kenric, Kenricks, Kenrik

Kent (Welsh) white; bright. (English) a short form of Kenton. Geography: a county in England.

Kentaro (Japanese) big boy.

Kenton (English) from Kent, England.
Kent, Kenten, Kentin, Kentonn

Kentrell (English) king's estate.

Kenward (English) brave; royal guardian.

Kenya (Hebrew) animal horn. (Russian) a form

of Kenneth. Geography: a country in Africa.
Kenyata, Kenyatta

Kenyon (Irish) white haired, blond.
Kenyan, Kenynn

Kenzie (Scottish) wise leader. See also Mackenzie.
Kensie

Keoki (Hawaiian) a form of George.

Keola (Hawaiian) life.

Keon (Irish) a form of Ewan.
Keeon, Keion, Keionne, Keondre, Keone, Keontae, Keontrye, Keony, Keyon, Kian, Kion

Keoni (Hawaiian) a form of John.

Kerbasi (Basque) warrior.

Kerel (Afrikaans) young.

Kerem (Turkish) noble; kind.

Kerey (Gypsy) homeward-bound.
Ker

Kerman (Basque) from Germany.

Kermit (Irish) an alternate form of Dermot.
Kermey, Kermie, Kermy

Kern (Irish) a short form of Kieran.
Kearn, Kerne

Kerr (Scandinavian) an alternate form of Carr.
Karr

Kerrick (English) king's rule.

Kerry (Irish) dark, dark haired.
Keary, Keri, Kerrey, Kerri, Kerrie

Kers (Todas) Botany: an Indian plant.

Kersen (Indonesian) cherry.

Kerstan (Dutch) a form of Christian.

Kerwin (Irish) little; dark. (English) friend of the marshlands.
Kervin, Kervyn, Kerwinn, Kerwyn, Kerwynn, Kirwin, Kirwyn

Kesar (Russian) a form of Caesar.
Kesare

Keshawn (American) a combination of the prefix Ke + Shawn.
Kesean, Keshaun, Keshon

Kesin (Hindi) long-haired beggar.

Kesse (Ashanti, Fanti) chubby baby.
Kessie

Kester (English) a form of Christopher.

Kestrel (English) falcon.
Kes

Keung (Chinese) universe.

Kevan (Irish) an alternate form of Kevin.
Kavan

Keven (Irish) an alternate form of Kevin.
Keve

Kevin (Irish) handsome. See also Cavan.
Keevin, Keevon, Kev, Kevan, Keven, Keveon, Keverne, Kévin, Kevinn, Kevins, Kevion, Kevis, Kevn, Kevon, Kevron, Kevvy, Kevyn

Key (English) key; protected.

Khachig (Armenian) small cross.

Khaim (Russian) a form of Chaim.

Khaldun (Arabic) forever.
Khaldoon

Khalfani (Swahili) born to lead.
Khalfan

Khälid (Arabic) eternal.
Khaled

Khalíl (Arabic) friend.
Kahlil, Kaleel, Kalil, Khalee, Khali, Khalial, Khaliyl

Khaliq (Arabic) creative.
Kaliq, Khalique

Khamisi (Swahili) born on Thursday.
Kham

Khan (Turkish) prince.
Khanh

Kharald (Russian) a form of Gerald.

Khayru (Arabic) benevolent.
Khiri, Khiry, Kiry

Khoury (Arabic) priest.
Khory

Khristian (Greek) an alternate form of Christian, Kristian.
Khris, Khristin

Khristos (Greek) an alternate form of Christopher, Christos.
Khris, Khristophe, Khristopher, Kristo, Kristos

Kibbe (Nayas) night bird.

Kibo (Uset) worldly; wise.

Kibuuka (Luganda) brave warrior. History: a brave Buganda warrior.

Kidd (English) child; young goat.

Kiel (Irish) an alternate form of Kyle.

Kiele (Hawaiian) gardenia.

Kieran (Irish) little and dark; little Keir.
Keiran, Keiren, Keiron, Kern, Kernan, Kiernan, Kieron, Kyran

Kiet (Thai) honor.

Kifeda (Luo) only boy among girls.

Kiho (Dutooro) born on a foggy day.

Kijika (Native American) quiet walker.

Kika (Hawaiian) a form of Keith.

Kiki (Spanish) a form of Henry.

Killian (Irish) little Kelly.
Kilian, Killie, Killy

Kim (English) a short form of Kimball.
Kimie, Kimmy

Kimball (Greek) hollow vessel. (English) warrior chief.
Kim, Kimbal, Kimbell, Kimble

Kimo (Hawaiian) a form of James.

Kimokeo (Hawaiian) a form of Timothy.

Kin (Japanese) golden.

Kincaid (Scottish) battle chief.

Kindin (Basque) fifth.

King (English) king. A short form of names beginning with "King."

Kingsley (English) king's meadow.
King, Kingslea, Kingslie, Kingsly, Kinslea, Kinslee, Kinsley, Kinslie, Kinsly

Kingston (English) king's estate.
King, Kinston

Kingswell (English) king's well.
King

Kini (Hawaiian) a short form of Iukini.

Kinnard (Irish) tall slope.

Kinsey (English) victorious royalty.

Kinton (Hindi) crowned.

Kioshi (Japanese) quiet.

Kipp (English) pointed hill.
Kip, Kippar, Kipper, Kippie, Kippy

Kir (Bulgarian) a familiar form of Cyrus.

Kiral (Turkish) king; supreme leader.

Kiran (Sanskrit) beam of light.

Kirby (Scandinavian) church village. (English) cottage by the water.
Kerbey, Kerbie, Kerby, Kirbey, Kirbie, Kirkby

Kiri (Cambodian) mountain.

Kiril (Slavic) a form of Cyril.
Kirill, Kiryl, Kyrillos

Kiritan (Hindi) wearing a crown.

Kirk (Scandinavian) church.
Kerk

Kirkland (English) church land.

Kirkley (English) church meadow.

Kirkwell (English) church well; church spring.

Kirkwood (English) church forest.

Kirton (English) church town.

Kistna (Hindi) sacred, holy. Geography: a sacred river in India.

Kistur (Gypsy) skillful rider.

Kit (Greek) a familiar form of Christian, Christopher, Kristopher.
Kitt, Kitts

Kito (Swahili) jewel; precious child.

Kitwana (Swahili) pledged to live.

Kiva (Hebrew) a short form of Akiva, Jacob.
Kiba, Kivi

Kiyoshi (Japanese) quiet; peaceful.

Kizza (Fanti) born after twins.
Kizzy

Kjell (Swedish) a form of Karl.

Klaus (German) a short form of Nicholas. An alternate form of Claus.
Klaas, Klaes, Klas, Klause

Kleef (Dutch) cliff.

Klement (Czech) a form of Clement.
Klema, Klemenis, Klemens, Klemet, Klemo, Klim, Klimek, Kliment, Klimka

Kleng (Norwegian) claw.

Knight (English) armored knight.
Knightly

Knoton (Native American) an alternate form of Nodin.

Knowles (English) grassy slope.
Knolls, Nowles

Knox (English) hill.

Knute (Scandinavian) an alternate form of Canute.
Knud, Knut

Koby (Polish) a familiar form of Jacob.
Kobi

Kody (English) an alternate form of Cody.
Kodey, Kodi, Kodie, Koty

Kofi (Twi) born on Friday.

Kohana (Lakota) swift.

Koi (Hawaiian) a form of Troy.

Kojo (Akan) born on Monday.

Koka (Hawaiian) Scotsman.

Kokayi (Shona) gathered together.

Kolby (English) an alternate form of Colby.
Kelby, Kole, Kollby

Kolton (English) an alternate form of Colton.
Kolt, Kolten, Koltin

Kolya (Russian) a familiar form of Nikolai.
Kola, Kolenka

Kona (Hawaiian) a form of Don.
Konala

Konane (Hawaiian) bright moonlight.

Kondo (Swahili) war.

Kong (Chinese) glorious; sky.

Konnor (Irish) an alternate form of Connor.

Kono (Moquelumnan) squirrel eating a pine nut.

Konrad (German) a form of Conrad.
Khonrad, Koen, Koenraad, Kon, Konn, Konney, Konni, Konnie, Konny, Konrád, Konrade, Konrado, Kord, Kort, Kunz

Konstantin (German, Russian) a form of Constantine. See also Dinos.
Konstancji, Konstandinos, Konstantinas, Konstantine, Konstantinos, Konstantio,

Konstanty, Konstanz, Kostantin, Kostas, Kostenka, Kostya, Kotsos

Kontar (Akan) only child.

Korb (German) basket.

Korbin (English) a form of Corbin.

Kordell (English) a form of Cordell.

Korey (Irish) an alternate form of Corey, Kory.
Kore, Korio, Korria, Korrye

Kornel (Latin) a form of Cornelius, Kornelius.
Kees, Kornél, Korneli, Kornelisz, Krelis, Soma

Kornelius (Latin) an alternate form of Cornelius. See also Kees, Kornel.
Karnelius, Korneilius, Korneliaus, Kornelious, Kornellius

Korrigan (Irish) an alternate form of Corrigan.
Korigan, Korigan, Korrigon, Korrigun

Kort (German, Dutch) an alternate form of Cort, Kurt.

Korudon (Greek) helmeted one.

Kory (Irish) an alternate form of Corey.
Korey, Kori, Korie, Korrey, Korrie, Korry

Kosey (African) lion.
Kosse

Kosmo (Greek) an alternate
form of Cosmo.
Kosmy

Kostas (Greek) a short
form of Konstantin.

Kosti (Finnish) a form
of Gustave.

Kosumi (Moquelumnan)
spear fisher.

Koukalaka (Hawaiian)
a form of Douglas.

Kovit (Thai) expert.

Kraig (Irish, Scottish)
an alternate form of Craig.
Kraggie, Kraggy

Krikor (Armenian) a form
of Gregory.

Kris (Greek) an alternate
form of Chris. A short
form of Kristian, Kristofer,
Kristopher.
Kriss, Krys

Krischan (German) a form
of Christian.

Krishna (Hindi) delightful,
pleasurable. Religion: one
of the human incarnations
of the Hindu god.
**Kistna, Kistnah, Krisha,
Krishnah**

Krispin (Latin) an alternate
form of Crispin.
Krispian, Krispino, Krispo

Krister (Swedish) a form
of Christian.
Krist, Kristar

Kristian (Greek) an alter-
nate form of Christian,
Khristian.
**Kerstan, Khristos, Kit,
Kris, Krischan, Krist,
Kristar, Kristek, Krister,
Kristjan, Kristo, Kristos,
Krists, Krystek, Krystian,
Khrystiyan**

Kristo (Greek) a short
form of Khristos.

Kristofer (Swedish)
a form of Kristopher.
**Kristef, Kristoffer,
Kristofor, Kristus**

Kristophe (French) a form
of Kristopher.

Kristopher (Greek) Christ-
bearer. An alternate form
of Christopher. See also
Topher.
**Kit, Kris, Kristfer, Kristfor,
Kristo, Kristóf, Kristofer,
Kristoforo, Kristoph,
Kristophe, Kristophor,
Kristos, Krists, Krisus,
Krystupas, Krzysztof**

Kruz (Spanish) an alternate
form of Cruz.

Krystian (Polish) a form
of Christian.
Krys, Krystek

Kuba (Czech) a form
of Jacob.
Kubo, Kubus

Kueng (Chinese) universe.

Kugonza (Dutooro) love.

Kuiril (Basque) lord.

Kumar (Sanskrit) prince.

Kunle (Yoruba) home filled with honors.

Kuper (Yiddish) copper.

Kurt (Latin, German, French) courteous; enclosure. A short form of Kurtis. An alternate form of Curt.
Kort, Kuno

Kurtis (Latin, French) an alternate form of Curtis.
Kurt, Kurtice, Kurtiss

Kuruk (Pawnee) bear.

Kutaaka (Lugisu) baby who follows one who died.

Kuzih (Carrier) good speaker.

Kwacha (Ngoni) morning.

Kwako (Akan) born on Wednesday.

Kwam (Zuni) a form of John.

Kwame (Akan) born on Saturday.
Kwamin

Kwan (Korean) strong.

Kwasi (Akan) born on Sunday. (Swahili) wealthy.
Kwesi

Kwayera (Ngoni) dawn.

Kwende (Ngoni) let's go.

Kyele (Irish) an alternate form of Kyle.

Kyle (Irish) narrow piece of land; place where cattle graze. (Yiddish) crowned with laurels.
Kiel, Kilan, Kile, Kilen, Kiley, Ky, Kye, Kyele, Kylan, Kylen, Kyler, Kylie, Kyrell

Kyler (English) a form of Kyle.

Kynan (Welsh) chief.

Kyne (English) royal.

Kyros (Greek) master.

Laban (Hawaiian) white.

Labib (Arabic) sensible; intelligent.

Labrentsis (Russian) a form of Lawrence.
Labhras, Labhruinn, Labrencis

Lachlan (Scottish) land of lakes.
Lache, Lachlann, Lachunn, Lakelan, Lakeland

Ladd (English) attendant.
Lad, Laddey, Laddie, Laddy

Ladislav (Czech) a form of Walter.
Laco, Lada, Ladislaus

Lado (Fanti) second-born son.

Lafayette (French) History: Marquis de Lafayette was a French soldier and politician who aided the American Revolution.
Lafaiete, Lafayett

Laird (Scottish) wealthy landowner.

Lais (Arabic) lion.

Lajos (Hungarian) famous; holy.
Lajcsi, Laji, Lali

Lal (Hindi) beloved.

Lamar (German) famous throughout the land. (French) sea, ocean.
Lamair, Lamario, Lamaris, Lamarr, Lamarre, Larmar, Lemar

Lambert (German) bright land.
Bert, Lambard, Lamberto, Lambirt, Lampard, Landbert

Lamond (French) world.
Lammond, Lamondre, Lamund, Lemond

Lamont (Scandinavian) lawyer.

Lamaunt, Lamonte, Lamontie, Lemont

Lance (German) a short form of Lancelot.
Lancy, Lantz, Lanz, Launce

Lancelot (French) attendant. Literature: the knight who loved King Arthur's wife, Queen Guinevere.
Lance, Lancelott, Launcelet, Launcelot

Landen (English) an alternate form of Landon.

Lander (Basque) lion man. (English) landowner.
Landers, Landor

Lando (Portuguese, Spanish) a short form of Orlando, Rolando.

Landon (English) open, grassy meadow.
Landan, Landen, Landin

Landry (French, English) ruler.
Landre, Landré, Landrue

Lane (English) narrow road.
Laney, Lanie, Layne

Lang (Scandinavian) tall man.
Lange

Langdon (English) long hill.
Landon, Langsdon, Langston

Langford (English) long ford.
Lanford, Lankford

Langley (English) long meadow.
Langlea, Langlee, Langleigh, Langly

Langston (English) long, narrow town.
Langsden, Langsdon

Langundo (Native American) peaceful.

Lani (Hawaiian) heaven.

Lanny (American) a familiar form of Lawrence, Laurence.
Lannie, Lennie

Lanu (Moquelumnan) running around the pole.

Lanz (Italian) a form of Lance.
Lanzo, Lonzo

Lao (Spanish) a short form of Stanislaus.

Lap (Vietnamese) independent.

Lapidos (Hebrew) torches.
Lapidoth

Laquintin (American) a combination of the prefix La + Quintin.
Laquentin, Laquenton, Laquintas, Laquintiss, Laquinton

Laramie (French) tears of love. Geography: a town in Wyoming on the Overland Trail.

Larkin (Irish) rough; fierce.
Larklin

Larnell (American) a combination of Larry + Darnell.

Laron (French) thief.
Laran, La'ron, La Ron, Laronn, La Ruan

Larrimore (French) armorer.
Larimore, Larmer, Larmor

Larry (Latin) a familiar form of Lawrence.
Larrie, Lary

Lars (Scandinavian) a form of Lawrence.
Laris, Larris, Larse, Larsen, Larson, Larsson, Lasse, Laurans, Laurits, Lavrans, Lorens

LaSalle (French) hall.
Lasalle, Lascell, Lascelles

Lash (Gypsy) a form of Louis.
Lashi, Lasho

Lashawn (American) a combination of the prefix La + Shawn.
Lasean, Lashajaun, Lashon, Lashonne

Lasse (Finnish) a form of Nicholas.

László (Hungarian) famous ruler.
Laci, Lacko, Laslo, Lazlo

Lateef (Arabic) gentle; pleasant.
Latif, Letif

Latham (Scandinavian) barn. (English) district.

Latham (cont.)
Laith, Lathe, Lay

Lathan (American)
a combination of the
prefix La + Nathan.
**Lathaniel, Lathen, Lathyn,
Leathan**

Lathrop (English) barn,
farmstead.
Lathe, Lathrope, Lay

Latimer (English)
interpreter.
**Lat, Latimor, Lattie, Latty,
Latymer**

Latravis (American)
a combination of the
prefix La + Travis.
**Latavious, Latraviaus,
Latravious, Latrivis**

Laudalino (Portuguese)
praised.
Lino

Laughlin (Irish) servant
of Saint Secundinus.
**Lanty, Lauchlin,
Leachlainn**

Laurence (Latin) crowned
with laurel. An alternate
form of Lawrence.
See also Rance, Raulas,
Raulo, Renzo.
**Lanny, Lauran, Laurance,
Laureano, Lauren,
Laurencho, Laurencio,
Laurens, Laurent,
Laurentij, Laurentios,
Laurentiu, Laurentius,
Laurentzi, Laurenz,
Laurie, Laurin, Lauris,**

**Laurits, Lauritz, Laurnet,
Lauro, Laurus, Lavrenti,
Lurance**

Laurencio (Spanish)
a form of Laurence.

Laurens (Dutch) a form
of Laurence.

Laurent (French) a form
of Laurence.
Laurente

Laurie (English) a familiar
form of Laurence.
Lorry

Lauris (Swedish) a form
of Laurence.

Lauro (Filipino) a form
of Laurence.

LaValle (French) valley.
**Lavail, Laval, Lavalei,
Lavalle**

Lavan (Hebrew) white.
Lavaughan, Lavon, Levan

Lavaughan (American)
a form of Lavan.
**Lavaughn, Levaughan,
Levaughn**

Lave (Italian) lava.
(English) lord.

Lavi (Hebrew) lion.

Lavon (American) a form
of Lavan.
Lavonne, Lavonte

Lavrenti (Russian) a form
of Lawrence.
**Larenti, Lavrentij,
Lavrusha, Lavrik, Lavro**

Lawford (English) ford
on the hill.
Ford, Law

Lawler (Irish) mutterer.
Lawlor, Lollar, Loller

Lawrence (Latin) crowned
with laurel. See also
Brencis, Chencho.
**Labrentsis, Laiurenty,
Lanny, Lanty, Larance,
Laren, Larian, Larien,
Laris, Larka, Larrance,
Larrence, Larry, Lars,
Larya, Laurence, Lavrenti,
Law, Lawerance,
Lawrance, Lawren,
Lawrey, Lawrie, Lawron,
Lawry, Lencho, Lon,
Lóránt, Loreca, Loren,
Loretto, Lorenzo, Lorne,
Lourenco, Lowrance**

Lawson (English) son
of Lawrence.

Lawton (English) town
on the hill.
Laughton, Law

Lazaro (Italian) a form
of Lazarus.
**Lazarillo, Lazarito,
Lazzaro**

Lazarus (Greek) a form
of Eleazar. Bible: Lazarus
was raised from the dead.
**Lazar, Lázár, Lazare,
Lazaro, Lazaros, Lazarusie**

Leander (Greek) lion-man;
brave as a lion.
Ander, Leandro

Leandro (Spanish) a form
of Leander.
**Leandra, Léandre,
Leandrew, Leandros**

Leben (Yiddish) life.

Lee (English) a short form
of Farley and names
containing "lee."
Leigh

Lefty (American) left-
handed.

Leggett (French) one who
is sent; delegate.
Legate, Leggitt, Liggett

Lei (Chinese) thunder.
(Hawaiian) a form of Ray.

Leib (Yiddish) roaring lion.
Leibel

Leif (Scandinavian)
beloved.
Laif, Lief

Leigh (English) an alternate
form of Lee.

Leighton (English)
meadow farm.
Lay, Layton, Leigh, Leyton

Leith (Scottish) broad river.

Lek (Thai) small.

Lekeke (Hawaiian) powerful ruler.

Leks (Estonian) a familiar
form of Alexander.
Leksik, Lekso

Lel (Gypsy) taker.

Leland (English) meadow-land; protected land.
Lealand, Lee, Leeland, Leigh, Leighland, Lelan, Lelann, Leyland

Lemar (French) an alternate form of Lamar.
Lemario, Lemarr

Lemuel (Hebrew) devoted to God.
Lem, Lemmie, Lemmy

Len (German) a short form of Leonard. (Hopi) flute.

Lencho (Spanish) a form of Lawrence.
Lenci, Lenzy

Lennart (Swedish) a form of Leonard.
Lennerd

Lenno (Native American) man.

Lennon (Irish) small cloak; cape.

Lennor (Gypsy) spring; summer.

Lennox (Scottish) with many elms.
Lenox

Lenny (German) a familiar form of Leonard.
Lennie, Leny

Leo (Latin) lion. (German) a short form of Leopold.
Lavi, Leão, Lee, Leib, Leibel, Leos, Leosko, Léo, Léocadie, Leos, Leosoko, Lev, Lio, Lion, Liutas, Lyon, Nardek

Leon (Greek, German) a short form of Leonard, Napoleon.
Leo, Léon, Leonas, Léonce, Leoncio, Leondris, Leone, Leonek, Leonetti, Leoni, Leonid, Leonidas, Leonirez, Leonizio, Leonon, Leons, Leontes, Leontios, Leontrae, Liutas

Leonard (German) brave as a lion.
Leanard, Lee, Len, Lena, Lenard, Lennard, Lennart, Lenny, Leno, Leon, Leonaldo, Léonard, Leonardis, Leonardo, Leonart, Leonerd, Leonhard, Leonidas, Leontes, Lernard, Lienard, Linek, Lnard, Lon, Londard, Lonnard, Lonya, Lynnard

Leonel (English) little lion. See also Lionel.

Leonhard (German) an alternate form of Leonard.
Leonhards

Leonid (Russian) a form of Leonard.
Leonide, Lyonechka, Lyonya

Leonidas (Greek) a form of Leonard.
Leonida, Leonides

Leopold (German) brave
people.
**Leo, Leopoldo, Leorad,
Lipót, Lopolda, Luepold,
Luitpold, Poldi**

Leor (Hebrew) my light.
Leory, Lior

Lequinton (American)
a combination of the
prefix Le + Quinton.
**Lequentin, Lequenton,
Lequinn**

Leron (French) round,
circle. (American)
a combination of the
prefix Le + Ron.
**Le Ron, Lerone, Liron,
Lyron**

Leroy (French) king.
See also Delroy, Elroy.
**Lee, Leeroy, LeeRoy, Leigh,
Lerai, Leroi, LeRoi, LeRoy,
Roy**

Les (Scottish, English)
a short form of Leslie,
Lester.
Lessie

Lesharo (Pawnee) chief.

Leshawn (American)
a combination of the
prefix Le + Shawn.
Lesean, Leshaun, Leshon

Leslie (Scottish) gray
fortress.
**Lee, Leigh, Les, Leslea,
Leslee, Lesley, Lesly,
Lezlie, Lezly**

Lester (Latin) chosen
camp. (English) from
Leicester, England.
Leicester, Les

Lev (Hebrew) heart.
(Russian) a form of Leo.
A short form of Levi,
Leverett.
**Leb, Leva, Levka, Levko,
Levushka**

Leverett (French) young
hare.
**Lev, Leveret, Leverit,
Leveritt**

Levi (Hebrew) joined in
harmony. Bible: the son
of Jacob; the priestly tribe
of Israel.
**Leavi, Leevi, Lev, Levey,
Levie, Levin, Levitis, Levy,
Lewi**

Levon (American) an alter-
nate form of Lavon.
**Leevon, Levone, Levonn,
Lyvonne**

Lew (English) a short form
of Lewis.

Lewin (English) beloved
friend.

Lewis (English) a form of
Louis. (Welsh) an alternate
form of Llewellyn.
Lew, Lewes, Lewie, Lewy

Lex (English) a short form
of Alexander.
Lexi, Lexie, Lexin

Leyati (Moquelumnan) shape of an abalone shell.

Lí (Chinese) strong.

Liam (Irish) a form of William.

Liang (Chinese) good, excellent.

Liberio (Portuguese) liberation.
Liberaratore

Lidio (Greek, Portuguese) ancient. Geography: an ancient province in Asia Minor.

Ligongo (Yao) who is this?

Likeke (Hawaiian) a form of Richard.

Liko (Chinese) protected by Buddha. (Hawaiian) bud.
Like

Lin (Burmese) bright. (English) a short form of Lyndon.
Linh, Linn, Linny, Lyn, Lynn

Linc (English) a short form of Lincoln.
Link

Lincoln (English) settlement by the pool. History: Abraham Lincoln was the sixteenth U.S. president.
Linc, Lincon

Lindberg (German) mountain where linden trees grow.

Lindbergh, Lindburg, Lindy

Lindell (English) valley of the linden trees.
Lendall, Lendel, Lendell, Lindall, Lindel, Lyndale, Lyndall, Lyndel, Lyndell

Lindley (English) linden field.
Lindlea, Lindlee, Lindleigh, Lindly

Lindon (English) an alternate form of Lyndon.
Lin, Lindan, Linden

Lindsay (English) an alternate form of Lindsey.
Linsay

Lindsey (English) linden-tree island.
Lind, Lindsay, Lindsee, Lindsy, Linsey, Lyndsay, Lyndsey, Lyndsie, Lynzie

Linford (English) linden-tree ford.
Lynford

Linfred (German) peaceful, calm.

Linley (English) flax meadow.
Linlea, Linlee, Linleigh, Linly

Linton (English) flax town.
Lintonn, Lynton, Lyntonn

Linu (Hindi) lily.

Linus (Greek) flaxen haired.
Linas, Linux

Lio (Hawaiian) a form of Leo.

Lionel (French) lion cub. See also Leonel.
Lional, Lionell, Lionello, Lynel, Lynell, Lyonel

Liron (Hebrew) my song.
Lyron

Lise (Moquelumnan) salmon's head coming out of the water.

Lisimba (Yao) lion.
Simba

Lister (English) dyer.

Litton (English) town on the hill.
Liton

Liu (African) voice.

Liuz (Polish) light.
Lius

Livingston (English) Leif's town.
Livingstone

Liwanu (Moquelumnan) growling bear.

Llewellyn (Welsh) lionlike.
Lewis, Llewelin, Llewellen, Llewelleyn, Llewellin, Llywellyn, Llywelyn

Lloyd (Welsh) gray haired; holy. See also Floyd.
Loy, Loyd, Loyde, Loydie

Lobo (Spanish) wolf.

Lochlain (Irish, Scottish) land of lakes.
Laughlin, Lochlann

Locke (English) forest.
Lock, Lockwood

Loe (Hawaiian) a form of Roy.

Logan (Irish) meadow.
Logen

Lok (Chinese) happy.

Lokela (Hawaiian) a form of Roger.

Lokni (Moquelumnan) raining through the roof.

Lomán (Irish) bare. (Slavic) sensitive.

Lombard (Latin) long bearded.
Bard, Barr

Lon (Spanish) a short form of Alonzo, Leonard, Lonnie. (Irish) fierce.
Lonn

Lonan (Zuni) cloud.

Lonato (Native American) flint stone.

London (English) fortress of the moon. Geography: the capital of Great Britain.

Long (Chinese) dragon. (Vietnamese) hair.

Lonnie (German, Spanish) a familiar form of Alonzo.
Lonnell, Lonniel, Lonny

Lono (Hawaiian) Mythology: a god of peace and farming.

Lonzo (German, Spanish) a short form of Alonzo.
Lonso

Lootah (Lakota) red.

Lopaka (Hawaiian) a form of Robert.

Loránd (Hungarian) a form of Roland.

Lóránt (Hungarian) a form of Lawrence.
Lorant

Lorcan (Irish) little; fierce.

Lord (English) noble title.

Loren (Latin) a short form of Lawrence.
Lorin, Lorren, Lorrin, Loryn

Lorenzo (Italian, Spanish) a form of Lawrence.
Larinzo, Lerenzo, Lorenc, Lorence, Lorenco, Lorencz, Lorens, Lorentz, Lorenz, Lorenza, Loretto, Lorinc, Lörinc, Lorinzo, Loritz, Lorrenzo, Lorrie, Lorry, Renzo, Zo

Loretto (Italian) a form of Lawrence.
Loreto

Lorimer (Latin) harness maker.
Lorrie, Lorrimer, Lorry

Loring (German) son of the famous warrior.
Lorrie, Lorring, Lorry

Loris (Dutch) clown.

Loritz (Latin, Danish) laurel.
Lauritz

Lorne (Latin) a short form of Lawrence.
Lorn, Lornie

Lorry (English) an alternate form of Laurie.
Lori, Lorri, Lory

Lot (Hebrew) hidden, covered. Bible: Lot fled from Sodom, but his wife glanced back upon its destruction and was transformed into a pillar of salt.

Lothar (German) an alternate form of Luther.
Lotaire, Lotarrio, Lothair, Lothaire, Lothario

Lou (German) a short form of Louis.

Louie (German) a familiar form of Louis.

Louis (German) famous warrior. See also Aloisio, Aloysius, Clovis, Luigi.
Lash, Lashi, Lasho, Lewis, Lou, Loudovicus, Louie, Lucho, Lude, Ludek, Ludirk, Ludis, Ludko, Ludwig, Lughaidh, Lui, Luigi, Luis, Luki, Lutek

Loudon (German) low valley.
Loudan, Louden, Loudin, Lowden

Lourdes (French)
from Lourdes, France.
Geography: a town in
France. Religion: a place
where the Virgin Mary was
said to have appeared.

Louvain (English) Lou's
vanity. Geography:
a city in Belgium.

Lovell (English) an alternate
form of Lowell.
Lovel, Lovelle, Lovey

Lowell (French) young
wolf. (English) beloved.
Lovell, Lowe, Lowel

Loyal (English) faithful,
loyal.
Loy, Loye, Lyall, Lyell

Lubomir (Polish) lover
of peace.

Luboslaw (Polish) lover
of glory.
Lubs, Lubz

Luc (French) a form
of Luke.
Luce

Lucas (German, Irish,
Danish, Dutch) a form
of Lucius.
Lucassie, Luckas, Lucus

Lucian (Latin) an alternate
form of Lucius.
**Liuz, Lucan, Lucanus,
Luciano, Lucianus, Lucias,
Lucjan, Lukianos, Lukyan**

Luciano (Italian) a form
of Lucian.
Luca, Lucca, Lucio

Lucien (French) a form
of Lucius.

Lucius (Latin) light; bringer
of light.
**Loukas, Luc, Luca, Lucais,
Lucanus, Lucas, Lucca,
Luce, Lucian, Lucien,
Lucio, Lucious, Luke,
Lusio**

Lucky (American)
fortunate.
Luckie, Luckson

Ludlow (English) prince's
hill.

Ludwig (German)
an alternate form of
Louis. Music: Ludwig Van
Beethoven was a famous
nineteenth-century
German composer.
**Ludovic, Ludovico, Ludvig,
Ludvik, Ludwik, Lutz**

Lui (Hawaiian) a form
of Louis.

Luigi (Italian) a form
of Louis.
Lui, Luigino

Luis (Spanish) a form
of Louis.
Luise, Luiz

Lukas (Greek, Czech,
Swedish) a form of Luke.
**Loukas, Lukash, Lukasha,
Lukass, Lukasz**

Luke (Latin) a form of Lucius. Bible: author of the Gospel of Saint Luke and Acts of the Apostles—two New Testament books.
Luc, Luchok, Luck, Lucky, Luk, Luka, Lúkács, Lukas, Luken, Lukes, Lukus, Lukyan, Lusio

Lukela (Hawaiian) a form of Russel.

Luken (Basque) bringer of light.
Luk

Luki (Basque) famous warrior.

Lukman (Arabic) prophet.
Luqman

Lulani (Hawaiian) highest point in heaven.

Lumo (Ewe) born face-downward.

Lundy (Scottish) grove by the island.

Lunn (Irish) warlike.
Lon, Lonn

Lunt (Swedish) grove.

Lusila (Hindi) leader.

Lusio (Zuni) a form of Lucius.

Lutalo (Luganda) warrior.

Lutfi (Arabic) kind, friendly.

Luther (German) famous warrior. History: the Prot-estant reformer Martin Luther was one of the central figures of the Reformation.
Lothar, Lutero, Luthor

Lutherum (Gypsy) slumber.

Luyu (Moquelumnan) head shaker.

Lyall, Lyell (Scottish) loyal.

Lyle (French) island.
Lisle, Ly, Lysle

Lyman (English) meadow.
Leaman, Leeman

Lynch (Irish) mariner.
Linch

Lyndal (English) valley of lime trees.
Lyndale, Lyndall, Lyndel, Lyndell

Lyndon (English) linden-tree hill. History: Lyndon B. Johnson was the thirty-sixth U.S. president.
Lin, Lindon, Lyden, Lydon, Lyn, Lynden, Lynn

Lynn (English) waterfall; brook.
Lyn, Lynell, Lynette, Lynnard, Lynoll

Lyron (Hebrew) an alter-nate form of Leron, Liron.

Lysander (Greek) liberator.
Sander

Mac (Scottish) son.
Macs

Macadam (Scottish) son
of Adam.
MacAdam, McAdam

Macallister (Irish) son
of Alistair.
**Macalaster, MacAlister,
McAlister, McAllister**

Macario (Spanish) happy;
blessed.

Macarthur (Irish) son
of Arthur.
MacArthur, McArthur

Macaulay (Scottish) son
of righteousness.
Macauley, McCauley

Macbride (Scottish) son of
a follower of Saint Brigid.
**Macbryde, Mcbride,
McBride**

Maccoy (Irish) son of
Hugh. See also Coy.
MacCoy, Mccoy, McCoy

Maccrea (Irish) son
of grace.
**MacCrae, MacCray,
Macrae, MacCrea, Mccrea,
McCrea**

Macdonald (Scottish)
son of Donald.
**MacDonald, Mcdonald,
McDonald, Mcdonna,
Mcdonnell, McDonnell**

Macdougal (Scottish)
son of Dougal. See also
Douglas.
**MacDougal, Mcdougal,
McDougal, McDougall,
Dougal**

Mace (French) club.
(English) a short form
of Macy, Mason.
**Macean, Macer, Macey,
Macy**

Machas (Polish) a form
of Michael.

Mack (Scottish) a short
form of names beginning
with "Mac" and "Mc."
**Macke, Mackey, Mackie,
Macklin, Macks**

Mackenzie (Irish) son
of Kenzie.
**Mackenxo, Mackenzey,
Mackenzi, MacKenzie,
Mackenzly, Mackenzy,
Mackienzie, Mackinsey,
Makenzie, McKenzie**

Mackinnley (Irish) son
of the learned ruler.
**MacKinnley, Mckinnely,
Mckinnlee, Mckinnley,
McKinnley**

Maclean (Irish) son
of Leander.

Maclean *(cont.)*
**MacLain, MacLean,
McLaine, McLean**

Macmahon (Irish) son
of Mahon.
MacMahon, McMahon

Macmurray (Irish) son
of Murray.
McMurray

Macnair (Scottish) son
of the heir.
Macknair

Maco (Hungarian) a form
of Emmanuel.

Macon (German, English)
maker.

Macy (French) Matthew's
estate.
Mace, Macey

Maddock (Welsh)
generous.
Madoc, Madock, Madog

Maddox (Welsh, English)
benefactor's son.
Madox

Madhar (Hindi) god;
godlike. Religion: another
name for the Hindu god
Shiva.

Madison (English) son
of Maude; good son.
**Maddie, Maddison,
Maddy, Madisson,
Son, Sonny**

Madongo (Luganda)
uncircumcised.

Madu (Ibo) people.

Magar (Armenian) groom's
attendant.
Magarious

Magee (Irish) son of Hugh.
MacGee, MacGhee, McGee

Magen (Hebrew) protector.

Magnar (Norwegian)
strong; warrior.
Magne

Magnus (Latin) great.
**Maghnus, Magnes,
Manius, Mayer**

Magomu (Luganda)
younger of twins.

Maguire (Irish) son of
the beige one.
**MacGuire, McGuire,
McGwire**

Mahdi (Arabic) guided
to the right path.

Mahesa (Hindi) great lord.
Religion: another name
for the Hindu god Shiva.

Mahi'ai (Hawaiian) a form
of George.

Mahir (Arabic, Hebrew)
excellent; industrious.
Maher

Mahkah (Lakota) earth.

Mahmúd (Arabic) an alter-
nate form of Mohammed.
**Mahmed, Mahmood,
Mahmoud**

Mahomet (Arabic) an alternate form of Mohammed.
Mehemet, Mehmet

Mahon (Irish) bear.

Mahpee (Lakota) sky.

Maimun (Arabic) lucky.
Maimon

Mairtin (Irish) a form
of Martin.
Martain, Martainn

Maitias (Irish) a form
of Mathias.
Maithias

Maitiú (Irish) a form
of Matthew.

Maitland (English)
meadowland.

Majid (Arabic) great,
glorious.
Majdi, Majed, Majeed

Major (Latin) greater;
military rank.
**Majar, Maje, Majer,
Mayer, Mayor**

Makaio (Hawaiian) a form
of Matthew.

Makalani (Mwera) writer.

Makani (Hawaiian) wind.

Makarios (Greek) happy;
blessed.
**.Macario, Macarios,
Maccario, Maccarios**

Makin (Arabic) strong.

Makis (Greek) a form
of Michael.

Makoto (Japanese) sincere.

Maks (Hungarian) a form
of Max.
Makszi

Maksim (Russian) a form
of Maximilian.
Maksimka, Maxim

Maksym (Polish) a form
of Maximilian.
**Makimus, Maksim,
Maksymilian**

Makyah (Hopi) eagle
hunter.

Mal (Irish) a short form
of names beginning with
"Mal."

Malachi (Hebrew) angel of
God. Bible: the last canon-
ical Hebrew prophet.
**Maeleachlainn, Mal,
Malachia, Malachie,
Malachy, Malchija,
Malechy, Málik**

Malachy (Irish) a form
of Malachi.

Malajitm (Sanskrit) garland
of victory.

Malcolm (Scottish)
follower of Saint Columba,
an early Scottish saint.
(Arabic) dove.
**Mal, Malcolum, Malcom,
Malcum, Malkolm**

Malden (English) meeting
place in a pasture.
Mal, Maldon

Maleko (Hawaiian) a form
of Mark.

Málik (Arabic) a form of
Malachi. (Punjabi) lord,
master.
**Maalik, Malak, Malik,
Malikh, Maliq, Malique,
Mallik**

Malin (English) strong,
little warrior.
Mal, Mallin, Mallon

Mallory (German) army
counselor. (French) wild
duck.
**Lory, Mal, Mallery,
Mallori, Mallorie, Malory**

Maloney (Irish) church
going.
Malone, Malony

Malvern (Welsh) bare hill.
Malverne

Malvin (Irish, English)
an alternate form of
Melvin.
**Mal, Malvinn, Malvyn,
Malvynn**

Mamo (Hawaiian) yellow
flower; yellow bird.

Manchu (Chinese) pure.

Manco (Peruvian)
supreme leader. History:
a thirteenth-century Incan
king.

Mandala (Yao) flowers.
Manda, Mandela

Mandeep (Punjabi) mind
full of light.
Mandieep

Mandel (German) almond.
Mandell

Mandek (Polish) a form
of Armand, Herman.
Mandie

Mander (Gypsy) from me.

Manford (English) small
ford.

Manfred (English) man
of peace. See also Fred.
**Manfrid, Manfried,
Mannfred, Mannfryd**

Manger (French) stable.

Mango (Spanish) a familiar
form of Emmanuel,
Manuel.

Manheim (German)
servant's home.

Manipi (Native American)
living marvel.

Manius (Scottish) a form
of Magnus.
Manus, Manyus

Manley (English) hero's
meadow.
Manlea, Manleigh, Manly

Mann (German) man.
Manin

Manning (English) son
of the hero.

Mannix (Irish) monk.
Mainchin

Manny (German, Spanish) a familiar form of Manuel.
Mani, Manni, Mannie

Mano (Hawaiian) shark. (Spanish) a short form of Manuel.
Manno, Manolo

Manoj (Sanskrit) cupid.

Mansa (Swahili) king. History: a fourteenth-century emperor of Mali.

Mansel (English) manse; house occupied by a clergyman.
Mansell

Mansfield (English) field by the river; hero's field.

Man-Shik (Korean) deeply rooted.

Mansür (Arabic) divinely aided.
Mansoor, Mansour

Manton (English) man's town; hero's town.
Mannton, Manten

Manu (Hindi) lawmaker. History: the writer of the Hindi code of conduct. (Hawaiian) bird. (Ghanian) second-born son.

Manuel (Hebrew) a short form of Emmanuel.
Maco, Mango, Mannuel, Manny, Mano, Manolón, Manual, Manue, Manuelli, Manuelo, Manuil, Manyuil, Minel

Manville (French) worker's village. (English) hero's village.
Mandeville, Manvil

Man-Young (Korean) ten thousand years of prosperity.

Manzo (Japanese) third son.

Maona (Winnebago) creator, earth maker.

Mapira (Yao) millet.

Marar (Watamare) mud; dust.

Marc (French) a form of Mark.

Marcel (French) a form of Marcellus.
Marcell, Marsale, Marsel

Marcello (Italian) a form of Marcellus.
Marcelo, Marchello, Marsello, Marselo

Marcellus (Latin) a familiar form of Marcus.
Marceau, Marcel, Marceles, Marcelin, Marcelino, Marcelis, Marcelius, Marcelleous, Marcellin, Marcellino, Marcello, Marcellous, Marcelluas, Marcely, Marciano, Marcilka, Marcsseau

March (English) dweller by a boundary.

Marciano (Italian) a form
of Martin.
Marci, Marcio

Marcilka (Hungarian)
a form of Marcellus.
Marci, Marcilki

Marcin (Polish) a form
of Martin.

Marco (Italian) a form of
Marcus. History: Marco
Polo was the thirteenth-
century Venetian traveler
who explored Asia.
Marcko, Marko

Marcos (Spanish) a form
of Marcus.
Markos, Markose

Marcus (Latin) martial,
warlike.
**Marc, Marcas, Marcellus,
Marcio, Marckus, Marco,
Marcos, Marcous, Marek,
Mark, Markov, Markus**

Marek (Slavic) a form
of Marcus.

Maren (Basque) sea.

Mareo (Japanese)
uncommon.

Marian (Polish) a form
of Mark.

Mariano (Italian) a form
of Mark.

Marid (Arabic) rebellious.

Marin (French) sailor.
**Marine, Mariner, Marino,
Marius, Marriner**

Marino (Italian) a form
of Marin.
Mario, Mariono

Mario (Italian) an alternate
form of Marino.
Marios, Marrio

Marion (French) bitter; sea
of bitterness. A masculine
form of Mary.
Mariano

Marius (Latin) a form of
Marin. History: a Roman
clan name.
Marious

Mark (Latin) an alternate
form of Marcus. Bible:
author of the New
Testament book, the
*Gospel According to
Saint Mark*. See also
Maleko.
**Marc, Marek, Marian,
Mariano, Marke, Markee,
Markel, Markell, Markey,
Marko, Markos, Márkus,
Markusha, Marque,
Martial, Marx**

Marke (Polish) a form
of Mark.

Markes (Portuguese) an
alternate form of Marques.
Markess, Markest

Markese (French) an alter-
nate form of Marquis.
**Markease, Markeece,
Markees, Markeese,
Markei, Markeice,
Markeis, Markice,**

Markies, Markiese, Markise

Markham (English) homestead on the boundary.

Markis (French) an alternate form of Marquis.
Markist

Marko (Latin) an alternate form of Marco, Mark.
Markco

Markus (Latin) an alternate form of Marcus.
Markas, Markcus, Markcuss, Marqus

Marland (English) lake land.

Marley (English) lake meadow.
Marlea, Marleigh, Marly, Marrley

Marlin (English) deep-sea fish.
Marlion

Marlon (French) a form of Merlin.

Marlow (English) hill by the lake.
Mar, Marlo, Marlowe

Marmion (French) small.
Marmyon

Marnin (Hebrew) singer; bringer of joy.

Maro (Japanese) myself.

Marques (Portuguese) nobleman.
Markes, Markques,

Marquest, Markqueus, Marquez, Marqus

Marquis (French) nobleman.
Marcquis, Marcuis, Markis, Markuis, Marquee, Marqui, Marquie, Marquist

Marr (Spanish) divine. (Arabic) forbidden.

Mars (Latin) bold warrior. Mythology: the Roman god of war.

Marsden (English) marsh valley.
Marsdon

Marsh (French) a short form of Marshall. (English) swamp land.

Marshall (French) caretaker of the horses; military title.
Marschal, Marsh, Marshal, Marshel, Marshell

Marston (English) town by the marsh.

Martell (English) hammerer.
Martel

Marten (Dutch) a form of Martin.

Marti (Spanish) a form of Martin.
Martee, Martez, Martie, Marties, Martiez, Martis, Martise

Martial (French) a form of Mark.

Martin (Latin) martial, warlike. (French) a form of Martinus. History: Martin Luther King, Jr. led the civic rights movement and won the Nobel Peace Prize. See also Tynek.
Maartin, Mairtin, Marciano, Marcin, Marinos, Marius, Mart, Martan, Marten, Martijn, Martinas, Martine, Martinez, Martinho, Martiniano, Martinien, Martinka, Martino, Martins, Marto, Marton, Márton, Marts, Marty, Martyn, Mattin, Mertin, Morten, Moss

Martinez (Spanish) a form of Martin.

Martinho (Portuguese) a form of Martin.

Martino (Italian) a form of Martin.
Martinos

Martins (Latvian) a form of Martin.

Martinus (Latin) martial, warlike.
Martin

Marty (Latin) a familiar form of Martin.
Martey, Marti, Martie

Marut (Hindi) Religion: the Hindu god of the wind.

Marv (English) a short form of Marvin.
Marve, Marvi, Marvis

Marvin (English) lover of the sea.
Marv, Marvein, Marven, Marwin, Marwynn, Mervin

Marwan (Arabic) history personage.

Marwood (English) forest pond.

Masaccio (Italian) twin.
Masaki

Masahiro (Japanese) broad minded.

Masamba (Yao) leaves.

Masao (Japanese) righteous.

Masato (Japanese) just.

Mashama (Shona) surprising.

Maska (Native American) powerful.

Maslin (French) little Thomas.
Maslen, Masling

Mason (French) stone worker.
Mace, Maison, Sonny

Masou (Native American) fire god.

Massey (English) twin.
Massi

Massimo (Italian) greatest.
Massimiliano

Masud (Arabic, Swahili) fortunate.
Masood, Masoud, Mhasood

Matai (Basque, Bulgarian) a form of Matthew.
Máté, Matei

Matalino (Filipino) bright.

Mateo (Spanish) a form of Matthew.
Matías, Matteo

Mateusz (Polish) a form of Matthew.
Matejs, Mateus

Mathe (German) a short form of Matthew.

Mather (English) powerful army.

Matheu (German) a form of Matthew.
Matheau, Matheus, Mathu

Mathew (Hebrew) an alternate form of Matthew.

Mathias (German, Swedish) a form of Matthew.
Maitias, Mathi, Mathia, Mathis, Matías, Matthia, Matthias, Mattia, Mattias, Matus

Mathieu (French) a form of Matthew.
Mathie, Mathieux, Mathiew, Matthieu, Matthiew, Mattieu, Mattieux

Matías (Spanish) a form of Mathias.

Mato (Native American) brave.

Matope (Rhodesian) our last child.

Matoskah (Lakota) white bear.

Mats (Swedish) a familiar form of Matthew.
Matts, Matz

Matson (Hebrew) son of Matt.
Matison, Mattison, Mattson

Matt (Hebrew) a short form of Matthew.
Mat

Matteen (Afghani) disciplined; polite.

Matteus (Scandinavian) a form of Matthew.

Matthew (Hebrew) gift of God. Bible: author of the New Testament book, the Gospel According to Saint Matthew.
Mads, Makaio, Maitiú, Mata, Matai, Matek, Mateo, Mateusz, Matfei, Mathe, Matheson, Matheu, Mathew, Mathian, Mathias, Mathieson, Mathieu, Matro, Mats, Matt, Matteus, Matthaeus, Matthaios, Matthaus, Matthäus, Mattheus,

Matthew *(cont.)*
**Matthews, Mattmias,
Matty, Matvey, Matyas,
Mayhew**

Matty (Hebrew) a familiar
form of Matthew.
Mattie

Matus (Czech) a form
of Mathias.

Matvey (Russian) a form
of Matthew.
**Matviy, Matviyko,
Matyash, Motka, Motya**

Matyas (Polish) a form
of Matthew.
Mátyás

Mauli (Hawaiian) a form
of Maurice.

Maurice (Latin) dark
skinned; moor; marshland.
See also Seymour.
**Mauli, Maur,
Maurance, Maureo,
Mauricio, Maurids,
Mauriece, Maurikas,
Maurin, Maurino,
Maurio, Maurise, Mauritz,
Maurius, Maurizio, Mauro,
Maurrel, Maurtel, Maury,
Maurycy, Meurig, Moore,
Morice, Moritz, Morrel,
Morrice, Morrie, Morrill,
Morris**

Mauricio (Spanish) a form
of Maurice.

Mauritz (German) a form
of Maurice.

Maurizio (Italian) a form
of Maurice.

Maury (Latin) a familiar
form of Maurice.
Maurey, Maurie, Morrie

Maverick (American)
independent.
Mavrick

Mawuli (Ewe) there is
a God.

Max (Latin) a short form
of Maximilian, Maxwell.
**Mac, Mack, Maks, Maxe,
Maxx, Maxy, Miksa**

Maxfield (English) Mack's
field.

Maxi (Czech, Hungarian,
Spanish) a familiar form
of Maximilian, Máximo.
**Makszi, Maxey, Maxie,
Maxis, Maxy**

Maxime (French) most
excellent.
Maxim

Maximilian (Latin)
greatest.
**Mac, Mack, Maixim,
Maksym, Massimiliano,
Max, Maxamillion,
Maxemilian, Maxemilion,
Maxi, Maximalian,
Maxime, Maximili,
Maximilia, Maximilianus,
Maximilien, Maximillian,
Maximillion, Máximo,
Maximos, Maxmilian,
Maxmillion, Maxon,**

Maxymilian, Maxymillian, Mayhew, Miksa

Máximo (Spanish) a form of Maximilian.
Massimo, Maxi, Maximiano, Maximiliano, Maximino, Máximo

Maximos (Greek) a form of Maximilian.

Maxwell (English) great spring.
Max, Maxwel, Maxwill, Maxy

Maxy (English) a familiar form of Max, Maxwell.
Maxi

Mayer (Hebrew) an alternate form of Meir. (Latin) an alternate form of Magnus, Major.
Mahyar, Mayeer, Mayor, Mayur

Mayes (English) field.
Mayo, Mays

Mayhew (English) a form of Matthew.

Maynard (English) powerful; brave. See also Meinhard.
May, Mayne, Maynhard, Ménard

Mayo (Irish) yew-tree plain. (English) an alternate form of Mayes. Geography: a county in Ireland.

Mayon (Hindi) god. Religion: ancient name for the Hindu god Krishna.

Mayonga (Luganda) lake sailor.

Mazi (Ibo) sir.

Mazin (Arabic) proper.
Mazen, Mazinn

Mbita (Swahili) born on a cold night.

Mbwana (Swahili) master.

McGeorge (Scottish) son of George.
MacGeorge

Mckay (Scottish) son of Kay.
Mackay, MacKay, McKay

McKenzie (Irish) an alternate form of Mackenzie.
Mckensey, Mckensie, Mckenson, Mckensson, Mckenzi

Mead (English) meadow.
Meade, Meed

Medgar (German) a form of Edgar.

Medwin (German) faithful friend.

Mehetabel (Hebrew) who God benefits.

Mehrdad (Persian) gift of the sun.

Mehtar (Sanskrit) prince.
Mehta

Meinhard (German)
strong, firm. See also
Maynard.
**Meinhardt, Meinke,
Meino, Mendar**

Meinrad (German) strong
counsel.

Meir (Hebrew) one who
brightens, shines; enlight-
ener. History: a leading
second-century scholar.
Mayer, Meyer, Muki, Myer

Meka (Hawaiian) eyes.

Mel (English, Irish) a familiar form of Melvin.

Melbourne (English)
mill stream.
**Melborn, Melburn, Melby,
Milborn, Milbourn,
Milbourne, Milburn,
Millburn, Millburne**

Melchior (Hebrew) king.
Meilseoir, Melker, Melkior

Meldon (English) mill hill.
Melden

Melrone (Irish) servant
of Saint Ruadhan.
Maolruadhand

Melvern (Native American)
great chief.

Melville (French) mill
town. Literature: Herman
Melville was a well-known
nineteenth-century
American writer.
Milville

Melvin (Irish) armored
chief. (English) mill friend;
council friend. See also
Vinny.
**Malvin, Mel, Melvino,
Melvon, Melvyn, Melwin,
Melwyn, Melwynn**

Menachem (Hebrew)
comforter.
Menahem, Nachman

Menassah (Hebrew) cause
to forget.
**Menashe, Menashi,
Menashia, Menashiah,
Menashya, Manasseh**

Mendel (English)
repairman.
**Mendeley, Mendell,
Mendie, Mendy**

Mengesha (Ethiopian)
kingdom.

Menico (Spanish) a short
form of Domenico.

Mensah (Ewe) third son.

Menz (German) a short
form of Clement.

Mercer (English)
storekeeper.
Merce

Mered (Hebrew) revolter.

Meredith (Welsh) guardian
from the sea.
**Meredyth, Merideth,
Meridith, Merry**

Merion (Welsh) from
Merion, England.
Merrion

Merle (French) a short form
of Merlin, Merrill.
Meryl

Merlin (English) falcon.
Literature: the wizard
in King Arthur's court.
**Marlon, Merle, Merlen,
Merlinn, Merlyn, Merlynn**

Merrick (English) ruler
of the sea.
**Merek, Meric, Merrik,
Meyrick, Myrucj**

Merrill (Irish) bright sea.
(French) famous.
**Meril, Merill, Merle,
Merrel, Merrell, Merril,
Meryl**

Merritt (Latin, Irish)
valuable; deserving.
Merit, Meritt, Merrett

Merton (English) sea town.
Murton

Merv (Irish) a short form
of Mervin.

Merville (French) sea
village.

Mervin (Irish) a form
of Marvin.
**Merv, Mervyn, Mervynn,
Merwin, Merwinn,
Merwyn, Murvin, Murvyn,
Myrvyn, Myrvynn,
Myrwyn**

Meshach (Hebrew) artist.
Bible: one of Daniel's three
friends who were rescued
from a fiery furnace by
an angel.

Mesut (Turkish) happy.

Metikla (Moquelumnan)
reaching a hand under
water to catch a fish.

Mette (Greek, Danish)
pearl.
Almeta, Mete

Meurig (Welsh) a form
of Maurice.

Meyer (Hebrew) an alter-
nate form of Meir.
(German) farmer.
Mayer, Meier, Myer

Mhina (Swahili) delightful.

Micah (Hebrew) an alter-
nate form of Michael.
Bible: a Hebrew prophet.
**Mic, Micaiah, Michiah,
Mika, Mikah, Myca,
Mycah**

Micha (Hebrew) a short
form of Michael.
Michah

Michael (Hebrew) who is
like God? See also Micah,
Miguel, Miles, Mika.
**Machael, Machas, Mahail,
Maichail, Maikal, Makael,
Makal, Makel, Makell,
Makis, Meikel, Mekal,
Mekhail, Mhichael,
Micael, Micah, Micahel,
Mical, Micha, Michaele,
Michaell, Michail, Michak,
Michal, Michale,
Michalek, Michalel,
Michau, Micheal, Micheil,
Michel, Michele, Michelet,**

Michael *(cont.)*
Michiel, Micho, Michoel, Mick, Mickael, Mickey, Mihail, Mihalje, Mihkel, Mika, Mikael, Mikáele, Mikal, Mike, Mikeal, Mikel, Mikelis, Mikell, Mikhail, Mikkel, Mikko, Miksa, Milko, Miquel, Misi, Miska, Mitchell, Mychael, Mychajlo, Mychal, Mykal, Mykhas

Michail (Russian) a form of Michael.
Mihas, Mikail, Mikale, Misha

Michal (Polish) a form of Michael.
Michak, Michalek

Micheal (Irish) a form of Michael.

Michel (French) a form of Michael.
Michaud, Miche, Michee, Michon

Michelangelo (Italian) a combination of Michael + Angelo. Art: Michelangelo Buonarroti was one of the greatest Italian Renaissance painters.
Michelange, Miguelangelo

Michele (Italian) a form of Michael.

Michio (Japanese) man with the strength of three thousand.

Mick (English) a short form of Michael, Mickey.
Mickerson

Mickael (English) a form of Michael.
Mickeal, Mickel, Mickelle, Mickle

Mickey (Irish) a familiar form of Michael.
Mick, Mickie, Micky, Miki, Mique

Micu (Hungarian) a form of Nick.

Miguel (Portuguese, Spanish) a form of Michael.
Migeel, Migel, Miguelly, Migui

Mihail (Greek, Bulgarian, Romanian) a form of Michael.
Mihailo, Mihal, Mihalis

Mika (Hebrew) an alternate form of Micah. (Russian) a familiar form of Michael. (Ponca) raccoon.
Miika

Mikael (Swedish) a form of Michael.
Mikaeel, Mikaele

Mikáele (Hawaiian) a form of Michael.
Mikele

Mikal (Hebrew) an alternate form of Michael.
Mekal

Mikasi (Omaha) coyote.

Mike (Hebrew) a short
form of Michael.
Mikey, Myk

Mikeal (Irish) a form
of Michael.

Mikel (Basque) a form
of Michael.
Mekel, Mekell, Mikell

Mikelis (Latvian) a form
of Michael.
Mikus, Milkins

Mikhail (Greek, Russian)
a form of Michael.
**Mekhail, Mihály, Mikhael,
Mikhalis, Mikhalka,
Mikhial, Mikhos**

Miki (Japanese) tree.
Mikio

Mikkel (Norwegian) a form
of Michael.
Mikkael, Mikle

Mikko (Finnish) a form
of Michael.
**Mikk, Mikka, Mikkohl,
Mikkol, Miko, Mikol**

Mikolaj (Polish) a form
of Nicholas.

Mikolas (Greek) an alternate form of Nicholas.
Miklós, Mikolai, Milek

Miksa (Hungarian) a form
of Max.
Miks

Milan (Italian) northerner.
Geography: a city in
northern Italy.

**Milen, Millan, Millen,
Mylan, Mylen, Mylon**

Milap (Native American)
giving.

Milborough (English)
middle borough.
Milbrough

Milek (Polish) a familiar
form of Nicholas.

Miles (Greek) millstone.
(Latin) soldier. (German)
merciful. (English) a short
form of Michael.
**Milas, Milles, Milo, Milson,
Myles**

Milford (English) mill
by the ford.

Mililani (Hawaiian)
heavenly caress.

Milko (Czech) a form
of Michael. (German)
a familiar form of Emil.
Milkins

Millard (Latin) caretaker
of the mill.
**Mill, Millar, Miller,
Millward, Milward, Myller**

Miller (English) miller,
grain grinder.
Mellar, Millard, Millen

Mills (English) mills.

Milo (German) an alternate
form of Miles. A familiar
form of Emil.
Mylo

Milos (Greek, Slavic)
pleasant.

Miloslav (Czech) lover
of glory.
Milda

Milt (English) a short form
of Milton.

Milton (English) mill town.
Milt, Miltie, Milty, Mylton

Mimis (Greek) a familiar
form of Demetrius.

Min (Burmese) king.
Mina

Mincho (Spanish) a form
of Benjamin.

Minel (Spanish) a form
of Manuel.

Miner (English) miner.

Mingan (Native American)
gray wolf.

Mingo (Spanish) a short
form of Domingo.

Minh (Vietnamese) bright.
**Minhao, Minhduc,
Minhkhan, Minhtong,
Minhy**

Minkah (Akan) just, fair.

Minor (Latin) junior;
younger.
Mynor

Minoru (Japanese) fruitful.

Mique (Spanish) a form
of Mickey.
Mequel, Mequelin, Miquel

Miron (Polish) peace.

Miroslav (Czech) peace;
glory.

Mirek, Miroslawy

Mirwais (Afghani) noble
ruler. History: a famous
king who lived in 900 A.D.

Misha (Russian) a short
form of Michail.
**Misa, Mischa, Mishael,
Mishal, Mishe, Mishenka,
Mishka**

Miska (Hungarian) a form
of Michael.
Misi, Misik, Misko, Miso

Mister (English) mister.
Mistur

Misu (Moquelumnan)
rippling water.

Mitch (English) a short
form of Mitchell.

Mitchell (English) a form
of Michael.
**Mitch, Mitchael, Mitchall,
Mitchel, Mitchele,
Mitchelle, Mitchem,
Mytch, Mytchell**

Mitsos (Greek) a familiar
form of Demetrius.

Modesto (Latin) modest.

Moe (English) a short form
of Moses.
Mo

Mogens (Dutch) powerful.

Mohamet (Arabic) an alter-
nate form of Mohammed.
**Mahomet, Mehemet,
Mehmet**

Mohammad (Arabic)
an alternate form
of Mohammed.
**Mahammad, Mohamad,
Mohamid, Mohammadi,
Mohammd, Mohammid,
Mohanad, Mohmad**

Mohammed (Arabic)
praised. See also Ahmad,
Hamid.
**Mahammed, Mahmúd,
Mahomet, Mohamed,
Mohamet, Mohammad,
Mohaned, Mouhamed,
Muhammad**

Mohan (Hindi) delightful.
Religion: another name
for the Hindu god Krishna.

Moises (Portuguese,
Spanish) a form of Moses.
Moisés, Moisey, Moisis

Moishe (Yiddish) a form
of Moses.
Moshe

Mojag (Native American)
crying baby.

Molimo (Moquelumnan)
bear going under shady
trees.

Momuso (Moquelumnan)
yellow jackets crowded in
their nests for the winter.

Mona (Moquelumnan)
gathering jimsonweed
seed.

Monahan (Irish) monk.
Monaghan, Monoghan

Mongo (Yoruba) famous.

Monroe (Irish) Geography:
the mouth of the Roe
River.
Monro, Munro, Munroe

Montague (French)
pointed mountain.
Montagu, Monte

Montana (Spanish) mountain. Geography: a U.S.
state. Culture: name popu-
larized by football player
Joe Montana.
Montaine

Montaro (Japanese) big
boy.
Montero

Monte (Spanish) a short
form of Montgomery.
**Montae, Montaé, Montay,
Montee, Monti, Montoya,
Monty**

Montez (Spanish) dweller
in the mountains.
**Monteiz, Monteze,
Montisze**

Montgomery (English)
rich man's mountain.
**Monte, Montgomerie,
Monty**

Montre (French) show.
**Montray, Montres,
Montrez**

Montreal (French) royal
mountain. Geography:
a city in Quebec.
Montrail, Montrale,

Montreal *(cont.)*
Montrall, Montrel, Montrell

Montsho (Tswana) black.

Monty (English) a familiar form of Montgomery.

Moore (French) dark; moor; marshland. See also Maurice.
Moor, Mooro, More

Mordecai (Hebrew) martial, warlike. Mythology: Marduk was the Babylonian god of war.
Mord, Mordechai, Mordy, Mort

Mordred (Latin) painful. Literature: the nephew of King Arthur.
Modred

Morel (French) an edible mushroom.

Moreland (English) moor; marshland.
Moorland, Morland

Morell (French) dark; from Morocco.
Moor, Moore, Morill, Morrell, Morrill, Murrel, Murrell

Morey (Greek) a familiar form of Moris. (Latin) an alternate form of Morrie.
Morrey, Morry

Morgan (Scottish) sea warrior.
Morgen, Morgun, Morrgan

Mori (Madi) born before father finished paying wife's dowry.

Morio (Japanese) forest.

Moris (Greek) son of the dark one. (English) an alternate form of Morris.
Morisz, Moriz

Moritz (German) a form of Maurice, Morris.
Morisz

Morley (English) meadow by the moor.
Moorley, Moorly, Morlee, Morleigh, Morlon, Morly, Morlyn, Morrley

Morrie (Latin) a familiar form of Maurice, Morse.
Maury, Morey, Morie

Morris (Latin) dark skinned; moor; marshland. (English) a form of Maurice.
Moris, Moriss, Morriss, Morry, Moss

Morse (English) son of Maurice.
Morresse, Morrie, Morrison, Morrisson

Mort (French, English) a short form of Morten, Mortimer, Morton.
Mortey, Mortie, Mortty, Morty

Morten (Norwegian) a form of Martin.
Mort

Mortimer (French) still
water.
Mort, Mortymer

Morton (English) town
near the moor.
Mort

Morven (Scottish) mariner.
Morvien, Morvin

Mose (Hebrew) a short
form of Moses.

Moses (Hebrew) drawn
out of the water.
(Egyptian) son, child.
Bible: the Hebrew
leader who brought the
Ten Commandments
down from Mount Sinai.
**Moe, Moise, Moïse,
Moisei, Moises, Moishe,
Mose, Mosese, Mosiah,
Mosie, Moss, Mosya,
Mosze, Moszek, Mousa,
Moyses, Moze**

Moshe (Hebrew, Polish) an
alternate form of Moses.
Mosheh

Mosi (Swahili) first-born.

Moss (Irish) a short form of
Maurice, Morris. (English)
a short form of Moses.

Moswen (African) light
in color.

Motega (Native American)
new arrow.

Mouhamed (Arabic)
an alternate form
of Mohammed.

**Mouhamadou,
Mouhamoin**

Mousa (Arabic) a form
of Moses.

Moze (Lithuanian) a form
of Moses.
Mozes, Mózes

Mpasa (Ngoni) mat.

Mposi (Nyakusa)
blacksmith.

Mpoza (Luganda) tax
collector.

Msrah (Akan) sixth-born.

Muata (Moquelumnan)
yellow jackets in their nest.

Mugamba (Runyoro) talks
too much.

Mugisa (Rutooro) lucky.
Mugisha, Mukisa

Muhammad (Arabic)
an alternate form of
Mohammed. History:
the founder of the
Islamic religion.
**Muhamad, Muhamet,
Muhammadali,
Muhammed**

Muhannad (Arabic) sword.
Muhanad

Muhsin (Arabic) benefi-
cent; charitable.

Muhtadi (Arabic) rightly
guided.

Muir (Scottish) moor;
marshland.

Mujahid (Arabic) fighter in the way of Allah.

Mukasa (Luganda) God's chief administrator.

Mukhtar (Arabic) chosen.
Mukhtaar

Mukul (Sanskrit) bud, blossom; soul.

Mulogo (Musoga) wizard.

Mundan (Rhodesian) garden.

Mundo (Spanish) a short form of Edmundo.

Mundy (Irish) from Reamonn, Ireland.

Mungo (Scottish) amiable.

Mun-Hee (Korean) literate; shiny.

Munir (Arabic) brilliant; shining.

Munny (Cambodian) wise.

Muraco (Native American) white moon.

Murali (Hindi) god. Religion: another name for the Hindu god Krishna.

Murat (Turkish) wish come true.

Murdock (Scottish) wealthy sailor.
Murdo, Murdoch, Murtagh

Murphy (Irish) sea-warrior.
Murfey, Murfy

Murray (Scottish) sailor.
Macmurray, Moray, Murrey, Murry

Murtagh (Irish) a form of Murdock.
Murtaugh

Musád (Arabic) untied camel.

Musoke (Rukonjo) born while a rainbow was in the sky.

Mustafa (Arabic) chosen; royal.
Mostafa, Mostaffa, Moustafa, Mustafah, Mustapha

Muti (Arabic) obedient.

Mwaka (Luganda) born on New Year's Eve.

Mwamba (Nyakusa) strong.

Mwanje (Luganda) leopard.

Mwinyi (Swahili) king.

Mwita (Swahili) summoner.

Mychajlo (Latvian) a form of Michael.
Mykhaltso, Mykhas

Mychal (American) a form of Michael.
Mychall, Mychalo, Mycheal

Myer (English) a form of Meir.
Myers, Myur

Mykal (American) a form of Michael.
Mykael, Mykel, Mykell

Myles (Latin) soldier. (German) an alternate form of Miles.

Myo (Burmese) city.

Myron (Greek) fragrant ointment.
Mehran, Mehrayan, My, Myran, Myrone, Ron

Myung-Dae (Korean) right; great.

Mzuzi (Swahili) inventive.

Naaman (Hebrew) pleasant.

Nabiha (Arabic) intelligent.

Nabil (Arabic) noble.
Nabeel, Nabiel

Nachman (Hebrew) a short form of Menachem.
Nachum, Nahum

Nada (Arabic) generous.

Nadav (Hebrew) generous; noble.
Nadiv

Nadidah (Arabic) equal to anyone else.

Nadim (Arabic) friend.
Nadeem

Nadir (Afghani, Arabic) dear, rare.
Nader

Nadisu (Hindi) beautiful river.

Naeem (Arabic) benevolent.
Naim, Naiym, Nieem

Naftali (Hebrew) wreath.
Naftalie

Nagid (Hebrew) ruler, prince.

Nahele (Hawaiian) forest.

Nahma (Native American) sturgeon.

Nailah (Arabic) successful.

Nairn (Scottish) river with alder trees.
Nairne

Naji (Arabic) safe.
Najee

Najíb (Arabic) born to nobility.
Najib, Nejeeb

Najji (Muganda) second child.

Nakos (Arapaho) sage, wise.

Naldo (Spanish) a familiar form of Reginald.

Nalren (Dene) thawed out.

Nam (Vietnamese) scrape off.

Namaka (Hawaiian) eyes.

Namid (Chippewa) star dancer.

Namir (Hebrew) leopard.
Namer

Nandin (Hindi) god; destroyer. Religion: another name for the Hindu god Shiva.

Nando (German) a familiar form of Ferdinand.
Nandor

Nangila (Abaluhya) born while parents traveled.

Nangwaya (Mwera) don't mess with me.

Nansen (Swedish) son of Nancy.

Nantai (Navajo) chief.

Nantan (Apache) spokesman.

Naoko (Japanese) straight, honest.

Napayshni (Lakota) he does not flee; courageous.

Napier (Spanish) new city.
Neper

Napoleon (Greek) lion of the woodland. (Italian) from Naples, Italy. History: Napoleon Bonaparte was a famous nineteenth-century French emperor.
Leon, Nap, Napoléon, Napoleone, Nappie, Nappy

Narain (Hindi) protector. Religion: another name for the Hindu god Vishnu.
Narayan

Narcisse (French) a form of Narcissus.
Narkis, Narkissos

Narcissus (Greek) daffodil. Mythology: the youth who fell in love with his own reflection.
Narcisse

Nard (Persian) chess player.

Nardo (German) strong, hardy. (Spanish) a short form of Bernardo.

Narve (Dutch) healthy, strong.

Nashashuk (Fox, Sauk) loud thunder.

Nashoba (Choctaw) wolf.

Nasim (Persian) breeze, fresh air.
Naseem

Nasser (Arabic) victorious.
Naseer, Nasir, Nassor

Nat (English) a short form of Nathan, Nathaniel.
Natt, Natty

Natal (Spanish) a form of Noël.
Natale, Natalino, Natalio, Nataly

Natan (Hebrew, Hungarian, Polish, Russian, Spanish) God has given.
Nataneal, Nataniel

Nate (Hebrew) a short form of Nathan, Nathaniel.

Natesh (Hindi) destroyer. Religion: another name for the Hindu god Shiva.

Nathan (Hebrew) a short form of Nathaniel. Bible: an Old Testament prophet who saved Solomon's kingdom.
Naethan, Nat, Nate, Nathann, Nathean, Nathen, Nathian, Nathin, Nathon, Natthan, Naythan

Nathanael (Hebrew) an alternate form of Nathaniel.
Nathanae

Nathanial (Hebrew) an alternate form of Nathaniel.

Nathanie (Hebrew) a familiar form of Nathaniel.
Nathania, Nathanni

Nathaniel (Hebrew) gift of God. Bible: one of the Twelve Apostles.
Nat, Natanael, Nataniel, Nate, Nathan, Nathanael, Nathanal, Nathaneal, Nathaneil, Nathanel, Nathaneol, Nathanial, Nathanie, Nathanielle, Nathanuel, Nathanyal, Nathanyel, Natheal, Nathel, Nathinel, Nethaniel, Thaniel

Nathen (Hebrew) an alternate form of Nathan.

Nav (Gypsy) name.

Navarro (Spanish) plains.
Navarre

Navin (Hindi) new, novel.

Nawat (Native American) left-handed.

Nawkaw (Winnebago) wood.

Nayati (Native American) wrestler.

Nayland (English) island dweller.

Nazareth (Hebrew) born in Nazareth, Israel.
Nazaire, Nazaret, Nazarie, Nazario

Nazih (Arabic) pure, chaste.
Nazim, Nazir, Nazz

Ndale (Ngoni) trick.

Neal (Irish) an alternate form of Neil.
Neale, Neall, Nealle, Nealon, Nealy

Neci (Latin) a familiar form of Ignatius.

Nectarios (Greek) saint. Religion: a recent saint in the Greek Orthodox church.

Ned (English) a familiar form of Edward.
Neddie, Neddym, Nedrick

Nehemiah (Hebrew)
compassion of Jehovah.
Bible: a Hebrew prophet.
**Nahemiah, Nechemya,
Nehemias, Nehmiah,
Nemo, Neyamia**

Nehru (Hindi) canal.

Neil (Irish) champion.
**Neal, Neel, Neihl, Neile,
Neill, Neille, Nels, Nial,
Niall, Nialle, Niele, Niels,
Nigel, Nil, Niles, Nilo, Nils,
Nyle**

Neka (Native American)
wild goose.

Nelek (Polish) a form
of Cornelius.

Nellie (English) a familiar
form of Cornell, Nelson.
Nell, Nelly

Nelius (Latin) a short form
of Cornelius.

Nelo (Spanish) a form
of Daniel.
Nello

Nels (Scandinavian) a form
of Neil, Nelson.
Nelse, Nelson, Nils

Nelson (English) son
of Neil.
**Nealson, Neilson, Nellie,
Nels, Nelsen, Nilson,
Nilsson**

Nemesio (Spanish) just.
Nemi

Nemo (Greek) glen, glade.
(Hebrew) a short form
of Nehemiah.

Nen (Egyptian) ancient
waters.

Neptune (Latin) sea ruler.
Mythology: the Roman
god of the sea.

Nero (Latin, Spanish) stern.
Neron, Nerone, Nerron

Nesbit (English) nose-
shaped bend in a river.
**Naisbit, Naisbitt, Nesbitt,
Nisbet, Nisbett**

Nestor (Greek) traveler;
wise.
Nester

Nethaniel (Hebrew)
an alternate form
of Nathaniel.
**Netanel, Netania,
Netaniah, Netanya,
Nethanel, Nethanial,
Nethaniel, Nethanyal**

Neto (Spanish) a short form
of Ernesto.

Nevada (Spanish) covered
in snow. Geography:
a U.S. state.
Navada

Nevan (Irish) holy.

Neville (French) new town.
**Nev, Nevil, Nevile, Nevill,
Nevyle**

Nevin (Irish) worshiper of
the saint. (English) middle;
herb.

Nefen, Nev, Nevan, Neven, Nevins, Niven

Newbold (English) new tree.

Newell (English) new hall.
Newall, Newel, Newyle

Newland (English) new land.
Newlan

Newlin (Welsh) new lake.
Newlyn

Newman (English) newcomer.

Newton (English) new town.

Ngai (Vietnamese) herb.

Nghia (Vietnamese) forever.

Ngozi (Ibo) blessing.

Ngu (Vietnamese) sleep.
Nguyen

Nhean (Cambodian) self-knowledge.

Niall (Irish) an alternate form of Neil. History: Niall of the Nine Hostages was a famous Irish ruler who founded the clan O'Neill.
Nial

Nibal (Arabic) arrows.

Nibaw (Native American) standing tall.

Nicabar (Gypsy) stealthly.

Nicho (Spanish) a form of Dennis.

Nicholas (Greek) victorious people. Religion: the patron saint of children. See also Caelan, Claus, Cola, Colar, Cole, Colin, Colson, Klaus, Lasse, Mikolaj, Mikolas, Milek.
Niccolas, Nichalas, Nichelas, Nichele, Nichlas, Nichlos, Nichola, Nichole, Nicholl, Nichols, Nick, Nicklaus, Nickolas, Nicky, Niclas, Niclasse, Nicolai, Nicolas, Nicoles, Nicolis, Nicoll, Nicolo, Nikhil, Nikili, Nikita, Niklas, Nikolas, Nikolos, Nils, Nioclás, Niocol, Nycholas

Nichols, Nicholson (English) son of Nicholas.
Nicolls, Nickelson, Nickoles

Nick (English) a short form of Dominic, Nicholas. See also Micu.
Nic, Nik

Nicklaus (Greek) an alternate form of Nicholas.
Nicklas, Nickolau, Nickolaus, Nicolaus, Niklaus, Nikolaus

Nickolas (Greek) an alternate form of Nicholas.
Nickolaos, Nickolus

Nicky (Greek) a familiar form of Nicholas.
Nickey, Nickie, Niki, Nikki

Nicodemus (Greek)
conqueror of the people.
Nicodem, Nikodema

Nicolai (Norwegian,
Russian) a form of
Nicholas.
**Nicolaj, Nicolau, Nicolay,
Nicoly**

Nicolas (Italian) a form
of Nicholas.
**Nico, Nicola, Nicolaas,
Nicolás**

Nicolo (Italian) a form
of Nicholas.
**Niccolo, Niccolò, Nicol,
Nicolao**

Niels (Danish) a form
of Neil.
**Niel, Nielsen, Nielson,
Niles, Nils**

Nien (Vietnamese) year.

Nigan (Native American)
ahead.
Nigen

Nigel (Latin) dark night.
**Niegel, Nigal, Nigiel, Nigil,
Nigle, Nijel, Nye, Nygel**

Nika (Yoruba) ferocious.

Nike (Greek) victorious.

Niki (Hungarian) a familiar
form of Nicholas.
**Nikia, Nikiah, Nikki,
Nikko, Niko**

Nikita (Russian) a form
of Nicholas.
Nakita, Nakitas, Nikula

Nikiti (Native American)
round and smooth like
an abalone shell.

Niklas (Latvian, Swedish)
a form of Nicholas.
Niklaas

Nikolai (Estonian, Russian)
a form of Nicholas.
**Kolya, Nikolais, Nikolajs,
Nikolah, Nikolay, Nikoli,
Nikolia, Nikula, Nikulas**

Nikolas (Greek) an alter-
nate form on Nicholas.
**Nicanor, Nikalus, Nikola,
Nikolaas, Nikolao,
Nikolaos, Nikolis, Nikolos,
Nikos, Nilos, Nykolas**

Nikolos (Greek) an alter-
nate form of Nicholas.
See also Kolya.
**Niklos, Nikolaos, Nikolò,
Nikolous, Nikos, Nilos**

Nil (Russian) a form of Neil.
Nilya

Nila (Hindi) blue.

Niles (English) son of Neil.
Nilesh

Nilo (Finnish) a form
of Neil.

Nils (Swedish) a short
form of Nicholas.

Nimrod (Hebrew) rebel.
Bible: a great-grandson
of Noah.

Niño (Spanish) young child.

Niran (Thai) eternal.

Nishan (Armenian) cross, sign, mark.

Nissan (Hebrew) sign, omen; miracle.
Nisan, Nissim

Nitis (Native American) friend.
Netis

Nixon (English) son of Nick.
Nixson

Nizam (Arabic) leader.

Nkunda (Runyankore) loves those who hate him.

N'namdi (Ibo) his father's name lives on.

Noach (Hebrew) an alternate form of Noah.

Noah (Hebrew) peaceful, restful. Bible: the patriarch who built the ark to survive the Great Flood.
Noach, Noak, Noe, Noé, Noi

Noam (Hebrew) sweet; friend.

Noble (Latin) born to nobility.
Nobe, Nobie, Noby

Nodin (Native American) wind.
Knoton, Noton

Noe (Czech, French) a form of Noah.

Noé (Hebrew, Spanish) quiet, peaceful.

Noël (French) day of Christ's birth. See also Natal.
Noel, Noél, Nole, Noli, Nowel, Nowell

Nohea (Hawaiian) handsome.

Nokonyu (Native American) katydid's nose.
Noko, Nokoni

Nolan (Irish) famous; noble.
Noland, Nolen, Nolin, Nollan, Nolyn

Nollie (Latin, Scandinavian) a familiar form of Oliver.
Noll, Nolly

Norbert (Scandinavian) brilliant hero.
Bert, Norberto, Norbie, Norby

Norman (French) norseman. History: a name for the Scandinavians who conquered Normandy in the tenth century, and who later conquered England in 1066.
Norm, Normand, Normen, Normie, Normy

Norris (French) northerner. (English) Norman's horse.
Norice, Norie, Noris, Norreys, Norrie, Norry, Norrys

Northcliff (English) northern cliff.
Northcliffe, Northclyff, Northclyffe

Northrop (English) north farm.
North, Northup

Norton (English) northern town.

Norville (French, English) northern town.
Norval, Norvel, Norvell, Norvil, Norvill, Norvylle

Norvin (English) northern friend.
Norvyn, Norwin, Norwinn, Norwyn, Norwynn

Norward (English) protector of the north.
Norwerd

Norwood (English) northern woods.

Notaku (Moquelumnan) growing bear.

Nowles (English) a short form of Knowles.

Nsoah (Akan) seventh-born.

Numa (Arabic) pleasant.

Numair (Arabic) panther.

Nuncio (Italian) messenger.
Nunzio

Nuri (Hebrew, Arabic) my fire.
Nery, Noori, Nur, Nuris, Nurism, Nury

Nuriel (Hebrew, Arabic) fire of the Lord.
Nuria, Nuriah, Nuriya

Nuru (Swahili) born in daylight.

Nusair (Arabic) bird of prey.

Nwa (Nigerian) son.

Nwake (Nigerian) born on market day.

Nye (English) a familiar form of Aneurin, Nigel.

Nyle (Irish) an alternate form of Neil. (English) island.

Oakes (English) oak trees.
Oak, Oakie, Oaks, Ochs

Oakley (English) oak-tree field.
Oak, Oakes, Oakie, Oaklee, Oakleigh, Oakly, Oaks

Oalo (Spanish) a form of Paul.

Oba (Yoruba) king.

Obadele (Yoruba) king arrives at the house.

Obadiah (Hebrew) servant of God.
Obadias, Obed, Obediah, Obie, Ovadiach, Ovadiah, Ovadya

Obed (English) a short form of Obadiah.

Oberon (German) noble; bearlike. Literature: the king of the fairies in the Shakespearean play *A Midsummer Night's Dream*. See also Auberon, Aubrey.
Oberron, Oeberon

Obert (German) wealthy; bright.

Obie (English) a familiar form of Obadiah.
Obbie, Obe, Oby

Ocan (Luo) hard times.

Octavio (Latin) eighth. See also Tavey.
Octave, Octavian, Octavien, Octavious, Octavis, Octavius, Octavo, Octavous, Octavus, Ottavio

Odakota (Lakota) friendly.
Oda

Odd (Norwegian) point.
Oddvar

Ode (Benin) born along the road. (Irish, English) a short form of Odell.
Odey, Odie, Ody

Oded (Hebrew) encouraging.

Odell (Greek) ode, melody. (Irish) otter. (English) forested hill.
Dell, Odall, Ode

Odin (Scandinavian) ruler. Mythology: the chief Norse god.

Odion (Benin) first of twins.

Odo (Norwegian) a form of Otto.

Odolf (German) prosperous wolf.
Odolff

Odom (Ghanian) oak tree.

Ödön (Hungarian) wealthy protector.
Odi

Odran (Irish) pale green.
Odhrán, Oran, Oren, Orin, Orran, Orren, Orrin

Odysseus (Greek) wrathful. Literature: the hero of Homer's epic *The Odyssey*.

Ofer (Hebrew) young deer.

Og (Aramaic) king. Bible: the king of Basham.

Ogaleesha (Lakota) red shirt.

Ogbay (Ethiopian) don't take him from me.

Ogbonna (Ibo) image of his father.

Ogden (English) oak valley. Literature: Ogden Nash was a twentieth-century American writer.
Ogdan, Ogdon

Ogima (Chippewa) chief.

Ogun (Nigerian) Mythology: the god of war.
Ogunkeye, Ogunsanwo, Ogunsheye

Ohanko (Native American) restless.

Ohannes (Turkish) a form of John.

Ohanzee (Lakota) comforting shadow.

Ohin (African) chief.
Ohan

Ohitekah (Lakota) brave.

Oistin (Irish) a form of Austin.
Osten, Ostyn, Ostynn

OJ (American) a combination of the initials O. + J.
O.J., Ojay

Ojo (Yoruba) difficult delivery.

Okapi (Swahili) giraffe-like animal with a long neck.

Oke (Hawaiian) a form of Oscar.

Okechuku (Ibo) God's gift.

Okeke (Ibo) born on market day.

Okie (American) from Oklahoma.
Okee

Oko (Ga) older twin. (Yoruba) god of war.

Okorie (Ibo) an alternate form of Okeke.

Okpara (Ibo) first son.

Okuth (Luo) born in a rain shower.

Ola (Yoruba) wealthy, rich.

Olaf (Scandinavian) ancestor. History: a patron saint and king of Norway.
Olaff, Olafur, Olav, Ole, Olef, Olof, Oluf

Olajuwon (Yoruba) wealth and honor are God's gifts.
Olajuan, Olajuwan, Oljuwoun

Olamina (Yoruba) this is my wealth.

Olatunji (Yoruba) honor reawakens.

Olav (Scandinavian) an alternate form of Olaf.
Ola, Olave, Olavus, Ole, Olen, Olin, Olle, Olov, Olyn

Ole (Scandinavian) a familiar form of Olaf, Olav.
Olay, Oleh, Olle

Oleg (Latvian, Russian) holy.
Olezka

Oleksandr (Russian) a form of Alexander.
Olek, Olesandr, Olesko

Olés (Polish) a familiar form of Alexander.

Olin (English) holly.
Olen, Olney, Olyn

Olindo (Italian) from Olinthos, Italy.

Oliver (Latin) olive tree. (Scandinavian) kind; affectionate.
Nollie, Oilibhéar, Oliverio, Oliverios, Olivero, Olivier, Oliviero, Oliwa, Ollie, Olliver, Ollivor, Olvan

Olivier (French) a form of Oliver.

Oliwa (Hawaiian) a form of Oliver.

Ollie (English) a familiar form of Oliver.
Olie, Olle, Olley, Olly

Olo (Spanish) a short form of Orlando, Rolando.

Olubayo (Yoruba) highest joy.

Olufemi (Yoruba) wealth and honor favors me.

Olujimi (Yoruba) God gave me this.

Olushola (Yoruba) God has blessed me.

Omar (Arabic) highest; follower of the Prophet. (Hebrew) reverent.
Omair, Omari, Omarr, Omer, Umar

Omari (Swahili) a form of Omar.

Omolara (Benin) child born at the right time.

On (Burmese) coconut. (Chinese) peace.

Onan (Turkish) prosperous.

Onaona (Hawaiian) pleasant fragrance.

Ondro (Czech) a form of Andrew.
Ondre

O'neil (Irish) son of Neil.
Oneal, O'neal, Oneil, Onel, Oniel, Onil

Onkar (Hindi) pure being. Religion: another name for the Hindu god Shiva.

Onslow (English) enthusiast's hill.
Ounslow

Onofrio (German) an alternate form of Humphrey.
Oinfre, Onfre, Onfrio, Onofredo

Onufry (Polish) a form of Humphrey.

Onur (Turkish) honor.

Ophir (Hebrew) faithful. Bible: an Old Testament character.

Opio (Ateso) first of twin boys.

Oral (Latin) verbal, speaker.

Oran (Irish) green.
Odhran, Odran, Ora,
Orane, Orran

Oratio (Latin) an alternate
form of Horatio.
Orazio

Orbán (Hungarian) born
in the city.

Ordell (Latin) beginning.
Orde

Oren (Hebrew) pine tree.
(Irish) light skinned, white.
Oran, Orin, Oris, Orren,
Orrin

Orestes (Greek) mountain
man. Mythology: the son
of the Greek leader
Agamemnon.
Aresty, Oreste

Ori (Hebrew) my light.

Orien (Latin) visitor from
the east.
Orie, Orin, Oris, Oron,
Orono, Orrin

Orion (Greek) son of fire.
Mythology: a hunter who
became a constellation.
See also Zorion.

Orji (Ibo) mighty tree.

Orlando (German)
famous throughout the
land. (Spanish) a form
of Roland.
Lando, Olando, Olo,
Orlan, Orland, Orlanda,

Orlandus, Orlo, Orlondo,
Orlondon

Orleans (Latin) golden.
Orlin

Orman (German) mariner,
seaman. (Scandinavian)
serpent, worm.
Ormand

Ormond (English) bear
mountain; spear protector.
Ormon, Ormonde

Oro (Spanish) golden.

Orono (Latin) a form
of Oren.
Oron

Orrick (English) old oak
tree.
Orric

Orrin (English) river.
Geography: a river in
England.
Orin

Orris (Latin) an alternate
form of Horatio.
Oris, Orriss

Orry (Latin) from the
Orient.
Oarrie, Orrey, Orrie

Orsino (Italian) a form
of Orson.

Orson (Latin) bearlike.
Orscino, Orsen, Orsin,
Orsini, Orsino, Son, Sonny,
Urson

Orton (English) shore
town.

Ortzi (Basque) sky.

Orunjan (Yoruba) born under the midday sun.

Orval (English) an alternate form of Orville.

Orville (French) golden village. History: Orville Wright and his brother Wilbur were the first men to fly an airplane.
Orv, Orval, Orvell, Orvie, Orvil

Orvin (English) spear friend.
Orwin, Owynn

Osahar (Benin) God hears.

Osayaba (Benin) God forgives.

Osaze (Benin) whom God likes.

Osbert (English) divine; bright.

Osborn (Scandinavian) divine bear. (English) warrior of God.
Osbern, Osbon, Osborne, Osbourn, Osbourne, Osburn, Osburne, Oz, Ozzie

Oscar (Scandinavian) divine spearman.
Oke, Oskar, Osker, Oszkar

Osei (Fanti) noble.
Osee

Osgood (English) divinely good.

O'Shea (Irish) son of Shea.
Oshai, O'Shane, Oshaun, Oshay, Oshea

Osip (Russian, Ukrainian) a form of Joseph.

Oskar (Scandinavian) an alternate form of Oscar.
Osker, Ozker

Osman (Turkish) ruler. (English) servant of God.
Osmanek, Osmen, Otthmor, Ottmar

Osmar (English) divine; wonderful.

Osmond (English) divine protector.
Osmand, Osmonde, Osmont, Osmund, Osmunde, Osmundo

Osric (English) divine ruler.
Osrick

Ostin (Latin) an alternate form of Austin.
Osten, Ostyn

Osvaldo (Spanish) a form of Oswald.
Osvald, Osvalda

Oswald (English) God's power; God's crest. See also Waldo.
Osvaldo, Oswaldo, Oswall, Oswell, Oswold, Oz, Ozzie

Oswin (English) divine friend.
Osvin, Oswinn, Oswyn, Oswynn

Osya (Russian) a familiar form of Osip.

Ota (Czech) prosperous.
Otik

Otadan (Native American) plentiful.

Otaktay (Lakota) kills many; strikes many.

Otek (Polish) a form of Otto.

Otello (Italian) a form of Othello.

Otem (Luo) born away from home.

Othman (German) wealthy.

Othello (Spanish) a form of Otto. Literature: the title character in the Shakespearean tragedy *Othello*.
Otello

Otis (Greek) keen of hearing. (German) son of Otto.
Oates, Odis, Otes, Otess, Ottis, Otys

Ottah (Nigerian) thin baby.

Ottar (Norwegian) point warrior; fright warrior.

Ottmar (Turkish) an alternate form of Osman. History: the founder of the Ottoman Empire.
Otomars, Ottomar

Otto (German) rich.
Odo, Otek, Otello,
Otfried, Othello, Otho,
Othon, Otik, Otilio,
Otman, Oto, Otón,
Otton, Ottone

Ottokar (German) happy warrior.
Otokars, Ottocar

Otu (Native American) collecting seashells in a basket.

Ouray (Native American) arrow. Astrology: born under the sign of Sagittarius.

Oved (Hebrew) worshiper, follower.

Owen (Irish) born to nobility; young warrior. (Welsh) a form of Evan.
Owain, Owens, Owin,
Uaine

Owney (Irish) elderly.
Oney

Oxford (English) place where oxen cross the river.
Ford

Oya (Moquelumnan) speaking of the jacksnipe.

Oystein (Norwegian) rock of happiness.
Ostein, Osten, Ostin,
Øystein

Oz (Hebrew) a short form of Osborn, Oswald.

Ozturk (Turkish) pure; genuine Turk.

Ozzie (English) a familiar form of Osborn, Oswald.
Ossie, Ossy, Ozi, Ozzi, Ozzy

Paavo (Finnish) a form of Paul.
Paaveli

Pablo (Spanish) a form of Paul.
Pable, Paublo

Pace (English) a form of Pascal.
Payce

Pacifico (Filipino) peaceful.

Paco (Italian) pack. (Spanish) a familiar form of Francisco. (Native American) bald eagle. See also Quico.
Pacorro, Panchito, Pancho, Paquito

Paddy (Irish) a familiar form of Padraic, Patrick.
Paddey, Paddie

Padget (English) a form of Page.
Padgett, Paget, Pagett

Padraic (Irish) a form of Patrick.
Paddrick, Paddy, Padhraig, Padrai, Pádraig, Padriac, Padric, Padron, Padruig

Page (French) youthful assistant.
Padget, Paggio, Paige, Payge

Paige (English) a form of Page.

Pakelika (Hawaiian) a form of Patrick.

Paki (African) witness.

Pal (Swedish) a form of Paul.

Pál (Hungarian) a form of Paul.
Pali, Palika

Palaina (Hawaiian) a form of Brian.

Palani (Hawaiian) a form of Frank.

Palash (Hindi) flowery tree.

Palben (Basque) blond.

Palladin (Native American) fighter.
Pallaton, Palleten

Palmer (English) palm-bearing pilgrim.
Pallmer, Palmar

Palti (Hebrew) God liberates.
Palti-el

Panas (Russian) immortal.

Panayiotis (Greek) an alternate form of Peter.

Panayiotis *(cont.)*
**Panagiotis, Panayioti,
Panayoti**

Pancho (Spanish) a familiar
form of Francisco, Frank.
Panchito

Panos (Greek) an alternate
form of Peter.
Petros

Paolo (Italian) a form
of Paul.

Paquito (Spanish) a familiar form of Paco.

Paramesh (Hindi) greatest.
Religion: another name for
the Hindu god Shiva.

Paris (Greek) lover.
Geography: the capital
of France. Mythology:
the prince of Troy who
started the Trojan War
by abducting Helen.
Paras, Paree, Parris

Park (Chinese) cypress tree.
(English) a short form of
Parker.
Parke, Parkes, Parkey

Parker (English) park
keeper.
Park

Parkin (English) little Peter.
Perkin

Parlan (Scottish) a form
of Bartholomew.

Parnell (French) little Peter.
History: Charles Stewart
Parnell was a famous Irish
politician.
**Nell, Parle, Parnel,
Parrnell, Pernell**

Parr (English) cattle enclosure, barn.

Parrish (English) church
district.
Parish, Parrie, Parrisch

Parry (Welsh) son of Harry.
Parrey, Parrie, Pary

Parthalán (Irish)
plow-man.
Parlan

Parthenios (Greek)
virgin. Religion: a Greek
Orthodox saint.

Pascal (French) born
on Easter or Passover.
**Pace, Pascale, Pascalle,
Paschal, Paschalis, Pascoe,
Pascow, Pascual, Pasquale**

Pascual (Spanish) a form
of Pascal.

Pasha (Russian) a form
of Paul.
Pashenka, Pashka

Pasquale (Italian) a form
of Pascal.
Pascuale, Pasquel

Pastor (Latin) spiritual
leader.

Pat (English) a short
form of Patrick. (Native
American) fish.
Pattie, Patty

Patakusu (Moquelumnan) ant biting a person.

Patamon (Native American) raging.

Patek (Polish) a form of Patrick.

Patrice (French) a form of Patrick.

Patricio (Spanish) a form of Patrick.
Patricius, Patrizio

Patrick (Latin) nobleman. Religion: the patron saint of Ireland. See also Fitzpatrick, Ticho.
Paddy, Padraic, Pakelika, Pat, Patek, Paton, Patric, Patrice, Patricio, Patrik, Patrique, Patrizius, Patryck, Patryk, Pats, Patsy

Patrin (Gypsy) leaf trail.

Patterson (Irish) son of Pat.
Patteson

Pattin (Gypsy) leaf.

Patton (English) warrior's town.
Paten, Patin, Paton, Patten, Pattin, Patty, Payton, Peyton

Patwin (Native American) man.

Patxi (Basque, Teutonic) free.

Paul (Latin) small. Bible: Saul, later renamed Paul, was the first to bring the teachings of Christ to the Gentiles.
Oalo, Paavo, Pablo, Pal, Pál, Pall, Paolo, Pasha, Pasko, Pauli, Paulia, Paulin, Paulino, Paulis, Paulo, Pauls, Paulus, Pavel, Pavlos, Pawel, Pol

Pauli (Latin) a familiar form of Paul.
Pauley, Paulie, Pauly

Paulin (German, Polish) a form of Paul.

Paulino (Spanish) a form of Paul.

Paulo (Portuguese, Swedish, Hawaiian) a form of Paul.

Pavel (Russian) a form of Paul.
Paavel, Pasha, Pavils, Pavlik, Pavlo, Pavlusha, Pavlushenka, Pawl

Pavit (Hindi) pious, pure.

Pawel (Polish) a form of Paul.
Pawelek, Pawl

Pax (Latin) peaceful.
Paz

Paxton (Latin) peaceful town.
Packston, Pax, Paxon, Paxten, Paxtun

Payat (Native American) he is on his way.
Pay, Payatt

Payne (Latin) man from the country.
Paine

Paytah (Lakota) fire.
Pay, Payta

Payton (English) an alternate form of Patton.
Paiton, Pate, Payden, Paydon, Peyton

Paz (Spanish) a form of Pax.

Pearson (English) son of Peter.
Pearsson, Pehrson, Peterson, Pierson, Piersson

Peder (Scandinavian) a form of Peter.
Peadar, Pedey

Pedro (Spanish) a form of Peter.
Pedrin, Pedrín, Petronio

Peers (English) a form of Peter.
Peerus, Piers

Peeter (Estonian) a form of Peter.
Peet

Peirce (English) a form of Peter.
Pearce, Pearse, Peirs

Pekelo (Hawaiian) a form of Peter.
Pekka

Peleke (Hawaiian) a form of Frederick.

Pelham (English) tannery town.

Pelí (Latin, Basque) happy.

Pell (English) parchment.
Pall

Pello (Greek, Basque) stone.
Peru, Piarres

Pelton (English) town by a pool.

Pembroke (Welsh) headland. (French) wine dealer. (English) broken fence.
Pembrook

Peniamina (Hawaiian) a form of Benjamin.
Peni

Penley (English) enclosed meadow.

Penn (Latin) pen, quill. (German) a short form of Penrod. (English) enclosure.
Pen, Penna, Penney, Pennie, Penny

Penrod (German) famous commander.
Penn, Pennrod, Rod

Pepa (Czech) a familiar form of Joseph.
Pepek, Pepik

Pepe (Spanish) a familiar form of José.
Pepillo, Pepito, Pequin, Pipo

Pepin (German)
determined; petitioner.
History: Pepin the short,
an eighth-century king of
the Franks, was the father
of Charlemagne.
Pepi, Peppie, Peppy

Peppe (Italian) a familiar
form of Joseph.
Peppi, Peppo, Pino

Per (Swedish) a form
of Peter.

Perben (Greek, Danish)
stone.

Percival (French) pierce
the valley; pierce the
veil of religion mystery.
Literature: a name
invented by Chrétien
de Troyes for the
knight-hero of his epic
about the Holy Grail.
**Parsafal, Parsefal,
Parsifal, Parzival, Perc,
Perce, Perceval, Percevall,
Percivall, Percy, Peredur,
Purcell**

Percy (French) a familiar
form of Percival.
**Pearcey, Pearcy, Percey,
Percie, Piercey, Piercy**

Peregrine (Latin) traveler;
pilgrim; falcon.
**Peregrin, Peregryne,
Perine, Perry**

Pericles (Greek) just leader.
History: an Athenian
statesman and general.

Perico (Spanish) a form
of Peter.
Pequin, Perequin

Perine (Latin) a short form
of Peregrine.
Perino, Perrin, Perryn

Perkin (English) little Peter.
**Perka, Perkins, Perkyn,
Perrin**

Perry (English) a familiar
form of Peregrine, Peter.
Parry, Perrie

Perth (Scottish) thornbush
thicket. Geography:
a county in Scotland;
a city in Australia.

Pervis (Latin) passage.

Pesach (Hebrew) spared.
Religion: another name
for the Jewish holiday
Passover.
Pessach

Pete (English) a short
form of Peter.
**Peat, Peet, Petey, Peti,
Petie, Piet, Pit**

Peter (Greek, Latin) small
rock. Bible: Simon,
renamed Peter, was
the leader of the Twelve
Apostles. See also Boutros,
Ferris, Takis.
**Panayiotos, Panos,
Peadair, Peder, Pedro,
Peers, Peeter, Peirce,
Pekelo, Per, Perico,
Perion, Perkin, Perren,
Perry, Petar, Pete, Péter,**

Peter *(cont.)*
**Peteris, Peterke, Peterus,
Petr, Petras, Petros,
Petru, Petruno, Petter,
Peyo, Piaras, Pierce, Piero,
Pierre, Pieter, Pietrek,
Pietro, Piotr, Piter, Piti,
Pjeter, Pyotr**

Petiri (Shona) where
we are.
Petri

Petr (Bulgarian) a form
of Peter.

Petras (Lithuanian) a form
of Peter.
Petrelis

Petros (Greek) an alternate
form of Peter.
Petro

Petru (Romanian) a form
of Peter.
Petrukas, Petrus, Petruso

Petter (Norwegian) a form
of Peter.

Peverell (French) piper.
Peverall, Peverel, Peveril

Peyo (Spanish) a form
of Peter.

Peyton (English) an alter-
nate form of Patton,
Payton.
Peyt

Pharaoh (Latin) ruler.
History: a title for the
ancient rulers of Egypt.
**Faroh, Pharo, Pharoah,
Pharoh**

Phelan (Irish) wolf.

Phelipe (Spanish) a form
of Philip.

Phelix (Latin) an alternate
form of Felix.

Phelps (English) son
of Phillip.

Phil (Greek) a short form
of Philip, Phillip.
Fil, Phill

Philander (Greek) lover
of mankind.

Philbert (English) an alternate form of Filbert.
Philibert, Phillbert

Philemon (Greek) kiss.
Phila, Philamina, Philmon

Philip (Greek) lover of
horses. Bible: one of the
Twelve Apostles. See also
Felipe, Felippo, Fillipp,
Filya, Fischel, Flip.
**Phelps, Phelipe, Phil,
Philipp, Philippe,
Philippo, Phillip, Phillipos,
Phillp, Philly, Phlip, Piers,
Pilib, Pilipo, Pippo**

Philipp (German) a form
of Philip.

Philippe (French) a form
of Philip.
Philipe, Phillepe

Phillip (Greek) an alternate
form of Philip.
**Phil, Phillipos, Phillipp,
Phillips, Philly**

Phillipos (Greek) an alternate form of Phillip.

Philly (American) a familiar form of Philip, Phillip.
Phillie

Philo (Greek) love.

Phinean (Irish) an alternate form of Finian.
Phinian

Phineas (English) a form of Pinchas.
Fineas, Phinehas, Phinny

Phirun (Cambodian) rain.

Phuok (Vietnamese) good.
Phuoc

Pias (Gypsy) fun.

Pickford (English) ford at the peak.

Pickworth (English) woodcutter's estate.

Pierce (English) a form of Peter.
Pearce, Pears, Pearson, Pearsson, Peerce, Peers, Peirce, Piercy, Piers, Pierson, Piersson

Piero (Italian) a form of Peter.
Pero, Pierro

Pierre (French) a form of Peter.
Peirre, Piere, Pierrot

Pierre-Luc (French) a combination of Pierre + Luc.

Piers (English) a form of Philip.

Pieter (Dutch) a form of Peter.
Pietr

Pietro (Italian) a form of Peter.

Pilar (Spanish) pillar.

Pili (Swahili) second born.

Pilipo (Hawaiian) a form of Philip.

Pillan (Native American) supreme essence.
Pilan

Pin (Vietnamese) faithful boy.

Pinchas (Hebrew) oracle. (Egyptian) dark skinned.
Phineas, Pincas, Pinchos, Pincus, Pinkas, Pinkus, Pinky

Pinky (American) a familiar form of Pinchas.
Pink

Pino (Italian) a form of Joseph.

Piñon (Tupi-Guarani) Mythology: the hunter who became the constellation Orion.

Pio (Latin) pious.

Piotr (Bulgarian) a form of Peter.
Piotrek

Pippin (German) father.

Piran (Irish) prayer.
Religion: the patron
saint of miners.
Peran, Pieran

Pirro (Greek, Spanish)
flaming hair.

Pista (Hungarian) a familiar
form of István.
Pisti

Piti (Spanish) a form
of Peter.

Pitin (Spanish) a form
of Felix.
Pito

Pitney (English) island of
the strong-willed man.
Pittney

Pitt (English) pit, ditch.

Placido (Spanish) serene.
Placidus, Placyd, Placydo

Plato (Greek) broad shoul-
dered. History: a famous
Greek philosopher.
Platon

Platt (French) flat land.
Platte

Pol (Swedish) a form
of Paul.
Pól, Pola, Poul

Poldi (German) a familiar
form of Leopold.
Poldo

Pollard (German) close-
cropped head.
Poll, Pollerd, Pollyrd

Pollock (English) a form
of Pollux.
Pollack, Polloch

Pollux (Greek) crown.
Astronomy: one of
the twins in the Gemini
constellation.
Pollock

Polo (Greek) a short form
of Apollo. (Tibetan) brave
wanderer. Culture: a game
played on horseback.
History: Marco Polo was
a Venetian explorer who
traveled throughout Asia
in the thirteenth and
fourteenth centuries.

Pomeroy (French) apple
orchard.
Pommeray, Pommeroy

Ponce (Spanish) fifth.
History: Juan Ponce de
León of Spain searched
for the fountain of youth
in Florida.

Pony (Scottish) small horse.
Poni

Porfirio (Greek, Spanish)
purple stone.
Porphirios, Prophyrios

Porter (Latin) gatekeeper.
Port, Portie, Porty

Poshita (Sanskrit)
cherished.

Po Sin (Chinese) grand-
father elephant.

Poul (Danish) a form of Paul.
Poulus

Pov (Gypsy) earth.

Powa (Native American) wealthy.

Powell (English) alert.
Powel

Pramad (Hindi) rejoicing.

Pravat (Thai) history.

Prem (Hindi) love.

Prentice (English) apprentice.
Prent, Prentis, Prentiss, Printiss

Prescott (English) priest's cottage. See also Scott.
Prescot, Prestcot, Prestcott

Presley (English) priest's meadow.
Presleigh, Presly, Presslee, Pressley, Prestley, Priestley, Priestly

Preston (English) priest's estate.
Prestin

Prewitt (French) brave little one.
Preuet, Prewet, Prewett, Prewit, Pruit, Pruitt

Price (Welsh) son of the ardent one.
Brice, Bryce, Pryce

Pricha (Thai) clever.

Primo (Italian) first; premier quality.
Preemo, Premo

Prince (Latin) chief; prince.
Prence, Princeton, Prinz, Prinze

Proctor (Latin) official, administrator.
Prockter, Procter

Prokopios (Greek) declared leader.

Prosper (Latin) fortunate.
Prospero, Próspero

Pryor (Latin) head of the monastery, prior.
Prior, Pry

Pumeet (Sanskrit) pure.

Purdy (Hindi) recluse.

Purvis (French, English) providing food.
Pervis, Purves, Purviss

Putnam (English) dweller by the pond.
Putnem

Pyotr (Russian) a form of Peter.
Petenka, Petinka, Petrusha, Petya, Pyatr

Qabil (Arabic) able.

Qadim (Arabic) ancient.

Qadir (Arabic) powerful.
Qadeer, Quadeer, Quadir

Qamar (Arabic) moon.

Qasim (Arabic) divider.

Qimat (Hindi) valuable.

Quaashie (Ewe) born on Sunday.

Quan (Comanche) a short form of Quanah.

Quanah (Comanche) fragrant.
Quan

Quant (Greek) how much?
Quanta, Quantae, Quantai, Quantay, Quantea, Quantey, Quantez

Qudamah (Arabic) courage.

Quenby (Scandinavian) an alternate form of Quimby.

Quennell (French) small oak.
Quenell, Quennel

Quentin (Latin) fifth. (English) Queen's town.

Qeuntin, Quantin, Quent, Quenten, Quenton, Quientin, Quienton, Quintin, Quinton, Qwentin

Quico (Spanish) a familiar form of many names.
Paco

Quigley (Irish) maternal side.
Quigly

Quillan (Irish) cub.
Quill, Quillen, Quillon

Quimby (Scandinavian) woman's estate.
Quenby, Quinby

Quincy (French) fifth son's estate.
Quincey, Quinn, Quinnsy, Quinsey

Quinlan (Irish) strong; well shaped.
Quindlen, Quinlen, Quinlin, Quinn, Quinnlan

Quinn (Irish) a short form of Quincy, Quinlan, Quinton.

Quintin (Latin) an alternate form of Quentin.

Quinton (Latin) an alternate form of Quentin.
Quinn, Quinneton, Quint, Quintan, Quintann, Quinten, Quintin, Quintus, Quitin, Quiton, Qunton, Qwinton

Quiqui (Spanish) a familiar
form of Enrique.
Quinto, Quiquin

Quitin (Latin) a short form
of Quinton.
Quiten, Quito, Quiton

Quito (Spanish) a short
form of Quinton.

Quon (Chinese) bright.

Raanan (Hebrew) fresh;
luxuriant.

Rabi (Arabic) breeze.
**Rabbi, Rabee, Rabiah,
Rabih**

Race (English) race.
Racel

Racham (Hebrew)
compassionate.
**Rachaman, Rachamim,
Rachim, Rachman,
Rachmiel, Rachum,
Raham, Rahamim**

Rad (English) advisor.
(Slavic) happy.
**Radd, Raddie, Raddy,
Radell, Radey**

Radbert (English) brilliant
advisor.

Radburn (English) red
brook; brook with reeds.
**Radborn, Radborne,
Radbourn, Radbourne,
Radburne**

Radcliff (English) red cliff;
cliff with reeds.
Radcliffe, Radclyffe

Radford (English) red ford;
ford with reeds.

Radley (English) red
meadow; meadow
of reeds.
**Radlea, Radlee, Radleigh,
Radly**

Radman (Slavic) joyful.
Radmen, Radusha

Radnor (English) red shore;
shore with reeds.

Radomil (Slavic) happy
peace.

Radoslaw (Polish) happy
glory.
**Radik, Rado, Radzmir,
Slawek**

Rafael (Spanish) a form of
Raphael. See also Falito.
**Rafaelle, Rafaello,
Rafaelo, Rafal, Rafeal,
Rafeé, Rafel, Rafello,
Raffael, Raffaelo, Raffeal**

Rafaele (Italian) a form
of Raphael.
Raffaele

Rafal (Polish) a form
of Raphael.

Rafe (English) a short form of Rafferty, Ralph.
Raff

Rafer (Irish) a short form of Rafferty.
Raffer

Rafferty (Irish) rich, prosperous.
Rafe, Rafer, Raferty, Raffarty, Raffer

Rafi (Hebrew) a familiar form of Raphael. (Arabic) exalted.
Raffee, Raffi, Raffy

Rafiq (Arabic) friend.
Rafeeq, Rafic, Rafique

Raghib (Arabic) desirous.
Raquib

Raghnall (Irish) wise power.

Ragnar (Norwegian) powerful army.
Ragnor, Rainer, Rainier, Ranieri, Rayner, Raynor, Reinhold

Rago (Hausa) ram.

Raheem (Punjabi) compassionate God.

Rahim (Arabic) merciful.
Raheem, Raheim, Rahiem, Rahiim

Rahman (Arabic) compassionate.
Rahmatt, Rahmet

Rahul (Arabic) traveler.

Raíd (Arabic) leader.

Raiden (Japanese) Mythology: the thunder god.

Raimondo (Italian) a form of Raymond.
Raymondo

Raimund (German) a form of Raymond.
Rajmund

Raimundo (Portuguese, Spanish) a form of Raymond.
Mundo, Raimon, Raimond, Raimonds, Raymundo

Raine (English) lord; wise.
Rain, Raines

Rainer (German) counselor.
Rainar, Rainey, Rainor

Rainey (German) a familiar form of Rainer.
Raine, Rainie, Rainy

Raini (Tupi-Guarani) Religion: the Native American god who created the world.

Rajabu (Swahili) born in the seventh month of the Islamic calendar.

Rajah (Hindi) prince, chief.
Raj, Raja, Rajae

Rajak (Hindi) cleansing.

Rakin (Arabic) respectable.
Rakeen

Raktim (Hindi) bright red.

Raleigh (English) an alternate form of Rawleigh.
Ralegh

Ralph (English) wolf counselor.
Radolphus, Rafe, Ralf, Ralpheal, Ralphel, Ralphie, Ralston, Raoul, Raul, Rolf

Ralphie (English) a familiar form of Ralph.

Ralston (English) Ralph's settlement.

Ram (Hindi) god; godlike. Religion: another name for the Hindu god Shiva. (English) male sheep.
Rami, Ramie, Ramy

Ramadan (Arabic) ninth month of the Arabic year.
Rama

Ramanan (Hindi) god; godlike. Religion: another name for the Hindu god Shiva.
Raman, Ramandeep, Ramanjit, Ramanjot

Ramiro (Portuguese, Spanish) supreme judge.
Rameriz, Rami, Ramirez, Ramos

Ramón (Spanish) a form of Raymond.
Ramon, Remone, Romone

Ramone (Dutch) a form of Raymond.
Ramonte, Remone

Ramsden (English) valley of rams.

Ramsey (English) ram's island.
Ram, Ramsay, Ramsy, Ramzee, Ramzi

Rance (English) a short form of Laurence, Ransom. (American) a familiar form of Laurence.
Rancel, Rancell, Rances, Rancey, Rancie, Rancy, Ransel, Ransell

Rand (English) shield; warrior.
Randy

Randal (English) an alternate form of Randall.
Randale, Randel, Randle

Randall (English) an alternate form of Randolph.
Randal, Randell, Randy

Randolph (English) shield-wolf.
Randall, Randol, Randolf, Randolfo, Randolpho, Randy, Ranolph

Randy (English) a familiar form of Rand, Randall, Randolph.
Randey, Randi, Randie, Ranndy

Ranger (French) forest keeper.
Rainger, Range

Rangle (American) cowboy.
Rangler, Wrangle

Rangsey (Cambodian)
seven kinds of colors.

Rani (Hebrew) my song;
my joy.
Ranen, Ranie, Ranon, Roni

Ranieri (Italian) a form
of Ragnar.
Raneir

Ranjan (Hindi) delighted;
gladdened.

Rankin (English) small
shield.
Randkin

Ransford (English) raven's
ford.

Ransley (English) raven's
field.

Ransom (Latin) redeemer.
(English) son of the shield.
Rance, Ransome, Ranson

Raoul (French) a form of
Ralph, Rudolph.
Raol, Raul, Raúl, Reuel

Raphael (Hebrew) God has
healed. Bible: one of the
archangels. Art: a promi-
nent painter of the Italian
Renaissance. See also
Falito, Rafi.
**Rafael, Rafaele, Rafal,
Raphaél, Raphale,
Raphaello, Rapheal,
Raphel, Raphello, Ray,
Rephael**

Rapier (French) blade-
sharp.

Rashad (Arabic) wise
counselor.
**Raashad, Rachad,
Rachard, Rachaud,
Raeshad, Raishard,
Rashaad, Rashaud,
Rashaude, Rashid,
Rashod, Rashoda,
Rashodd, Rayshod,
Reshad, Rhashad,
Rhashod, Rishad,
Roshad**

Rashawn (American)
a combination of the
prefix Ra + Shawn.
**Rashann, Rashaun,
Rashaw, Rashon, Rashun,
Raushan, Raushawn,
Rhashan, Rhashaun,
Rhashawn**

Rashean (American)
a combination of the
prefix Ra + Sean.
**Rashane, Rasheen,
Rashien, Rashiena**

Rashid (Arabic) an alter-
nate form of Rashad.
**Rasheed, Rasheid,
Rasheyd, Rashida,
Rashidah, Rashied,
Rashieda, Raushaid**

Rashida (Swahili)
righteous.

Rashidi (Swahili) wise
counselor.

Rasmus (Greek, Danish)
a short form of Erasmus.

Raul (French) a form
of Ralph.

Raulas (Lithuanian) a form
of Laurence.

Raulo (Lithuanian) a form
of Laurence.
Raulas

Raven (English) a short
form of Ravenel.
Ravin, Ravon, Ravone

Ravenel (English) raven.
Raven, Ravenell, Revenel

Ravi (Hindi) sun. Religion:
another name for the
Hindu sun god Surya.
Ravee, Ravijot

Ravid (Hebrew) an alternate form of Arvid.

Raviv (Hebrew) rain, dew.

Rawdon (English) rough
hill.

Rawleigh (English) deer
meadow.
Raleigh, Rawley, Rawly

Rawlins (French) a form
of Roland.
Rawlinson, Rawson

Ray (French) kingly, royal.
(English) a short form
of Rayburn, Raymond.
See also Lei.
Rae, Raye

Rayburn (English) deer
brook.
**Burney, Raeborn,
Raeborne, Raebourn, Ray,**

**Raybourn, Raybourne,
Rayburne**

Rayhan (Arabic) favored
by God.

Rayi (Hebrew) my friend,
my companion.

Raymond (English)
mighty; wise protector.
See also Aymon.
**Radmond, Raemond,
Raemondo, Raimondo,
Raimundo, Ramón,
Ramond, Ramonde,
Ramone, Ray, Rayman,
Raymand, Rayment,
Raymon, Raymont,
Raymund, Raymunde,
Reamonn, Redmond**

Raynaldo (Spanish) an
alternate form of Renaldo,
Reynold.
Raynal, Raynald, Raynold

Raynard (French) an alternate form of Renard,
Reynard.

Raynor (Scandinavian)
a form of Ragnar.
**Rainer, Rainor, Ranier,
Ranieri, Raynar, Rayner**

Rayshod (American) a form
of Rashad.
Raychard, Rayshard

Rayshawn (American)
a combination of
Ray + Shawn.
**Rayshaan, Rayshan,
Rayshaun, Raysheen,**

Rayshawn *(cont.)*
Rayshon, Rayshone, Rayshun, Rayshunn

Razi (Aramaic) my secret.
Raz, Raziel, Raziq

Read (English) an alternate form of Reed, Reid.
Raed, Raede, Raeed, Reaad, Reade

Reading (English) son of the red wanderer. Geography: a city in Pennsylvania.
Redding, Reeding, Reiding

Reagan (Irish) little king. History: Ronald Wilson Reagan was the fortieth U.S. president.
Raegan, Regan, Reagen, Reegan, Reegen, Regen

Rebel (American) rebel.
Reb

Red (American) red, redhead.
Redd

Reda (Arabic) satisfied.
Ridha

Redford (English) red river crossing.
Ford, Radford, Reaford, Red, Redd

Redley (English) red meadow; meadow with reeds.
Radley, Redlea, Redleigh, Redly

Redmond (German) protecting counselor. (English) an alternate form of Raymond.
Radmond, Radmund, Reddin, Redmund

Redpath (English) red path.

Reece (Welsh) enthusiastic; stream.
Reese, Reice, Rice

Reed (English) an alternate form of Reid.
Raeed, Read, Reyde

Reese (Welsh) an alternate form of Reece.
Rees, Reis, Rhys, Riess

Reeve (English) steward.
Reave, Reaves, Reeves

Reg (English) a short form of Reginald.

Reggie (English) a familiar form of Reginald.

Reginal (English) a form of Reginald.

Reginald (English) king's advisor. An alternate form of Reynold.
Reg, Reggie, Reggis, Reginal, Reginaldo, Reginale, Reginalt, Reginauld, Reginault, Reginel, Regnauld, Ronald

Regis (Latin) regal.

Rehema (Kiswahili) second-born.

Rei (Japanese) rule, law.

Reid (English) redhead.
Read, Reed, Reide, Ried

Reidar (Norwegian) nest warrior.

Reilly (Irish) an alternate form of Riley.
Reilley, Rielly

Reinhart (German) a form of Reynard.
Rainart, Rainhard, Rainhardt, Rainhart, Reinart, Reinhard, Reinhardt, Renke

Reinhold (Swedish) a form of Ragnar.
Reinold

Reku (Finnish) a form of Richard.

Remi, Rémi (French) alternate forms of Remy.
Remie, Remmie

Remington (English) raven estate.
Rem, Tony

Remus (Latin) speedy, quick. Mythology: Remus and his twin brother Romulus founded Rome.

Remy (French) from Rheims, France.
Ramey, Remee, Remi, Rémi, Remmy

Renaldo (Spanish) a form of Reynold.
Raynaldo, Reinaldo, Reynaldo, Rinaldo

Renard (French) an alternate form of Reynard.
Ranard, Raynard

Renardo (Italian) a form of Reynard.

Renato (Italian) reborn.

Renaud (French) a form of Reynard, Reynold.
Renauld, Renauldo, Renould

Rendor (Hungarian) policeman.

René (French) reborn.
Renat, Renato, Renatus, Renault, Renee, Renny

Renfred (English) lasting peace.

Renfrew (Welsh) raven woods.

Renjiro (Japanese) virtuous.

Renny (Irish) small but strong. (French) a familiar form of René.
Ren, Renn, Renne, Rennie

Reno (American) gambler. Geography: a gambling town in Nevada.
Renos, Rino

Renshaw (English) raven woods.
Renishaw

Renton (English) settlement of the roe deer.

Renzo (Latin) a familiar form of Laurence. (Italian) a short form of Lorenzo.

Reshad (American) a form
of Rashad.
**Reshade, Reshard,
Resharrd, Reshaud,
Reshod**

Reshawn (American)
a combination of the
prefix Re + Shawn.
**Reshaun, Reshaw, Reshon,
Reshun**

Reshean (American)
a combination of the
prefix Re + Sean.
**Reshane, Reshay, Resheen,
Reshey**

Reuben (Hebrew) behold
a son.
**Reuban, Reubin, Reuven,
Rheuben, Rube, Ruben,
Rubey, Rubin, Ruby,
Rueben**

Reuven (Hebrew) an alternate form of Reuben.
Reuvin, Rouvin, Ruvim

Rex (Latin) king.

Rexford (English) king's
ford.

Rexton (English) king's
town.

Rey (Spanish) a short form
of Reynard, Reynaldo,
Reynold.
Reyes

Reyhan (Arabic) favored
by God.
Reyham

Reymundo (Spanish)
a form of Raymond.
**Reimond, Reimonde,
Reimundo, Reymon**

Reynaldo (Spanish) a form
Reynold.
Renaldo

Reynard (French) wise;
bold, courageous.
**Raynard, Reinhard,
Reinhardt, Renard,
Renardo, Renaud,
Rennard, Rey, Reynardo**

Reynold (English) king's
advisor.
**Rainault, Rainhold,
Ranald, Raynald,
Raynaldo, Reinald,
Reinaldo, Reinaldos,
Reinhart, Reinhold,
Reinold, Reinwald,
Renald, Renaldi, Renaldo,
Renauld, Renault, Rey,
Reynald, Reynaldo,
Reynaldos, Reynol,
Reynolds, Rinaldo, Ronald**

Réz (Hungarian) copper;
redhead.
Rezsö

Rhett (Welsh) an alternate
form of Rhys. Literature:
Rhett Butler was the hero
of Margaret Mitchell's
novel *Gone with the Wind.*

Rhodes (Greek) where
roses grow. Geography:
an island off the coast
of Greece.
Rhoads, Rhodas, Rodas

Rhys (Welsh) an alternate
form of Reece.
Rhett, Rice

Rian (Irish) little king.

Ric (Italian, Spanish) a short
form of Rico.
Ricca, Ricci, Ricco

Ricardo (Portuguese,
Spanish) a form of
Richard.
**Racardo, Recard, Ricaldo,
Ricard, Ricardos,
Riccardo, Ricciardo,
Richardo**

Rice (Welsh) an alternate
form of Reece. (English)
rich, noble.

Rich (English) a short
form of Richard.
Ritch

Richard (English) rich and
powerful ruler. See also
Aric, Dick, Juku, Likeke.
**Reku, Ricardo, Rich,
Richar, Richards,
Richardson, Richart,
Richer, Richerd, Richie,
Richshard, Rick, Rickard,
Rickert, Rickey, Ricky,
Rico, Rihardos, Rihards,
Rikard, Riocard, Riócard,
Risa, Risardas, Rishard,
Ristéard, Ritchard, Rostik,
Rye, Rysio, Ryszard**

Richart (German) rich and
powerful ruler. The original
form of Richard.

Richie (English) a familiar
form of Richard.
**Richey, Richi, Rishi,
Ritchie**

Richman (English)
powerful.

Richmond (German)
powerful protector.
Richmon, Richmound

Rick (German) a short
form of Richard.
**Ric, Ricke, Rickey, Ricks,
Ricky, Rik, Riki, Rykk**

Rickard (Swedish) a form
of Richard.

Ricker (English) powerful
army.

Rickey (English) a familiar
form of Richard, Rick.

Rickward (English) mighty
guardian.
Rickwerd, Rickwood

Ricky (English) a familiar
form of Richard, Rick.
**Ricci, Rickey, Ricki, Rickie,
Riczi, Riki, Rikki, Rikky,
Riqui**

Rico (Spanish) a familiar
form of Richard. (Italian)
a short form of Enrico.
Ric

Rida (Arabic) favor.

Riddock (Irish) smooth
field.

Rider (English) horseman.
Ridder, Ryder

Ridge (English) ridge of
a cliff.
Ridgy, Rig, Rigg

Ridgeley (English) meadow
near the ridge.
**Ridgeleigh, Ridglea,
Ridglee, Ridgleigh,
Ridgley**

Ridgeway (English) path
along the ridge.

Ridley (English) meadow
of reeds.
**Riddley, Ridlea, Ridleigh,
Ridly**

Riel (Spanish) a short form
of Gabriel.

Rigby (English) ruler's
valley.

Rigel (Arabic) foot.
Astronomy: one of
the stars in the Orion
constellation.

Rigg (English) ridge.
Rigo

Rikard (Scandinavian)
a form of Richard.
Rikárd

Riki (Estonian) a form
of Rick.
Rikki, Riks

Riley (Irish) valiant.
**Reilly, Rilley, Rilye, Rylee,
Ryley, Rylie**

Rinaldo (Italian) a form
of Reynold.
Rinald

Ring (English) ring.
Ringo

Ringo (Japanese) apple.
(English) a familiar
form of Ring.

Rio (Spanish) river. Geography: Rio de Janeiro
is a seaport in Brazil.

Riordan (Irish) bard,
royal poet.
**Rearden, Reardin,
Reardon**

Rip (Dutch) ripe, full-
grown. (English) a short
form of Ripley.
Ripp

Ripley (English) meadow
near the river.
Rip, Ripleigh, Ripply

Riqui (Spanish) a form of
Rickey.

Rishad (American) a form
of Rashad.
Rishaad

Rishawn (American)
a combination of the
prefix Ri + Shawn.
Rishan, Rishaun, Rishon

Rishi (Hindi) sage.

Risley (English) meadow
with shrubs.
**Rislea, Rislee, Risleigh,
Risly, Wrisley**

Risto (Finnish) a short form
of Christopher.

Riston (English) settlement near the shrubs.
Wriston

Ritchard (English) an alternate form of Richard.
Ritcherd, Ritchyrd, Ritshard, Ritsherd

Ritchie (English) an alternate form of Richie.
Ritchy

Rithisak (Cambodian) powerful.

Ritter (German) knight; chivalrous.
Rittner

Riyad (Arabic) gardens.
Riad, Riyaz

Roald (Norwegian) famous ruler.

Roan (English) a short form of Rowan.
Rhoan

Roar (Norwegian) praised warrior.
Roary

Roarke (Irish) famous ruler.
Roark, Rorke, Rourke, Ruark

Rob (English) a short form of Robert.
Robb, Robe

Robbie (English) a familiar form of Robert.
Robie, Robbi

Robby (English) a familiar form of Robert.
Robbey, Robhy, Roby

Robert (English) famous brilliance. See also Bobek, Dob, Lopaka.
Bob, Rab, Rabbie, Raby, Riobard, Riobart, Rob, Robars, Robart, Robbie, Robby, Rober, Roberd, Robers, Roberto, Roberts, Robin, Robinson, Roibeárd, Rosertas, Rubert, Ruberto, Rudbert, Rupert

Roberto (Portuguese, Spanish) a form of Robert.

Roberts, Robertson (English) son of Robert.
Robertson, Robeson, Robinson, Robson

Robin (English) a short form of Robert.
Robben, Robbin, Robbins, Robbyn, Roben, Robinet, Robinn, Robins, Robyn, Roibín

Robinson (English) son of Robert. An alternate form of Roberts, Robertson.
Robbinson, Robson, Robynson

Rocco (Italian) rock.
Rocca, Rocky, Roko, Roque

Rochester (English) rocky fortress.
Chester

Rock (English) a short form of Rockwell.
Rocky

Rockford (English) rocky ford.

Rockland (English) rocky land.

Rockledge (English) rocky ledge.

Rockley (English) rocky field.
Rockle

Rockwell (English) rocky spring. Art: Norman Rockwell was a well-known twentieth-century American illustrator.
Rock

Rocky (American) a familiar form of Rocco, Rock.
Rockey, Rockie

Rod (English) a short form of Penrod, Roderick, Rodney.
Rodd

Rodas (Greek, Spanish) an alternate form of Rhodes.

Roddy (English) a familiar form of Roderick.
Roddie, Rody

Roden (English) red valley.

Roderich (German) an alternate form of Roderick.

Roderick (German) famous ruler. See also Broderick.
Rhoderick, Rod, Rodderick, Roddrick, Roddy, Roderic, Roderich, Roderigo, Roderik, Roderyck, Rodgrick,

Rodric, Rodrich, Rodrick, Rodricki, Rodrigo, Rodrigue, Rodrik, Rodrique, Rodrugue, Rodryck, Rodryk, Roodney, Rory, Rurik, Ruy

Rodger (German) an alternate form of Roger.
Rodge, Rodgy

Rodman (German) famous man, hero.
Rodmond

Rodney (English) island clearing.
Rhodney, Rod, Rodnee, Rodni, Rodnie, Rodnne

Rodolfo (Spanish) a form of Rudolph.
Rodolpho, Rodulfo

Rodrigo (Italian, Spanish) a form of Roderick.

Rodriguez (Spanish) son of Rodrigo.
Rodrigues

Rodrik (German) famous ruler.

Roe (English) roe deer.
Row, Rowe

Rogan (Irish) redhead.

Rogelio (Spanish) famous warrior.

Roger (German) famous spearman. See also Lokela.
Rodger, Rog, Rogelio, Rogerick, Rogerio, Rogers, Rogiero, Rojelio, Rüdiger, Ruggerio, Rutger

Rogerio (Portuguese, Spanish) a form of Roger.
Rogerios

Rohan (Hindi) sandalwood.

Rohin (Hindi) upward path.

Rohit (Hindi) big and beautiful fish.

Roi (French) an alternate form of Roy.

Roja (Spanish) red.
Rojay

Roland (German) famous throughout the land.
Loránd, Orlando, Rawlins, Rolan, Rolanda, Rolando, Rolek, Rolland, Rolle, Rollie, Rollin, Rollo, Rowe, Rowland, Ruland

Rolando (Portuguese, Spanish) a form of Roland.
Lando, Olo, Roldan, Roldán

Rolf (German) a form of Ralph. A short form of Rudolph.
Rolfe, Rolle, Rolph, Rolphe

Rolle (Swedish) a familiar form of Roland, Rolf.

Rollie (English) a familiar form of Roland.
Roley, Rolle, Rolli, Rolly

Rollin (English) a form of Roland.
Rolin, Rollins

Rollo (English) a familiar form of Roland.
Rolla, Rolo

Rolon (Spanish) famous wolf.

Romain (French) a form of Roman.
Romane

Roman (Latin) from Rome, Italy.
Roma, Romain, Romanos, Romman, Romochka, Romy

Romanos (Greek) a form of Roman.

Romeo (Italian) pilgrim to Rome; Roman. Literature: the title character of the Shakespearean play *Romeo and Juliet*.
Roméo, Romero

Romney (Welsh) winding river.
Romoney

Romulus (Latin) citizen of Rome. Mythology: Romulus and his twin brother Remus founded Rome.
Romolo, Romono, Romulo

Romy (Italian) a familiar form Roman.
Rommie, Rommy

Ron (Hebrew) a short form of Aaron, Ronald.
Ronn

Ronald (Scottish) a form of Reginald.
Ranald, Ron, Ronal, Ronaldo, Ronney, Ronnie, Ronnold, Ronoldo

Ronaldo (Portuguese) a form of Ronald.

Rónán (Irish) seal.
Renan, Ronan, Ronat

Rondel (French) short poem.
Rondale, Rondall, Rondeal, Rondell, Rondey, Rondie, Rondrell, Rondy, Ronel

Ronel (American) a form of Rondel.
Ronell, Ronelle, Ronnel, Ronnell, Ronyell

Roni (Hebrew) my song; my joy.
Rani, Roneet, Ronit, Ronli

Ronnie (Scottish) a familiar form of Ronald.
Roni, Ronie, Ronney, Ronnie, Ronny

Ronson (Scottish) son of Ronald.
Ronaldson

Ronté (American) a combination of Ron + the suffix -te.
Rontae, Ronte, Rontez

Rooney (Irish) redhead.

Roosevelt (Dutch) rose field. History: Theodore and Franklin D. Roosevelt were the twenty-sixth and thirty-second U.S. presidents, respectively.
Rosevelt

Roper (English) rope maker.

Rory (German) a familiar form of Roderick. (Irish) red king.
Rorey

Rosario (Portuguese) rosary.

Roscoe (Scandinavian) deer forest.
Rosco

Roshad (American) a form of Rashad.
Roshard

Roshean (American) a combination of the prefix Ro + Sean.
Roshan, Roshane, Roshay, Rosheen, Roshene

Rosito (Filipino) rose.

Ross (Latin) rose. (Scottish) peninsula. (French) red.
Rosse, Rossell, Rossi, Rossie, Rossy

Rosswell (English) springtime of roses.
Rosvel

Rostislav (Czech) growing glory.
Rosta, Rostya

Roswald (English) field of roses.
Ross, Roswell

Roth (German) redhead.

Rothwell (Scandinavian) red spring.

Rover (English) traveler.

Rowan (English) tree with red berries.
Roan, Rowe, Rowen, Rowney

Rowell (English) roe deer well.

Rowland (German) an alternate form of Roland. (English) rough land.
Rowlands, Rowlandson

Rowley (English) rough meadow.
Rowlea, Rowlee, Rowleigh, Rowly

Rowson (English) son of the redhead.

Roxbury (English) rook's town or fortress.
Roxburghe

Roy (French) king. A short form of Royal, Royce. See also Conroy, Delroy, Fitzroy, Leroy, Loe.
Rey, Roi, Ruy

Royal (French) kingly, royal.
Roy, Royale, Royall

Royce (English) son of Roy.
Roice, Roy

Royden (English) rye hill.
Royd, Roydan

Ruben (Hebrew) an alternate form of Reuben.
Rube, Rubin, Ruby

Rubert (Czech) a form of Robert.

Ruby (Hebrew) a familiar form of Reuben, Ruben.

Rudd (English) a short form of Rudyard.

Ruda (Czech) a form of Rudolph.
Rude, Rudek

Rudi (Spanish) a familiar form of Rudolph.
Ruedi

Rudo (African) love.

Rudolf (German) an alternate form of Rudolph.
Rodolf, Rodolfo, Rudolfo

Rudolph (German) famous wolf. See also Dolf.
Raoul, Rezsó, Rodolfo, Rodolph, Rodolphe, Rolf, Ruda, Rudek, Rudi, Rudolf, Rudolpho, Rudolphus, Rudy

Rudolpho (Italian) a form of Rudolph.

Rudy (English) a familiar form of Rudolph.
Ruddy, Ruddie, Rudey

Rudyard (English) red enclosure.
Rudd

Ruff (French) redhead.

Rufin (Polish) redhead.

Ruford (English) red ford; ford with reeds.
Rufford

Rufus (Latin) redhead.
Rayfus, Rufe, Ruffis, Ruffus, Rufino, Rufo, Rufous

Rugby (English) rook fortress. History: a famous British school after which the sport of rugby was named.

Ruggerio (Italian) a form of Roger.
Rogero, Ruggero, Ruggiero

Ruhakana (Rukiga) argumentative.

Ruland (German) an alternate form of Roland.
Rulan, Rulon

Rumford (English) wide river crossing.

Runako (Shona) handsome.

Rune (German, Swedish) secret.

Runrot (Thai) prosperous.

Rupert (German) a form of Robert.
Ruperth, Ruperto, Ruprecht

Ruperto (Italian) a form of Rupert.

Ruprecht (German) an alternate form of Rupert.

Rush (French) redhead. (English) a short form of Russell.
Rushi

Rushford (English) ford with rushes.

Rusk (Spanish) twisted bread.

Ruskin (French) redhead.
Rush, Russ

Russ (French) a short form of Russell.

Russell (French) redhead; fox colored. See also Lukela.
Roussell, Rush, Russ, Russel, Russelle, Rusty

Rusty (French) a familiar form of Russell.
Rustie, Rustin, Rustyn

Rutger (Scandinavian) a form of Roger.
Ruttger

Rutherford (English) cattle ford.
Rutherfurd

Rutland (Scandinavian) red land.

Rutledge (English) red ledge.

Rutley (English) red meadow.

Ruy (Spanish) a short form of Roderick.
Rui

Ryan (Irish) little king.
**Rhyan, Rhyne, Ryane,
Ryann, Ryen, Ryin, Ryne,
Ryon, Ryuan, Ryun**

Rycroft (English) rye field.
Ryecroft

Ryder (English) an alternate
form of Rider.
Rye

Rye (English) a short
form of Ryder. A grain
used in cereal and
whiskey. (Gypsy)
gentleman.
Ry

Ryerson (English) son
of Rider, Ryder.

Rylan (English) land where
rye is grown.
**Ryeland, Ryland, Rylin,
Rylund**

Ryle (English) rye hill.
Ryal, Ryel

Ryman (English) rye seller.

Ryne (Irish) an alternate
form of Ryan.

Saber (French) sword.
Sabir, Sabre

Sabin (Basque) ancient
tribe of central Italy.
Saben, Sabino

Sabiti (Rutooro) born
on Sunday.

Sabola (Ngoni) pepper.

Saburo (Japanese)
third-born son.

Sachar (Russian) a form
of Zachariah.

Saddam (Arabic) powerful
ruler.

Sadiki (Swahili) faithful.
Saadiq, Sadiq, Sadique

Sadler (English) saddle
maker.
Saddler

Safari (Swahili) born while
traveling.
Safa

Safford (English) willow-
river crossing.

Sahale (Native American)
falcon.
Sael, Sahel, Sahil

Sahen (Hindi) above.

Sahir (Hindi) friend.

Sa'id (Arabic) happy.
Saeed, Sa'ied, Sajid, Sajjid,
Sayeed, Sayid, Seyed

Sajag (Hindi) watchful.

Saka (Swahili) hunter.

Sakeri (Danish) a form
of Zachariah.

Sakima (Native American)
king.

Sakuruta (Pawnee)
coming sun.

Sal (Italian) a short form
of Salvatore.

Salam (Arabic) lamb.

Salamon (Spanish) a form
of Solomon.
Salomon, Salomón,
Salomone

Salaun (French) a form
of Solomon.

Sálih (Arabic) right, good.
Saleeh, Saleh, Salehe

Salim (Swahili) peaceful.

Salím (Arabic) peaceful,
safe.
Saleem, Salem, Saliym,
Salman

Salmalin (Hindi) taloned.

Salman (Czech) a form
of Salím, Solomon.
Salmaine, Salmon

Salton (English) manor
town; willow town.

Salvador (Spanish) savior.
Salvadore

Salvatore (Italian) savior.
See also Xavier.
Sal, Salbatore, Sallie,
Sally, Salvator, Salvidor,
Sauveur

Sam (Hebrew) a short form
of Samuel.
Samm, Sammy, Sem,
Shem, Shmuel

Sambo (American) a familiar form of Samuel.

Samír (Arabic) entertaining
companion.

Samman (Arabic) grocer.
Sammon

Sammy (Hebrew) a familiar
form of Samuel.
Saamy, Sameeh, Sameh,
Samey, Samie, Sammee,
Sammey, Sammie, Samy

Samo (Czech) a form of
Samuel.
Samho, Samko

Samson (Hebrew) like the
sun. Bible: a strong man
betrayed by Delilah.
Sampson, Sansao,
Sansom, Sansón, Shem,
Shimshon

Samuel (Hebrew) heard
God; asked of God. Bible:
a famous Old Testament
prophet and judge. See
also Kamuela, Zamiel,
Zanvil.

**Sam, Samael, Samaru,
Samauel, Samaul, Sambo,
Sameul, Samiel, Sammail,
Sammel, Sammuel,
Sammy, Samo, Samouel,
Samu, Samual, Samuele,
Samuelis, Samuello,
Samuil, Samuka, Samule,
Samuru, Samvel, Sanko,
Saumel, Schmuel, Shem,
Shmuel, Simão, Simuel,
Somhairle, Zamuel**

Samuele (Italian) a form
of Samuel.

Samuru (Japanese) a form
of Samuel.

Sanat (Hindi) ancient.

Sanborn (English) sandy
brook.
**Sanborne, Sanbourn,
Sanbourne, Sanburn,
Sanburne, Sandborn,
Sandbourne**

Sancho (Latin) sanctified;
sincere. Literature: Sancho
Panza was Don Quixote's
faithful companion.
**Sanchaz, Sanchez,
Sauncho**

Sandeep (Punjabi)
enlightened.

Sander (English) a short
form of Alexander,
Lysander.
Sandor, Sándor, Saunder

Sanders (English) son
of Sander.

**Sanderson, Saunders,
Saunderson**

Sándor (Hungarian) a short
form of Alexander.
Sanyi

Sandro (Greek, Italian)
a short form of Alexander.
**Sandero, Sandor,
Saundro, Shandro**

Sandy (English) a familiar
form of Alexander.
Sande, Sandey, Sandie

Sanford (English) sandy
river crossing.
Sandford

Sani (Hindi) Saturn.

Sanjiv (Hindi) long lived.
Sanjeev

Sankar (Hindi) god.
Religion: another name
for the Hindu god Shiva.

Sansón (Spanish) a form
of Samson.
Sanson, Sansone, Sansun

Santana (Spanish) History:
Antonio Santa Ana was a
revolutionary general and
president of Mexico.
Santanna

Santiago (Spanish) a form
of James.

Santo (Italian, Spanish)
holy.
Santos

Santon (English) sandy
town.

Santonio (Spanish) Geography: a short form of San Antonio, a town in Texas.
Santino, Santon

Santosh (Hindi) satisfied.

Sanyu (Luganda) happy.

Saqr (Arabic) falcon.

Sarad (Hindi) born in the autumn.

Sargent (French) army officer.
Sargant, Sarge, Sarjant, Sergeant, Sergent, Serjeant

Sarito (Spanish) a form of Caesar.
Sarit

Sariyah (Arabic) clouds at night.

Sarngin (Hindi) archer; protector.

Sarojin (Hindi) like a lotus.
Sarojun

Sasha (Russian) a short form of Alexander.
Sacha, Sascha, Sashenka, Sashka, Sashok, Sausha

Sasson (Hebrew) joyful.
Sason

Satordi (French) Saturn.
Satori

Saul (Hebrew) asked for, borrowed. Bible: in the Old Testament, a king of Israel and the father of Jonathan; in the New Testament, Saint Paul's original name was Saul.
Saül, Shaul, Sol, Solly

Saverio (Italian) a form of Xavier.

Saville (French) willow town.
Savil, Savile, Saviil, Savylle, Seville, Siville

Saw (Burmese) early.

Sawyer (English) wood worker.
Sawyere

Sax (English) a short form of Saxon.
Saxe

Saxon (English) swordsman. History: the Roman name for Germanic people who fought with short swords.
Sax, Saxen

Sayer (Welsh) carpenter.
Say, Saye, Sayers, Sayre, Sayres

Sayyid (Arabic) master.
Sayed, Sayid, Sayyad, Sayyed

Scanlon (Irish) little trapper.
Scanlan, Scanlen

Schafer (German) shepherd.
Schaefer, Shaffar, Shäffer

Schmidt (German)
blacksmith.
Schmid, Schmit, Schmitt

Schneider (German) tailor.
Schnieder, Snider, Snyder

Schön (German)
handsome.
Schönn, Shon

Schuyler (Dutch)
sheltering.
**Schuylar, Schylar, Schyler,
Scoy, Scy, Skuyler, Sky,
Skylar, Skyler, Skylor**

Scorpio (Latin) dangerous,
deadly. Astronomy:
a southern constellation
between Libra and
Sagittarius resembling
a scorpion. Astrology: the
eighth sign of the zodiac.
Scorpeo

Scott (English) from
Scotland. A familiar
form of Prescott.
Scot, Scotto, Scotty

Scotty (English) a familiar
form of Scott.
Scotie, Scotti, Scottie

Scoville (French) Scott's
town.

Scully (Irish) town crier.

Seabert (English) shining
sea.
Seabright, Sebert, Seibert

Seabrook (English) brook
near the sea.

Seamus (Irish) a form of
James.
Seamas, Seumas

Sean (Hebrew) God is
gracious. (Irish) a form
of John.
**Seaghan, Séan, Seán,
Seanán, Seane, Seann,
Shaan, Shane, Shaun,
Shawn, Shon, Siôn**

Searlas (Irish, French)
a form of Charles.
Séarlas, Searlus

Searle (English) armor.

Seasar (Latin) an alternate
form of Caesar.
**Seasare, Seazar, Sesar,
Sesear, Sezar**

Seaton (English) town near
the sea.
Seeton, Seton

Sebastian (Greek) venera-
ble. (Latin) revered.
**Bastian, Sabastian,
Sabastien, Sebastiano,
Sebastien, Sébastien,
Sebastin, Sebastion,
Sebbie, Sebestyén, Sebo,
Sepasetiano**

Sebastien, Sébastien
(French) forms of
Sebastian.
Sebasten

Sedgely (English) sword
meadow.
Sedgeley, Sedgly

Sedric (Irish) a form of Cedric.
Seddrick, Sederick, Sedrick

Seeley (English) blessed.
Sealey, Seely, Selig

Sef (Egyptian) yesterday. Literature: an Egyption lion god in *The Book of the Dead.*

Sefton (English) village of rushes.

Sefu (Swahili) sword.

Seger (English) sea spear; sea warrior.
Seager, Seeger, Segar

Segun (Yoruba) conqueror.

Segundo (Spanish) second.

Seibert (English) bright sea.
Seabert, Sebert

Seif (Arabic) religion's sword.

Seifert (German) an alternate form of Siegfried.

Sein (Basque) innocent.

Sekaye (Shona) laughter.

Selby (English) village by the mansion.
Shelby

Seldon (English) willow tree valley.
Selden, Sellden, Shelden, Sheldon

Selig (German) a form of Seeley.
Seligman, Seligmann, Zelig

Selwyn (English) friend from the palace.
Selvin, Selwin, Selwinn, Selwynn, Selwynne, Wyn

Semanda (Luganda) cow clan.

Semer (Ethiopian) a form of George.

Semon (Greek) a form of Simon.

Sempala (Luganda) born in prosperous times.

Sen (Japanese) wood fairy.
Senh

Sener (Turkish) bringer of joy.

Senior (French) lord.

Sennett (French) elderly.
Sennet

Senon (Spanish) living.

Senwe (African) dry as a grain stalk.

Sepp (German) a form of Joseph.
Seppi

Septimus (Latin) seventh.

Serafino (Portuguese) a form of Seraphim.

Seraphim (Hebrew) fiery, burning. Bible: the fiery angels who guard the throne of God.

Saraf, Saraph, Serafim, Serafin, Serafino, Seraphimus, Seraphin

Sereno (Latin) calm, tranquil.

Serge (Latin) attendant.
Seargeoh, Serg, Sergei, Sergio, Sergios, Sergius, Sergiusz, Serguel, Sirgio, Sirgios

Sergei (Russian) a form of Serge.
Sergey, Sergeyuk, Sergi, Sergie, Sergo, Sergunya, Serhiy, Serhiyko, Serjiro, Serzh

Sergio (Italian) a form of Serge.
Serginio, Serigo, Serjio

Seth (Hebrew) appointed. Bible: the third son of Adam.
Set, Sethan, Sethe, Shet

Setimba (Luganda) river dweller. Geography: a river in Uganda.

Seumas (Scottish) a form of James.

Severiano (Italian) a form of Séverin.

Séverin (French) severe.
Seve, Sevé, Severan, Severian, Severiano, Severo, Sevien, Sevrin

Severn (English) boundary. Geography: a river in southern England.

Sevilen (Turkish) beloved.

Seward (English) sea guardian.
Sewerd, Siward

Sewati (Moquelumnan) curved bear claws.

Sexton (English) church offical, sexton.

Sextus (Latin) sixth.
Sixtus

Seymour (French) prayer. Religion: name honoring Saint Maur. See also Maurice.
Seamor, Seamore, Seamour, See

Shabouh (Armenian) king, noble. History: a Persian king.

Shad (Punjabi) happy-go-lucky.
Shadd

Shadi (Arabic) singer.
Shaddy, Shade, Shadee, Shadeed, Shadey, Shadie, Shady, Shydee, Shydi

Shadrach (Babylonian) god; godlike. Religion: another name for Aku, the sun god. Bible: one of Daniel's three companions in captivity.
Shad, Shadrack, Shadrick, Shederick, Shedrach, Shedrick

Shadwell (English) shed by a well.

Shah (Persian) king.
History: a title for rulers
of Iran.

Shai (Hebrew) a short form
of Yeshaya.

Shaiming (Chinese) life;
sunshine.

Shaka (Zulu) founder, first.
History: Shaka Zulu was
the founder of the Zulu
empire.

Shakir (Arabic) thankful.
Shakeer

Shalom (Hebrew) peace.
**Shalum, Shlomo, Sholem,
Sholom**

Shalya (Hindi) throne.

Shaman (Sanskrit) holy
man, mystic, medicine
man.
**Shamaine, Shamine,
Shamon, Shamone**

Shamir (Hebrew) precious
stone. Bible: a hard,
precious stone used to
build Solomon's temple.
**Shahmir, Shameer,
Shamyr**

Shamus (Irish) an alternate
form of Seamus.
(American) slang for
detective.
Seamus, Shemus

Shanahan (Irish) wise,
clever.

Shandy (English)
rambunctious.
Shandey, Shandie

Shane (Irish) an alternate
form of Sean.
Shaine, Shayn, Shayne

Shangobunni (Yoruba) gift
from Shango.

Shanley (Irish) small;
ancient.
Shannley

Shannon (Irish) small
and wise.
**Shanan, Shannan,
Shannen, Shanon**

Shantae (French) an alter-
nate form of Chante.
**Shant, Shantell, Shantelle,
Shanti, Shantie, Shanton,
Shanty**

Shap (English) an alternate
form of Shep.

Shaquille (Arabic)
handsome.

Sharad (Pakistani) autumn.

Sharif (Arabic) honest;
noble.
**Shareef, Sharef, Shareff,
Shariff, Shariyf, Sharyif**

Sharron (Hebrew) flat area,
plain. Bible: the area from
Mount Carmel south to
Jaffa, covered with oak
trees.
Sharone, Sharonn

Shattuck (English) little
shad fish.

Shaun (Irish) an alternate
form of Sean.
**Shaughan, Shaughn,
Shauna, Shaunahan,
Shaune, Shaunn**

Shavar (Hebrew) comet.
Shavit

Shaw (English) grove.

Shawn (Irish) an alternate
form of Sean.
**Shawen, Shawne,
Shawnee, Shawnn,
Shawon**

Shawnta (American)
a combination of
Shawn + suffixes
beginning with a t.
**Shawntae, Shawntel,
Shawnti**

Shea (Irish) courteous.
**Shae, Shai, Shayan, Shaye,
Shey**

Sheehan (Irish) little;
peaceful.
Shean

Sheffield (English) crooked
field.
**Field, Shef, Sheff, Sheffie,
Sheffy**

Shel (English) a short form
of Shelby, Sheldon,
Shelton.

Shelby (English) ledge
estate.
**Shel, Shelbey, Shelbie,
Shell, Shelley, Shelly**

Sheldon (English) farm
on the ledge.
**Shel, Shelden, Sheldin,
Shell, Shelley, Shelly,
Shelton**

Shelley (English) a familiar
form of Shelby, Sheldon,
Shelton. Literature:
Percy Bysshe Shelly was
a British poet.
Shell, Shelly

Shelton (English) town
on a ledge.
Shel, Shelley

Shem (Hebrew) name;
reputation. (English)
a short form of Samuel.
Bible: Noah's oldest son.

Shen (Egyptian) sacred
amulet. (Chinese)
meditation.

Shep (English) a short form
of Shepherd.
Shap, Ship, Shipp

Shepherd (English)
shepherd.
**Shep, Shepard, Shephard,
Shepp, Sheppard,
Shepperd**

Shepley (English) sheep
meadow.
**Sheplea, Sheplee, Shepply,
Shipley**

Sherborn (English) clear
brook.
**Sherborne, Sherbourn,
Sherburn, Sherburne**

Sheridan (Irish) wild.
Dan, Sheredan, Sheridon, Sherridan

Sherill (English) shire on a hill.
Sheril, Sherril, Sherrill

Sherlock (English) light haired. Literature: Sherlock Holmes was Sir Arthur Conan Doyle's famous British detective character.
Sherlocke, Shurlock, Shurlocke

Sherman (English) sheep shearer; resident of a shire.
Scherman, Schermann, Sherm, Shermann, Shermie, Shermy

Sherrod (English) clearer of the land.
Sherod, Sherrad, Sherrard, Sherrodd

Sherwin (English) swift runner, one who cuts the wind.
Sherwind, Sherwinn, Sherwyn, Sherwynd, Sherwynne, Win

Sherwood (English) bright forest.
Sherwoode, Shurwood, Woody

Shihab (Arabic) blaze.

Shilín (Chinese) intellectual.
Shilan

Shiloh (Hebrew) God's gift.
Shi, Shile, Shiley, Shilo, Shy, Shyle

Shimon (Hebrew) an alternate form of Simon.

Shimshon (Hebrew) an alternate form of Samson.
Shimson

Shing (Chinese) victory.
Shingae, Shingo

Shipton (English) sheep village; ship village.

Shiro (Japanese) fourth-born son.

Shiva (Hindi) life and death. Religion: the most common name for the god of destruction and reproduction.
Shiv, Shivan, Siva

Shlomo (Hebrew) an alternate form of Solomon.
Shelmu, Shelomo, Shelomoh, Shlomi, Shlomot

Shmuel (Hebrew) an alternate form of Samuel.
Shem, Shemuel, Shmelke, Shmiel, Shmulka

Shneur (Yiddish) senior.
Shneiur

Shon (German) an alternate form of Schön. (American) a form of Sean.
Shondae, Shondale, Shondel, Shonntay,

Shontae, Shontarious, Shouan, Shoun

Shunnar (Arabic) pheasant.

Si (Hebrew) a short form of Silas, Simon.
Sy

Sid (French) a short form of Sidney.
Cyd, Siddie, Siddy, Sidey, Syd

Siddel (English) wide valley.
Siddell

Siddhartha (Hindi) History: the original name of Buddha, an Indian mystic and founder of Buddhism.
Sida, Sidh, Sidharth, Sidhartha, Sidhdharth

Sidney (French) from Saint Denis, France.
Cydney, Sid, Sidnee, Sidon, Sidonio, Sydney, Sydny

Sidonio (Spanish) a form of Sidney.

Sidwell (English) wide stream.

Siegfried (German) victorious peace. Literature: a dragon-slaying hero. See also Zigfrid, Ziggy.
Seifert, Seifried, Siegfred, Siffre, Sig, Sigefriedo, Sigfrid, Sigfried, Sigfroi, Sigfryd, Siggy, Sigifredo, Siguefredo, Sigvard,

Singefrid, Sygfried, Szygfrid

Sierra (Irish) black. (Spanish) saw toothed. Geography: a range of mountains with a saw-tooth appearance.
Siera

Sig (German) a short form of Siegfried, Sigmund.

Siggy (German) a familiar form of Siegfried, Sigmund.

Sigmund (German) victorious protector. See also Ziggy, Zsigmond, Zygmunt.
Siegmund, Sig, Siggy, Sigismond, Sigismondo, Sigismund, Sigismundo, Sigismundus, Sigmond, Sigsmond, Szygmond

Sigurd (German, Scandinavian) victorious guardian.
Sjure, Syver

Sigwald (German) victorious leader.

Silas (Latin) a short form of Silvan.
Si, Sias, Sylas

Silvan (Latin) forest dweller.
Silas, Silvain, Silvano, Silvanos, Silvanus, Silvaon, Silvie, Silvio, Sylvain, Sylvan, Sylvanus, Sylvio

Silvester (Latin) an alternate form of Sylvester.
Silvestr, Silvestre, Silvestro, Silvy

Silvestro (Italian) a form of Sylvester.

Silvio (Italian) a form of Silvan.

Simão (Portuguese) a form of Samuel.

Simba (Swahili) lion. (Yao) a short form of Lisimba.
Sim

Simcha (Hebrew) joyful.
Simmy

Simeon (French) a form of Simon.
Simone

Simms (Hebrew) son of Simon.
Simm, Sims

Simmy (Hebrew) a familiar form of Simcha, Simon.
Simmey, Simmi, Simmie, Symmy

Simon (Hebrew) he heard. Bible: in the Old Testament, the second son of Jacob and Leah; in the New Testament, one of the Twelve Disciples. See also Symington, Ximenes.
Saimon, Samien, Semon, Shimon, Si, Sim, Simao, Simen, Simeon, Simion, Simm, Simmon, Simmonds, Simmons,
Simms, Simmy, Simonas, Simone, Simson, Simyon, Síomón, Symon, Szymon

Simpson (Hebrew) son of Simon.
Simonson, Simson

Sinclair (French) prayer. Religion: name honoring Saint Clair.
Sinclare, Synclair

Sinjon (English) saint, holy man. Religion: name honoring Saint John.
Sinjun, Sjohn

Sipatu (Moquelumnan) pulled out.

Sipho (Zulu) present.

Siraj (Arabic) lamp, light.

Siseal (Irish) a form of Cecil.

Sisi (Fanti) born on Sunday.

Siva (Hindi) an alternate form of Shiva.
Siv

Sivan (Hebrew) ninth month of the Jewish year.

Siwatu (Swahili) born during a time of conflict.
Siwazuri

Siwili (Native American) long fox's tail.

Skah (Lakota) white.

Skee (Scandinavian) projectile.
Ski

Skeeter (English) swift.
Skeat, Skeet, Skeets

Skelly (Irish) storyteller.
Shell, Skelley, Skellie

Skelton (Dutch) shell town.

Skerry (Scandinavian) stony island.

Skip (Scandinavian) a short form of Skipper.

Skipper (Scandinavian) shipmaster.
Skip, Skipp, Skippie, Skipton

Skiriki (Pawnee) coyote.

Skule (Norwegian) hidden.

Skye (Dutch) a short form of Skylar, Skyler, Skylor.
Sky

Skylar (Dutch) an alternate form of Schuyler.
Skye, Skyelar

Skyler (Dutch) an alternate form of Schuyler.
Skye, Skyeler, Skylee

Skylor (Dutch) an alternate form of Schuyler.
Skye, Skyelor, Skylour

Slade (English) child of the valley.
Slaide, Slayde

Slane (Czech) salty.
Slan

Slater (English) roof slater.

Slava (Russian) a short form of Stanislav.
Slavik, Slavoshka

Slawek (Polish) a short form of Radoslaw.

Slevin (Irish) mountaineer.
Slaven, Slavin, Slawin

Sloan (Irish) warrior.
Sloane

Smedley (English) flat meadow.
Smedleigh, Smedly

Smith (English) blacksmith.
Schmidt, Smid, Smidt, Smitt, Smitty, Smyth, Smythe

Snowden (English) snowy hill.
Snowdon

Socrates (Greek) wise, learned. History: a great ancient Greek philosopher.
Socratis, Sokrates, Sokratis

Sofian (Arabic) devoted.

Sohrab (Persian) ancient hero.

Soja (Yoruba) soldier.

Sol (Hebrew) a short form of Saul, Solomon.
Soll, Sollie, Solly

Solly (Hebrew) a familiar form of Saul, Solomon.
Sollie, Zollie

Solomon (Hebrew) peaceful. Bible: a king of Israel famous for his wisdom. See also Zalman.
Salamen, Salamon, Salamun, Salaun, Salman, Salomo, Selim, Shelomah, Shlomo, Sol, Solamh, Solaman, Solly, Solmon, Soloman, Solomonas, Sulaiman

Solon (Greek) wise. History: a sixth-century Athenian lawmaker noted for his wisdom.

Somerset (English) place of the summer settlers. Literature: William Somerset Maugham was a well-known British writer.
Sommerset, Sumerset, Summerset

Somerville (English) summer town.
Somerton, Summerton, Summerville

Son (Vietnamese) mountain. (Native American) star. (English) son, boy. A short form of Madison, Orson.
Sonny

Songan (Native American) strong.
Song

Sonny (English) a familiar form of Grayson, Madison, Orson, Son.
Sonnie

Sono (Akan) elephant.

Sören (Danish) thunder; war. Mythology: Thor was the Norse god of thunder and war.

Sorrel (French) reddish brown.
Sorel, Sorrell

Soroush (Persian) happy.

Soterios (Greek) savior.

Southwell (English) south well.

Sovann (Cambodian) gold.

Sowande (Yoruba) wise healer sought me out.

Spalding (English) divided field.
Spaulding

Spangler (German) tinsmith.
Spengler

Spark (English) happy.
Sparke, Sparkie, Sparky

Spear (English) spear carrier.
Speare, Spears, Speer, Speers, Spiers

Speedy (English) quick; successful.
Speed

Spence (English) a short form of Spencer.
Spense

Spencer (English) dispenser of provisions.
Spence, Spencre, Spenser

Spenser (English)
an alternate form of
Spencer. Literature:
Edmund Spenser was
the British poet who
wrote *The Faerie Queene*.
Spanser, Spense

Spike (English) ear of grain;
long nail.
Spyke

Spiro (Greek) round basket;
breath.
**Spiridion, Spiridon,
Spiros, Spyridon, Spyros**

Spoor (English) spur maker.
Spoors

Sproule (English) energetic.
Sprowle

Spurgeon (English) shrub.

Spyros (Greek) an alternate
form of Spiro.

Squire (English) knight's
assistant; large landholder.

Stacey, Stacy (English)
familiar forms of Eustace.
Stace, Stacee

Stafford (English) river-
bank landing.
**Staffard, Stafforde,
Staford**

Stamford (English) an
alternate form of Stanford.

Stamos (Greek) an alternate form of Stephen.
Stamatis, Stamatos

Stan (Latin, English) a short
form of Stanley.

Stanbury (English) stone
fortification.
**Stanberry, Stanbery,
Stanburghe, Stansbury**

Stancio (Spanish) a form
of Constantine.
Stancy

Stancliff (English) stony
cliff.
Stanclife, Stancliffe

Standish (English) stony
parkland. History: Miles
Standish was a prominent
pilgrim in colonial
America.

Stane (Slavic) a short form
of Stanislaus.

Stanfield (English) stony
field.
Stansfield

Stanford (English) rocky
ford.
**Sandy, Stamford, Stan,
Standford, Stanfield**

Stanislaus (Latin) stand of
glory. See also Lao, Tano.
**Slavik, Stana, Standa,
Stane, Stanislao, Stanislas,
Stanislau, Stanislav,
Stanislus, Stannes, Stano,
Stasik, Stasio**

Stanislav (Slavic) a form of
Stanislaus. See also Slava.
Slava, Stanislaw

Stanley (English) stony
meadow.
**Stan, Stanlea, Stanlee,
Stanleigh, Stanly**

Stanmore (English) stony
lake.

Stannard (English) hard
as stone.

Stanton (English) stony
farm.
Stan, Stanten, Staunton

Stanway (English) stony
road.

Stanwick (English)
stony village.
Stanwicke, Stanwyck

Stanwood (English) stony
woods.

Starbuck (English)
challenger of fate.
Literature: a character
in Herman Melville's
novel *Moby Dick*.

Stark (German) strong,
vigorous.
Stärke, Starkie

Starling (English) bird.
Sterling

Starr (English) star.
**Star, Staret, Starlight,
Starlon, Starwin**

Stasik (Russian) a familiar
form of Stanislaus.
**Stas, Stash, Stashka,
Stashko, Stasiek**

Stasio (Polish) a form
of Stanislaus.
**Stas, Stasiek, Stasiu,
Staska, Stasko**

Stavros (Greek) an alternate form of Stephen.

Steadman (English) owner
of a farmstead.
**Steadmann, Stedman,
Steed**

Steel (English) like steel.
Steele

Steen (German, Danish)
stone.
Stein

Stefan (German, Polish,
Swedish) a form of
Stephen.
**Staffan, Staffon,
Steafeán, Stefanson,
Stefaun, Stefawn,
Steffan, Steffon**

Stefano (Italian) an alternate form of Stephen.

Stefanos (Greek) a form
of Stephen.
**Stefans, Stefos, Stephano,
Stephanos**

Stefen (Norwegian) a form
of Stephen.
Steffen, Steffin, Stefin

Stein (German) an alternate form of Steen.
Steine, Steiner

Steinar (Norwegian) rock
warrior.

Stepan (Russian) a form
of Stephen.
Stepa, Stepanya, Stepka

Steph (English) a short
form of Stephen.

Stephan (Greek) an alter-
nate form of Stephen.
**Stephanas, Stephano,
Stephanos, Stephanus**

Stéphane (French) a form
of Stephen.
Stefane, Stepháne

Stephen (Greek) crowned.
See also Estéban, Estebe,
Estevao, Étienne, István,
Szczepan, Tapani, Teb,
Teppo, Tiennot.
**Stamos, Stavros, Stefan,
Stefano, Stefanos, Stefen,
Stenya, Stepan, Stepanos,
Steph, Stephan,
Stephanas, Stéphane,
Stepháne, Stephano,
Stephanos, Stephanus,
Stephens, Stephenson,
Stephfan, Stephin,
Stephon, Stephone,
Stepven, Steve, Steven,
Stevie**

Stephon (Greek) an alter-
nate form of Stephen.
**Stefon, Stefone, Stepfon,
Stephone**

Sterling (English) valuable;
silver penny. An alternate
form of Starling.
Sterling

Stern (German) star.

Sterne (English) austere.
Stearn, Stearne, Stearns

Steve (Greek) a short form
of Stephen, Steven.
**Steave, Steeve, Stevie,
Stevy**

Steven (Greek) crowned.
An alternate form of
Stephen.
**Steevan, Steeven, Steiven,
Stevan, Steve, Stevens,
Stevie**

Stevens (Greek) son of
Steven.
Stevenson

Stevie (English) a familiar
form of Stephen, Steven.
Stevey, Stevy

Stewart (English) an alternate form of Stuart.
Steward, Stu

Stian (Norwegian) quick
on his feet.

Stig (Swedish) mount.

Stiggur (Gypsy) gate.

Stillman (English) quiet.
Stillmann

Sting (English) spike
of grain.

Stockman (English) tree-
stump remover.

Stockton (English) tree-
stump town.

Stockwell (English) tree-

Stoddard (English) horse keeper.

Stoffel (German) a short form of Christopher.

Stoker (English) furnace tender.
Stoke, Stokes

Stone (English) stone.
Stoney, Stony

Storm (English) tempest, storm.
Stormi, Stormy

Storr (Norwegian) great.
Story

Stover (English) stove tender.

Stowe (English) hidden, packed away.

Strahan (Irish) minstrel.
Strachan

Stratford (English) bridge over the river. Literature: Stratford-upon-Avon was Shakespeare's birthplace.

Stratton (Scottish) river valley town.

Strephon (Greek) one who turns. Literature: a character in Gilbert and Sullivan's play *Iolanthe*.

Strom (Greek) bed, mattress. (German) stream.

Strong (English) powerful.

Stroud (English) thicket.

Struthers (Irish) brook.

Stu (English) a short form of Stewart, Stuart.
Stew

Stuart (English) caretaker, steward. History: the Scottish and English royal dynasty.
Stewart, Stu, Stuarrt

Studs (English) rounded nail heads; shirt ornaments; male horses used for breeding. History: Studs Terkel, a famous American radio journalist.
Stud, Studd

Styles (English) stairs put over a wall to help cross it.
Stiles

Subhi (Arabic) early morning.

Suck Chin (Korean) unshakable rock.

Sudi (Swahili) lucky.
Su'ud

Sued (Arabic) master, chief.

Suffield (English) southern field.

Sugden (English) valley of sows.

Suhail (Arabic) gentle.
Sohail, Sohayl, Souhail, Sujal

Suhuba (Swahili) friend.

Sukru (Turkish) grateful.

Sulaiman (Arabic) a form of Solomon.

**Sulaman, Sulay,
Sulaymaan, Sulayman,
Suleiman, Suleman,
Suleyman**

Sullivan (Irish) black eyed.
Sullavan, Sullevan, Sully

Sully (Irish) a familiar form
of Sullivan. (French) stain,
tarnish. (English) south
meadow.
Sulleigh, Sulley

Sultan (Swahili) ruler.
Sultaan

Sum (Thai) appropriate.

Summit (English) peak,
top.
Summet, Summitt

Sumner (English) church
officer, summoner.
Summer

Sundeep (Punjabi) light;
enlightened.
Sundip

Sunreep (Hindi) pure.
Sunrip

Sutcliff (English) southern
cliff.
Sutcliffe

Sutherland (Scandinavian)
southern land.
Southerland, Sutherlan

Sutton (English) southern
town.

Sven (Scandinavian) youth.
**Svein, Svend, Swen,
Swenson**

Swaggart (English) one
who sways and staggers.
Swaggert

Swain (English) herdsman;
knight's attendant.
Swaine, Swanson

Swaley (English) winding
stream.
**Swail, Swailey, Swale,
Swales**

Sweeney (Irish) small hero.
Sweeny

Swinbourne (English)
stream used by swine.
**Swinborn, Swinborne,
Swinburn, Swinburne,
Swinbyrn, Swynborn**

Swindel (English) valley
of the swine.
Swindell

Swinfen (English) swine's
mud.

Swinford (English) swine's
crossing.
Swynford

Swinton (English) swine
town.

Sy (Latin) a short form
of Sylas, Symon.
Si

Sydney (French) an alternate form of Sidney.
Syd

Syed (Arabic) happy.

Sying (Chinese) star.

Sylas (Latin) an alternate form of Silas.
Sy

Sylvain (French) a form of Silvan, Sylvester.

Sylvester (Latin) forest dweller.
Silvester, Silvestro, Sly, Syl, Sylvain, Sylverster, Sylvestre

Symington (English) Simon's town, Simon's estate.

Symon (Greek) a form of Simon.
Sy, Syman, Symeon, Symms, Symon, Symone

Szczepan (Polish) a form of Stephen.

Szygfrid (Hungarian) a form of Siegfried.
Szigfrid

Szymon (Polish) a form of Simon.

Taamiti (Lunyole) brave.

Taaveti (Finnish) a form of David.
Taavi, Taavo

Tab (German) shining, brilliant. (English) drummer.
Tabb, Tabbie, Tabby

Tabari (Arabic) he remembers. History: a Muslim historian.
Tabarus

Tabib (Turkish) physician.
Tabeeb

Tabo (Spanish) a short form of Gustave.

Tabor (Persian) drummer. (Hungarian) encampment.
Tabber, Taber, Taboras, Taibor, Tayber, Taybor, Taver

Tad (Greek, Latin) a short form of Thaddeus. (Welsh) father.
Tadd, Taddy, Tade, Tadek, Tadey

Tadan (Native American) plentiful.

Taddeo (Italian) a form of Thaddeus.
Tadeo

Taddeus (Greek, Latin) an alternate form of Thaddeus.
Taddeusz, Taddius, Tadeas, Tades, Tadio, Tadious

Tadi (Omaha) wind.

Tadzi (Carrier) loon.

Tadzio (Polish, Spanish) a form of Thaddeus.
Taddeusz

Taffy (Welsh) a form of David. (English) a familiar form of Taft.

Taft (English) river.
Taffy, Tafton

Tage (Danish) day.
Tag

Taggart (Irish) son of the priest.

Tahír (Arabic) innocent, pure.
Taheer

Tai (Vietnamese) weather; prosperous; talented.

Taima (Native American) born during a storm.

Taiwan (Chinese) island; island dweller. Geography: a country off the coast of mainland China.
Taywan

Tait (Scandinavian) an alternate form of Tate.
Taite, Taitt

Taiwo (Yoruba) first-born of twins.

Taj (Urdu) crown.
Taji

Tajo (Spanish) day.
Taio

Tajuan (American) a combination of the prefix Ta + Juan.
Tájuan, Tajwan, Taquan, Tyjuan

Takeo (Japanese) strong as bamboo.
Takeyo

Takis (Greek) a familiar form of Peter.
Takius

Takoda (Lakota) friend to everyone.

Tal (Hebrew) dew; rain.
Tali, Talia, Talley, Talor, Talya

Talbert (German) bright valley.

Talbot (French) boot maker.
Talbott, Tallbot, Tallbott, Tallie, Tally

Talcott (English) cottage near the lake.

Tale (Tswana) green.

Talib (Arabic) seeker.

Taliesin (Welsh) radiant brow.
Tallas, Tallis

Taliki (Hausa) fellow.

Talli (Lenape) legendary hero.

Talmadge (English) lake between two towns.

Talmai (Aramaic) mound; furrow. Bible: a king of Geshur and father-in-law of King David.
Telem

Talman (Aramaic) injured; oppressed.
Talmon

Talon (French, English) claw, nail.
Tallin, Tallon

Talor (English) a form of Tal. An alternate form of Taylor.

Tam (Hebrew) honest. (English) a short form of Thomas. (Vietnamese) number eight.
Tama, Tamas, Tamás, Tameas, Tamlane, Tammany, Tammas, Tammen, Tammy

Taman (Slavic) dark, black.
Tama, Tamann

Tamar (Hebrew) date; palm tree.
Tamarr, Timur

Tambo (Swahili) vigorous.

Tamir (Arabic) tall as a palm tree.

Tammy (English) a familiar form of Thomas.
Tammie

Tamson (Scandinavian) son of Thomas.
Tamsen

Tan (Burmese) million. (Vietnamese) new.
Than

Tanek (Greek) immortal. See also Atek.

Taneli (Finnish) God is my judge.
Tanella

Tanguy (French) warrior.

Tani (Japanese) valley.

Tanner (English) leather worker, tanner.
Tan, Tanery, Tann, Tannor, Tanny

Tanny (English) a familiar form of Tanner.
Tana, Tanney, Tannie

Tano (Spanish) camp glory. (Russian) a short form of Stanislaus. (Ghanian) Geography: a river in Ghana.
Tanno

Tanton (English) town by the still river.

Tapani (Finnish) a form of Stephen.
Tapamn, Teppo

Täpko (Kiowa) antelope.

Tarell (German) an alternate form of Terrell.
Tarelle, Tarrel, Tarrell, Taryl

Tarif (Arabic) uncommon.
Tareef

Táriq (Arabic) conqueror. History: Tarik was the Muslim general who conquered Spain.
Tareck, Tareek, Tarek, Tarick, Tarik, Tarreq, Tereik

Tarleton (English) Thor's settlement.
Tarlton

Taro (Japanese) first-born male.

Taron (American) a combination of Tad + Ron.
Taeron, Tahron, Tarone, Tarren, Tarun

Tarrant (Welsh) thunder.
Terrant

Tarver (English) tower; hill; leader.
Terver

Tas (Gypsy) bird's nest.

Tass (Hungarian) ancient mythology name.

Tasunke (Dakota) horse.

Tate (Scandinavian, English) cheerful. (Native American) long-winded talker.
Tait, Tayte

Tatius (Latin) king, ruler. History: a Sabine king.
Tatianus, Tazio, Titus

Tau (Tswana) lion.

Tauno (Finnish) a form of Donald.

Taurean (Latin) strong; forceful. Astrology: born under the sign of Taurus.
Tauris, Taurus

Tavaris (Aramaic) an alternate form of Tavor.
Tarvaris, Tarvarres, Tavar, Tavaras, Tavares, Tavari, Tavarian, Tavarius, Tavarres, Tavarri, Tavarris, Tavars, Tavarse, Tavarus, Taveress, Tevaris, Tevarus

Tavey (Latin) a familiar form of Octavio.

Tavi (Aramaic) good.

Tavish (Scottish) a form of Thomas.
Tav, Tavi, Tavis

Tavo (Slavic) a short form of Gustave.

Tavor (Aramaic) misfortune.
Tarvoris, Tavaris, Tavores, Tavorious, Tavoris, Tavorris, Tavuris

Tawno (Gypsy) little one.
Tawn

Tayib (Hindi) good; delicate.

Taylor (English) tailor.
Tailer, Tailor, Talor, Tayler,

Taylor *(cont.)*
Taylour, Teyler

Taz (Arabic) shallow ornamental cup.

Tazio (Italian) a form of Tatius.

Teague (Irish) bard, poet.
Teagan, Teagun, Teak, Tegan, Teige

Tearlach (Scottish) a form of Charles.

Tearle (English) stern, severe.

Teasdale (English) river dweller. Geography: a river in England.

Teb (Spanish) a short form of Stephen.

Ted (English) a short form of Edward, Theodore.
Tedd, Tedek, Tedik, Tedson

Teddy (English) a familiar form of Edward, Theodore.
Teddey, Teddie

Tedmund (English) protector of the land.
Tedman, Tedmond

Tedorik (Polish) a form of Theodore.
Teodoor, Teodor, Teodorek

Tedrick (American) a combination of Ted + Rick.
Tedric

Teetonka (Lakota) big lodge.

Tefere (Ethiopian) seed.

Tekle (Ethiopian) plant.

Telek (Polish) a form of Telford.

Telem (Hebrew) mound; furrow.
Talmai, Tel

Telford (French) iron cutter.
Telek, Telfer, Telfor, Telfour

Teller (English) storyteller.
Tell, Telly

Telly (Greek) a familiar form of Teller, Theodore.

Telmo (English) tiller, cultivator.

Telutci (Moquelumnan) bear making dust as it runs.

Tem (Gypsy) country.

Teman (Hebrew) on the right side; southward.

Tembo (Swahili) elephant.

Tempest (French) storm.

Temple (Latin) sanctuary.

Templeton (English) town near the temple.
Temp, Templeten

Tennant (English) tenant, renter.
Tenant, Tennent

Tennessee (Cherokee)
mighty warrior.
Geography: a state in
the American south.
**Tennessee, Tennesy,
Tennysee**

Tennyson (English)
an alternate form
of Dennison.
**Tenney, Tenneyson,
Tennie, Tennis, Tenny**

Teo (Vietnamese) a form
of Tom.

Teobaldo (Italian, Spanish)
a form of Theobald.

Teodoro (Italian, Spanish)
a form of Theodore.

Teppo (French) a familiar
form of Stephen.

Teremun (Tiv) father's
acceptance.

Terence (Latin) an alternate
form of Terrence.
Teren, Teryn

Terencio (Spanish) a form
of Terrence.

Terran (Latin) a short form
of Terrance.
**Teran, Teren, Terin,
Terran, Terren, Terrin**

Terrance (Latin) an alter-
nate form of Terrence.
**Tarrance, Tearance,
Tearrance, Terance,
Terran**

Terrell (German) thunder
ruler.
**Tarell, Terrail, Terral,
Terrale, Terrall, Terreal,
Terrelle, Terrill, Terryal,
Terryel, Tirel, Tirrell,
Turrell, Tyrel**

Terrence (Latin) smooth.
**Tarrance, Terence,
Terencio, Terrance,
Terren, Terry, Torrence,
Tyreese**

Terrill (German) an alternate form of Terrell.
Terril, Terryl, Terryll, Tyrill

Terris (Latin) son of Terry.

Terron (American) a form
of Tyrone.
Terone, Terrone, Terryon

Terry (English) a familiar
form of Terrence. See also
Keli.
Tarry, Terrey, Terri, Terrie

Tertius (Latin) third.

Teva (Hebrew) nature.

Tevel (Yiddish) a form
of David.

Tevis (Scottish) a form
of Thomas.
Tevish

Tewdor (German) a form
of Theodore.

Tex (American) from Texas.
Tejas

Thabit (Arabic) firm,
strong.

Thad (Greek, Latin) a short form of Thaddeus.
Thadd, Thadee, Thady

Thaddeus (Greek) courageous. (Latin) praiser. Bible: one of the Twelve Apostles. See also Fadey.
Tad, Taddeo, Taddeus, Tadzio, Thad, Thaddaeus, Thaddaus, Thaddeau, Thaddeaus, Thaddeo, Thaddiaus, Thaddius, Thadeaou, Thadeous, Thadeus, Thadieus, Thadious, Thadius, Thadus

Thady (Irish) praise.
Thaddy

Thai (Vietnamese) many, multiple.

Thaman (Hindi) god; godlike. Religion: another name for the Hindu god Shiva.

Than (Burma) million.
Tan

Thane (English) attendant warrior.
Thain, Thaine, Thayne

Thang (Vietnamese) victorious.

Thanh (Vietnamese) finished.

Thaniel (Hebrew) a short form of Nathaniel.

Thanos (Greek) nobleman; bear-man.
Athanasios, Thanasis

Thatcher (English) roof thatcher, repairer of roofs.
Thacher, Thatch, Thaxter

Thaw (English) melting ice.

Thayer (French) nation's army.
Thay

Thel (English) upper story.

Thenga (Yao) bring him.

Theo (English) a short form of Theodore.

Theobald (German) people's prince. See also Dietbald.
Teobaldo, Thebault, Theòbault, Thibault, Tibalt, Tibold, Tiebold, Tiebout, Toiboid, Tybald, Tybalt, Tybault

Theodore (Greek) gift of God. See also Feodor, Fyodor.
Téadóir, Teador, Ted, Teddy, Tedor, Tedorek, Telly, Teodomiro, Teodoro, Teodus, Teos, Tewdor, Theo, Theodor, Theódor, Theodors, Theodorus, Theodosios, Theodrekr, Tivadar, Todor, Tolek, Tudor

Theodoric (German) ruler of the people. See also Derek, Dietrich, Dirk.

Teodorico, Thedric, Thedrick, Thierry, Till

Theophilus (Greek) loved by God.
Teofil, Théophile

Theron (Greek) hunter.
Theran, Theren, Therin, Therron

Thian (Vietnamese) smooth.
Thien

Thibault (French) a form of Theobald.
Thibaud, Thibaut

Thierry (French) a form of Theodoric.
Theirry, Theory

Thom (English) a short form of Thomas.
Thomy

Thoma (German) a form of Thomas.

Thomas (Greek, Aramaic) twin. Bible: one of the Twelve Apostles. See also Chuma, Foma, Maslin.
Tam, Tammy, Tavish, Tevis, Thom, Thoma, Thomason, Thomeson, Thomison, Thompson, Thomson, Tom, Toma, Tomas, Tomasso, Tomcy, Tomey, Tomi, Tomey, Tommy, Toomas

Thompson (English) son of Thomas.
Thomison, Thomson

Thor (Scandinavian) thunder. Mythology: the Norse god of thunder and war.
Thorin, Tor, Tyrus

Thorald (Scandinavian) Thor's follower.
Terrell, Terrill, Thorold, Torald

Thorbert (Scandinavian) Thor's brightness.
Torbert

Thorbjorn (Scandinavian) Thor's bear.
Thorburn, Thurborn, Thurburn

Thorgood (English) Thor is good.

Thorleif (Scandinavian) Thor's beloved.
Thorlief

Thorley (English) Thor's meadow.
Thorlea, Thorlee, Thorleigh, Thorly, Torley

Thorndike (English) thorny embankment.
Thorndyck, Thorndyke, Thorne

Thorne (English) a short form of names beginning with "Thorn."
Thorn, Thornie, Thorny

Thornley (English) thorny meadow.
Thorley, Thorne, Thornlea, Thornleigh, Thornly

Thornton (English) thorny town.
Thorne

Thorpe (English) village.
Thorp

Thorwald (Scandinavian) Thor's forest.
Thorvald

Thuc (Vietnamese) aware.

Thurlow (English) Thor's hill.

Thurmond (English) defended by Thor.
Thormond, Thurmund

Thurston (Scandinavian) Thor's stone.
Thorstan, Thorstein, Thorsten, Thurstain, Thurstan, Thursten, Torsten, Torston

Tiago (Spanish) a form of Jacob.

Tiberio (Italian) from the Tibor River region.
Tiberius, Tibius

Tibor (Hungarian) holy place.
Tiburcio

Tichawanna (Shona) we shall see.

Ticho (Spanish) a short form of Patrick.

Tiennot (French) a form of Stephen.
Tien

Tiernan (Irish) lord.

Tierney (Irish) lordly.
Tiarnach, Tiernan

Tige (English) a short form of Tiger.
Ti, Tig, Ty, Tyg, Tyge

Tiger (American) tiger; powerful and energetic.
Tige, Tyger

Tiimu (Moquelumnan) caterpiller coming out of the ground.

Tilden (English) tilled valley.

Tiktu (Moquelumnan) bird digging up potatoes.

Tilford (English) prosperous ford.

Till (German) a short form of Theodoric.
Thilo, Til, Tillman, Tilman, Tillmann, Tilson

Tilton (English) prosperous town.

Tim (Greek) a short form of Timothy.
Timmie, Timmy

Timin (Arabic) born near the sea. Mythology: sea serpent.

Timmy (Greek) a familiar form of Timothy.

Timo (Finnish) a form of Timothy.
Timio

Timofey (Russian) a form
of Timothy.
Timofei, Timofej, Timofeo

Timon (Greek) honorable.
History: a famous Greek
philosopher.

Timoteo (Portuguese,
Spanish) a form of
Timothy.

Timothy (Greek) honoring
God. See also Kimokeo.
**Tadhg, Taidgh, Tiege,
Tim, Tima, Timithy,
Timka, Timkin, Timmathy,
Timmothy, Timmoty,
Timmthy, Timmy, Timo,
Timofey, Timok, Timon,
Timontheo, Timonthy,
Timót, Timote, Timotei,
Timoteo, Timoteus,
Timothé, Timothée,
Timotheo, Timotheos,
Timotheus, Timothey,
Timthie, Tiomóid, Tisha,
Tomothy, Tymon,
Tymothy**

Timur (Hebrew) an alter-
nate form of Tamar.
(Russian) conqueror.
Timour

Tin (Vietnamese) thinker.

Tino (Greek) a short form
of Augustine. (Spanish)
venerable, majestic.
(Italian) small. A familiar
form of Antonio.
Tion

Tinsley (English) fortified
field.

Tisha (Russian) a form
of Timothy.
Tishka

Tito (Italian) a form of
Titus.
Titas, Titis, Titos

Titus (Greek) giant. (Latin)
hero. Bible: a recipient
of one of Paul's New
Testament letters.
Tite, Titek, Tito, Tytus

Tivon (Hebrew) nature
lover.

TJ (American) a combina-
tion of the initials T. + J.
**Teejay, Tj, T.J., T Jae,
Tjayda**

Tobal (Spanish) a short
form of Christopher.
Tabalito

Tobar (Gypsy) road.

Tobi (Yoruba) great.

Tobias (Hebrew) God is
good.
**Tobia, Tobiah, Tobiás,
Tobin, Tobit, Toby, Tobyn,
Tovin, Tuvya**

Toby (Hebrew) a familiar
form of Tobias.
Tobby, Tobe, Tobey, Tobie

Todd (English) fox.
Tod, Toddie, Toddy

Todor (Basque, Russian) a form of Theodore.
Teodor, Todar, Todas, Todos

Toft (English) small farm.

Tohon (Native American) cougar.

Tokala (Dakota) fox.

Toland (English) owner of taxed land.
Tolan

Tolbert (English) bright tax collector.

Toller (English) tax collector.

Tom (English) a short form of Tomas, Thomas.
Teo, Thom, Tommey, Tommie, Tommy

Toma (Romanian) a form of Thomas.
Tomah

Tomas (German) a form of Thomas.
Tom, Tomaisin, Tomaz, Tomcio, Tome, Tomek, Tomelis, Tomico, Tomik, Tomislaw, Tomo, Tomson

Tomás (Irish, Spanish) a form of Thomas.
Tomas, Tómas, Tomasz

Tomasso (Italian) a form of Thomas.
Tomaso, Tommaso

Tombe (Kakwa) northerners. Geography: a village in northern Uganda.

Tomey (Irish) a familiar form of Thomas.
Tome, Tomie, Tomy

Tomi (Japanese) rich. (Hungarian) a form of Thomas.

Tomlin (English) little Tom.
Tomkin, Tomlinson

Tommie (Hebrew) an alternate form of Tommy.
Tommi

Tommy (Hebrew) a familiar form of Thomas.
Tommie

Tonda (Czech) a form of Tony.
Tonek

Tong (Vietnamese) fragrant.

Toni (Greek, German, Slavic) a form of Tony.
Tonie, Tonio, Tonis, Tonnie

Tonio (Portuguese) a form of Tony. (Italian) a short form of Antonio.
Tono

Tony (Greek) flourishing. (Latin) praiseworthy. (English) a short form of Anthony. A familiar form of Remington.
Tonda, Tonek, Toney, Toni, Tonik, Tonio

Tooantuh (Cherokee) spring frog.

Toomas (Estonian) a form of Thomas.
Toomis, Tuomas, Tuomo

Topher (Greek) a short form of Christopher, Kristopher.
Tofer, Tophor

Topo (Spanish) gopher.

Topper (English) hill.

Tor (Norwegian) thunder. (Tiv) royalty, king.
Thor

Torin (Irish) chief.
Thorfin, Thorstein

Torkel (Swedish) Thor's cauldron.

Tormey (Irish) thunder spirit.
Tormé, Tormee

Tormod (Scottish) north.

Torn (Irish) a short form of Torrence.
Toran

Torquil (Danish) Thor's kettle.
Torkel

Torr (English) tower.
Tory

Torrence (Latin) an alternate form of Terrence. (Irish) knolls.
Tawrence, Torance, Toreence, Toren, Torin, Torn, Torr, Torren, Torreon, Torrin, Torry, Tory, Tuarence, Turance

Torrey (English) an alternate form of Tory.
Toreey, Torre, Torri, Torrie, Torry

Toru (Japanese) sea.

Tory (English) a familiar form of Torr, Torrence.
Tori, Torrey

Toshi-Shita (Japanese) junior.

Tovi (Hebrew) good.
Tov

Townley (English) town meadow.
Townlea, Townlee, Townleigh, Townlie, Townly

Townsend (English) town's end.
Town, Towney, Townie, Townshend, Towny

Trace (Irish) an alternate form of Tracy.

Tracy (Greek) harvester. (Latin) courageous. (Irish) battler.
Trace, Tracey, Tracie, Treacy

Trader (English) well-trodden path; skilled worker.

Trahern (Welsh) strong as iron.
Traherne, Tray

Tramaine (Scottish)
an alternate form of
Tremaine, Tremayne.
Tramain, Tramayne

Traugott (German) God's
truth.

Travell (English) traveler.
**Travelis, Travelle, Trevel,
Trevell, Trevelle**

Travers (French)
crossroads.
**Travaress, Travaris,
Travarius, Travarus,
Traver, Traverez, Travis,
Travoris, Travorus**

Travis (English) a form
of Travers.
**Travais, Traves, Traveus,
Travious, Traviss, Travus,
Travys, Trevais**

Trayton (English) town
full of trees.

Tredway (English) well-
worn road.
Treadway

Tremaine, Tremayne
(Scottish) house of stone.
**Tramaine, Tremain,
Treymaine, Trimaine**

Trent (Latin) torrent,
rapid stream. (French)
thirty. Geography:
a city in northern Italy.
**Trente, Trentino, Trento,
Trentonio**

Trenton (Latin) town
by the rapid stream.
Geography: a city
in New Jersey.
**Trendon, Trendun,
Trenten, Trentin, Trinton**

Trev (Irish, Welsh) a short
form of Trevor.

Trevelyan (English) Elian's
homestead.

Trevor (Irish) prudent.
(Welsh) homestead.
**Trefor, Trev, Trevar,
Trevares, Trevaris,
Trevarus, Trever, Trevoris,
Trevorus, Treyvor**

Trey (English) three; third.
Trae, Trai, Tray

Trigg (Scandinavian) trusty.

Trini (Latin) a short form
of Trinity.

Trinity (Latin) holy trinity.
Trenedy, Trini, Trinidy

Trip, Tripp (English)
traveler.

Tristan (Welsh) bold.
Literature: a knight in the
Arthurian legends who
fell in love with his
uncle's wife.
**Trestan, Treston, Tris,
Trisan, Tristano, Tristen,
Tristian, Tristin, Triston,
Trystan**

Tristano (Italian) a form of
Tristan.

Tristram (Welsh) sorrowful. Literature: the title character in Laurence Sterne's eighteenth-century novel *Tristram Shandy*.
Tristam

Trot (English) trickling stream.

Trowbridge (English) bridge by the tree.

Troy (Irish) foot soldier. (French) curly haired. (English) water. See also Koi.
Troi, Troye, Troyton

True (English) faithful, loyal.

Truesdale (English) faithful one's homestead.

Truitt (English) little and honest.
Truett

Truman (English) honest. History: Harry S Truman was the thirty-third U.S. president.
Trueman, Trumaine, Trumann

Trumble (English) strong; bold.
Trumball, Trumbell, Trumbull

Trustin (English) trustworthy.
Trustan, Trusten, Truston

Trygve (Norwegian) brave victor.

Trystan (Welsh) an alternate form of Tristan.
Tryistan, Trysten, Trystian, Trystin, Tryston

Tse (Ewe) younger of twins.

Tu (Vietnamese) tree.

Tuaco (Ghanian) eleventh-born.

Tuan (Vietnamese) goes smoothly.

Tuari (Laguna) young eagle.

Tucker (English) fuller, tucker of cloth.
Tuck, Tuckie, Tucky

Tudor (Welsh) a form of Theodore. History: an English dynasty.
Todor

Tug (Scandinavian) draw, pull.

Tuketu (Moquelumnan) bear making dust as it runs.

Tukuli (Moquelumnan) caterpillar crawling down a tree.

Tulio (Italian, Spanish) lively.

Tullis (Latin) title, rank.
Tullius, Tullos, Tully

Tully (Latin) a familiar form of Tullis. (Irish) at peace with God.
Tull, Tulley, Tullie, Tullio

Tumaini (Mwera) hope.

Tumu (Moquelumnan) deer thinking about eating wild onions.

Tung (Vietnamese) stately, dignified. (Chinese) everyone.

Tupi (Moquelumnan) pulled up.

Tupper (English) ram raiser.

Turi (Spanish) a short form of Arthur.

Turk (English) from Turkey.

Turner (Latin) lathe worker; woodworker.

Turpin (Scandinavian) Finn named after Thor.

Tut (Arabic) strong and courageous. History: a short form of Tutankhamen, an Egyptian pharoah. **Tutt**

Tutu (Spanish) a familiar form of Justin.

Tuvya (Hebrew) an alternate form of Tobias. **Tevya, Tuvia, Tuviah**

Tuwile (Mwera) death is inevitable.

Tuyen (Vietnamese) angel.

Twain (English) divided in two. Literature: Mark Twain (whose real name was Samuel Clemens) was one of the most prominent nineteenth-century American writers. **Tawine, Twaine, Tway, Twayn, Twayne**

Twia (Fanti) born after twins.

Twitchell (English) narrow passage. **Twytchell**

Twyford (English) double river crossing.

Txomin (Basque) like the Lord.

Ty (English) a short form of Tyler, Tyrone, Tyrus. **Tye**

Tyee (Native American) chief.

Tyger (English) a form of Tiger. **Tige, Tyg, Tygar**

Tyler (English) tile maker. **Tiler, Ty, Tyel, Tylar, Tyle, Tylee, Tylere, Tyller, Tylor**

Tylor (English) an alternate form of Tyler.

Tymon (Polish) a form of Timothy. **Tymeik, Tymek**

Tymothy (English) a form of Timothy. **Tymithy, Tymmothy, Tymoteusz, Tymothee, Timothi**

Tynan (Irish) dark.
 Ty

Tynek (Czech) a form
 of Martin.
 Tynko

Tyquan (American) a combination of Ty + Quan.
 Tyquann

Tyree (Scottish) island
 dweller. Geography: Tiree
 is an island off the west
 coast of Scotland.
 **Tyra, Tyrae, Tyrai, Tyray,
 Tyre, Tyrea, Tyrée**

Tyreese (American) a form
 of Terrence.
 **Tyreas, Tyrease, Tyrece,
 Tyreece, Tyreice**

Tyrel, Tyrell (American)
 forms of Terrell.
 Tyrelle, Tyrrel, Tyrrell

Tyrick (American) a combi-
 nation of Ty + Rick.
 **Tyreck, Tyreek, Tyreik,
 Tyrek, Tyreke, Tyric,
 Tyriek, Tyrik, Tyriq,
 Tyrique**

Tyron (American) a form
 of Tyrone.
 Tyronn, Tyronna, Tyronne

Tyrone (Greek) sovereign.
 (Irish) land of Owen.
 **Teirone, Terron, Ty,
 Tyerone, Tyron, Tyroney,
 Tyroon, Tyroun**

Tyrus (English) a form
 of Thor.
 Ty, Tyruss

Tyshawn (American)
 a combination of
 Ty + Shawn.
 **Tyshan, Tyshaun, Tyshinn,
 Tyshon**

Tyson (French) son of Ty.
 **Tison, Tiszon, Tyce, Tyesn,
 Tyeson, Tysen, Tysie,
 Tysne, Tysone**

Tytus (Polish) a form
 of Titus.
 Tyus

Tywan (Chinese) an alternate form of Taiwan.
 Tywon, Tywone

Tzadok (Hebrew)
 righteous.
 Tzadik, Zadok

Tzion (Hebrew) sign from
 God.
 Zion

Tzuriel (Hebrew) God is
 my rock.
 Tzuriya

Tzvi (Hebrew) deer.
 Tzevi, Zevi

Uaine (Irish) a form of Owen.

Ubadah (Arabic) serves God.

Ubaid (Arabic) faithful.

Uberto (Italian) a form of Hubert.

Uche (Ibo) thought.

Udell (English) yew-tree valley.
Dell, Eudel, Udale, Udall, Yudell

Udo (Japanese) ginseng plant. (German) a short form of Udolf.

Udolf (English) prosperous wolf.
Udo, Udolfo, Udolph

Ugo (Italian) an alternate form of Hugh.

Ugutz (Basque) a form of John. Religion: name honoring John the Baptist.

Uilliam (Irish) a form of William.
Uileog, Uilleam, Ulick

Uinseann (Irish) a form of Vincent.

Uistean (Irish) intelligent.
Uisdean

Uja (Sanskrit) growing.

Uku (Hawaiian) flea, insect; skilled ukulele player.

Ulan (African) first-born twin.

Ulbrecht (German) an alternate form of Albert.

Ulf (German) wolf.

Ulfred (German) peaceful wolf.

Ulger (German) warring wolf.

Ullock (German) sporting wolf.

Ulmer (English) famous wolf.
Ullmar, Ulmar

Ulmo (German) from Ulm, Germany.

Ulrich (German) wolf ruler; ruler of all. See also Alaric.
Uli, Ull, Ullric, Ulrick, Ulrik, Ulrike, Ulu, Ulz, Uwe

Ultman (Hindi) god; godlike. Religion: another name for the Hindu god Shiva.

Ulysses (Latin) wrathful. A form of Odysseus.
Ulick, Ulises, Ulishes, Ulisse, Ulisses, Ulysse

Umar (Arabic) an alternate form of Omar.
Umarr, Umayr, Umer

Umberto (Italian) a form of Humbert.
Uberto

Umi (Yao) life.

Umit (Turkish) hope.

Unai (Basque) shepherd.

Uner (Turkish) famous.

Unika (Lomwe) brighten.

Unwin (English) nonfriend.
Unwinn, Unwyn

Upshaw (English) upper wooded area.

Upton (English) upper town.

Upwood (English) upper forest.

Urban (Latin) city dweller; courteous.
Urbain, Urbaine, Urbane, Urbano, Urbanus, Urvan, Urvane

Urbane (English) a form of Urban.

Urbano (Italian) a form of Urban.

Uri (Hebrew) a short form of Uriah.
Urie

Uriah (Hebrew) my light. Bible: the husband of Bathsheba and a captain in David's army. See also Yuri.
Uri, Uria, Urias, Urijah

Urian (Greek) heaven.

Uriel (Hebrew) God is my light.
Urie

Urson (French) a form of Orson.
Ursan, Ursus

Urtzi (Basque) sky.

Usamah (Arabic) like a lion.
Usama

Useni (Yao) tell me.
Usene, Usenet

Usi (Yao) smoke.

Ustin (Russian) a form of Justin.

Utatci (Moquelumnan) bear scratching itself.

Uthman (Arabic) companion of the Prophet.

Uwe (German) a familiar form of Ulrich.

Uzi (Hebrew) my strength.

Uziel (Hebrew) God is my strength; mighty force.
Uzie, Uzziah, Uzziel

Uzoma (Nigerian) born during a journey.

Uzumati (Moquelumnan) grizzly bear.

Vachel (French) small cow.
Vache, Vachell

Vaclav (Czech) wreath of glory.
Vasek

Vadin (Hindi) speaker.

Vail (English) valley.
Vaile, Vaill, Vale, Valle

Val (Latin) a short form of Valentine.

Valborg (Swedish) mighty mountain.

Valdemar (Swedish) famous ruler.

Valentine (Latin) strong; healthy.
Val, Valencio, Valenté, Valentijn, Valentin, Valentino, Valentyn, Velentino

Valentino (Italian) a form of Valentine.

Valerian (Latin) strong; healthy.
Valeriano, Valerii, Valerio, Valeryn

Valerii (Russian) a form of Valerian.
Valera, Valerij, Valerik

Valfrid (Swedish) strong peace.

Valin (Hindi) an alternate form of Balin. Mythology: a tyrannical monkey king.

Vallis (French) from Wales, England.

Valter (Lithuanian, Swedish) a form of Walter.
Valters, Valther, Valtr, Vanda

Van (Dutch) a short form of Vandyke.
Vander, Vane, Vann, Vanno

Vance (English) thresher.

Vanda (Lithuanian) a form of Walter.
Vander

Vandyke (Dutch) dyke.
Van

Vanya (Russian) a familiar form of Ivan.
Vanechka, Vanek, Vanka, Vanusha

Vardon (French) green knoll.
Varden, Verdan, Verdon, Verdun

Varian (Latin) variable.

Varick (German) protecting ruler.
Warrick

Vartan (Armenian) rose producer; rose giver.

Varun (Hindi) rain god.
Varron

Vashawn (American)
a combination of the
prefix Va + Shawn.
**Vashae, Vashan, Vashann,
Vashaun, Vashon, Vishon**

Vasilis (Greek) an alternate
form of Basil.
**Vas, Vasaya, Vaselios,
Vashon, Vasil, Vasile,
Vasileior, Vasileios,
Vasilios, Vasilius, Vasilos,
Vasilus, Vasily, Vasylko,
Vasyltso, Vazul**

Vasily (Russian) a form
of Vasilis.
**Vasilek, Vasili, Vasilii,
Vasilije, Vasilik, Vassili,
Vassilij, Vasya, Vasyenka**

Vasin (Hindi) ruler, lord.

Vasyl (German, Slavic)
a form of William.
**Vasos, Vassily, Vassos,
Vasya, Vasyuta, VaVaska,
Wassily**

Vaughn (Welsh) small.
**Vaughan, Vaughen, Vaun,
Von, Voughn**

Veasna (Cambodian) lucky.

Vedie (Latin) sight.

Vegard (Norwegian)
sanctuary; protection.

Velvel (Yiddish) wolf.

Vencel (Hungarian) a short
form of Wenceslaus.
Venci, Vencie

Venedictos (Greek) a form
of Benedict.
**Venedict, Venediktos,
Venka, Venya**

Veniamin (Bulgarian)
a form of Benjamin.
Verniamin

Venkat (Hindi) god;
godlike. Religion: another
name for the Hindu god
Shiva.

Venya (Russian) a familiar
form of Benedict.
Venedict, Venka

Vere (Latin, French) true.

Vered (Hebrew) rose.

Vergil (Latin) an alternate
form of Virgil.
Verge

Vern (Latin) a short form
of Vernon.
**Verna, Vernal, Verne,
Vernell, Vernine, Vernis,
Vernol**

Vernados (German)
courage of the bear.

Verner (German) defend-
ing army.
Varner

Verney (French) alder
grove.
Vernie

Vernon (Latin) springlike;
youthful.
**Vern, Vernen, Verney,
Vernin**

Verrill (German) mascu-
line. (French) loyal.
**Verill, Verrall, Verrell,
Verroll, Veryl**

Vian (English) full of life.
A masculine short form
of Vivian.

Vic (Latin) a short form
of Victor.
Vick, Vicken, Vickenson

Vicente (Spanish) a form
of Vincent.
Vicent, Visente

Vicenzo (Italian) a form
of Vincent.

Victoir (French) a form
of Victor.

Victor (Latin) victor,
conqueror.
**Vic, Victa, Victer,
Victoir, Victoriano,
Victorien, Victorin,
Victorio, Viktor, Vitin,
Vittorio, Wiktor**

Victorio (Spanish) a form
of Victor.
Victorino

Vida (Spanish) a form
of Vitas.
Vidal

Vidar (Norwegian) tree
warrior.

Vidor (Hungarian) cheerful.

Viho (Cheyenne) chief.

Vijay (Hindi) victorious.
Religion: another name
for the Hindu god Shiva.

Vikas (Hindi) growing.

Viktor (German,
Hungarian, Russian) a form
of Victor.
Viktoras, Viktors

Vilhelm (German) a form
of William.
**Vilhelms, Vilho, Vilis,
Viljo, Villem**

Vili (Hungarian) a short
form of William.
Vilmos

Viliam (Czech) a form
of William.
**Vila, Vilek, Vilém, Vilko,
Vilous**

Viljo (Finnish) a form
of William.

Ville (Swedish) a short
form of William.

Vin (Latin) a short form
of Vincent.
Vinn

Vinay (Hindi) polite.

Vince (English) a short
form of Vincent.
Vence, Vint

Vincent (Latin) victor,
conqueror. See also
Binkentios, Binky.
**Uinseann, Vencent,
Vicente, Vicenzo, Vikent,
Vikenti, Vikesha, Vin,
Vince, Vincence, Vincens,**

Vincente, Vincentius, Vincents, Vincenty, Vincenzo, Vinci, Vincien, Vincient, Vinciente, Vinny, Wincent

Vincente (Spanish) a form of Vincent.
Vencente

Vincenzo (Italian) a form of Vincent.
Vincenz, Vincenzio, Vinzenz

Vinci (Hungarian, Italian) a familiar form of Vincent.
Vinci, Vinco, Vincze

Vinny (English) a familiar form of Calvin, Vincent. See also Melvin.
Vinnie

Vinson (English) son of Vincent.
Vinnis

Virgil (Latin) rod bearer, staff bearer. Literature: a Roman poet best known for his epic *Aenid*.
Vergil, Virge, Virgial, Virgie, Virgilio

Virgilio (Spanish) a form of Virgil.

Virote (Thai) strong, powerful.

Vishnu (Hindi) protector.

Vitas (Latin) alive, vital.
Vida

Vitya (Russian) a form of Victor.
Vitenka, Vitka

Vito (Latin) a short form of Vittorio.
Veit, Vidal, Vital, Vitale, Vitalis, Vitas, Vitin, Vitis, Vitus, Vitya, Vytas

Vittorio (Italian) a form of Victor.
Vito, Vitor, Vitorio, Vittore, Vittorios

Vivek (Hindi) wisdom.
Vivekinan

Vladimir (Russian) famous prince. See also Dima, Waldemar, Walter.
Vimka, Vlad, Vladamir, Vladik, Vladimar, Vladimeer, Vladimire, Vladjimir, Vladka, Vladko, Vladlen, Volodya, Volya, Vova, Wladimir

Vladislav (Slavic) glorious ruler.
Vladik, Vladya, Vlas, Vlasislava, Vyacheslav, Wladislav

Vlas (Russian) a short form of Vladislav.

Volker (German) people's guard.
Folke

Volney (German) national spirit.

Von (German) a short form of many German names.

Vova (Russian) a form
of Walter.
Vovka

Vuai (Swahili) savior.

Vyacheslav (Russian)
a form of Vladislav.
See also Slava.

Waban (Native American)
east wind.
Wabon

Wade (English) ford; river
crossing.
**Wadesworth, Wadie,
Waide, Wayde, Waydell**

Wadley (English) ford
meadow.
Wadleigh, Wadly

Wadsworth (English)
village near the ford.
Waddsworth

Wafula (Samia) rain;
born during the rain.

Wagner (German)
wagoner, wagon maker.
Music: Richard Wagner
was a famous German
composer.
Waggoner

Wahid (Arabic) single;
exclusively unequaled.
Waheed

Wahkan (Lakota) sacred.

Wahkoowah (Lakota)
charging.

Wain (English) a short form
of Wainwright. An alter-
nate form of Wayne.

Wainwright (English)
wagon maker.
**Wain, Wainright, Wayne,
Wayneright,
Waynewright, Waynright,
Wright**

Waite (English) watchman.
**Waitman, Waiton, Waits,
Wayte**

Wakefield (English) wet
field.
Field, Wake

Wakely (English) wet
meadow.

Wakeman (English)
watchman.
Wake

Wakiza (Native American)
determined warrior.

Walcott (English) cottage
by the wall.
**Wallcot, Wallcott,
Wolcott**

Waldemar (German)
powerful; famous.
See also Vladimir.
**Valdemar, Waldermar,
Waldo**

Walden (English) wooded valley. Literature: Henry David Thoreau made Walden Pond famous with his book *Walden*.
Waldi, Waldo, Waldon, Welti

Waldo (German) a familiar form of Oswald, Waldemar, Walden.
Wald, Waldy

Waldron (English) ruler.

Waleed (Arabic) newborn.
Waled, Walid

Walerian (Polish) strong; brave.

Wales (English) from Wales, England.
Wael, Wail, Wali, Walie, Waly

Walford (English) Welshman's ford.

Walfred (German) peaceful ruler.

Wali (Arabic) all-governing.

Walker (English) cloth walker; cloth cleaner.
Wallie, Wally

Wallace (English) from Wales.
Wallach, Wallas, Wallie, Wallis, Wally, Walsh, Welsh

Wallach (German) a form of Wallace.
Wallache

Waller (German) powerful. (English) wall maker.

Wally (English) a familiar form of Walter.
Walli, Wallie

Walmond (German) mighty ruler.

Walsh (English) an alternate form of Wallace.
Welch, Welsh

Walt (English) a short form of Walter, Walton.
Waltey, Waltli, Walty

Walter (German) army ruler, general. (English) woodsman. See also Gualberto, Gualtiero, Ladislav, Vladimir.
Valter, Vanda, Vova, Walder, Wally, Walt, Waltli, Walther, Waltr, Wat, Waterio, Watkins, Watson

Walther (German) an alternate form of Walter.

Walton (English) walled town.
Walt

Waltr (Czech) a form of Walter.

Walworth (English) fenced-in farm.

Walwyn (English) Welsh friend.
Walwin, Walwinn, Walwynn, Walwynne, Welwyn

Wamblee (Lakota) eagle.

Wang (Chinese) hope; wish.

Wanikiya (Lakota) savior.

Wapi (Native American) lucky.

Warburton (English) fortified town.

Ward (English) watchman, guardian.
Warde, Warden, Worden

Wardell (English) watchman's hill.

Wardley (English) watchman's meadow.
Wardlea, Wardleigh

Ware (English) wary, cautious.

Warfield (English) field near the weir; fishtrap.

Warford (English) ford near the weir; fishtrap.

Warley (English) meadow near the weir; fishtrap.

Warner (German) armed defender. (French) park keeper.
Werner

Warren (German) general; warden; rabbit hutch.
Ware, Waring, Warrenson, Warrin, Warriner, Worrin

Warton (English) town near the weir; fishtrap.

Warwick (English) buildings near the weir; fishtrap.
Warick, Warrick

Washburn (English) overflowing river.

Washington (English) town near water. History: George Washington was the first U.S. president.
Wash

Wasili (Russian) a form of Basil.
Wasyl

Wasim (Arabic) graceful; good looking.
Waseem

Watende (Nyakyusa) there will be revenge.

Waterio (Spanish) a form of Walter.
Gualtiero

Watford (English) wattle ford; dam made of twigs and sticks.

Watkins (English) son of Walter.
Watkin

Watson (English) son of Walter.
Wathson

Waverly (English) quaking aspen-tree meadow.
Waverlee, Waverley

Waylon (English) land by the road.
Wallen, Walon, Way,

Waylan, Wayland, Waylen, Waylin, Weylin

Wayman (English) road man; traveler.
Waymon

Wayne (English) wagon maker. A short form of Wainwright.
Wain, Wanye, Wayn, Waynell, Wene

Wazir (Arabic) minister.

Webb (English) weaver.
Web, Weeb

Weber (German) weaver.
Webner

Webley (English) weaver's meadow.
Webbley, Webbly, Webly

Webster (English) weaver.

Weddel (English) valley near the ford.

Wei-Quo (Chinese) ruler of the country.
Wei

Welborne (English) spring-fed stream.
Welborn, Welbourne, Welburn, Wellborn, Wellborne, Wellbourn, Wellburn

Welby (German) farm near the well.
Welbey, Welbie, Wellbey, Wellby

Weldon (English) hill near the well.

Welfel (Yiddish) a form of William.
Welvel

Welford (English) ford near the well.

Wells (English) springs.

Welsh (English) an alternate form of Wallace, Walsh.
Welch

Welton (English) town near the well.

Wemilat (Native American) all give to him.

Wemilo (Native American) all speak to him.

Wen (Gypsy) born in winter.

Wenceslaus (Slavic) wreath of honor. Music: "Good King Wenceslaus" is a popular Christmas Carol.
Vencel, Wenceslas, Wenzel, Wiencyslaw

Wendell (German) wanderer. (English) good dale, good valley.
Wandale, Wendall, Wendel, Wendle, Wendy

Wene (Hawaiian) a form of Wayne.

Wenford (English) white ford.
Wynford

Wentworth (English) pale man's settlement.

Wenutu (Native American) clear sky.

Werner (English) a form of Warner.
Wernhar, Wernher

Wes (English) a short form of Wesley.
Wess

Wesh (Gypsy) woods.

Wesley (English) western meadow.
Wes, Weslee, Wesleyan, Weslie, Wesly, Wessley, Westleigh, Westley

West (English) west.

Westbrook (English) western brook.
Brook, West, Westbrooke

Westby (English) western farmstead.

Westcott (English) western cottage.
Wescot, Wescott, Westcot

Westley (English) an alternate form of Wesley.

Weston (English) western town.
West, Westen, Westin

Wetherby (English) wether-sheep farm.
Weatherbey, Weatherbie, Weatherby, Wetherbey, Wetherbie

Wetherell (English) wether-sheep corner.

Wetherly (English) wether-sheep meadow.

Whalley (English) woods near a hill.

Wharton (English) town on the bank of a lake.
Warton

Wheatley (English) wheat field.
Whatley, Wheatlea, Wheatleigh, Wheatly

Wheaton (English) wheat town.

Wheeler (English) wheel maker; wagon driver.

Whistler (English) whistler, piper.

Whit (English) a short form of Whitman, Whitney.
Whitt, Whyt, Whyte, Wit, Witt

Whitby (English) white house.

Whitcomb (English) white valley.
Whitcombe, Whitcumb

Whitelaw (English) small hill.
Whitlaw

Whitey (English) white skinned; white haired.

Whitfield (English) white field.

Whitford (English) white ford.

Whitley (English) white meadow.
Whitlea, Whitlee, Whitleigh

Whitman (English) white-haired man.
Whit

Whitmore (English) white moor.
Whitmoor, Whittemore, Witmore, Wittemore

Whitney (English) white island; white water.
Whit, Whittney, Widney, Widny

Whittaker (English) white field.
Whitacker, Whitaker, Whitmaker

Wicasa (Dakota) man.

Wicent (Polish) a form of Vincent.
Wicek, Wicus

Wichado (Native American) willing.

Wickham (English) village enclosure.
Wick

Wickley (English) village meadow.
Wilcley

Wid (English) wide.

Wies (German) renowned warrior.

Wikoli (Hawaiian) a form of Victor.

Wiktor (Polish) a form of Victor.

Wilanu (Moquelumnan) pouring water on flour.

Wilbert (German) brilliant; resolute.
Wilberto, Wilburt

Wilbur (English) wall fortification; bright willows.
Wilber, Wilburn, Wilburt, Willbur, Wilver

Wilder (English) wilderness, wild.

Wildon (English) wooded hill.
Wilden, Willdon

Wile (Hawaiian) a form of Willie.

Wiley (English) willow meadow; Will's meadow.
Wildy, Willey, Wylie

Wilford (English) willow-tree ford.

Wilfred (German) determined peacemaker.
Wilferd, Wilfredo, Wilfrid, Wilfride, Wilfried, Wilfryd, Will, Willfred, Willfried, Willie, Willy

Wilfredo (Spanish) a form of Wilfred.
Fredo, Wifredo, Willfredo

Wilhelm (German) determined guardian.

The original form of
William.
Wilhelmus, Willem

Wiliama (Hawaiian)
a form of William.
Pila, Wile

Wilkie (English) a familiar
form of Wilkins.
Wikie

Wilkins (English)
William's kin.
**Wilkens, Wilkes, Wilkie,
Wilkin, Willkes, Willkins**

Wilkinson (English)
son of little William.
Willkinson

Will (English) a short
form of William.
Wilm, Wim

Willard (German) determined and brave.

Willem (German) a form
of William.

William (English) deter-
mined guardian. See also
Gilamu, Guglielmo,
Guilherme, Guillaume,
Guillermo, Gwilym, Liam,
Uilliam, Wilhelm.
**Bil, Vasyl, Vilhelm, Vili,
Viliam, Viljo, Ville,
Villiam, Welfel, Wilek,
Wiliama, Wiliame,
Wiliame, Willaim, Willam,
Willeam, Willem,
Williams, Willie, Willil,
Willis, Williw, Willyam,
Wim**

Williams (German) son
of William.
Williamson

Willie (German) a familiar
form of William.
**Wile, Wille, Willey, Willi,
Willia, Willy, Wily**

Willis (German) son of
Willie.
Willice, Wills, Willus

Willoughby (English)
willow farm.
Willoughbey, Willoughbie

Wills (English) son of Will.

Wilmer (German) deter-
mined and famous.
**Willimar, Willmer, Wilm,
Wilmar, Wylmar, Wylmer**

Wilmot (Teutonic) resolute
spirit.
Willmot, Wilm, Wilmont

Wilny (Native American)
eagle singing while flying.

Wilson (English) son of
Will.
Wilkinson, Willson

Wilt (English) a short form
of Wilton.

Wilton (English) farm by
the spring.
Will, Wilt

Wilu (Moquelumnan)
chicken hawk squawking.

Win (Cambodian) bright.
(English) a short form
of Winston.
Winn, Winnie, Winny

Wincent (Polish) a form of Vincent.
Wicek, Wicenty, Wicus, Wince, Wincenty

Winchell (English) bend in the road; bend in the land.

Windsor (English) riverbank with a winch. History: the surname of the British royal family.
Wincer, Winsor, Wyndsor

Winfield (English) friendly field.
Field, Winifield, Winnfield, Wynfield, Wynnfield

Winfried (German) friend of peace.

Wing (Chinese) glory.
Wing-Chiu, Wing-Kit

Wingate (English) winding gate.

Wingi (Native American) willing.

Winslow (English) friend's hill.

Winston (English) friendly town; victory town.
Win, Winsten, Winstonn, Winton, Wynstan, Wynston

Winter (English) born in winter.
Winterford

Winthrop (English) victory at the crossroads.

Winton (English) an alternate form of Winston.
Wynten, Wynton

Winward (English) friend's guardian; friend's forest.

Wit (Polish) life. (English) an alternate form of Whit. (Flemish) a short form of DeWitt.
Witt, Wittie, Witty

Witek (Polish) a form of Victor.

Witha (Arabic) handsome.

Witter (English) wise warrior.

Witton (English) wise man's estate.

Wladislav (Polish) a form of Vladislav.
Wladislaw

Wolcott (English) cottage in the woods.

Wolf (German, English) a short form of Wolfe, Wolfgang.
Wolff, Wolfie, Wolfy

Wolfe (English) wolf.
Wolf, Woolf

Wolfgang (German) wolf quarrel. Music: Wolfgang Amadeus Mozart was a famous eighteenth-century Austrian composer.
Wolf, Wolfgans

Wood (English) a short form of Woodrow. See also Elwood, Garwood.
Woody

Woodfield (English) forest meadow.

Woodford (English) ford through the forest.

Woodrow (English) passage in the woods. History: Thomas Woodrow Wilson was the twenty-eighth U.S. president.
Wood, Woodman, Woody

Woodruff (English) forest ranger.

Woodson (English) son of Wood.

Woodward (English) forest warden.
Woodard

Woodville (English) town at the edge of the woods.

Woody (American) a familiar form of Woodrow.
Wooddy, Woodie

Woolsey (English) victorious wolf.

Worcester (English) forest army camp.

Wordsworth (English) wolf-guardian's farm. Literature: William Wordsworth was a famous English poet.
Worth

Worie (Ibo) born on market day.

Worth (English) a short form of Woodsworth.
Worthey, Worthington, Worthy

Worton (English) farm town.

Wouter (German) powerful warrior.

Wrangle (American) an alternate form of Rangle.
Wrangler

Wray (Scandinavian) corner property. (English) crooked.

Wren (Welsh) chief, ruler. (English) wren.

Wright (English) a short form of Wainwright.

Wrisley (English) an alternate form of Risley.
Wrisee, Wrislie, Wrisly

Wriston (English) an alternate form of Riston.
Wryston

Wuliton (Native American) will do well.

Wunand (Native American) God is good.

Wuyi (Moquelumnan) turkey vulture flying.

Wyatt (French) little warrior.
Wiatt, Wyat, Wyatte, Wye, Wyeth

Wybert (English)
battle-bright.

Wyborn (Scandinavian)
war bear.

Wyck (Scandinavian)
village.

Wycliff (English) white
cliff; village near the cliff.
Wycliffe

Wylie (English) charming.
Wiley, Wye

Wyman (English) fighter,
warrior.

Wymer (English) famous
in battle.

Wyn (Welsh) light skinned,
white. (English) friend.
A short form of Selwyn.
Win, Wynn, Wynne

Wyndham (Scottish)
village near the winding
road.
Windham, Wynndham

Wynono (Native American)
first-born son.

Wythe (English) willow
tree.

Xabat (Basque) savior.

Xan (Greek) a short form
of Alexander.
Xande, Xander

Xanthus (Latin) golden
haired.
Xanthos

Xarles (Basque) a form
of Charles.

Xavier (Arabic) bright.
(Basque) owner of the
new house. See also Javier,
Salvatore, Saverio.
**Xabier, Xaiver, Xaver,
Xavian, Xavon, Xever,
Xizavier, Xzaiver,
Xzavaier, Xzaver, Xzavier,
Xzavion, Zavier**

Xenophon (Greek) strange
voice.
Xeno, Zennie

Xenos (Greek) stranger;
guest.
Zenos

Xerxes (Persian) ruler.
History: a name used by
many Persian emperors.
Zerk

Ximenes (Spanish) a form of Simon.
Ximenez, Ximon, Ximun, Xymenes

Xylon (Greek) forest.

Yadid (Hebrew) friend; beloved.
Yedid

Yadon (Hebrew) he will judge.
Yadin, Yadun

Yael (Hebrew) an alternate form of Jael.

Yafeu (Ibo) bold.

Yagil (Hebrew) he will rejoice.

Yago (Spanish) a form of James.

Yahto (Lakota) blue.

Yahya (Arabic) living.

Yair (Hebrew) he will enlighten.

Yakecen (Dene) sky song.

Yakez (Carrier) heaven.

Yakov (Russian) a form of Jacob.
Yaacob, Yaacov, Yaakov, Yachov, Yacov, Yakob, Yashko

Yale (German) productive. (English) old.

Yan (Russian) a form of John.
Yanichek, Yanik, Yanka

Yana (Native American) bear.

Yancy (Native American) Englishman, Yankee.
Yan, Yance, Yancey, Yanci, Yantsey

Yanka (Russian) a form of John.
Yanic, Yanick, Yanikm, Yannick, Yonnik

Yanni (Greek) a form of John.
Ioannis, Yani, Yannakis, Yannis, Yiannis

Yanton (Hebrew) an alternate form of Johnathon, Jonathon.

Yao (Ewe) born on Thursday.

Yawo (Akan) born on Thursday.

Yaphet (Hebrew) an alternate form of Japheth.
Yapheth, Yefat, Yephat

Yarb (Gypsy) herb.

Yardan (Arabic) king.

Yarden (Hebrew) an alternate form of Jordan. Geography: another name for the Jordan River, which flows through Israel.

Yardley (English) enclosed meadow.
Lee, Yard, Yardlea, Yardlee, Yardleigh, Yardly

Yarom (Hebrew) he will raise up.
Yarum

Yaron (Hebrew) he will sing; he will cry out.
Jaron, Yairon

Yasashiku (Japanese) gentle; polite.

Yasha (Russian) a form of Jacob, James.
Yascha, Yashka, Yashko

Yasin (Arabic) prophet. Religion: another name for Muhammed.

Yasir (Afghani) humble; takes it easy. (Arabic) wealthy.
Yasar, Yaser, Yashar, Yasser

Yasuo (Japanese) restful.

Yates (English) gates.
Yeats

Yavin (Hebrew) he will understand.
Jabin

Yazid (Arabic) his power will increase.

Yechiel (Hebrew) God lives.

Yedidya (Hebrew) an alternate form of Jedidiah. See also Didi.

Yadai, Yedidia, Yedidiah, Yido

Yegor (Russian) a form of George. See also Egor, Igor.
Ygor

Yehoshua (Hebrew) an alternate form of Joshua.
Yoshua, Y'shua, Yushua

Yehoyakem (Hebrew) an alternate form of Joachim.
Yakim, Yehayakim, Yokim, Yoyakim

Yehudi (Hebrew) an alternate form of Judah.
Yechudi, Yechudit, Yehuda, Yehudah, Yehudit

Yelutci (Moquelumnan) bear walking silently.

Yeoman (English) attendent; retainer.
Yoeman, Youman

Yeremey (Russian) a form of Jeremiah.
Yarema, Yaremka, Yerik

Yervant (Armenian) king, ruler. History: an Armenian king.

Yeshaya (Hebrew) gift. See also Shai.

Yeshurun (Hebrew) right way.

Yeska (Russian) a form of Joseph.
Yesya

Yestin (Welsh) just.

Yevgenyi (Russian) a form of Eugene.
Gena, Yevgeni, Yevgenij

Yigal (Hebrew) he will redeem.
Yagel, Yigael

Yirmaya (Hebrew) an alternate form of Jeremiah.
Yirmayahu

Yishai (Hebrew) an alternate form of Jesse.

Yisrael (Hebrew) an alternate form of Israel.
Yesarel, Yisroel

Yitro (Hebrew) an alternate form of Jethro.

Yitzchak (Hebrew) an alternate form of Isaac. See also Itzak.
Yitzak, Yitzchok, Yitzhak

Yngve (Swedish) ancestor; lord, master.

Yo (Cambodian) honest.

Yoakim (Slavic) a form of Jacob.
Yoackim

Yoav (Hebrew) an alternate form of Joab.

Yochanan (Hebrew) an alternate form of John.
Yohanan

Yoel (Hebrew) an alternate form of Joel.

Yogesh (Hindi) ascetic. Religion: another name for the Hindu god Shiva.

Yohance (Hausa) a form of John.

Yohann (German) a form of Johann.
Yohane, Yohannes, Yohn

Yonah (Hebrew) an alternate form of Jonah.
Yonas

Yonatan (Hebrew) an alternate form of Jonathan.
Yonathan, Yonathon

Yong (Chinese) courageous.

Yong-Sun (Korean) dragon in the first position; courageous.

Yoofi (Akan) born on Friday.

Yooku (Fanti) born on Wednesday.

Yoram (Hebrew) high God.
Joram

York (English) boar estate; yew-tree estate.
Yorick, Yorke, Yorker, Yorkie, Yorrick

Yorkoo (Fanti) born on Thursday.

Yosef (Hebrew) an alternate form of Joseph. See also Osip.
Yoseff, Yosif, Yosyf, Yousef, Yusif

Yóshi (Japanese) adopted son.
Yoshiki, Yoshiuki

Yoshiyahu (Hebrew) an alternate form of Josiah.
Yoshia, Yoshiah, Yoshiyah

Yoskolo (Moquelumnan) breaking off pinecones.

Yosu (Hebrew) an alternate form of Jesus.

Yotimo (Moquelumnan) yellow jacket carrying food to its hive.

Yottoko (Native American) mud at the water's edge.

Young (English) young.

Young-Jae (Korean) pile of prosperity.

Young-Soo (Korean) keeping the prosperity.

Yousef (Yiddish) a form of Joseph.
Yousaf, Youseef, Yousef, Yousif, Yousuf

Youssel (Yiddish) a familiar form of Joseph.
Yussel

Yov (Russian) a short form of Yoakim.

Yovan (Slavic) an alternate form of Jovan.
Yovani, Yovanny, Yovany

Yoyi (Hebrew) a form of George.

Yrjo (Finnish) a form of George.

Ysidro (Greek) a short form of Isidore.

Yu (Chinese) universe.
Yue

Yudell (English) an alternate form of Udell.
Yudale, Yudel

Yuki (Japanese) snow.
Yukiko, Yukio, Yuuki

Yul (Mongolian) beyond the horizon.

Yule (English) born at Christmas.

Yuli (Basque) youthful.

Yuma (Native American) son of a chief.

Yunus (Turkish) a form of Jonah.

Yurcel (Turkish) sublime.

Yuri (Russian, Ukrainian) a form of George. (Hebrew) a familiar form of Uriah.
Yehor, Youri, Yura, Yurchik, Yure, Yurii, Yurij, Yurik, Yurko, Yurochka, Yurri, Yury, Yusha

Yusif (Russian) a form of Joseph.
Yusup, Yuzef, Yuzep

Yustyn (Russian) a form of Justin.
Yusts

Yusuf (Arabic, Swahili) a form of Joseph.
Yusef, Yusuff

Yutu (Moquelumnan) coyote out hunting.

Yuval (Hebrew) rejoicing.

Yves (French) a form
of Ives.
Yvens, Yvon

Yvon (French) an alternate
form of Ivar, Yves.
Ivon

Zac (Hebrew) a short form
of Zacharia, Zachary.
Zacc

Zacarias (Portuguese,
Spanish) a form of
Zachariah.
Zacaria, Zacariah

Zacary (Hebrew) an alter-
nate form of Zachary.
**Zac, Zacaras, Zacariah,
Zacarias, Zacarious,
Zacory, Zacrye**

Zaccary (Hebrew) an alter-
nate form of Zachary.
**Zac, Zaccaeus, Zaccari,
Zaccaria, Zaccariah,
Zaccary, Zaccea, Zaccury**

Zaccheus (Hebrew) innocent, pure.
Zacceus, Zacchaeus

Zach (Hebrew) a short form
of Zacharia, Zachary.

Zachariah (Hebrew) God
remembered.
**Zacarias, Zacarius, Zacary,
Zaccary, Zacharias,
Zachary, Zachory,
Zachury, Zako, Zaquero,
Zecharia, Zechariah,
Zecharya, Zeggery, Zeke,
Zhachory**

Zacharias (German)
a form of Zachariah.
**Zacarías, Zakarias,
Zekarias**

Zacharie (Hebrew)
an alternate form of
Zachary.
Zachare, Zacharee

Zachary (Hebrew) God
remembered. A familiar
form of Zachariah.
History: Zachary Taylor
was the twelfth U.S.
president. See also
Sachar, Sakeri.
**Zacary, Zaccary,
Zach, Zacha, Zachaios,
Zacharey, Zachari,
Zacharia, Zacharias,
Zacharie, Zachaury,
Zachery, Zachry, Zack,
Zackary, Zackery,
Zakary, Zeke**

Zachery (Hebrew) an alter-
nate form of Zachary.
**Zacherey, Zacheria,
Zacherias, Zacheriah,
Zacherie, Zacherius**

Zachry (Hebrew) an alternate form of Zachary.

Zachre, Zachrey, Zachri

Zack (Hebrew) a short form of Zachariah, Zachary.
Zach, Zak, Zaks

Zackary (Hebrew) an alternate form of Zachary.
Zack, Zackari, Zacharia, Zackariah, Zackarie, Zackery, Zackie, Zackorie, Zackory, Zackree, Zackrey, Zackry

Zackery (Hebrew) an alternate form of Zachery.

Zadok (Hebrew) a short form of Tzadok.
Zaddik, Zadik, Zadoc, Zaydok

Zadornin (Basque) Saturn.

Zafir (Arabic) victorious.
Zafar, Zafeer, Zaffar

Zahid (Arabic) self-denying, ascetic.

Zahir (Arabic) shining, bright.
Zahair, Zaheer, Zahi, Zayyir

Zahur (Swahili) flower.

Zaid (Arabic) increase, growth.

Zaide (Hebrew) older.

Zaim (Arabic) brigadier general.

Zakariyya (Arabic) prophet. Religion: an Islamic prophet.

Zakary (Hebrew) an alternate form of Zachery.
Zak, Zakarai, Zakareeyah, Zakari, Zakaria, Zakarias, Zakarie, Zakariya, Zakariyyah, Zakary, Zake, Zakerie, Zakery, Zakhar, Zaki, Zakir, Zakkai, Zako, Zakqary, Zakree, Zakri, Zakris, Zakry

Zaki (Arabic) bright; pure. (Hausa) lion.
Zakia

Zakia (Swahili) intelligent.

Zako (Hungarian) a form of Zachariah.

Zale (Greek) sea-strength.
Zayle

Zalmai (Afghani) young.

Zalman (Yiddish) a form of Solomon.
Zaloman

Zamiel (German) a form of Samuel.
Zamal, Zamuel

Zamir (Hebrew) song; bird.

Zan (Italian) clown.
Zanni

Zander (Greek) a short form of Alexander.
Zandrae, Zandy

Zane (English) a form of John.
Zain, Zayne

Zanis (Latvian) an alternate form of Janis.
Zannis

Zanvil (Hebrew) an alternate form of Samuel.
Zanwill

Zareb (African) protector.

Zared (Hebrew) ambush.

Zarek (Polish) may God protect the king.

Zavier (Arabic) an alternate form of Xavier.
Zavior, Zayvius, Zxavian

Zayit (Hebrew) olive.

Zdenek (Czech) follower of Saint Denis.

Zeb (Hebrew) a short form of Zebediah, Zebulon.
Zev

Zebediah (Hebrew) God's gift.
Zeb, Zebadia, Zebadiah, Zebedee, Zebedia, Zedidiah

Zebedee (Hebrew) a familiar form of Zebediah.
Zebadee

Zebulon (Hebrew) exalted, honored; lofty house.
Zabulan, Zeb, Zebulen, Zebulun, Zebulyn, Zev, Zevulon, Zevulun, Zubin

Zechariah (Hebrew) an alternate form of Zachariah.
Zecharia, Zekarias, Zeke, Zekeriah

Zed (Hebrew) a short form of Zedekiah.

Zedekiah (Hebrew) God is mighty and just.
Zed, Zedechiah, Zedekias

Zedidiah (Hebrew) an alternate form of Zebediah.

Zeeman (Dutch) seaman.

Zeév (Hebrew) wolf.
Zeévi, Zeff, Zif

Zeheb (Turkish) gold.

Zeke (Hebrew) a short form of Ezekiel, Zachariah, Zachary, Zechariah.

Zeki (Turkish) clever, intelligent.

Zelgai (Afghani) heart.

Zelig (Yiddish) a form of Selig.
Zeligman, Zelik

Zelimir (Slavic) wishes for peace.

Zemar (Afghani) lion.

Zen (Japanese) religious. Religion: a form of Buddhism.

Zenda (Czech) a form of Eugene.
Zhek

Zeno (Greek) cart; harness. History: a Greek philosopher.
Zenan, Zenas, Zenon, Zino, Zinon

Zephaniah (Hebrew) treasured by God.

Zaph, Zaphania, Zeph, Zephan

Zephyr (Greek) west wind. **Zeferino, Zeffrey, Zephram, Zephran**

Zero (Arabic) empty, void.

Zeroun (Armenian) wise and respected.

Zeshawn (American) a combination of the prefix Za + Shawn. **Zeshan, Zeshaun, Zeshon**

Zesiro (Luganda) older of twins.

Zeus (Greek) living. Mythology: chief god in the Greek pantheon who ruled from Mount Olympus.

Zeusef (Portuguese) a form of Joseph.

Zev (Hebrew) a short form of Zebulon.

Zevi (Hebrew) an alternate form of Tzvi. **Zhvie, Zhvy, Zvi**

Zhek (Russian) a short form of Evgeny. **Zhenechka, Zhenka, Zhenya**

Zhixin (Chinese) ambitious. **Zhi, Zhihuán, Zhipeng, Zhi-yang, Zhìyuan**

Zhora (Russian) a form of George.

Zhorik, Zhorka, Zhorz, Zhurka

Zia (Hebrew) trembling; moving.

Zigfrid (Latvian, Russian) a form of Siegfried. **Zegfrido, Zigfrids, Ziggy, Zygfryd, Zygi**

Ziggy (American) a familiar form of Siegfried, Sigmund. **Ziggie**

Zigor (Basque) punishment.

Zilaba (Luganda) born while sick. **Zilabamuzale**

Zikomo (Ngoni) thank you.

Zimra (Hebrew) song of praise. **Zemora, Zimrat, Zimri, Zimria, Zimriah, Zimriya**

Zimraan (Arabic) praise.

Zindel (Yiddish) a form of Alexander. **Zindil, Zunde**

Zion (Hebrew) sign, omen; excellent. Bible: name used to refer to the land of Israel and to the Hebrew people. **Tzion**

Ziskind (Yiddish) sweet child.

Ziv (Hebrew) shining brightly. (Slavic) a short form of Ziven.

Ziven (Slavic) vigorous, lively.
Zev, Ziv, Zivka, Zivon

Ziyad (Arabic) increase.
Zayd

Zohar (Hebrew) bright light.

Zollie, Zolly (Hebrew) alternate forms of Solly.
Zoilo

Zoltán (Hungarian) life.

Zorba (Greek) live each day.

Zorion (Basque) a form of Orion.
Zorian

Zorya (Slavic) star.

Zotikos (Greek) saintly, holy. Religion: a recent saint in the Greek Orthodox church.

Zsigmond (Hungarian) a form of Sigmund.
Ziggy, Zigmund, Zsiga

Zuberi (Swahili) strong.

Zubin (Hebrew) a short form of Zebulon.

Zuhayr (Arabic) brilliant, shining.

Zuka (Shona) sixpence.

Zuriel (Hebrew) God is my rock.

Zygmunt (Polish) a form of Sigmund.

Familiarity Breeds Children

selected by Bruce Lansky

This collection is a treasury of the most outrageous and clever things ever said about raising children by world-class humorists, including Roseanne, Erma Bombeck, Bill Cosby, Dave Barry, Mark Twain, Fran Lebowitz, and others. Filled with entertaining photographs, it makes the perfect gift for any parents you know—including yourself. Originally entitled *The Funny Side of Parenthood.*

The Baby Name Personality Survey

by Bruce Lansky and Barry Sinrod

Based on a national consumer survey of 75,000 parents, this revolutionary baby name book presents personality profiles of 1,400 common names. Parents will understand what images and stereotypes are associated with each name—before they pick one.

Pregnancy, Childbirth, and the Newborn
Revised and Expanded Edition

by Simkin, Whalley, and Keppler

More complete and up-to-date than any other pregnancy guide, this remarkable book is "the bible" for childbirth educators from coast to coast. Called "excellent" by the *American Journal of Nursing*.

Getting Organized for Your New Baby

by Maureen Bard

The fastest way to get ready for pregnancy, childbirth, and new-baby care. Busy expectant parents will love the checklists, forms, schedules, charts, and hints.

Order #1229 $9.00

The Maternal Journal

by Matthew Bennett
illustrated by Breck Wilson
This colorful pregnancy planner/
calendar offers a quick and
delightful way for expectant moth-
ers to learn what to expect and do
during the nine months of pregnancy and first three months of
parenthood.

Order #3171 $10.00

First-Year Baby Care

edited by Paula Kelly, M.D.
For new parents: an illustrated,
step-by-step guide to caring for
baby during the first 12 months.
Complete, authoritative, and
easy to use.

Order #1119 $9.00

Feed Me! I'm Yours

by Vicki Lansky

Now expanded, updated, and revised for the '90s! This best-selling baby- and toddler-food cookbook has sold over 3 million copies. It's a must-have book for all new parents. More than 200 child-tested recipes. A baby-care classic. Comb-bound so it lays flat.

Order #1109 $9.00

Practical Parenting Tips

by Vicki Lansky

Here's the #1-selling tricks-of-the-trade book for new parents. Includes tips on toilet training, discipline, travel, temper tantrums, childproofing, and more. It's revised and updated for the '90s, with more than 400 new ideas that have worked for parents.

Order Form

Qty	Title	Author	Order No.	Unit Cost (US $)	Total
	15,000+ Baby Names	Lansky, B.	1210	$3.95	
	35,000+ Baby Names	Lansky, B.	1225	$5.95	
	Baby & Child Emergency First-Aid Handbook	Einzig, M.	1381	$8.00	
	Baby & Child Medical Care	Hart, T.	1159	$9.00	
	Baby Name Personality Survey	Lansky/Sinrod	1270	$8.00	
	Best Baby Shower	Cooke, C.	1239	$7.00	
	Child Care A to Z	Woolfson, R.	1010	$11.00	
	Discipline w/out Shouting, Spanking	Wyckoff/Unell	1079	$6.00	
	Eating Expectantly	Swinney, B.	1135	$12.00	
	Familiarity Breeds Children	Lansky, B.	4015	$7.00	
	Feed Me! I'm Yours	Lansky, V.	1109	$9.00	
	First-Year Baby Care	Kelly, P.	1119	$9.00	
	Gentle Discipline	Lighter, D.	1085	$6.00	
	Getting Organized for Your New Baby	Bard, M.	1229	$9.00	
	Grandma Knows Best	McBride, M.	4009	$7.00	
	How to Pamper Your Pregnant Wife	Schultz/Schultz	1140	$7.00	
	Joy of Parenthood	Blaustone, J.	3500	$7.00	
	Maternal Journal	Bennett, M.	3171	$10.00	
	Practical Parenting Tips	Lansky, V.	1180	$8.00	
	Pregancy, Childbirth, and the Newborn	Simkin/Whalley/Keppler	1169	$12.00	
	Sweet Dreams	Lansky, B.	2210	$15.00	
	Very Best Baby Name Book	Lansky, B.	1030	$8.00	
				Subtotal	
			Shipping and Handling (see below)		
			MN residents add 6.5% sales tax		
				Total	

YES, please send me the books indicated above. Add $2.00 shipping and handling for the first book and $.50 for each additional book. Add $2.50 to total for books shipped to Canada. Overseas postage will be billed. Allow up to four weeks for delivery. Send check or money order payable to Meadowbrook Press. No cash or C.O.D.'s please. Prices subject to change without notice.
Quantity discounts available upon request.

Send book(s) to:

Name _____

Address _____

City _____ State _____ Zip _____

Phone (_____) _____

☐ Check enclosed for $ _____ payable to Meadowbrook Press

☐ Charge to my credit card (for purchases of $10.00 or more only)

☐ Phone Orders call: (800) 338-2232 (for purchases of $10.00 or more only)

Account #_____ ☐ Visa ☐ MasterCard

Signature _____ Expiration Date _____

A *FREE* Meadowbrook Press catalog is available upon request.

Meadowbrook Press, 5451 Smetana Drive, Minnetonka, MN 55343
Phone (612) 930-1100   Toll free (800) 338-2232   FAX (612) 930-1940